Sri Chaitanya: *His Life & Associates*

MANDALA
PUBLISHING

San Rafael

Sri Chaitanya: *His Life & Associates*

Swami B. B. Tirtha

Mandala Publishing

San Rafael

SRI CHAITANYA MAHAPRABHU

Sri Nityananda Prabhu

MANDALA
PUBLISHING

2240-B 4th Street
San Rafael, CA 94901
telephone. 415.460.6112
fax. 415.460.5218
orders. 800.688.2218
web site. www.mandala.org
e-mail. mandala@mandala.org

ISBN: 1-886069-28-X

Designed and printed
through Palace Press International

Printed in China

dedication

This volume is dedicated to the divine lotus feet of my beloved gurudeva, **Oṁ Viṣṇupāda Śrī Śrīmad Bhakti Dayita Mādhava Goswāmī Mahāraja,** and also to the lotus feet of my most revered śikṣa guru, **Oṁ Viṣṇupāda Śrī Śrīmad Bhakti Promode Puri Goswāmī Mahāraja,** who greatly inspired this publication in English for the benefit of devotees all over the world.

FOREWORD
by
SRILA BHAKTI PROMODE PURI GOSWAMI MAHARAJ

Our divine master, Om Vishnupada 108 Sri Srimad Bhaktisiddhanta Saraswati Goswami Thakur, who has now entered into the eternal pastimes of the Supreme Lord, founded the Sri Chaitanya Math in Mayapur in Nabadwip, whose branch Gaudiya Maths have now spread throughout the world. His dear associate and successor in the disciplic succession, Srimad Bhakti Dayita Madhava Goswami Maharaj, an exemplary monk in the Tridandi order, founded the Chaitanya Gaudiya Math, which also has branches throughout India. After he went to join the pastimes of the Lord, he left his dear disciple, Srimad Bhakti Ballabh Tirtha Maharaj, also a monk in the Tridandi order, as the current president and acharya of Sri Chaitanya Gaudiya Math.

In this jewel-like volume, the venerable Tirtha Maharaj recounts the nectarean activities of the associates of Lord Gauranga and the acharyas of the Gaudiya Vaishnava religion. Tirtha Maharaj has previously written commentaries on the life of the devotee Dhruva, a guide to the Vrindavan parikrama, a summary of the procedures involved in deity worship, as well as a biography in two volumes of his spiritual master, Srimad Madhava Goswami Maharaj. These have all been published in Bengali. He is also the editor of the Chaitanya Gaudiya Math's monthly magazine, Sri Chaitanya Vāṇī, in which his biography of Madhava Maharaj as well as the biographies found in this volume first appeared in installments.

Tirtha Maharaj has shown a force of intelligence beyond the capacities of an ordinary man, for at seventy years of age he not only edits a monthly magazine and writes books such as this one, but also takes responsibility for managing a large organization like the Chaitanya Gaudiya Maths through which he preaches the gospel of Sri Chaitanya Deva to devotees speaking a variety of languages throughout India, from the Himalayas to Cape Cormorin. Even at his advanced age it has been possible for him to find the energy and the enthusiasm to apply himself to tasks that tax his body, mind, speech and intelligence, and still achieve unimaginable results. This is proof that the inexhaustible affectionate blessings of the Supreme Lord, the guru and the Vaishnavas have poured down upon him and that unlimited divine powers have descended upon him through their transcendental mercy. We pray to the lotus feet of Sri Guru, the Vaishnavas, and the Supreme Lord that he will live many more years so that he may continue to serve Krishna and His devotees in the same enthusiastic and unyielding manner. We also humbly submit our prayer to the Srimad Bhagavatam and the devotee Bhagavata that these sweet biographies of Mahaprabhu's associates will flood the ears and touch the hearts of the devotees like a nectar tonic, bringing them all unending joy.

Lord Gaurasundara Mahaprabhu is the most generous incarnation, who descended to bestow upon the world the unique love of Vraja, a mood of devotion to Himself that had never before been given. The lives of the saintly are rich with the sweetness of loving service and are worth repeated study because they are most dear to Gaurasundara. Without such study, we will never be able to understand the nature of devotional service. When we relish the lives of the great devotees we become attracted by their compassion and develop affection without artifice for their lotus feet. Since the Lord is so kind to his devotees, this is the road to becoming the object of his mercy.

Scripture has said that the Lord's mercy follows that of His devotees. Lord Krishna Himself has said in the Bhagavatam that the worship of His devotee is dearer to Him than His own worship (*mad-bhakta-pūjābhyadhikā*). Vrindavan Das paraphrases this statement in the Chaitanya Bhagavata: "The worship of My devotee is even greater than Me; this has been confirmed by the Lord in the Veda and the Bhagavatam."

No matter how great a show of commitment one makes to Krishna's worship, Krishna will never pay the slightest attention to it if one disregards the service of His devotees. Indeed, Krishna will refuse such worship because of the performer's pride. In no way can one be engaged in the worship of the Lord without following in the footsteps of the devotees. Thus the scriptures have ordained that one should begin one's puja with the worship of the guru, who is the best of the devotees and most dear to Krishna. Krishna stated as much to his foremost devotee and associate Uddhava, when He said, "O Uddhava! Know that it is I who am the acharya. Never show disrespect for the acharya by thinking that he is an ordinary man, for all the gods reside within him." The compassion of the Lord has become incarnate in the form of the guru. Worship to the Lord can have no meaning if one disregards the spiritual master.

Tirtha Maharaj has gathered a great deal of information about the lives of the devotees from numerous sources, and has made this information more relishable by virtue of his own insight. It is my wish that these biographies of Mahaprabhu's devotees be read on their appearance and disappearance days, for this will bring great joy to both those who hear and those who read them. It is for this reason that we pray for the wide distribution of this work. In this English translation, it will be possible for devotees around the world to enjoy it.

In this volume, the author delights in the life stories of Jagannath Mishra, Madhavendra Puri, Ishvara Puri, Advaita Acharya, Srivas Pandit, Chandrasekhar Acharya, Pundarika Vidyanidhi, Gadadhar Pandit, Vakresvara Pandit, Gadadhar Das, Shivananda Sen, Paramananda Puri, Murari Gupta, and many others. Every letter of these accounts is drenched with the juice of devotion. We will never be able to enter the transcendental kingdom nor to advance in the devotional life unless we also discover this delight. We should repeatedly discuss the lives of the devotees because they are saturated with loving service to the Lord and this will melt our stonelike hearts. It will awaken in us a genuine remorse for all the time we have wasted in activities outside the life of devotion, thus readying our minds for the mercy of the pure devotee, which invests us with receptivity to devotion.

The devotees of the Lord are oceans of mercy; they feel distress at the pain of others; they are endowed with amazing powers of forgiveness; their hearts are entirely pure, free from enviousness, hate and jealousy. When they see the misery of persons like myself, the lowest of souls who, bound by illusion and forgetful of their eternal identities, have become disinterested in Krishna, they pray to Krishna's lotus feet for their salvation, shedding tears in intense feelings of compassion. After hearing this prayer, Krishna turns His merciful glance towards us.

vaiṣṇavera āvedane kṛṣṇa dayāmay
mo hena pāmara prati habena saday

The merciful Lord Krishna, upon hearing the Vaishnava's supplications, will become merciful to those, who like myself, are most fallen. (Bhaktivinoda Thakur)

The Lord, the ocean of compassion, cannot resist the heart-rending tears of those whose lives are totally dedicated to Him. The Lord quickly appears in the world when he hears the intense pleas of a surrendered devotee. All living beings attain the great fortune of the Lord's mercy through the mercy of such devotees. Therefore one should take shelter of a pure devotee before doing anything else.

śuddha-bhakata-caraṇa-reṇu bhajana-anukūla
bhakata-sevā parama-siddhi prema-latikāra mūla

"The dust of the pure devotee's lotus feet has the most positive effect on one's worship of the Lord. Service to the devotee is the greatest perfection, it is the root of the creeper of love for Krishna." (Bhaktivinoda Thakur)

At the beginning of his collection of devotional songs, *Śaraṇāgati*, Bhaktivinoda Thakur wrote: "Lord Sri Krishna Chaitanya, out of compassion for the people of this world, descended into this world along with His eternal associates and His abode. In order to give *prema* most rare, He taught the process of surrender that is the life of devotion."

In every age for all eternity, the Lord takes a body in each of the unlimited universes. This does not cause a disruption in the Lord's eternal pastimes. Thus, when the Supreme Lord, the *līlā-puruṣottama*, son of Nanda, the king of Vraja, appears in Nabadwip as Gauranga, the son of Jagannath Mishra, all of His associates from His Vraja-lila join Him as companions for these pastimes. Narottam Das Thakur sings: "He who was the son of the King of Vraja has become the son of Sachi, Balaram has become Nitai."

Krishna Das Kaviraj states as much in the Chaitanya Charitamrita: "Krishna appeared with all of Vraja at the end of the Dvapara Yuga of the twenty-eighth four-yuga cycle in the seventh Manvantara, named Vaivasvata." (1.3.9-10)

Jiva Goswami explains the Bhagavata verses that begin with the words *kṛṣṇa-varṇaṁ tviṣākṛṣṇam* (11.5.32) and *āsan varṇās trayo hy asya* (10.8.13) in his *Krama-sandarbha* commentary: "Thus the same Krishna who descended at the end of the Dvapara Yuga, appears as Gaura in the age of Kali that immediately follows it. From this understanding it is evident that Gauranga is a special incarnation of Krishna. This is the only way to avoid the apparent contradictions in the Bhagavatam verses, which state that 'in the Kali Age Krishna appears in a color other than black,' and that He appears in the four ages in four colors, red, black, white and gold.

The Supreme Personality of Godhead Krishna displays activities characterized by magnanimity (*audārya*) predominated by the character of *mādhurya,* sweetness. The pastimes of the Lord in Nabadwip, however, though non-different from those of Vraja, are characterized by *mādhurya* predominated by His magnanimity. Just as all of Krishna's qualities are manifest in His devotees, so too are Gaura's qualities in their entirety manifest in His devotees. Since Gaura is the most magnanimous and generous of incarnations, these qualities are the primary characeristics of His divine pastimes and are therefore also present in all the participants in His lila. It is thus natural that constant rereading of the activities of the devotees who have dedicated themselves to Gaura's service will wash all of the dirt and sin from our hearts and we will become free from envy, hatred and jealousy. Then, in the same way that it is said of Gaura that "He taught the world by following the practices and principles Himself" (Chaitanya Charitamrita 1.3.20, 1.4.41), we will be able to enthusiastically preach the message of Lord Chaitanya to every corner of the world. Should we be successful by the mercy of the beneficent Lord, a supreme peace will establish itself everywhere, the victory banner of the Holy Name will fly, the skies of the world will ring with the glorious sound of Krishna's name being sung, and the sweetness of the Holy Name that Lord Chaitanya Himself called out will flood the world with divine love. For, as Bhaktivinoda Thakur exclaimed, "What power is contained in the name of Krishna!"

Bhakti Varidhi Parivrajaka Maharaj, a monk who is particularly dear to me, took on himself the responsibility for printing the Bengali edition of this book. He worked with dedication both day and night to finish the job, and even if I could sing his glories with a hundred tongues I would not feel satisfied. He produced not only this volume, but works tirelessly and with unflagging enthusiasm to put out all of the Math publications. His gurus have noticed this service and will pour unlimited affectionate blessings on him. We pray to the Lord's lotus feet with all our heart that his eager efforts to serve the Lord, the guru, and all the Vaishnavas constantly increase, that he receive their unlimited blessings and enjoy good health and long life.

Srila Prabhupada Bhaktisiddhanta Saraswati Goswami Thakur used to call the printing press the big drum, the *brihat mridanga,* because through books and magazines filled with the authoritative message of pure devotion, the worldwide preaching mission can have a stable and far-reaching effect. Therefore the beating of the "big drum" is a major element in serving Mahaprabhu in preaching His message. Mahaprabhu himself said, "Wherever you go, give the fruits of love to whomever you see" (Chaitanya Charitamrita 1.9.36); "Those who have taken a human birth in India (*Bhārata-bhūmi*) should perfect their own lives and then do good for others" (Chaitanya Charitamrita 1.9.41); "Spread this command of mine wherever you go: "Chant Krishna, worship Krishna, study Krishna's teachings'" (Chaitanya Bhagavata 2.13.7-8); "Explain Krishna consciousness to whomever you meet" (Chaitanya Charitamrita 2.7.128); "My name shall be heard in all the towns and villages of the world" (Chaitanya Bhagavata 3.4.126). As we try to fulfill these commands of the Lord in as sustained and far-reaching way as possible, we will get most help from the "big mridanga."

Therefore, in making the preaching of Chaitanya Mahaprabhu's message through printing books a prominent part of the Math's service activities, Parivrajaka Maharaj and Bhakti Ballabha Tirtha Maharaj are insuring that they will receive the affection of their spiritual masters and all pure devotees, not only those who have preceded them, but those who will follow.

In conclusion, we would like to sincerely thank as much as possible all those who have aided through financial contributions or volunteer work to help bring this and other books and magazines of the Math to publication. We humbly pray to everyone who reads this work to kindly forgive any errors that may have been missed in proofreading.

Praying for the dust of the
pure devotees' lotus feet,
I am the servant of the servant
of the Vaishnavas,

Sri Bhakti Promode Puri.

23 Bhadra 1399 (Bengali year)
9 September 1992.

Srila Bhakti Promode Puri Goswami Maharaj

Contents.

Parishads.

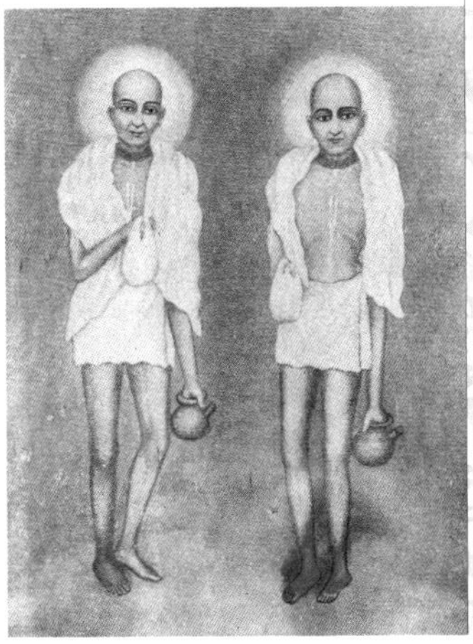

Introduction

by

SRILA BHAKTI BALLABH TIRTHA MAHARAJ

The contents of this book first appeared as a series of articles in Sri Chaitanya Vāṇī ("The Gospel of Lord Chaitanya"), a monthly magazine exclusively devoted to spiritual subject matters. Those articles have been brought together here to form a single book, though they were originally published in Bengali in two separate volumes. I hope that this publication will facilitate the devotees' relishing of the activities of the Lord's associates.

The contents of this book first appeared as a series of articles in *Sri Chaitanya Vāṇī* ("The Gospel of Lord Chaitanya"), a monthly magazine exclusively devoted to spiritual subject matters. Those articles have been brought together here to form a single book, though they were originally published in Bengali in two separate volumes. I hope that this publication will facilitate the devotees' relishing of the activities of the Lord's associates.

Sri Gauranga Mahaprabhu is the supreme truth and his associates are also transcendental, beyond matter. They are thus not accessible to the material senses, mind and intelligence. Since the transcendent is by nature self-manifest, one can only understand their glories through their causeless mercy. Just as the glories of the Lord are unlimited, so too are the glories of His devotees without end. Those who are not surrendered have no right of entry into these mysteries.

Amongst those who have abandoned themselves to the Lord, too, there are varying degrees of surrender producing varying degrees of ability to perceive the devotees' glories. The jiva who is covered by an assortment of anarthas cannot approach an understanding of the glories of Vishnu and the Vaishnavas. And even if such persons try to glorify them, the inevitable result is a discourtesy. Nevertheless, if one recognizes one's own unworthiness and humbly glorifies them in a prayerful attitude, the Vaishnavas will forgive any flaws in their expression.

The satisfied glance of the Vaishnavas frees the jiva from his anarthas and brings him all auspiciousness. Even though the neophyte is inadequate in so many ways and thus unable to glorify Krishna and His devotees in a satisfactory manner, if he does not do so his inadequacies will only remain. The only hope for the fallen souls is that the Vaishnavas will be merciful and not find any fault with them. Those who engage honestly in service find that by the mercy of the Vaishnavas, all obstacles are eliminated and all desired goals attained.

The pure devotee is very rare in this world; it is only due to great fortune that one can meet and associate with such a devotee. In the Chaitanya Charitamrita (1.1.20-1), it is said, "By meditating on the guru, the Vaishnava and the Lord, all obstacles are destroyed and all desires are fulfilled." "All perfections come from the mercy of the Vaishnavas." "I have heard from my guru and from the saintly persons that the jiva who glorifies the qualities of the devotees is liberated."

Chaitanya Mahaprabhu's direct associates, the Six Goswamis, daily paid thousands of obeisances to the Vaishnavas. Indeed, one should spend some time meditating on the Vaishnavas every single day. An important element of devotional service is the regular observance of Vaishnavas' appearance and disappearance days. On these occasions, one should remember them, pray to them for their mercy and glorify their qualities in kirtan. We at the Chaitanya Gaudiya Math annually publish a Vaishnava calendar in which all the different fasting days and feasts are indicated; all the known appearance and disappearance days which have been noted therein. The purpose of this book is to assist the devotees who wish to remember the Vaishnavas, to pray to them, and especially to glorify them in kirtan.

We should chant the glories of the merciful devotees of Sri Chaitanya because we wish to rid ourselves of all tendencies that lead away from devotional service and to develop attachment for Krishna. Sometimes, however, we find that there is absolutely no change in our nature. We do not attain the desired result because we are not able to adequately glorify them due to our incapacities. Nevertheless, one cannot give it the effort because the lotus feet of the Vaishnavas are the only recourse for the fallen.

In researching the holy activities of Chaitanya's associates, I became aware that many details of their lives are unavailable. Many of their appearance and disappearance tithis (lunar dates) and years are unknown, as are their places of birth, the names of their parents and their ancestors. This information could thus not be given in all cases. Some readers may find that the language used to describe the devotees' lives is not sufficiently poetic and thus not find the joy in reading these accounts as they had hoped.

The chief editor and president of *Chaitanya Vāṇī* magazine, my siksha guru, the most venerable Bhakti Promode Puri Goswami Maharaj, has rained down countless blessings on me in order to encourage me to perform this service. He has made many personal contributions to this volume by way of making corrections, and in some instances adding new information about certain of the associates' lives.

We thank everyone who contributed for the publication of this book. I pray that the blessings of the guru, the Vaishnavas and the Supreme Lord fall upon them.

I pay thousands of prostrated obeisances to the lotus feet of my most worshipable Gurudeva, the purifier of the sinful, to the lotus feet of my *parama gurudeva*, Srila Prabhupada Bhaktisiddhanta Saraswati Thakur, to the feet of my siksha guru, Srila Bhakti Promode Puri Goswami Maharaj, and to all the other disciples of Srila Prabhupada, who are all *siksha gurus*, and I pray for their causeless mercy and blessings.

Servant of the servant
of the Vaishnavas,

Bhakti Ballabh Tirtha

Srila Bhakti Ballabh Tirtha Maharaj

Srila Bhakti Dayita Madhava Goswami Mahraj

Srila Gaura Kishora Das Babaji Maharaj

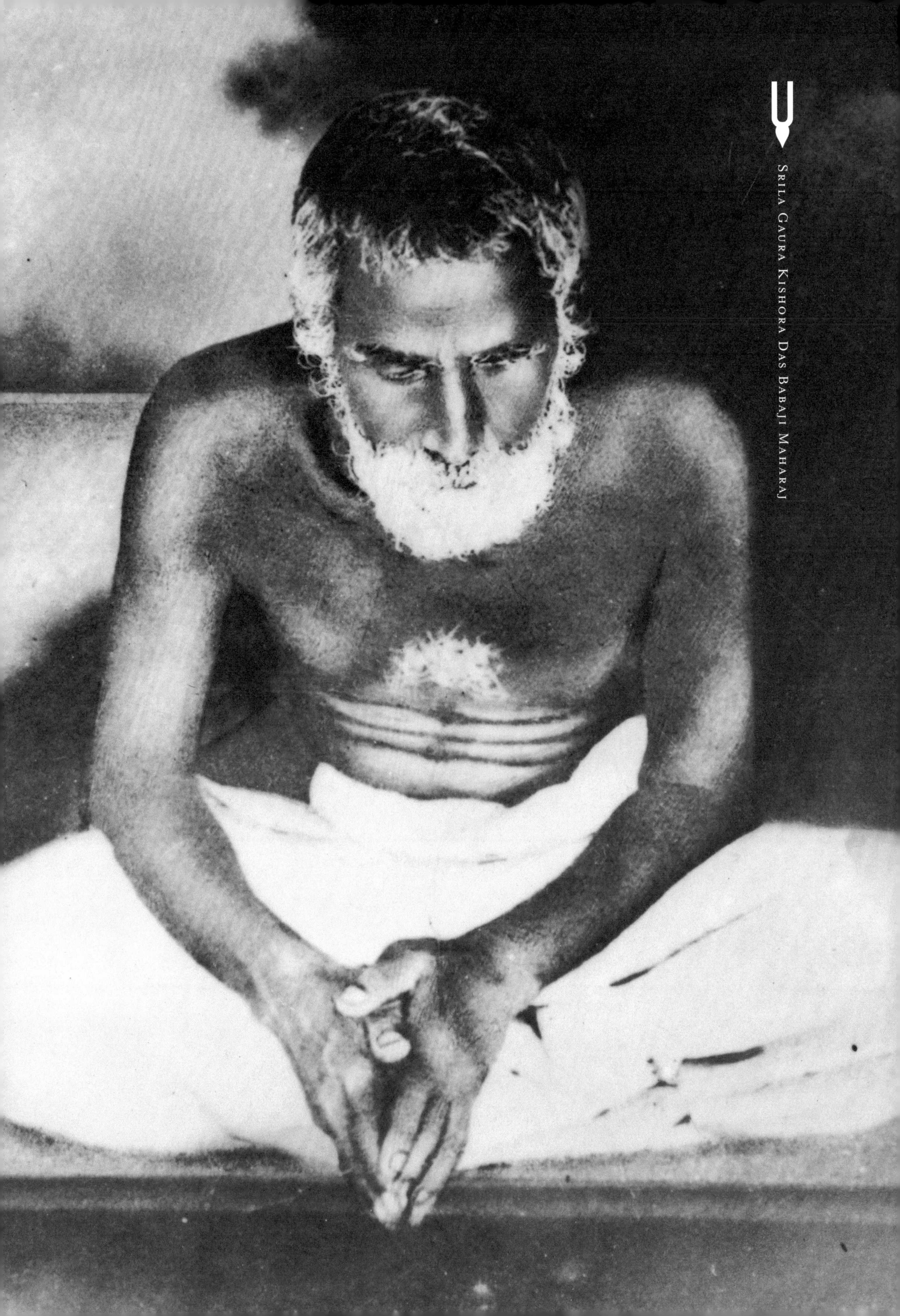

Srila Gaura Kishora Das Babaji Maharaj

Srila Satchitananda Bhaktivinode Thakur

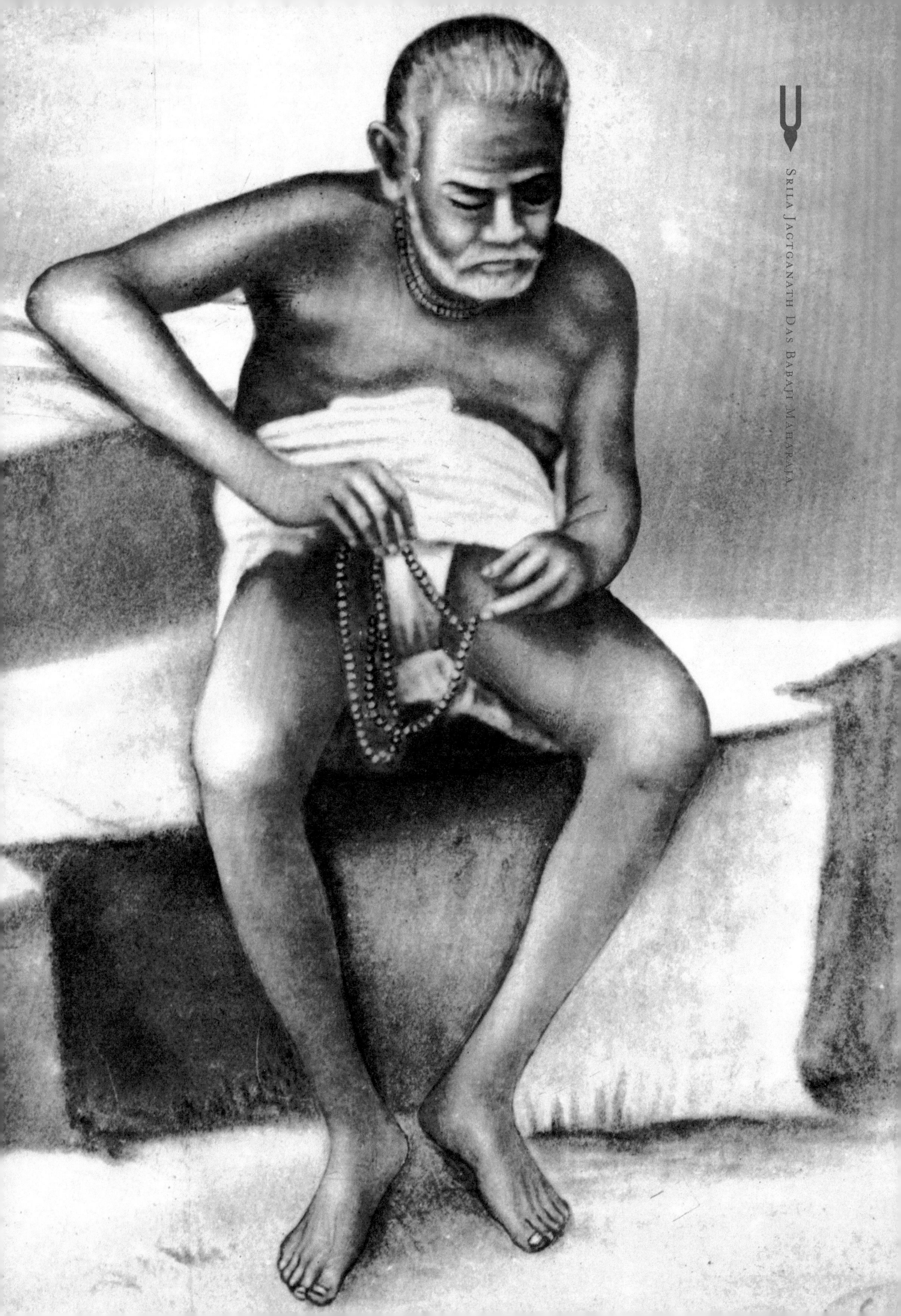
Srila Jagtganath Das Babaji Maharaja

B.G. Sharma

The Associates

{parishads}

SRI JAYADEVA

Srila Jayadeva Goswami appeared in either the eleventh or twelfth century of the Shaka era. There is a difference of opinion about his place of birth. The majority opinion holds that he hailed from the village of Kendubilva, presently in the district of Birbhum. Others claim that he was born in either Orissa or south India.

Kendubilva is situated about twenty miles south of Siuri on the banks of the Ajaya River. In the *Gauḍīya Vaiṣṇava Abhidhāna*, it is stated that Jayadeva found his Radha Madhava deities in this river's waters. It is also stated there that he used to rest and worship at the temple of Shiva known as Kusheshwar, which is also on the banks of the Ajaya River. Jayadeva's father was named Bhojadeva and his mother, Vama Devi.

JAYADEVA'S LIFE IN NABADWIP

Jayadeva lived for a long time in Nabadwip during the reign of the king of Bengal, Lakshman Sen, making his home not far from the king's palace. At that time, the king's chief scholar was Govardhan Acharya. According to Ashutosh Deb's Bengali dictionary, Jayadeva was Lakshman Sen's court poet.

Srila Bhaktivinoda Thakur writes in his *Nabadvīpa-dhāma-māhātmya* that Lakshman Sen was delighted when he heard Jayadeva's hymn to the ten incarnations, the *Daśāvatāra-stotra*. When Govardhan Acharya notified the king that it was Jayadeva who had composed the hymn, he became desirous to meet the poet. He went incognito to Jayadeva's house and when he saw him, he noticed that Jayadeva possessed all the characteristics of a great and powerful spiritual personality. Deeply impressed and attracted by Jayadeva, the king revealed his identity to him and invited him to come and live in the royal palace. Jayadeva was leading a very renounced life and was therefore unwilling to live in the opulent environment of the palace. He told the king that he preferred to live in Jagannath Puri.

Lakshman Sen was disappointed by Jayadeva's intentions. He quickly suggested that he take up residence in the village of Champa Hati, saying that it was a place suitable for a person who wished to lead a meditative life. He also promised him that he would never come to disturb him again. When Jayadeva agreed, Lakshman Sen had a cottage built for him in the village that was formerly known as Champaka-hatta, named after the beautiful garden of champa trees and the village market where its flowers were sold. It was in this village that Mahaprabhu's associate Dvija Baninath received a vision of Him in the Satya Yuga, seeing Him in the form of a Brahmin whose skin was the color of a champa flower. Similarly, Jayadeva had a vision here, first of Radha-Madhava, then of Their combined form as the golden champa-colored Gauranga Mahaprabhu.

After the Lord gave Jayadeva this vision, He told him to go to Jagannath Puri. Although Jayadeva was sad to leave the future abode of his Lord, he obeyed the Lord's command and made his way to Puri where it is said that he was engaged as the king of Orissa's court poet. He spent the remainder of his life in the abode of Lord Jagannath, where he wrote the transcendental poem based on the sentiment of love in separation known as *Gīta-govinda* or *Aṣṭapadī*. Indeed, Mahaprabhu told Jayadeva while giving him the vision in Nabadwip that after appearing there, He would take sannyas and go to Jagannath Puri where He would relish the *Gīta-govinda*.

Further information about the life of Jayadeva is found in the preface to the Calcutta Basumati Sahitya Mandir edition of *Gīta-govinda*: "Sometime prior to the Muslim conquest of Delhi, King Manikya Chandra ordered the writing of the book *Alaṅkāra-śekhara*, in which Jayadeva is mentioned as the court poet of the king of Orissa. Sridhar Das, the son of one of the chief courtiers of Lakshman Sen, included many of Jayadeva's verses in his anthology *Sad-ukti-karṇāmṛta*, citing a work named *Amiyābha-kāvya*. The colophon to one ancient manuscript of the *Gīta-govinda* states, "Jayadeva had a great reputation as a poet during the time of Lakshman Sen."

JAYADEVA'S MARRIAGE TO PADMAVATI

According to legend, Jagannath Himself ordered Jayadeva to marry his wife, Padmavati. The story is told in the *Viśvakoṣa* as follows: There once was a Brahmin who was without offspring despite having worshiped Jagannath for many years in the hope of having a son. Finally, he and his wife had a daughter and they named her Padmavati. When she came of marriageable age, the Brahmin brought her to Lord Jagannath to offer her to his lotus feet.[1] When He saw them, Jagannath said to the Brahmin, "I have a servant whose name is Jayadeva. He has given up family life and has dedicated himself to chanting My names. Give your daughter to him in marriage."

The Brahmin took his daughter to Jayadeva and asked him to marry his daughter. However, since Jayadeva had no desire to get married, he refused to agree to any such arrangement. The Brahmin then told him that it was Jagannath Himself who had arranged this marriage; and without another word, he left, leaving his daughter behind. Jayadeva found himself totally unprepared for this situation and told the girl, "Tell me where you want to go and I will take you and leave you there. You cannot stay here."

Padmavati started to cry and said, "My father brought me here to marry you on Jagannath Deva's order. You are my husband, my all in all. If you do not accept me, then I will fall down at your feet and die right here. You are my only hope, my Lord."

The poet and scholar Jayadeva could not abandon her after such a heartfelt plea. So he became a householder.

THE LORD HELPS JAYADEVA WRITE GITA-GOVINDA

Jayadeva took up the worship of a Narayan deity and, in the waves of love he felt for Him, began writing *Gīta-govinda*, with its incomparable ambrosia. It is said that though Jayadeva is responsible for all the moods and sentiments that appear in the *Gīta-govinda*, he had some reticence about writing that Krishna fell down at Radharani's feet to beg Her forgiveness when She was angry with Him for having deceived Her.

On that day, when Jayadeva left the house to take his bath in the ocean, Lord Jagannath Himself came inside, disguised as Jayadeva, opened his manuscript and completed the verse he had started smara-garala-khaṇḍanaṁ mama śirasi maṇḍanaṁ with the words dehi pada-pallavam udāram: "Make the noble blossom of Your foot an ornament on My head, as it dispels the poison of love in separation." (Gita-govinda 10.8)

Padmavati was surprised to see her husband back so soon from his bath and asked, "What are you doing here? You just left a minute ago." The disguised Jagannath answered, "I thought of something I had forgotten while on my way. I was afraid I might forget so I came back to write it down."

Not long after Jagannath had left, the real Jayadeva returned. This time, Padmavati was really astonished to see him. She said, "You just left to go and take your bath. Just a few moments ago you were writing in your manuscript and then you left. How could you have finished and come back so quickly? I am beginning to wonder who that was and who you are."

Jayadeva was clever enough to guess what had happened and he went and looked at his unfinished text and saw the words that the Lord Himself had written. The hair stood on end all over his body and tears came pouring from his eyes. He called Padmavati and said to her, "You are so fortunate. Your life has been made worthy. You have had the good fortune to see the Lord Himself. I am so lowly that I did not have that opportunity!"

JAGANNATH'S LOVE FOR GITA-GOVINDA

There is a legend told in Jagannath Puri that there was a flower gardener's daughter who had learned *Gīta-govinda* and would sing it with great emotion. Jagannath was attracted by her singing and would go to listen to her, only returning to the temple after she had finished her singing.

One day, when the king of Orissa came to see the deity, he saw that the Lord's body was covered in dust and his clothes filled with thorns. He asked the pujaris the reason for the Lord's disheveled condition, but no one could explain how it had come about. The servants of the deity were afraid that they would be punished, but that night Jagannath appeared to the king in a dream and explained that no one was to blame for his clothes being soiled that day. He had gone to listen to the gardener's daughter and had become covered with dust and thorns while hiding in the garden.

The king was struck with wonder by his dream and immediately sent for the gardener's daughter to be brought to the court in a palanquin. After making inquiries from her, he decided that she should sing for Jagannath in the temple, rather than obliging the Lord to leave the temple and get all dirty. This was the beginning of the tradition of the temple engaging girls named *deva-dāsīs* to sing *Gīta-govinda* for Jagannath's pleasure.

MAHAPRABHU APPRECIATES GITA-GOVINDA

In the last twelve years of His lila, Mahaprabhu was absorbed in Radha's mood and constantly relished this hidden spirit of love. During this time, he would savor the songs of the *Gīta-govinda*.

Day and night, the Lord would speak as though He were Radha meeting Uddhava. He would also relish the poems of Chandi Das, Jayadeva and Vidyapati.

(Chaitanya Charitamrita 1.13.41-2)

Mahaprabhu was never pleased to hear books or verses that contradicted siddhanta, nor did He like hearing *rasābhāsa*, an improper mixture of devotional sentiments. It was the practice of Svarupa Damodar Goswami to examine all works of literature to find out whether their conclusions were correct. Only then would he allow them to be heard by the Lord. Sri Svarupa Damodar used to make Mahaprabhu very happy by singing the songs of Vidyapati, Chandi Das and *Gīta-govinda*.

(Chaitanya Charitamrita 2.10.113-5)

Svarupa Damodar would sing songs that reflected the moods of the Lord whenever they arose; Ramananda Raya also selected verses from Vidyapati, Chandi Das and *Gīta-govinda* according to the Lord's mood..

(Chaitanya Charitamrita 2.17.5-6)

The Lord returned to external consciousness for a moment and told Svarupa to sing some sweet songs. Svarupa sang one of Vidyapati's lyrics and then songs from the *Gīta-govinda*, which were greatly appreciated by the Lord.

(Chaitanya Charitamrita 3.17.62)

caṇḍi dāsa vidyāpati rāyera nāṭaka gīti
karṇāmṛta śrī gīta-govinda

svarūpa rāmānanda sane mahāprabhu rātri-dine
gāya, śune parama ānanda

Day and night, Mahaprabhu ecstatically relished the songs of Chandi Das, Vidyapati and Ramananda Raya's plays, as well as *Kṛṣṇa-karṇāmṛta* and *Gīta-govinda* in the company of Svarupa and Ramananda.

(Chaitanya Charitamrita 2.2.77)

JAYADEVA AND THE ROBBERS

Many other such marvelous and miraculous events were scattered through Jayadeva's life. He used to serve his deities Radha-Madhava in a trance of divine love. It is said that just as the devotee dedicates himself to the Lord, the Lord also dedicates Himself to His devotee. One day, as Jayadeva was thatching his roof under the merciless, mid-day sun, Jagannath saw His devotee's discomfort and decided to help him quickly finish the work by handing him the rope needed to bale the straw and removing the finished bundles and placing them on the roof. Jayadeva thought that it was Padmavati who was helping him in this way. But when he came down from the roof after finishing much earlier than expected, he saw no one there. He asked his wife and she told him that she had been busy elsewhere at the time. He was curious about what had happened, but struck with wonder when he went into the deity room and saw that Madhava's hands were black from handling the straw. He was thus able to understand that it was Madhava himself who had come to help him thatch the roof. He fell down before his Lord and started to cry.

On another occasion, Jayadeva wished to put on a festival for his deities Radha-Madhava, but he was short of money. He decided to travel in order to collect some funds by making use of his poetic skills. On his return journey, he was stopped by a band of thugs who not only stole his money but cut off his hands and feet and threw him down a well to die. Despite the pain, Jayadeva shouted out the names of the Lord as loudly as he could.

After Jayadeva had spent three days in this way, the king happened to pass that way on a hunting expedition and heard the sound of the Holy Names coming from the hole in the ground. The king approached the sound out of curiosity and was horrified to see Jayadeva in such a serious condition. He had him pulled out of the well and brought back to his palace where he had him treated. Under the queen's care, Jayadeva gradually returned to health.

Both the king and queen were charmed by Jayadeva's sweet singing of the *Gīta-govinda* as well as by his saintly character. They sent for Padmavati and had her brought to their home to help take care of him. The royal couple heard about Krishna from Jayadeva and took initiation from him and started to make their lives successful by service of the Lord and His devotees. One day, the robbers who had attacked Jayadeva came to the king's palace as guests in the guise of devotees. Even though Jayadeva recognized who they were, he offered them the appropriate honor due to their outward appearance and arranged for the king's hospitality to be extended to them. The robbers, however, did not understand Jayadeva's forgiving and generous nature and, fearing capture and punishment, thought it best to leave without accepting the royal invitation. Jayadeva understood their fear and asked the king to give them a large sum of money, an escort, and send them on their way.

After they had gone a certain distance, the robbers said to the soldiers accompanying them, "You need not go any further. However, we would like to give you a secret message to convey to the king. Prior to becoming Vaishnavas we were the servants of a certain king who for very good reason ordered us to murder this priest, Jayadeva. That is why we cut off his hands and feet and left him to die. The reason this priest gave us a lot of money and asked us to leave quickly is because he was afraid that this secret would come out."

Unable to tolerate the telling of such a great lie, the Earth herself opened up and swallowed the entire gang of thieves.The goddess of the Earth was unable to support the weight of these sinful liars and so she swallowed them up. As they blasphemed the great devotee of the Lord, they met their doom in the bowels of the earth. When Shukracharya, the guru of the demons, told Bali Maharaj not to give the three feet of land demanded by Vạmana Deva, Bali answered that he was the grandson of Prahlad Maharaj. How could he go back on his word like a miser once he had committed himself to giving in charity? He substantiated this by quoting the Earth,

na hy asatyāt paro'dharma
iti hovāca bhūr iyam
sarvaṁ soḍhum alaṁ manye
ṛte'līka-paraṁ naram

"There is no greater irreligiousness than untruth," says the Earth. "I can bear any burden other than that of a person who constantly lies." (Srimad Bagavatam 8.20.4)

The servants of the king who had accompanied these robbers were astonished to see them punished for their offence to Jayadeva right before their very eyes. When they came back to the king's palace, they told him everything they had witnessed. The king inquired from Jayadeva about the robbers and he told the entire story. He said, "O king! A saintly man does not seek revenge from those who have done evil toward him. He attempts to satisfy them by polite behavior. Even so, the Lord's flawless will makes them suffer the consequences of their own sin, as He did in this case."

PADMAVATI IS TESTED

Jayadeva's wife became a close friend to the queen. In those days, the practice of *satī*, where a wife would enter the funeral pyre along with her husband, was an accepted custom. After her brother's death, the queen was mortified that her sister-in-law would have to die on the funeral pyre with him. Padmavati said to the queen, "A faithful wife's life airs leave her body the very moment that her husband dies."

When the queen heard this, she decided to test Padmavati herself. One day she announced to Padmavati that her husband Jayadeva had suddenly died. As soon as this news entered Padmavati's ears, she instantly gave up her life. Padmavati's sudden death shocked the queen who began to cry out of a sense of guilt for having caused it. The king went to Jayadeva and begged him to return the life to Padmavati's corpse. The great devotee Jayadeva whispered the name of Krishna into his wife's ear and she opened her eyes as though she had just awakened. Upon seeing this manifestation of both Jayadeva and Padmavati's glories, the king and queen as well as all their courtiers and servants paid obeisances at their feet.

JAYADEVA GOES TO VRINDAVAN

After this, Jayadeva wished to see Vrindavan. He took leave of the king and queen and then, taking his deities Radha and Madhava with him, set off on the long journey. Once in Vrindavan, he began to serve his deities in an area near Keshi Ghat. When the residents of the Dham heard Jayadeva sing the *Gīta-govinda* in his sweet voice, they were entranced. One merchant built a large temple for the deities on that site.

It is said that Jayadeva returned to his birthplace in Kendubilva after living in Vrindavan for many years. He spent the rest of his life there, worshiping his deities and performing his bhajan. He would make the long walk to the Ganges every day to take his bath there. One day, for some reason or another, he was unable to make it. Ganga Devi was so kind to him that she came personally to the village of Kendubilva so that he could bathe in her holy waters. It is said that Jayadeva died in Kendubilva and every year on the first day of the month of Magh a large festival is held there in his memory.

There is, however, a difference of opinion about where Jayadeva finished his life. Though some say he returned to Kendubilva, others claim it was Puri, and still others say that he went to Vrindavan. Srila Bhaktisiddhanta Saraswati Goswami Thakur has stated his opinion that Jayadeva left this world from Jagannath Puri. Though some people say that Jayadeva returned to Kendubilva to spend his last days, there is no indication anywhere that he brought his Radha-Madhava deities with him. In fact, these deities were taken by the king of Jaipur to a place named Ghati sometime after Jayadeva's passing way and they are still being served in the Jaipur area. Jayadeva's disappearance day is on the sixth day of the waning moon of the month of Paush.

[1] Many people in Orissa still follow the custom of offering their daughters in marriage to Jagannath before they marry anyone else.

Sri Madhavendra Puri

Mahaprabhu's seniors, His parents and gurus, are all his servants and eternal associates and they take their birth prior to His appearance in order to serve Him in their own way.

Whenever Krishna descends to the earth, He first sends down His elders. These include His father, mother, guru and all the other persons He considers to be the objects of His respect. He arranges that these persons should accept birth before He does. Madhavendra Puri, Ishvara Puri, Sachi, Jagannath, and Advaita Acharya are amongst those who appeared in this way.

(Chaitanya Charitamrita 1.3.92-4)

Later in the Chaitanya Charitamrita (1.13.52-55), the same thing is stated in the following way:

Whenever the son of the king of Vraja decides to appear on earth in order to fulfill a particular desire, He first sends down His seniors. I will briefly name some of them as it is not possible to mention everyone: Sachi Devi, Jagannath Mishra, Madhava Puri, Keshava Bharati, Ishvara Puri, Advaita Acharya, Srivas Pandit, Acharyaratna, Pundarika Vidyanidhi, Hari Das Thakur.

THE DISCIPLIC SUCCESSION

Srila Madhavendra Puri appeared in the 14th century. He was a guru of the Brahma or Madhva sampradaya, one of the four (Brahma, Sri, Rudra and Sanaka) Vaishnava lineages that purify the world in the age of Kali. The Madhva lineage has been transcribed in books like *Gaura-gaṇoddeśa-dīpikā*, *Prameya-ratnāvalī* and the writings of Gopal Guru Goswami. The same set of verses is found with some slight differences in the *Bhakti-ratnākara* (5.2149-2162). The following is the version as found in the *Gaura-gaṇoddeśa-dīpikā*:

paravyomeśvarasyāsīc chiṣyo brahmā jagat-patiḥ
tasya śiṣyo nārado 'bhūt vyāsas tasyāpa śiṣyatām
śuko vyāsasya śiṣyatvaṁ prāpto jñānāvabodhanāt
vyāsāl labdha-kṛṣṇa-dīkṣo madhvācāryo mahāyaśaḥ
tasya śiṣyo 'bhavat padmanābhācāryo mahāśayaḥ
tasya śiṣyo naraharis tacchiṣyo mādhava-dvijaḥ
akṣobhyas tasya śiṣyo 'bhūt tac-chiṣyo jayatīrthakaḥ
tasya śiṣyo jñāna-sindhus tasya śiṣyo mahānidhiḥ
vidyānidhis tasya śiṣyo rājendras tasya sevakaḥ
jayadharmā munis tasya śiṣyo yad-gaṇa-madhyataḥ
śrīmad-viṣṇu-purī yas tu bhaktiratnāvalī-kṛtiḥ
jayadharmasya śiṣyo 'bhūd brahmaṇyaḥ puruṣottamaḥ
vyāsatīrthas tasya śiṣyo yaś cakre viṣṇusaṁhitām
śrīmān lakṣmīpatis tasya śiṣyo bhaktirasāśrayaḥ
tasya śiṣyo mādhavendro yad-dharmo 'yaṁ pravartitaḥ
tasya śiṣyo "bhavat śrīmān īśvarākhya-purī-yatiḥ
kalayāmāsa śṛṅgāraṁ yaḥ śṛṅgāra-phalātmakaḥ

advaitaṁ kalayāmāsa dāsya-sākhye phale ubhe
īśvarākhya-purīṁ gaura urarīkṛtya gaurave
jagad āplāvayāmāsa prākṛtāprākṛtātmakam

Brahma, the master of this universe, was the disciple of the Lord of the spiritual world. His disciple was Narada and Vyasa became the disciple of Narada. Suka became the disciple of Vyasa through the endowment of spiritual knowledge. Madhvacharya took initiation in the Krishna mantra from Vyasa. His disciple was Padmanabhacarya, whose disciple was Narahari, who was followed by Madhava Dvija. Akshobhya was his disciple, then Jayatirtha, Jnanasindhu, Mahanidhi, Vidyanidhi and Rajendra followed. Jayadharma Muni was one of Rajendra's many disciples and Vishnu Puri, the author of *Bhakti-ratnāvalī* and Purushottam, the lover of Brahmin culture became his disciples. Vyasa Tirtha, the author of *Viṣṇu-saṁhitā*, was the disciple of Purushottam. Lakshmipati Tirtha, a reservoir of devotion, was Vyasa Tirtha's disciple. Madhavendra Puri was the disciple of Lakshmipati, and it is by him that this religion was founded. His disciple, the sannyasi Ishvara Puri, took up the mood of conjugal devotion, while Advaita Acharya [also the disciple of Madhavendra] took up the moods of servitude and friendship. Gaura accepted Ishvara Puri as his guru, and then flooded the material and spiritual worlds [with love].

Thus, Madhavendra Puri was the disciple of Lakshmipati Tirtha. Madhavendra Puri's disciples included Ishvara Puri, Advaita Acharya, Paramananda Puri (a Brahmin from the Tirhut area), Brahmananda Puri, Sri Ranga Puri, Pundarika Vidyanidhi, Raghupati Upadhyaya, and others. Nityananda Prabhu is said by some to be Madhavendra Puri's disciple, others say that Lakshmipati was his guru, while the *Prema-vilāsa* states that he was Ishvara Puri's disciple.

Bhaktivinoda Thakur writes: "Madhavendra Puri was a well known sannyasi of the Madhva sampradaya. His granddisciple was Sri Chaitanya Mahaprabhu. Prior to his appearance, there was no evidence of prema bhakti in the Madhva line. In his verse, *ayi dīna-dayārdra-nātha* (Chaitanya Charitamrita 2.4.197), the seed of the religious doctrines of Chaitanya Mahaprabhu can be found."

To this, Bhaktisiddhanta Saraswati Goswami Prabhupada adds, "Madhavendra Puri was the first shoot of the desire tree of divine love that came out of the Madhva lineage. Prior to his appearance, there was no sign of the conjugal mood of devotion in the Madhva line."

MADHAVENDRA AND NITYANANDA PRABHU

Nityananda met Madhavendra Puri while wandering through the pilgrimage sites in Western India. As soon as they saw each other they were overcome with the symptoms of ecstatic love. Vrindavan Das Thakur describes this event in the ninth chapter of the *Ādi-khaṇḍa*:

While Nityananda Prabhu was wandering [through Southern India] in this way, he suddenly encountered Madhavendra Puri. Madhavendra was the embodiment of love, as were all his associates. He consumed nothing other than Krishna rasa, and Krishna dwelt in his body. How can I sufficiently glorify him whose disciple was Advaita Acharya? When Nityananda saw Madhavendra Puri, he fainted and became motionless with love. As soon as Madhava Puri saw Nityananda, he too completely forget himself and lost consciousness. No wonder Gauranga repeatedly said that Madhavendra Puri was the harbinger of the ecstatic mood of devotion.

Nityananda Prabhu said, "I have visited many holy sites, but today I have been fulfilled by the sight of Madhavendra Puri. I have finally achieved the true reward of visiting the holy places. I have never seen symptoms of such divine love anywhere else. Madhavendra loses consciousness simply upon seeing a cloud in the sky."

Madhavendra embraced Nityananda Prabhu and wet him with his tears. He began to describe Nityananda's glories and became completely absorbed in this description. He took Nityananda to his breast; his throat was so choked with tears that he could not speak. He felt such deep affection for Nityananda that he would not let him go. He finally spoke, saying, "I know that Krishna is merciful to me, for He has given me a companion like Nityananda. Anyone who feels even the slightest enmity for Nityananda can never be dear to Krishna, no matter how much of a devotee he appears to be."

(Chaitanya Bhagavata 1.9.154-169)

The Bhakti-ratnākara also describes the glories of Madhavendra Puri and states that Nityananda treated him as a guru:

Madhavendra Puri is the embodiment of ecstatic loving devotion; simply by remembering his name, all perfections are achieved. Ishvara Puri, Ranga Puri and so many of his other disciples were intoxicated with the wine of devotion in the way he was. Madhavendra had many disciples throughout Bengal and Orissa, all of whom were devotees and fixed in prema bhakti.

(Bhakti-ratnākara 5.2272-4)

A few days later, in a holy place on the west coast of India, Nityananda met Madhavendra Puri. Who can describe the manifestations of love that arose upon their meeting? Only those who were there can know. Madhavendra treated Nityananda as a friend, an equal, but Nitai treated him like a superior. Madhavendra said, "I know that Krishna has been merciful toward me, for he has given me a companion like Nityananda." Even so, Nityananda never treated Madhavendra as anything but a guru.

(Bhakti-ratnākara 5.2330-2334)

GIRIDHARI GOPAL

After taking sannyas in Katwa, Mahaprabhu went to Shantipur and spent some time at Advaita Acharya's house. Then He proceeded from there to Sri Purushottam (Puri), following the path through Chatrabhog along the banks of the Ganges. He traveled through Atisar, Panihati, and Baranagar until finally He arrived at the border of the kingdom of Utkala (Orissa) at the place called Vriddha Mantreshwar. Nityananda Prabhu, Mukunda Datta, Jagadananda and Damodar were His companions on this journey. They came to the town of Remuna in the district of Baleshwar where they visited the deity Khirchora Gopinath. Afterward, Mahaprabhu recounted to His companions the story of Madhavendra Puri as He had heard it from His guru Ishvara Puri, at the same time telling how Khirchora Gopinath had earned His name:

One day Madhavendra Puri was circumambulating Govardhan in a state of total intoxication and absorption in love for Krishna. When he arrived at Govinda Kund, he took his bath and sat down beneath a tree to perform his evening *sandhyā* meditation and rituals. While he was so doing, a young cowherd boy carrying a pot of milk approached him and said with a smile, "What have you been thinking? Why don't you ask for something to eat? I have brought you some milk. Drink it."

When Madhavendra Puri saw the beautiful lad, he was so overcome that he completely forgot his hunger and thirst. Instead, he asked him, "Who are you? Where do you live? How did you know that I had not eaten?" The cowherd boy answered, "I am a cowherd and I live in this village. In our village, no one ever goes hungry. Some people beg for food, but if someone doesn't ask, then I bring him something to eat. The womenfolk came here to fetch water and saw that you had not eaten. They sent me here with this milk for you. But it is nearly milking time and I will have to leave. I'll come back later to fetch the pot."

Madhavendra Puri was astonished to see the boy walk away and disappear. He drank the milk and then, washed the pot and put it aside, waiting for the cowherd boy to return. He sat under the tree chanting the Holy Names until the end of the night when he started to doze. While asleep, he had a dream in which the cowherd youth came to him and led him by the hand to a wooded bower. The boy said, "I live here in this bower, but I am very uncomfortable due to the summer heat, the rains and the winter cold. Go and tell the village folk to help you uncover Me, and take Me to the top of the hill and build a shelter for Me. Then bathe Me with cool, clear water. I have been waiting for you for a long time, wondering when you would come to serve Me. I was waiting for your loving service so that I could show Myself and thereby save the entire universe.

"My name is Gopal, the lifter of Govardhan. Krishna's great grandson, Aniruddha's son Vajra, established My service so many years ago, but the pujari in charge of My service hid Me here when he fled out of fear of the Muslims. Since then I have been here. It is good that you have finally come here, now please dig Me up."

When Madhavendra awoke, he began to cry from his intense feelings of love, thinking, "Alas! Krishna himself came to me in the form of a cowherd boy and I was unable to recognize Him!" However, after a few moments he brought himself under control in order to carry out Gopal's orders. He took his morning bath and then gathered the village folk together and said, "Gopal, the lifter of Govardhan, is the deity of this village, but He is buried in this bower. Go and bring shovels, we have to dig Him up and release Him."

The village people enthusiastically started to clear the bower and soon discovered a large deity covered in earth and weeds. The strongest of the villagers lifted the deity and carried Him to the top of the hill where he placed Him on a large rock throne. In order to carry out the grand abhishek (bathing ceremony), the local Brahmins had water from Govinda Kund filtered and carried to the site in a hundred new jugs. When word got out about the discovery of the deity and it was announced that His puja and abhishek would soon be held, a joyful noise arose in all directions, musicians played on their instruments and the people danced and sang. The mountain was covered with all kinds of offerings, ghee, milk, yogurt and *sandeśa*, all gifts from the local people.

Madhavendra Puri himself performed the abhishek bathing ceremony. First of all, he cleaned the accumulated dirt from the body of the deity according to the regulations. The scriptures say that barley and wheat flour, and a powder made from *symplocos racemosa*, as well as the powder of pistachio nuts, saffron and pulses, are to be used to clean the deity's body. He also used a brush made from long *uṣīra* grasses and the hair of a cow's tail. Afterwards, he polished Gopal's body and made it shiny with oil, and then bathed Him again, first in *pañca-gavya* (milk, yogurt, clarified butter, cow's urine and dung) and then in *pañcāmṛta* (milk, yogurt, clarified butter, honey and sugar). This procedure is described in the *Hari-bhakti-vilāsa's* sixth chapter, where it is said,

tataḥ śaṅkhabhūtenaiva
kṣīreṇa snapayet kramāt
dadhnā ghṛtena madhunā
khaṇḍena ca pṛthak pṛthak

First bathe the deity with milk poured from a conch shell, then with yogurt, clarified butter, honey and finally sugar, each one separately. (Hari-bhakti-vilasa 6.30)

After this, Gopal was bathed with the hundred jugs of water. This was the great bathing ceremony—the *mahā-snāna*, in which ghee and water are used in equal parts, and a total of a hundred seers of water are needed. A seer is approximately equal to a liter. After bathing the deity in this way and then oiling Him once again, Madhavendra Puri bathed Him again in water scented with sandalwood and perfumes poured from a conch. The *Hari-bhakti-vilāsa* prescribes 100 *palas*[2] of water for the bath, another 25 of oil for the body, and then 2,000 *palas* for the *mahā-snāna*.

After the great bath was completed, the deity's entire body was dried with a cloth and He was dressed in a clean cloth and decorated with sandalwood, tulasi and flower garlands. Just as Krishna instructed the cowherds at the end of the Dvapara Yuga to worship Govardhan with a mountain of foodstuffs, so in the Kali Yuga, Madhavendra Puri ordered a mountain of food to be prepared for Giridhari Gopal. Ten Brahmins were engaged in preparing the rice, another five in cooking vegetable preparations, another five or six Brahmins prepared various types of breads, all of which was brought together in one place to be heaped up in the shape of a mountain. A pile of rice was surrounded by many clay pots filled with soups, cooked vegetable preparations, milk, yogurt, whey, *śikhariṇī* (a drink made of yogurt, milk, sugar, camphor and pepper), rice pudding, butter, and cream. When the mountain of food was ready, Madhavendra Puri made the offering along with many jugs filled with water. Gopal, who had not eaten for such a long time, hungrily ate everything He was offered. Even so, by His merciful touch, all the pots were again filled. Only Madhavendra saw how the Lord did this.

Afterwards, Madhavendra offered the deity a mouthwash and then pan. Then he performed the arati ceremony, after which he brought a new bed for Gopal to rest upon. When Gopal was finally taking rest, Madhavendra Puri fed the prasad of the *anna-kūṭa* festival, first to all the Brahmins and then to all the men, women and children, of the village.

Word spread to all the villages of the area that Gopal had made His appearance and people from each village took turns having their own feast on different days in His honor. "The people of Vraja are naturally affectionate toward Krishna. And Krishna, too, is affectionate to them."

(Chaitanya Charitamrita 2.4.95)

In time, the rich kshatriyas had a temple built for Gopal and gave Him ten thousand cows. Madhavendra Puri remained there for two years in Gopal's service until one day he again had a dream in which Gopal told him that He still suffered from the heat and that it was only by smearing Malayan sandalwood that He would be freed of the problem. Madhavendra was overjoyed to receive the Lord's direct order, and after engaging a qualified person to serve Him, started off on a journey to the east to find Malayan sandalwood.

Malaya refers to the Malabar Coast in Kerala at the very south of India, in what is known as the Western Ghats. This area is also known as Nilgiri or Malaya Parvata. Sandalwood is so closely associated with this area that the word *malayaja* ("born of Malaya") is a synonym for the perfumed wood.

THE STORY OF KHIRCHORA GOPINATH

While on his way to the South, Madhavendra stopped at Advaita Acharya's house in Shantipur and initiated him. From there he went on until he arrived at Remuna. Seeing the beautiful image of Gopinath in Remuna, Madhavendra was overwhelmed with love and started singing His names and danced for some time in ecstasy. He asked one of Gopinath's Brahmin servants what foods were offered to the deity. The Brahmin answered: "In the evening we give Gopinath twelve bowls of *amṛta-keli*, a thickened milk preparation that is like the nectar of the gods. It is famous everywhere as Gopinath's kṣīra, and no offering anywhere in the world is its equal."

(Chaitanya Charitamrita 2.4.119)

As the Brahmin spoke, other servants of Gopinath started to make the *amṛta-keli* offering to their deity. Madhavendra thought that if he could just get a taste of this preparation, he would be able to one day make it himself and offer it to his own Gopal. However, this very thought shamed him, as it is improper to desire the food intended for the Lord. After watching the arati ceremony, Madhavendra went outside and sat in the empty marketplace, chanting the Holy Names. Madhavendra followed *ayācaka-vṛtti*, which means he would never ask for food from anyone and only accepting the food that was spontaneously offered him. He was able to do this because he never felt hunger or thirst, as he was constantly engaged in drinking the nectar of prema and that kept him satisfied.

In the meantime, the pujari had finished his duties and was taking rest when he had a vision of the deity in a dream telling him, "Get up! Open the door. I have put a bowl of kṣīra aside for the sannyasi. It is hidden behind the pleats of my dhoti. You did not see me put it there because of my maya. The sannyasi, whose name is Madhava Puri, is sitting in the marketplace. Quickly take this kṣīra to him." (Chaitanya Charitamrita 2.4.127-129)

The pujari was startled by the dream and immediately got up. He bathed, opened the door to the altar and found a bowl of the *kṣīra* behind the deity's cloth, just as he had been told. He took the bowl and went to find Madhavendra Puri. He wandered through the market, shouting, "I have *kṣīra* here for Madhava Puri. Gopinath has stolen it for you. Take it and eat it with joy, for there is no person as fortunate as you in the three worlds."

(Chaitanya Charitamrita 2.4.133)

When Madhavendra heard the pujari shouting in this way, he approached him and identified himself. The pujari gave him the *kṣīra* and then fell at his feet. He recounted the whole story to Madhavendra, sending him into paroxysms of divine love for Krishna. He respectfully ate the prasad and then, after washing the clay bowl, broke it into many small pieces and wrapped them up in his outer garment. Each day thereafter, he would eat a piece of the clay bowl and once again feel the same ecstatic love. Knowing that word of this miracle would spread by morning, Madhavendra Puri became fearful of the celebrity that would inevitably befall him and the crowds of people that would then surround him. So, he paid his obeisance to Gopinath and left for Puri before dawn.

When Madhavendra arrived in Jagannath Puri, he visited Lord Jagannath and became ecstatic with love at seeing Him. News of the miracle at Remuna had reached Puri even before he had and countless people came to see him and pay him their respects. "The nature of fame in this world is well known: even if one does not seek it, it comes anyway as a result of one's destiny. Though Madhavendra Puri was afraid of being distracted by celebrity and ran away from it, when one has love for God, then celebrity comes flowing to him without being sought."

(Chaitanya Charitamrita 2.4.146)

Even though Madhavendra Puri wanted to avoid the attention that Krishna bestowed on him, he was not able to flee because he was committed to finding the sandalwood he had promised to bring Gopal. He went to the servants and directors of the Jagannath temple and explained his mission. Those who had contacts with the king interceded and collected both sandalwood and camphor on his behalf. They then arranged for another Brahmin and a servant to travel with him and help him carry the load. The king also gave him an official exemption paper to help him avoid customs duties.

On his return route, Madhavendra Puri stopped in Remuna again. Once again he danced and sang kirtan before Gopinath in a state of loving absorption and accepted the *kṣīra* prasad from the pujari. That night he slept in the temple. Once again he had a vision of Gopal, who spoke to him as follows: "Listen, Madhava. I have already received all the sandalwood and camphor. Now grind it into a paste and smear it on Gopinath's body. Gopinath and I are one and the same person; if you give Him the sandalwood, I will feel the cooling effect. Don't hesitate; don't doubt this message at all. Just believe Me and give Gopinath the sandalwood on my order."

(Chaitanya Charitamrita 2.4.158-161)

After having this dream, Madhavendra Puri summoned Gopinath's pujaris and servants to let them know what Gopal had told him. The pujaris were very happy to hear that Gopinath would be getting sandalwood paste, as it was the middle of summer. Madhavendra had his two companions, as well as two other people from the temple, daily grind the sandalwood into a paste. He stayed in Remuna until it had all been used up in Gopinath's service. At the end of the summer season, with the coming of the rains, Madhavendra returned to Puri where he observed Chaturmasya and demonstrated the exemplary character of his love for Krishna.

Gopal gave Madhavendra Puri the order to bring Him sandalwood paste to show the world the depth of his love. It was a great effort for Madhavendra to bring the sandalwood as far as Remuna, but he experienced it as a joy and not a difficulty. Gopal gave Madhavendra this commission in order to test him; but when he passed the test, He was merciful to His devotee.

(Chaitanya Charitamrta Madhya 4.187-189)

THE SANORIYA BRAHMIN

Madhavendra Puri mercifully bestowed love for Krishna on a Sanoriya Brahmin in Mathura. He accepted food from this Brahmin, knowing him to be a Vaishnava. By so doing, he showed how the *daiva-varṇāśrama* system is meant to operate. According to Srila Bhaktivinoda Thakur, members of the business community (*vaiśyas*) in the west of India are divided into several castes including Agrawalas, Kanwars, and Sanwars. Of these, the Agrawalas are considered to be very pure, while the two other groups, who are gold and jewelry merchants, are considered fallen as a result of their own actions. Those Brahmins who perform ritual activities for the Kanwars and Sanwars are known as Sanoriya Brahmins. Because of this low caste association, they are also considered to be fallen as a caste and sannyasis refuse to accept food in their homes.

Later on, when Mahaprabhu was traveling in northern India, He went to take food at this Sanoriya Brahmin's house between His visits to Kashi and Prayag because He knew that Madhavendra Puri had been merciful to him. He even showed him the respect that was due to senior personality, saying, "You are my guru, and I am practically your disciple. It is not fitting for a guru to pay obeisances to a disciple." (Chaitanya Charitamrita 2.17.170) This was the example that Mahaprabhu set.

MADHAVENDRA AND ISHVARA PURI

There is one last important incident from Madhavendra Puri's immaculate life left to be told. Ramachandra Puri and Ishvara Puri were two of Madhavendra's initiated disciples. However, Ramachandra was unable to receive his spiritual master's mercy because he showed him disrespect, whereas Ishvara Puri was blessed through his single-minded devotion to him and was thus able to attain the highest level of pure love for Krishna. Ramachandra was unable to understand the sweetness and supremacy of his gurudeva's feelings of separation and had the audacity to give him advice based on knowledge of Brahman. Madhavendra Puri became so angry that he shunned him completely. Even though he was such a great loving devotee, Madhavendra Puri became angry with his own disciple when he became offensive and chastised him severely, using harsh words. When Ramachandra told him to remember that he was a spiritual being, Madhavendra lost his temper and said:

"Get away from me, you most sinful rascal! I am dying from the distress of not having received Krishna's mercy, of not having attained Mathura, and you come to add to my misery! Go wherever you like, but don't show your face to me again! If I see you while I am dying, I will take a lower birth. I am dying from the distress of not having attained Krishna and this lowly fool is teaching me about Brahman."

As a result, Madhavendra Puri withdrew his blessings from his disciple, Ramachandra Puri, who then started to develop material desires. He became a dry philosopher without any interest in Krishna. Not only that, but he became critical of everyone and devoted himself to faultfinding. (Chaitanya Charitamrita 3.8.20-25)

Srila Prabhupada Bhaktisiddhanta Saraswati Thakur comments on this incident in his *Anubhāṣya*: "Even though Ramachandra Puri saw his own guru suffering of separation from Krishna, he was incapable of recognizing the transcendental nature of his transport of emotions. He judged his guru to be an ordinary man and took his mood to be mundane, the result of some material insufficiency. As a result Ramachandra tried to explain to him the value of experiencing the oneness of Brahman. Madhavendra Puri reacted unfavorably to his disciple's stupidity and disregard for his teachings and thus stopped wishing for his well-being. He abandoned him and drove him away." The words "material desires" (*vāsanā*) means "the desire for dry knowledge" and from that arose the tendency to criticize the devotees.

On the other hand, Ishvara Puri not only adhered to his guru's teachings, but served him physically and thus received his mercy. He served the lotus feet of his spiritual master, even to the point of personally cleaning his urine and feces, as well as helping him to perform shravan of Krishna's name and pastimes. In this way he satisfied him completely.

He continuously repeated the name of Krishna and recounted Krishna's pastimes to him. Madhavendra Puri was so pleased with Ishvara Puri that he embraced him and blessed him, saying, "May you have the treasure of love for Krishna!"

From that time onward, Ishvara Puri became an ocean of love for Krishna, while Ramachandra Puri became a mine of insults. These two personalities thus bear witness to the results of pleasing or displeasing a great soul. Madhavendra Puri taught this truth through them.

He was the spiritual master of the whole world and he gave the gift of love of God. He left this world while repeating this verse:

ayi dīnadayārdra nātha he,
mathurānātha kadāvalokyase
hṛdayaṁ tvad-aloka-kātaraṁ
dayita bhrāmyati kiṁ karomy aham

"O Lord, whose heart softens at seeing the condition of the unfortunate! Oh Lord of Mathura, when will I ever see you? My heart is filled with pain from not seeing you, my love, and I am confused. What can I do?"

When Mahaprabhu recited this verse, He became so intoxicated with divine love that Nityananda had to hold Him to calm Him down.

(Chaitanya Charitamrta 3.8.26-31)

Prabhupada Bhaktisiddhanta Saraswati writes, "The feeling of separation from Krishna, or transcendental *vipralambha* is the only practice by which the spirit soul can achieve perfection. Material feelings of separation give rise to a despondency that reveals the attachment one has for matter, whereas the despondency that results from the feelings of separation for Krishna are the best proof of one's desire to bring pleasure to His senses. The desire to bring pleasure to Krishna's senses shown by Madhavendra Puri, the great soul who is the root of this movement, is the ideal example to follow for anyone who wishes to serve the Lord. It is especially worth remarking that Mahaprabhu and His closest followers later adopted this example and made it their standard."

Madhavendra Puri's disappearance day is the *śuklā dvādaśī* of the month of Phalgun.

[2] A pala is a smaller measure of weight, about equal to 1.5 oz. or 45 grams. 25 palas of oil or ghee is thus about a liter, 2,000 palas of water about 80 liters.

ISHVARA PURIPADA

Ishvara Puri was born in the town of Kumara Hatta on the full moon day of the month of Jyestha to a family of Brahmins hailing from Rarha. Kumara Hatta is in the 24 Paraganas district about two miles from the Halisahar train station. The town is also important for Gaudiya Vaishnavas because Srivas Pandit and his brothers moved here after Mahaprabhu took sannyas because they were unable to tolerate all the painful reminders of Him in Nabadwip. Their house is not far from the place in the Mukhopadhyaya Para neighborhood where Ishvara Puri was born.

Ishvara Puri's birthplace is popularly known by the name "Chaitanya Doba." The word *ḍobā* means "a pool of water." When Chaitanya Mahaprabhu passed through Kumara Hatta on His way to Puri, He showed respect for His spiritual master by picking up some earth from the place of his birth, wrapping it in his cloth and taking it with him. Thousands of pilgrims have since followed His example, thus forming a pit that has since filled with water.

THE MERCY OF THE SPIRITUAL MASTER

Ishvara Puri is a sannyas name. Though his name prior to taking sannyas is unknown, we do know that his father's name was Shyamasundara Acharya. Ishvara Puri took initiation from Madhavendra Puri, the embodiment of nectarean devotional love. Madhavendra Puri was pleased with Ishvara Puri's guileless, sincere and affectionate service and thus showered him with blessings, so that he too became immersed in the ocean of love for Krishna. If a disciple can satisfy his spiritual master, then he will be fortunate and attain all auspiciousness and the fulfillment of all his desires. On the other hand, if the guru is unhappy with his disciple, then he will only know inauspiciousness. These teachings have been highlighted in the exemplary life of Madhavendra Puri.

Ramachandra Puri was another of Madhavendra Puri's initiated disciples, but because of his arrogance he was bereft of his guru's grace. Krishna Das Kaviraj has described the incident with great beauty in the Chaitanya Charitamrita (1.8.16-30) as follows:

Previously, when Madhavendra Puri was on his deathbed, Ramachandra Puri came to see him. Madhavendra Puri was singing the names of the Lord and crying out, "I have not attained Mathura!" Ramachandra then began to instruct him— he had no compunction about doing so, even though he was a disciple. He said, "Remember that you are completely full of the bliss of

Brahman. Why are you crying like this despite being knowledgeable of your own Brahma-nature?"

When Madhavendra Puri heard this, he became angry and began to rebuke Ramachandra saying, "Get away, get away, you most sinful rascal! I am dying from the distress of not having received Krishna's mercy, of not having attained Mathura, and you come to add to my misery! Go wherever you like, but don't show your face to me again! If I see you while I am dying I will take a lower birth. I am dying from the distress of not having attained Krishna and this lowly fool is teaching me about Brahman."

As a result, Madhavendra Puri withdrew his blessings from his disciple who thenceforth started to develop material desires. He became a dry philosopher without any interest in Krishna. Not only that, but he became critical of everyone and devoted himself to faultfinding.

Ishvara Puri, on the other hand, served his guru, even personally cleaning his urine and feces. He continuously repeated the name of Krishna and recounted Krishna's pastimes to him. Madhavendra Puri was so pleased with Ishvara Puri that he embraced him and blessed him, saying, "May you have the treasure of love for Krishna!"

From that time onward, Ishvara Puri became an ocean of love for Krishna, while Ramachandra Puri became a mine of insults. These two personalities thus bear witness to the results of pleasing or displeasing a great soul. Madhavendra Puri taught this truth through them.

In this connection Bhaktisiddhanta Saraswati Goswami Prabhupada has written in his *Anubhāṣya*, "Even though Ramachandra Puri saw his own guru suffering of separation from Krishna, he was incapable of recognizing the transcendental nature of this transport of emotions. He judged his guru to be an ordinary man and took his mood to be mundane, the result of some material insufficiency. As a result he tried to explain to him the value of experiencing the oneness of Brahman. Madhavendra Puri reacted to his disciple's stupidity and disregard for his instructions and thus stopped wishing for his welfare. He abandoned him and drove him away."

MAHAPRABHU TAKES INITIATION FROM ISHVARA PURI

Mahaprabhu is the Supreme Personality of Godhead and has no need of any teacher. Even so, He wishes to teach the world that it is absolutely necessary to take shelter of a bonafide spiritual master. For this reason, He played the role of a disciple by taking initiation from Ishvara Puri when He met him at Gaya. This in itself shows beyond a doubt Ishvara Puri's greatness and importance.

Then the Lord went to Gaya where He met Ishvara Puri. After taking initiation from him, He started to display the signs of love of God, and when He returned to His homeland He began to engage in the pastimes of divine love. (Chaitanya Charitamrita 1.17.8-9)

When they met, Mahaprabhu and Ishvara Puri were overcome by the ecstasy of love and drenched each other in tears of prema that fell from their eyes. The Lord said, "My pilgrimage to Gaya is successful, for today I have seen your lotus feet. When one makes the *piṇḍa* (offering to the ancestors at a holy place), then that ancestor is delivered. But simply by seeing you, ten million ancestors are delivered from all forms of bondage in a single moment. Therefore no holy place is your equal, and you are the primary source of auspiciousness for even the holy places. Please lift Me up from the ocean of material suffering; I offer this body up to your service. The only gift I ask of you is that you give Me the nectar of Krishna's lotus feet to drink."

(Chaitanya Bhagavata 1.17.49-55)

Mahaprabhu was acting the role of an ordinary mortal, a pilgrim who had come to Gaya to offer the *śrāddha* oblations for His deceased father. On the day that He performed these rituals, He returned to His room and began to cook. When Ishvara Puri came and placed his holy feet in Mahaprabhu's room, Mahaprabhu personally served him the rice and vegetables that He Himself had cooked with great satisfaction. In so doing, Mahaprabhu demonstrated most perfectly how to serve the guru.

ISHVARA PURI IN NABADWIP

Ishvara Puri had met Mahaprabhu in Nabadwip even prior to giving him the ten-syllable mantra in Gaya. He also met with Advaita Acharya, who had similarly played the role of Madhavendra Puri's disciple. Vrindavan Das Thakur has described this meeting in the Chaitanya Bhagavata.

Once, Ishvara Puri passed through Nabadwip when Nimai was still engaged in His pastimes as a student. He stayed there for a few months in the house of Gopinath Acharya as his guest. One day he saw Nimai and was most impressed and attracted by His bodily beauty. Nimai invited Ishvara Puri to his house to eat and had His mother Sachi cook and serve Him Krishna prasad. Then He and Ishvara Puri began talking about Krishna.

Ishvara Puri also met Gadadhar Pandit and was pleased when he saw the depth of his renunciation. He started to affectionately give him lessons from *Śrī-Kṛṣṇa-līlāmṛta*, a book of his own composition. Nimai would also come daily to Gopinath Acharya's house to visit Ishvara Puri while he was teaching Gadadhar and offer him His obeisances. One day, Ishvara Puripada asked Nimai to correct any mistakes that were in his book. Nimai answered:

"Anyone who finds any fault with a devotee's description of Krishna is a sinner. If a devotee writes a poem, no matter how poorly he does it, it will certainly contain his love for Krishna. A fool says 'viṣṇāya' while a scholar knows the correct form is 'viṣṇave', but Krishna accepts the sentiment in either case. If anyone sees a fault in this, the fault is his, for Krishna is pleased with anything the pure devotee says. You too describe the Lord with words of love, so what arrogant person would dare criticize anything that you have written?" (Chaitanya Bhagavata 1.11.105-110)

The same incident is described in the *Bhakti-ratnākara* in the following way:

Look here, this is the house of Gopinath Acharya where Visvambhara would visit from time to time. Ishvara Puri stayed here for a while and composed his book Śri-Kṛṣṇa-līlāmṛta. He had great affection for Gadadhar Pandit and when he saw the symptoms of love for Krishna in him, he taught him that book. (Bhakti-ratnākara 12.2205-7)

When Nityananda Prabhu was traveling in the west of India, he incidentally met Madhavendra Puri there. When the two met, they fainted. Nityananda was overcome by love and started to describe Madhavendra Puri's glories while Madhavendra Puri himself embraced Nityananda and wet him with his tears. Ishvara Puripada understood that Nityananda was extremely dear to his spiritual master and so, like his guru's other disciples, held him in great affection and felt a deep love for him.

All glories to Madhava Puri, the ocean of love for Krishna! He was the first shoot of the desire tree of devotion. That first shoot was nourished and grew in the form of Ishvara Puri and from him the thick trunk of Chaitanya lila took shape. (Chaitanya Charitamrita 1.9.10-11)

Before he left this world, Ishvara Puri sent two of his disciples, Kashisvara and Govinda, to serve Mahaprabhu. Even though they were His godbrothers, Mahaprabhu still obeyed the order of His spiritual master and accepted them as His servants.

Sri Ranga Puri

Mahaprabhu met Sri Ranga Puri and put an end to the sufferings of Rama Das. (Chaitanya Charitamrita 2.1.113)

During His travels through South India, Mahaprabhu came to the town Pandharpur on the banks of the Bhima River. Pandharpur is in the Sholapur district of Maharashtra and is the home of the four-armed deity of Narayan, Vitthaladeva, who is so beloved of the Marathi people. Pandharpur is also well known as the home of the famous Marathi Vaishnava saint Tukarama, who lived there in the 15th century of the Shaka era.

(Anubhasya 2.9.282)

While in Pandharpur, Mahaprabhu was invited by a Brahmin to his home where He was lavishly fed. While there, He heard that Madhavendra Puri's disciple, Sri Ranga Puri, was staying nearby in another Brahmin's house. Mahaprabhu immediately went there to meet him. He prostrated himself before his guru's godbrother and was immediately inspired by a mood of ecstatic love. Sri Ranga Puri was also impressed by the sight of Mahaprabhu's ecstatic symptoms. He guessed that the Lord must have some relation to the spirit of devotion promulgated by his own spiritual master, without which such symptoms would be impossible. He lifted the Lord up and embraced Him and the two of them began to cry in devotional ecstasy.

Krishna Das Kaviraj's account of this meeting is given as follows:

From there Sri Chaitanya Mahaprabhu went to Pandharpur, where He joyfully saw the temple of Vitthala Thakur. A local Brahmin was delighted when he saw the Lord chanting and dancing in ecstatic love and invited Him to his home for lunch. The Brahmin offered Mahaprabhu food with great respect and love. After the Lord finished His lunch, He heard the auspicious news that Sri Ranga Puri, one of Sri Madhavendra Puri's disciples, was currently residing in Pandharpur at the home of another Brahmin. The Lord immediately went to that Brahmin's home and, upon entering, saw Sri Ranga Puri. He was overwhelmed with ecstatic love and prostrated Himself in obeisance. All the symptoms of ecstatic transformation were visible in His body—tears, jubilation, trembling and perspiration.

(Chaitanya Charitamrita 2.9.282-7)

Upon learning that Mahaprabhu was Ishvara Puripada's disciple, Sri Ranga Puri was filled with great affection for Him. Just by touching each other, they were both flooded with ecstatic feelings. They passed seven days together in discussions of Krishna consciousness. Sri Ranga Puri was overjoyed to hear that the Lord's birthplace was in Nabadwip. He told the Lord that he had previously been to Nabadwip with his spiritual master and that they had eaten at Jagannath Mishra's house. He recalled that Jagannath's wife Sachi had fed them a delicious banana flower curry. She had served the sannyasis as though they were her own sons as if the Mother of the Universe had become incarnate in her. Sri Ranga Puri continued to tell Mahaprabhu that Sachi and Jagannath had a worthy son who took sannyas, taking on the name Shankararanya, but who had died there in Pandharpur.

Upon hearing all this, Mahaprabhu was overcome with feelings of separation and He told Sri Ranga Puri that Shankararanya was His very own brother and that Jagannath and Sachi were His father and mother. After they finished their conversation, Sri Ranga Puri went on to Dvaraka while the Lord continued following the Krishnavenva River.

Madhavendra Puri is an abode of divine loving sentiments. Simply by remembering his name one achieves all perfection. All of his disciples, such as Ishvara Puri and Sri Ranga Puri, were similarly intoxicated with moods of sacred rapture. (Bhakti-ratnākara 5.2272-3)

Some people say that Sri Ranga Puri later came to Jagannath Puri to join the Lord and spend the remainder of his life in His association.

SRI JAGANNATH MISHRA

Jagannath Mishra was born in the village of South Dhaka in Sylhet. His grandfather, Madhu Mishra had four sons: Upendra, Rangada, Kirtida, and Kirtivasa. His father and mother, Upendra Mishra and Kalavati, had seven sons: Kamsari, Paramananda, Padmanabha, Sarveshvara, Jagannath Mishra, Janardana and Trailokyanath.

(*Prema-vilāsa*, 24).

purā yaśodā-vrajarāja-nandau
vṛndāvane prema-rasākarau yau
śacī-jagannath-purandarābhidhau
babhūvatus tau na ca saṁśayo'tra

amū āviśatām eva devāvaditi-kaśyapau
śrī-kauśalyā-daśarathau tathā śrī-pṛṣni-tatpatī

According to the *Gaura-gaṇoddeśa-dīpikā*, Upendra was Krishna's grandfather, the cowherd Parjanya, while Jagannath was Nanda Maharaj in Krishna's Vraja pastimes (*Gaura-gaṇoddeśa-dīpikā* 37). Other parents of the Lord's incarnations, such as Kashyapa, Dasharath, Sutapa and Vasudeva and their wives, entered into Jagannath and Sachi for the Lord's pastimes.

The king of Vraja has become Chaitanya's father, Jagannath; the queen of Vraja is His mother Sachi. The son of Nanda is Chaitanya Gosai and Baladeva is His brother Nityananda. (Chaitanya Charitamrita 1.17.94-295)

In the Chaitanya Charitamrita it is also stated that Jagannath Mishra was known by his title Purandara, which is an epithet of Indra. His wife Sachi Devi's father was named Nilambara Chakravarti.

(Chaitanya Charitamrita 1.13.59-60)

THE BIRTH OF MAHAPRABHU

At first, eight baby girls were born to Jagannath and Sachi, but each of them died at birth. Jagannath then performed a special ceremony to have a son, and not long afterward a boy, Vishvarupa, was born. Vishvarupa is a manifestation of Baladeva and belongs to the same ontological category in the spiritual world, named Sankarshan. Vishvarupa took sannyas at the age of twelve, adopting the name Shankararanya. He left this world in the year 1509 in Pandharpur, in the Solapur district of Maharashtra.

Jagannath Mishra and Sachi Devi are eternally liberated companions of Krishna; thus, it is clear that their heart and body are made of pure goodness or *śuddha-sattva*. Another name for pure goodness is *vasudeva*. Krishna is named *Vāsudeva* because He takes pleasure in the spiritual nature and makes His appearance through pure goodness or *vasudeva*.

At sundown on the full moon day of the month of Phalgun in 1486, at the auspicious moment of a lunar eclipse, amidst the joyful sounds that filled the sky the cries of "Hari!" and "Krishna!" made by the townspeople, the *uludhvani* of the womenfolk, and the divine instruments of the gods in heaven—Gauranga Mahaprabhu accepted Jagannath Mishra and Sachi Devi as His father and mother and appeared in the holy dham of Sri Mayapur.

It is said that witches, evil female spirits and other powerful demonic specters cannot go near a neem tree. Out of their feelings of maternal love, Sachi and the other women named the Lord "Nimai" in order that He be protected from any inauspiciousness. Later, when Nimai took the renounced order of life, He was given the name Sri Krishna Chaitanya. Some of the other names by which He is known are Visvambhara, Nabadwip Chandra, Gaura Hari, Gauranga and Mahaprabhu.

When Sachi and Jagannath saw their child's face, they forgot themselves in their excitement. Nilambar Chakravarti was a great astrologer and when he examined the constellations at the baby's birth, he divined that He was to be a king among kings, that He was to possess all virtues, indeed that He was Narayan Himself. Jagannath and his entire household were immersed in the ocean of ecstasy upon hearing these predictions.

This ocean only increased in fullness as the baby Nimai began to display His childhood pastimes. Whenever Nimai cried, the adults would sing the Holy Names in order to pacify Him. When He was only four months old, He started throwing various household articles about, but as soon as He caught sight of His mother, He would lie down and start to cry. Sachi would sing the Holy Names to stop Him from crying, and only when He had stopped would she notice the mess the baby had made of the room. Because He was so young, she never suspected Him of creating the disorder; rather, she thought that it must have been some evil spirit whose efforts to harm the baby had failed due to the protective incantations she was always making over Him.

When the time came for Nimai's name-giving ceremony, Nilambar Chakravarti and other learned men in the community called him Vishvambhar, which is thus his principal name, while the women gave him the name Nimai. This latter name was given because neem leaves have a bitter taste and are said to keep death away, and they wished to bless Nimai with a long life. The name-giving ceremony is also the occasion when a child's tastes and tendencies are tested. Jagannath placed rice, puffed rice, gold, silver and a manuscript of the Srimad Bhagavatam before the child, who ignored everything to reach out for the Holy Scripture. All were delighted by Nimai's choice. The philosophers amongst them began to say, "Nimai will be a great scholar." In fact, Nimai wished to show even at this young age that the Bhagavatam is the supreme authority in spiritual matters. This is the lesson hidden within this lila.

NIMAI'S CHILDHOOD

As Nimai grew, he began to crawl, giving pleasure to His mother and father and all their neighbors. One day, the child saw the god Sesha in the form of a cobra in the garden. He played with him for a while in the mood of a golden Narayan, and then like Narayan, curled up on the coiled snake and fell asleep. When Jagannath Mishra came upon this scene, he feared the worst for the child and started to shout and cry, frightening the beast, which then slithered away. Nevertheless, Sachi and Jagannath had seen the wondrous form that the child had displayed and became convinced that He was a divine personality.

The neighborhood women found that whenever they loudly chanted the names of the Lord, Nimai would stop crying and start dancing in ecstasy, even rolling about in the dust. So every morning they would surround Him and sing the Holy Names. Whether they knew Him or not, people would be attracted by His beautiful appearance and affectionately give Him *sandeśa* sweets or bananas. Nimai would take all these sweets and fruits and give them to the women who sang for Him as prasad.

When Nimai was able to walk, He would go into the neighbors' houses and take milk and rice, and if He found nothing to eat, He would break various household items. This naughty behavior is a source of delight for His devotees. On one occasion, as Nimai was playing in front of Jagannath Mishra's house, two thieves saw that he was wearing valuable ornaments and became greedy. They charmed the child by offering Him a ride on their shoulders and then started to carry Him away. However, they were bewildered by Vishnu's illusory power and shortly found themselves back in front of Nimai's own home. Frightened by this unexpected turn of events, the two scoundrels ran away. Meanwhile, Jagannath had been searching anxiously for Nimai. When he saw that his child had returned, he held Him tightly to his heart and felt as though his life had also been returned him.

One day Jagannath Mishra asked Nimai to bring him a book from inside the house. When Nimai ran to fetch it, Sachi was surprised to hear the wondrous jingling of ankle bells. After Nimai had given His father the book and gone off to play, Sachi was amazed to see that His footprints held the auspicious signs of the flag, lightning bolt, elephant rod and banner. Under the influence of parental love, Jagannath and Sachi were not able to accept that these were Nimai's own footprints, but took them rather to be the traces of Damodar, their household Shalagram Shila deity, and so they performed a special ceremony for the deity, bathing Him, peforming the puja and offering food.

BABY NIMAI STEALS GOPAL'S OFFERINGS

On another day, a Brahmin pilgrim passed through Nabadwip with Bala Gopal, his deity of the baby Krishna. Jagannath offered the Brahmin a place to perform his puja as well as food to cook for an offering. When the pilgrim had finished cooking, he sat down to offer the bhoga to his deity. But as soon as he started meditation on his mantra, Nimai came and began eating the offering. The Brahmin saw this and started to shout in distress. Jagannath Mishra was extremely disturbed by the incident and the Brahmin had to intercede to stop him from giving the child a spanking.

Although the Brahmin did not want to cook again, Jagannath begged him to do so. Before he recommenced preparing the offering, Jagannath took Nimai to a neighbor's house so that He would not do any more mischief. Once again, when the Brahmin sat down to meditate on his Bala Gopal mantra to make his offering, Gaura Gopal appeared out of nowhere and started to enjoy the foodstuffs. The Brahmin again began to shout in frustration, "Everything's ruined. Everything's ruined!" For a second time, Jagannath was devastated and once again was about to punish the child, only to be stopped by his guest. The Brahmin said, "He's only a child and doesn't understand anything. It's not His fault. It seems that it is not my destiny to eat today."

This time, Nimai's older brother Vishvarupa begged the Brahmin to try a third time, and so finally, on his insistence, he began to cook again. It was quite late at night and Nimai was fast asleep in His room so no one suspected there would be any more trouble. Even so, the Brahmin waited until the entire household had gone to bed before making his offering; but once again, contrary to all expectation, Gaura Gopal came to consume it. This time however, He gave the Brahmin a vision of an extraordinary eight-armed form. In four of these hands, He held the conch, discus, mace and lotus flower of Narayan; but in the palm of another hand, He held a lump of butter from which he was taking morsels with another. The last two hands were engaged in playing a flute. When the pilgrim Brahmin saw this wonderful vision, he fainted completely away.

When he came to consciousness, Nimai told him not to reveal this pastime to anyone. He told him, "You have been My servant for many, many births. Indeed, this very same lila also took place at Nanda's house in Gokula."

The Brahmin decided to stop his travels and remain forever in Nabadwip to be close to his Lord. Every evening, after finishing his daily activities, he would return to Nimai's house to behold his worshipable Lord.

NIMAI'S EDUCATION

Nimai underwent the three rituals (*saṁskāras*) in which a child's ears are pierced, his hair is shorn and his education is begun. Jagannath Mishra himself performed all these rituals. It took Nimai only three days to learn the entire alphabet and He started to read and write all of Krishna's names.

The little Gaura Gopal would often ask His parents to bring Him birds, even the stars or the moon, and would cry if they could not do so. When they chanted the Holy Names, He would stop crying, otherwise there was no way to quiet Him. One day however, though they repeatedly sang the names of Hari, the child's tears did not stop flowing. When pressed to tell them why He was crying so insistently, Nimai said that though it was Ekadasi, He wanted to eat the offerings that the Brahmins Jagadish and Hiranya had made to their Vishnu deity. Jagannath was astonished to hear this unusual request, but went to the house of his two friends. He told them what had happened, and they were delighted to give him the offering. When Jagannath brought the prasad home and gave it to

Nimai, He finally stopped crying.

Nimai continued his naughty behavior and the males in the community reported it to his father, while the girls and women would complain to Sachi. Though Jagannath would be angry and want to punish his child, he would be quite astonished to see Him completely calm and free from any guilty demeanor. Both parents wondered, "Who is this child? Has Nandanandan Krishna secretly appeared here as our son?"

Vishvambhar's older brother Vishvarupa had been indifferent to material life throughout his childhood. After studying at Advaita Acharya's school, (Tol), he came to understand that the ultimate conclusion of the scriptures was devotion to Krishna. When he was twelve years old and his parents started making arrangements for his marriage, Vishvarupa left home and was initiated as a sannyasi, taking the name Shankararanya. This event traumatized Sachi and Jagannath, who were greatly pained by separation from their oldest son. As a result, Jagannath was afraid that Nimai too would become detached from family life through studying the scriptures, so he stopped His education. Better that He should remain a fool at home than become a scholar only to abandon His family!

This decision did not please Nimai and He started to misbehave again. One day, He went and sat down in the rubbish heap where used and contaminated pottery was thrown. When Sachi saw this, she became angry and told Him several times to leave this filthy area. Nimai answered her in the spirit of the divine philosopher Dattatreya, "How can a fool tell the difference between what is pure and what is not? How can the pots that have been used to cook for Vishnu possibly be contaminated? What is more, how can any place be considered impure if I am there? Ideas of purity and impurity from the *karma-kāṇḍa* have no place in devotion to the Lord. Such concepts are just the imaginings of people who know nothing but the material world."

Seeing that the boy would in no way heed her order to leave the unclean spot, Sachi finally dragged Him away by force, made Him bathe and then took a bath herself. After this, she and other members of the community approached Jagannath Mishra and entreated him to allow Nimai to resume His studies. Thus Jagannath was forced to relent.

Some time after this incident, Nimai's sacred thread ceremony was held. After the fire sacrifice, Nimai went out to beg alms, just as Vaman did. Jagannath then entrusted Him to Ganga Das Pandit, who is none other than the same Sandipani Muni who gave Krishna His education. Ganga Das Pandit was overjoyed to accept the handsome and virtuous child as his student. Nimai would ask him and his fellow students trick questions based on logic and the ensuing arguments would be a source of amazement to everyone.

Jagannath was pleased to see his son take up a disciplined life in which He would bathe daily in the Ganges, perform puja to Vishnu strictly according to the regulations, and offer water to the sacred tulasi plant before finally taking prasad. Nimai would then go to a place where He could be undisturbed and study. Jagannath prayed to Krishna for Nimai's continued welfare, but at the same time was always afraid that He would come to understand the emptiness of the cycle of *saṁsāra* and eventually leave home. One day Jagannath had a dream in which he saw Mahaprabhu's beautiful form as a sannyasi, performing sankirtan, dancing, singing, laughing, and crying while surrounded by His devotees. After this, he began to think it inevitable that Nimai would one day leave home. Sachi Devi tried to convince Jagannath that because Nimai had become so attached to His studies, He would never leave, but she failed. As it happened, Nimai's father left this world before He became a sannyasi. On the death of His father, Gaurasundara lamented just like Ramachandra did upon hearing of the death of Dasharath, but still showed great strength of character to console His heartbroken mother.

SRILA JAGADISH PANDIT

apare yajña-patnyau śrī-jagadīśa-hiraṇyakau
ekādaśyāṁ yayor annaṁ prārthayitvā'ghasat prabhuḥ

The wives of the sacrificing Brahmins in Vraja took birth as Jagadish and Hiranya. The Lord (Mahaprabhu) asked for and ate their prasad on the Ekadasi day.

(*Gaura-gaṇoddeśa-dīpikā* 192)

āsīd vraje chandrahāso nartako rasa-kovidaḥ
so'yaṁ nṛtya-vinodī śrī-jagadīśākhyaḥ paṇḍitaḥ

In Vraja there was a dancer named Chandrahasa who was very expert in the tasting of rasa. In Chaitanya-lila he became Jagadish Pandit, who also took great pleasure in dancing for the Lord.

(Gaura-gaṇoddeśa-dīpikā 143)

Jagadish Pandit is simultaneously considered to be both Nityananda-*śākhā* and Chaitanya-*śākhā*, that is, a branch both of Chaitanya as well as Nityananda in the desire tree of devotion. He took birth in the town of Gauhati (Pragjyotishpur) in modern Assam. His father's name was Kamalaksha Bhatta. Both of his parents were devotees of Vishnu. When they died, he came with his wife Duhkhini and his brother Hiranya to Mayapur on the shores of the Ganga where they built a home near to that of Jagannath Mishra. Jagadish Pandit subsequently became Jagannath Mishra's very close friend.

Jagadish and his wife Duhkhini had the same kind of parental affection for little Nimai as Jagannath and Sachi. Duhkhini was like a mother to Him and even sometimes acted as His wet-nurse. Nimai, the son of Sachi, is none other than the son of Yashoda, the supreme Lord Krishna incarnate. It is not possible for anyone but an eternal associate of the Lord to have the good fortune to treat Him like a son in this way.

NIMAI BEGS FOR JAGADISH'S OFFERING

Mahaprabhu showed through His pastimes just how dear He considered Jagadish Pandit to be. Sriman Mahaprabhu is the father of sankirtan and even as a child He tricked everyone into chanting the Holy Names. Sachi and all the neighbors would clap their hands and sing the names of the Lord to make Him stop crying. One Ekadasi day, however, Nimai kept on crying despite Sachi Mata and Jagannath Mishra's chanting the Names in the usual way. Confused and anxious, His parents finally asked Him out of desperation, "What do you want, child? What must we give you to make you to stop crying?"

Nimai answered, "They have made a rice offering to Vishnu at Jagadish's house today. I want to eat some of that prasad. Give Me some of that prasad and I will stop crying."

Jagannath Mishra was surprised to hear Nimai say such things. How could He know that Jagadish Pandit was making a rice offering on Ekadasi? Jagannath Mishra immediately went to his neighbor's house and was surprised to see that a large offering of rice and other dishes had indeed been made to their Vishnu deity. Jagannath told Jagadish of Nimai's request, adding that he was worried that it would not be correct for him to eat rice on Ekadasi day. But Gauranga's eternal associate Jagadish Pandit knew that it was little Gopal in the form of Nimai who was hungry. Without any hesitation he gave the entire offering to Jagannath Mishra. As soon as Nimai received the plate, He immediately stopped crying and joyfully started to eat.

Jagadish Pandit and Hiranya [are Chaitanya's branches of the desire tree of devotion]. The merciful Lord gave them His grace when He was a little boy. He ate the offerings to Vishnu at their house on the Ekadasi day.

(Chaitanya Charitamrita 1.10.70-71)

Jagadish Pandit purifies the entire universe, for the nectar of love for Krishna pours from him like torrents of rain.

(Chaitanya Charitamrita 1.11.30)

The abovementioned pastime is described in the Chaitanya Bhagavata, *Ādi-khaṇḍa*, chapter 4.

The Lord grabs the things of the devotee even if he doesn't offer them, but He shows no interest whatsoever in the gifts of the non-devotee.

Just as Mahaprabhu was conquered by the devotion of Jagadish Pandit, so too was His dearest companion Nityananda Prabhu who considered him to be one of His own intimate associates. Nityananda Prabhu was Jagadish's life and soul. Jagadish was present in Panihati for the Chira-dadhi Mahotsava (the great chipped rice and yogurt festival).

JAGADISH AND JAGANNATH DEVA

Before taking sannyas, Mahaprabhu ordered Jagadish to go to Nilachala to preach Krishna bhakti and the religious practice of the age, Harinam sankirtan. The son of Nanda, Sri Krishna and the son of Jagannath Mishra, Sri Gaurasundar, are the same supreme divinity as Jagannath. When Jagadish arrived in Puri, he went for Lord Jagannath's darshan and melted with love when he saw Him. On his way back to Bengal, however, he felt extreme separation from Jagannath. Thousands and thousands of people go on pilgrimage to Puri every single day. All of them take darshan of Jagannath, but how many of them are overcome by feelings of separation when returning home? Perhaps once in a while some fortunate individual is able to feel such emotions. If one truly feels such pangs of separation, then this is a sign of Jagannath's mercy; if not, then one has not truly received the grace of the Lord.

Jagannath Deva saw Jagadish crying and mercifully appeared to him in a dream and told him to take His *vigraha* and serve it. Simultaneously, He appeared to the king of Orissa and ordered him that at the time of the *nava-kalevara*, when the wooden deity of Jagannath is renewed, the outgoing form should be given to Jagadish Pandit. As a result of this dream, the Maharaj considered it to be a great honor to give Jagadish Lord Jagannath's outgoing form, which is known as the *samādhi-stha-vigraha*.

Jagadish prayed to Jagannath, asking Him how he could possibly carry the deity's heavy body all the way back to Bengal. Jagannath answered that for his sake He would become as light as cork. Then Jagadish was to cover Him with a piece of new cloth and then carry Him suspended on the end of a staff. Jagannath further told him that he would have to make permanent arrangements to stay wherever He was set down on the ground. Jagadish enlisted the aid of two Brahmins and they took turns carrying Jagannath as far as the village of Jashora on the banks of the Ganges, near the town of Chakdaha. Jagadish left Jagannath with one of the Brahmins and went to take his bath in the Ganges and to perform oblations of Ganga water. While he was gone, the Brahmin found that Jagannath was suddenly becoming very heavy and that he was no longer able to hold Him up. When Jagadish came back from his bath, he saw Jagannath sitting on the ground and realized that the Lord wanted to stay in that very spot.

Chakdaha is a historical site and an ancient holy place. During the Puranic age, it was known as Rathavarma. Pradyumna killed the demon Sambara there during Krishna's incarnation at the end of the Dvapara age and thus it was known as Pradyumna-nagara. Prior to that, when Bhagiratha was bringing down the Ganga in order to save the Sagara dynasty, he buried the wheel of his chariot here. Thus the town was also given the name Chakradaha, which in time has been corrupted into Chakdaha. When the local people heard that the Jagannath deity from Puri had come to stay in Jashora, they flocked there in the thousands to seek His darshan. This is how Jagadish decided to remain in Jashora rather than return to to his home in Mayapur.

Being attracted by Jagadish Pandit and his wife's parental devotion, Nityananda Prabhu and Chaitanya

Mahaprabhu both visited the Jagannath temple in Jashora on two different occasions. The two Prabhus held sankirtan and a feast both times. As the Lord was about to leave Jashora to go to Puri, Duhkhini began to cry from the imminent separation so intensely that the Lord agreed to remain behind in the form of the Gaura Gopal deity. In the course of the couple's householder life, they also had a son named Ramabhadra.

THE JASHORA TEMPLE AFTER JAGADISH PANDIT

At first the deity was kept under a Bata tree near the Ganges, and later the king of Krishnagar, Krishna Chandra, had a temple built there for Him. When the temple became old and dilapidated, Umesh Chandra Majumdar's wife Mokshada Devi arranged for repairs to be made. The temple building has no spire, but has been constructed in the manner of an ordinary house. Along with Jagannath, it houses Sri Sri Radha Vallabha and Gaura Gopal. The staff that Jagadish Pandit used to carry the deity from Puri continues to be kept there. Devotees for the service of the Jagannath deity donated a large amount of land, but over the course of time, Jagadish Pandit's descendants sold it all off in order to keep the service of the deity alive. No Rathayatra festival is held here, though his Snana Yatra is celebrated with great pomp. On that occasion, the deity is carried from the temple to an altar built in a large field not far from the temple for the purpose of the bathing ritual. A mela or fair is also held in the field, attracting countless people. This Jashora Jagannath Snana Yatra fair is still very well known. There is also a 500 year-old dais (wooden platform) for Dola Yatra at the site that is used to swing Radha Vallabha on Phalguni purnima.

Siddha Bhagavan Das Babaji of Khalna stayed in Jashora for some time to do his bhajan. There is an annual festival celebrating Jagadish Pandit's disappearance day on the third day of the waxing moon (*śuklā tṛtīyā*) in the month of Paush (December-January). His appearance day is the twelfth day of the waxing moon (*śuklā dvādaśī*) in the same month.

Jagadish Pandit's temple is currently under the management of the Sri Chaitanya Gaudiya Math. How this came to pass was described in the *Chaitanya Vāṇī* magazine (2.9) in the following way:

"The Supreme Lord is most affectionate to His devotees and is conquered by their love. How many different stratagems He engages in just to accept the service of His devotee! Though served in Goloka by hundreds of thousands of goddesses of fortune, Govinda still seems to not have enough people to serve Him. It is as though He feels that the service is not being conducted as it should. How many tricks He plays in order to engage the devotee He wants in His service!

Just look at the ploy that Govardhan-dhari Gopal used to engage Madhavendra Puri. His previous pujari had buried Him in the jungle on top of Govardhan out of fear of Muslim marauders. Gopal waited there patiently until Puripada happened by. He said to him, "I have been waiting impatiently for you for many days, just wondering when Madhavendra will come to render Me service." The Lord plays His cosmic game and these are all different aspects of His pastime.

So now, the very same Jagannath and Gaura Gopal deities who were worshiped by Nityananda Prabhu's dear associate, Jagadish Pandit, have similarly displayed the wonderful pastime of voluntarily offering Themselves to the great devotee, Tridandi Swami Srimad Bhakti Dayita Madhava Maharaj, in order to accept his service."

Due to increasing monetary difficulties three of Jagadish Pandit's descendants, Vishvanath Goswami, Shambhunath Mukhopadhyaya and Mrityunjaya Mukhopadhyaya, had come to realize that they were no longer able to maintain the day-to-day service nor undertake the annual festivals of their ancestral deities. The condition of the temple buildings had also deteriorated and they were unable to make the necessary repairs. As a result, they decided to take the counsel of Sri Panchu Thakur of Jashora and Santosh Kumar Mallik of Ranaghat and eventually surrender the temple, without conditions, to my spiritual master, the founder and acharya of Sri Chaitanya Gaudiya Math, Om 108 Sri Srimad Bhakti Dayita Madhava Goswami Maharaj. Guru Maharaj immediately spent a large sum of money on making the needed repairs and improvements to the temple, adding electric lighting and a new hostel building.

In the first year after taking over Jagannath's service, Guru Maharaj came to the annual festival and personally sat several thousand men and women in the neighboring field and fed them with maha prasad. I still feel goose bumps when I remember the ecstasy that flooded over Jashora on that day.

SRIMAD ADVAITA ACHARYA

vraje āveśa-rūpatvād vyūho yo'pi sadāśivaḥ
sa evādvaita-gosvāmī caitanyābhinna-vigrahaḥ
yaś ca gopāla-dehaḥ san vraje kṛṣṇasya sannidhau
nanarta śrī-śivā-tantre bhairavasya vaco yathā
ekadā kārttike māsi dīpa-yātrā-mahotsave

sa-rāmaḥ saha-gopālaḥ kṛṣṇo nṛtyati yatnavān
nirīkṣya mad-gurur devo gopa-bhāvābhilāṣavān
priyeṇa nartitum ārabdhaś cakra-bhramaṇa-līlayā
śrī-kṛṣṇasya prasādena dvi-vidho'bhūt sadāśivaḥ
ekas tatra śivaḥ sākṣād anyo gopāla-vigrahaḥ

Sadashiva, an expansion of the supreme Lord in Vraja, is here known as Advaita Acharya. He is non-different from Chaitanya. In Vraja, he took the form of a cowherd boy and danced alongside Krishna. This is stated by Bhairava in the *Śivātantra*: "Once, during the Divali festival in the month of Karttik, my guru Shankaradeva saw Krishna dancing with Balaram and the cowherd boys. He then wished to become a cowherd boy himself and began to dance, spinning like a whirling wheel for Krishna's pleasure." Thus, by Krishna's mercy, Sadashiva plays two different roles in Vraja, in one he is Shiva himself, in the other, he is a cowherd boy.

(*Gaura-gaṇoddeśa-dīpikā* 76-80)

ADVAITA-TATTVA

In Chaitanya Charitamrita, Krishna Das Kaviraj Goswami quotes the following evidence from the diary of Svarupa Damodar to describe the ontological principle of Advaita Acharya:

mahā-viṣṇur jagat-kartā māyayā yaḥ sṛjaty adaḥ
tasyāvatāra evāyam advaitācārya īśvaraḥ
advaitaṁ hariṇādvaitād ācāryaṁ bhakti-śāsanāt
bhaktāvatāram īśaṁ tam advaitācāryam āśraye

Maha Vishnu is the master of the universe, which he creates through his power of Maya. Advaita Acharya is the incarnation of this form of the Supreme Lord. He is known as Advaita because he is none other than Hari, as Acharya because he is the preceptor of devotion. I take shelter of the Supreme Lord Advaita Acharya, who is the incarnation of a devotee. (Chaitanya Charitamrita 1.1.12-13)

Srila Bhaktivinoda Thakur has written, "Maya has two functions, and Maha Vishnu appears in two ways according to those functions. When he is within the material world as creator, he is the universe's effective cause (*nimitta-kāraṇa*) in his form as Vishnu. In the unmanifest material energy (*pradhāna*), appearing in the form of Rudra, he has a second identity as Advaita."

Bhaktisiddhanta Saraswati Goswami Thakur has also written about Advaita Acharya in his *Anubhāṣya* to Chaitanya Charitamrita 1.6.12: "Lord Advaita Acharya is Maha Vishnu. He is the supreme preceptor. Vishnu's activities are auspicious because of his existence as the owner or master of the universe. He is the root source of all auspiciousness.... Anyone who cannot understand that the complications that are ever present in the material universe are beneficial in a way that is pure, eternal, complete and free is deprived of his true spiritual activity, devotion to Krishna." Advaita Acharya was also known as Kamalaksha:

Advaita embodies universal welfare. He is the abode of all auspicious qualities. His activities are the eternal source of the world's well-being, so he was given the name Mangala. (Chaitanya Charitamrita 1.6.12)

Advaita, the abode of virtue, is a portion (*aṁśa*) of Maha Vishnu. Because he is not different from Vishnu, Advaita is his most perfect name.

(Chaitanya Charitamrita 1.6.26)

He is the noblest personality in the universe, the spiritual master of the Vaishnavas; he thus has two names that come together as Advaita Acharya. Because in appearance he has eyes like lotus flowers, he also has the name Kamalaksha. (Chaitanya Charitamrita 1.6.30-31)

Vrindavan Das Thakur has also described Advaita as both the foremost of the Vaishnavas and as Shiva:

Residing in Nabadwip is the foremost and the most fortunate of all Vaishnavas, Sri Advaita Acharya. He heads all spiritual masters in knowledge, devotion and renunciation. He especially teaches devotion to Krishna in the same way that Lord Shankara did.

(Chaitanya Bhagavata 1.2.78-9)

ADVAITA'S APPEARANCE

Advaita Acharya appeared in the village of Navagram near the city of Sylhet as the son of the Varendra Brahmin Kubera Pandit and his wife Nabha Devi, on the seventh day of the waxing moon in the month of Magh. Kubera Pandit is identified in the *Gaura-gaṇoddeśa-dīpikā* (91) with the god Kubera, Mahadeva's friend and leader of the Guhyakas.

Kubera Pandit, a devotee of Nrisingha, resided in the village of Navagram near Sylhet in Bangladesh. He was a greatly fortunate follower of the path of devotion; he knew nothing other than the lotus feet of Krishna. His devoted and faithful wife was named Nabha Devi. She is worshipable to the whole world for she is the mother of Advaita Prabhu. (Bhakti-ratnākara 5.2041-3)

On the seventh day of the waxing moon in the month of Magh, the great ocean of joy overflowed. In that auspicious moment, the moon of Advaita descended in the blessed womb of Nabha Devi. In his ecstasy, Kubera Pandit made gifts to the Brahmins and the poor. He tiptoed to the birthing room and his heart was filled with gladness upon seeing his son's face. All the villagers came running to his house and said to each other, "What pious works did this Brahmin do that in his old age he has been blessed with such a jewel of a son?" The gods rained down flowers without being seen. There is nothing with which this scene can compare. Ghanashyama sings of this great auspicious occasion when a joyous uproar rang around the earth.

(*Bhakti-ratnākara* 12.1759-62)

In the *Gauḍīya Vaiṣṇava Abhidhāna*, Advaita's birthplace is given as Laura. It is also said there that Advaita Prabhu left Laura to reside in Sylhet and from there moved to Shantipur. He also had a home in Nabadwip. His full name was Sri Kamalaksha or Kamala Kanta Vedapanchanan. His birth took place in 1434 AD and he disappeared in the year 1559, at the age of 125 years. The *Advaita-vilāsa* confirms this: "The Lord [Advaita] remained on this earth for a century and a quarter, performing unlimited pastimes."

Jahnava Mata's diksha disciple Nityananda Das gives a third opinion. He writes in his *Prema-vilāsa* that Advaita was born in Shantipur. He also writes that Advaita studied the Veda and other scriptures with the scholar Shantacharya, who lived in the Phullabati section of Shantipur and earned from him the title *ācārya*.

Advaita's life has been described in several Bengali books, including *Advaita-maṅgala, Advaita-vilāsa* and *Sītā-caritra.* The great scholar Sarvabhauma Bhattacharya also wrote several Sanskrit poems glorifying Advaita—*Advaita-dvādaśa-nāma-stotra, Advaitāṣṭakam* and *Advaitāṣṭottara-śata-nāma-stotra.*

ADVAITA PRABHU'S TRAVELS

When Kubera Pandit and Nabha Devi disappeared, Advaita went to Gaya on the pretext of performing the appropriate rituals of mourning, and thence continued on a pilgrimage of all of India's holy places. When he came to Vrindavan, he became absorbed in the worship of Krishna, but through his meditation was able to understand that Krishna was about to appear in Nabadwip. While on this pilgrimage, he stopped in Mithila where he met the poet Vidyapati. This encounter is beautifully described in *Advaita-vilāsa.* Advaita Prabhu finally returned from Vrindavan to Shantipur after spending several days in Nabadwip. The people of Shantipur had been suffering from his separation for a long time and were very happy to see him again.

Lord Vishnu is always accompanied by three aspects or shaktis—Sri, Bhu, and Nila (Lila). Advaita Acharya's own divine persona would not be fully manifest without all these three aspects of his identity. Therefore, Advaita accepted two wives; one was named Sri, the other Sita. Both appeared as daughters of the great Brahmin devotee, Sri Nrisingha Baduri. In the *Gaura-gaṇoddeśa-dīpikā* (86), it is written that the divine Yogamaya took the form of Advaita's wife Sita, and that Sri is her *prakāśa* expansion.

Advaita Acharya had two residences, one in Shantipur, the other not far from Srivas' home in Nabadwip-Mayapur. His heart was greatly pained at seeing that the people of the world were devoid of any devotion to Vishnu and, as a consequence, greatly suffering the torments of material life. Overwhelmed with compassion, he began to teach the Bhagavad Gita and Srimad Bhagavatam, explaining that the purport of the scriptures was to engage in devotional service to Krishna.

At about the same time, Madhavendra Puri had a dream in which Govardhandhari Gopal commanded him to find sandalwood paste for the deity service. Madhavendra then started out for Puri, taking the road through western Bengal. While there, he stopped at Advaita's house in Shantipur. Advaita became convinced that Madhavendra Puri was his guru when he saw his devotional ecstasies. Even though he himself is an expansion of the Supreme Lord, he underwent the ritual of initiation in order to demonstrate to the conditioned souls the necessity of accepting a spiritual master.

Madhavendra Puri arrived at Advaita Acharya's house. When Advaita saw Puripada's prema, he felt a deep inner joy. So he took care to receive the mantra from him, after which Madhavendra left to continue his voyage to the South. (Chaitanya Charitamrita 2.4.110-1)

It is said that Mahaprabhu is the main trunk of the wish-fulfilling tree of devotion, as well as the gardener who enjoys and distributes the tree's fruits. Though the tree was planted in Nabadwip, it grew in Purushottam Dham (Puri) and Vrindavan, expanding into an entire orchard producing many, many fruits of love. Madhavendra Puri is said to be the first seedling, which eventually grew into this tree. Ishvara Puri was the sprouted form of this seedling. Mahaprabhu, though Himself the gardener, also became the tree's main trunk through His inconceivable energies. Advaita and Nityananda were the two secondary trunks into which the main trunk divided.

(Chaitanya Charitamrita 1.9.21)

THE CAUSE OF THE LORD'S INCARNATION

Sri Krishna Chaitanya Mahaprabhu is the main body of the devotional movement, and Advaita and Nityananda are its limbs. All three of Them advented with Srivas and other devotees in order to preach devotion to Hari. All those who were senior to Gauranga appeared on earth prior to Him. Advaita appeared along with the other elderly members of Chaitanya's retinue and when he did so, he observed that the sinfulness of the age of Kali had reached a disturbing extreme and that the world was entirely devoid of devotion to Lord Krishna. He thought that a partial incarnation of the Lord would not be sufficient to completely remedy the situation. He felt, "The world will only benefit if the Supreme Personality of Godhead Himself descends to the earth." So he began to worship Krishna's lotus feet with Ganges water and tulasi leaves, shouting and pleading to the Lord to incarnate. With roars of love (*prema-huṅkāra*) Advaita showed his desire for the Lord of Goloka to descend to the earth.

He constantly offered water from the Ganges and tulasi manjaris while meditating on Krishna's lotus feet, at the same time calling to Krishna with loud roars. This is the way he brought about Krishna's descent. This is the chief reason that Krishna Chaitanya became incarnate on earth. The Lord, the bridge of justice, descends at the wish of the devotee. (Chaitanya Charitamrita 1.3.107-9)

Advaita Acharya lived in Shantipur. His body is the

reservoir of devotional nectar and is not different from that of Chaitanya. He brought Sri Krishna Chaitanya, whose spotless fame has filled the world, down to this earth. My Advaita is not different from Gauranga, and his wife Sita is the mother of the universe. First he brought Gauranga into this world with his roars, and then he glorified him everywhere.

(*Bhakti-ratnākara* 12.3753-6)

All glories to Advaita Acharya, the most merciful, whose roars brought about Gauranga's incarnation. Whoever takes shelter of his lotus feet will obtain the great wealth of love for Gaura.

(Bhakti-ratnākara 12.3761, 3764)

He constantly served Krishna with great enthusiasm, offering Ganges water and tulasi manjaris. Absorbed in thoughts of Krishna, he worshiped Him by roaring His name, the sound of which filled the entire universe, reaching up to Vaikuntha. Lord Krishna heard the sound of these roars of love and made Himself visible to humanity, for He is controlled by His devotee.

(Chaitanya Bhagavata 1.2.81-3)

Nityananda Prabhu also descended prior to Mahaprabhu's appearance, on the thirteenth day of the waxing moon in the month of Magh. He appeared in the family of Harai Pandit and Padmavati in the village of Ekachakra in Rarha, bestowing upon them the opportunity to serve him in the *vātsalya-rasa*. Meanwhile, eight daughters were born to Jagannath Mishra and Sachi Devi, all of whom died before their son, Vishvarupa, Nityananda Prabhu's other self, took birth. Subsequently, on the full moon evening of the month of Phalgun, the source of all avatars, Gaurachandra, made His appearance. After the appearance of Sri Chaitanya, Sita Devi took Advaita's permission to come with gifts to Nabadwip from Shantipur to see the most wonderful child. When she saw Him, she blessed Him by placing unhusked rice and *dūrvā* grass on his head.

After taking permission from her husband, Sita Thakurani, Advaita Acharya's respectable and noble wife, went to Nabadwip to see the crown jewel of infants, taking gifts with her. (Chaitanya Charitamrita 1.13.112)

Advaita Acharya established a Tol for teaching Sanskrit in Nabadwip-Mayapur and started to engage in a deep study of the scriptures. Every day after bathing in the Ganges, Mahaprabhu's older brother Vishvarupa used to go to Advaita's house to listen to him lecture. On certain occasions, when Advaita was engaged in performing his puja, Vishvarupa would explain to everyone present there that devotion to Krishna was the ultimate purport of all the scriptures. When Advaita heard him speaking in this way, he got up from worshiping his deity and embraced him. Sachi regularly sent little Nimai at noon with something for Vishvarupa's lunch. When Advaita Prabhu saw Nimai's beautiful face he became enchanted, but was unable to recognize him as his worshipable Lord, the Supreme Truth.

In the meantime, Vishvarupa had secretly decided that he would renounce family life in the knowledge that the material world is temporary and that a human being's only real duty is to worship the Lord. When he saw that his parents were starting to make wedding plans for him, he quickly left home and took sannyas, after which he was known by the name Shankararanya. Sachi, Jagannath and other devotees all lamented his loss. Advaita was pained by Vishvarup's departure, but pacified everyone by saying that Krishna Himself would appear soon to eradicate everyone's distress.

After Vishvarupa left home, Sachi and Jagannath feared that Nimai would follow his example and so they put a stop to His education. Later, however, when they heard Nimai speaking sweetly in the mood of Dattatreya, they decided it would be better to send Him back to school. Jagannath Mishra left this world not long after Nimai was given the sacred thread and had become fully absorbed in his studies. While Mahaprabhu was still fully devoted to His pastimes as a scholar, His mother arranged His marriage to Lakshmipriya, the daughter of Ballabha.

In those days, Advaita was holding Bhagavata lectures and kirtan at his house in Nabadwip. All the devotees including Advaita were very enthused about the singer Mukunda Datta's fine voice. On one occasion Ishvara Puri came to Advaita's house while visiting Nabadwip. From his vigorous appearance, Advaita was able to recognize that he was a Vaishnava sannyasi. Later, Gauranga also met Ishvara Puri there.

At that time, Ishvara Puri arrived in Nabadwip in a most discrete manner. Ishvara Puri was single-minded in his constant preoccupation with relishing Krishna devotion; he was dear to Krishna and compassionate. No one was able to recognize him because he was not dressed as a sannyasi, until he arrived by chance one day at Advaita's house. (Chaitanya Bhagavata 1.11.70-72)

ADVAITA TESTS MAHAPRABHU

When Gauranga returned from Gaya, His mood had changed. Advaita, Srivas and the other devotees were overjoyed to see that He had become a devotee. In due course, Nityananda Prabhu arrived in Nabadwip after having toured the sacred pilgrimage sites and there he met Nimai. One day at Srivas' house, Mahaprabhu indicated that He wanted to perform the Vyasa Puja to Nityananda. On the eve of this puja, Mahaprabhu showed everyone that Nityananda was Baladeva and then, repeating the words, "*Nāṛā, Nāṛā*", revealed that Advaita had caused Him to descend to the earth by calling Him.

It is due to Advaita that I have become incarnate, for *Nāṛā's* roars rang in My ears. I was lying in the Milk Ocean, but *Nāṛā's* roar woke Me up and brought Me down here.

(Chaitanya Bhagavata 2.9.297-8)

After the Vyasa Puja had come to an end, Mahaprabhu took on the mood of the Supreme Lord and sent Ramai Pandit, Srivas Pandit's brother, to fetch Advaita from his house in Shantipur. He told him of the

Lord's divine manifestation: "Advaita Prabhu has brought Hari, the Lord of Goloka, to this earth by his cries and by worshiping Him with Ganges water and tulasi. Nityananda Prabhu has also made his auspicious appearance in Nabadwip. So Advaita Acharya and his wife should immediately come to Srivas Angan, bringing all the paraphernalia for worship." Ramai promptly carried out Mahaprabhu's order and took His message to Advaita Prabhu.

As soon as Advaita heard that Mahaprabhu had publicly revealed His divinity, He and Sita Devi immediately set off, bringing their son Achyutananda and some other associates. But rather than going directly to Srivas' house, Advaita decided to test Mahaprabhu by hiding in Nandanacharya's house. He told Ramai not to tell Mahaprabhu, but the Lord, who knows the heart of all, was able to see through Advaita's plan. As Mahaprabhu sat on the altar and revealed to everyone His divine identity, Nityananda held the royal parasol while Gadadhar and the other devotees engaged in a variety of services. When Mahaprabhu sent Ramai to Nandanacharya's house to fetch Advaita, Advaita realized that Mahaprabhu was omniscient and hesitated no longer.

In the company of his wife, Advaita joyfully prostrated himself before the Lord, speechless before the manifestation of the Lord's divine power. He washed the Lord's lotus feet and then worshiped Him with the five ingredients (*pañcopacāra*), using the following mantra to do so:

namo brahmaṇya-devāya go-brāhmaṇa-hitāya ca
jagad-dhitāya kṛṣṇāya govindāya namo namaḥ

I offer my obeisances to Krishna Govinda, the Lord of brahminical society, to Him who is the source of the cows' and the Brahmins' welfare, and who is the source of the entire universe's well-being.

Mahaprabhu then commanded Advaita Prabhu to get up and dance. Advaita started to dance madly until he was completely intoxicated in a way that astonished all the devotees.

Krishna Das Kaviraj has written:

There is one Mahaprabhu or Supreme Lord, and two other prabhus, or masters. The two other prabhus serve the lotus feet of Mahaprabhu. These three personalities belong to the category of the all-worshipable; the fourth category is the devotee who is the worshiper. Srivas and the millions of other devotees belong to this category of pure devotees. Gadadhar Pandit and others are considered to be incarnations of the Lord's energies or shaktis. They are counted as His most intimate devotees.

(Chaitanya Charitamrita 1.7.94-7)

Pancha Tattva, the five-fold aspect of divinity, includes Gauranga Mahaprabhu, who accepted the form of a devotee; Nityananda Prabhu, who is the *bhakta-svarūpa*; and Advaita Acharya, the Lord's incarnation as a devotee. These three are considered to be *prabhu-tattva* or *Viṣṇu-tattva,* the ontological category of Godhead. Advaita is an incarnation of Maha Vishnu, so he belongs to the category of *Viṣṇu-tattva,* but because he took on the mood of a devotee he is called *bhaktāvatāra*, "the Lord's incarnation as a devotee." Because Gauranga, Nityananda and Advaita all belong to the category of *Viṣṇu-tattva,* tulasi leaves are offered to their feet. Without Advaita's mercy, one can never attain the service of Chaitanya and Nityananda.

dayā koro sītāpati advaita gosāñi
tava kṛpā-bale pāi caitanya-nitāi

Be merciful, Advaita Prabhu, husband of Sita! On the strength of your mercy, I will attain Chaitanya and Nitai.

(Narottam Das Thakur)

Advaita Acharya's glories and activities have been extensively described in Krishna Das Kaviraj Goswami's Chaitanya Charitamrita, Vrindavan Das' Chaitanya Bhagavata, Narahari Chakravarti's *Bhakti-ratnākara, Advaita-vilāsa*, and other works. Those who wish to have a deeper knowledge of his life should consult these books. We can only give an abbreviated biography in this book and such an extensive account cannot be given here. We have only set out to remember the main pastimes of Sri Advaita.

ADVAITA AND HARI DAS THAKUR

By his deeds, Advaita Prabhu revealed that a Vaishnava is praiseworthy and worthy of worship regardless of his family background. Namacharya Hari Das Thakur was born in a Muslim family in Burhan village in the district of Jessore. Later he came to live in the village of Phuliya and was staying in a grotto engaged in solitary devotional practices, but would sometimes come to associate with Advaita Prabhu in nearby Shantipur. This was after he had spent time preaching the glories of the Holy Names at the Chandpur house of Raghunath Das Goswami's father and uncle, Govardhan and Hiranya Majumdar.

Advaita used to invite Hari Das to come to his house in Shantipur to take prasad. This made Hari Das Thakur feel somewhat uneasy. However, Advaita Prabhu, the world teacher, claimed that his behavior comformed with all the scriptures, for to feed a great devotee like Hari Das is equal to feeding millions of Brahmins. In order to demonstrate this, he honored Hari Das by giving him the plate offered in the *śrāddha* ceremony. On the annual date set aside for offering oblations to the forefathers, householder Vaishnavas offer all kinds of foodstuffs to the Lord. They then invite Brahmins and Vaishnavas to honor prasad. The maha prasad is given to the guest of honor and Advaita Prabhu chose Hari Das for this special treatment.

Advaita said, "Please don't be afraid. I shall only do what is accepted in scripture. If you accept this prasad it is as though I had fed ten million Brahmins." After saying these words, he gave him the *śrāddha* plate to eat.

(Chaitanya Charitamrita 3.3.219-20)

One of the branches of the Chaitanya tree is Hari Das Thakur, whose activities are amazing. He would unfailingly chant 300,000 names of the Lord every day. I only give an indication here of his unlimited virtues; Advaita Acharya honored him by giving him the *śrāddha* plate.

(Chaitanya Charitamrita 1.10.43-4)

THE SONS OF ADVAITA

Although six sons were born to Advaita Acharya, the incarnation of Maha Vishnu, he indicated that some of them had understood the essence of spiritual life and some had not. Those who simply claimed to be his followers but showed no affection for Gauranga were the latter; those who were attached to Mahaprabhu in ever-increasing affection were the former. These included Achyutananda, Sri Krishna Mishra and Gopal Mishra, while Balaram, Svarupa and Jagadish belonged to the category of those who did not give recognition to Sri Chaitanya. Achyutananda was the oldest brother and Sri Krishna Mishra and Gopal Mishra followed his lead. The Chaitanya Charitamrita (1.12.12) compares the two groups to wheat and chaff.

Bhaktisiddhanta Saraswati also writes in his *Gauḍīya-bhāṣya* to the Chaitanya Bhagavata (2.10.162), "If someone takes Advaita Acharya to be the best of all the Vaishnavas, then he can be called a Vaishnava. On the other hand, if someone considers him to be the object of all religious life, the *viṣaya* Krishna, and Sri Krishna Chaitanya Mahaprabhu to be his devotee, or *āśraya,* then he will never be able to attain Krishna's lotus feet."

THE LORD PUNISHES ADVAITA

It is also said that Mahaprabhu taught Advaita the real meaning of the Bhagavad Gita.

Vishvambhar explained the true understanding of the Gita to Advaita, withdrawing the gates that conceal the nature of bhakti. (Chaitanya Bhagavata 2.10.166)

Another wonderful pastime was prepared by Advaita in order to show the fallen jivas how auspicious it is to receive punishment from the Lord, the guru or a Vaishnava. How fortunate is a devotee who is chastised by his guru! This is described in the seventeenth chapter of the Chaitanya Charitamrita, *Ādi-līlā*, where Bhaktivinoda Thakur has made the following comments in his *Amṛta-pravāha-bhāṣya*: "Advaita Acharya is the godbrother of Mahaprabhu's guru, Ishvara Puri. For this reason, Mahaprabhu treated Advaita as his elder and spiritual master even though Advaita considered himself to be Mahaprabhu's servant. Advaita was pained to see Mahaprabhu treat him with such respect and so, in order to seek out the merciful punishment of the Lord, he returned to Shantipur and began to explain the path of knowledge to a few unfortunate individuals. When the Lord caught wind of this, He became extremely angry and went to Shantipur to give him a good thrashing. When he was chastised in this way, Advaita danced for joy, saying, 'Just see, My desires have been fulfilled today! Mahaprabhu was previously miserly with me, treating me as His respectful elder, but now He has acted toward me as though I were His servant or disciple by trying to save me from the heresy of mayavada.' When the Lord understood that this had all been a ruse on Advaita's part, He was embarrassed but pleased with him."

The Lord treated Advaita with the respect deserved by a guru. This caused the Acharya great distress, so he adopted a ruse of teaching the path of knowledge. Mahaprabhu became angry and scorned Advaita, causing him great bliss. When He saw his satisfaction with the turn of events, the Lord became ashamed and was merciful to him.

(Chaitanya Charitamrita 1.17.66-8)

"Previously Mahaprabhu would honor me. This made me unhappy, so I thought that if I started giving lectures on the *Yoga-vaśiṣṭha*, teaching *mukti* as the supreme goal of life, the Lord would become angry and insult me.

(Chaitanya Charitamrita 1.12.39-40)

SACHI DEVI AND ADVAITA

Because of Advaita's compassion and sympathy for the plight of the conditioned souls, Mahaprabhu could not forgive even His mother when she looked askance at him. On one occasion, through chastising her, He warned all devotees of the danger of offences to the Vaishnavas. If Sachi, who is the essence of motherly affection, the incarnation of Yashoda Devi, cannot be forgiven an offence to the Vaishnava, then what chance do others have? By the same lila, Mahaprabhu also showed that in order to become free of *vaiṣṇavāparādha*, one should beg for forgiveness from the Vaishnava one has offended.

When Vishvarupa came to the conclusion, after studying with Advaita Prabhu, that the world is a temporary place and the only real duty of humankind is to worship the Supreme Lord, he left home and took sannyas. Sachi Mata, though troubled by his departure, was wary of insulting Advaita for the role he had played in it, knowing him to be a Vaishnava, and took solace in Nimai's presence at home. But when she saw that Nimai too was constantly going to associate with Advaita, leaving his wife Lakshmipriya alone at home, she began to think that Advaita's name was really unsuitable, that rather than unifying people as it would indicate, he split them apart. "Dvaita" would thus be a more appropriate name, she thought. "This old gosai goes by the name Advaita, but he should be called Dvaita. One son of mine, as beautiful as the moon, has left home because of him, and he hasn't let me keep the other one settled. No one has mercy on me. I am now alone in this world. He may be one (*advaita*) with the world, but I see him as Maya (*dvaita*)."

(Chaitanya Bhagavata 2.22.114-6)

Because of her affection for her son, Sachi mentally criticized Advaita in this way, but no one knew except for her son, Gaura Hari, who is the indweller of all beings. On the day of the *mahāprakāśa* in the house of Srivas,

Mahaprabhu was fulfilling the desires of every one of His devotees by allowing them to see His divine form for twenty-one hours. Srivas asked Him whether Śachi Devi could also be blessed with this divine vision. Mahaprabhu answered, "My mother has committed an offence against Advaita Prabhu, so I will not show her this form."

When the devotees told Sachi what her son had said, she immediately went to Advaita and begged him for forgiveness. After Advaita had heard Sachi's confession, he began to glorify her as the one who had carried the Supreme Lord of all creation in her womb. He continued until he became unconscious from the overwhelming love that he felt. Only when he fell unconscious could Sachi finally take the dust of his lotus feet and thus be free from her offence. Mahaprabhu was satisfied with His mother and showed her His glorious, divine form. Another important lesson we can draw from this story is that Vaishnavas are never proud. Even though she had given birth to Lord Gaura Hari, Sachi felt no pride in her exalted status. As soon as she became aware of having committed an offence, she went to Advaita without any hesitation and prayed to be pardoned.

THE LORD COMES TO SHANTIPUR

Advaita Acharya was Mahaprabhu's associate in sankirtan, both in Srivas' house and in the streets of Nabadwip and along the shores of the Ganges.

> Everyone joyfully sang in unison, "Krishna, Rama, Mukunda, Murari, Vanamali!" Holding on to Nityananda and Gadadhar, Advaita, ran in every direction like a lion.
>
> (Chaitanya Bhagavata 2.23.29-30)

> The Lord danced along the banks of the Bhagirathi while around him all the people sang the names of Hari. Advaita Acharya preceded him, dancing ecstatically with a small group of devotees.
>
> (Chaitanya Bhagavata 2.23.202-3)

After Mahaprabhu had taken sannyas from Keshava Bharati in Katwa, He became overwhelmed with love for Krishna and started to run toward Vrindavan. With the help of some cowherd boys, Nityananda Prabhu tricked Him into coming to the banks of the Ganges. Nityananda wanted to show Him to the people of Nabadwip and to bring Him to Shantipur. When Mahaprabhu saw the Ganges, He thought that it was the Yamuna and became overwhelmed with ecstasy. Meanwhile, Advaita heard that Nityananda had brought Mahaprabhu there and came by boat across the river with new clothes for Him. Mahaprabhu was astonished to see Advaita, wondering how he could have known that He was in Vrindavan. Advaita answered by saying that Vrindavan was wherever Mahaprabhu went and the western flow of the Ganges was the Yamuna. When He heard these words, Mahaprabhu realized that He had been tricked into coming to the western bank of the Ganges across from the town of Shantipur. Advaita had Mahaprabhu take a bath, dressed Him in the new cloth, and then took Him to his house where the Lord stayed for several days.

When Sachi and the people of Nabadwip heard that Gaura Hari was at Advaita's they all came there to visit him. Seeing Him in His dress as a sannyasi, they felt joy mixed with separation. Sita Thakurani prepared an immense meal and served it on whole leaves from seed-banana trees.[3] As Mahaprabhu and Nityananda ate, Advaita Prabhu talked and joked with them. This has been extensively described in the Chaitanya Charitamrita's *Madhya-līlā*, chapter 3. Mahaprabhu afterwards also ate foodstuffs prepared by his mother Sachi Devi in order to ease the suffering He had caused her by His departure. The reunion of devotees turned into a great festival, and Advaita's house in the town of Shantipur was transformed into the city of Vaikuntha.

> Since everyone was dancing and singing the names of Hari, Advaita's house became Vaikuntha Puri.
>
> (Chaitanya Charitamrita 2.3.156)

ADVAITA GOES TO PURI ON THE ANNUAL PILGRIMAGE

When Mahaprabhu was saying his goodbyes to the devotees, he set off to Puri or Nilachala to live there at the behest of his mother. Advaita and the residents of Nabadwip were once again hurled into the ocean of separation from their Lord. These events took place in the year 1510. It was probably three more years before the devotees went to Puri during the Chaturmasya period to visit him there at the time of the Rathayatra.

> The first year, Advaita and the other devotees went to Nilachala to see Mahaprabhu's lotus feet. They witnessed the Rathayatra and then stayed for four months, passing the time in kirtan and dancing in great joy. When the time came for them to depart, the Lord told everyone to return each year to see the Rathayatra festival. And so the yearly trips to Puri to see the Lord became a tradition.
>
> (Chaitanya Charitamrita 2.1.46-49)

Of the last twenty-four years of Mahaprabhu's life, six were spent in traveling to and from Puri, while He spent the last eighteen in Puri without ever leaving. During the six years that he spent traveling, the Bengali devotees would first find out whether He was present in Puri before going. During the eighteen years of Mahaprabhu's permanent stay in Puri, the annual trips became an annual event.

> After Mahaprabhu arrived in Puri from Vrindavan, He never again left for the eighteen remaining years of His life. The devotees came from Bengal every year, meeting with the Lord and staying for the four months of the rainy season.
>
> (Chaitanya Charitamrita 2.1.249-50)

All of Mahaprabhu's servants, Advaita, Nityananda, Mukunda, Srivas, Vidyanidhi, Vasudeva and Murari went every year to meet with the Lord, staying in Puri for four months. The Lord enjoyed a multitude of pastimes with these devotees during this time.

(Chaitanya Charitamrita 2.1.255-6)

The time for Rathayatra came again and the devotees started on the annual pilgrimage to Nilachala. They were following the Lord's order to come every year to see the Rathayatra festival. With Advaita Acharya at their head, all the devotees set off toward Nilachala.

(Chaitanya Charitamrita 3.8.4-6)

Advaita Acharya would go every year to Puri and stay for the full four months, participating with Mahaprabhu in lilas such as the cleaning of the Gundicha temple, the water sports in Narendra Sarovar and Jagannath's Rathayatra. The best of Advaita's three orthodox sons, Achyutananda, who was totally devoted to Gauranga, was also present there, as is attested by the mentioning of him as the leader of the sixth kirtan group at the Rathayatra, which was from Shantipur. Another of Advaita's sons, Gopal Mishra, is also named in this list. Advaita himself was the principal dancer in the first kirtan group led by Svarupa Damodar.

In the third year of this tradition, the wives of the Bengali devotees accompanied them, bringing various gifts for Mahaprabhu's service.

In the third year, all the devotees from Bengal decided to go to Nilachala. They went in a group to Advaita Acharya's house, and he happily agreed to go with them to see the Lord. That year, all the wives of these saints went also, the mother of Achyuta accompanying Advaita Acharya. (Chaitanya Charitamrita 2.16.12-13, 21)

Advaita went first to Sachi Mata's house to take her leave. Then he departed with the assembly of devotees. They brought with them all the edibles they knew formerly brought pleasure to the Lord. They performed sankirtan the entire length of the route, purifying everything and everyone on their path. All the people of the three worlds were sanctified by the devotees' joyful calls of Hari! Hari! In a mood of ecstasy, they were all going to see Chaitanya, accompanied by their wives and sons, their male and female servants. (Chaitanya Charitamrita 3.8.39-43)

Krishna Das Kaviraj has written about a wonderful pastime with Advaita's son Gopal Mishra in the twelfth chapter of Chaitanya Charitamrita's *Ādi-līlā*. During the cleaning of the Gundicha temple, both Advaita and Mahaprabhu were satisfied to see Gopal's deep absorption in dancing and singing before them. When Gopal Mishra suddenly fell unconscious, Advaita became very anxious and took his inert body on his lap, chanting the Nrisingha mantra. Despite the various mantras that Advaita uttered, Gopal did not return to consciousness. All the devotees began to cry for him, but Mahaprabhu, who takes away the distress of his devotees, touched Gopal over the heart and said, "Rise up Gopal and chant Hari Hari!" Gopal immediately awoke and stood up. The devotees shouted the names of the Lord in relief and joy.

KAMALA KANTA VISHWAS

Advaita Acharya had a disciple named Kamala Kanta Vishwas who wrote to King Prataparudra explaining that Advaita was the Supreme Lord, but that he was in debt and needed money. He asked Prataparudra to give Advaita the amount needed to pay his creditors. When Mahaprabhu heard about this, He punished Kamala Kanta by refusing him access to the Gambhira. Kamala Kanta was disturbed by this punishment, but Advaita explained to him that to be punished by Mahaprabhu was a cause for rejoicing and that he was most fortunate.

Bhaktivinoda Thakur has made the following comment on this story, which is found in the twelfth chapter of the *Ādi-līlā*: "Kamala Kanta first proved that Advaita was the supreme Lord, but then begged for money from the king on Advaita's behalf. This action was very displeasing to Mahaprabhu. Even though Advaita Acharya is God Himself, he is in this world playing the part of a man in order to teach. For an acharya to go begging to a king in order to free himself from a debt is considered to be shameless behavior. One should entirely abandon the desire for material gain and if the desire for material well-being is taken to the point of begging from a foreign king in order to become free of a debt, then one's spiritual life will certainly go to ruin. Kings are by nature materialistic. If one eats the food of a materialistic person, his mind becomes clouded over. When one's mind is clouded over, then he can no longer remember Krishna and his life is wasted.

"Such begging from materialistic men is therefore prohibited for everyone, but it is especially so for those who are in the position of acharya. It is the acharya's duty to instruct people in the Holy Names, but he should not take money in return for such instruction. If he does so, he becomes an offender to the Holy Name rather than an initiator in the Name. If an instructor of the Holy Names becomes a money collector, then it is a matter of shame and his religious reputation will be ruined."

MAHAPRABHU GLORIFIES ADVAITA PRABHU

In the third year when the Bengali devotees came with their wives and gifts of various food preparations dear to the Lord, He mercifully ate all these offerings out of His affection for them. One day, Mahaprabhu was invited to eat at Advaita's residence. This time, Advaita himself did the cooking and his wife assisted him by cutting the vegetables and gathering the ingredients. It was Advaita's secret wish to be able to feed Mahaprabhu alone. It so happened that on that day the weather turned bad and due to a storm, all the sannyasis who normally came with Mahaprabhu on such occasions were unable to accompany Him. Mahaprabhu thus arrived by Himself to Advaita's great satisfaction, for he was thus able to serve Him the meal in complete privacy. He praised the god Indra as a servant of Krishna who fulfilled the wishes of his devotees. Mahaprabhu was aware of Advaita's mood and praised him by saying, "Krishna Himself fulfills your desires, so what is unusual about Indra carrying out your orders?"

(Chaitanya Bhagavata 3.9.60-72)

On another occasion, Mahaprabhu glorified Advaita and described the underlying truth of his nature in the following way:

> Advaita Acharya is God himself. As a result of his association, I have become purified. Because there is no one equal to him in devotion to Krishna, nor in knowledge of the scriptures, he is called Advaita Acharya. By his mercy, even the mlecchas become devotees of Krishna, who can describe the extent of his powers or devotion?
> (Chaitanya Charitamrita 3.7.17-9)

Mahaprabhu had Rupa and Sanatan meet with Sri Advaita and Nityananda Prabhu in Puri and asked them to bless the brothers. Raghunath Das Goswami received Mahaprabhu's leftovers by the grace of Advaita Prabhu. He was the object of Advaita's affection because his father, Govardhan Majumdar, had served him honestly.

> His father always rendered service to Advaita Acharya, therefore the acharya was pleased with him. By the grace of the acharya, Raghunath obtained the Lord's leftover plate and was able to have darshan of the Lord for five or six days. (Chaitanya Charitamrita 2.16.225-6)

The words that Mahaprabhu spoke to Advaita when He was about to leave Puri show just how much affection He had for him:

> Acharya Gosai came here to show Me his mercy. I am bound in debt to his love and there is no way that I can repay him. He has abandoned his wife, children and home for My sake, traveling a long and difficult way to come here. I am living here in Nilachala without moving. I make no effort on your behalf. I am a monk and I have no wealth—what could I give you to make good on My debt? My only possession is My body, which I give you. I will sell it to whomever you wish.
> (Chaitanya Charitamrita 3.12.70-74)

ADVAITA'S RIDDLE

When Advaita Acharya returned to Nabadwip from Puri, he met Jagadananda Pandit who had been sent there earlier by Mahaprabhu. Advaita was very happy to have his association. When Jagadananda finally asked permission of Advaita Prabhu to return to Nilachala, Advaita gave him a message in the form of a riddle to take back to Mahaprabhu. The riddle was comprehensible to no one but Mahaprabhu Himself. The message read as follows:

> Tell the Lord that I pay Him a million obeisances and that I humbly submit to Him the following: Tell the madman that everyone has gone mad. Tell the madman that they are no longer selling rice in the market. Tell the madman that the crazies are no longer good for anything. Tell the madman that this is what the madman said.
> (Chaitanya Charitamrita 3.19.19-21)

Bhaktivinoda Thakur explains this riddle in this way: "Tell Mahaprabhu that everyone has become intoxicated with love for Krishna and so in the marketplace of love, no one is buying the rice of Krishna prema any longer. Tell Mahaprabhu that the crazies (*āul*) are so intoxicated with love that they are no longer doing their material duties. Tell Mahaprabhu that Advaita said this in a state of complete intoxication with prema. In short, the message was that the purpose for which Advaita had called Mahaprabhu to earth had been achieved. Now the Lord may do as He wishes."

Advaita, the avatar of Maha Vishnu, appeared in this world on the seventh day of the waxing moon (*śuklā saptamī*) in the month of Magh. This *tithi* is also known as *advaita-saptamī*.

[3] A type of banana that has large seeds. It is cultivated for its leaves rather than its fruit.

Srila Namacharya Hari Das Thakur

ṛcīkasya muneḥ putro nāmnā brahmā mahātapāḥ
prahlādena samaṁ jāto haridāsākhyako'pi san
murāri-gupta-caraṇaiś caitanya-caritāmṛte
ukto muni-sutaḥ prātas tulasi-patram āharan
adhautam abhiśaptas taṁ pitrā yavanatāṁ gataḥ
sa eva haridāsaḥ san jātaḥ parama-bhaktimān

Hari Das Thakur is a combined incarnation of Brahma Mahatapa, the son of Richika Muni, and Prahlad. The respected Murari Gupta has written in his Caitanya-carita-mahākāvya that this muni's son picked a tulasi leaf and offered it to Krishna without having washed it first. His father then cursed him to become a mleccha in his next life. He was thus born as Hari Das, a great devotee.
(*Gaura-gaṇoddeśa-dīpikā* 93-95)

HARI DAS' BIRTH AS A MUSLIM

In his book *Nabadwip-dhama-māhātmya*, Bhaktivinoda Thakur has written the following account of how Brahma became Hari Das Thakur:

Once, in the Dvapara Yuga, when Nandanandana Sri Krishna was herding the cows through Vraja Dham in the company of his cowherd boyfriends, Brahma desired to see the Lord's majestic form and opulences and decided to test Him. He stole Krishna's cows and calves as well as His friends and hid them for a year in the caves of Sumeru Mountain. But when Brahma returned to Vraja a year later, he was astonished to see that Krishna was still there with both His friends and His kin. Brahma immediately understood his error and began to regret his rash action. He fell down at Krishna's feet and begged for forgiveness; Krishna responded by mercifully revealing His divine opulence.

He who appears in the Dvapara Yuga as Nandan andana Sri Krishna, descends again in the Kali Yuga as Gauranga, taking on the mood and bodily luster of Radharani in order to display the most magnanimous pastimes. Brahma was afraid that he might commit the same offence during Gaura's incarnation, so he went to Antardwip, the central island of Nabadwip, and began to meditate. The Lord was able to understand his mind and came to him in the form of Gauranga and said, "During My incarnation as Gaura, you will be born in a family of mlecchas and will preach the glories of the Holy Name, bringing auspiciousness to all the living beings."

From this above description, it is understood that Hari Das Thakur was an incarnation of the creator god Brahma. It is said that in order to avoid coming under the influence of *ahaṁkāra*, false ego, in Gauranga lila, he prayed to Krishna to take birth in a lowly family. The same idea is found in the *Advaita-vilāsa*.

A Vaishnava may appear in any family in any class of

society. Mahaprabhu wished to show that even though he may be born in a lowly family, a Vaishnava is the ideal member of human society. In order to do so, He had His associates appear in a variety of castes. Vrindavan Das Thakur has written the following in Chaitanya Bhagavata:

> Hari Das Thakur was born in a low-caste family on the Lord's order in order to show that caste and class have no importance at all. All the scriptures say that a devotee of Vishnu, though born in a lowly family, is still worshipable by all. What will one's pedigree do for one who is born in a high caste but does not worship Krishna? He will go to hell in spite of his noble birth. Hari Das took a low birth just to bear witness to these scriptural statements. He is comparable to Prahlad who was born in a family of demons, or Hanuman, who was born a monkey. They only superficially belong to low classes.
>
> (Chaitanya Bhagavata 1.16.237-240)

Namacharya Hari Das Thakur appeared in Burhan village. Burhan is currently an administrative region containing 65 blocks (groups of villages) in the Satkhira subdivision of Khulna in Bangladesh. It is not clear exactly where Burhan village itself lies. Some people hold that it is in West Bengal in the district known as 24 Paraganas, while others say that it is in Jessore district in Bangladesh. Benapole, where many of Hari Das' pastimes took place is the first railway station after Bongaon on the line to Khulna on the Bangladesh side of the border. It is thus likely that Burhan is also on the Bangladesh side of the border.

According to some sources, Hari Das Thakur was born in a Brahmin family. His father's name was Sumati and his mother Gauri. These parents died when he was young, so he went to live with a Muslim couple named Khan in the village of Halimpur about five miles from his birthplace on the other bank of the Salai River. He was thus brought up in an Islamic environment. According to the *Advaita-vilāsa*, however, Hari Das Thakur was born in 1372 of the Shaka era (1451 AD) in the month of Agrahayan and his father's name was Khanaulla Kazi. However, Hari Das was orphaned young according to this version as well.

HARI DAS' PARTICIPATION IN THE SANKIRTAN MOVEMENT

It was Mahaprabhu's wish that Hari Das should appear long before He did. If we accept the *Advaita-vilāsa's* version, Hari Das was 35 years older than Mahaprabhu, who was born in 1407 Shaka. It is known that Nityananda was twelve years older than Mahaprabhu, so Hari Das was also 23 years older than He. Hari Das first entered into Mahaprabhu's association when the Lord returned to Nabadwip after being initiated by Ishvara Puri in Gaya and had begun preaching the sankirtan movement. When Mahaprabhu began His sankirtan pastimes in Nabadwip, He was 23 years old. From this we can reckon that Hari Das was 58 years old when he first met the Lord. Even before meeting the Lord, however, Hari Das had already started to reveal the glories of the Holy Names in many wondrous ways. He is one of the Lord's most important associates in his role as the initiator of the yuga dharma, which is Harinam sankirtan. Vrindavan Das Thakur has described Hari Das' spotless and glorious pastimes extensively in his Chaitanya Bhagavata and Krishna Das Kaviraj Goswami has supplemented this with extra information about his life and character.

> Hari Das Thakur was an extraordinary personality and a major branch of the desire tree of devotion. He would unfailingly chant 300,000 names of the Lord each day. His virtues are unlimited and I can only give a brief summary here. Advaita Acharya gave him the place of honor at his father's *śrāddha* ceremony. Hari Das Thakur possessed the same qualities as Prahlad, being undisturbed even when being beaten by the Muslims. When he entered the Lord's eternal pastimes, Mahaprabhu danced ecstatically with Hari Das' mortal remains in His arms. Vrindavan Das Thakur has described his pastimes extensively, I will simply take up what he has left unsaid.
>
> (Chaitanya Charitamrita 1.10.43-47)

It is not known exactly when Hari Das Thakur performed the various lilas that have been described, nevertheless we will try to follow a chronological order as far as possible. In the *Ādi-khaṇḍa* of the Chaitanya

Bhagavata, Vrindavan Das Thakur writes about Mahaprabhu's life from His birth until His return from Gaya. Some of Hari Das' pastimes before meeting Mahaprabhu are described there. The *Madhya-khaṇḍa* describes the period after He came back from Gaya, His ecstatic transformations in separation from Krishna, His Krishna conscious instructions to His students, His beginning the sankirtan movement with His students, His kirtan pastimes in the houses of Chandrasekhar and Srivas Pandit, and other activities up until He took sannyas.

Hari Das was an eternal associate of the Lord and he incarnated in a Muslim household in order to serve Him; from a very early age he showed a natural proclivity for the chanting of the Holy Names. His life is a brilliant example of how a devotee who chants constantly without ulterior motivation and without offences, cannot be swayed from his goal of attaining pure devotional service by any kind of worldly temptation, not even if Maya Devi herself comes to lure him. The following is a summary of what Krishna Das Kaviraj Goswami has written in the third chapter of the *Antya-līlā* of Chaitanya Charitamrita.

TEMPTATION BY THE PROSTITUTE LAKSHAHIRA

After Hari Das Thakur had left his home in Burhan, he came to the Benapole jungle, which after the pastime about to be described was given the name "the prostitute Hira's jungle." Hari Das would have been in his early youth at this time, and these events took place before Mahaprabhu had appeared. He took up residence in a cottage in a secluded part of the jungle, worshiping Tulasi Devi and daily chanting three lakhs of Names. He would beg for food at a Brahmin's house. All the people of the surrounding country observed Hari Das' spotless character and staunch devotion to the Holy Name and gave him their respect.

At the time, an atheistic Vaishnava-hater named Ramachandra Khan was the area's principal landowner. He became jealous of Hari Das Thakur's increasing reputation and decided to ruin it by showing a flaw in his character. To this end he devised numerous tactics, none of which were successful. Finally, he called some prostitutes together and asked them to seduce Hari Das. One of these prostitutes, a very beautiful young girl named Lakshahira, claimed to be able to accomplish the task within three days. Hence, Ramachandra engaged her for this mission.

Ramachandra proposed sending an armed guard with Lakshahira to take Hari Das Thakur prisoner as soon as he had been brought down, but she refused, saying that it would be better to wait until she was sure that Hari Das was ready to succumb. That night, she dressed and decorated herself in a most attractive manner and went to Hari Das' hut. The first thing she did was to pay obeisances to the Tulasi plant, showing that she was still influenced by her pious Hindu upbringing.

She then went and stood beside Hari Das. She began to use all the wiles at her command, flirting with him by saying, "You are a very handsome man, Thakur, in the full bloom of youth. What woman would be able to resist you? I have come here because I am filled with desire for you. If you do not embrace me, I will kill myself."

In answer to this, Hari Das Thakur said, "I have just begun chanting my regular number of Holy Names. As soon as I am finished I will do whatever you wish. In the meantime, please sit down and wait and listen to the sound of the Holy Name." He kept on chanting until morning, when the prostitute finally became impatient and left. She returned to Ramachandra Khan and reported Hari Das' promise to him.

That night Lakshahira returned to Hari Das' hut, and he expressed his regret at having been unable to fulfill her desires due to his inability to complete his quota of Holy Names. Once again, however, he assured her that as soon as he was finished, he would do as she wished. Lakshahira paid her obeisances to Tulasi Devi as she had the previous evening and sat down. Once again she spent the night waiting for Hari Das to finish his chanting. When morning came, she again grew restless. Hari Das said to her, "I have taken a vow to chant 10,000,000 Holy Names before the end of the month. I have almost completed this number. As a matter of fact, I should finish it this very night. Don't worry, as soon as I have fulfilled my obligation, I will be able to sleep with you."

On the third night, Lakshahira returned, again paying obeisances to the tulasi plant and sitting down beside Hari Das Thakur to listen to him chant. As she continued to listen to him repeat the Holy Names, the contaminations in her mind began to melt away and she began to regret her mission. She finally fell down at his feet and begged forgiveness of him. She told him of Ramachandra Khan's evil intentions, but Hari Das answered her, "I know all about them. I would have left here on the very first day you came, but I wanted to show you my mercy and so I stayed for three days."

Lakshahira then asked Hari Das to instruct her so that she might be saved. He told her that whatever money she had earned by sinful means should be given in charity to the Brahmins and that she should then come and take up residence in his hut, where she should worship Tulasi Devi and chant the Holy Names constantly.

Lakshahira did exactly as her guru instructed her, giving all her riches to the Brahmins and shaving her head before returning to the hut dressed in a single piece of cloth. She then started to chant three lakhs of names as Hari Das did. By virtue of her service to Tulasi and her chanting of the Holy Name, she became very renounced. All her senses were conquered and she attained pure love for Krishna. Through Hari Das Thakur's mercy, the prostitute became a great Vaishnavi.

> The prostitute became very advanced in spiritual life and a celebrated devotee. Many stalwart Vaishnavas would come to see her. (Chaitanya Charitamrta 3.3.141)

Srila Bhaktisiddhanta Saraswati Goswami Thakur has commented on Hari Das Thakur's instructions to Lakshahira in the following way: "Even though the guru has a legitimate claim on all of his disciple's worldly possessions, he does not ask for them for his own use. Those who take *dakṣiṇā*, or alms, are opening the door to the house of Yamaraj. A Vaishnava guru is not bound for the house of Yama, but is a traveler on a higher road. For this reason, there is an arrangement for giving donations to Brahmins on the *karma-mārga*. By not accepting his disciple's possessions, which are after all intended for sense gratification, the Vaishnava guru remains independent of his disciple and does not compromise his integrity. He renounces them because he knows that they will awaken in him a disinterest in the service of the Lord. Hari Das Thakur's teaching here is that the guru's duty is to rid his disciple of his mundane pride and not himself accept the material possessions his disciple has renounced."

(*Anubhāṣya* to Chaitanya Charitamrita 3.3.139)

THE FATE OF RAMACHANDRA KHAN

A Vaishnava does not take offence from anyone, for he does not even consider himself to be a Vaishnava. He accepts that all the suffering he undergoes is a result of his own sinful past and thus does not blame it on anyone else. Nevertheless, he is so dear to Krishna that the Lord never tolerates offences at his feet. The Lord never forgives offences at the feet of a devotee who is constantly engaged in acts that benefit all living beings. As a result, there is no source of self-destruction and misfortune more powerful than an offence to a Vaishnava. The results of such offences may come immediately or they may be delayed, but they are inevitable.

In the case of Ramachandra Khan, the seeds he had sown in committing offences to Hari Das Thakur grew into a great tree that bore fruit one day when Nityananda Prabhu came to his house during a preaching tour in the area. As the indwelling soul of all beings, Nityananda was perfectly aware of Ramachandra's record and had in fact come to his house because he was angry and intended to punish him. Though Nityananda Prabhu is known to be the most compassionate, merciful to even the lowliest people, saving sinners like Jagai and Madhai and giving them love of God, he too becomes angry with one who offends a Vaishnava.

As a result of his offences to Hari Das Thakur, Ramachandra Khan had become a complete demon. He thus could not give Nityananda and his companions the respect due such exalted guests, but arranged quarters for them in a cowshed. Nityananda became even more displeased with Ramachandra Khan as a result of this insult and immediately left the place. He said, "This place is not fit for us, but for cow-slaughtering meat-eaters." Not long thereafter, the Muslim revenue officer came with his soldiers to collect Khan's overdue taxes. He and his men stayed in the Durga Mandapa at Ramachandra Khan's house and killed a cow there. They took him and his family prisoner and looted the house and village, destroying his caste, his wealth and his family in one fell swoop.

Any town or country in which a great soul is insulted, even if by only one of its inhabitants, is destroyed on account of that offence. (Chaitanya Charitamrita 3.3.163)

HARI DAS IS IMPRISONED AND TORTURED

From Srila Vrindavan Das Thakur's Chaitanya Bhagavata, it is known that before meeting Advaita Prabhu in Shantipur, Hari Das lived in Phuliya. Phuliya is on the Eastern Railway line in Nadia district between Ranaghat and Shantipur, about five miles north of Ranaghat. When the Brahmins of the village saw his dedication to the chanting of the Holy Names as well as his ecstatic symptoms of love, they concluded that he was a Vaishnava of the highest order.

The local magistrate (Kazi), however, knowing that Hari Das had been born in a Muslim household, and now was showing such a taste for chanting the Holy Names of Krishna, began to fear that he might convert others to Vaishnavism. He took his complaint to the governor (Nawab), suggesting that Hari Das be punished as soon as possible. The governor ordered his officers to place Hari Das under arrest. The other prisoners already knew Hari Das' glories and thought that the sight and blessings of such a great spiritual personality would surely bring them merit to insure their early release from jail. But Hari Das told them that they were better off in jail and he blessed them that they stay there. The prisoners were naturally unhappy to hear such a "benediction," but then Hari Das explained it to them:

> "I don't mean to say that you should remain prisoners, but that you forget sense gratification and chant the names of Hari. This was the meaning of my blessing; please don't be troubled for a moment on that account."
>
> (Chaitanya Bhagavata 1.16.63-64)

In other words, while in jail the prisoners could forget the entanglements of material life and simply concentrate on chanting the Holy Name.

One day, the Nawab asked Hari Das why he had abandoned the pure religion of Islam to embrace Hinduism. Hari Das Thakur answered, "God is one. The same God is present in every religion; He is the non-dual absolute truth. In the different faiths, it is simply the name that differs, but on the absolute plane, there is no distinction. The same God sits in the heart of every living being and engages everyone in His service in different ways. We all worship in the way we are made to worship by Him. As a result, some Hindu Brahmins convert to Islam. In the same way, though I was born in a Muslim family, the Lord has engaged me in chanting the holy names of Krishna. The living being has no independence in such matters. If this is a fault, then please punish me."

The Nawab rebuked Hari Das, saying, "Chant the names of God as they are found in your own religion and stop practicing that of other people. If you don't, you will have to face a very severe punishment." Hari Das Thakur answered with conviction:

> *khaṇḍa khaṇḍa haṅ deha jāy jadi prāṇa*
> *tabu āmi vadane nā chāṛi hari-nāma*

"You may cut my body to pieces, and the life may leave it. But I will never abandon the Holy Name which my tongue will ever continue to chant."

(Chaitanya Bhagavata 16.91)

This statement demonstrated Hari Das' unswerving determination in his worship of the Name. The ordinary living entity is bound up in Maya and considers the well-being of the body to be more important than worshiping the Lord. Those who are transcendentalists recognize that the body and its interests are fleeting, and so they put them aside and concentrate on their real self interest, that of the soul, and worship the Lord.

When the Nawab saw that Hari Das Thakur's determination to continue chanting the names of Krishna was unbreakable, he asked the Kazi what should be done. The Kazi answered, "He should be given such a severe punishment that other Muslims will be afraid to convert. He should be flogged publicly in twenty-two market places until he is dead. If he is still alive after that, we will know that he really has some kind of spiritual power and has been telling the truth!"

The Nawab gave the order and several infantrymen took Hari Das Thakur from marketplace to marketplace, giving him a cruel flogging with a cane in each one. Even so, he did not die. Just like Prahlad, Krishna's mercy protected his body and kept him conscious only of the joys of the Holy Name, so that he felt not the slightest pain. The pious people of the area who witnessed the merciless beating of Hari Das were greatly distressed, but he himself did not stop praying to the Lord for the well-being of his torturers despite being ruthlessly flogged by them.

"Be merciful to all these poor souls, O Lord! Though they treat me like an enemy, do not consider this to be an offence." (Chaitanya Bhagavata 16.110)

Normally, the type of beating that was being given to Hari Das would have killed an ordinary man after only two or three marketplaces. When his torturers saw that he was still alive after twenty-two, they began to worry. The Kazi would not believe that they had really flogged him if Hari Das remained alive, and would order them to be killed in punishment for their failure. When Hari Das saw that they were inconvenienced by his remaining alive, he went into a deep trance of meditation on Krishna, appearing to everyone as though dead.

The infantrymen took the body to the Nawab who ordered it to be buried. But the Kazi objected, saying that because Hari Das had engaged in such reprehensible activities, he should not be given a Muslim burial but thrown into the water. So on the Kazi's order, the soldiers flung Hari Das' body into the Ganges. To everyone's surprise, Hari Das floated to the other shore where he climbed onto dry land and started walking in the direction of Phuliya, chanting the Holy Names in a loud voice. Both the Nawab and the Kazi realized that he was a real saint or *pīr* and they fell to the ground in obeisances and begged him for forgiveness. By Hari Das' grace, they were forgiven their wicked misdeeds. The Nawab gave Hari Das official permission to go wherever he pleased and to chant the Holy Names.

In the tenth chapter of the *Madhya-khaṇḍa*, Vrindavan Das Thakur writes that while Hari Das was being cruelly beaten, Mahaprabhu descended with His discus, intending to destroy the demons, but was unable to do so on account of Hari Das' prayers. So He shielded Hari Das' body with His own. The Lord then revealed to Hari Das the cane marks on His own back. The main reason for the Lord's appearance is His devotee. When such an outrage was being perpetrated on His devotee, He immediately appeared to protect him.

When Hari Das heard the Lord recount this story, he immediately fainted. The Lord then showed him His divine form. He glorified Hari Das himself: "Anyone who even sees Hari Das becomes free from all bondage. Even great gods like Brahma and Shiva desire Hari Das' company and the Ganges desires his touch."

The Brahmins of Phuliya were overjoyed to see Hari Das again. They had been paralyzed by the news that he was being flogged in all the district marketplaces. Hari Das told them that he had had to submit to these events because he had heard the blasphemy of Vaishnavas, which in itself is a great offence. Indeed, the punishment that he had received could be considered minimal.

HARI DAS MEETS ADVAITA ACHARYA

Later, Hari Das came into contact with Advaita Acharya. Advaita was born in 1434, 52 years before the appearance of Chaitanya Mahaprabhu, so he was 17 years older than Hari Das. Hari Das was attracted to Advaita's discourses on Vaishnava philosophy, while Advaita recognized Hari Das' exalted character as a *bhajanānandī* devotee dedicated to constant chanting of the Holy Name.

In recognition of his exalted status, Advaita Prabhu gave Hari Das the *śrāddha* plate that was normally given only to Brahmins. When Hari Das objected to the honor, Advaita said, "Feeding you is the equivalent of giving thousands of Brahmins food to eat." Thenceforward Hari Das daily took his midday meal at Advaita's house at his invitation. From Krishna Das Kaviraj Goswami's account, it is apparent that these events took place before Mahaprabhu's appearance. The primary reason for Mahaprabhu's incarnation was the devotion and the heartfelt prayers of both Advaita Acharya and Hari Das Thakur.

Advaita began to wonder how the world could be saved. How can this world without devotion for the Supreme Lord ever achieve liberation. Determined to make Krishna descend, he worshiped Krishna with Ganges water and tulasi leaves. Meanwhile, Hari Das Thakur was in his grotto chanting the Holy Names and also praying for Krishna to appear. Chaitanya Mahaprabhu's appearance, by which He saved the world through preaching the chanting of the Holy Names and love of Krishna, was the result of both these persons' devotion.

(Chaitanya Charitamrita 3.3.221-4)

MAYA DEVI TRIES TO TEMPT HARI DAS

While Hari Das Thakur was sitting in his grotto in Phuliya and chanting the Holy Names with exclusive devotion, Maya Devi the presiding deity of the material manifestation, the Lord's illusory potency, came herself to test him. She took on the form of a beautiful woman and called out to him in a sweet voice that would have shaken the resolve of even great sages, imploring him to embrace her. Once again, Hari Das told her that he would complete his vow of chanting a fixed number of Harinam, and only then he would satisfy her desires. Although she came three nights in a row, Maya Devi was astonished to see that there was not the slightest wavering in Hari Das Thakur's resolve to chant the Holy Name. She admitted defeat and prayed to him for his mercy. Hari Das then gave her initiation in the Maha Mantra and thus Maya Devi left, feeling that she had been fulfilled. Before she disappeared, she said,

"Previously I received the name of Rama from Shiva, but I had the desire to hear the name of Krishna from you. Rama's name is the tāraka-nāma that gives liberation, whereas Krishna's name is called the pāraka-nāma because it gives prema. You have made me fortunate by initiating me in Krishna's name, for I feel a flood of love for Him washing over me." (Chaitanya Charitamrita 3.3.254-6)

A devotee who chants the Holy Name without artifice cannot be swayed from the path of pure devotion, not even by the personification of Maya herself. Once again, Hari Das Thakur is an outstanding example. There was no object of enjoyment in this entire world that could tempt him. If one sees a person who is apparently taking shelter of the Holy Name but at the same time succumbs to the temptations of women, wealth and power, it can be understood that he is not truly surrendering to the Name. *Phalena phala-kāraṇam anumīyate*: one can guess the cause by examining the results. Although we see the Holy Names being chanted in many places, we do not often see the desired results. The reason is that those who are chanting are not doing it in a fashion that is sincere, single-minded and offenceless.

HARI DAS, THE SNAKE AND THE SNAKE-CHARMER

In the grotto where Hari Das performed his bhajan lived a poisonous snake. Those who came to visit Hari Das' residence were placed in some discomfort because of the poisonous fumes emanating from this beast. Some local doctors, who were particularly expert in dealing with snakebite, warned Hari Das of the danger and advised him to leave his place of worship. At the persistent pleadings of all the people, Hari Das finally agreed to move. However, as he was about to leave just before sunset, the great serpent itself left the grotto of its own accord.

Another lesson that can be taken from Hari Das' life is that making a public display of love of Krishna in order to gain public prestige is very detrimental to one's devotional life. One day, a snake charmer from Phuliya village went to a rich man's house to sing Krishna's pastime of taming the serpent Kaliya. Hari Das was present and when he heard the lilas of Krishna, he became so affected by love that he fainted and the various manifestations of ecstatic love became present on his body. All the people present took the dust of Hari Das' feet and smeared it on their bodies.

A certain Brahmin who was present there saw the respect that the people were showing Hari Das and became jealous. The shameless fellow had such a strong desire for prestige that when the snake charmer continued his song, he too fell to the ground and started to make a show of all kinds of false ecstasies. The snake charmer could recognize the faker for what he was and started to hit him with a cane. The Brahmin began to scream and plead and then ran away. The snake charmer explained to everyone present the spontaneity of Hari Das' love and the falseness of the Brahmin's pretense. This shows that even a humble snake charmer can have enough common sense to distinguish between real and faked ecstatic symptoms.

THE LOUD CHANTING OF THE HOLY NAMES

Hari Das Thakur constantly chanted the Holy Name and called to the Lord in a loud voice. At that time, not many people were able to understand the value of this practice. Prior to Gaurasundara's appearance, most people were simply interested in sense gratification and inimical to devotion for Krishna and the chanting of His holy names. Advaita Acharya and Hari Das Thakur were saddened by this terrible situation. When the non-devotees heard them chanting loudly, they would say, "The Lord sleeps during the four months of the rainy season. If you call to Him out loud in this way, you will wake Him up and that will be a grave offence. There will be famine in the country if you keep on with it. Some Brahmins have taken up this chanting business as a way of worshiping their own bellies, no doubt." They would criticize Hari Das and Advaita by joking in this way. Even though such criticism pained Hari Das, he never stopped chanting Hare Krishna in a loud voice.

One day, a Brahmin from a village named Harinadi in Jessore district started a debate with Hari Das on this subject. He argued that the names of the Lord should be meditated upon and that there was no reason to chant them aloud. He wanted to know in which scripture it was stated that one should chant aloud. In answer to these questions, Hari Das Thakur gave a detailed account of the glories of the Holy Name. He said that loud chanting of the Holy Names was a hundred times more powerful than japa. Through the loud chanting of the Names, even the birds, animals and other creatures are also saved.

Animals, birds, insects and other creatures are unable to speak, but if they just hear the Holy Name, they can all cross over the ocean of nescience. If you chant the Holy Names silently, then you yourself will be saved, but if you chant aloud, then you will benefit others. Therefore, all the scriptures state that by the loud chanting of the Name, a hundred times greater result can be obtained.

(Chaitanya Bhagavata 1.16.280-2)

japato hari-nāmāni
sthāne śata-guṇādhikaḥ
ātmānaṁ ca punāty uccair
japan śrotṝn punāti ca

Someone who chants the Holy Names aloud is a hundred times better than one who performs japa, because the one who is chanting japa simply benefits himself, while the person who chants japa aloud not only does good for himself, but for all those who hear him as well.

(*Nāradīya Purāṇa*)

Who is better, the person who earns money and spends it all on himself, or the one who uses his money to help thousands of others? Through silent japa, one takes care of his own spiritual needs, whereas all living beings are benefited through loud *sankirtan*. This is why it is considered to be superior.

Even though he heard Hari Das quote scripture in support of his idea, the Brahmin from Harinadi village was unconvinced. Indeed, he became angry and began to verbally abuse Hari Das by bringing up his low birth. He said, "If everything that you say about the Holy Name is not found in scripture, then I will publicly cut off your nose and ear as a punishment." As a result of this offensive behavior, the Brahmin contracted smallpox not long afterward and his own nose and ear fell off.

THE OFFENCES OF GOPAL CHAKRAVARTI

Once Hari Das Thakur came to Hooghly and stayed in the village of Chandpur, near Saptagram-Triveni, at the house of Hiranya and Govardhan Majumdar's family priest, Balaram Acharya. He was given a straw hut to live in, and there he chanted the Holy Names all day long, taking food at Balaram Acharya's house. Govardhan's son Raghunath Das Goswami was a young boy at the time and would often visit Hari Das, whose merciful glance made it possible for him to eventually come into Mahaprabhu's direct company.

Hiranya and Govardhan Majumdar would regularly arrange for discussions of the Bhagavata and other scriptures at their house. One day Balaram Acharya brought Hari Das Thakur to this assembly. When Raghunath's father heard about Hari Das Thakur's various qualities and that he chanted three lakhs of Names every day, he was very impressed.

While discussing the scriptures at the meeting, the scholars present brought up the subject of the glories of the Holy Names. One pandit said that the Holy Name destroys sins; another claimed it bestows liberation. Hari Das said that the primary fruit of chanting the Holy Name is love for the lotus feet of Sri Krishna, and the destruction of accumulated sinful karmas and liberation from the material condition are only its secondary effects. He gave the following example: with the dawn's first light, the darkness is dissipated and with it goes the fear of thieves, ghosts and demons. With the full rising of the sun, one can set about doing one's daily duties. Similarly, even before one has experienced the full manifestation of the Holy Name, one's sins are destroyed and one becomes liberated. With its full manifestation, one attains Krishna prema. The reflection of the Holy Name (*nāmābhāsa*) brings liberation, the devotee considers liberation such an inconsequential benefit that he does not accept it even if the Lord wants to give it him.

One of the people who heard Hari Das speak was a Brahmin named Gopal Chakravarti, a handsome and learned young scholar who worked as a tax collector for the Muslim government. When he heard that simply the shadow of the Holy Name could bring liberation, he got angry and said, "Fellow scholars! These are the statements of a sentimentalist. Even after millions of births of cultivating knowledge, one may or may not attain liberation. Yet this fellow says that just a glimpse of the Holy Name will bring that result!"

Hari Das Thakur answered, "The pleasure of liberation is insignificant when compared to the ecstasy of devotion. Just a shadow of devotion, just a shadow of the Holy Name, will easily produce liberation."

The Brahmin became even angrier and said, "Hari Das must swear that he will cut off his nose if one is not liberated by *nāmābhāsa*."

Hari Das Thakur had no trouble agreeing to this, but the rest of the people in the assembly were shocked by Gopal's breach of proper etiquette toward a great spiritual personality. Hiranya and Govardhan rebuked the tax collector. Balaram Acharya also chastised him saying, "You are a foolish logician. What do you know about devotion? You have insulted Hari Das Thakur. Nothing positive will come of that. You will be ruined on account of it." All the other members of the assembly fell at Hari Das' feet and asked for forgiveness for Gopal's behavior, but he only said, "Neither he nor you are at fault. The Brahmin is ignorant and addicted to argument. One cannot understand the glories of the Holy Name through logic. May the Lord bless you all. Don't worry about me." The Majumdars ostracized Gopal Chakravarti, banning him from their home.

Though Hari Das Thakur took no offence at Gopal Chakravarti's words and even forgave him, Krishna does not take the blasphemy of a devotee lightly and so he punished the Brahmin. Three days later he contracted leprosy and his prominent nose decayed and melted off. Everyone was terrified by the Brahmin's misfortune and glorified Hari Das Thakur's spiritual power, but it was a source of distress to Hari Das himself.

HARI DAS COMES TO NABADWIP

After this, Hari Das Thakur went to live in Nabadwip out of a desire to be with pure devotees like Advaita Acharya. He was thus present there when Mahaprabhu began to reveal the purpose of His divine incarnation. Hari Das' participation in these pastimes is described in the *Madhya-khaṇḍa* where it is said that he was a participant in the sankirtan festivities in the houses of Chandrasekhar and Srivas Pandit.

When the Vaishnavas heard that the Lord had begun His sankirtan pastimes, they all were overjoyed. Every night He would hold kirtan in the house of Srivas Pandit, or sometimes at the house of Chandrasekhar Acharya. Nityananda, Gadadhar, Advaita, Srivas, Vidyanidhi, Murari, Hiranya and Hari Das were all there.
(Chaitanya Bhagavata 2.8.110-112)

Hari Das and Nityananda Prabhu were the first preachers of the Holy Name. Mahaprabhu ordered them to go from door to door to beg people to chant the names of Krishna, to worship Him and to study the Vaishnava scriptures.

One day, the Lord suddenly had an idea and He called Nityananda and Hari Das to tell them: "Listen, listen, Nityananda. Listen, Hari Das. I wish you to go and tell everyone of My order. Knock on every door and beg people to chant the names of Krishna, worship Krishna, and learn about Krishna. Speak of nothing but this and inspire others to do the same. At the end of the day, come here and tell me the results of your preaching. If people do not comply after you implore them in this way, I will come and destroy them with the discus in My hand."
(Chaitanya Bhagavata 2.13.7-11)

Nityananda Prabhu and Hari Das Thakur followed the Lord's order and began preaching throughout Nabadwip town. One day they went up to two feared drunken bandits named Jagai and Madhai, and asked them to chant the Holy Name as the Lord had instructed them. Seeing their fallen condition, Nityananda was particularly merciful toward them, but Jagai and Madhai were so inebriated that they simply became angry when they heard his appeal, and turned on him and Hari Das, intending to give them a beating. They both started to run away, but Hari Das, being already quite advanced in age, was unable to keep up with Nityananda. Nevertheless, he somehow managed to escape with his life.

That evening, Hari Das told Advaita Acharya about the day's events, saying that he would not go out preaching with Nityananda any more, since his behavior was rash and unpredictable. The all-powerful Lord Nityananda's running away is certainly a mysterious pastime, but it is to be remembered that he later went out on his own and managed to deliver the two rascals, Jagai and Madhai.

Hari Das Thakur also engaged in water sports with the Lord in Nabadwip. One day, overcome by a mood of love, the Lord tried to drown Himself in the Ganges, but Hari Das and Nityananda jumped in to save Him. They then hid Mahaprabhu in the house of Nandan Acharya because of his wish for seclusion. When Advaita Acharya and the other devotees felt the distress of separation from the Lord, Hari Das went and brought Srivas to Nandan Acharya's house, bringing about the reunion of the devotees and the Lord.

When Mahaprabhu put on a play about Krishna's Vrindavan pastimes in the house of Chandrasekhar Acharya, Hari Das played the part of the town constable. He came onto the scene, dressed as a policeman, carrying a stick in his hand. The other actors in the play were Mahaprabhu as *Ādyā śakti*, Nityananda as an old cowherd woman, Advaita as the clown, Gadadhar Pandit as a cowherd girl, and Srivas Pandit as Narada Muni. Hari Das' duty in the play was to announce its beginning, telling everyone to wake up to the service of Krishna. He cried out, "Wake up! Wake up! Wake up, for Srivas will dance dressed as Narada Muni." (Chaitanya Bhagavata 2.18.100)

When the Lord took His sankirtan party along the banks of the Bhagirathi, Hari Das joined Him.

Then Hari Das, the ocean of Krishna-rasa danced beautifully on Mahaprabhu's order.
(Chaitanya Bhagavata 2.23.204)

The night before Mahaprabhu left to take sannyas, Hari Das stayed at his home. He and all the other devotees were devastated by the Lord's intention to take the renounced order. Not long after the Lord went to Puri, Hari Das followed Him. He went with the other Bengali devotees to see the Rathayatra and never left.

HARI DAS THAKUR IN PURI

After Mahaprabhu's tour of South India, He returned to Jagannath Puri and centred His life of worship around the Jagannath temple and its annual cycle of festivals. After the Snana Yatra, when Lord Jagannath was absent from the temple (*anavasara-kāla*), Mahaprabhu felt separation so intensely that he went to stay in Alalanath. In the meantime, when His devotees in Bengal heard that He was back, they immediately organized a pilgrimage to Jagannath Puri for the Rathayatra. Hari Das was amongst these devotees.

When Mahaprabhu heard that the more than 200 devotees from Bengal had arrived, He returned to Puri where He met them at Kashi Mishra's house. At first He did not see Hari Das Thakur, and so He inquired after him. In fact, Hari Das was standing in the roadway, paying his obeisances from there. The devotees went to Hari Das and told him that Mahaprabhu wanted to see him, but Hari Das answered,

"I am a low-born person with no good qualities. I have no right to go near the temple. If I can find a solitary place to stay in some garden somewhere, then I will pass my time there alone. That way there is no danger that the servants of Jagannath will accidentally touch me. This is my wish." (Chaitanya Charitamrita 2.11.165-7)

The devotees came back to Mahaprabhu to report what Hari Das had said, and this wish pleased Him. He asked for Kashi Mishra to arrange for a solitary cottage for Hari Das in a garden not far from His own place of worship, the Gambhira. Kashi Mishra was happy to have the chance to serve the Lord by making these arrangements according to His order.

After everyone was settled in their own quarters, the

Lord went to see Hari Das, who was ecstatically chanting the Holy Names. When Hari Das saw the Lord, he immediately fell to the ground again in respectful obeisances. The Lord lifted him from the ground and embraced him, but Hari Das said, "Lord, I am an untouchable. You should not touch me." The Lord answered:

"I touch you for my own purification, for you have reached a level of holiness that I haven't. At every moment, you are engaged in every pious activity: you are constantly bathing in the water of every holy place; you are constantly engaged in all the sacrifices, penances and charity. You are constantly studying the Vedic scriptures. You are thus holi-

er than any Brahmin or sannyasi."

After saying this, the Lord took him to the flower garden and gave him the solitary room there as a place to stay. "Stay here and chant the Holy Names. I will come every day to visit you. You can see the discus (chakra) on the pinnacle of the temple tower from here. Pay your obeisances when you see it. I will arrange for Jagannath's prasad to be brought to you here every day."

(Chaitanya Charitamrita 2.11.189-95)

This flower garden is now known as Siddha Bakula. Previously it was named Mudra Math. There is a legend connected with the Siddha Bakula tree. Lord Jagannath's pujaris have a tradition of giving some fortunate person the twig used to clean Jagannath's teeth as prasad. One day they gave Mahaprabhu a bakula twig that had been so used. The Lord planted this twig in the ground at Hari Das' place of bhajan. This twig eventually grew into a large tree. It is said that the Lord planted the twig on the first day of the month of Chaitra also known as *Mahāviṣuva Saṅkrānti*, the day when the sun enters into the sign of Aries. For this reason, a festival named *Danta-kāṣṭha-ropaṇa mahotsava* is held every year on that day to celebrate the occasion.

Though Hari Das was not officially banned from going into the Jagannath temple or the house of Kashi Mishra (where Mahaprabhu was staying), he never went there out of humility for his lowly birth. Like Hari Das, Rupa and Sanatan Goswami never entered the Jagannath temple. Even though they were born in a very high-caste Brahmin family. Rupa and Sanatan considered themselves to be no better than mlecchas because of their long association with the Muslim court. When in Puri, they would stay with Hari Das and go for darshan of neither Jagannath nor Mahaprabhu. On the other hand, Mahaprabhu Himself would go to see them every day.

Hari Das, Rupa and Sanatan never entered the Jagannath temple, but when Mahaprabhu went to see the Upala-bhoga in the morning, He would regularly go to Hari Das' cottage where they were staying. It was the Lord's regular practice to visit Rupa and Sanatan whenever they were staying in Puri. (Chaitanya Charitamrita 2.1.63-65)

Srila Hari Das Thakur participated in the kirtan during the Rathayatra festival as the main dancer in one of the seven kirtan sampradayas. He was in the third group, whose lead singer was Mukunda Datta.

HARI DAS' TEACHINGS ON THE HOLY NAME

Mahaprabhu taught the glories of the Holy Name through Hari Das Thakur. One day, the Lord was feeling particularly unhappy about the lot of the conditioned souls. He came to Siddha Bakula and said to the Thakur: "Hari Das, in the age of Kali, the non-Hindus kill the cow and are inimical to the Brahmins. How will these Muslims ever be saved?" Hari Das answered, "Don't be distressed at seeing the pitiable condition of the Muslims. They will be liberated by the *nāmābhāsa*, the shadow of the Holy Name, whenever they say *hārām*.[4] In the *Nṛsiṁha-purāṇa*, it is said,

daṁṣṭri-dantāhato mleccho hārāmeti punaḥ punaḥ
uktvāpi muktim āpnoti kiṁ punaḥ śraddhayā gṛṇan

When wounded by the tusks of a boar, the Muslim cries out "Hārāma, Hārāma!" again and again. If he attains liberation by so doing, then just think what will be the result if one chants the name of Rama with faith.

(Chaitanya Charitamrita 3.3.56)

Bhaktivinoda Thakur says that if any Muslim dies while saying this word, he is immediately liberated. This is *nāmābhāsa* or *nāma-saṅketa* because the speaker makes the correct sound even though he does not intend the Lord Rama by it. When the Holy Name is such a powerful sound, it is impossible to say just what fruits await the sincere and faithful chanter. The example is given of Ajamila who called the name of his son Narayan as he was dying, but attained liberation through this *nāmābhāsa*.

When he heard Hari Das' explanation, Mahaprabhu was very pleased, but again He asked him, "But how will the dumb animals and the trees and plants be delivered?" Hari Das answered:

"You yourself have instituted the loud chanting of the Holy Names, which both the moving and non-moving creatures can hear. The mobile creatures are freed from their bondage to repeated birth and death by hearing the Holy Name. As for the immobile, they perform kirtan themselves by echoing its sound. By your indescribable mercy, the entire universe is engaged in kirtan and the mobile and immobile beings dance when they hear it... You preached the loud chanting of the Holy Names by which the repeated births and deaths of all living beings come to an end."

(Chaitanya Charitamrita 3.3.68-71, 75)

THE DISAPPEARANCE OF HARI DAS THAKUR

Rupa and Sanatan Goswami first met Hari Das when he accompanied Mahaprabhu to Ramakeli on His aborted pilgrimage to Vrindavan. They thus knew each other's virtues quite well. One day in Puri, after Hari Das recited the glories of Sanatan Goswami, Sanatan returned the favor by praising him as follows:

"Is anyone your equal? You are the most fortunate member of Mahaprabhu's entourage. The purpose of the Lord's incarnation is the preaching of the Holy Name; but He accomplishes His personal mission through you. Every single day you chant three lakhs of Holy Names and you glorify the Holy Name to everyone you meet. Some people act properly but do not deliver the message of Krishna consciousness, while others preach but do not meet the behavioral standards. You both demonstrate ideal behavior and you preach the chanting of the Holy Names. You are a perfect human being and the spiritual master of everyone in the universe." (Chaitanya Charitamrita 3.4.99-103)

In the eleventh chapter of the Chaitanya Charitamrita's *Antya-līlā*, Krishna Das Kaviraj Goswami describes Hari Das Thakur's disappearance in a most captivating way. This account should be read by in its entirety to commemorate that day. A brief summary is given here:

namāmi hari dāsaṁ taṁ caitanyaṁ taṁ ca tat-prabhum
saṁsthitām api yan-mūrtiṁ skāndhe kṛtvā nanarta yaḥ

I offer my obeisances to Hari Das as well as to his worshipable Lord, Chaitanya Mahaprabhu, who placed his body on His shoulders and danced.

(Chaitanya Charitamrta 3.11.1)

As Hari Das Thakur grew old, it became more and more difficult for him to maintain his vow of chanting three lakhs of Names every day. Thus, he had no appetite when Govinda came with Jagannath's prasad and would eat only a single grain of rice just to avoid disrespecting the holy food. Out of His affection for Hari Das, Mahaprabhu told him that he was a perfected being and that there was no need for him to show such attachment for devotional service in practice; he could thus reduce the number of Holy Names that he chanted every day.

Hari Das then revealed what was really bothering him. He knew that Mahaprabhu would soon be ending His pastimes in this world and he wished to leave before Him. The affectionate Lord granted Hari Das his wish, even though He felt desolate at the prospect of losing his company.

Hari Das Thakur sat in front of Mahaprabhu, who was standing, and gazed at His lotus face. As the tears flowed from his eyes, he took the Lord's lotus feet on his chest and, with the names "Krishna Chaitanya" on his lips, voluntarily left his body like Bhishma.

All around them, the devotees were being swept away by a kirtan that grew louder and louder. The Lord spontaneously lifted Hari Das' body and started to dance around the courtyard, holding him to His chest. In the accompaniment of the loud singing of the Holy Names, He and the devotees took Hari Das' remains to the beach. There they washed the body in the sea and then dug a hole in the sand where they placed it. Mahaprabhu was the first to throw sand into the samadhi. This was the samadhi ritual of Hari Das Thakur and by virtue of his continued presence, the seashore has become a great place of pilgrimage.

Mahaprabhu circumambulated the burial place and then went personally to the Jagannath temple to beg prasad for a feast in honor of Hari Das. Svarupa Damodar Goswami would not let Mahaprabhu carry the prasad, but took personal responsibility for organizing the festival. At the feast, all the devotees were given enough food to eat to their fill. In a mood of absorption in divine love, Mahaprabhu said to them:

"All those who witnessed Hari Das Thakur's disappearance festival, who participated in it by dancing or singing the Holy Names, who threw sand on his samadhi or took maha prasad on this occasion, will quickly attain Krishna. This is the fruit of seeing a great personality like Hari Das Thakur. The Supreme Lord was so merciful that He gave Me Hari Das' association, and now the independent Lord has again deprived Me of that association. When Hari Das decided that he wanted to leave, there was nothing I could do to keep him back. He left his body at the very moment he desired to do so, just as we have heard that Bhishma did. Hari Das was the exemplar of humanity in this world, and now that he is gone, the world has lost a jewel. All glories to Hari Das Thakur! Sing the Lord's names!" Having finished His eulogy, the Lord began once again to dance. (Chaitanya Charitamrita 3.11.91-98)

Hari Das Thakur's *tirodhāna-lila* took place on the fourteenth day of the waxing moon in the month of Bhadra.

---

[4] The Arabic word harām (hārām in Bengal) means anything which is impure according to the Islamic religion. For Bengali Muslims, it particularly refers to the pig or boar which is an untouchable animal in Islam.

Ganga Das Pandit

GANGA DAS' PREVIOUS IDENTITY

purāsīd raghunāthasya yo vaśiṣṭha-munir guruḥ
sa prakāśa-viśeṣeṇa gaṅgā-dāsa-sudarśanau

Ramachandra's guru, Vasishtha Muni, appeared in two expansions in Gaura lila as Ganga Das Pandit and Sudarshana. (Gaura-gaṇoddeśa-dīpikā 53)

ācāryaḥ śrī-jagannātho gaṅgā-dāsa prabhu-priyaḥ
āsīn madhu-vane prāg yo durvāsā gopikā-priyaḥ

Jagannath Acharya and Ganga Das Pandit were previously Durvasa, who was so dear to the gopis in Madhuvana. (Gaura-gaṇoddeśa-dīpikā 199)

Ganga Das was very dear to Lord Chaitanya Mahaprabhu. Anyone who remembers him will be freed from all material bondage.
(Chaitanya Charitamrita 1.10.29)

In his Chaitanya Bhagavata, Vrindavan Das Thakur identifies Ganga Das Pandit as Krishna's guru Sandipani Muni:

There was a wonderful professor in Nabadwip named Ganga Das Pandit, who resembled Krishna's guru, Sandipani Muni. (Chaitanya Bhagavata, 1.8.26)

In the *Gauḍīya Vaiṣṇava Abhidhāna*, Haridas Das suggests that Ramachandra's guru Vasishtha entered into Sandipani Muni during Krishna lila. Thus, these apparently conflicting statements can be true. In verse 52 of *Gaura-gaṇoddeśa-dīpikā*, however, Kavi Karnapur identifies Sandipani Muni with Keshava Bharati.

Advaita Acharya is the incarnation of Maha Vishnu. Out of a desire to see the salvation of all creatures in this world, he prayed and called to Krishna to descend to this earth. Indeed, it was through the heartfelt cries of Advaita that Chaitanya Mahaprabhu felt obliged to descend. It was the Lord's desire that all His eternally perfected associates from His previous incarnations who played the role of His seniors descend prior to His own appearance. Ganga Das Pandit was one of these elders (*guru-varga*) who preceded the Lord.

Nityananda Prabhu appeared in the land of Rarha while Ganga Das Pandit, Murari Gupta and Mukunda also appeared elsewhere. (Chaitanya Charitamrita 1.13.61)

Many other associates of the Lord remained hidden in Nabadwip, taking birth there prior to Him on His order. They included Chandrasekhar, Jagadish, Gopinath, Sriman, Murari, Sri Garuda and Ganga Das.
(Chaitanya Bhagavata 1.9.98-9)

NIMAI'S STUDENT LIFE

Jagannath took little Nimai to Ganga Das when the child expressed his desire to study with him. Ganga Das lived in the neighborhood known as Ganganagar. It is said that when Bhagiratha brought down the Ganges, the goddess waited on this spot for the arrival of Gauranga Mahaprabhu. During the parikrama of Nabadwip Dham, the devotees sit down at a spot near the Yoga Pith temple to hear the glories of Ganga Das' home, even though it is in fact situated in Simantadwip.

In his commentary to Chaitanya Bhagavata, Srila Bhaktisiddhanta Saraswati Goswami Thakur writes: "Gaura-Narayan is the Lord of Vaikuntha, the Supreme Personality of Godhead. He is therefore the only reservoir of all scriptural knowledge, as well as the embodiment of the opulence of wisdom. Even so, He accepts human-like conditions during His incarnation and thus desired to learn grammar and other arts and sciences just as Krishna did when He studied with Sandipani Muni. He did this to show that those who make a living as teachers should have genuine learning and not make a pretense of possessing knowledge." (Gauḍīya-bhāṣya, 1.8.24)

When Jagannath Mishra brought Nimai to Ganga Das, the scholar was overjoyed to accept Him as his student. He began to teach Him with as much care as if He were his own son. He was astounded by Nimai's powerful memory and His intelligence. Though he had taught thousands of students, he had never had a pupil of such caliber. A student of quality brings glory to his teacher.

Nimai would ask trick questions of his fellow students Murari Gupta, Krishnananda, Kamala Kanta and others. He was able to explain a sutra in one way and then again in a completely different way, baffling His classmates while impressing them with His scholarship. Thus, the Lord's education pastimes took place in the home of Ganga Das Pandit.

This is the house of Ganga Das Pandit, where the son of Sachi studied grammar. He took delight in study daily, even making his own explanatory comments on the sutras. With a twinkle in His eye, He would ask tricky questions of Murari Gupta, Krishnananda, Kamala Kanta, and his classmates. Gaurasundara immersed Himself completely in the joys of learning—such pastimes are beyond the ken of the great gods themselves. (Bhakti-ratnākara 12.2185-8)

The Lord studied grammar with Ganga Das Pandit. He would only have to hear a lesson once in order to learn both the sutra and its explanation by heart.
(Chaitanya Charitamrita 1.15.5)

MAHAPRABHU AFTER HIS RETURN FROM GAYA

After Nimai's return from Gaya in 1509, all the Nabadwip devotees, Srivas Pandit, Sriman Pandit, Gadadhar Pandit, Sadashiva, and Shuklambara

Brahmachari were amazed to see the transformation in His character. They also felt great joy to see how He had abandoned His attachment to studies to turn to devotion to Krishna and preaching.

Even so, on His return, Mahaprabhu continued to set the proper example of how to serve one's teacher, going to Ganga Das' house and paying obeisances to his feet. Ganga Das also displayed the suitable behavior of a guru toward his dear disciple by embracing Him with respect and affection. If one's education does not lead to devotion to Krishna, it is a waste of time. Through devotion to Krishna, one's ancestors on both the father and mother's side are delivered. Ganga Das Pandit was also happy to see Nimai's transformation, but he told Him to continue teaching.

Nimai's guru said, "Your life is blessed, my child. Your mother and father's forefathers have all been delivered. Neither You nor Your students should open a book today, even if Brahma himself tells You to do so. You have come now and everyone has seen You, so go home for today. Come back tomorrow, however, and continue teaching."
(Chaitanya Bhagavata 2.1.122-4)

I pay my obeisances to Ganga Das Pandit's feet, for he has the Lord of the Vedas and the husband of the Goddess of Learning as his disciple. What goals are left for Ganga Das to achieve? His disciple is worshipable to the fourteen worlds.
(Chaitanya Bhagavata 2.1.283-4)

GANGA DAS AT SRIVAS ANGAN

Nityananda Prabhu, the savior of the most fallen, also visited Ganga Das Pandit one day after having been worshiped in Srivas Pandit's house. At the time He was wandering through Nabadwip in the mood of a child, playing with the boys of the town.

On the day that Mahaprabhu sat on Vishnu's throne in the house of Srivas Pandit, displaying his effulgent form for twenty-one hours in the *Mahā-prakāśa*, He called all His devotees one by one, to give them His blessings. On this occasion He called Ganga Das as well, reminding him of the following event from the past.

One day, Ganga Das had left his home with his wife and children out of fear for the Muslim rulers. He was standing by the banks of the Ganges with his family, waiting for a ferry to come to take them across the river, but none came. This was causing him no small amount of anxiety, but even after waiting almost the whole night, no ferry docked at the quay. He began to weep in the fear that the Muslims would touch his family members and contaminate them. He thought that he would have to drown himself in the Ganges if this ever happened.

At that very moment, Mahaprabhu himself took the form of a ferryman and arrived at the riverbank. Ganga Das was so glad to see him that he said:

Oh brother! Please save me. My caste, my life, my wealth and my body are all dependent on you. Help me by taking my family and me across the river right now. I will give you a silver coin and a pair of new garments.
(Chaitanya Bhagavata 2.9.116)

The Lord then took them on board and across the river, after which he returned to his abode in Vaikuntha. When Ganga Das heard the Lord recount this event, of which only he had known, he fainted in ecstasy.

GANGA DAS PANDIT IN PURI

After the Lord took sannyas at Katwa, Nityananda Prabhu tricked Him into going to Advaita's house in Shantipur. Ganga Das came there to see Him along with the rest of the Nabadwip devotees. He was also one of the first Bengali devotees to go to Puri to see the Lord there. The first time that the devotees went to Puri, the Lord was in Alalanath due to his feelings of separation from Jagannath, who cannot be seen for a period following the Snana Yatra. On hearing that the Bengali devotees had come, the Lord immediately returned to Puri to meet them. Sarvabhauma Bhattacharya pointed out these devotees to King Prataparudra, naming them one by one, including Ganga Das (Chaitanya Charitamrita 2.11.85).

When the Lord met Ganga Das on that occasion, He praised him to the Orissan devotees and embraced him respectfully (Chaitanya Charitamrita 2.11.159-60). Ganga Das also participated in the kirtan before the Jagannath cart as a member of the chorus in the second kirtan group, which had Srivas Pandit as its lead singer and Nityananda as its chief dancer. Hari Das Thakur, Sriman Pandit, Shubhananda and Srirama Pandit were some of the others in the same group (Chaitanya Charitamrita 2.13.38-9).

SRIVAS PANDIT

śrīvāsa-paṇḍito dhīmān yaḥ purā nārado muniḥ
parvatākhyo muni-varo ya āsīn nārada-priyaḥ
śri-rāma-paṇḍitaḥ śrīmān tat-kaniṣṭha-sahodaraḥ
nāmnāmbikā vraje dhātrī stanya-dātrī sthitā purā
saiveyaṁ Malini nāmnī śrīvāsa-gṛhiṇī matā

Srivas is Narada, who plays such an important part in Krishna's lila. Narada Muni's friend Parvata Muni appeared as Srivas' younger brother Ramai. Srivas' wife Malini Devi was Krishna's wet nurse in Vraja, Ambika.
(*Gaura-gaṇoddeśa-dīpikā* 90)

THE PANCHA TATTVA

pañcatattvātmakaṁ kṛṣṇaṁ
bhakta-rūpa-svarupakam
bhaktāvatāraṁ bhaktākhyaṁ
namāmi bhaktaśaktikam

I pay obeisances to the Supreme Lord Krishna who

has appeared in five aspects: as a devotee, as the expansion of a devotee, as the incarnation of a devotee, as a pure devotee and as the devotional energy.

(Chaitanya Charitamrta 1.1.14)

Srila Bhaktisiddhanta Saraswati Thakur comments: "The supremely potent is revealed in five different manifestations according to His desire to experience five different pastimes. Ontologically there is no difference between them: they are one truth expressed according to five dispositions. Thus Sri Gauranga, Sri Nityananda, Sri Advaita, Sri Gadadhar and Srivas and the other devotees, are ontologically non-different from one another. Nevertheless, that one truth is manifest as a devotee (*bhakta-rūpa*), the expansion of a devotee (*bhakta-svarūpa*), the incarnation of a devotee (*bhaktāvatāra*), the energy of a devotee (*bhakta-śakti*) and the pure devotee (*bhaktākhya*), according to the desire to relish different tastes of divine relationship.

"Of these five truths, the Supreme Lord himself, the son of Nanda, takes on the devotional mood to become *bhakta-rūpa*. His full expansion (*svayaṁ prakāśa*), Balaram, takes on the devotional mood and appears as the *bhakta-svarupa*, Nityananda. The *puruṣāvatāra* Maha Vishnu takes on the devotional mood and appears as the *bhaktāvatāra* incarnation of a devotee, Advaita Acharya. These three are all Prabhus, that is, they are Vishnu-tattva. The devotional energy (*bhakta-śakti*) and the pure devotee (*śuddha-bhakta*) are classified as energies of Vishnu-tattva, which are considered non-different because of their dependent relationship to it."

The principal devotional energies are Gadadhar, Svarupa Damodar, and Ramananda Raya. The pure devotees include Srivas and others who are in the moods of friendship or servitude. Srivas is thus a member of the Pancha Tattva.

SRIVAS PANDIT'S ORIGINS

Srivas Pandit hailed from Sylhet. He later came to live in Nabadwip where he made an immense contribution to Gauranga lila. From the Chaitanya Bhagavata and Chaitanya Charitamrita we learn that Srivas had three brothers living with him in Nabadwip: Srirama Pandit, Sripati Pandit and Srikanta or Srinidhi Pandit. All four were participants in Mahaprabhu's lila.

Gauḍīya Vaiṣṇava Abhidhāna cites *Prema-vilāsa* in saying that Srivas' father was a Vedic Brahmin of the name Sri Jaladhar Pandit. Srivas was the second of five sons. The eldest son, Sri Nalina Pandit, had a daughter named Narayani, the mother of the author of the Chaitanya Bhagavata, Vrindavan Das. Narayani's husband Vaikuntha Das Vipra died while she was pregnant with Vrindavan Das, so she left her husband's house in Kumarahatta (Halisahar) and came to live with Srivas in Nabadwip.

SRIVAS AND NIMAI PANDIT

During his student life, Nimai would engage Gadadhar and Mukunda and other devotees in debate, first defeating all their arguments and then showing how they could have been defended. The devotees were astonished at His prowess, but thought that His learning would bear fruit only if He became a devotee of Krishna. Nimai would pay obeisances to devotees such as Srivas whenever He saw them and they in turn would bless Him, saying "May You have devotion to Krishna."

One day Srivas Pandit was out walking when he encountered Nimai on the street. He said, "People study in order to become devotees of Krishna. What is the use of all their studies if they don't become devotees? Don't waste Your time. Start worshiping Krishna as soon as possible."

Mahaprabhu felt great joy on hearing such words from the mouth of His own devotee and answered, "You are a devotee. By your mercy I will surely have devotion for Krishna some day." Even though they could not help but be attracted to Nimai, the devotees were unable to recognize Him as their own worshipable Lord due to the force of His Yogamaya *līlā-śakti*. This is a most astonishing and attractive pastime.

NIMAI BECOMES A DEVOTEE

When Mahaprabhu returned from Gaya, He began to display all the symptoms of one who is intoxicated with love of God. Though nothing could have been more auspicious than this, Sachi Mata became terrified, thinking that her son had gone mad. Word of her anxiety came to Srivas and he came to see her and Nimai. When Srivas came near Him, Mahaprabhu was immediately overcome with divine ecstasy on seeing a devotee of Krishna. When he had recovered, the Lord said, "Everyone thinks that I have gone crazy. They say my humors are disturbed. What do you think has happened to Me?" Srivas laughed and answered,

"If your humors have become disturbed, then I want some of that, too. I see that powerful devotional feelings have entered your body. This means that Krishna has been merciful to you."

A relieved Mahaprabhu joyfully embraced Srivas and said, "If you too had said that I was going mad, I would have drowned Myself in the Ganges."

(Chaitanya Bhagavata 2.2.113-7)

When Mahaprabhu instituted the loud chanting of the Holy Names in His own house and in that of Srivas, all the atheistic neighbors began to complain that they were losing sleep because of the noise. They looked for ways to counter the movement and even started false rumors that the king would come soon to punish the devotees. The impressionable Srivas Pandit believed these stories and was filled with anxiety. He began to worship Nrisingha Deva for protection.

Understanding that Srivas was afraid, the Lord, who takes away the distress of His devotees, went to His house. He kicked open the door and said, "Who are you worshiping? Who are you meditating on? Behold! He whom you are worshiping is standing before you! I will save the righteous and destroy the wicked. You should worry no longer!" So saying, He sat down in the heroic posture (*vīrāsana*) and revealed the divine form of Nrisingha, holding conch, discus, club and lotus.

When Srivas saw this extraordinary manifestation of the Lord, he was overcome with feelings of love and began to recite hymns of praise. Mahaprabhu was pleased with Srivas' recital and told him to call his wife and family members to see His divine form. He gave His prasad to Narayani and showed His mercy to her by making her utter the Holy Name. Just as the devotee is dear to the Lord, the Lord is also dear to His devotee.

NITYANANDA'S VYASA PUJA

When Nityananda came to Nabadwip, Mahaprabhu knew that he was staying at Nandanacharya's house and so He went there in the company of the devotees where they met for the first time. In order to reveal Nityananda's glories to His associates, He had Srivas recite a verse from the Bhagavatam:

barhāpīḍaṁ naṭa-vara-vapuḥ karṇayoḥ karṇikāraṁ
bibhrad vāsaḥ kanaka-kapiśaṁ vaijayantīṁ ca mālām
randhrān veṇor adhara-sudhayā pūrayan gopa-vṛndair
vṛndāraṇyaṁ svapada-ramaṇaṁ prāviśad gīta-kīrtiḥ

Krishna, whose glories are sung to the world by the cowherd boys, is dressed as a dancing performer, a peacock feather decorating his topknot, karnikara flowers behind his ears, a golden cloth covering his body, and a victory garland around his neck. Dressed in this way, He entered Vrinda's forest, the pleasure garden of His auspiciously marked feet, while filling the holes of His flute with the nectar of His lips. (Srimad Bhagavatam 10.21.5)

As soon as Nityananda Prabhu heard the verse, he fainted and the eight ecstatic symptoms appeared on his body. Vishvambhar clasped Nityananda to his bosom.

A few days later, Mahaprabhu indicated that He wished Nityananda to perform the Vyasa Puja ceremony, so preparations were made for this ritual to be held at Srivas' house. On the eve of the ceremony, when the *adhivāsa* kirtan was being sung, Mahaprabhu Himself was possessed by the spirit of Baladeva, thus revealing Nityananda's identity with Balaram. Then he called out Advaita's name "*Nāṛā, Nāṛā!*" (meaning, "one who makes something move"), revealing how he had made Him descend by his prayers.

On the following day, Srivas Pandit, took the role of the ceremony's acharya. After completing the puja, he placed a flower garland in Nityananda's hand and told him to offer it to Vyasadeva while chanting the appropriate mantras. Nityananda hesitated and looked around, until Mahaprabhu told him to hurry up and complete the ceremony by offering the garland to Vyasadeva. The ever-independent Nityananda, however, put the garland around Mahaprabhu's neck instead of giving it to the deity. Mahaprabhu immediately gave Nityananda a vision of a six-armed form, with Balaram's club and plough along with the usual four symbols of Vishnu.

At the end of the Vyasa Puja, Mahaprabhu ordered the devotees to sing the Holy Names and as they did so, He asked Srivas for the prasad, which He personally distributed to all the devotees as well as to Srivas' servants. Everyone ate the offerings with great pleasure.

When Mahaprabhu saw Srivas' devotion to Nityananda, He blessed him as follows:

jadi lakṣmī bhikṣā kare nagare nagare
tathāpiha dāridrya tora nahibeka ghare
biṛāla-kukkura-ādi tomāra bāṛīra
sabāra āmāte bhakti haibeka sthira
nityānande samarpiluṅ tomā sthāne
sarva-mate sambaraṇa karibā āpane

Even if the Goddess of Fortune should be forced to beg from town to town, there will never be any poverty in your home. Even the dogs and cats in your home will have enduring devotion to the Lord. I have turned Nityananda over to you, so take responsibility for him.

(Chaitanya Bhagavata 2.8.20-22)

KIRTANA AT SRIVAS ANGAN

When Mahaprabhu's desired to begin His sankirtan pastimes, He held them in the house of Srivas with only His intimate associates present. It all began on an Ekadasi, with Mahaprabhu revealing many transformations of ecstatic love as soon as the chanting began.

śrī hari vāsare hari-kīrtana vidhāna
nṛtya ārambhilā prabhu jagatera prāṇa
puṇyavanta śrīvāsāṅgane śubhārambha
uṭhila kīrtana-dhvani "gopāla! govinda!"

The scriptural injunction is that one should engage in Hari kirtan on Ekadasi evening, also known as *hari-vāsara*. On that night, Mahaprabhu, the life of the world, began to dance. This auspicious beginning for the sankirtan movement took place in the pious Srivas' courtyard, where the sound of Krishna's names Gopal and Govinda rose to the sky.

(Chaitanya Bhagavata 2.8.77-8)

Mahaprabhu ordered that the doors should remain closed, and the wicked and hard-hearted persons who were refused entry began to criticize Mahaprabhu and His devotees. Mahaprabhu's followers ignored their insults and continued to ecstatically sing the Holy Names. Just as the long night of the *rāsa-līlā* seemed to the gopis to last only a few moments, the nights of kirtan at Srivas' house seemed brief to Mahaprabhu and his followers.

At the end of one such night, Mahaprabhu placed all the Shalagram Shilas on his lap and sat down on the altar where He revealed His divine nature in a wonderful form and accepted all the food offerings given Him by His devotees.

On another occasion, Mahaprabhu engaged in His *Mahā-prakāśa-līlā*, "the pastime of the great epiphany" at Srivas Angan. This is recounted in chapter nine of

Chaitanya Bhagavata's *Madhya-khaṇḍa*. On that occasion, He withdrew His devotional mood, stopped all His divine trances, and openly revealed His divinity, sitting on Vishnu's throne for twenty-one hours. At His signal, the devotees performed the abhishek ceremony reserved for the king of kings according to the scriptural regulations. The devotees made their offerings of flowers and gifts and Mahaprabhu stretched out His feet and accepted them without artifice. He then gave all present a blessing, fulfilling their personal desires. In the course of this twenty-one-hour (*sāt prahariyā*) pastime, Mahaprabhu appeared in the forms of all the previous avatars.

One evening, Srivas' mother-in-law hid in a corner of the courtyard from where she hoped to be able to see the Lord's sankirtan pastimes. Being the indweller of all beings, the Lord was aware of her presence and kept repeating to His companions that on that day He felt no joy in singing the Holy Name. This was very disquieting to the devotees who, suspecting that some outsider might be hiding there, started to search through the house. When Srivas found his mother-in-law, he was mortified and, taking her by the hair, led her out of the courtyard. Only those who have received the mercy of Sri Chaitanya Mahaprabhu have the right to witness His pastimes.

On another occasion, a certain brahmachari who subsisted on milk alone asked Srivas for permission to see Mahaprabhu's kirtan. Srivas knew that he was *sāttvika* in his habits and so he invited him in. Srivas had the brahmachari hide inside the house, but Mahaprabhu, the indweller of all beings, was well aware of what was taking place. He said, "I don't know what is wrong with the kirtan today, but I am feeling no pleasure in it. I think that there must be an outsider here somewhere." Srivas became afraid and said, "A brahmachari who takes only milk asked if he could watch you dance. He was so eager and I knew him to be austere so I let him in." Mahaprabhu became angry and answered, "One cannot attain devotion to Krishna without surrendering to Him, and certainly not by eating a milk diet and engaging in other superficial austerities. Make him leave." The Brahmin fearfully left the house, but still asked if he could have a partial look at the Lord. The most merciful Lord called him to His side and placed His lotus feet on his head, telling him not to make a show of his austere practices out of pride.

When Mahaprabhu put on a play about His Vrindavan pastimes at Chandrasekhar's house in Mayapur, Srivas played the part of Narada Muni. Advaita took on the role of the clown, or *vidūṣaka*, and Hari Das Thakur played the police officer. Mahaprabhu Himself first played Krishna's wife, Rukmini, and then the *Ādyā śakti*, while Nityananda played the part of an old woman. The Lord again sat on the altar in the mood of the goddess of fortune, Lakshmi, and later as the mother of the universe. In a spirit of affection for His devotees, He gave them His breast to drink from.

OFFENSES TO SRIVAS

Mahaprabhu's kirtans went on at Srivas' house with the doors locked every night for a full year. During this time, many non-devotee Brahmins tried to make fun of Mahaprabhu and His associates. Several of these pashandis became envious because they were unable to see what was going on and insulted the devotees. One of them was a Bhattacharya Brahmin named Gopal Chapala, who decided to destroy Srivas' reputation by placing a plate of offerings intended for Kali on his doorstep. These included liquor and meat, red hibiscus (*jabā phūl*) flowers, and red sandalwood. In the morning, when Srivas opened the door, he saw these items and started to laugh. He loudly proclaimed, "Look everyone! I am a Shakta. I have been worshiping the Goddess all night long." His better-behaved neighbors were pained to see what had taken place. They removed the offending items and then purified the doorstep with cow dung.

As a result of this offence to Srivas, Gopal Chapala was afflicted with leprosy. One day, when Mahaprabhu came to the banks of the Ganges to bathe, Gopal Chapala approached Him and prayed to be freed from his disease. Mahaprabhu angrily answered him:

> "O sinner! Enemy of the devotees! I will not save you. I will have you eaten by worms like this for a million births. You made it seem as though Srivas had worshiped Kali, so you will dwell for a million lifetimes in the hell known as Raurava." (Chaitanya Charitamrita 1.17.51-2)

After Mahaprabhu had taken sannyas, He came once to Kuliya, the site where offences are forgiven. Kuliya is the present-day town of Nabadwip, also known as Koladwip. This time, when Gopal Chapala begged him again to be forgiven, Mahaprabhu was compassionate and told him to ask forgiveness of Srivas Pandit. One has to ask forgiveness of the very devotee one has offended if one wishes to be freed of the offence. When Srivas forgave Gopal Chapala, he was liberated from the effects of his offence.

The unfortunate Devananda Pandit, though a great lecturer on the Srimad Bhagavatam, was devoid of devotion. One day, Srivas Pandit went to listen to him lecture and, being a great devotee, was deeply affected by the Bhagavata's verses and started to cry in midst of the assembly. Devananda's students, who were all pashandis, forcibly dragged Srivas outside for disturbing the audience. Even though he saw his students acting in this way, Devananda did nothing to stop them. Thus, he too became an offender to a Vaishnava. Mahaprabhu later roundly rebuked Devananda for his inaction on this occasion. However, Devananda had the good fortune to come into the association of Vakresvara Pandit who taught him Chaitanya Mahaprabhu's true identity. He thus became sorry for the offence he had committed and received Mahaprabhu's mercy. According to *Gaura-gaṇoddeśa-dīpikā*, Devananda is Nanda Maharaj's court pandit, Bhandari Muni, in Vraja lila.

THE KAZI TRIES TO BREAK UP THE KIRTAN

Mahaprabhu was always *amānī mānada*—He asked for no honors for Himself, but always showed respect to others. He would embrace everyone and with great feeling ask them to chant the names of the Lord. These converts would then engage in the loud chanting of the Holy Names in the accompaniment of mridanga and conch shells. Materialistic persons considered them to be nothing other than musicians who were worshiping Mahamaya on the wrong day and would insult them with various blasphemous statements. One day the local magistrate or Kazi, known as Sirajuddin Chand Kazi, was walking by and saw the scene. Hearing the loud noise of the kirtan he became irritated and angry. He went to Srivas' house and broke the mridanga and had some of the devotees beaten as a warning. He said, "If anyone does this sankirtan again, he will be punished even more severely." This prohibition brought great satisfaction to all the pashandis of the town, and they joyfully continued to mock the devotees.

When Mahaprabhu received word of the incident, He became very angry. He ordered the devotees to take torches and musical instruments and join Him for a demonstration against the Kazi's edict. Telling them to be fearless, He separated the devotees into several groups and then led the procession along the banks of the Ganges, Himself dancing at its head. Thousands of men, women and children put aside their housework to join Him and follow the sankirtan procession. When the miscreants heard the sound of the kirtan, their hearts began to tremble. Meanwhile, when Chand Kazi heard that thousands of Hindus were approaching his house, he ran inside to hide, trembling with fear.

Upon his arrival, Mahaprabhu asked some respectable persons from the neighborhood to kindly inform the Kazi that He was there and that He meant him no harm. When the Kazi heard the polite way in which Mahaprabhu had addressed him, he was attracted and came outside. He addressed Mahaprabhu as "nephew," since by village relationship he was Nilambara Chakravarti's brother. After a few moments of cordial conversation, the Kazi recounted the following story: "The night I broke the mridanga, I had a dream in which I saw a most frightening figure, half-man half-lion. He came and sat on my chest and threatened to rend it asunder the way I had broken the drum. When he saw how afraid I was, he calmed me down and told me that he would forgive me if I promised never to interfere with the kirtan again."

Chand Kazi then showed the scratch marks that had been imprinted on his chest by Nrisingha Deva's claws. He then promised that neither he nor anyone from his family would ever stop sankirtan again. He also became Mahaprabhu's devotee. The tomb of Chand Kazi is in Baman Pukur, by which stands a very old Goloka Champa tree. Both Hindus and Muslims offer their respects to the tomb of the Chand Kazi.

MORE KIRTAN PASTIMES AT SRIVAS ANGAN

After a night of kirtan at Srivas' house, when Mahaprabhu returned to external awareness, He would go with all the devotees to bathe in the Ganges. Sometimes the devotees would ceremonially bathe the Lord at Srivas Angan. One of Srivas' servant girls named Dukhi would watch Mahaprabhu's ecstatic dancing with tears in her eyes. She also performed the service of filling jugs of water from the Ganges for Mahaprabhu's morning bath. One day, Mahaprabhu observed her devotion and was pleased; He changed her name from Dukhi ("unhappy") to Sukhi ("happy").

Another day, Srivas' only son died while sankirtan was being performed in his house. Srivas was afraid that the sounds of mourning from the women's quarters would disturb Mahaprabhu while He was engaged in singing the Holy Names. So he went directly into the house and tried to quiet the women by explaining spiritual truths to them. When they still didn't stop their loud lamentations, Srivas threatened to throw himself into the river and drown if they did not stop making noise. This had the desired result.

Later on that night, however, the kirtan came to a stop and Mahaprabhu said, "Something doesn't seem right. Has some tragedy taken place in the pandit's house?" Srivas answered, "How can anything be wrong, when I have Your smiling face in my home?"

However, some of the other devotees said, "Prabhu, Srivas' only son died in the evening about an hour after sunset."

Mahaprabhu asked, "Why did no one say anything before now?"

The devotees answered, "Lord, Srivas told us not to, because he was afraid that it would interfere with Your pleasure in kirtan."

Mahaprabhu said, "How could I ever abandon devotees who love Me to this extent!" and started to cry. After this, He went inside and sat down beside the child's dead body and brought him back to consciousness. He asked, "Child! Why do you want to leave the house of such a great devotee as Srivas?"

The dead child answered, "The few days that I was to spend in Srivas' house are over, and now I am following Your wishes in going elsewhere. I am a living being without any independence; I cannot go against Your wishes. Please be merciful to me that I never forget Your lotus feet, wherever I go."

When Srivas' family members heard the child speak such wisdom, they immediately forgot their distress and stopped mourning. Mahaprabhu said to Srivas, "From this day on, Nityananda and I will be your sons. We will never leave you."

SRIVAS' VISITS TO PURI

After Mahaprabhu had taken sannyas and was living in Puri, Srivas would come with the other devotees each year to stay with Him for the four months of the rainy season.

Advaita, Nityananda, Mukunda Datta, Srivas, Vidyanidhi, Vasudeva Datta, Murari Gupta and all of Mahaprabhu's other devoted servants met with Him in Puri every year and stayed four months. Mahaprabhu engaged in various pastimes in their company.
(Chaitanya Charitamrita 2.9.255-6)

Srivas was a participant with Mahaprabhu in His lilas of cleaning the Gundicha temple and Rathayatra. He was the principal singer in the second kirtan group or sampradaya, whose chief dancer was Nityananda Prabhu himself. Svarupa Damodar was the lead singer and Advaita Acharya the dancer in the first kirtan group; in the third, Mukunda Datta sang, while Hari Das Thakur danced. Govinda Ghosh sang in the fourth, with Vakresvara Pandit dancing. The fifth sampradaya came from the village of Kulina, and Ramananda and Satyaraja were its principal dancers. The sixth group was from Shantipur in which Achyutananda danced. The seventh group was composed of the residents of Srikhanda, in which Narahari and Raghunandan took the lead roles.

When Mahaprabhu wished to dance, the seven groups all came together. On one such occasion, the king Prataparudra was watching Mahaprabhu's wild dancing while leaning on his servant Harichandan's shoulder. In the meantime, Srivas came and stood in front of Harichandan to watch Mahaprabhu himself. The king's servant kept pushing the deeply absorbed Srivas, telling him to move so that the king could see. Srivas became irritated at the repeated disturbance and finally turned around and slapped Harichandan. Harichandan became angry and was about to hit him back when the king stopped him, telling him how fortunate he was to have been touched by the hand of a devotee such as Srivas.

One day, Srivas and the other devotees led by Advaita Prabhu were glorifying Mahaprabhu's name, form, qualities and activities. Mahaprabhu became angry and left the scene, but later accepted defeat and acquiesced to their desire to glorify Him.

SRIVAS MOVES TO KUMARAHATTA

After Mahaprabhu took sannyas in Katwa, Srivas and his brothers found it impossible to remain in Nabadwip where everything was full of painful reminders of the Lord. They moved to Kumarahatta (Halisahar) near the birthplace of Ishvara Puri. Even so, Srivas and his brothers made annual trips from Kumarahatta both to Nilachala to see Mahaprabhu and to Mayapur to visit Sachi Mata.

On one occasion Mahaprabhu came to His guru's birthplace and showed His respects by taking some dust and wrapping it in His cloth. From there, He went to Srivas' house. All the members of the household joyfully received Him and His companions and became absorbed in their service. Mahaprabhu noticed this and said to Srivas, "You are a householder with a large family. You have to earn money in order to maintain your family, otherwise how will you be able to do so?" Srivas first replied that he had no wish to make money and then clapped his hands three times. Mahaprabhu asked him what he meant by clapping his hands and Srivas answered, "I will fast one, two, three days. Then if I still get nothing to eat, I will tie a jug to my neck and jump in the Ganges." Mahaprabhu responded to Srivas' statement by giving a roar and repeated the blessing He had given him before in Nabadwip, "Even if the Goddess of Fortune has to go begging, you will never know want in your home. Lord Krishna himself provides everything that His exclusive devotees need."

ananyāś cintayanto māṁ
ye janā paryupāsate
teṣāṁ nityābhiyuktānāṁ
yoga-kṣemaṁ vahāmy aham

I personally assume the whole responsibility of acquiring and protecting the necessities for My fully dependent devotees who are always absorbed in thoughts of Me and who worship Me exclusively. (Gita 9.22)

Even after Mahaprabhu remained permanently in Puri, it is said that His divine apparitions took place in four places: in Sachi Devi's house, wherever Nityananda was dancing, in Srivas' kirtan, and in the home of Raghava Pandit. These apparitions took place because the Lord is naturally attracted by the love of His devotees.
(Chaitanya Charitamrita 3.2.34-5)

Srivas Pandit's appearance day is the eighth day of the waning moon (*kṛṣṇā aṣṭamī*) in the month of Chaitra, and his disappearance day is celebrated on the tenth day of the waning moon (*kṛṣṇā daśamī*) in Asharh.

Sri Murari Gupta

murāri-gupto hanumān
aṅgadaḥ śrī-purandaraḥ
yaḥ śrī-sugrīva-nāmāsīd
govindānanda eva saḥ

Murari Gupta was Hanuman in Ramachandra's lila; Purandara was Angada and Govindananda, Sugriva.
(*Gaura-gaṇoddeśa-dīpikā* 91)

The word *gupta* means "hidden, so the name Murari Gupta indicates that Murari (Sri Chaitanya Deva) had secretly taken up permanent residence in his heart.
(Chaitanya Bhagavata 2.10.31)

Murari Gupta took birth in a family of Ayurvedic physicians in the district of Sylhet.

Murari Gupta is a physician for the disease of material life. He was amongst the many associates of Mahaprabhu who appeared in Sylhet. (Chaitanya Bhagavata 1.2.35)

The names of Murari's parents are unknown. He was somewhat older than Mahaprabhu. The Chaitanya Bhagavata includes his name in the list of associates who appeared prior to Mahaprabhu's incarnation.

There were many devotees hidden in Nabadwip who had previously taken birth at the Lord's command. They included Sri Chandrasekhar, Jagadish, Gopinath, Sriman, Murari, Sri Garuḍa and Ganga Das.
(Chaitanya Bhagavata 1.2.98-99)

When Murari's family moved from Sylhet to Nabadwip, they lived in the same neighborhood as Sri Chaitanya, so Murari was Nimai's companion in many of His childhood pastimes. The Chaitanya Charitamrita confirms that he observed Mahaprabhu's childhood pastimes.

MURARI'S STUDENT LIFE IN NABADWIP

Murari Gupta was also a student at Ganga Das Pandit's Tol along with Nimai. When the Lord was engaged in His pastimes of learning and study, He would often engage Murari in joking and mock debate. Murari was amazed at his fellow student's wonderful intelligence and learning. He also observed that just the touch of Nimai's hand would immerse him in ecstasy. All these things convinced him early on that Nimai was no ordinary human being.

Murari Gupta became a good scholar by the Lord's mercy. One day, Nimai was very pleased with the solution Murari Gupta gave to a certain problem. He touched Murari with his lotus hand, filling his companion's entire body with ecstasy. Murari Gupta thought privately that this person could in no way be an ordinary human being. Can an ordinary human attain such scholarship so quickly? And his mere touch brings such ecstatic pleasure!
(Chaitanya Bhagavata 1.10.30-33)

The Vaishnava's ornament is humility. Mahaprabhu would feel strong emotions when he saw Murari Gupta display this ornament.

Murari Gupta, the twenty-first branch of the Chaitanya tree, was a storehouse of love. The Lord's heart would melt when he saw Murari's meekness and humility.
(Chaitanya Charitamrita 1.10.49)

MAHAPRABHU'S SPECIAL MERCY TO MURARI

When Mahaprabhu returned from Gaya, He saw Murari at the house of Shuklambar Brahmachari. Murari had heard of Mahaprabhu's transformations from Sriman Pandit. Mahaprabhu was pleased with Murari and one day gave him a vision of His form as the Varaha avatar; the Lord lifted Murari's water jug on His nose as He gave a loud roar. Murari considered his life to have been fulfilled by this vision and he composed a hymn in glorification of the Lord. This event has been beautifully described by Vrindavan Das Thakur in the Chaitanya Bhagavata, *Madhya-khaṇḍa*, chapter 3.

The Lord took on the mood of Varaha in the house of Murari. The Lord climbed on his shoulders and danced in the courtyard. (Chaitanya Charitamrita 1.17.19)

Murari Gupta was a worshiper of Lord Ramachandra, and Mahaprabhu's affection for him resembled that of Rama for his servant, Hanuman.

The Lord Gaura Hari felt great love for Murari. It was just like Lord Ramachandra's love for Hanuman.
(Chaitanya Bhagavata 2.3.11)

During the twenty-one-hour great epiphany (*mahā-prakāśa*) at Srivas Angan, the Lord gave Murari a vision of Himself as Rama. When Murari saw his worshipable deity before him, he fainted away. He then glorified the Lord in a way that so much pleased Him that He gave Murari a benediction to have all his desires fulfilled.

Mahaprabhu ordered Murari: "Behold My form!" Lo, Murari saw the form of Raghunath directly before him. He saw the Lord of the Universe with the swarthy color of durba grass, sitting in the *vīrāsana*, the posture of a great bowman. He saw Sita and Lakshman standing on either side of Him, and His army of monkeys surrounding Him singing hymns of praise. It seemed to Murari that he was himself one of the monkeys, and as soon as he saw this, he fainted. The best of the physicians, Murari, lay unconscious on the ground, completely under Mahaprabhu's spell.
(Chaitanya Bhagavata 2.10.7-11)

On one occasion, when Mahaprabhu heard Murari Gupta recite the glories of Ramachandra, he wrote

Rama Das, "servant of Rama," on his forehead (Chaitanya Charitamrita 1.17.61). On another occasion, Mahaprabhu displayed a four-armed Narayan form in the house of Srivas, and began calling the name of Garuda. Murari Gupta heard the call and, giving a loud roar, took the form of the king of birds. Mahaprabhu then climbed on his shoulders. This lila is described both in the 20th chapter of the *Madhya-khaṇḍa* of Chaitanya Bhagavata and the 12th wave of *Bhakti-ratnākara*.

MURARI AND NITYANANDA PRABHU

Mahaprabhu taught the spiritual truths about Himself, Nityananda Prabhu, and matters of etiquette through Murari. One day, Murari Gupta came to Srivas' house. Upon arriving, he first paid obeisances to Mahaprabhu and then to Nityananda, but Mahaprabhu told him that he had not followed the proper procedure. Murari could not understand what He meant. That night when he returned home, he had a dream in which he saw Nityananda as Balaram, fanning Mahaprabhu, Krishna, with a fly wisk. Murari then understood what Mahaprabhu had been telling him and from then on always paid obeisances first to Nityananda and afterwards to Mahaprabhu.

Srila Bhaktisiddhanta Saraswati Goswami Thakur writes in his *Gauḍīya-bhāṣya*, "Sri Murari was a worshiper of Balaram. Therefore to worship the Supreme Lord without first worshiping the guru and jagad-guru is an error of protocol."

The lotus-eyed Mahaprabhu was sitting down with the smiling Nityananda at his right hand side. Murari paid obeisances first to Nityananda and then to the feet of Vishvambhar. (Chaitanya Bhagavata 2.20.22-3)

THE LORD GIVES MURARI HIS PAN

Mahaprabhu had great affection for Murari Gupta and so sometimes gave him His own pan, which Murari would eat with relish. When Mahaprabhu told Murari to wash his hands, Murari would simply wipe his hands on his head. It was at this time that Mahaprabhu suddenly began to criticize the false views of the Smarta Brahmins and Prakashananda's mayavada philosophy.

The Lord said, "O foolish one, you have lost your caste status. My remnants are all over your body." As he spoke, the Lord went into a trance in which He took on His identity as the Supreme Person. He ground his teeth and started to say something special, "There is a sannyasi named Prakashananda in Kashi who is cutting Me into little bits. He teaches the Vedanta, but does not accept My form. I have caused him to become leprous, but still he does not understand. The fool does not realize that the unlimited universes are contained within My body; what arrogance that he should deny it! I tell you the truth Murari, for You are My servant: anyone who does not accept My form is bound for ruin."

(Chaitanya Bhagavata 2.20.31-36)

MURARI CURES THE LORD'S INDIGESTION

The Lord is very happy to accept a devotee's offering no matter how it is made. When Murari returned home, he told his wife that he wished to eat. His devoted wife carefully prepared rice with ghee and gave it to her husband. But Murari, absorbed in contemplation on Krishna, took handful after handful of the food and threw it on the ground, offering it to the Lord in this way. The amazing thing is that even though Mahaprabhu was not physically present there at that time, He accepted the offering. The next day He came to Murari's house and said to him, "I have come to you for medicine. Yesterday, you kept insisting that I eat. You made me eat so much that now I have indigestion. You must give Me some water, that will be the remedy for my stomach problem." Mahaprabhu took water from a jug in Murari's house, drinking down its entire contents. Seeing this, Murari fainted and all the devotees began to cry.

Murari would cure anyone who came to him, whether their disease was of the body or the soul.

(Chaitanya Charitamrita 1.10.51)

MURARI'S FEAR OF THE LORD'S DEPARTURE

Murari Gupta analyzed the pastimes of many incarnations of the Lord and came to the conclusion that in each one of the Lord's appearances, He always arranged for His associates to leave the world before He did. Thus, Ramachandra destroyed Ravana to save Sita, but then abandoned her. Lord Krishna arranged for the destruction of the Yadus. Murari thus thought that since Mahaprabhu would inevitably be disappearing at a certain moment, it would be better for him to depart before that day arrived, for it would be far too painful for him to witness such an event. For this reason, Murari purchased a sharp knife and kept it hidden in his home. The Lord knew of his intention and immediately came to his house and asked Murari to hand over the knife. Both the abovementioned lilas are found described in the *Bhakti-ratnākara's* twelfth wave.

Murari Gupta would also go on the annual pilgrimage with the other devotees to see Mahaprabhu in Puri. Accompanied by his wife, he would feed Mahaprabhu with many preparations they had prepared themselves. Murari would participate in the Rathayatra festival as a member of the third sankirtan group in which Mukunda Datta sang and Hari Das Thakur danced.

MURARI'S EXCLUSIVE DEVOTION TO RAMA

Mahaprabhu taught the principle of devotion to one's worshipable deity through Murari Gupta. One cannot advance in devotional service without a particular devotion to a worshipable deity, or *iṣṭa-devatā*. Murari was an incarnation of Hanuman, and he saw Chaitanya Mahaprabhu as Ramachandra. On one occasion, Mahaprabhu desired to test his loyalty to his worshipable deity Rama by telling him to worship Krishna instead. The Lord explained to Murari that Krishna was the Supreme Personality of Godhead, the fountainhead of all the other incarnations. Because Krishna is the ocean of all devotional mellows, the joy to be had in worshiping Him cannot be had in the service of any other form of the Lord. Murari promised Mahaprabhu that he would do as He advised and worship Krishna, but when he returned to his home, he could not give up the lotus feet of Ramachandra. Just the thought of it made him upset and he stayed awake the entire night. In the morning, he went to Mahaprabhu and fell at His feet with tears in his eyes and made the following humble submission:

> I have sold my head to Ramachandra. I cannot remove it from his feet, for as soon as I try, it causes me great pain. I cannot give up the lotus feet of Raghunath, even though this means disobeying you. What can I do? O merciful one, please allow me to give up my life here before You rather than suffer this fate.
>
> (Chaitanya Charitamrita 2.15.149-151)

Hanuman is famous for a verse, in which he shows his single-minded devotion for Rama.

śrī-nāthe jānakī-nāthe
cābhede paramātmani
tathāpi mama sarvasvo
rāmaḥ kamala-locanaḥ

> Both Narayan, the husband of Lakshmi, and Ramachandra, the husband of Sita are equally the supreme personality of Godhead. Even so, the lotus-eyed Rama alone is everything to me.

Mahaprabhu was greatly satisfied to hear this exclusive devotional attitude to the worshipable deity. He said, "You are Hanuman himself, the eternal servant of Ramachandra. Indeed, why should you give up worshiping His feet?"

Sri Jiva Goswami's father Anupama was similarly devoted to Rama. Mahaprabhu compared him to Murari when Sanatan told him that Anupama was not able to give up worshiping Rama despite his brothers' exhortations.

> Mahaprabhu said, "Previously, I tested Murari Gupta and found him to be devoted to Rama in the same way. That devotee who does not abandon his worshipable deity's lotus feet is truly glorious. Glorious too is that Lord who does not abandon His devotee."
>
> (Chaitanya Charitamrita 3.4.45-46)

Murari Gupta disappeared on the same full-moon day as the autumn *rāsa-līlā* festival, *śarat-pūrṇimā*.

SRI VASUDEVA DATTA THAKUR

vraje sthitau gāyakau yau
madhukaṇṭha-madhuvratau
mukunda-vāsudevau tau
dattau gaurāṅga-gāyakau

> In Vraja there were two singers named Madhukaṇṭha and Madhuvrata. They appeared in Chaitanya lila as Mukunda and Vasudeva Datta, who were singers in the society of Lord Chaitanya Mahaprabhu.
>
> (*Gaura-gaṇoddeśa-dīpikā* 140)

Sri Vasudeva Datta was born in the Chittagong district of modern Bangladesh, in the village of Chanhara, which is under the jurisdiction of the police station named Patiya. This village is situated ten kosas, or about twenty miles, from the village of Mekhala where Pundarika Vidyanidhi made his home. Mahaprabhu's associate Mukunda Datta was Vasudeva Datta's younger brother.

In the book *Prema-vilāsa*, it is said that Vasudeva was the older of the two and that they were born in an Ambashtha family:

In the district of Chittagong, there is a village named Cakrashala where there lives a respectable family of Ambashtha physicians named Datta. Two great devotees named Mukunda Datta and Vasudeva Datta were born into this family. Both Vasudeva the older and Mukunda the younger came to Nabadwip to live.

Vasudeva Datta Thakur had a beautiful voice and was also well versed in the *Saṅgīta-śāstra*. He was one of the chief associates of Mahaprabhu, participating in sankirtan in the home of Srivas and the streets of Nabadwip. Mahaprabhu enjoyed his association because of his Vaishnava qualities.

> Vasudeva Datta is a respected servant of the Lord. A thousand tongues are insufficient to sing his glories.
>
> (Chaitanya Charitamrita 1.10.41)

> Mahaprabhu said, "Even though Mukunda has been My companion since childhood, I get even more pleasure when I see You." (Chaitanya Charitamrita 2.11.138)

Vasudeva had a particularly close friendship with Srivas Pandit and Shivananda Sen. He lived near Kumarahatta and Kanchra Para, which were the homes of these two great associates of the Lord. Vasudeva was very generous by nature. Never thinking of himself, he spent his money liberally for others. Mahaprabhu saw this and asked Shivananda Sen to become his *sarkhel* and supervise His affairs.

VASUDEVA'S COMPASSION

Vasudeva was so distressed by the suffering of the living beings that he was ready to accept their sins and suffer in hell, and he prayed emotionally to Mahaprabhu for such a boon:

"My Lord! You have appeared in this world to save it, so please accept my prayer. You are omnipotent and all-merciful, so if You agree to fulfill my request, it can be easily done. When I see the suffering of the world, my heart is torn apart. So I ask you, Lord, give their sins to me. I will take their sins and suffer in hell on their behalf, but please deliver them from their material disease."
(Chaitanya Charitamrita 2.15.160-163)

Vasudeva wished to take the sins of every single living being and suffer in hell in their place so that they could be liberated. (Chaitanya Charitamrita 1.10.42)

When Mahaprabhu heard this heartfelt plea on behalf of the living beings of the world, He said to Vasudeva:

"You have desired the liberation of all the living beings in the entire universe, so be it. They will be saved without having to suffer the consequences of their sins. Krishna is not incapable of doing it; He has all powers, so why should He make you suffer for their sins? Those whose welfare you desire will all become Vaishnavas, and Krishna removes the sins of all Vaishnavas."
(Chaitanya Charitamrita 2.15.167-169)

Srila Bhaktisiddhanta Saraswati Goswami Thakur writes in his *Anubhāṣya* to the Chaitanya Charitamrita: "In the Western world, Christians believe that only their guru, Jesus Christ, appeared in this world out of a desire to suffer on behalf of the people of the world by accepting their sins. But here we see that amongst Mahaprabhu's associates, Vasudeva Datta Thakur, like Hari Das Thakur, showed a compassion millions of times greater and more generous, as he was willing to suffer in the place of all creatures in the universe. By so doing, he taught the world the unlimited nature of the Vaishnava's selfless love."

Raghunath Das Goswami's diksha guru, Yadunandan Acharya, was blessed by Vasudeva Datta. The author of Chaitanya Bhagavata, Vrindavan Das Thakur, was born in Mamgachi in Modadrumadwip, one mile from the Purvasthali station on the Howrah-Katwa line of the Eastern Railway. Vasudeva Datta consecrated the worship of the Madan Gopal deity that is still being worshiped at his birthplace.

We can see just how dear Vasudeva Datta was to Mahaprabhu by the Lord's statements made when He was visiting Srivas Pandit's house in Kumarahatta :

Gaurachandra repeated again and again, "This body of mine belongs to Vasudeva. If he wants to sell Me, I allow myself to be sold; I will not do otherwise. I announce this truth to all of you. If someone has even come into the briefest contact with Vasudeva Datta, he will be protected by Krishna. Listen all you Vaishnavas! I tell you the truth: My body belongs to Vasudeva alone."
(Chaitanya Bhagavata 3.5.27-30)

Srila Gadadhar Pandit Goswami

śrī-rādhā-prema-rūpā yā purā vṛndāvandeśvarī
sā śrī-gadādharo gaura-vallabhaḥ paṇḍitākhyakaḥ
nirṇītaḥ śrī-svarupair yo vraja-lakṣmītayā yathā
purā vṛndāvane lakṣmīḥ śyāmasundara-vallabhā
sādya gaura-prema-lakṣmīḥ śrī-gadādhara-paṇḍitaḥ
rādhām anugatā yat tal lalitāpy anurādhikā
ataḥ prāviśad eṣā taṁ gaura-candrodaye yathā

The incarnation of love who was previously the queen of Vrindavan, Radha, is now the beloved of Gaura named Srila Gadadhar Pandit. Svarupa Damodar himself indicated that Gadadhar was Vraja's goddess of fortune, the Lakshmi who was previously the beloved of Shyamasundara in Vrindavan. She has today become the goddess of fortune and love for Gaura and is known as Srila Gadadhar Pandit. Lalita, who is also known as Anuradha, is Radha's closest friend and confidante. She has also entered into Gadadhar, as was shown in the play Chaitanya-candrodaya.(Gaura-gaṇoddeśa-dīpikā 147-150)

GADADHAR-TATTVA

gadādhara paṇḍitādi prabhura nija-śakti
tān sabhāra caraṇe mora sahasra praṇati

Gadadhar Pandit and others are the Lord's own energies. I pay thousands of obeisances to their feet.
(Chaitanya Charitamrita 1.1.41)

"Chaitanya Mahaprabhu appears in six features, namely as the two types of guru, the devotees of the Lord, the Lord Himself, His incarnation, His expansion and His energy. According to the principle of simultaneous oneness and difference, they are all identified with Chaitanya Mahaprabhu Himself." (*Anubhāṣya* to Chaitanya Charitamrita 1.1.37-45)

She who was Radha in Krishna's pastimes became Srila Gadadhar Pandit Goswami in Gaura lila. When Gaura manifests His identity with Narayan, His shaktis are His wives Lakshmipriya and Vishnupriya. When identifying with Krishna, His shakti is Srila Gadadhar Pandit Goswami.

pañcatattvātmakaṁ kṛṣṇaṁ
bhakta-rūpa-svarupakam
bhaktāvatāraṁ bhaktākhyaṁ
namāmi bhaktaśaktikam

I offer my obeisances to Krishna who appears in five features, as a devotee, as the expansion of a devotee, as an incarnation of a devotee, as the pure devotee and as the devotional energy.

These five features all appeared with Chaitanya Mahaprabhu in His incarnation, and in their association,

He joyfully performed the congregational chanting of the Holy Names. Though He appears in these five forms, there is in fact no difference between them. The distinctions arise due to His desire to relish different devotional flavors.

Sri Gauranga, Nityananda, Advaita, Gadadhar and Srivas, etc., make up the Pancha Tattva and there is spiritually no difference between them. The supreme truth has unlimited different pastimes in order to relish the different tastes of transcendental relationship and thus he separates into these five forms as the devotee, the devotional manifestation, the devotional incarnation, the devotional energy and the pure devotee.

jaya jaya nityānanda-gadādharera jivana
jaya jaya advaitādi bhaktera śaraṇa

All glories, all glories, to the life of Nityananda and Gadadhar! All glories, all glories, to the shelter of all the devotees, headed by Advaita!

Srila Bhaktisiddhanta Saraswati Goswami Thakur comments on words "the life of Gadadhar" as follows: "Srila Gadadhar Pandit Goswami is chief amongst the most intimate devotees of Sri Chaitanya. He is the fountainhead of the entire *śakti-tattva* and is thus present equally in Mahaprabhu's lilas in Nabadwip and in Nilachala. His childhood home was in Nabadwip; later, when He took sannyas, He went to live in Jagannath Puri, in a garden or *ṭoṭā* by the seashore. Pure devotees who wish to enter into worship of Radha and Govinda in the *madhura-rasa* take shelter of Gadadhar Pandit and are known as Gauranga Mahaprabhu's intimate devotees. Those devotees who are not so inclined take shelter of Nityananda Prabhu and engage in pure devotional service according to his mood. Some of Mahaprabhu's devotees, such as Narahari, were followers of Srila Gadadhar Pandit Goswami. They took refuge in him because they knew him to be Mahaprabhu's dearest associate and thus worthy of their service. Some devotees therefore call Chaitanya 'the life of Nityananda' while others called him 'the life of Gadadhar'."

GADADHAR'S EARLY LIFE

Srila Gadadhar Pandit Goswami was born in the village of Beleti in the Chittagong district of modern Bangladesh in 1408 of the Shaka era (1486 AD) on the dark moon day of the month of Vaishakh. His father was Madhava Mishra, a Varendra Brahmin in the Kashyapa gotra, and his mother Ratnavati Devi. He also had a younger brother named Baninath. The family remained in Beleti Gram until Gadadhar was twelve and then moved to Nabadwip.

Gadadhar Pandit was a brahmachari for his entire life. Indeed, his indifference to the pleasures of the world was such that Ishvara Puripada was very impressed when he visited Nabadwip. Ishvara Puri gave Gadadhar instruction in a book he had himself written, *Kṛṣṇa-līlāmṛta*.

While Mahaprabhu was delighting in His pastimes as a student, there was no scholar in the entire town of Nabadwip who was unafraid of entering into debate with Him. Mahaprabhu would defeat one's position and then show how the same position could be defended. Mukunda, Srivas and others who knew the joys of the devotional sentiment were afraid of getting involved in such useless debates with Nimai Pandit and so they would avoid Him. One day, Nimai Pandit saw Gadadhar and asked him to give the definition of liberation. Gadadhar answered according to the Nyaya philosophy, that liberation consisted in the final and absolute eradication of all miseries (*ātyantika-duḥkha-nivṛtti*). Nimai then proceeded to show how this definition was inadequate. The other devotees listening to Him speak thought how wonderful it would be if such a brilliant scholar only became a devotee.

When Mahaprabhu returned from Gaya, He began to reveal the amazing transformations of divine love. Sriman Pandit was the first to see Mahaprabhu's ecstatic symptoms and he reported what he had seen to all the other devotees, who were overjoyed at the news. When Mahaprabhu decided to reveal His true identity to the devotees, He told them to come to the house of Shuklambar Brahmachari. Gadadhar was amongst those who went there, but remained discrete about his presence until he saw Mahaprabhu become intoxicated with the power of the Holy Names. Gadadhar himself was overcome by the ecstatic emotions known as *sāttvikas* and fainted. Mahaprabhu then said to him:

"Gadadhar! You have such good fortune. From your early childhood, your mind has been fixed on Krishna's lotus feet while I have been wasting My life in useless activities. Despite obtaining the great treasure of a human birth, by My misfortune, I was able to make no use of it."
(Chaitanya Bhagavata 2.1.98-99)

Subsequently, Gadadhar would calm Mahaprabhu whenever He was overly affected by His ecstasies. One day, Mahaprabhu was crying out in separation, "Where is Krishna? Where is Krishna?" Gadadhar said to Him, "Your Lord Krishna is hidden in Your heart." As soon as He heard this, Mahaprabhu began to claw at His chest, but luckily Gadadhar was able to stop Him by holding His hands. He then pacified Him by saying, "Krishna will come to You shortly. Be patient." When Sachi saw how clever Gadadhar was in handling her son, she asked him to always stay near Nimai to protect Him. (Chaitanya Bhagavata 2.2.198-210)

GADADHAR TAKES INITIATION FROM PUNDARIKA

Once, Mahaprabhu suddenly started calling out the name of His dear associate, Pundarika Vidyanidhi, saying, "Pundarika, My father!" and crying. None of the devotees present knew Pundarika, who was formerly Radharani's father Vrishabhanu, and were thus unable to understand what the Lord meant. When they asked Him, He glorified Pundarika Vidyanidhi and told them that he would shortly be coming to Nabadwip Mayapur. However, when Pundarika arrived in Nabadwip, no one recognized him because he disguised himself as a great sense enjoyer in order to mask his profound devotional feeling.

Mukunda Datta was a former resident of Chittagong and knew Pundarika very well. One day, he told Srila Gadadhar Pandit Goswami that he wanted to introduce him to a very advanced Vaishnava and took him to Pundarika's house. Mukunda introduced the two of them and Vidyanidhi happily engaged Gadadhar in conversation. Gadadhar, however, had been indifferent to sensual pleasures since he was very young and could not help doubting Pundarika Vidyanidhi when he saw the expensive furnishings by which he was surrounded, from the fine silk sheets as white as milk foam and the perfumes in the air to the pan he was chewing. Mukunda saw the doubt written on Gadadhar's face and decided to reveal Pundarika's true devotional nature to him. He recited a verse in glorification of Krishna from the Bhagavatam:

aho bakīyaṁ stana-kāla-kūṭaṁ
jighāṁsayāpāyayad apy asādhvī
lebhe gatiṁ dhātry-ucitaṁ tato'nyaṁ
kaṁ vā dayāluṁ śaraṇaṁ vrajema

How truly amazing! The sister of Bakasura, the evil Putana, was sent on a mission to kill Krishna. Despite her evil intentions, He drank the kālakūṭa poison that was mixed with her breast milk and awarded her the position of a wet nurse (as Ambika Kilimba in Goloka). Is there anyone else I can take shelter of who is more merciful than this Krishna? (Srimad Bhagavatam 3.2.23)

The instant that Pundarika Vidyanidhi heard this quatrain, he began to cry, "Ha Krishna!" and fell to the ground in a faint. Extraordinary ecstatic symptoms began to show on his body. Srila Gadadhar Pandit Goswami was amazed to see this reaction and began to regret the offensive thoughts he had been having just moments before. Later, Mahaprabhu advised Gadadhar that the best way to become free of this offence was to ask Pundarika Vidyanidhi for initiation. So this is how Gadadhar became his disciple.

THE LORD'S CONSTANT COMPANION

Srila Gadadhar Pandit Goswami was Mahaprabhu's constant companion. He participated in Mahaprabhu's water sports after the conversion of Jagai and Madhai; he acted in the play about Krishna lila in Chandrasekhar's house; he observed the great epiphany (*mahā-prakāśa*) in Srivas Angan; he was there when the Kazi was converted and when Mahaprabhu took sannyas; he accompanied Mahaprabhu to Puri where he joined Him in cleaning the Gundicha temple, bathing in Narendra Sarovar, and so many other pastimes.

At Chandrasekhar's house, in the first act of the play about Krishna's pastimes in Vrindavan that Mahaprabhu staged, Hari Das played the part of the village constable, Srivas Pandit played Narada Muni and Mahaprabhu Rukmini. In the second act, Gadadhar also dressed as a woman, at which time Mahaprabhu said, "Gadadhar is a part of my Vaikuntha family." Afterward, Mahaprabhu dressed as the primal energy and gave joy to everyone in the form of the mother of the universe; the devotees too glorified Him with hymns addressed to the Divine Mother.

GADADHAR'S KÑETRA-SANNYĀSA

Srila Gadadhar Pandit Goswami went to live in Puri as a *kṣetra-sannyāsī*. Mahaprabhu gave him the service of the Tota Gopinath deity and told him to live in Yameshwar Tota, or garden adjoining the Yameshwar Shiva temple. On one occasion, when Gadadhar heard that Nityananda had come to Puri, he invited him to come and take Tota Gopinath's prasad. Nityananda accepted his invitation and brought some fine rice from Bengal as an offering for Gopinath. Gadadhar cooked the rice along with leaves and vegetables from the Yameshwar garden. When he was offering the foodstuffs to the deity, Mahaprabhu also appeared there, giving him great pleasure. The three of them joyfully took prasad together.

(Chaitanya Bhagavata, *Antya* 10)

When Mahaprabhu wanted to go to Vrindavan, Ramananda Raya and Sarvabhauma Bhattacharya used all the means at their disposal to make Him stay in Puri. On the third Chaturmasya after his departure from Nabadwip, all the Bengali devotees came to Puri with their wives to see him. After the Gundicha temple cleansing and the Rathayatra, the devotees returned home. As they were leaving, the devotees from Kulina village asked Mahaprabhu to describe the characteristics of a devotee. Mahaprabhu then described the differences between a Vaishnava, a more advanced Vaishnava and the most advanced Vaishnava.

(Chaitanya Charitamrita 2.16.69-75)

When Mahaprabhu showed even more determination to go to Vrindavan, the devotees finally gave Him permission to leave after Vijaya-daśamī. King Prataparudra gave a great deal of official help to smooth His journey. When Mahaprabhu crossed the Chitrotpala River to leave Puri, Raya Ramananda, Mardaraja, and Harichandana continued on in His company. Because of his *kṣetra-sannyāsa*, Srila Gadadhar Pandit Goswami was not permitted to go any further. He was unable to tolerate the idea of separation from the Lord, however, and wanted to continue on with Him. Mahaprabhu had to remind him of his vow to remain in Jagannath Puri and forbade him to go onward to Vraja. Gadadhar retorted, "To hell with my vows to remain in Puri. As far as I am concerned, Jagannath Puri is wherever You are." Mahaprabhu insisted and told Gadadhar not to abandon his service to Gopinath. Gadadhar stubbornly argued, "Just seeing your lotus feet is worth a million times more than any service to Gopinath."

Mahaprabhu said, "If you abandon your duties to Gopinath, then it will be considered My fault." Gadadhar said, "No, I will take all the responsibility for any offence to Gopinath. I am going alone, not with You. I am going to Bengal to see Sachi Mata, and not for Your sake." So Mahaprabhu continued on His way north to meet the

Jharikhanda path, which He intended to take to Vrindavan, while Gadadhar trailed behind, walking alone.

Other than Mahaprabhu's intimate associates, no one is able to understand the extent of Gadadhar Prabhu's rebellious devotion to Gauranga. Love on the path of spontaneous devotion is not easy to comprehend. Gadadhar was ready to abandon his vows, his service, everything for the sake of Mahaprabhu.

When Mahaprabhu's party arrived at Cuttack, a hundred kilometers north of Puri, Mahaprabhu called Gadadhar and said, "You have realized your objective to break your vows and leave your service. If you come with Me, that will make you happy. But do you want your own happiness or Mine? It will make Me unhappy if your vows to remain in Puri and to serve Gopinath are broken. If you want My happiness, return to Puri and take up your vows again. That is all I have to say."

When he heard Mahaprabhu's words, Gadadhar fell to the ground and fainted. Mahaprabhu told Sarvabhauma Bhattacharya to comfort him and accompany him back to Puri. He Himself then continued to Vrindavan on His own.

GADAI-GAURANGA

Due to her amiable simplicity, Krishna's wife Rukmini was not always able to understand His joking words and would become frightened. Like her, Gadadhar was also unable to always understand Mahaprabhu's witticisms or his feigned indifference, all of which would cause him anxiety. Srila Gadadhar Pandit Goswami was by nature simple and affectionate. On one occasion, Vallabha Bhatta came to see Mahaprabhu and engaged Him in jocular conversation. When Mahaprabhu saw that Vallabha Bhatta was proud of his scholarship, however, He became somewhat distant from him and started to find flaws in everything that he said.

Vallabha responded to Mahaprabhu's indifference by starting to visit Gadadhar and making a show of attachment to him. Mahaprabhu did not particularly care for Gadadhar's relation with Vallabha and began to demonstrate a certain coolness toward him also. This behavior made Gadadhar fear that Mahaprabhu would ostracize him, so he came and fell at the Lord's feet and started to cry. Mahaprabhu laughed and embraced Gadadhar. He said,

"I wanted to tease you, but you were not flustered. You said nothing in anger, but patiently bore everything. Your mind was not agitated by My tricks. By remaining fixed in your simple nature, you have purchased Me." No one can fully describe the nature of Gadadhar's ecstatic love. Mahaprabhu has thus been given the name *Gadadhara-prāṇanātha*, "Gadadhar's life and soul." No one can describe the Lord's mercy toward Gadadhar; thus people sing their names together: Gadai-Gauranga.

(Chaitanya Charitamrita 3.7.157-160)

Srila Gadadhar Pandit Goswami remained on this earth for only eleven months after Mahaprabhu's disappearance. In *Bhakti-ratnākara*, Narahari Chakravarti has described the terrible suffering of Gadadhar in Mahaprabhu's separation. He remained alive only in order to be able to see Srinivas Acharya.

Repeating the name of Gaurasundar with his eyes closed, his sighs were as hot as flames. No one but the Lord can know how Gadadhar Pandit suffered in the absence of Gauranga. His motionless body remained alive only so that he could bestow his mercy on Srinivas Acharya.

(*Bhakti-ratnākara* 3.142-4)

Srila Gadadhar Pandit Goswami disappeared at Puri on the dark moon day of Jyestha in 1456 of the Shaka era (1535 AD).

Sri Buddhimanta Khan

Buddhimanta Khan was very dear to Lord Chaitanya Mahaprabhu. He was one of the Lord's greatest servants who obeyed Him from the time of His birth.

(Chaitanya Charitamrita 1.10.74)

BUDDHIMANTA'S PREVIOUS LIFE

Buddhimanta Khan is considered to be one of Chaitanya's branches. In his *Navadvīpa-dhāma-māhātmya*, Srila Bhaktivinoda Thakur has written the following in connection with the village of Suvarna Bihar in Godrumadwip: "In the Satya Yuga, a pious king named Suvarna Sen lived in this village of Suvarna Bihar. Through the blessings of Narada Muni, this king obtained love for Radha and Krishna as well as for Their joint form, Sri Gauranga Mahaprabhu. One night, Suvarṇa Sen saw Gaura and Gadadhar with all their associates in a dream. When he awoke, the King cried out in distress from the loss of the vision. Suddenly, he heard a voice from the sky which told him that when Mahaprabhu appeared again in the Age of Kali, then he would also take birth as Buddhimanta Khan in order to expand the Lord's pastimes."

BUDDHIMANTA'S CHARITABLE WORKS

Buddhimanta lived in Nabadwip. He and Mukunda Sanjaya were amongst the richest people in the town. They performed charitable works such as providing medicines and treatment for the poor who fell ill. Once, when Mahaprabhu was still a householder, He was undergoing ecstatic transformations of love for Krishna. His relatives and friends thought that He had been afflicted by some kind of mental disorder and called Buddhimanta Khan to see to His treatment.

Buddhimanta paid for all the costs of Mahaprabhu's wedding when He married for the second time, to Vishnupriya, the daughter of a local zamindar's priest,

Sanatan Mishra. Buddhimanta also participated in all of Mahaprabhu's Nabadwip pastimes—in the kirtans at Srivas Angan, at Chandrasekhar's house, and on the streets of Nabadwip, in the liberation of Jagai and Madhai and the water sports in the Ganges.

BUDDHIMANTA AT CHANDRASEKHAR'S HOUSE

One day, Mahaprabhu revealed His desire to put on a play about Vraja lila and dance in the mood of Maha Lakshmi. He told Buddhimanta Khan that He wanted him to take responsibility for the costumes and decorations. Buddhimanta himself dressed Mahaprabhu.

[Mahaprabhu said,] "Buddhimanta Khan! Go quickly and arrange for costumes for today I shall dance." Upon receipt of the order, Sadashiva and Buddhimanta Khan immediately returned home, feeling unlimited joy. The devotees quickly put up an awning of bamboo and cloth and there started dressing the actors for the play. Buddhimanta brought the costumes and presented them to the Lord. (Chaitanya Bhagavata 2.18.13-16)

"Look here. This is the house of Chandrasekhar Acharya. The Lord came here with his dearest associates. Sadashiva and Buddhimanta Khan took charge of the costumes and dressing the actors. (*Bhakti-ratnākara* 12.2902-3)

After Mahaprabhu took sannyas in Katwa, He went to Shantipur where He met with all the Nabadwip devotees, including Buddhimanta Khan. Buddhimanta also accompanied the Bengali devotees to Puri to see the Lord. The Lord also lovingly accepted his and the other Bengali devotees' gifts of foodstuffs, which they brought to Puri for Him.

Buddhimanta Khan, whose only interest from his very birth had been to serve the Lord's order, also went [on the pilgrimage to Puri]. (Chaitanya Bhagavata 3.8.30)

Sri Nandan Acharya

According to both Chaitanya Bhagavata and Chaitanya Charitamrita, Nandan Acharya's father was named Caturbhuja and he had two brothers, Vishnu Das and Ganga Das. (Chaitanya Bhagavata 3.5.74; Chaitanya Charitamrita 1.11.43) They were a family of Bhattacharya Brahmins residing in Nabadwip. Both Vishnu Das and Ganga Das stayed in Nilachala with Mahaprabhu for a while. Mahaprabhu, Nityananda Prabhu and Advaita Acharya all hid in Nandan Acharya's house at one time or another. Nityananda Prabhu even stayed at his house while in Nabadwip.

Nandan Acharya is a branch of the Chaitanya tree that is celebrated throughout the world because two of the three Prabhus hid in his house.

(Chaitanya Charitamrita 1.10.39)

In the *Gauḍīya Vaiṣṇava Abhidhāna*, a different family tree is given for Nandan Acharya. The author of that dictionary writes: "Nandan Acharya came from a family of astrologer Brahmins. His father's name was Lakshmi Narayan. Lakshmi Narayan had two sons: Nandan Acharya and Bhagavan Adhikari Sarvabhauma. Lakshmi Narayan had a reputation as a seer and astrologer. He was present when Mahaprabhu was born. Nandan Acharya is included as a branch of the Chaitanya tree. He was lame. When Mahaprabhu returned from South India, all the devotees were overjoyed to see Him. Even though Nandan Acharya was lame, he went ahead of everyone else to perform puja to the Lord.

"Sri Nandan Acharya came from a family of Shakdwipi Brahmins descended from Shanti Muni, the son of Parashara. He belonged to the Bharata branch of the Vatsya gotra from Rarha. He lived for some time in Bahirkhanda village near Tarakeshwar in present-day Birbhum before moving to Nabadwip where he made his home in Srihatiya or Dakshin Para."

It is also written in the *Gauḍīya Vaiṣṇava Abhidhāna*: "The Nandan mentioned in the Chaitanya Charitamrita as the brother of Ganga Das and Vishnu Das is a different person. He is counted as a branch of Nityananda Prabhu. He is a writer of poetry and songs, but little else is known about him. He is not Nandan Acharya."

NITYANANDA PRABHU IN THE HOUSE OF NANDAN ACHARYA

When Sriman Nityananda Prabhu was in a mood of separation, he wandered all over India looking for Krishna until finally he came to Vrindavan. There he heard that Krishna had already appeared in Nabadwip Mayapur: the son of Nanda, Sri Krishna, had appeared as Gaura Hari, the son of Sachi. Nityananda Prabhu, who is none other than Balaram himself, quickly came to Nabadwip and started to live incognito in the house of Nandan Acharya. As soon as he laid eyes on Nityananda and gained the opportunity to serve him, Nandan Acharya felt that his life had been fulfilled. Mahaprabhu knew of Nityananda's coming through a dream. He told the other devotees that Nityananda Prabhu had arrived in town and sent Srivas Pandit and Hari Das Thakur out to look for him. These two searched through the entire town but could not find him anywhere. When Mahaprabhu heard from Srivas Pandit and Hari Das Thakur that Nityananda was not in Nabadwip, He slightly smiled in His omniscience and took the devotees with Him to Nandan Acharya's house.

The devotees were astonished to behold a personality effulgent as a million suns. In order to reveal Nityananda's true identity to all his devotees, Mahaprabhu signaled Srivas Pandit to sing a verse from the Bhagavatam (10.21.5):

barhāpīḍaṁ naṭa-vara-vapuḥ karṇayoḥ karṇikāraṁ
vibhrad-vāsaḥ kanaka-kapiśaṁ vaijayantīṁ ca mālām

randhrān veṇor adhara-sudhayā pūrayan gopa-vṛndai-
rvṛnāraṇyaṁ sva-pada-ramaṇaṁ prāviśad gīta-kīrtiḥ

Krishna, whose glories are sung to the world by the cowherd boys, is dressed as a dancing performer, a peacock feather decorating His topknot, *karṇikāra* flowers behind His ears, a golden cloth covering His body and a victory garland around His neck.

In this costume, He entered Vrinda's forest, the pleasure garden of His auspiciously marked feet, while filling the holes of His flute with the nectar of His lips.

As soon as he heard this verse, Nityananda Prabhu uttered the words "Ha Krishna!" and fainted, the eight ecstatic symptoms manifesting in his body. Mahaprabhu became anxious to be reunited with His brother and He clutched Nitai to His bosom while glorifying him to the assembled devotees.

Sri Nandan Acharya was fortunate, indeed. Just look, Srinivas, this is his home. The Lord came to this house with all the devotees and found Nityananda sitting here in meditation. The devotees stood here gazing upon his incomparable beauty. (Bhakti-ratnākara 12.2422-4)

ADVAITA ACHARYA HIDES IN SRI NANDAN ACHARYA'S HOUSE

When the Vyasa Puja at Srivas Angan had been completed, Mahaprabhu, Nityananda Prabhu and their other associates became fully absorbed in the ecstasies of sankirtan. One day, Mahaprabhu was absorbed in His identity as the Supreme Person. He ordered Ramai Pandit to go to Advaita's house and tell him that He had manifested His presence. He also said to Ramai, "Sri Advaita Acharya called to the Lord of Goloka in order to bring Him down to this earth, while performing puja with Ganges water and tulasi leaves. This Lord has now appeared in Nabadwip along with Nityananda Prabhu. Therefore, Advaita should immediately come to Srivas Angan with his wife and all the paraphernalia needed to worship Him."

Ramai acted according to Mahaprabhu's instruction and went to Advaita Acharya's house. When Advaita heard from Ramai that Mahaprabhu had manifested in Nabadwip, he and his wife Sitadevi, his son Achyutananda, and a number of his other followers all shed tears of joy. Advaita excitedly did as he had been instructed, gathering up the paraphernalia for worship, and made for Nabadwip with his entourage. Even so, he still wished to test Mahaprabhu first and so he stopped at Nandan Acharya's house and waited there. He sent Ramai ahead, but told him to keep his presence at Nandan's house secret and to tell Mahaprabhu instead that he had refused to come.

As the Supersoul, Vishvambhar Mahaprabhu could understand exactly what Advaita was trying to do. He revealed a majestic divine form on the altar of Srivas' house. He indicated to Nityananda Prabhu to hold the parasol over His head and the other devotees to engage in various services. Mahaprabhu then announced to all the devotees, "Advaita Acharya has decided to test Me. He is hiding at Nandan Acharya's house with all the paraphernalia for my puja." He again sent Ramai to tell Advaita that He was aware of his plan and to quickly come. When Advaita got this direct order from Mahaprabhu a second time, he joyfully went to Srivas' house. As soon as he saw the Lord, he fell to the ground at some distance to pay obeisance to His lotus feet and recite hymns of glorification. Seeing the Lord's opulent form, Advaita became motionless and then began to praise the unequalled mercy of the Lord. Advaita then washed the Lord's lotus feet and worshiped Him with the five ingredients (*pañcopacāra*), using the following mantra to do so:

namo brahmaṇya-devāya
go-brāhmaṇa-hitāya ca
jagad-dhitāya kṛṣṇāya
govindāya namo namaḥ

I pay my obeisances to Krishna Govinda, the Lord of the Brahminical society, to Him Who is the source of the cows' and the Brahmins' welfare, and Who is the source of the welfare of the entire universe.

Mahaprabhu then commanded Advaita Prabhu to get up and dance. Advaita started to dance madly until he became completely intoxicated, immersing all the watching devotees in a flood of ecstasy.

MAHAPRABHU HIDES IN THE HOUSE OF NANDAN ACHARYA

The local atheists started to plot against Mahaprabhu after having been beaten in debates by His talent and learning. They fabricated complaints and went to the local administrator. That day, when He returned home, Mahaprabhu started sankirtan in order to put an end to the atheists' blasphemous ways. However, on that day, Mahaprabhu noticed that He was not feeling the usual emotion in the divine names and made public His distress. Advaita Acharya gave the following reasons for His lack of ecstasy on that day: "You have made Nityananda the keeper of the storehouse of love. You have deprived Srivas and myself of this love. On the other hand, You have given it to everyone else, even to those in the lower castes. So, I have dried up the ocean of Your prema. That is why you are not feeling anything today."

When Mahaprabhu heard this, He decided that He could not bear to live another minute in a useless body devoid of prema, and so He went and jumped into the Ganges, intending to drown Himself. Nityananda and Hari Das immediately jumped in after Him and pulled Him out. Mahaprabhu then revealed to these two his intention to go and stay for a while at Nandan

Acharya's house, out of sight of the other devotees. Nitai and Hari Das were thus the only ones to know that He was staying there.

The other devotees found no sign of Mahaprabhu anywhere and began to feel intense separation from Him. Advaita Prabhu even undertook a fast. Meanwhile, Mahaprabhu sat down on the deity's throne in Nandan Acharya's house and engaged its owner in various kinds of service. Mahaprabhu also instructed Him not to tell anyone that He was at his place, but Nandan answered, "You are the wealth of the devotees' hearts. The devotees are the ones who reveal You to the world. How will You ever manage to remain hidden from them?"

Indeed, the Lord was aware that the devotees were unable to tolerate the pain of His absence, and so He asked Nandan Acharya to bring Srivas Pandit there. Srivas described how upset Advaita was and that he was fasting. Mahaprabhu immediately accompanied Srivas to Advaita's residence and when He saw him lying faint and weak on the floor, He felt Himself to be a great offender. Advaita rose up from his faint and prayed to the Lord again and again to be forgiven for his rash statements and begged a place at the Lord's lotus feet so that he could serve Him birth after birth. (Chaitanya Bhagavata 2.17)

NANDAN ACHARYA'S PARTICIPATION IN OTHER LILAS

After taking sannyas in Katwa, Mahaprabhu was brought to the house of Advaita in Shantipur by Nityananda's trickery. Sachi and other residents of Nabadwip came to see Him there; Nandan Acharya was amongst them. The year that Raghava Pandit first brought his famous bags of food (*rāghavera jhali*) to Mahaprabhu in Puri, Nandan Acharya also gave the Lord food preparations that pleased Him greatly. Nandan Acharya was also among those devotees whose invitations to lunch were accepted by the Lord at Puri. His name is also mentioned by Sarvabhauma Bhattacharya when he described the Lord's devotees to King Prataparudra.

(Chaitanya Charitamrita 2.11.89).

Nandan Acharya was also amongst the participants in the nightly kirtan at Srivas Angan and in the procession to the Kazi's house. In Puri, he participated in the cleaning of the Gundicha temple and the Nrisingha temple and the Lord's bathing pastimes in Indradyumna Sarovar. He also took part in the feast in the Ai Tota gardens and, of course, the Rathayatra festival.

Srila Bhakti Saranga Goswami Maharaj, the founder of the Gaudiya Sangha and who has now entered the eternal pastimes of the Lord, constructed a temple at the site of Nandan Acharya's house in Ishodyan, Mayapur. The temple houses deities of Sri Chaitanya Mahaprabhu and Nityananda Prabhu.

The dates and places of Nandan Acharya's appearance and disappearance are unknown.

Chandrasekhar Acharya

candraśekhara ācāryaś
candro jñeyo vicakṣaṇaiḥ
śrīmān uddhava-dāso'pi
candrāveśāvatārakaḥ

The wise know that Chandrasekhar Acharya is an incarnation of the moon god, while Uddhava Das is also a partial incarnation of the moon.

(*Gaura-gaṇoddeśa-dīpikā* 112)

One of the great branches of the Chaitanya tree is called Acharyaratna, also known as Chandrasekhar; his entourage forms another group of branches and sub-branches. Mahaprabhu danced in his house in the mood of the goddess. (Chaitanya Charitamrita 1.10.12-13)

Srila Bhaktisiddhanta Saraswati Goswami Thakur writes: "Chandrasekhar was one of the nine treasures, or the god Chandra. His home is known as Vraja-pattana [i.e., the place where Mahaprabhu enjoyed his pastimes of putting on a play about Vrindavan]."

Srila Bhaktivinoda Thakur writes in his *Amṛta-pravāha-bhāṣya* that according to some sources, Acharyaratna was Chaitanya Mahaprabhu's *meso*, i.e., the husband of his mother's sister. The *Gauḍīya Vaiṣṇava Abhidhāna* explains that he married Sachi Devi's sister Sarvajaya.

In the book called Śākhā-nirṇayāmṛta by Srila Gadadhar Pandit Goswami's disciple Yadunath Das, Chandrasekhar Acharya's identity is revealed in the following way:

paurṇamāsī-pṛthu-prema-
pātraṁ śrī-candraśekharam
apāra-karuṇā-pūra-
paurṇamāsīti saṁjñakam

Chandrasekhar was the recipient of Paurnamasi Devi's deepest love. He is known as the full moon of unlimited compassion.

Chandrasekhar Acharya was also born in Sylhet.

Srivas Pandit, Sri Rama Pandit and Chandrasekhar Deva are worshipable throughout the three worlds; they, as well as Murari Gupta, the physician who cures one of the disease of worldliness, all appeared in Sylhet.

(Chaitanya Bhagavata 1.2.34-5)

All of Mahaprabhu's elders appear on this earth prior to His birth.

There were many devotees hidden in Nabadwip who had previously taken birth at the Lord's command. They included Chandrasekhar, Jagadish, Gopinath, Sriman, Murari, Sri Garuḍa, and Ganga Das.

(Chaitanya Bhagavata 1.2.98-9)

Sri Chandrasekhar lived just next door to Jagannath Mishra in Mayapur. The Chaitanya Math established by Srila Bhaktisiddhanta Saraswati Goswami Thakur now stands on this site. Prior to Mahaprabhu's appearance, Chandrasekhar and his wife would visit the Mishra household regularly and helped them to manage their affairs out of an interest in their well-being. When Jagannath departed from this world, Chandrasekhar took complete responsibility for Sachi Devi's household affairs.

PASTIMES IN CHANDRASEKHAR'S HOUSE

After Mahaprabhu's return from Gaya, when He commenced His sankirtan movement in the company of His devotees, He would sometimes hold nightly kirtans in the house of Chandrasekhar, just as He would in the house of Srivas Pandit.

> All the Vaishnavas felt great enthusiasm when they heard that Mahaprabhu had begun His sankirtan movement. Every night, these kirtans took place in the house of Srivas Pandit, and on certain occasions, in the house of Chandrasekhar Acharya.
>
> (Chaitanya Bhagavata 2.8.110-1)

Jagai and Madhai were two brothers who, though born in a high caste Brahmin family, had nevertheless adopted robbery as their livelihood. By Mahaprabhu's causeless mercy, all of their sins were cleansed and they were given the opportunity to engage in sankirtan with the rest of His devotees. Chandrasekhar Acharya was amongst the associates of the Lord who witnessed these wonderful events. "Vakresvara Pandit and Chandrasekhar Acharya both know all the glories of Chaitanya Mahaprabhu."

(Chaitanya Bhagavata 2.13.240)

Mahaprabhu put on a play about Vraja lila in the house of Chandrasekhar Acharya. This lila has been described in great detail by Vrindavan Das Thakur in his Chaitanya Bhagavata, in the eighteenth chapter of the Madhya-khaṇḍa. Krishna Das Kaviraj Goswami has briefly mentioned the event in his Chaitanya Charitamrita:

> Then Mahaprabhu performed Krishna lila in the house of Chandrasekhar. He Himself took on the role of Rukmini and others as well, becoming in turn Durga, Lakshmi and the Divine Energy. Then He sat down on the deity throne and distributed love of God to all the assembled devotees. (Chaitanya Charitamrita 1.17.241-2)

Here is a brief summary of the story as found in the Chaitanya Bhagavata: One day Mahaprabhu revealed his desire to put on a play with His devotees about His pastimes in Vrindavan. He told Sadashiva and Buddhimanta Khan who would play which role and what they should wear.

> Then Sachi's son, completely absorbed in the kirtan of the Lord's names, called out to Sadashiva and Buddhimanta Khan. "Today I will go to Chandrasekhar's house where I will dance in the dress of Lakshmi. Arrange for conch bracelets, saris, bodices, golden ornaments and other paraphernalia we can use for our costumes." Having so ordered him, Mahaprabhu and His companions went down the path that led to Chandrasekhar's house.
>
> (Bhakti-ratnākara 12.1949-52)

According to his instruction, Buddhimanta then arranged for appropriate dress and makeup for those who would be in the play, pleasing Mahaprabhu immeasurably. Mahaprabhu announced that He would dance in the role of Lakshmi, but that only those whose senses were controlled would be able to sit in the audience. Advaita Acharya, Srivas Pandit and others sadly said that since they had no control over their senses they would be ineligible to watch. Mahaprabhu laughed slightly at hearing this and said that for that day at least everyone would become a great yogi and would not be bewildered by His performance.

Sachi Mata and Vishnupriya Devi also came to see Mahaprabhu dance as Lakshmi, and so did all the other devotees with their families. Advaita Acharya took the role of the vidūṣaka, or clown, while Hari Das Thakur played the role of the town constable and Srivas Pandit dressed up as Narada Muni. The performance began when Mukunda sang Krishna kirtan. Hari Das Thakur came dancing in, twirling his baton, and told everyone to watch the play and the Lord's dancing attentively.

Srivas Pandit in the role of Narada Muni said, "I have been wandering throughout the universes hoping to get a glimpse of Krishna. I went to Vaikuntha, but found the door closed and the house empty. Then I heard that Krishna had come to Nadia and had dressed up as Lakshmi and was about to dance just as she would." When Sachi saw Srivas in his identity as Narada she fainted in amazement, but the other women brought her back to consciousness by chanting the name of Krishna.

In the next act, Mahaprabhu came out dressed as Rukmini. Totally absorbed in the mood of Rukmini, He recited from the Bhagavatam the letter she wrote to Krishna, and as He did so, He cried and wrote on the ground with His toes. When the Vaishnavas saw this scene, they were overwhelmed by the ecstasy of divine love.

Later on in the evening, Srila Gadadhar Pandit Goswami came onto the stage dressed as a gopi and began to dance like a woman in love. Mahaprabhu and Nityananda then entered the stage area, Mahaprabhu in the dress of the Ādyā śakti and Nityananda as an old woman, Radha's maternal grandmother. As the members of the audience looked at Mahaprabhu, each beheld Him according to his or her own mood: some as Kamala, some as Lakshmi, others as Sita and yet others as Mahamaya. Even those who had known Nimai since His birth, including Sachi, were unable to recognize Him. In the guise of playing the roles of all the different female divinities, Mahaprabhu revealed His divine energies and taught the proper respect due to each one of them. While the Lord was thus dancing as the Ādyā śakti, Nityananda fainted and all the other devotees began to cry loudly.

Then the Lord revealed another amazing pastime: He took on the mood of Maha Lakshmi, sat down on the deity throne and placed the Gopinath deity on His lap. When the devotees saw this they began to sing hymns of praise to Maha Lakshmi. As this was going on, dawn broke and the devotees were saddened to know that the wonderful night had suddenly come to an end. When the Lord saw their sadness, He took the form of the Mother of the Universe and one by one, took all the devotees on His lap and gave them His breast to drink. The devotees' sadness disappeared in a moment.

By the Lord's inconceivable potencies, there remained a divine light in Chandrasekhar's house for seven days and nights afterward. It was so bright that people were unable to open their eyes to look at it. When people asked what this light was, the Vaishnavas would only smile in response.

PARTICIPATION IN OTHER PASTIMES

Chandrasekhar Acharya was also present in the sankirtan procession Mahaprabhu led through Nabadwip to Chand Kazi's house to deliver him. He was also present when Mahaprabhu took sannyas in Katwa, and he performed all the rituals on His behalf at that time.

> So saying, Keshava Bharati went to Katwa. Mahaprabhu followed later to take sannyas. Nityananda, Mukunda Datta and Chandrasekhar accompanied Him and performed all the rituals.
>
> (Chaitanya Charitamrita 1.17.272-3)

Afterwards, Mahaprabhu became frantic to see Vrindavan and set off in that direction. However, Nityananda tricked him into going to the bank of the Ganges opposite Shantipur, in the meantime, sending Chandrasekhar with a message for the people of Nabadwip that Mahaprabhu had taken sannyas and was in Shantipur.

> The children showed Mahaprabhu the way to the Ganges, and He set off in that direction, completely absorbed in consciousness of Krishna. Nityananda Prabhu said to Chandrasekhar, "Go immediately to Advaita Acharya and tell him that I am coming there with the Lord. Tell him to wait for us with a boat. Then go to Nabadwip and fetch Sachi Mata and the devotees."
>
> (Chaitanya Charitamrita 2.3.19-22)

Chandrasekhar did as he was commanded and brought Sachi Mata to Advaita's house in a palanquin. The Nabadwip devotees also accompanied them.

> In the morning, Acharyaratna put Sachi in a palanquin and set off to Shantīpur in the company of the other devotees. (Chaitanya Charitamrita 2.3.137)

Later, when Mahaprabhu came back from South India to Puri, He sent Kala Krishna Das (whom he had rescued from the Bhattahari women) with Nityananda and some other devotees to inform the Bengali Vaishnavas of His return. Kala Krishna Das met with Chandrasekhar on that occasion. Chandrasekhar also regularly accompanied the other devotees to Puri to spend Chaturmasya with Mahaprabhu. He participated with Him in all the pastimes there, such as cleaning the Gundicha temple and playing watersports in Narendra Sarovar.

SRI PUNDARIKA VIDYANIDHI

vṛṣabhānutayā khyātaḥ purā yo vraja-maṇḍale
adhunā puṇḍarīkākṣo vidyānidhi-mahāśayaḥ
svakīya-bhāvam āsvādya rādhā-viraha-kātaraḥ
caitanyaḥ puṇḍarīkākṣam aye tātāvadat svayam
prema-nidhitayā khyātiṁ gauro yasmai dadau sukhī
mādhavendrasya śiṣyatvāt gauravaṁ ca sadākarot
tat-prakāśa-viśeṣo'pi miśraḥ śrī-mādhavo mataḥ
ratnāvatī tu tat-patnī kīrtidā kīrtitā budhaiḥ

> He who was previously known in Vraja as Vrishabhanu, is known here as Sri Pundarikaksha Vidyanidhi. When Mahaprabhu was in his own mood as Krishna and felt the pain of separation from Radha, he would call him "father." Gaurachandra was happy with Pundarika and named him Premanidhi, or "the treasure house of love." Mahaprabhu always treated him with respect because he was the disciple of Madhavendra Puri. Madhava Mishra is said to be his expansion and his wife Ratnavati was Kirtida in Vraja.
>
> (Gaura-gaṇoddeśa-dīpikā 54)

Pundarika Vidyanidhi's father was named Banesvara and his mother, Ganga Devi. He was born on vasanta-pañcamī, the fifth day of the waxing moon in the month of Magh in Chakrashala in Chittagong. His home, or śrīpāṭ, used to stand in the village of Mekhala, two miles east of the Hat Hajari police station and about twelve miles north of the city of Chittagong. Vidyanidhi's father was a Varendra Brahmin who hailed from the town of Baghiya in the district of Dhaka. Pundarika Vidyanidhi himself was a wealthy landowner in Chakrashala.

> He is an extremely rich zamindar from Chakrashala, but is very pure in his actions. He is a Varendra Brahmin, whose lineage is extremely respectable. His name is Sri Pundarika Vidyanidhi. Sometimes he stays in Chittagong and sometimes in Nabadwip. He is a disciple of Madhavendra Puri. (Prema-vilāsa, 22)

THE LORD GLORIFIES PUNDARIKA

> Sri Pundarika Vidyanidhi came to Nabadwip because he wished to live by the banks of the Ganges. Mahaprabhu, the indweller of all beings, knew prior to his coming that he had such a desire, and one day in the assembly of devotees started calling out, "Pundarika, My friend, My father!" and crying.

When His associates asked Him why He was crying in this way, the Lord described Pundarika Vidyanidhi to them in the following way: "His character is quite extraordinary. Just by hearing his name, the whole world is purified, but he dresses and looks just like a materialistic person in the midst of the accoutrements of the life of pleasure. No one is able to recognize him as a Vaishnava, yet he remains constantly merged in the deep ocean of devotion for Krishna. He never bathes in the Ganges because he is afraid to touch the holy waters with his feet, which would show disrespect. He only goes to take darshan of the Ganges at night and from a distance. He cannot bear to see people engaged in offensive behavior to the Ganges by gargling, cleaning their teeth, washing their hair in her waters, so he never goes there during the daytime. He never engages in worship of the deity without having taken a drink of Ganges water. He has homes in both Chittagong and in Nabadwip and will soon be arriving here. Because of his apparently materialistic behavior, you will not be able to recognize him, but I feel unwell because I am not able to see him."

The Supreme Lord has appeared in Nabadwip, but He heaves long sighs because He doesn't see Pundarika Vidyanidhi. Lord Gauranga stands up and starts to dance, calling out loudly, "Pundarika, My father! Pundarika, My friend, My father! When will I see you?"
(Chaitanya Bhagavata 2.7.11-3)

It is thought that Pundarika Vidyanidhi took initiation from Madhavendra Puripada at the same time that Advaita Acharya did. Mahaprabhu always showed him the respect that was due the godbrother of his own guru. In the Chaitanya Charitamrita, Krishna Das Kaviraj Goswami writes:

I know Sri Pundarika Vidyanidhi to be a major branch, for the Lord Himself cried while spontaneously calling out his name. (Chaitanya Charitamrita 1.10.14)

GADADHAR BECOMES PUNDARIKA'S DISCIPLE

Srila Gadadhar Pandit Goswami, Mukunda Datta and Vasudeva Datta were also originally from Chittagong and so they were acquainted with Pundarika Vidyanidhi. Indeed Gadādhar Pandit's father Madhava Mishra was his good friend. Mukunda Datta knew his transcendental personality and that he was a Vaishnava, but Gadadhar did not, even though he was from the same town. This was, of course, a pretense for the sake of the lila.

When Pundarika was living in Nabadwip, Mukunda Datta told Gadādhar one day that he wanted to introduce him to a great Vaishnava. Srila Gadadhar Pandit Goswami was a brahmachari from childhood and extremely detached from the senses and ascetic in his lifestyle. When he saw Pundarika sitting on comfortable cushions covered in sheets as white as the foam of milk, and wearing very expensive clothes and perfumes, smoking from a hookah, and generally surrounded by all the trappings of a sensual lifestyle, he was unable to recognize him as a Vaishnava. Indeed, he felt let down.

Mukunda could see from Gadadhar's face what was going through his head, and in order to bring out Pundarika's inner mood, he recited two verses from the Bhagavatam that ignited flames of love for Krishna.

aho bakīyaṁ stana-kāla-kūṭaṁ
jighāṁsayāpāyayad apy asādhvī
lebhe gatiṁ dhātry-ucitaṁ tato'nyaṁ
kaṁ vā dayāluṁ śaraṇaṁ prapadye

How truly amazing! The sister of Bakasura, the evil Putana, was sent on a mission to kill Krishna. He drank the kālakūṭa poison mixed with her breast milk, and despite her evil intentions, awarded her the position of a wet nurse (as Ambika Kilimba in Goloka). Who is more merciful than he that I should take shelter of him?
(Srimad Bhagavatam 3.2.23)

pūtanā loka-bālaghnī rākṣasī rudhirāśanā
jighāṁsayāpi haraye stanaṁ dattvāpa sad-gatim

That Rakshasi Putana was a blood-drinking killer of infants. Even though she wanted to kill Krishna, she attained the auspicious goal of a nurse in Goloka because she had given Him her breast to drink.
(Srimad Bhagavatam 10.6.35)

As soon as he heard these two verses in glorification of Krishna's mercy, Sri Pundarika Vidyanidhi cried out "Ha Krishna!" and fell to the floor in a swoon. He began to roll on the floor in ecstasy, knocking over the hookah and tearing his clothes.

When he saw these transcendental symptoms of love on Pundarika's body, Gadadhar realized that he had committed an offence, which he began to regret. He decided that the only way to rid himself of this offence would be to take initiation from Pundarika, and he related this idea to

Mukunda. Mukunda then communicated his desire to Pundarika who happily set a date for the auspicious act. Mahaprabhu also gave His approval and so Gadadhar took mantra initiation from Pundarika Vidyanidhi.

In Krishna lila, Sri Pundarika Vidyanidhi is Vrishabhanu and Srila Gadadhar Pandit Goswami is Radha. Because of Pundarika's identity as Vrishabhanu, Mahaprabhu would call out to him as "father!" when He was Himself in the mood of Srimati Radharani. The deep affection from their previous life's relation became apparent between Pundarika and Gadadhar. No one can understand the pastimes of the Vaishnavas without their mercy.

vaiṣṇava cinite nāre devera śakati
mui kon chāra śiśu alpa-mati

Even the gods are unable to recognize a Vaishnava, so how can a foolish, fallen child like myself do so?

Even though Pundarika Vidyanidhi was a great Vaishnava, he kept it a secret and went about just like a materialistic person. Srila Bhaktisiddhanta Saraswati Goswami Thakur warns us in his Gauḍīya-bhāṣya to the Chaitanya Bhagavata that one cannot recognize a Vaishnava through any superficial examination: "Krishna lila is not accessible to limited sensory understanding. Krishna's servants occasionally go unrecognized due to their apparently materialistic surroundings. In this way they deceive the conditioned souls. Many scholars take Krishna's activities to be those of a material lover because of their own obsession with sensuality, and thus they have no faith in Him. Others consider Krishna to be an ordinary man who is born, undergoes transformation and dies; thus they have no idea of who He really is. Krishna's devotees are also sometimes reluctant to reveal their real selves to the unworthy and thus make a pretense of being ordinary materialistic persons. Gauranga Mahaprabhu is also sometimes called the pracchanna-avatāra or hidden incarnation. In the same spirit, Pundarika put on the show of being sensualist for those who were capable of being deceived by someone's external appearance."

Once Pundarika Vidyanidhi came to see Mahaprabhu when it was already quite late at night. As soon as he saw the Lord, he was so overcome by love that he could not even pay his obeisances. Mahaprabhu was similarly anxious to see His dearmost devotee, Pundarika, and immediately took him to His breast and washed him with tears of love. When the other devotees heard Mahaprabhu cry and call Pundarika "father" and "treasure of love," they knew just how dear he was to Him. Pundarika Vidyanidhi was also known to Mahaprabhu's associates as Acharyanidhi.

The Supreme Lord cried and called out "Pundarika! Father! Today I have seen My own father! Today I rose from My sleep at an auspicious moment, and I saw Premanidhi standing before Me.
(Chaitanya Bhagavata 2.7.131, 143)

Sri Pundarika Vidyanidhi participated in the nightly sankirtan festival in Srivas Pandit's house along with Mahaprabhu and His other associates. On Mahaprabhu's order, Nityananda and Hari Das went door to door to spread the chanting of the Holy Names and thus to liberate the conditioned souls, succeeding in converting Jagai and Madhai. Later, when Jagai and Madhai were sitting amongst the devotees before Mahaprabhu, they also displayed the ecstatic symptoms of prema. Sri Pundarika Vidyanidhi was also present there and he became completely submerged in loving ecstasy to see their great fortune. It is stated in the Bhakti-ratnākara that Mahaprabhu celebrated the birth of Radharani at Sri Pundarika Vidyanidhi's house. (Bhakti-ratnākara 12.3177).

PUNDARIKA IN PURI

On Mahaprabhu's order, the devotees led by Advaita Acharya went each year to see the Rathayatra. Krishna Das Kaviraj Goswami describes him as being one of the leaders of the party of pilgrims as they made the annual trip:

All of Mahaprabhu's servants such as Advaita, Nityananda, Mukunda, Srivas, Vidyanidhi, Vasudeva and Murari came together each year to meet with him and they would stay four months. The Lord enjoyed many pastimes in their company. (Chaitanya Charitamrita 2.1.255-6)

Sri Pundarika Vidyanidhi was also present at Jagannath's Chandana Yatra festival when Mahaprabhu and all His devotees played in the water of Narendra Sarovar, also known as Chandan Pukur. Pundarika and Svarupa Damodar were close friends and they laughed and splashed each other as a part of these pastimes.
(Chaitanya Bhagavata 3.8.124)

Pundarika Vidyanidhi also participated with Mahaprabhu and His associates in the cleaning of the Gundicha temple, relishing maha prasad with them afterwards.

GADADHAR WISHES TO RECEIVE THE MANTRA AGAIN

One day, Srila Gadadhar Pandit Goswami asked Mahaprabhu if he could hear his initiation mantra from Him. He said,

"Ever since I repeated my iṣṭa-mantra to someone, I have been unable to concentrate when I chant. Please repeat the mantra to me, then my mind will be calmed."

Mahaprabhu answered,

"You already have a mantropadeśaka guru. Be careful, otherwise you will become an offender to him. Everything I have is yours, even My life, what to speak of the mantra. But as long as your guru is alive it is improper for Me to repeat it to you." (Chaitanya Bhagavata 3.10.23-6)

Gadadhar answered, saying, "He isn't here. Please do it in his place."

Mahaprabhu replied: "Destiny will bring your guru Vidyanidhi to you." The omniscient Mahaprabhu continued, "Sri Pundarika Vidyanidhi will be coming to Puri to see Me and will be here in ten days." And that is what came to pass. Mahaprabhu became ecstatic, crying, "Father has come! Father has come!" Gadadhar went to Vidyanidhi upon his arrival.

Gadadhar Deva asked Premanidhi to again initiate him in the iṣṭa-mantra, which he lovingly did. How can I sufficiently glorify Sri Pundarika Vidyanidhi, who has a loving disciple like Gadadhar Pandit!
(Chaitanya Bhagavata 3.10.79-80)

Our most worshipable Srila Prabhupada commented one of the above verses (3.10.24) in the following way: "The mantra is śabda brahma, the divine sound that destroys the mental aptitude for sense gratification. If one instructs a faithless person in the divine sound, one's mind becomes contaminated. If one's divine understanding (divya-jñāna) is destroyed, then one must seek the same again. Gadadhar Pandit understood this and so he asked Gaurasundar Mahaprabhu to reinitiate him. Mahaprabhu's judgment, however, was that he should go to his own guru to hear the mantra again."

The lesson to be learned here is this: Srila Gadadhar Pandit Goswami is Mahaprabhu's eternal associate; it is thus impossible that any contamination could have entered his mind. Through Gadadhar, Mahaprabhu was instructing those who would be guru that if one instructs an unqualified person in the mantra, it loses its potency and no longer brings the same joy to the heart of the practitioner. When this happens, it is necessary to go to the guru and hear the mantra from him again. It is against custom to hear the mantra again from someone who is not one's guru, because one cannot change initiating spiritual masters in this way. Gadadhar was only saying, "I cannot concentrate like before" (nā sphure bhālo mati), i.e., "The ecstatic feelings no longer come when I chant," out of an exemplary humility designed to teach humanity how to act.

JAGANNATH SLAPS PUNDARIKA

On the Oṛana Ṣaṣṭhī festival, Jagannath's servants dress him in a cloth that still has starch in it. According to Bhaktivinoda Thakur, Oṛana Ṣaṣṭhī takes place at the beginning of winter. This is the first day that Jagannath is dressed in winter clothes. The winter cloth is called māṛuwā vastra, because it has not been washed and still has māṛa (weaver's starch) in it. Sri Pundarika Vidyanidhi was a pure sad-ācārī, attached to the proper etiquette of Vaishnavism. When he observed this custom, he did not feel happy about it and said to his friend, Svarupa Damodar, "Why do they give this unwashed cloth to the Lord? The people of this country know the rules in the Smritis and the Srutis, so why do they give māṛuwā cloth to Jagannath?"

Svarupa Damodar answered that the Supreme Lord is beyond the rules and regulations that have become general custom and that therefore there was no fault. Vidyanidhi did not find this conclusion satisfying and he countered by saying, "That may be true for the Lord Himself. But His servants should follow the rules of the scripture. The śrī-vigraha of the Lord is beyond the material qualities, so you can say this of Him, but His servants are not of the same nature as He. So we are permitted to judge whether their behavior is proper or not."

Vidyanidhi is Mahaprabhu's dear associate and beyond any fault, but once again we see that the Lord teaches particular lessons through His devotees. Here He wished to show that we have no right to make judgments or to find fault with the behavior of Jagannath's devotees. That night an angry Jagannath came to Pundarika Vidyanidhi and gave him a dream vision. Vidyanidhi was frightened when he saw the anger of the Lord. Jagannath and Balaram slapped him on each of his cheeks and Pundarika started to cry out, "Krishna save me! Krishna, save me! Forgive me my offence!" Jagannath said,

"There is no end to your offensiveness. Just as there is no question of pure and impure in My case, the same holds true for My servants. You are staying here; you should know all this. If you thought that it was impure, then why did you stay at all? Go home then, if you want to maintain your purity." (Chaitanya Bhagavata 3.10.131-2)

When Pundarika woke up in the morning, the devotees saw the marks of the Lords' slaps on his cheeks, which had swollen as a result, and they started to laugh. This pastime shows just how dear Sri Pundarika Vidyanidhi was to Jagannath and to Mahaprabhu, for the Lord only comes to His dearest devotees to punish them personally in this way.

That night Jagannath and Balaram came to him and, laughing all the while, slapped him on the cheeks. Pundarika Vidyanidhi felt a secret joy at his swollen cheeks, as has been described by Vrindavan Das in detail.
(Chaitanya Charitamrita 2.16.80-1)

Vrindavan Das Thakur concludes the Chaitanya Bhagavata with the following glorification of Sri Pundarika Vidyanidhi:

The Supreme Lord Gauranga called out the name of this devotee, crying "Pundarika, My father. Anyone who hears about his life and activities will undoubtedly attain Krishna's lotus feet." (Chaitanya Bhagavata 3.10.183-4)

Sri Shuklambar Brahmachari

śuklāmbaro brahmacārī purāsīd yajñapatnikā
prārthayitvā yad-annaṁ śrī-gaurāṅgo bhuktavān prabhuḥ
kecid āhur brahmacārī yājñika-brāhmaṇaḥ purā

Shuklambar Brahmachari was previously one of the wives of the sacrificial priests in Vraja. Mahaprabhu begged food from him and ate it. Some people say that he was one of the sacrificial Brahmins. (Gaura-gaṇoddeśa-dīpikā 191)

SHUKLAMBAR BRAHMACHARI, A POOR MENDICANT

Shuklambar Brahmachari is counted among the branches of Chaitanya Mahaprabhu. He was a resident of Nabadwip town, manifesting the pastimes of a poor Brahmin who begged for a living. Nevertheless, he had an abiding affection for the Lord. Though to an ordinary conditioned soul he appeared to be a poverty-stricken mendicant, to transcendental eyes he was rich because of his love for Mahaprabhu.

prema-dhana vinā vyartha daridra jīvana
dāsa kari betana more deha prema-dhana

Without the wealth of love of God, my life is poverty-stricken and worthless. Employ me as Your servant and pay me with the coin of ecstatic love of God.
(Chaitanya Charitamrita 3.20.37)

When Mahaprabhu returned from Gaya, He first met with the devotees in Shuklambar Brahmachari's house.

Sriman Pandit then left along the banks of the Ganges to the house of Shuklambar Brahmachari, where the Lord had announced He would meet with the devotees that night. Having heard Sriman make this announcement, Gadadhar Pandit quickly followed him there. He hid in Shuklambar's house thinking that he would eavesdrop, as Mahaprabhu would surely talk about Krishna. All the loving devotees of the Lord, such as Sadashiva, Murari, Sriman and Shuklambar, had gathered there when Vishvambhar suddenly appeared on the scene.
(Chaitanya Bhagavata 2.1.78-82)

Srila Gadadhar Pandit Goswami, Sadashiva, Murari, Srivas Pandit, Sriman Pandit and others all witnessed the Lord's ecstatic transformations in Shuklambar's house.

THE LORD SNATCHES RICE FROM SHUKLAMBAR'S BEGGING BAG

Shuklambar Brahmachari was very fortunate, for the Lord snatched his food from him and ate it Himself.
(Chaitanya Charitamrita 1.10.38)

Shuklambar Brahmachari kept body and soul together by offering and eating the foodstuffs which he daily accumulated by begging. Since he was constantly absorbed in the joys of chanting the names of the Lord and remembering his qualities and pastimes, he never suffered from his poverty. Ignorant people thought he was just an ordinary beggar. No one can recognize Mahaprabhu's servants unless they receive the Lord's mercy.

One day, Mahaprabhu was sitting alone in a devotional trance when Shuklambar Brahmachari happened by, his begging bag flung over his shoulder. When he saw the Lord, he started to dance ecstatically. The Lord was pleased to see the depth of Shuklambar's feeling and he began to glorify him. He then plucked a handful of the dry rice from his bag and began to chew it. Shuklambar Brahmachari was troubled to see the Lord eating the uncleaned and broken fragments of low-quality rice and felt that he had committed an offence. The Lord calmed him and said that He always ate His devotee's food with great enthusiasm, but that He had no interest whatsoever in the finest foods of the non-devotee. The devotees were delighted to see the Lord's mercy on Shuklambar Brahmachari, who was then given a blessing by the Lord.

The Lord said, "Listen, Shuklambar Brahmachari. I reside permanently in your heart. Whenever you eat, I eat. When you go on your begging rounds, I accompany you. I have descended to distribute love of Godhead and you are My servant, lifetime after lifetime. I hereby bestow upon you prema bhakti, which is My very soul." When the devotees heard the Lord's blessing, they made a joyful noise, shouting "Jaya, jaya!" (Chaitanya Bhagavata 2.16.133-8)

Srila Bhaktisiddhanta Saraswati Goswami Thakur paraphrases Mahaprabhu's blessing in his Gauḍīya-bhāṣya: "You are My poor servant lifetime after lifetime. You have no desire to enter into this world to become the head of a household. Rather, you remain a bachelor and beg from house to house, making an offering to Me of whatever you amass in this way. Your vow of celibacy is unbreakable. You are free of the mundane egoism that is prominent in householders and retired householders. You are thus factually fixed in the highest state of spiritual life, the highest stage of the renounced order. You are a de facto sannyasi, a completely surrendered carrier of the triple staff, because you have successfully engaged every action of your body, mind and speech in My service. I pray constantly for your offerings for you have no interest in enjoying anything that has not been offered to Me. It is for this reason that I have made a show of My power and taken everything away from you, making you poor." (Chaitanya Bhagavata 2.16.123)

The Lord was sitting here on this altar of Vishnu, absorbed in the sound of the Holy Name, when Shuklambar Brahmachari passed by on his begging rounds. Mahaprabhu lovingly put His hand on Shuklambar's begging bag and took a handful of unwashed rice, calling him

Sudama. Shuklambar Brahmachari made repeated humble comments and danced in the kirtan with the bag still on his shoulder. The Lord and his devotees felt the intensity of their emotions increase as they watched Shuklambar's ecstatic transformations. This is one of the pastimes of the Lord in the house of Srivas Pandit, after which He went through the town back to His own house.

(Bhakti-ratnākara 12.2754-8)

THE LORD EATS AT SHUKLAMBAR'S HOUSE

In the Chaitanya Bhagavata, it is also said that Mahaprabhu ate cooked food in the house of Shuklambar Brahmachari, being attracted by his love. When the Lord announced to Shuklambar that he wished to eat at His house, the brahmachari felt nervous because he was afraid that he was unable to provide suitable fare for the Lord with his begged rice. However, the Lord repeatedly told him that this was indeed his desire, and so Shuklambar went to the other devotees to ask their advice. The devotees suggested that he cook without touching the food and that this would be satisfactory.

On the day of the invitation, Shuklambar bathed and dressed. He then lit the stove and put water to boil. Then, without touching the rice, he poured it into the water along with the core of the plantain tree (thoṛ), all the while emotionally chanting the names, "Jaya Krishna Gopal, Govinda, Vanamali!" At that moment, Lakshmi Devi blessed the food cooked by the devotee by glancing at it. When Mahaprabhu came to Shuklambar's house with His associates, He offered the rice and vegetables to Vishnu by His own hand. When it came time to eat it, He praised its flavor, saying, "In my entire life, I have never eaten anything so delicious." Once again the devotees cried at the sight of the Lord's merciful attitude to Shuklambar.

When the devotees saw the wealth of blessings the Lord bestowed upon Shuklambar Brahmachari, they all began to cry. The Lord continued to eat joyfully, greatly relishing its taste. May all the rich millionaire non-devotees observe the mercy received by the beggar Shuklambar. No one can attain the Lord's mercy through wealth, high birth or scholarship. The scriptures repeatedly tell us that the Lord is only attracted by the taste of devotion.

(Chaitanya Bhagavata 2.26.28-31)

Srila Bhaktisiddhanta Saraswati Goswami Thakur comments on this passage in Gauḍīya-bhāṣya: "Vishnu is the Lord of the Sacrifice who only eats that which is offered by Brahma in sacrifice. Shuklambar Brahmachari gathered rice by begging from a variety of households. This rice is often parboiled rather than sun-dried rice. Householder Brahmins thus normally consider it contaminated and refuse to accept it. However, Vaishnavas hold that rice received from begging is superior to any other rice because it has been obtained by the mercy of the Lord. Though superficially this rice appears to be contaminated by the touch of non-devotees and offering it is thus a deviation from the usual rules and regulations, in Mahaprabhu's path, the purity of a devotee's heart is the most important ingredient in maha prasad. One should not think that a millionaire is the only person who can offer foods suitable for the Lord. Shuklambar was poverty-stricken, but the Lord was satisfied with the food he had gathered through begging. Those who are sinful and without an aptitude of service cannot understand this at all."

One day, the Lord asked Shuklambar to cook lunch for Him. This is the street that the devotees took to go to his house. What can I say? The Lord ate Shuklambar's cooking and a wonderful pastime took place there.

(Bhakti-ratnākara 12.3467-8)

Shuklambar is also named in the Chaitanya Bhagavata as being amongst the Bengali devotees who went to Puri on the annual pilgrimage.

Shuklambar Brahmachari, whose rice had been eaten by Lord Gaurasundar, joyfully went along.

(Chaitanya Bhagavata 3.8.23)

SRI SADASHIVA PANDIT

Sadashiva Pandit is considered a Chaitanya branch of the tree of divine love. He was a resident of Nabadwip who participated in the beginnings of the sankirtan movement. When Nityananda Prabhu first arrived in Nabadwip, he stayed in his house.

Sadashiva Pandit placed all his hopes at the Lord's feet. His house was Nityananda Prabhu's first residence in Nabadwip. (Chaitanya Charitamrita 1.10.34)

Sadashiva Pandit, in whose home Nityananda had previously been domiciled, also went [with the party of devotees to Jagannath Puri].(Chaitanya Bhagavata 3.8.19)

In Vrindavan Das Thakur's Chaitanya Bhagavata, Sadashiva Pandit's name is included in the list of devotees who were present in the kirtan in the house of Srivas Pandit, along with Gopinath, Jagadish, Sriman, Sridhar, Vakresvara, Srigarbha and Shuklambar.

(Chaitanya Bhagavata 2.8.115)

He was also one of the Lord's companions when He engaged in water sports in the Ganges. He was also one of the first to witness the Lord's displays of ecstatic love after He returned from Gaya. Mahaprabhu also told him to be present in Shuklambar's house where He publicly announced the transformation that had taken place.

[The Lord said,] "You [Sriman Pandit] and Sadashiva Pandit should also come tomorrow to Shuklambar's house.

(Chaitanya Bhagavata 2.1.40)

Sadashiva, Murari, Sriman and Shuklambar, and all

the Lord's other devoted followers assembled there.
(Chaitanya Bhagavata 2.1.81)

On the same occasion, the Lord revealed to the world how dear He considered Sadashiva to be by unveiling his secret pain to him.

"I will reveal all my sadness to you [Sriman Pandit], Sadashiva and Murari Gupta."
(Chaitanya Bhagavata 2.1.70)

When Mahaprabhu decided to put on a performance of Vraja lila in the house of Chandrasekhar Acharya, He gave the responsibility for costumes and makeup to Sadashiva and Buddhimanta Khan. Sadashiva was ecstatic to receive this order from the Lord.

The Lord called Buddhimanta Khan and Sadashiva and told them to go immediately to arrange for the actors' costumes. (Chaitanya Bhagavata 2.18.7)

Overjoyed, Buddhimanta and Sadashiva immediately went home to fulfill the duties given them by the Lord.
(Chaitanya Bhagavata 2.18.14)

Here [at the house of Chandrasekhar Acharya], Buddhimanta Khan and Sadashiva Pandit made all kinds of costume arrangements to help Lord Gauranga put on a performance as Lakshmi, so that the entire universe will become intoxicated by the singing of the Holy Names.
(Bhakti-ratnākara 12.2903-4)

Sridhar Pandit

kholā-becatayā khyātaḥ paṇḍitaḥ śrīdharo dvijaḥ
āsīd vraje hāsya-karo yo nāmnā kusumāsavaḥ

One of the twelve Gopals in Krishna lila was named Kusumasava. He appeared in Gaura lila as Sridhar Pandit, who was given the nickname kholā-becā, "bark-seller."
(Gaura-gaṇoddeśa-dīpikā 133)

Sridhar Pandit was a resident of Nabadwip. Nabadwip is composed of nine islands, of which the central island is known as Antardwip. He used to live at the northern extremity of Mayapur and to the southeast of the Chand Kazi's samadhi, in the place that now goes by the name of Sridhar Angan. During his lifetime, it was a banana orchard, which nowadays is no longer the case, at least not to our mortal eyes. During this incarnation, Sridhar played the role of a poor Brahmin who made his living selling the produce of his banana garden. In order to keep the memory of Sridhar Pandit alive, the founder of the world-wide Chaitanya and Gaudiya Maths, nitya-līlā-praviṣṭa Om Vishnupada Srila Bhaktisiddhanta Saraswati Goswami Prabhupada, discovered and revealed this site of Chaitanya Mahaprabhu's pastimes. Deity worship was established there and it continued until after Srila Bhaktisiddhanta Saraswati Goswami Thakur's disappearance. Now, because of problems with the local people, the beauty of this place is once again being covered over. Even so, during the Nabadwip parikrama, devotees still pay their obeisances to the memory of Sridhar Pandit at that spot.

Srila Bhaktivinoda Thakur says in his Navadvīpa-dhāma-māhātmya that Sridhar's house was on the other side of the weaver district. Mahaprabhu often stopped the kirtan here so that the devotees could rest. Nityananda Prabhu says the following to Jiva Goswami:

"Out of His mercy, Mahaprabhu Gauranga Hari would end the kirtan here so that the devotees could rest. It is therefore known as viśrāma-sthāna, or the Lord's place of rest. So let us also repose a while here at the house of Sridhar Pandit." (Navadvīpa-dhāma-māhātmya)

According to Bhaktivinoda in the same book, there was previously a large pond near Sridhar's banana orchard, but this too is no longer visible.

SRIDHAR'S POVERTY

Material wealth and prosperity are not the truest signs of the Lord's mercy on someone. Those who worship the gods and goddesses are generally seen to prosper materially, but one who is rich in the wealth of devotion to the Lord is the one who has truly benefited from His mercy. Mahaprabhu gave this teaching to His associates through Sridhar Pandit: a devotee of Vishnu is free from attachments to material possessions and enjoyments.

One day, the Lord went to Sridhar's place and asked him why he was so poor. He was worshiping the husband of the goddess of fortune, Lakshmi, yet he never had enough money for food or clothing and his house was dilapidated. On the other hand, those who worshiped the bloodthirsty Kali always seemed to have an abundance of material wealth. Sridhar answered that a bird who made its nest in the trees and wandered from place to place to find food was passing the time of day in the same way as a king in his palace who enjoyed the best objects of gratification. There was no difference of degree or amount of pleasure experienced by the two. The Lord then said to Sridhar: "Externally, though you appear to be poor, you are actually the true rich man. I will shortly reveal to the entire foolish world that devotees are qualified to possess the greatest wealth, indeed they are the owners of all things."

Generally we call someone deprived of wealth, possessions and a home "poor" or "unfortunate." One who has these things is called rich or fortunate. People try to accumulate wealth in order to find happiness, not distress. But it is the happiness they find that is the real wealth, not the external possessions through which they hope to find it. Sri Krishna is the personification of happiness. The real difference between wealth and poverty is that one who has love for Krishna is rich; one who does not is poor. By way of example, during Krishna's lila, Vidura played the part of a poor man, but one who was rich in love for Krishna. On the other hand, Duryodhana possessed unlimited riches but had no love for Krishna, and thus was truly poor. The Supreme Lord used Khola-becha Sridhar to show the world who was truly wealthy and fortunate. The Lord is conquered by loving devotion alone, and by nothing else.

bhaktyāham ekayā grāhyaḥ
śraddayātmā priyaḥ satām
bhaktiḥ punāti man-niṣṭhā
śvapākān api sambhavāt

I, who as the supreme soul am the ultimate object of affection and love, can be attained only through exclusive devotion born of faith. Such devotion performed with single-minded attention purifies even a dog-eater and outcaste. (Srimad Bhagavatam 11.1.4.21)

patraṁ puṣpaṁ phalaṁ toyaṁ
yo me bhaktyā prayacchati
tad ahaṁ bhakty-upahṛtam
aśnāmi prayatātmanaḥ

I accept whatever anyone offers Me with devotion, whether it be a leaf, a flower, a fruit or water, because of his pure consciousness. (Bhagavad Gita 6.29)

The Lord accepts and eats whatever is given to Him with devotion, but does not accept things given Him by a non-devotee. He would not accept the invitation to eat the finest, most expensive foods with Duryodhana in order to take a humble meal prepared for him by Vidura and his wife.

THE LORD STEALS SRIDHAR'S GOODS

The Supreme Lord Chaitanya Mahaprabhu showed the charming pastime of hungrily taking Sridhar's foodstuffs without being invited to do so. While the Lord was still a student, Sridhar used to make his living by selling banana flowers (mocā) and the core of the banana plant (thoṛa). He would spend half of whatever little money he made in this way on worshiping the Ganges, the other half on his own necessities. Like Yudhisthira, he was a great devotee of the truth and would always tell the real price of the items he sold. Everyone in Nabadwip knew this and so would not haggle with him. But Mahaprabhu would come to Sridhar and give him only half the amount he was asking for his bananas, banana flowers or thoṛa and then walk off with them. Every day, the two of them would pull back and forth on a bunch of bananas or something else, arguing for an hour or more over the price that was to be paid.

Every day they would argue for an hour and a half; then finally Mahaprabhu would walk away with the goods, leaving only half the asked price. Sridhar would always tell the truth and give the real price of each item, but the Lord would still only give him half of the amount he asked for and then take it. Sridhar would jump up and grab the item, trying to take it back, even pushing and shoving the Lord. (Chaitanya Bhagavata 2.9.163-5)

Even though the Lord argued with Sridhar, He only took his wares when He saw that Sridhar was not angry. From a superficial point of view, it appears that Mahaprabhu was mistreating Sridhar by stealing from him, but the fact of the matter is that Sridhar allowed Him to get away with it. Upon seeing the Lord's beauty, he would become completely enchanted and immersed in an ocean of joy, so how could he get angry with Him? While arguing with Sridhar, Mahaprabhu would delight in calling him names and insulting him, and sometimes even hinted at His own divine identity:

"Every day you buy things to offer to the Ganges. Why don't you just give something to Me without charging anything? Don't you know that I am the father of the Ganges you worship? I assure you that this is the absolute truth!" (Chaitanya Bhagavata 2.9.178-9)

They finally came to a settlement and Sridhar agreed to daily give Mahaprabhu some bananas or other items from the banana tree for free. From then on, the Lord daily ate with great satisfaction from the little bowls made of banana bark given him by Sridhar.

The Lord said, "Very well. There is no reason for you to give me anything else." And from that day on, He ate with great contentment on the banana leaves Sridhar had given Him. The Lord thus eats anything that the devotee offers Him, but rejects even luxurious items given Him by a non-devotee. (Chaitanya Bhagavata 2.9.184-6)

SRIDHAR BLESSED AT THE MAHĀ-PRAKĀÇA

On that eventful night the Lord sat on the altar in Srivas' home and revealed His divine form to His devotees for twenty-one hours. After showing them all the different incarnations of Vishnu, one after the other, He ordered them to summon Sridhar also. Sridhar would regularly stay up the whole night chanting the Holy Names and calling out to the Lord. This was a source of happiness to the devotees, but the non-devotees would complain that he was keeping them awake with his noise and would regularly criticize and rebuke him. As the devotees were going to his house on the Lord's order, they could hear his loud chanting from a considerable distance.

When Sridhar arrived at Srivas Angan, he beheld the Lord's glorious form and fell to the ground in a faint. He was brought back to consciousness by the Lord's voice and then, with the power that was given him through the Lord's mercy, began to recite hymns of glorification. Satisfied with Sridhar's hymns of praise, Mahaprabhu offered him the eight mystic powers[5] as a benediction, but Sridhar refused, saying that he only wanted service to the Lord's lotus feet.

Lord Vishvambhar repeatedly urged Sridhar to ask for a boon. Finally Sridhar said, "Lord, if You must give me something, then I ask for this: May that Brahmin boy who used to pinch my banana leaves and bark be my Lord, lifetime after lifetime. May I ever serve the lotus feet of that Brahmin boy who always used to argue with me."

(Chaitanya Bhagavata 2.9.223-5)

Who can recognize the servants of the Lord who want nothing of wealth, followers, or scholarship? Of what use are learning, wealth, beauty, fame or high birth? All of these things simply increase one's pride and are ultimately valueless. A millionaire may try for millions of years to achieve what Sridhar did while selling bananas and banana products, and still not be able to do so.

(Chaitanya Bhagavata 2.9.233-5)

Srila Bhaktisiddhanta Saraswati Goswami Thakur comments on these verses as follows: "Through empirical knowledge or external analysis, no one can recognize the true character of a devotee. It should not be thought that the ability to collect great amounts of money is a function of devotion, nor that someone who is able to accumulate a great number of followers is a better Vaishnava than someone who cannot. Furthermore, even if someone is a great religious scholar, this does not mean that he is a devotee of the Lord. A servant of Sri Chaitanya might have very little money, may show no signs of having a great number of followers, and have no talent for argument or debate. Ordinary people are unable to understand why he is indifferent to these externals. The answer is that these devotees consider service to Sri Chaitanya something more valuable than the accumulation of wealth, followers or learning. Thus, there is no possibility of the depth of their wisdom, their glories and their superiority being perceived by the general public."

Who is capable of recognizing a devotee? He may possess all perfections, but we see only his poverty. The seller of banana products, Sridhar Pandit, is a living example of this. He disregarded the eight mystic perfections in order to accept only devotion as a benediction. However much misery you see in a devotee's life, you should know that in fact he is enjoying divine pleasure in devotional service. Those who are absorbed in sense gratification and intoxicated by learning or wealth can never recognize a Vaishnava. (Chaitanya Bhagavata 2.9.238-41)

MAHAPRABHU DRINKS FROM SRIDHAR'S WATERPOT

On the day He delivered Chand Kazi, Mahaprabhu led His sankirtan party through the conch shell merchant and weaver districts to Sridhar Pandit's house. There He took a long drink of water from Sridhar's old, beaten iron water pot. When Sridhar saw Mahaprabhu do this, he was mortified and fell unconscious.

Mahaprabhu's action was meant to teach us that we can attain devotion by drinking a devotee's water. He wanted to show that the water from a devotee's water jug, even though it is old and rusty, is still like nectar to the Supreme Lord Himself. By way of contrast, He ignores the proud non-devotee's water, even if offered in a jeweled goblet.

When the Lord saw Sridhar's tumbledown shack of a home from a distance, He laughed quietly from the inner joy He felt. He led the company of devotees along the path to Sridhar's hut, where He spotted an iron water pot full of holes. There was still a little water in it, and the Lord drank it thirstily. The Lord is bhakta-vatsala, ever affectionate toward His devotees, and this act overwhelmed Him with feelings of love. Tears poured from His eyes like the currents of the Ganges, and a wonderful kirtan began in Sridhar's courtyard in which all the devotees led by Nityananda and Advaita Prabhus were crying. Ah, my heart breaks when I think of the great joy they all experienced on that day here at Sridhar's house.

(Bhakti-ratnākara 12.3136-41)

The Lord drank water from Sridhar's iron water pot and fulfilled the desires of every single devotee.

(Chaitanya Charitamrita 1.17.70)

On the very day before He took sannyas, Mahaprabhu happily accepted a gift of a gourd from Sridhar. Sachi Mata cooked the gourd with milk, making one of the Lord's favorite preparations.

The pious Sridhar came to see the Lord carrying a gourd (lāu). When Gaurasundar saw the gift He laughed and asked, "Where did you get it?" He knew He would be leaving the next day and would not be able to eat it after He had gone. He did not want to see the gift go unused and so determined to have it prepared that very day.

(Chaitanya Bhagavata 2.28.33-6)

After taking sannyas, Mahaprabhu wandered in the land of Rarha for three days in a intoxicated state of love for Krishna until Nityananda tricked him into coming to Shantipur to Advaita Acharya's house. When the Lord met Sachi Mata and the other Nabadwip devotees, He also met with Sridhar. Sridhar came every year to Puri to meet with the Lord at the time of the Rathayatra.

[5] The eight mystic powers or siddhis are listed in the Narada-pañcarātra: aṇimā laghimā vyāptiḥ prākāmyā mahimā tathā īśitvaṁ ca vaśītvaṁ ca tathā kāmāvasāyitā. Three of these mystic powers are physical: becoming very small (aṇimā), light (laghimā) or large (mahimā); vyāpti means to possess the powers of the tutelary deities of the senses; prākāmya is the power to do anything within the scope of the material nature; īśitva is the perfection through which one can control the maya energy; vaśitā is the perfection of detachment from sense enjoyment; kāmāvasāyitā is the power to be able to enjoy anything that one can imagine through his desires.

Vakresvara Pandit

vyūhas turyo'niruddho yaḥ sa vakreśvara-paṇḍitaḥ
kṛṣṇāveśaja-nṛtyena prabhoḥ sukham ajījanat
sahasra-gāyakān mahyaṁ dehi tvaṁ karuṇā-maya
iti caitanya-pāde sa uvāca madhuraṁ vacaḥ
sva-prakāśa-vibhedena śaśirekhā tam āviśat

Vakresvara Pandit is the fourth member of the *catur-vyūha*, Aniruddha. He brought happiness to the Lord by dancing in the mood of Krishna. He would sweetly say to Mahaprabhu, "O merciful Lord, give me a thousand singers so that I can dance!" Radha's dear sakhi Sasirekha also entered into him.
(*Gaura-gaṇoddeśa-dīpikā* 71)

Sri Vakresvara Pandit revealed such great potency that he danced non-stop for three days. Krishna Das Kaviraj Goswami writes the following summary of Vakresvara:

Vakresvara Pandit is the Lord's dear servant, who danced without rest for seventy-two hours. One day Mahaprabhu was singing and dancing Himself and Vakresvara fell down at His feet and said, "O moon-faced Lord. Give me ten thousand Gandharvas! It will make me happy if I can dance as they sing." The Lord answered, "I have only one wing like you. If I had another, I could fly in the sky!" (Chaitanya Charitamrita 1.10.17-20)

Vakresvara and Devananda Pandit

Vakresvara was also present in the kirtans at the houses of Srivas and Chandrasekhar, where he would dance ecstatically. Vakresvara was so dear to Mahaprabhu that Devananda Pandit was freed of his offenses to Srivas Pandit and received Mahaprabhu's mercy through serving him. In answer to a Brahmin's question Mahaprabhu explained how to atone for offenses to the Vaishnavas:

Listen Brahmin, if you want to be cured after consuming poison, you must ingest ambrosia through the very same mouth you took the poison. That way, not only will the poison be digested, but your body will become immortal through the ambrosia's divine power. Now let me answer your question. Whatever blasphemies you have unknowingly made are exactly like a poison that you have eaten. Now you must use the same mouth to constantly glorify Krishna's name and qualities, which are like ambrosia. You have used your tongue to insult the devotees, now use it to glorify them. Glorify the devotees in songs and poetry as the best of humanity. I will destroy all the poison of blasphemy through the ambrosia of the ecstasies of Krishna's glories. Everyone has unknowingly committed offenses; this is the truth. If you should stop all kinds of offensive activity and simply engage in praising Krishna and His devotees, then you will be free from all the sins you have committed, however numerous they may be. You will not be able to achieve the same results through millions of atonements.
(Chaitanya Bhagavata 3.3.449-458)

Srila Bhaktisiddhanta Saraswati Goswami Thakur comments: "An offensive person will only attain the ultimate good by using the tongue with which he made his blasphemous comments to acknowledge his offense and then to glorify Krishna and His devotees. If you take poison it will disrupt the body's functioning, but you can remedy the situation by taking a medicine that destroys its effects. Similarly, the way to become free from the effects of Vaishnava-ninda is to first of all stop the poisonous activity; then, rather than performing thousands of other ineffective atonement rituals, one should glorify the Vaishnava.

"Through serving the devotee, Kuliya's Devananda Pandit became a believer in Mahaprabhu's lotus feet. This good fortune visited him when Vakresvara came to stay in his house. Devananda was a follower of the Smarta path, but was nevertheless a great scholar and very austere. He read no scripture other than the Bhagavatam. He was devoted to the Supreme Lord and was free from the domination of his senses. Nevertheless, he was not a believer in Sri Chaitanya Mahaprabhu. By Vakresvara's mercy, this foolish misunderstanding was dispelled and he developed faith in the Lord."
(*Gauḍīya-bhāṣya* to Chaitanya Bhagavata 3.3.453, 481)

Vakresvara Pandit was very dear to Chaitanya Mahaprabhu. Anyone who remembers him will purify the entire creation. He is the embodiment of Krishna prema and both gods and demons are enchanted by his dancing. (Chaitanya Bhagavata 3.3.469-70)

Mahaprabhu Himself described Vakresvara's glories to Devananda Pandit:

The Lord said, "You have served Vakresvara and have thus come into My presence. Vakresvara Pandit is the Lord's complete energy, so whoever pays homage to him attains Krishna. Krishna has made His home in Vakresvara's heart. Krishna dances in order to make Vakresvara dance. If any place becomes associated with Vakresvara, it immediately becomes the equivalent of Vaikuntha and equal to all the holy places.
(Chaitanya Bhagavata 3.3.493-6)

After Mahaprabhu had absolved Devananda of his offenses, He affectionately gave him many instructions. Those vain egoists who are proud of their scholarship cannot understand the meaning of the Bhagavatam; that is the prerogative of the surrendered devotee, the *śaraṇāgata*. The word *bhāgavata* can refer to either the holy scripture that describes the Supreme Lord, Bhagavan, or to the devotees of Bhagavan. The only object of the scriptural Bhagavatam is to elucidate pure devotion, so it is not different from the pure devotee. One who speaks from the Bhagavatam with this knowledge will attain the supreme auspiciousness.

One who thinks, "I understand the Bhagavatam," does not really know the Bhagavatam's central meaning. On the other hand, an ignorant person who takes shelter of the Bhagavatam will directly perceive its meaning. The Bhagavatam is pure love, it is the incarnation of Krishna Himself. It recounts Krishna's most intimate activities. After recounting the Vedas and the Puranas, Vedavyasa felt unsatisfied, but as soon as the Bhagavatam manifested on his tongue, his mind was immediately satisfied.
(Chaitanya Bhagavata 3.3.514-8)

GOPAL GURU GOSWAMI

When Vakresvara came to live at Puri, he would accompany Mahaprabhu, Advaita Acharya and other devotees to Tota Gopinath to hear Gadadhar Pandit give discourses on the Bhagavatam. One should hear the book Bhagavatam from the devotee Bhagavatam.

Gopal Guru Goswami, whose previous name was Makaradhvaja Pandit, was Vakresvara Pandit's disciple. In his childhood, Gopal Guru personally served Chaitanya Mahaprabhu. It is said that he also displayed extraordinary powers. When Abhiram Thakur came to pay him obeisances, Mahaprabhu took Gopal on his lap to protect him. Mahaprabhu gave Gopal the name Guru because he instructed people to chant Krishna's names in all circumstances, whether pure or impure.

Before leaving his body, Gopal Guru turned over the service of his Radhakanta deity to his disciple, Dhyanachandra Goswami. After his death, when Gopal Guru's body was taken to the Svarga Dwar to be cremated, some representatives of the king came and closed the Radhakanta Math. Dhyanachandra was so distressed that he began to cry aloud. Gopal Guru arose from the funeral pyre, returned to Radhakanta's temple and resolved the problem before going back to the crematorium. Even after that, however, Gopal Guru appeared in Vrindavan, where devotees were amazed to witness him engaged in his devotions. A *mūrti* of Gopal Guru is still worshiped at the Radhakanta Math. Many people in Orissa are initiated in Vakresvara Pandit's line and consider themselves to be Gaudiya Vaishnavas.

During Rathayatra at Puri, Vakresvara was the chief dancer in the fourth kirtan sampradaya, whose lead singer was Govinda Ghosh. He is sometimes described as a branch of Chaitanya, or alternatively as a branch of Gadadhar Pandit.

Vakresvara's disappearance day is the sixth day of the waxing moon (*śuklā ṣaṣṭhī*) in the month of Asharh.

Sri Devananda Pandit

purāṇānām artha-vettā śrī devānanda-paṇḍitaḥ
purāsīn nanda-pariṣat-paṇḍito bhāṇḍarir muniḥ

The scholar Devananda Pandit knew the meaning of all the Puranas. Previously, he was Bhandari Muni, the scholar in Nanda Maharaj's court.
(*Gaura-gaṇoddeśa-dīpikā* 106)

Sarvabhauma Bhattacharya's father was named Mahesvara Visharada. Mahaprabhu visited his house, which was situated on an embankment. Devananda Pandit, a peaceful Brahmin who desired liberation, made his home nearby. (Chaitanya Bhagavata 2.21.6-7)

The Lord delivered Devananda Pandit in the town of Kuliya. (Chaitanya Charitamrita 2.1.153)

According to Bhaktisiddhanta Saraswati Prabhupada, Kuliya was a suburb of Nabadwip situated on the west bank of the Ganges. In that time, the central part of the town of Nabadwip, also known as Mayapur, was situated on the eastern bank of the river. The modern city of Nabadwip stands on the site of the former Kuliya, which is also known as "the place where offenses are forgiven" (*aparādha-bhañjaner pāṭa*). Proof of this is found in the old names of many neighborhoods, such as Koler Ganj, Koler Daha, and Gadkhali Kol.
(*Gauḍīya-bhāṣya* to Chaitanya Bhagavata 2.9.98)

Each of the nine islands of Nabadwip Dham represents one of the nine types of devotional service. Koladwip is the island of service to the Lord's lotus feet (*pada-sevana*). The word *kola* has been distorted into the popular speech as *Kuliya*.

Just look—this is Visharada's embankment. Here the Lord met Devananda Pandit and chastised him for the offense he had committed to Srivas Pandit, causing him to repent. (*Bhakti-ratnākara* 12.2976-7)

From the above evidence from Chaitanya Bhagavata, Chaitanya Charitamrita and *Bhakti-ratnākara*, it is clear that Devananda Pandit's house was somewhere near to the house of Sarvabhauma Bhattacharya's father, Mahesvara Visharada. It is thus clearly indicated that his school (*ṭol*) was situated somewhere in Kuliya village.

DEVANANDA'S OFFENSE

Devananda Pandit was a scholar and an ascetic who had been indifferent to the world from an early age. Although he had won a reputation for his erudition, he nevertheless had no real feeling of devotion to Krishna and so failed to understand that bhakti was the ultimate purport of the Srimad Bhagavatam. Being a *mumukṣu,* or one who seeks impersonal liberation, *mokṣa,* Devananda

Pandit praised dry austerities and renunciation in his discourses on the Bhagavatam and did not glorify devotional service.

One day, Srivas Pandit came to hear a Bhagavatam recital at Devananda's house. As he listened to the text of the Bhagavatam, Srivas Pandit became absorbed in a mood of loving devotion and started to cry. Devananda Pandit's faithless disciples threw him out of the assembly for causing a disturbance. Since Devananda did not object to the action of his students, he was responsible for their offense to a devotee. Mahaprabhu was thus angry with him.

The Lord said: "Whoever recites the Bhagavatam without glorifying devotional service is an ignorant fool who knows nothing. This rascal recites the Bhagavatam and never mentions bhakti. I will go and tear up his manuscript, just watch Me. (Chaitanya Bhagavata 2.21.20-21)

Srila Bhaktisiddhanta Saraswati Goswami Thakur comments on this verse as follows: "When those bereft of devotion forget their actual identity, they become completely indifferent to the service of the Lord. When they identify this indifference as the ultimate goal of life, they become a source of profound irritation to the Lord, even though He is by nature supremely merciful. Here Lord Gaurasundara shows His irritation and informs us that this attitude of the non-devotee is not only unnecessary, but reprehensible. He also indicates that both the acts of enjoying and renouncing the fruits of material actions are improper. The devotees find great satisfaction in seeing the Lord become angry in this way."

DEVANANDA GAINS FAITH IN THE LORD

Some time after Devananda Pandit committed this offense to Srivas Pandit, Mahaprabhu passed nearby his house and saw that he was engaged in giving a discourse on the Bhagavatam. He became angry and rebuked him severely for his lack of faith in the Vaishnavas. Just as blasphemy of the devotees is the best way to be deprived of the Lord's mercy and destined for downfall, glorifying them and engaging in their service is the best way to find the mercy of the Lord and become freed from all sinful activity.

"Listen, Brahmin, if you want to be cured after consuming poison, you must ingest ambrosia through the very same mouth you took the poison. In this way, not only will the poison be digested, but your body will become immortal through the ambrosia's divine power."

(Chaitanya Bhagavata 3.3.449-50)

Through great good fortune, Mahaprabhu's dear associate Vakresvara Pandit came to stay at Devananda Pandit's house. Because Devananda took excellent care of Vakresvara, Mahaprabhu softened towards him. Previously, Devananda had been completely without any faith in the Lord, but when he heard of Mahaprabhu's glories from Vakresvara, his attitude changed. Through the association of the Lord's devotee, he began to develop a taste for pure devotional service.

Srila Bhaktisiddhanta Saraswati Goswami Thakur writes in this regard, "For Devananda Pandit of Kuliya, the fruit of service to the Vaishnava was faith in Mahaprabhu's lotus feet. Vakresvara Pandit's visit to his house was the source of this auspiciousness. Although Devananda was a Smarta, he was a great scholar and self-controlled. He studied nothing but the Srimad Bhagavatam. He believed in God and had control of his senses. All he lacked was faith in Mahaprabhu. By the grace of Vakresvara Pandit, this faulty intelligence was wiped away and he became a believer in Lord Gaurasundara."

Devananda was a scholar of the Bhagavatam, but it was through Vakresvara's mercy that he was able to understand its meaning from Mahaprabhu.

(Chaitanya Charitamrita 1.10.77)

Mahaprabhu told Devananda to explain the Bhagavatam in terms of devotional service. It was Devananda Pandit's great fortune that he was able to receive the mercy of the Lord in the form of a chastisement.

Devananda Pandit was a great pious soul, for Mahaprabhu verbally punished him. The chastisement of Chaitanya Mahaprabhu is the greatest pious act. Even if one should die as a result of the Lord's punishment, he still goes to Vaikuntha. (Chaitanya Bhagavata 2.21.77-8)

Devananda received this mercy due to living in Kuliya or Koladwip, the place where offenses are forgiven. Gopal Chapal was also forgiven his offenses in Kuliya.

Devananda Pandit's disappearance day is celebrated on the *kṛṣṇā ekādaśī* of the month of Paush.

THE GHOSH BROTHERS

kalāvatī rasollāsā guṇatuṅgā vraje sthitāḥ
śrī-viśākhā-kṛtaṁ gītaṁ gāyanti smādya tā matāḥ
govinda-mādhavānanda-vāsudevā yathā-kramam

Govinda, Madhava and Vasudeva were gopis in Vraja, namely Kalavati, Rasollasa and Gunatunga, who used to sing the songs composed by Vishakha.

(*Gaura-gaṇoddeśa-dīpikā* 188)

The three Ghosh brothers were born in an upper class kayastha family from northern Rarha. All three were singers famed for the sweetness of their voices.

The meritorious Madhava Ghosh devoted himself to kirtan. There was no singer on earth who was his equal. It was said of him that he was a singer from Vrindavan. He was most dear to Nityananda Prabhu. The three brothers, Govinda, Madhava and Vasudeva sang while Lord Nityananda danced. (Chaitanya Bhagavata 3.5.257-9)

Chaitanya Mahaprabhu and Nityananda Prabhu danced to the kirtan of the three brothers, Govinda, Madhava and Vasudeva.

(Chaitanya Charitamrita 1.15.115)

When Nityananda returned from Puri to preach in Bengal, he was accompanied by Vasudeva and Madhava Ghosh, while Govinda remained with Mahaprabhu.

GOVINDA GHOSH

Govinda is counted amongst Chaitanya Mahaprabhu personal branches (Chaitanya Charitamrita 1.10.118). Eventually, he made his home in Agradwip, Vasudeva in Tamluk, and Madhava Ghosh in Dain Hat.[6] Govinda Ghosh Thakur's house is not far from Agradwip in Kashipur Vishnutala. Some are of the opinion that Vishnutala was his birthplace. Govinda Ghosh participated in Mahaprabhu's lilas in Srivas Angan, in the nagara-sankirtan to the Kazi's house, and in the house of Raghava Pandit. During the Rathayatra festival, he was the lead singer in the fourth kirtan group, accompanied by his two brothers, Chota Hari Das, Vishnu Das and Raghava Pandit. Vakresvara Pandit joined this group as the principal dancer.

On Mahaprabhu's direction, Govinda revealed the Gopinath deity from a black stone in Agradwip. Mahaprabhu also instructed him to get married. There is a legend that Govinda Ghosh's wife and son both died untimely. As he grew older, Govinda began to wonder who would perform his last rites, as it is considered important to have a son who can do the *śrāddha* ceremony on his behalf. Govinda had a dream in which Gopinath appeared to him and said, "Don't worry about this. I am your son, and I will perform the *śrāddha* ceremony for you Myself." When Govinda Ghosh finally left this world, Gopinath was true to His word and offered the *piṇḍa* on his behalf. Gopinath continues to perform this ceremony every year on the anniversary of Govinda Ghosh's departure from the world. This takes place on the *kṛṣṇā trayodaśī* of the month of Chaitra. Vasudeva Ghosh's disappearance day is on the second day of the waxing moon (*śuklā dvitīyā*) in the month of Karttik.

Two songs written by Govinda Ghosh

prāṇera mukunda he!
ki āji śunilu ācambite?
kahite parāṇa jāya mukhe nāhi bāhirāya
śrī gaurāṅga chāṛibe navadvīp

ihāto nā jāni mo rāsakāle milinuṅ gorā
avanata māthe āche basi
nijhare nayana jhare buka bahi dhārā paṛe
malina haiyāche mukha śaśi

dekhite takhana prāṇa sadā kare āna cāna
sudhāite nāhi avasara
kṣaṇeka sambita haila tabe mui nivedila
śuniyā dilena e uttara

āmi ta vivaśa haiyā tāre kichu nā kahiyā
dhāiyā āiluṅ tuwā pāśa
ei ta kahiluṅ āmije karite pāra tumi
mora nāhi jivanera āśa

śuniyā mukunda kānde hiyā thira nāhi bāndhe
gadādharer vadana heriyā
e govinda ghoṣa kaya ihā jena nāhi haya
tabe muñi jāinu mariyā

(Gadadhar says,) "O Mukunda! My life! Did I really hear what I think I heard today? If I say it I will surely die... the words do not want to come out of my mouth. Gauranga is really going to leave Nabadwip."

"We had no idea, but when we saw Gaura this morning, He was sitting with His head bowed in thought. Streams of tears flowed from His eyes and washed over His chest; His moon-like face had lost its luster."

"When we saw Him like that, our own hearts fluttered and we could not ask Him anything. For a moment, I regained consciousness and humbly asked Him the question and that is what He told me."

"I was so disturbed that I ran here to you right away without saying anything further to Him. I have told you this and now do what you can. As far as we are concerned, I don't think that we have any hope of continuing to live."

When he heard this news, Mukunda started to cry. He could no longer keep his composure when he looked at Gadadhar. Govinda Ghosh says, "Let it not be, for if He leaves, I will die."

hede re nadīyā vāsī kāra mukha cāo
bāhu pasāriyā gorācāṅde phirāo
to sabāre ke āra karibe nija kore
ke jāciyā dibe prema dekhiyā kātare
ki śela hiyāya hāya ki śel hiyāya
parāṇa putalī nabadwip chāṛi jāya
āra nā jāiba morā gaurāṅgera pāśa
āra nā kariba morā kīrtana vilāsa
kāṅdaye bhakata-gaṇa buka vidāriyā
pāṣāṇa govinda ghoṣa nā jāya miliyā

O people of Nabadwip, who are you staring at? Spread your arms to stop Gaurachandra; make Him come back! Who is there now who will clasp you to his chest? Who will come and beg you to take love of Krishna? I have been stabbed in the heart! I have been stabbed in the heart! The beloved of my life has abandoned Nabadwip and gone. No longer will we be able to go and sit with Gauranga; no longer will we be able to enjoy kirtan the way we did. All the devotees are crying, their hearts are bursting and, like a stone, Govinda Ghosh does not go to join them.

[6] Agradwip and Dain Hat are villages lying between Nabadwip and Katwa, while Tamluk is in Midnapur.

Sri Vishnupriya Devi

śrī-sanātana-miśro'yaṁ purā satrājito nṛpaḥ
viṣṇupriyā jagan-mātā yat-kanyā bhū-svarūpiṇī

King Satrajit in Krishna lila became Sanatan Mishra in Chaitanya lila. The mother of the universe, the incarnation of the Lord's *bhū-śakti*, is his daughter Vishnupriya.
(*Gaura-gaṇoddeśa-dīpikā* 47)

Krishna married Satyabhama, the daughter of King Satrajit and a Yadu princess. In Gaura lila, this same Satrajit became Sanatan Mishra and she became Vishnupriya Devi. All manifestations of Vishnu tattva have three energies, known as Sri, Bhu and Nila (or Lila). Lakshmipriya Devi is the *śrī-śakti* of Mahaprabhu in his majestic Gaura-Narayan attitude; Vishnupriya is his *bhū-śakti* and Nabadwip Dham is his *līlā-śakti*. Srila Gadadhar Pandit Goswami is the *śakti* of Gaura-Krishna, or Mahaprabhu in the mood of Krishna.

Knowledge is of two kinds, *aparā vidyā* or material knowledge and *parā vidyā* or transcendental knowledge. Vishnupriya Devi is the personification of transcendental knowledge. Devotees worship her on her appearance day on the *śuklā pañcamī* of the month of Magh. On the same day, materialistic persons seeking the perfection of worldly knowledge worship the goddess of learning, Saraswati. Vishnupriya Devi's grandfather was Durga Das Mishra. Some people believe that Durga Das was Vishnupriya's father. In the *Prema-vilāsa*, the family of Durga Das Mishra's descendants through Yadavacharya is known as Vishnupriya's *parivāra*.

Mahaprabhu's Marriage to Vishnupriya Devi

Vrindavan Das Thakur describes the birth of Gaura-Narayan's *śakti*, Vishnupriya Devi, in his Chaitanya Bhagavata. Krishna Das Kaviraj Goswami has also mentioned the event in his Chaitanya Charitamrita.

In the *Ādi-khaṇḍa*, the disappearence of Mahaprabhu's first wife is described, and then his second marriage to the daughter of the court pandit.
(Chaitanya Bhagavata 1.1.110)

Then the Lord was married to Vishnupriya Thakurani, after which He defeated the Digvijayi Pandit.
(Chaitanya Charitamrita 1.16.25)

For the materialistic person, the marriage of a man and woman is the source of bondage. When the Lord marries in imitation of ordinary mortals, it becomes something quite different: it is a transcendental affair. By chanting and hearing about the union of the Supreme Lord with His divine potency, one is liberated from the material energy.

Whoever hears about the holy pastime of the Lord's marriage will be liberated from his bondage to this world. Lakshmi sat beside the Lord and the house of Sachi was filled with light. (Chaitanya Bhagavata 1.10.110-1)

All who saw the Lord's effulgent form on that day were freed from their sins and went to Vaikuntha. This is why the Lord is known as the merciful Lord of the fallen.
(Chaitanya Bhagavata 1.15.216-7)

Mahaprabhu's first wife, Lakshmipriya, left the world prematurely. In order to support her and His mother, Mahaprabhu made a trip to eastern Bengal to teach some students. However, He was away longer than planned and Lakshmipriya Devi found it impossible to tolerate His absence. So, meditating on His lotus feet, she departed from this world. When Mahaprabhu finally arrived back in Nabadwip, He found His mother grieving for her daughter-in-law.

Though Mahaprabhu consoled her with spiritual instructions, soon afterwards, Sachi Mata started looking for another wife for her son. For that purpose, she consulted Kashinatha Pandit, a well-known matchmaker described in *Gaura-gaṇoddeśa-dīpikā* (50) as having been Kulaka in Krishna lila. Kulaka was the Brahmin who was sent by Satrajit to arrange the marriage between his daughter Satyabhama and Krishna. Kashinath went to the court pandit Sanatan Mishra to arrange for a marriage between Mahaprabhu and his daughter, the devotionally minded Vishnupriya. Kashinath persuaded Sanatan Mishra with the following words:

"Give your daughter to Vishvambhar Pandit; it is a perfect combination. She alone is worthy of such a divine husband, while He deserves just such a pious and chaste wife. Vishnupriya and Nimai Pandit are worthy of each

other, just as Rukmini and Krishna were."
(Chaitanya Bhagavata 1.15.57-59)

From her very early childhood, Vishnupriya Devi had been deeply devoted to her parents and to Vishnu. She would take bath in the Ganges three times daily. Sachi Mata would see her there and bless her when she saw her paying obeisances. Sachi thus already knew Vishnupriya's good qualities and happily agreed to accept her as a wife for her son.

Buddhimanta Khan was a rich and wise friend of Nimai's family who volunteered to bear the entire expense of His marriage. Once it had been decided that Vishnupriya and Vishvambhar would be married, an auspicious day and moment were fixed for the ceremony. With great pomp, the *adhivāsa* rituals were carried out on the eve of the marriage. The Lord arrived at Sanatan Mishra's house in a palanquin at dusk and Gaura and Vishnupriya's wedding ceremony was performed according to both scriptural and popular traditions.

On the following day, Vishnupriya joined her new husband on the palanquin and returned with Him to His house. Those who hear the eternal pastime of the wedding of Lakshmi and Narayan lose their desire for a material relationship of enjoyer and enjoyed, for they come to understand that Narayan alone is the supreme enjoyer of the entire universe. For his service, Buddhimanta Khan received Mahaprabhu's embrace and mercy.

Vrindavan Das describes how the pious women who saw the newly-weds compared them to various heavenly couples:

Some said, "They remind me of Gauri and Shiva." Others said, "It seems that they are Lakshmi and Narayan." Yet others said, "No, they rather resemble Rati and Kamadeva." Some compared them to Indra and Sachi, and others to Rama and Sita. (Chaitanya Bhagavata 1.15.205-8)

VISHNUPRIYA DEVI AFTER NIMAI'S SANNYAS

When Mahaprabhu left home to go to Katwa and take sannyas, He was only 24 years old. Lochan Das Thakur has described Vishnupriya's terrible feelings of separation in the days that followed His departure in the *Chaitanya-maṅgala*:

The earth split from the sound of Vishnupriya's crying: the birds and beasts, even the trees and stones shed tears when they heard it. Falling to the ground she would lament, crying out "Why does my sinful life not end?" In separation, her breath was like fire drying her lips and her body trembled constantly. (2.14.15-6)

The *Advaita-prakāśa* also describes how Vishnupriya lived her life in terrible separation from the Lord after His departure. Every morning, she would go for her bath in the Ganges with mother Sachi, after which she spent the entire day inside the house, never allowing the moon or sun to see her. Not even the devotees were allowed to see anything more than her feet, nor hear her voice. Constantly shedding tears and eating only Mother Sachi's remnants, she became pale and thin. She took intense delight in the Holy Name, chanting all day long in solitude before a portrait of Gauranga, serving it as though He were present in it and surrendering herself to His lotus feet. In this way, she demonstrated the ideal character of a devoted wife as well as the forbearance spoken of by the Lord in His verse, *tṛṇād api sunīcena taror iva sahiṣṇunā*.

Srinivas Acharya received Vishnupriya Devi's blessing. He personally witnessed her devotion to Mahaprabhu in separation. Narahari Chakravarti has described this in his *Bhakti-ratnākara*:

Every day Srinivas would come to see her. He observed her daily activities, which are beyond description. She had completely renounced sleep, and if ever she closed her eyes, it would be while lying on the bare ground. Her bodily luster, which had formerly glowed more brilliantly than gold, had become dull and she was as thin as the waning moon on its fourteenth day. She set aside grains of rice to count the Holy Names she chanted, and would cook only this rice and offer it to her Lord. Of this amount, she would only eat a small portion. No one understood how she managed to stay alive.
(*Bhakti-ratnākara* 4.47-51)

Jahnava Devi's disciple Nityananda Das has also described the standard Vishnupriya Devi set for bhajan in his *Prema-vilāsa*.

Listen, brothers, to the way which Isvari Vishnupriya would take the names of the Lord. By listening to this, you will get a feeling for the lila. Every day she would place two clay pots on either side of her, one filled with uncooked rice, the other empty. Each time she completed one mantra of sixteen names and thirty-two syllables, she would joyfully place a grain of rice into the empty container. She would chant in this way until three o'clock in the afternoon, and then would take whatever rice had accumulated and cook it. This is the only food that she prepared, drenching it with her tears before she offered it to the Lord. It is not possible to estimate how many names Mahaprabhu Himself chanted, for He chanted all day and night. Similarly, His beloved wife Vishnupriya chanted incessantly through the day and the night. Such dedication to the Holy Name was not impossible for her, for the Lord had planted the seed of His power in her.

It is said that Vishnupriya Devi was the first to establish worship of a *mūrti* of Gauranga. This has been stated in Murari Gupta's diary, *kaṛacā*:

prakāśa-rūpeṇa nija-priyāyāḥ
samīpam āsādya nijāṁ hi mūrtim
vidhāya tasyāṁ sthita eṣa kṛṣṇaḥ
sā lakṣmī-rūpā ca niṣevate prabhum

Krishna came to His beloved wife in this expansion form to remain by her side as the Mahaprabhu deity. Thus she, the incarnation of the goddess of fortune, was able to serve Him constantly.

The devotees of Mahaprabhu sometimes say that just as Ramachandra, who had taken the vow of monogamy, performed a sacrifice to a golden Sita made during His exile in the forest rather than marry a second time, so Vishnupriya repaid her debt to her Lord in the pastimes of Gaura-Narayan by having an image of Mahaprabhu created so she could perform the sacrifice of the Holy Name to Him. This deity is still present and worshiped in Nabadwip.

Sri Vamsivadana Thakur and Ishan Thakur were blessed by the service of caring for Vishnupriya Devi and Sachi Devi after Mahaprabhu took sannyas.

Sri Ishan Thakur

Ishan Thakur is counted as one of Chaitanya Mahaprabhu's branches:

Srinath Mishra, Subhananda, Sri Rama, Ishan, Srinidhi, Sri Gopikanta, Bhagavan Mishra [were branches of Chaitanya's tree]. (Chaitanya Charitamrita 1.10.110)

Ishan Thakur[7] was Jagannath Mishra's household servant. Only an eternal associate of the Supreme Lord could have the good fortune to render Him personal service in His own home. The Lord accepts the service of His own confidential associates. When Mahaprabhu was born, Ishan had the chance to take the Lord on his lap and to hold Him affectionately. He tolerated all of little Nimai's childhood pranks and answered His every whim. Nimai was unable to go without Ishan for even a moment.

How can I understand the activities of Ishan Thakur, whom Nimai used to lovingly call "father"? The son of Sachi, Nimai Chand, was his very life and Nimai would not go anywhere without him. In His childhood, Nimai was very naughty and would make all kinds of capricious demands that Ishan would do his best to fulfill.
(*Bhakti-ratnākara* 12.95-7)

Ishan Thakur also had the chance to serve Nityananda Prabhu, Sri Chaitanya Mahaprabhu's other self. The Lord would plead with His mother to be able to invite Nitai and when she finally agreed, would go Himself to invite Him. Before the two sat down to eat in Sachi's house, Ishan Thakur would bring water to wash their feet.

As one of the Lord's eternal associates, Ishan Thakur was fully aware of His divine nature. He knew that the worship of the devotee is more important than even the worship of the Lord Himself. Thus he performed all kinds of service to Sachi Devi, who is none other than Yashoda Devi, and was blessed by her affection. The Lord, too, blesses His devotees through His devotee's merciful attitude. The Lord's mercy follows upon the mercy of the devotee.

Ishan Thakur glories are described in the work known as the *Vaiṣṇava-vandanā*:

vandiba īśāna-dāsa kara-joṛa kari
śacī-ṭhākurāṇī jāre sneha kaila baṛi

I pay obeisances to Ishan Das with folded hands, for Sachi Thakurani was very affectionate towards him.
(quoted in *Bhakti-ratnākara* 12.94)

The Brahmin said, "Look, here comes Ishan. What can I say? No one really understands his great qualifications. He has the reputation of knowing all the truths about the Lord, and he served Sachi by doing whatever she needed. Because he rendered such service to the Lord's mother, Ishan is uniquely fortunate in the fourteen worlds. Even though I saw with my own eyes the affection she had for him, I am unable to find words to describe it.
(*Bhakti-ratnākara* 12.90-3)"

Ishan, who was most fortunate in the fourteen worlds, served the Lord's mother constantly.
(Chaitanya Bhagavata 2.8.74)

When Mahaprabhu took sannyas and left for Puri, Ishan was left with the responsibility of taking care of His mother Sachi and wife Vishnupriya Devi and supervising their household. In his commentary to the Chaitanya Bhagavata (2.8.73), where it is said that Ishan Thakur did all the cleaning of the house as well as other services, Srila Bhaktisiddhanta Saraswati Goswami Thakur writes: "Ishan was the servant in Mahaprabhu's house. He gathered up the rice that had been thrown all over [by Nityananda] and made the house proper. There was no limit to Ishan's good fortune. He was able to render service to the Lord's mother throughout his entire life. Even after the Lord took sannyas, he was engaged in the service of the Lord's mother and wife, showing the extent of the blessings he had received. He is therefore described as 'most blessed' or 'most fortunate among the blessed.'"

Ishan Thakur lived a very long life. He was still living even after the disappearance of Vishnupriya Devi and all the other devotees of Mahaprabhu in Nabadwip. Thus when Srinivas Acharya, Narottam Thakur and Ramachandra Kaviraj came to Nabadwip on pilgrimage, only Ishan was able to show them where all the places of the Lord's pastimes were. In the *Bhakti-ratnākara*, it is said that when Ishan showed these devotees the holy places, they were already old and in a state of disrepair. This gives some idea of how old he must have been.

Nearly everyone has disappeared from Nabadwip. No one but the Lord's servant Ishan remains here.
(*Bhakti-ratnākara* 11.721)

Srinivas Acharya, Narottam Thakur and Ramachandra Kaviraj received Ishan Thakur's blessings in Nabadwip Dham and were embraced by him before leaving to visit Srikhanda where they met with Raghunandan Thakur. When they arrived there, they received the news that Ishan had left the world.

I heard from some people while on my way here that Ishan has disappeared. (*Bhakti-ratnākara* 13.21)

After Mahaprabhu and Sachi Mata had disappeared, Vamsivadanananda Thakur served Vishnupriya Devi and Ishan Thakur.

---

[7] Other than this Ishan, there were several other associates of the Lord who had the same name. (1) Sanatan Goswami's servant was named Ishan. (2) There was a devotee in Vrindavan of that name. He is mentioned in the *Bhakti-ratnākara* as a member of the party of devotees who accompanied Rupa Goswami to the house of Vitthalesvara to have darshan of Govardhandhari Gopal. He also is said to have blessed Srinivas Acharya, Narottam Das Thakur and Shyamananda Prabhu when they started their voyage to Bengal with the Goswamis' books. (3) In the *Gauḍiya Vaiṣṇava Abhidhāna*, there is mention of a certain Ishan Acharya who is identified as Vraja's Yauna Manjari. (4) The author of the *Advaita-Prakāśa* was named Ishan Nagara.

SRI VAMSIVADANANANDA THAKUR

vaṁśī kṛṣṇa-priyā yāsīt sā vaṁśī-dāsa-ṭhakkuraḥ

Vamsivadanananda Thakur was Krishna's flute in Vraja. (*Gaura-gaṇoddeśa-dīpikā* 179)

The gopis praised the good fortune of Krishna's flute, for He was able to constantly drink the nectar of Krishna's lips. Everything in Vraja is spiritual, i.e., conscious, and so the flute could take human form as Sri Vamsivadanananda Thakur. His life story has been recounted by his grandson, Sri Ballabha Das, in the book *Vaṁśī-vilāsa*. Other books which contain details of his life are *Sripat-paryaṭana* and *Bhakti-ratnākara*, and the *Gauḍīya Vaiṣṇava Abhidhāna* also gives a brief biography.

VamsivadananandaThakur was known by five names in Gaudiya Vaishnava society: Vamsivadana, Vamsi Das, Vamsi, Vadana, and Vadanananda. He was a well-known writer of devotional songs. His appearance took place on the day of the spring full moon (in the month of Chaitra) in either 1416 (according to *Vamshi-śikṣā*) or 1427 of the Shaka era (1495 or 1506 AD).

VAMSIVADANANANDA'S HOME IN NABADWIP

In the *Śrīpāṭa-paryaṭana*, the following information is given:

The two villages known as Kuliya and Paharpur were side by side. Vamsivadana, Kavidatta and Saranga Thakur lived there. As the town grew, it was known as Kuliya Paharpur.

VamsivadananandaThakur's home was in Koladwip, the present-day town of Nabadwip formerly known as Kuliya Paharpur. Kuliya had four neighborhoods known as Teghari, Benchiara, Bedra Para and Chine Danga. Srikara Chattopadhyaya came from Bilvagrāma to live in Benchiara. Amongst the descendants of Srikara Chattopadhyaya was Yudhisthira Cattopadhyaya who had three sons: Madhava Das (nicknamed Chakori), Hari Das (Tinkori) and Krishna Sampatti (Dukori) Chattopadhyaya. Chakari Chattopadhyaya was Vamshivadana's father. His mother's name was Candrakalā Devi. When Mahaprabhu passed through Kuliya on His trip through Bengal that ultimately ended at Kanair Natshala, he stayed at Chakari Chattopadhyaya's house for seven days. During this time He gave His blessings to all the residents of Nabadwip and in particular to Devananda Pandit. This information comes from Kavi Karnapur's *Caitanya-candrodaya Nāṭaka*.

It is said that both Mahaprabhu and Advaita Acharya were present when Vamsivadanananda was born. After Mahaprabhu took sannyas, he was engaged as Sachi Mata and Vishnupriya's servant and protector. When Srinivas Acharya came to Nabadwip to see the Lord's family, Vamsi embraced him emotionally. This is described in the *Bhakti-ratnākara*:

Though he had not been introduced, Vamsivadanananda guessed that this must be Srinivas. He approached him and asked who he was. Srinivas told him everything about himself. Vamsi embraced him and washed his body with his tears. Srinivas wanted to fall to the ground and pay obeisances to Vamsi Thakur, but Vamsi would not let him. He then went and told Vishnupriya and Sachi Mata that Srinivas had come.

(*Bhakti-ratnākara* 4.20-24)

Vamsivadanananda Thakur lived as a householder. He had two sons, Chaitanya Das and Nityananda Das. His deity's name was Pranavallabha. Later, at Vishnupriya Devi's request, he established the worship of the Mahaprabhu deity. He also worshiped his forefathers' Gopinath deity. He spent the last part of life in his ancestral village of Bilva Gram. The Bhattacharyas of that village are said to be his descendants.

RAMAI THAKUR

Vamsivadanananda Thakur's grandson, the son of Chaitanya Das, was named Sri Ramachandra or Ramai Thakur. He found Rama and Krishna deities at Praskandan Tirtha[8] in Vrindavan and then brought them to Baghna Para in Burdwan district. They are known ar Sri Rama-Kanai.

Vamsivadanananda Thakur's family received the mercy of Jahnava Thakurani. The following comment is found in the *Gauḍīya* magazine (22.30-37): "Jahnava Mata asked for Ramachandra to be given to her. She gave him initation and then took him to Khardaha where she taught him Vaishnava philosophy."

A SONG BY VAMSHIVADANANANDA

The following is a song written by Vamsivadanananda Thakur:

āra nā heriba prasara kapāle alakā tilaka kāca
āra nā heriba sonāra kamale nayana khañjana nāca
āra nā nācibe śrīvāsa mandire bhakata cātaka laiyā
āra nā nācibe āpanāra ghare āmarā dekhiba cāiyā
āra ki du' bhāi nimāi nitāi nācibe ek ṭhāñi
nimāi kariyā phukari sadāi nimāi kothāo nāi
nidaya keśava bhāratī āsiyā māthāya paṛila bāja
gaurāṅga sundara nā dekhi kemane rahiba nadīyā māja
kebā hena jana ānibe ekhana āmāra gaurāṅga rāya
śāśuṛī vadhūra rodana śuniyā vaṁśī gaṛāgaṛi jāya

No more will I see his broad forehead, decorated with tilaka and sandalwood dots; no more will I see His eyes dance like hummingbirds in the golden lotus of his face. No longer will He dance in Srivas' house with His sparrow-like devotees; no more will He dance in His own home, while looking upon me. Will Nimai and Nitai, those two divine brothers ever dance together again? I call out Nimai's name, but Nimai is nowhere to be seen. The heartless Keshava Bharati came and threw a thunderbolt on all of our heads. How can we stay in Nabadwip any longer, now that we cannot see Gauranga here? Who here can now bring my Gauranga back? When Vamsi hears His young wife and her mother-in-law crying, he rolls on the ground in pain.

[8] Praskandan Tirtha is the Yamuna ghāṭa which is not far from Dvādaśāditya Ṭilā. It is said that when Krishna fought with Kāliya in the middle of the Yamuna, he became cold in the water. When he came out, all the twelve Ādityas appeared simultaneously and warmed him up. Krishna became so hot that he started to sweat. His sweat, and his sweat flowed down and merged with the water of the Yamuna. The place where this happened is known as Praskandana Tirtha.

Srila Narahari Sarkar Thakur

purā madhumatī prāṇa-sakhī vṛndāvane sthitā
adhunā narahary-ākhyaḥ sarakāraḥ prabhoḥ priyaḥ

Narahari Sarkar, The Lord's dear associate, was previously Radha's intimate girlfriend named Madhumati is today Narahari Sarkar. (*Gaura-gaṇoddeśa-dīpikā* 117)

Srila Narahari Sarkar Thakur is counted as one of Chaitanya's branches on the desire tree of pure devotional service. By Mahaprabhu's desire, he took birth in a physician (*vaidya*) family, blessing his family when he did so. He was foremost among the residents of the village of Srikhanda, all of who were the Lord's associates. On the Katwa-Burdwan rail line, the first station west of Katwa is Sripat Srikhanda, and the second Srikhanda. Narahari's home is about one mile from the station. Some of the other prominent residents of Srikhanda who were devotees of Lord Chaitanya were Sri Mukunda, Sri Raghunandan, Sri Chiranjiva, Sri Sulocana, Sri Damodar Kaviraj, Sri Ramachandra Kaviraj, Sri Govinda Kaviraj, Sri Balaram Das, Sri Ratikanta, Sri Ramagopala Das, Sri Pītambara Das, Sri Sachinandana, and Sri Jagadananda. Krishna Das Kaviraj Goswami mentions many of these names as Chaitanya's branches that generously distributed the fruits of love of God. (Chaitanya Charitamrita 1.10.78-9)

The scholar Bharat Mallik has written the following Sanskrit verses about Narahari's appearance in a *vaidya* family in his book *Candra-prabhā*:

śrīkhaṇḍa-nāma-nagarī rāḍhe baṅgeṣu viśrutā
sarveṣām eva vaidyānām āśrayo yatra vidyate
yatra goṣṭhī-bhūtā vaidyā yaḥ khaṇḍo'bhūd bhiṣak-priyaḥ
viśeṣataḥ kulīnānāṁ sarveṣām eva vāsa-bhūḥ

In Bengal, in the area known as Rarha (Burdwan, Birbhum), there is a famous town known as Srikhanda that gave shelter to all the physician clans. Since *vaidyas* gathered there, it became a favored residence for them, especially those who were of the noblest birth.

In the *Gauḍīya Vaiṣṇava Abhidhāna*, it is stated that Narahari Sarkar Thakur appeared in either the Shaka year 1401 or 1402 (1479-80 AD). His father's name was Sri Narayan Das, his mother Sri Goyi. Goyi was the daughter of Murari Sen. Narayan Das had three sons, Mukunda, Madhava and Narahari. Raghunandan Thakur was Mukunda's son. (*Bhakti-ratnākara* 11.730-1) Mukunda is said to have sometimes worked as the Shah of Bengal's family physician.

The author of *Caitanya-maṅgala*, Locana Das, who came from the village of Kogram, near Jhamatpur, was Narahari's disciple. For this reason, Locana Das writes that Srila Gadadhar Pandit Goswami and Narahari Sarkar Thakur were Mahaprabhu's dearest associates. On the other hand, in Chaitanya Bhagavata, Vrindavan Das Thakur has not spoken at any length about the devotees of Srikhanda.

Srila Locana Das Thakur has written the following about his guru in *Caitanya-maṅgala*:

Narahari Das Thakur is my worshipable master. He was the descendent of a pure line of physicians; his body was permeated by love for Krishna and he taught his disciples nothing other than Krishna prema. He was previously known as Madhumati, one of Radha's dearest sakhis in Vrindavan, a storehouse of sweetness. Now in the Age of Kali, with the appearance of Gauranga, he has become the keeper of the storehouse of love for Radha and Krishna.

After the death of his father Narayan, Narahari's older brother Mukunda arranged for him to study in Nabadwip. Narahari quickly became very learned as well as a connoisseur of the flavors of devotional sentiment. Even before becoming Mahaprabhu's associate, he composed songs glorifying Radha and Govinda's pastimes. When Srila Gadadhar Pandit Goswami was constantly by the Lord's side, engaged in his service, Narahari had the good fortune to enter into his association. Narahari Sarkar Thakur's personal service was to fan the Lord with the yak-tail whisk. Srila Bhaktivinoda Thakur, Mahaprabhu's personal representative, confirmed this in his *Gaura-ārati*:

narahari ādi kare cāmara ḍhulāy
sañjaya, mukunda, vāsu ghoṣa ādi gāy

Narahari and the other residents of Srikhanda fanned with the *cāmara*, while Sanjaya, Mukunda and Vasu Ghosh sang.

Narahari wrote several books, including *Bhakti-candrikā-paṭala, Śrī-Kṛṣṇa-bhajanāmṛta, Śrī-caitanya-sahasranāma, Śrī-Śacīnandanāṣṭaka, Śrī-Rādhāṣṭaka*, etc. All of these are well known and thought of highly by the devotees.

The following story is told about Narahari: Once when Mahaprabhu and Nityananda Prabhu came to his house in Srikhanda, they suddenly expressed a desire for honey. Narahari demonstrated his miraculous powers by transforming the water in a pond near his house into honey. Ever since he quenched the Lords' desire for honey with water from this pond, it has been known as *Madhu-puṣkariṇī*. The Lord gave Narahari the order in a dream to install the three deities of Himself that are currently worshiped in Srikhanda, Katwa and Ganganagar.

Narahari Sarkar Thakur also participated in the Lord's activities in Puri. He and the other residents of Srikhanda were amongst those who went every year with Shivananda Sen (Chaitanya Charitamrita 2.1.132). When Mahaprabhu returned to Puri after His pilgrimage to South India, where He had saved so many people by giving them love for Krishna, Nityananda sent Kala Krishna Das back to Bengal to tell everyone that He was back. The Bengali devotees immediately made arrangements to go to Jagannath Puri to see the Lord. The residents of Srikhanda (the Khaṇḍa-vāsīs) were counted amongst them.

Mukunda, Narahari, and Raghunandan from Srikhanda arrived at Advaita Acharya's house to go to Nilachala. (Chaitanya Charitamrita 2.10.90)

After the Snana Yatra, Jagannath would not be available for *darshan*. Mahaprabhu would go to Alalanath to get relief from not being able to see Jagannath. When Sarvabhauma Bhattacharya asked Gopinath Acharya to identify the Lord's devotees, he mentioned the names of Narahari, Mukunda Das, Raghunandan, Chiranjiva and Sulochan. (Chaitanya Charitamrita 2.11.92)

During the Rathayatra festival, the Lord formed seven kirtan groups with the devotees from Bengal. One of these was composed uniquely of the devotees from Srikhanda. Krishna Das Kaviraj Goswami writes that Narahari and Raghunandan were the dancers for this group, which sang separately from the others.
(Chaitanya Charitamrita 2.13.46)

When the Lord gave all the devotees directions for service, He told Narahari to remain in the association of devotees. (Chaitanya Charitamrita 2.15.132)

Many people confuse Narahari Sarkar Thakur with the author of *Bhakti-ratnākara*, Narahari Chakravarti. The latter, who is also known as Ghanashyama Das, was born two centuries later in the district of Murshidabad. His father's name was Jagannath Chakravarti and he was a disciple of Vishvanath Chakravarti. On Govindajī's order, he was engaged as the cook for the Govinda temple and was known as the "cooking pujari" (*rasuiyā pujari*) in Braj.

IF GAURA CAME BACK TO NADIA TOWN

The following is one of the many delectable songs composed by Narahari Sarkar Thakur:

āola gaura puna hi nadīyā pura
hoyata manahi ullāsa
aiche ānanda kanda kiye heraba
karabahi kīrtana vilāsa

hari hari,
kaba hāma heraba so mukha-c~āda
viraha payodhi kabahu dina pāṅ raba
ṭuṭaba hṛdayaka bāṅdha

kundana kanaka pāṅti keba heraba
yajña ki sutra virāja
bāhu-jugala tuli hari hari bolaba
naṭana bhakata-gaṇa mājha

eta kahi nayana mudi bahu saba jana
gaura prema bhela bhora
narahari dāsa āśa kaba pūraba
heraba gaura-kiśora

If Gaura came back to Nadia town, my mind would be filled with joy. I would see Him, the source of all joy, performing His kirtan pastimes.

Hari Hari! When will I again gaze upon that moon-like face? When will the day come when the dam holding the ocean of separation in my heart breaks?

When will I see the golden form of the Lord, wrapped in his *yajña-sutra*? Lifting my arms in the air, I will shout "Hari! Hari!" and dance in the midst of the devotees.

Saying such things, many of Gaura's devotees close their eyes and merge into love for Him. When will Narahari's desires be filled? When will he gaze again upon the form of the young Gaura?

Narahari disappeared in around 1570 AD, in the

month of Agrahayan on the *kṛṣṇā ekādaśī* day. Srinivas Acharya officiated at his funeral ceremony. Nityananda Prabhu's son Virachandra Goswami and many other important Vaishnavas were in Srikhanda to celebrate Narahari's disappearance feast, which is described in *Bhakti-ratnākara*:

Some people said, "Brothers! Do not leave right away. An ocean of prema will flood over in Srikhanda in a few days. On the thirteenth day of the waning moon of Agrahayan, when Narahari Thakur disappeared, a great festival will be held here." (*Bhakti-ratnākara* 9.512-4)

Srila Raghunandan Thakur

vyūhas tṛtīyaḥ pradyumnaḥ priya-narma-sakho'bhavat
cakre līlā-sahāyaṁ yo rādhā-mādhavayor vraje
śrī-caitanyādvaita-tanuḥ sa eva raghunandanaḥ

The third member of the *catur-vyūha*, Pradyumna, took part in Radha-Madhava's lila in Vraja as Krishna's intimate friend or *priya-narma-sakhā*. He has now appeared as Raghunandan, whose body is not different from that of Sri Chaitanya. (*Gaura-gaṇoddeśa-dīpikā* 70)

RAGHUNANDAN'S FATHER, MUKUNDA DAS

Raghunandan was born into a family of physicians[9] in the Shaka year 1432 (1510 AD). His father's name was Mukunda Das, his mother's name is unknown. Mukunda Das was Narahari Sarkar Thakur's older brother. In the fifteenth chapter of the *Madhya-līlā* of Chaitanya Charitamrita, it is clearly said that Mukunda Das was physician to the king.

Superficially, he appears to be engaged in government service as physician to the king. But in his inner life, he is filled with divine love. Who can know the extent of his love? (Chaitanya Charitamrita 2.15.120)

Once when Mukunda Das was engaged in treating the king, he saw a peacock feather and fainted. This incident is also described in the Chaitanya Charitamrita (2.15.121). Like Narahari, they made their home in Srikhanda. Mukunda Das' home is about one mile from the Srikhanda station. Raghunandan Thakur took birth on the Vasanta Panchami day. His uncle Narahari took a great deal of interest in raising Raghunandan, for whom he had much affection.

Chaitanya Mahaprabhu indicated that one's importance increases with the depth of devotion by telling Mukunda Das that his son was really his father.

The three most important devotees from Srikhanda were Mukunda Das, Raghunandan and Narahari. Mahaprabhu asked Mukunda Das, "Are you Raghunandan's father and he your son? Or, is he your father and you his son? Tell me so that I can put my doubts to rest." Mukunda answered, "Raghunandan is my father and I am his son, rest assured. Whatever devotion we have comes from him; therefore I see him as my father." When he heard Mukunda Das' answer, Mahaprabhu was thrilled and said, "He from whom we imbibe devotion should always be considered our senior."

(Chaitanya Charitamrita 2.15.112-117)

MAHAPRABHU GAVE RAGHUNANDAN THE SERVICE OF DEITY WORSHIP.

From his early childhood, Raghunandan Thakur would feed the family's Gopinath deity laddus. Uddhava Das has written a song in which this lila is described:

Mukunda Das lived in the village of Srikhanda where his household deity was named Gopinath. One day he had to go somewhere for work and he asked Raghunandan to do the service.

He said, "In this house we worship Krishna, so I want you to be sure to give Him something to eat." And then he left. Raghunandan did as his father had ordered and made the offering to the deity.

Raghunandan was just a child and in his simplicity, he said to Gopinath, "Eat! Eat!" Krishna is controlled by love, and so He did as the child told Him and ate everything on the plate without leaving even a grain of rice.

When Mukunda Das returned, he asked the boy to bring him the prasad from the offering he had made. The child answered, "Father, Krishna ate everything and left no remnants."

Mukunda was so astonished at his child's wondrous words that he asked him to make another offering. This time after he left the house, he returned and hid to watch what his son did.

Raghunandan joyfully placed a laḍḍu in Krishna's hand and said in a commanding voice, "Eat! Eat!" When Krishna had eaten half of the laddu, Raghunandan saw Mukunda Das in the doorway.

Mukunda saw that Krishna did not take another bite and that the half-eaten laddu remained in His hand. This caused him to be filled with love. He embraced his child and, as tears of joy rained from his eyes, spoke to him in a broken voice.

To this day, fortunate people come to Srikhanda to see the half-eaten laddu in Gopinath's hand. Raghunandan is not different from Cupid himself, says Uddhava Das with great feeling.

[All the mahantas] felt fascinated to see the Gopinath deity whom Raghunandan had fed laddus.

(*Bhakti-ratnākara* 9.525)

OTHER MIRACULOUS EVENTS

Narahari Sarkar Thakur gave mead to Nityananda Prabhu and Mahaprabhu from the pond right next to their home. This pond became known as Madhu Pushkarini. The legend is told that a kadamba tree that grew next to this pond always had two flowers blooming regardless of the season as a result of Raghunandan's miraculous powers.

According to the *Gauḍīya Vaiṣṇava Abhidhāna*, another miraculous event took place in Raghunandan's life: One day Abhiram Thakur came to Srikhanda and paid his obeisances to Raghunandan. Then he embraced him and melted with feelings of prema. Raghunandan started to dance and sing kirtan, and while doing so, one of his ankle bells slipped from his foot and went flying off, landing four miles away in Akai Hat near his disciple Krishna Das' house. Later, in order to commemorate the event, an artificial pond was excavated in that village and given the name Nupur Kund.

Mahaprabhu, the father of sankirtan, gave his adopted son Raghunandan Thakur the authority to offer the garland on the day before the sankirtan yajna (the *adhivāsa*) and to make the final offering at the yajna's end.

Raghunandan Thakur accompanied the Bengali devotees to Puri every year at Chaturmasya. He would dance with his uncle Narahari at the Rathayatra festival in the group formed by the residents of Srikhanda.

He participated in the Kheturi festival organized by Narottam Das Thakur, at Gadadhar Das' festival in Katwa and at the commemorative festival for Narahari Sarkar Thakur in Srikhanda.

Some people said, "Anyone who is dear to Raghunandan will win Mahaprabhu's mercy for life after life." Others said, "Raghunandan is so merciful that he gives life to the most humble and fallen." Some said, "What humility! There is no one who is his equal." And others, "He is as beautiful as Cupid himself!"
(*Bhakti-ratnākara* 9.660 ff.)

Srila Raghunandan Thakur had great affection for Srinivas Acharya. Prior to his disappearance he consoled Srinivas that despite the difficult times, he would be able to spread Vaishnavism in the future:

"A difficult time is coming in which people will succumb to various doubts. Narahari Prabhu wrote in his *Śrī-Kṛṣṇa-bhajanāmṛta*:

kṛṣṇa-caitanya-candreṇa nityānandena saṁhṛte
avatāre kalāv asmin vaiṣṇavāḥ sarva eva hi
bhaviṣyanti sadodvignāḥ kāle kāle dine dine
prāyaḥ sandigdha-hṛdayā uttametara-madhyamāḥ
(verses 3-4)

Once our Lord Krishna Chaitanya and his companion Nityananda Prabhu have ended their incarnation, the Vaishnavas in this age of Kali will become more anxious with every passing day. Whether very advanced, somewhat advanced or neophyte, their hearts will nearly always be filled with doubt.

But don't let this worry you. Lord Gauranga will accomplish many great works through you. I bless you that you remain long on this earth and that you and your followers protect our Lord's religion. Those who are opposed to devotion to Krishna will become devotees by your influence and they will take shelter of you.
(*Bhakti-ratnākara* 13.174-179)

Raghunandan Thakur bequeathed the service of his Gaura-Gopal deity to his son Kanai Thakur and then left this world on the fourth day of the waxing moon (*śuklā caturthī*) in the month of Shravan. Kanai Thakur gave a feast as a part of his father's last rites:

Raghunandan slowly became hidden to mortal eyes while repeating the names of Sri Krishna Chaitanya again and again. How glorious is that day of Shravan *śuklā caturthī*! Will anyone not sing the glories of Raghunandan Thakur? (*Bhakti-ratnākara* 13.183-4)

[9] See section on Narahari Sarkar Thakur.

Sri Shivananda Sen

purā vṛndāvane vīrā dūtī sarvāś ca gopikāḥ
nināya kṛṣṇa-nikaṭaṁ sedānīṁ janako mama

The go-between Vira, who previously brought all the gopis to Krishna, has now become my father.
(*Gaura-gaṇoddeśa-dīpikā* 176)

SHIVANANDA'S HOME AND FAMILY

Shivananda Sen's son, Paramananda Sen, also known as Kavi Karnapura, wrote the above verse in his *Gaura-gaṇoddeśa-dīpikā*. Just as Vira Duti acted to enrich the pastimes of Krishna and the gopis, Shivananda Sen appeared to enrich Gaura Hari's lila. A Vaishnava may take birth in any family. Shivananda Sen manifested his lila of being born in the Vaidya or physician caste to increase its glory. The names of his parents are not known, nor that of his wife. He had three sons: Sri Chaitanya Das, Sri Rama Das and Sri Paramananda(Kavi Karnapur).

Shivananda Sen made his home in the present day city of Halisahar, in Kumarahatta near Kanchra Para. This is the same town where Ishvara Puri, Mahaprabhu's guru, was born. Mahaprabhu took some earth from Ishvara Puri's birthplace and devotees have been taking earth from that spot ever since, leaving a hole in the ground big enough to form a pool that has taken the name of Sri Chaitanya Doba.

After Mahaprabhu took sannyas, Srivas Pandit and his family found impossible to remain in Nabadwip and so moved to Kumarahatta. Other notable residents of the town were Vasudeva Datta Thakur, Khanja Bhagavan Das and others. According to Chaitanya Bhagavata, Shivananda Sen was present when Mahaprabhu came to visit Srivas Pandit's house in Kumarahatta:

Vasudeva Datta came immediately, as did Shivananda Sen and his family members.(Chaitanya Bhagavata 3.5.18)

SHIVANANDA'S SERVICE

Shivananda was best known for managing the yearly trips to Puri, when the Bengali devotees went on pilgrimage to see Mahaprabhu. He would take responsibility for the route they took, the costs of both coming and going, and everyone's lodgings.

On the Lord's order, every single year all the devotees came to see the Rathayatra.... Among them were Krishna's own singer, Mukunda Datta and Shivananda Sen and others who were accompanied by their family members.

(Chaitanya Bhagavata 3.8.5, 15)

Shivananda Sen took care of the paying the customs duties and ferry fees for the group. He took personal care of everyone in the pilgrimage. He saw to all the devotees' necessities, especially making lodging arrangements. He knew the roads through Orissa and would show the way.

(Chaitanya Charitamrita 2.16.19-20)

In the third year, when Mahaprabhu's associates took their wives with them, Shivananda Sen also took his wife and son, Sri Chaitanya Das. The Chaitanya Charitamrita's description of that trip is as follows:

Malini accompanied Srivas Pandit, Shivananda Sen's wife travelled with him. Shivananda's little boy named Chaitanya Das also jubilantly came along with them to see the Lord... Shivananda Sen dealt with customs officials and made eating and lodging arrangements, ecstatically going on the road to see Mahaprabhu.

(Chaitanya Charitamrita 2.16.22-3, 26-7)

One of Mahaprabhu's dear devotees was Vasudeva Datta from Chittagong. He was very generous and somewhat prodigal in his spending. Mahaprabhu told Shivananda Sen to take charge of his affairs to help him cut back on his expenses, giving practical instructions on the necessity of earning money to run a household.

He respectfully said to Shivananda Sen, "Please take Vasudeva Datta to hand. He is too generous. He spends whatever he earns the very day he earns it. He is a householder and has to save some money; if he doesn't, he will not be able to maintain his wife and family. I want you to supervise his income and expenditures. Be his manager and resolve his difficulties.

(Chaitanya Charitamrita 2.15.93-96)

SHIVANANDA SEN AND THE DOG

Krishna Das Kaviraj Goswami has recounted an anecdote in the Chaitanya Charitamrita about the amazing relationship between Shivananda Sen and a dog.

One year, as the pilgrimage party made its way to Puri, a stray dog began to tag along behind it. When the pilgrims had to cross a certain river, the ferryman refused to allow the dog on board. Shivananda Sen considered the dog a devotee and a pilgrim and felt that he could not leave it behind. He finally paid the ferryman 10 *paṇas* of cowry shells to take it across. One day, when Shivananda was delayed in paying tolls for the party, his servant forgot to feed the dog its rice and it disappeared. Distressed at its loss, Shivananda sent ten men to find the animal, but they had no success. Shivananda was so upset that he did not eat his meal that evening.

As they approached Puri, the devotees became increasingly anxious to see Mahaprabhu and on their arrival, they went straight to His residence even before going to the temple to see Jagannath. They then went to take their meal with Mahaprabhu who, at the end of the meal, sent them all to their lodgings to rest.

The next day, when the devotees came to see Mahaprabhu, they were astonished to see the dog there. Mahaprabhu was laughing and feeding it coconut prasad and saying, "Chant Hare Krishna, Hare Rama!" The dog was clearly barking out the divine names and eating the prasad given him by the Lord. Everyone was completely amazed to see this extraordinary event. Shivananda Sen prostrated himself on the ground in obeisances to the dog and humbly begged him for forgiveness. The next day, the dog had disappeared once more and was never seen again. By Mahaprabhu's mercy, it had taken a spiritual body and gone to Vaikuntha.

These are the transcendental pastimes of Lord Sachinandana: he made a dog say the names of Krishna and then sent it to the spiritual world.

(Chaitanya Charitamrita 3.1.33)

SHIVANANDA SEN AND NAKULA BRAHMACHARI

During the period of Muslim rule, the county courthouse in the town of Kalna in the district of Burdwan was in the neighborhood named Ambika. This neighborhood was known then as Ambua Muluk, today as Pyari Ganj. A great Vaishnava named Nakula Brahmachari lived there. Mahaprabhu entered into Nakula's heart out of His desire to deliver the people of Bengal. The brahmachari began to behave just like someone possessed by celestial influences and would dance, sing and shout in a deep mood of divine love. Both his inner attitude and physical appearance took on Mahaprabhu's qualities.

When people heard about the miraculous occurrences surrounding Nakula Brahmachari, they flocked to see him. Everyone in his presence would be influenced by his absorption in Mahaprabhu's mood; they would sing Krishna's names and begin to experience the taste of Krishna prema.

When Shivananda Sen heard about all this, he could not at first believe that it was true and decided to test Nakula Brahmachari to eradicate his doubts. He came to Ambika, but kept himself at some distance from the brahmachari. His idea was that if Nakula were truly possessed by Mahaprabhu, he would call out to him and tell him what his own secret mantra was. In spite of the fact that Shivananda was invisible in the great crowd of innumerable devotees, Nakula called out his name and sent people to look for him. When he heard his name being called, Shivananda came forth and paid his obeisances to Nakula. The brahmachari said,

> "You doubted me, so listen carefully and I will put an end to your doubts. Your worshipable mantra is the four-syllable Gaura-Gopal mantra. Give up the uncertainty you held in your heart." (Chaitanya Charitamrita 3.2.30-31)

When he heard this, Shivananda became convinced that Nakula Brahmachari was indeed filled with the presence of Mahaprabhu. He paid his prostrated obeisances and acknowledged his faith and devotion to him. This is just one example of Mahaprabhu's inconceivable potencies.

SHIVANANDA SEN AND NRISINGHANANDA BRAHMACHARI

Shivananda Sen had a nephew, Srikanta Sen, who was so eager to see the Lord that one year he went to Puri alone. Mahaprabhu treated him warmly and kept him for two months before instructing him to return to Bengal. He told him to convey the message to the Bengali devotees that there was no need for them to come to Puri that year, for He Himself would be visiting Bengal in the month of Paush. He would then meet with them all and eat at Jagadananda's house. When Srikanta returned with the news, everyone was jubilant in expectation of the Lord's visit. But when the time of Mahaprabhu's expected arrival came, Shivananda, Jagadananda and others who had been waiting anxiously for Him were distressed to see that He did not come.

At that time, Pradyumna Brahmachari (who had been given the name Nrisinghananda by Mahaprabhu) happened by and asked why everyone was so unhappy. When he heard about their disappointment over Mahaprabhu not arriving, he assured them that he would bring Mahaprabhu there within three days. Everyone knew of Pradyumna's spiritual powers and so they believed that he could do it. Pradyumna sat down in meditation. After two days, he said, "Mahaprabhu has arrived in Panihati. By midday tomorrow he will be at Shivananda's house." Without showing the slightest doubt, he ordered Shivananda Sen to start making preparations for a feast in honor of Mahaprabhu's arrival. Nrisinghananda personally started cooking early in the morning, and made a large variety of preparations, which he distributed onto three separate plates to make offerings to Jagannath, Nrisingha Deva and Mahaprabhu. As soon as he sat down in meditation for the offering, Mahaprabhu personally appeared and ate all three plates without leaving any remnants.

Pradyumna was overjoyed to see the Lord accept his offerings. Nevertheless, though he well knew that on a higher level there is no distinction between Mahaprabhu, Nrisingha and Jagannath, in order to demonstrate the principle of devotion to one's personal worshipable deity, he said, "Nrisingha Deva has not eaten anything today." Shivananda asked why this was so and Pradyumna Brahmachari answered,

> "Mahaprabhu ate the offerings intended for all three deities. Therefore Nrisingha and Jagannath have gone hungry." (Chaitanya Charitamrita 3.2.71)

When he heard this, Shivananda felt a twinge of doubt. Nevertheless, he furnished Pradyumna with more raw foodstuffs so that he could prepare another offering for Nrisinghadeva. The next year, when Shivananda came to Nilachala, Mahaprabhu one day started to glorify Nrisinghananda's virtues to all the devotees.

> "Last year in the month of Paush, he gave Me such a nice meal. I have never tasted such delicious rice and vegetables!" (Chaitanya Charitamrita 3.2.77)

All the devotees were struck with wonder at hearing this, and Shivananda himself became confident that the incident was true. This is another example of Mahaprabhu's mercy to Shivananda.

NITYANANDA PRABHU PUNISHES SHIVANANDA

Shivananda Sen also received much mercy from Nityananda Prabhu. One day Nityananda kicked Shivananda, who thus received the touch of his lotus feet, a rare attainment for even Brahma and the demigods. Krishna Das Kaviraj Goswami has described this incident in the 12th chapter of the Chaitanya Charitamrita's *Antya-līlā*.

After the disappearance of Hari Das Thakur, Mahaprabhu's ecstatic transformations increased day by day. That year, the devotees gathered in Nabadwip as usual in preparation for the journey to Puri. This time, Nityananda Prabhu also joined the party, even though Mahaprabhu had expressly forbidden him to come to Puri. As usual, since he knew the roads of Orissa, Shivananda was in charge of the party and would take care of the customs agents and toll collectors along the way. On this occasion, he was accompanied by his wife and three sons.

Normally, Shivananda would cross a given tollgate last, after first insuring that all members of the party had gone through. On one occasion, the procedure took longer than usual and since he had not arranged for lodgings for the company in the nearby village, the devotees were obliged to loiter about under a tree until quite late at night. While waiting for Shivananda to come through the tollgate, Nityananda Prabhu appeared to take on the mood of a cowherd boy from Vraja overcome by hunger. He made a pretense of being angry at Shivananda, complaining, "Shiva has still not come and arranged for a place for us to stay and I am dying of hunger. I curse his three sons to die."

On hearing Nityananda make such a curse, Shivananda's wife started to cry. When Shivananda finally returned from paying the toll collector, he had to calm his wife. He said, "Foolish woman! Why are you crying needlessly? If they must, let our sons die for the inconvenience we have caused Nityananda Prabhu."

He then went to speak to Nityananda, who kicked him in the head as he paid his obeisances. Shivananda was overjoyed to receive the merciful touch of the Lord's foot and immediately went to arrange quarters for the night in the house of a milkman. When Shivananda brought Nityananda Prabhu to his lodgings, he glorified him and prayed to receive the touch of his feet again and again. He said,

"Today you have accepted me as your servant, for you have duly punished me as you would your own servant. You are so compassionate that even your punishments are a sign of your causeless mercy. Who in the three worlds can understand your personality? The dust of your feet is unattainable by even Brahma, yet it has fallen on my wretched body. My life, my family and my service have all become perfected today. Today I have attained devotion to Krishna, as well as all the other goals of human life."
(Chaitanya Charitamrita 3.12.27-30)

Nityananda was so pleased by Shivananda's prayers that he embraced him. However, Srikanta, Shivananda's nephew, had been upset by Nityananda's behavior. He thought, "Shivananda is Mahaprabhu's dear associate and respected by all the devotees, and yet Nityananda has kicked him in the head." He left the party and went ahead to Puri on his own. Upon his arrival, he went to Mahaprabhu and paid his prostrated obeisances. Mahaprabhu first told his servant Govinda to instruct Srikanta to take off his upper garment when paying obeisances. Then, knowing his thoughts, He said to His associates,

"Srikanta has come on his own because of some great mental distress. Don't tell him what to do, but allow him do as he pleases." (Chaitanya Charitamrita 3.12.38)

From these words, Srikanta could understand that Mahaprabhu was all-knowing and so said nothing about the incident to anyone. The Lord is so affectionate to His devotees that even their friends and relations are also dear to Him.

ahaṁ bhaktaparādhīno hy asvatantra iva dvija
sādhubhir grasta-hṛdayo bhaktair bhakta-janapriyaḥ

O Brahmin, I am under the control of my devotees as though I were completely lacking any independence. The saintly devotees have taken possession of My heart, for I am dear to them and they to Me.
(Srimad Bhagavatam 9.4.63)

MAHAPRABHU'S MERCY ON SHIVANANDA'S FAMILY

Because of their relation to Shivananda, his wife and three sons also received the Lord's unlimited mercy. Shivananda had named his youngest son Paramananda Das in accordance with Mahaprabhu's instruction. Mahaprabhu would jokingly call the child "Puri Das." When Shivananda presented the baby to Him, the Lord affectionately allowed him to suck on his toe.

Who can find the limits of the ocean of Shivananda's good fortune? The Lord accepted his entire family as His own. The Lord then sat down and ate with all the devotees. As He washed His mouth and hands after the meal, He instructed Govinda to give Shivananda Sen, his wife and child His remnants every day, for as long as they stayed in Puri.
(Chaitanya Charitamrita 3.12.51-3)

Mahaprabhu's unlimited mercy on Shivananda's youngest son, Puri Das, is described in the sixteenth chapter of the Antya-lila. One year, when Shivananda and his wife were in Puri for the Rathayatra, Mahaprabhu said to the little boy, "Say Krishna! Chant Krishna's names!" Though the Lord asked him to chant repeatedly, the boy refused to utter the Holy Name. His embarrassed father also tried to get him to chant, but the Puri Das was steadfast in his refusal. Mahaprabhu threw up His hands in frustration. He said, "I have induced everyone in the universe, even the lower forms of life, to chant the names of Krishna, but I am unable to make this little child do so. Whatever is the reason for his refusal?"

Svarupa Damodar alone realized what it was: "You have instructed him in the mantra consisting of Krishna's name. Now that he has received the mantra, he will not reveal it publicly, but only chants mentally. That is my guess."

In his *Anubhāṣya,* Srila Bhaktisiddhanta Saraswati Goswami Thakur has written: "The mantra that one receives from his guru is not to be revealed to anyone else, otherwise it will lose its potency. We have seen this previously from the story about Gadadhar Pandit."

Another day, Mahaprabhu asked Puri Das to recite a verse. Puri Das broke his silence and recited a verse of his own composition that thrilled all those who heard it. Even Brahma and the gods cannot understand the glories of Mahaprabhu's mercy. Puri Das, or Kavi Karnapura's verse:

śravasoḥ kuvalayam akṣnor
añjanam uraso mahendramaṇidāma
vṛndāvana-ramaṇīnāṁ
maṇḍanam akhilaṁ harir jayati

All glories to Hari, the ornament of all the lovely ladies of Vrindavan — a blue lotus for their ears, black collyrium for their eyes, and a necklace of blue sapphires to decorate their breasts. (Chaitanya Charitamrita 3.16.74)

SHIVANANDA AND RAGHUNATH DAS GOSWAMI

When Raghunath Das Goswami left home, using an errand for his guru Yadunandan Acharya as a pretext, his father Govardhan sent ten men to Shivananda, who was already on his way to Puri, asking him to send Raghunath Das back. They did not find Raghunath Das with Shivananda, however, and returned empty-handed. At the end of the rainy season, when Shivananda and the other devotees returned from Puri, Govardhan Majumdar heard from some of them that Raghunath Das was engaged in strict austere practices and begging near the Singha Dwar of the Jagannath temple. Raghunath's parents were greatly distressed by this news and the next year, Govardhan entrusted 400 rupees to Shivananda for his son. Raghunath refused to accept this money for himself, however. Shivananda Sen's son Kavi Karnapura glorified Raghunath Das extensively in his play, *Caitanya-candrodaya*.

The dates of Shivananda Sen's appearance and disappearance are not known. The Gaura Gopal deity he installed is still being worshiped in the Krishna Raya temple in Kanchra Para.

SRI ACHYUTANANDA

yogamāyā bhagavatī gṛhiṇī tasya sāmpratam
sītā-rūpeṇāvatīrṇā śrīnāmnā tat-prakāśataḥ
tasya putro'cyutānandaḥ kṛṣṇa-caitanya-vallabhaḥ
śrīmat-paṇḍita-gosvāmi-śiṣyaḥ priya iti śrutaḥ
yaḥ kārttikeyaḥ prāg āsīd iti jalpanti kecana
kecid āhū rasavido "cyutā-nāmnī tu gopikā
ubhayaṁ tu samīcīnaṁ dvayor ekatra saṅgatāt
kārttikeyaḥ kṛṣṇa-miśras tat-sāmyād iti kecana

The goddess Yogamaya was Advaita Acharya's wife, having appeared as Sita; his other wife Sri was her expansion. Advaita's son Achyutananda was very dear to Sri Krishna Chaitanya. He became a dear disciple of Srila Gadadhar Pandit Goswami. Some say that he was Karttikeya in his previous incarnation, while others who are knowledgeable about sacred rapture say that he was the gopi named Achyutā. Both opinions are reasonable because both identities are joined in him. Some people hold that his brother Krishna Mishra was also Karttikeya, due to his similarity to him. (*Gaura-gaṇoddeśa-dīpikā*, 81-84)

Achyutananda was born as the son of Advaita Acharya and Sitadevi in the town of Shantipur in the year 1428 Shaka (1506 AD). He was Advaita's oldest son and is counted as a Chaitanya branch of the tree of devotion.

śrī-caitanyāmara-taror dvitīya-skandha-rūpiṇaḥ
śrīmad-advaita-chandrasya śākhā-rūpān numaḥ

I offer my obeisances to all the branches of Sri Advaita Chandra, who is the second trunk of the eternal Chaitanya tree. (Chaitanya Charitamrita 1.12.3)

Achyutananda was one of Advaita Prabhu's major branches; from his very birth, he served Chaitanya's lotus feet. (Chaitanya Charitamrita 1.12.13)

ADVAITA'S SIX SONS

Advaita Acharya had six sons, of whom three, Achyutananda, Krishna Mishra and Gopal Mishra are considered to have understood the essence of spiritual life, while the other three, Balaram, Svarupa and Jagadish, did not. The book *Advaita-carita* describes this as follows:

acyutaḥ kṛṣṇa-miśraś ca gopāla-dāsa eva ca
ratna-trayam idaṁ proktaṁ sītāgarbhādi-sambhavam
ācārya-tanayeṣvete trayo gaura-gaṇāḥ smṛtāḥ |
caturtho balarāmaś ca svarupaḥ pañcamaḥ smṛtaḥ
ṣaṣṭhas tu jagadīśākhya ācārya-tanayo hi ṣaṭ

The three sons Achyuta, Krishna Mishra and Gopal Das were born in the womb of Sitadevi and are called the three jewels. Amongst Advaita's sons, these three were members of Gaura's inner circle. His fourth son was Balaram, his fifth son Svarupa and the sixth, Jagadish.

Srila Bhaktivinoda Thakur paraphrases Krishna Das Kaviraj's explanation of this problem in his *Amṛta-pravāha-bhāṣya*: "In the beginning, all of Advaita Prabhu's followers shared a common understanding, but in the course of time, some unfortunately adopted differing doctrines. Those who followed the opinions of Advaita himself are considered to be pure Vaishnavas, but those who under some fateful influence rejected his teachings and invented a new doctrine are considered useless. We have no need of knowing the names of the useless sons of Advaita Prabhu, but have listed them here in order to be able to distinguish them. Just as the useful rice grain is separated from the chaff by winnowing, so have the useful sons of Advaita been separated from the useless."

The doctrines of Advaita Acharya are the essential teachings of spiritual life; those who ignored his orders became useless. (Chaitanya Charitamrita 1.12.10)

All those who took Achyutananda's opinion belong to the group of Advaita Acharya's associates. They are great devotees who received his mercy and easily attained the lotus feet of Chaitanya Mahaprabhu.
(Chaitanya Charitamrita 1.12.73-4)

MAHAPRABHU'S MERCY ON THE CHILD ACHYUTANANDA

After taking sannyas in Katwa, Mahaprabhu descended on Shantipur. Achyutananda was either three or five years old at the time (as Vrindavan Das Thakur gives both ages in different places).

Advaita's son Achyutananda, though still young enough to go about without any clothes, glowed with good fortune. Omniscient by the Lord's inconceivable power, he was Advaita's worthy heir. His entire body was covered with dust, but on hearing that the Lord had arrived, he came to see Him, a smile on his face. He fell at the Lord's feet and the Lord picked him up, dust and all, and held him on His lap. (Chaitanya Bhagavata 3.1.213-6)

While holding him, Mahaprabhu said to Achyutananda: "Since Advaita is My father, you are My brother." When he heard this, Achyuta responded by displaying a profound understanding of Mahaprabhu's spiritual identity. He said, "You are the friend of every single living being and the scriptures say that You are the father of all creation." The devotees were astonished when they heard Achyuta show this understanding of the Lord's identity.

THE WISDOM OF ACHYUTANANDA AT FIVE

In the fourth chapter of the *Antya-khaṇḍa* of Chaitanya Bhagavata, Vrindavan Das Thakur writes about Achyutananda's single-minded devotion to Chaitanya Mahaprabhu in the following way: One day, a sannyasi came to visit Advaita Prabhu's house and asked him what the relationship between Chaitanya Mahaprabhu and Keshava Bharati was. Advaita answered in a conventional way that Keshava Bharati was the Lord's sannyas guru. The five-year-old child interjected angrily, "The Lord is the spiritual master of all the gurus of the world; He is the Supreme Lord Himself. How could anyone be His guru?" When Advaita heard this wisdom from the mouth of his child, he said, "This boy is my father and I am his son!" And he asked his son forgiveness for his offense—causing the lad to hang his head with embarrassment. Krishna Das Kaviraj Goswami has also summarized this story beautifully:

When Achyutananda heard from his father that Keshava Bharati was Lord Chaitanya Mahaprabhu's spiritual master, he was very unhappy. He told his father, "Your teaching about the supreme spiritual master, Chaitanya Mahaprabhu, will wreak havoc in the country. Lord Chaitanya Mahaprabhu is the teacher of the fourteen worlds, but you say that someone else is His spiritual master. This is not supported by any revealed scripture." Advaita Acharya felt great satisfaction to hear his five-year-old son Achyutananda display such an understanding of doctrine. (Chaitanya Charitamrita 1.12.14-7)

Mahaprabhu appeared at Advaita's house just when the entire household was becoming aware of Achyutananda's spiritual intelligence and gave him His blessings.

Prior to this occasion, Achyutananda had seen Mahaprabhu's glories at His great epiphany (*Mahāprakāśa*), for when the Lord had summoned Advaita through Srirama Pandit, Achyutananda had accompanied him to Nabadwip.

Achyutananda also witnessed the Lord's punishment of his father for teaching impersonalism. Srila Bhaktisiddhanta Saraswati Goswami Thakur writes the following in his *Anubhāṣya*: "Sri Achyuta was the Lord's devotee from childhood. There is no information on whether Achyutananda ever married, but he is described as the foremost of Advaita Acharya's disciples. On the other hand, in Yadunandan Das' book describing the disciples of Gadadhar Pandit Goswami, *Śākhā-nirṇayāmṛta,* it is said that Achyutananda was a disciple and branch of Gadadhar. The passage there is as follows:

mahārasāmṛtānandam
acyutānanda-nāmakam
gadādhara-priyatamaṁ
śrīmad-advaita-nandanam

[I offer obeisances to] Advaita Acharya's son named Achyutananda, who takes great joy in the ocean of nectarean sacred rapture. He is Gadadhar's dearest disciple.

ACHYUTANANDA IN PURI

Near the end of Mahaprabhu's life, Gadadhar remained permanently in Jagannath Puri. Achyutananda and Advaita's other sons also came to stay in Puri to be near Him.

Achyutananda, the son of Advaita Acharya, lived in Jagannath Puri, taking shelter of Lord Chaitanya Mahaprabhu. (Chaitanya Charitamrita 1.10.150)

Achyutananda came to Puri every year to celebrate the Rathayatra festival during which he danced in the sixth kirtan group that came from Shantipur. (Chaitanya Charitamrita 2.13.45) He also participated as a dancer in the *berā-sankirtan,* when the Lord danced around the temple.

The kirtan around the temple started and the seven groups began to sing. In each of the seven groups, one devotee was the designated dancer: Advaita Acharya, Nityananda Prabhu, Vakresvara, Achyutananda, Srivas Pandit, Satyaraj Khan, and Narahari Das. The Lord wandered from group to group, but all the devotees thought that He was with them alone.
(Chaitanya Charitamrita 3.10.58-61)

Achyutananda also participated in the cleaning of the Gundicha temple. When Lord Jagannath was in the Gundicha temple, Mahaprabhu would go there with the devotees to see him after his morning bath. They would go three times a day and perform sankirtan in the Gundicha temple courtyard. At the Lord's behest, either Advaita Acharya, Nityananda Prabhu, Vakresvara Pandit, Achyutananda, or Hari Das Thakur would dance.

After bathing in the morning, the Lord would go to see Jagannath, taking the devotees and dancing in sankirtan. He would sometimes make Advaita dance, sometimes Nityananda, sometimes Hari Das and sometimes Achyutananda, sometimes Vakresvara and sometimes other devotees. The Lord performed sankirtan three times a day in the courtyard of the Gundicha temple.

(Chaitanya Charitamrita 2.14.70-72)

According to Narahari Chakravarti's *Narottama-vilāsa*, Achyutananda remained in Puri until Mahaprabhu's disappearance, after which he spent the rest of his life living at the family home in Shantipur. He also participated in the Kheturi festival.

Raghava Pandit

dhaniṣṭhā bhakṣya-sāmagrīṁ kṛṣṇāyādād vraje'mitām
saiva sāmpratam gaurāṅga-priyo rāghava-paṇḍitaḥ
guṇamālā vraje yāsīd damayantī tu tat-svasā

The gopi Dhanishtha who brought unlimited amounts of food to Krishna in Vraja has now become Gauranga's dear servant, Raghava Pandit. His sister Damayanti was Gunamala in Krishna lila.

(*Gaura-gaṇoddeśa-dīpikā* 166-7)

In Krishna lila, Dhanishtha Devi would take Krishna's prasad to Radharani on Yashoda Mata's order. Radharani would then lovingly eat the prasad. Bhaktivinoda describes this in his *bhoga ārati*:

yaśomati ājñā peye dhaniṣṭhā ānīta
śrī-kṛṣṇa-prasad rādhā bhuñje haye prīta

Mahaprabhu, who was none other than Krishna in the mood of Radharani, similarly accepted the food offerings made by Dhanishtha's incarnation, Raghava Pandit.

MAHAPRABHU RESIDES PERMANENTLY IN RAGHAVA'S HOUSE

Raghava Pandit's home was in the town of Panihati. Panihati is on the eastern bank of the Ganges, one mile from the Sodhpur station on the Eastern Railway line out of Sealdah. It is only a few kilometers south of Kumarahatta. Krishna Das Kaviraj Goswami has written that Mahaprabhu was permanently resident in the house of Raghava Pandit.

The Lord's manifestations took place in the home of Sachi, during Nityananda's dancing, in Srivas' kirtan, and in the house of Raghava Pandit. It is the Lord's nature to be attracted by His devotee's love.

(Chaitanya Charitamrita 3.2.34-5)

Vrindavan Das Thakur's biography of the Lord indicates clearly how dear Raghava Pandit was to Mahaprabhu. When Raghava saw the Lord of his life coming from Srivas' house in Kumarahatta toward his own home, he fell down at His feet, overcome by love.

When the Lord of Vaikuntha saw Raghava Pandit's devotion, He blessed him with a look of favor. The Lord said, "I have come to Raghava's house and forgotten all distress simply by seeing him. I feel the same pleasure coming here as I do by taking a refreshing bath in the Ganges."

(Chaitanya Bhagavata 3.5.81-3)

The Lord often told Raghava Pandit to cook for Him because He enjoyed accepting his preparations, imbued as they were with deep devotion. Raghava cooked and fed the Lord with great enthusiasm. Balaram's other form, Nityananda Prabhu, would also come to eat at Raghava's house with his companions and all would praise his cooking. Mahaprabhu especially enjoyed his spinach platters.

While the Lord was there, Gadadhar Das, Purandara Pandit, Parameshvari Das, Raghunath Vaidya and other great Vaishnavas came to Raghava's house in Panihati in accordance with His desire. The Lord took Raghava aside in order to explain to him His oneness with Nityananda Prabhu. Mahaprabhu once told Makaradhvaja Kara that service to Raghava Pandit was the same as service to Himself.

RAGHAVERA JHALI

Rāghavera jhali or "Raghava's bags" were filled with various preparations that his sister Damayanti made throughout the year for Mahaprabhu. They have been mentioned in Abhiram Das Thakur's *Pāṭa-paryaṭana* and in the Chaitanya Charitamrita.

Raghava and Damayanti lived in Panihati. They were famous for the bags of food known as *Rāghavera jhali*. (*Pāṭa-paryaṭana*)

Raghava Pandit, Mahaprabhu's primary follower, is the Lord's seventh branch. An important sub-branch, Makaradhvaja Kara, proceeded from him. Raghava's sister Damayanti was the Lord's dear maidservant, who throughout the year gathered various ingredients for the Lord's bhoga. Raghava filled bags with the foods Damayanti prepared and secretly carried them to Puri for the Lord. The Lord then ate these gifts of food for an entire year. Those bags are still celebrated as *Rāghavera jhāli*.

(Chaitanya Charitamrita 1.10.24-27)

The generous Raghava Pandit, in whose house Mahaprabhu secretly stayed, also went with them.
(Chaitanya Bhagavata 3.8.32)

Krishna Das Kaviraj Goswami writes a complete description of these bags in his Chaitanya Charitamrita (*Antya*.10). Krishna's devotees in Vraja have no sense of awe and wonder in their attitude to the Lord. Damayanti would prepare *śuktā* for the Lord because she worried that He might have problems with His digestion. Mahaprabhu was overjoyed to receive these preparations because they were offered with such natural affection.

Raghava Pandit came with bags full of condiments prepared very nicely by his sister, Damayanti. Damayanti made a variety of unparalleled culinary concoctions suitable for the Lord. The Lord would then enjoy them for the entire year that followed. These are the names of some of the pickles and condiments in the bags of Raghava Pandit: mango mustard pickle, ginger mustard pickle, hot spicy mustard, lime and mango pickle, *āmra-koli*, dried ground mango, sliced dried mango, mangoes preserved in oil and dried mango. With great attention, Damayanti also made a powdered dried bitter vegetable preparation (*śuktā*). Do not disregard *śuktā* because of its bitter taste; the Lord derived more happiness from eating this *śuktā* than from drinking *pañcāmṛta* [a combination of milk, sugar, ghee, honey and curd]. Since Chaitanya Mahaprabhu is the Supreme Lord, He takes the spirit in which things are done; accepting the love in which a gift is given. He therefore derived great pleasure even from the dried bitter leaves of *śuktā* and *kāśandi* (mustard sauce). Because of her natural love for Mahaprabhu, Damayanti considered Him to be an ordinary human being and therefore worried that He might become sick from overeating and get dysentery. She prepared *śuktā* for Him, since it diminishes the mucus that accumulates in the digestive system and causes dysentery. Damayanti's affectionate attitude brought great pleasure to the Lord.
(Chaitanya Charitamrita 3.10.13-20)

Makaradhvaja Kara, a kayastha who also lived in Panihati, was Raghava Pandit's initiated disciple. It was he who annually carried the bags of food his spiritual master prepared for the Lord to Puri. He was named the *munsib* or "superintendent" of these bags.
(Chaitanya Charitamrita 3.10.40).

RAGHAVA PANDIT'S STRICT CLEANLINESS

Mahaprabhu joyfully praised the extent of Raghava Pandit's devotion to His entourage in Puri, especially lauding his coconut offerings. Though Raghava Pandit owned an ordchard with hundreds of coconut trees, he would have more expensive nuts brought from afar in order to offer coconut water and pulp offerings to the Lord. Mahaprabhu happily accepted them.

Raghava Pandit never offered anything to the Lord that was not pure and of the highest quality. Paying high prices for the best possible produce, he had mangoes, jackfruit, bananas and other fruit brought from distant villages to be offered to his Mahaprabhu deity. One day a servant touched the coconut offering after his hand had brushed against the doorframe. Raghava worried that dust from people's feet had contaminated the foodstuffs. Thus, he rejected them as unsuitable for the deity and threw them away.

Should anyone criticize Raghava Pandit for throwing fruit away, Srila Bhaktisiddhanta Saraswati Goswami Thakur has warned, "Raghava Pandit was an eternally perfected servant of Krishna and not some person with an obsessive-compulsive neurosis about cleanliness. Nor was he a low-level devotee who artificially projected transcendental qualities on matter. He served the object of his worship without the slightest hint of any materialistic attitude, completely absorbed in a transcendental mood of service."
(*Anubhāṣya*, 2.14.83)

NITYANANDA VISITS PANIHATI

Mahaprabhu ordered Nityananda Prabhu to take his associates and leave Puri to preach pure devotion in Bengal. While wandering through the Ganges valley, Nitai was attracted by Raghava Pandit's pure devotional attitude and came to his house in Panihati. Along with him came the three Ghosh brothers, Govinda, Madhava and Vasudeva, who were known for their abilities as kirtaniyas. When they started singing, Nityananda fell into a trance-like state and started to dance. When he had finished dancing, he sat on the deities' altar; Nityananda Prabhu's entourage and Raghava Pandit performed an elaborate *abhishek* ceremony to honor him. After the bathing ceremony, they dressed and garlanded him, whereupon Nityananda sat down again on the deities' throne while Raghava Pandit held the parasol.

At this moment, a miraculous event occurred. Nityananda Prabhu, still in a trance-like state, ordered Raghava Pandit to quickly bring him a garland of kadamba flowers. Raghava answered that kadamba trees were not yet in flower. Nityananda Prabhu told him to look around the grounds of his house and he would find the flowers. As Raghava searched, he was amazed to find kadamba flowers blossoming on a lime tree. He quickly picked the flowers and made a garland, which he placed around Nityananda's neck.

A few moments later, the house was filled with the fragrance of damanaka flowers. Nityananda Prabhu said that Mahaprabhu Himself had come from Puri wearing a damanaka garland to hear the kirtan. Narahari Chakravarti Thakur mentions this dance and kirtan in his *Bhakti-ratnākara*:

First Nityananda Prabhu came to Panihati with his associates. Raghava Pandit, Makaradhvaja Kara and the

other devotees of the village were overjoyed to see them. Who can describe the wonderful dancing and kirtan that took place in Raghava Pandit's house?
(*Bhakti-ratnākara* 12.3645-7)

Nityananda Prabhu came to Panihati along with Rama Das and Gadadhar Das, where he first visited Raghava Pandit's house. The kirtan that they began there filled the entire universe with transcendental joy. Panihati is the birthplace of the great devotee, Raghava Pandit. There is no limit to the glories of a great devotee's birthplace. (*Bhakti-ratnākara* 8.156-8)

CIDA-DADHI MAHOTSAVA

While Nityananda was there in Panihati, he ordered Raghunath Das Goswami to put on a feast of chipped rice and yogurt for his entourage. Raghava Pandit also participated by contributing various foods that had not been contaminated by the touch of cooked rice. He thus witnessed Nityananda's lila of picnicking by the riverbank in a mood of great amazement. After resting the afternoon by the Ganges, Nityananda went and spent the evening at Raghava Pandit's house in kirtan and dance. Mahaprabhu Himself manifested there, being attracted by Nityananda's dancing. In order to reveal the extent of Raghava Pandit's good fortune, Mahaprabhu and Nityananda sat down together and accepted his offerings of fine rice and various vegetable preparations, as well as cakes and sweet rice, all of which was like the nectar of the gods. Overcome with affection for Raghunath Das, Raghava Pandit gave him Mahaprabhu's remnants.

Raghava Pandit visited Puri on occasion and participated with Mahaprabhu in the cleaning of the Gundicha temple, the Rathayatra festival, water sports in the Indradyumna Sarovar and many others. He sang in the chorus with the first group of singers who were led by Svarupa Damodar and in which Advaita Acharya was the principal dancer.

Srila Bhaktisiddhanta Saraswati Goswami Thakur has written a few words about Raghava Pandit's samadhi tomb in Panihati: "A high platform was built over Raghava Pandit's tomb and it is now overgrown with vines. To the north of the samadhi is a broken down building in which his Madana Mohana deities are present, but much neglected. The service is managed by the principal landlord of Panihati, named Shivachandra Raya Chaudhuri." (*Anubhāṣya,* 1.10.24). Srila Prabhupada wrote these lines in 1932. Sixty years later, it appears that the situation has changed. A new temple and residential building have now been constructed on the site of Raghava Pandit's home.

Sri Kali Das and Jharu Thakur

pulinda-tanayā mallī kālidāso'dhunābhavat

Kali Das was previously the tribal girl named Malli in Vraja. (*Gaura-gaṇoddeśa-dīpikā* 190)

Mahaprabhu's devotee Kali Das was born in a kayastha family. His home was in the village of Bheda or Bhaduwa in Hooglhy district. This village is about three miles south of Raghunath Das Goswami's birthplace in Saptagram Krishnapura and one mile west of the present-day Bandel Junction train station. Jharu Thakur, who was born in a sweeper caste (*bhuṅi-mālī*), lived in the same village. These places are served by the Devanandapura post office. Kali Das' deities used to be worshiped in Shankhanagar village, but have since been moved to Triveni. Jharu Thakur's deity was named Madana Gopal and is still being worshiped in Bhaduwa.

Krishna Das Kaviraj Goswami has glorified these two devotees in his Chaitanya Charitamrita, in the sixteenth chapter of the *Antya-līlā*. There we learn that Kali Das was related to Raghunath Das Goswami as a distant uncle.

He was related to Raghunath Das as an uncle and he made a vow of eating the remnants of the Vaishnavas throughout his life. (Chaitanya Charitamrita 3.16.8)

KALI DAS' DEVOTION TO THE REMNANTS OF THE DEVOTEES

Kali Das was a great devotee who constantly chanted the Holy Names of Krishna. He uttered the words "Hare Krishna" throughout all his activities. His devotion to eating the remnants of the Vaishnavas resulted in his receiving extraordinary blessings from Sri Chaitanya Mahaprabhu. The Lord gives so much mercy to anyone who has faith in the Vaishnavas and eats their remnants that He has nothing left to give.

This is the extent of the glories of the remnants of the devotee's foodstuffs—through dedication to them, Kali Das was able to attain Sri Chaitanya Mahaprabhu's lotus feet. Therefore, set aside your shame and disgust and eat the Vaishnavas' remnants, for by so doing you will be able to fulfill all your desires. The remnants of Krishna's food are called *mahā-prasāda*, but the remnants of the devotee are given the name *mahā-mahā-prasāda*. The dust of a devotee's feet, the water that has washed his feet, and the remnants of his food are three very powerful aids to spiritual practice. All revealed scriptures loudly declare again and again that one can attain the supreme goal of ecstatic love for Krishna through the use of these three substances. So, my dear devotees, please listen to me, for I insist on this point: keep faith in these three substances and render service to them with complete faith. Through these three substances you will taste the joy of sacred love which is found in the holy name of Krishna and you will win Krishna's pleasure. This has been proved by the experience of Kali Das. (Chaitanya Charitamrta 3.16.58-63)

While living in Bengal, Kali Das ate the remnants of all devotees, without taking their caste status into consideration. He would go to their houses with gifts of the finest foodstuffs. After they had finished eating, he would ask for their remnants. If any were unwilling to give him their remnants, he would take them without their knowledge. He would hide and wait for them to throw away the leaf-plates on which they had eaten and lick them clean.

KALI DAS VISITS JHARU THAKUR

All Vaishnavas are worshipable, regardless of the caste in which they have been born. A Vaishnava is beyond the material qualities and is thus not to be identified with his nationality or caste. Anyone who makes a judgment of a devotee on the basis of caste is said to have a hellish mentality. Though Jharu Thakur was born into the Bhuimali, one of Bengal's untouchable castes, he was a great devotee. One day, Kali Das went to Jharu Thakur's house and paid him and his wife obeisances. He then made them a gift of ripe, sweet mangoes. Jharu Thakur recognized Kali Das to be a guest of the highest order. He showed him the appropriate respect and said, "Dear sir, I am of a low caste. Please let me know how I can serve you. Just say the word and I will arrange for food to be cooked for you in a Brahmin's house. If you take prasad there, I will consider myself most fortunate."

Kali Das recognized Jharu Thakur's humility as being appropriate to a Vaishnava and said, "I am extremely fallen. It is only as a result of great good fortune that I have been able to meet you today. If you would only be so kind as to place the dust of your feet on my head."

Jharu Thakur was embarrassed and felt uneasy. Kali Das recited a few verses that glorify the devotees of the Lord:

na me'bhaktaś catur-vedī
mad-bhaktaḥ śva-pacaḥ priyaḥ
tasmai deyaṁ tato grāhyaṁ
sa ca pūjyo yathā hy aham

A scholar learned in the four Vedas is not dear to Me if he is not My devotee, whereas someone born as a dog-eater who is My devotee is very dear to Me. All respect should be given to such a person, and one should accept his gifts, for such devotees are as worshipable as I am. (*Hari-bhakti-vilāsa* 10.29, Chaitanya Charitamrita 3.16.25)

viprād dvi-ṣaḍ-guṇa-yutād aravinda-nābha-
pādāravinda-vimukhāc chva-pacaṁ variṣṭham
manye tad-arpita-mano-vacanehitārtha-
prāṇaṁ punāti sa kulaṁ na tu bhūri-mānaḥ

A person born in a Brahmin family and possessing all twelve Brahminical qualities, but who is adverse to the lotus-navelled Lord Krishna's lotus feet, is inferior to a dog-eater who has dedicated his mind, words, activities, wealth and life to the service of the Lord. Such a person purifies not only his own being, but that of his entire family, whereas one who is proud of his qualifications cannot purify anything.(Srimad Bhagavatam 7.9.10, Chaitanya Charitamrita 3.16.26)

aho bata śva-paco'to garīyān
yaj-jihvāgre vartate nāma tubhyam
tepus tapas te juhuvuḥ sasnur āryā
brahmānūcur nāma gṛṇanti ye te

How wonderful it is! Even a dog-eater who always keeps Your holy name on his tongue is greater than a Brahmin! Despite his low caste, anyone who chants Your names is understood to have performed all kinds of austerities and the great Vedic sacrifices, to have studied all the Vedas, and to have bathed in all the holy places of pilgrimage. Such people belong to the truly noble class of man. (Srimad Bhagavatam 3.33.7, Chaitanya Charitamrita 3.16.27).

Though Jharu Thakur accepted the truth of these scriptural statements, he humbly stated that they were not applicable to him. Kali Das respectfully paid his obeisances and withdrew, and Jharu Thakur politely followed him a short distance before returning to his home. Kali Das took this opportunity to take the dust from Jharu Thakur's footprints and smear it over his entire body. Desiring to take the Thakur's remnants, he then hid not far from his house. When Jharu Thakur entered his house, he placed the mangoes in a banana-bark bowl and mentally offered them to Krishna. His wife then took the mango prasad from the bowl and gave them to her husband. Jharu Thakur ate the mango and, after sucking the seed, placed it back in the bowl. She herself took his remnants and then took the mango seeds and skins and threw the bowl into the refuse pit. When she had gone, Kali Das came and sucked on the seeds and even licked the outside of the skins. As he tasted the remnants of the Vaishnavas, Kali Das was overwhelmed with ecstatic symptoms.

This, then, was Kali Das' procedure as he paid obeisances to all the Vaishnavas in Bengal and ate their food remnants.

KALI DAS RECEIVES MAHAPRABHU'S MERCY IN PURI

Every year, the Bengali devotees went to Puri to visit Mahaprabhu. Kali Das went in the second year of this institution. As the Supersoul, the Lord knew of Kali Das' dedication to the devotees' remnants and so He bestowed profuse blessings upon him. When Mahaprabhu went on his daily visit to the Jagannath temple, He would be accompanied by Govinda who carried his kamandalu (water pot). Mahaprabhu would wash His feet before entering the temple and the water would run off into a pool situated at the bottom of the twenty-two steps at the northern entrance, known as the Singha Dwar. Mahaprabhu gave Govinda the strict order not to allow anyone to touch the water that had washed His feet. Everyone knew this, so no one dared to make the attempt. Only a few intimate devotees found ways to get some of this holy liquid.

One day, as Mahaprabhu was washing His feet as usual, Kali Das came there and stretched out his hand to take some of the water. He drank not just once, not twice, but three times as Mahaprabhu looked on. The Lord only stopped him when he cupped his hands for the fourth time.

The all-knowing Supreme Lord, Chaitanya Mahaprabhu, knew the faith that Kali Das had in the Vaishnavas. Happy with him for this great virtue, He allowed him to win a blessing unavailable to anyone else. (Chaitanya Charitamrita 3.16.48-9)

After visiting Jagannath, Mahaprabhu returned to Kashi Mishra's house to take His midday meal. Kali Das sat outside the door, hoping to receive some of the Lord's remnants. The Lord knew of his desire and, after He had finished eating, He signaled Govinda to bring Him prasad.

This is the wonderful result of eating Vaishnavas' remnants: through so doing, Kali Das attained Chaitanya Mahaprabhu's supreme mercy. Therefore, set aside your shame and disgust and eat the Vaishnavas' remnants, for by so doing you will be able to fulfill all your desires. (Chaitanya Charitamrita 3.16.57-8)

Sri Pradyumna Brahmachari or Sri Nrisinghananda

āveśaś ca tathā jñeyo miśre pradyumna-sañjñake

The Lord's *āveśa* manifestation took place in Pradyumna Mishra. (*Gaura-gaṇoddeśa-dīpikā* 74)

Srila Bhaktisiddhanta Saraswati Goswami Thakur has quoted the above verse in connection with Pradyumna Brahmachari and not for the Orissan Pradyumna Mishra who will be described later in chapter 63 of this volume. In the *Gauḍīya Vaiṣṇava Abhidhāna*, Haridas Das has also taken the same position, since Pradyumna Brahmachari was known to be the Lord's *āveśa*.

THE LORD'S AVIRBHAVA

sākṣāt-darśana, āra yogya-bhakta-jīve
āveśa karaye kāhāṅ, kāhāṅ āvirbhāve

Sri Chaitanya Maharabhu delivered the fallen souls in three different ways: in some places by appearing to them directly in His self-same body, in other places by entering into a worthy devotee (*āveśa*), and in still other places by divine epiphany. His principal method of giving salvation was to appear to the conditioned souls in his self-same body, but he also took possession of Nakula Brahmachari's body and made an apparition before Nrisinghananda Brahmachari. It is the Supreme Lord's nature to declare, "I shall deliver the people of the world."
(Chaitanya Charitamrita 3.2.4-6)

THE NAME NRISINGHANANDA

Mahaprabhu gave Pradyumna Brahmachari the epithet Nrisinghananda because of his absorption in the service of Nrisingha. He is considered to be one of Chaitanya's own branches. (Chaitanya Charitamrita 1.10.35, 3.2.53)

Pradyumna Brahmachari considered himself to be the servant of Nrisingha for Nrisinghadeva manifested himself in his body. He remained by Mahaprabhu's side in the consciousness that Nrisingha himself had appeared in the form of a sannyasi. (Chaitanya Charitamrita 3.3.286-7)

Vrindavan Das Thakur writes in the Chaitanya Bhagavata that Pradyumna conversed directly with Nrisingha Deva. This is mentioned particularly when Pradyumna joined the company of devotees on the annual pilgrimage to Jagannath Puri.

Pradyumna Brahmachari, who talked directly to Lord Nrisingha, walked along as a part of the company of devotees. (Chaitanya Bhagavata 3.8.92)

All those people who think that the body of the Lord is a product of the material nature are atheists who have been bewildered by the Lord's illusory energy. They think that these accounts are tall tales they can criticize out of their false sense of being learned. Anyone who lacks faith in the Supreme Lord is an unfortunate beggar who is cheated of any worthwhile achievement in life. He gains nothing but the birth and death that are the lot for the conditioned soul.

THE POWER OF PRADYUMNA'S MEDITATION

When Mahaprabhu took sannyas in Katwa, He made off for Vrindavan, but Nityananda Prabhu tricked Him into coming back to Shantipur to the house of Advaita Acharya. Afterwards, the Lord continued to Puri in the company of Nityananda Prabhu, Jagadananda Pandit, Mukunda Datta and Damodar Pandit. Shortly thereafter, He left Puri on a pilgrimage through southern India. On His return from South India, He planned a trip to Vrindavan that would take Him on the route along the Ganges through Bengal. On this trip, He stopped at the house of Sarvabhauma Bhattacharya's brother, Vidya Vachaspati, in Vidyanagara, delivered Devananda Pandit and Chapal Gopal from their offenses in Kuliya village, and then met Rupa and Sanatan Goswamis for the first time in Ramakeli.

As Mahaprabhu made this trip, Pradyumna Brahmachari meditated on Him, visualizing himself placing jeweled bricks on the road the Lord was following to make His journey more agreeable. When the Lord reached Kanair Natshala, about 200 miles north of Calcutta in the Santal Paragana district of Bihar state, five miles from the town of Raj Mahal, Pradyumna's meditation suddenly broke. He was immediately able to understand that the Lord would only go as far as Kanair Natshala and no further.

It is said that mental service like that performed by Nrisingha Brahmachari in his meditation is superior to service performed with actual ingredients. Rupa Goswami makes this point in his *Bhakti-rasāmṛta-sindhu* (1.2.182), where he gives the example of the Brahmin from Pratishthanpur who attained the association of Narayan in Vaikuntha as a result of mental service or *mānasī sevā*.

PRADYUMNA BRINGS THE LORD TO KUMARAHATTA

On one occasion, Mahaprabhu was attracted by Nrisinghananda's love to come to Kumarahatta and to appear in the house of Shivananda Sen. This story has been told beautifully by Krishna Das Kaviraj Goswami in the second chapter of the *Antya-līlā* of his Chaitanya Charitamrita.

One year, as Shivananda Sen's nephew Srikanta Sen left Puri, Mahaprabhu told him to convey the message to the Bengali devotees that there was no need for them to come to Puri that year, for He Himself would be visiting Bengal in the month of Paush. When Srikanta came with this news, all the devotees were jubilant in expectation of the Lord's visit. But when the month of Paush had almost come to an end and there was no sign of Mahaprabhu, Shivananda Sen, Jagadananda Pandit and the others who had been waiting anxiously were disheartened by not seeing Him.

At that time, Nrisinghananda happened by and asked everyone the reason for their unhappiness. When he heard that they were disappointed that the Lord had not come, he assured them that he would be able to make Mahaprabhu appear there within three days. Since Shivananda and Jagadananda knew Nrisinghananda's spiritual powers, they believed him.

Nrisinghananda sat down and stayed absorbed in meditation for two days, after which he told Shivananda that Mahaprabhu had arrived in Panihati and that by noon of the next day He would be in Kumarahatta. He ordered Shivananda Sen to supply him with the ingredients for a feast in honor of the Lord. He personally started cooking early in the morning and made a large variety of preparations that he distributed onto three plates to make offerings to Jagannath, Nrisinghadeva and Mahaprabhu. As soon as he sat down in meditation for the offerings, Mahaprabhu personally appeared and ate all three plates, leaving no remnants.

Although Nrisinghananda was overjoyed to see the Lord accept his offerings, he made a pretense of disappointment. He said, since Mahaprabhu and Jagannath are ontologically non-different, there was no fault in his eating the plate set out for Jagannath. But why had he taken the offering intended for Nrisingha? "Nrisinghadeva has fasted today," he said. Indeed, the Lord performed this pastime in order to show that He is not different from Jagannath or Nrisinghadeva.

After eating, Mahaprabhu left for Panihati. Nrisinghananda cried out in distress, causing Shivananda to inquire what was the cause of his troubles. Nrisinghananda answered that the Lord had alone eaten all three plates, leaving Jagannath and Nrisinghadeva to fast. Shivananda Sen had some doubts, but on his request provided him with foodstuffs to prepare a second offering. The brahmachari cooked once again and made an offering to Nrisinghadeva.

The next year, when Shivananda Sen went with the Bengali devotees to Puri, everyone was duly astonished to hear the Lord Himself volunteer the information that He had been to Shivananda's house in the month of Paush and had eaten the delicious offerings made by Nrisinghananda.

One day, the Lord was engaged in conversation in the presence of all the devotees and suddenly began to praise Nrisinghananda's qualities. He said, "Last year in the month of Paush, Nrisinghananda gave Me delicious sweetmeats and vegetables such as I had never eaten." Hearing this, all the devotees were struck with wonder and Shivananda was finally convinced that the incident was true.

(Chaitanya Charitamrita 3.2.76-78)

SRI GADADHAR DAS

rādhā-vibhūti-rūpā yā chandrakāntiḥ purā sthitā
sādya gaurāṅga-nikaṭe dāsa-vaṁśyo gadādharaḥ
pūrṇānandā vraje yāsīd baladeva-priyagraṇīḥ
sāpi kārya-vaś ād eva prāviśat taṁ gadādharam

She who during Krishna's incarnation was Chandrakanti, the manifestation of Radharani's opulence, has become Gadadhar Das by Gauranga's side. Balaram's beloved Purnananda has also entered into him for some special purpose. (*Gaura-gaṇoddeśa-dīpikā* 154-155)

Srila Bhaktisiddhanta Saraswati Goswami Thakur has made the following comments on Gadadhar Das' identity in Krishna lila: "He is Srimati Radharani's effulgence. Just as Srila Gadadhar Pandit Goswami is Srimati Radharani Herself, so Gadadhar Das is an incarnation of Her bodily luster. In the Lord's incarnation as Krishna with the emotions and bodily luster of Srimati Radharani, he is that bodily luster. In the *Gaura-gaṇoddeśa-dīpikā*, he is said to be the manifestation of Radha's opulence. He is counted amongst the followers of both Gaura and Nityananda. As a follower of Gaura, he relished the mood of conjugal love, while as a follower of Nityananda, he is in the mood of pure devotional service in friendship, etc. Although Gadadhar Das was an associate of Nityananda, his mood of friendship is not that of a cowherd boy, but is in the conjugal mood. He established the temple of Gauranga in Katwa." (*Anubhāṣya* to Chaitanya Charitamrita 1.10.53)

Gadadhar Das' home was in Eriyadaha, a village situated 8 miles north of Calcutta on the banks of the Bhagirathi River. After Mahaprabhu's disappearance, Gadadhar moved from Nabadwip to Katwa, and then later to Eriyadaha. In the *Gauḍīya Vaiṣṇava Abhidhāna*, it is said that Gadadhar Das supervised Sachi Mata and Vishnupriya Devi's affairs. When they disappeared, he moved to Katwa where he established the worship of the Gauranga deity on the site where Gadadhar Das' samadhi tomb is situated on the grounds of the Mahaprabhu Bari temple in Katwa, where Keshava Bharati gave Mahaprabhu sannyas. The temple is currently known in Katwa as Mahaprabhur Bari. Gadadhar Das first met with Mahaprabhu when the Lord was making His initial attempt to travel to Vrindavan by taking the route through Bengal, first stopping in Shantipur, then Kumarahatta and then at Raghava Pandit's house in Panihati. At this meeting, Mahaprabhu affectionately placed His lotus feet on Gadadhar's head:

When Gadadhar heard that Mahaprabhu had arrived at Raghava Pandit's house, he ran to see Him. Gadadhar is extremely dear to Mahaprabhu; his body is charged with the joy of devotion. When the Lord saw the pious Gadadhar, He lifted his feet and placed them on his head. (Chaitanya Bhagavata 3.5.92-4)

When Mahaprabhu sent Nityananda from Puri to Gauda Desh to preach the religion of love, Gadadhar Das, Rama Das, Krishna Das Pandit, Paremeshvari Das, Purandara Pandit, Raghunath Vaidya and others accompanied him. On the road from Nilachala, Nityananda and his associates made various extraordinary displays of divine love. Gadadhar Das, the eternal resident of Vraja, took on the transcendental mood of Srimati Radharani, and in the ecstasy of a cowherd girl began to laugh and shout, "Yogurt for sale! Yogurt for sale! Does anyone want to buy some yogurt?" In the mood of the cowherd boy, Abhiram Das Thakur stood for nine hours in the three-fold bending form. Krishna Das and Parameshvari Das also took the mood of cowherd boys, shouting "Hoi! hoi!" as though they were herding cattle. Purandara Pandit climbed up a tree and shouted, "I am Angada!" and then jumped down to the ground.

The mood of Radhika descended on Gadadhar Das. He began to call, "Who will buy yogurt?" and burst out laughing.... Krishna Das and Parameshvari both shouted "Hoi! hoi!" in the spirit of the cowherd boys. (Chaitanya Bhagavata 3.5.238, 240)

When Nityananda Prabhu arrived in Bengal, he visited villages on both banks of the Ganges. Gadadhar Das was still experiencing *gopī-bhāva* and took a jug full of Ganges water and called out to everyone, "Milk! Who wants to buy milk?" When Nityananda saw Gadadhar Das' *bhāva*, he took the Gopal deity from his house and danced, holding it to his chest.

In the mood of a gopi, Gadadhar Das had no consciousness of external reality. He constantly referred to himself as a gopi. (Chaitanya Bhagavata 3.5.381)

Srila Bhaktisiddhanta Saraswati Goswami Thakur writes in his commentary to this verse that though Gadadhar considered himself to be a gopi, he did not dress like a woman. His mood was expressed internally and he had no need to make any artificial, external display.

One day, Nityananda was in the audience at a performance of Krishna's *dāna-līlā* by Madhavananda Ghosh at the house of Gadadhar Das, and he went into a deep trance. For this reason, Gadadhar's house is also known as the place of the *dāna-lila*. The *dāna-līlā* is described elaborately in Rupa Goswami's *Dāna-keli-kaumudī*.

In Gadadhar Das' village of Eriyadaha, there were many people antagonistic to religion who hated the very sound of the congregational chanting of Krishna's names. One of these people was a powerful Muslim administrator, or Kazi. One day, Gadadhar was in a particulary ecstatic mood and walked right into the house of this Kazi, singing the Holy Names at the top of his voice. The Kazi was sitting there in the company of his inner circle and Gadadhar ordered him to chant the Holy Names. The Kazi became very angry at the affront, but when he saw that Gadadhar was in a trance-like state, he calmed down and asked him why he had come. Gadadhar Das answered, "Chaitanya Mahaprabhu and Nityananda Prabhu have descended to this earth to make everyone chant the Holy Names. You are the only one who has not yet done so, so I have come here to make you chant the name of Krishna. If you chant the Holy Names, all your sins will be eradicated."

Although the Kazi was by nature cruel, he laughed and said, "Alright, I will chant Krishna's name tomorrow. Now go home. Gadadhar Das danced jubilantly and said, "What tomorrow? You have just uttered the name of Krishna now! Now that you have taken the name of Hari, you will never again know any inauspiciousness!" (Chaitanya Bhagavata 3.5.409-10)

Gadadhar Das thus converted the irascible Kazi through his otherworldly power. This impossible task became possible because his body had been possessed by Krishna.

This is the glory of Gadadhar Das, who has been counted as one of Chaitanya Mahaprabhu's intimate associates. Just seeing him in his ecstatic devotional mood erases all of one's sinful reactions. (Chaitanya Bhagavata 3.5.413, 727)

Krishna Das Kaviraj Goswami has also written the following about Gadadhar Das in the Chaitanya Charitamrita:

Sri Rama Das and Gadadhar Das were both devotees of Sri Chaitanya Mahaprabhu and stayed with Him. When the Lord ordered Nityananda to return to Bengal, he told both of them to accompany him. Gadadhar Das was always in an ecstatic state in the devotional mood of a gopi. Nityananda put on the *dāna-līlā* performance in his house.
(Chaitanya Charitamrita 1.11.13-17)

Gadadhar was also present when Raghunath Das Goswami put on the yogurt and chipped-rice festival in Panihati on Nityananda's order. Yadunandan Das was Gadadhar Das' disciple. This is stated in the *Bhakti-ratnākara*:

Yadunandan Chakravarti was a very learned scholar whose guru and worshipable Lord was Gadadhar Das.
(*Bhakti-ratnākara* 9.352)

Gadadhar Das' disappearance day is on the eighth day of the waning moon (*kṛṣṇā aṣṭamī*) of the month of Karttik. Srinivas Acharya put on a huge festival on the occasion of Gadadhar Das' disappearance day. Like the one at Kheturi, this festival was greatly renowned throughout the Vaishnava community.

What can I say about Karttik *kṛṣṇā aṣṭamī*? My prabhu disappeared here on that day. (*Bhakti-ratnākara* 9.362)

Gadadhar Das' samadhi tomb is situated on the grounds of the Mahaprabhu Bari temple in Katwa.

Sri Vasudeva Datta Thakur

vraje sthitau gāyakau yau madhukaṇṭha-madhuvratau
mukunda-vāsudevau tau dattau gaurāṅga-gāyakau

The two singers in Vraja named Madhukantha and Madhuvrata appeared in Chaitanya lila as Mukunda and Vasudeva Datta, who were singers in the society of Lord Chaitanya Mahaprabhu. (*Gaura-gaṇoddeśa-dīpikā* 140)

VASUDEVA'S FAMILY BACKGROUND

Sri Vasudeva Datta was born in the Chittagong district of modern Bangladesh, in the village of Chanhara, which is under the jurisdiction of the police station named Patiya. This village is situated ten krośas, or about twenty miles, from the village of Mekhala where Pundarika Vidyanidhi made his home. Mahaprabhu's associate Mukunda Datta was Vasudeva Datta's brother.

In the book *Prema-vilāsa*, it is said that Vasudeva was the older of the two and that they were born in an Ambashtha family:

In the district of Chittagong, there is a village named Cakrashala where a respectable family of Ambashtha physicians named Datta lives. Two great devotees, Mukunda and Vasudeva Datta, were born into this family. Both Vasudeva the older and Mukunda the younger came to Nabadwip to live.

VASUDEVA THE KIRTANIYA

Vasudeva Datta Thakur had a beautiful voice and was also well versed in the *Saṅgīta-śāstra*. He was one of Mahaprabhu's chief associates in Nabadwip, participating in sankirtan in the home of Srivas and the streets of the town. Mahaprabhu enjoyed his association because of his Vaishnava qualities.

Vasudeva Datta is a respected servant of the Lord. A thousand tongues are insufficient to sing his glories.
(Chaitanya Charitamrita 1.10.41)

Mahaprabhu said, "Even though Mukunda has been My companion since childhood, I get even more pleasure when I see you." (Chaitanya Charitamrita 2.11.138)

Vasudeva had a particularly close friendship with Srivas Pandit and Shivananda Sen. He lived near Kumarahatta and Kanchra Para, which were the homes of these two great associates of the Lord. Vasudeva was very generous by nature. Never thinking of himself, he spent his money liberally for others. Mahaprabhu saw this and asked Shivananda Sen to become his *sarkhel* and supervise his affairs.

VASUDEVA'S COMPASSION

Vasudeva was so distressed by the suffering of the living beings that he was ready to accept their sins and suffer in hell for them, and he prayed emotionally to Mahaprabhu for such a boon:

"My Lord! You have appeared in this world to save it, so please accept my prayer. You are omnipotent and all-merciful, so if You agree to fulfill my request, it can be easily done. When I see the suffering of the world, my heart is torn apart. So I ask you, Lord, give their sins to me. I will take their sins and suffer in hell on their behalf, but please deliver them from their material disease."
(Chaitanya Charitamrita 2.15.160-163)

He wished to take the sins of every single living being and suffer in hell in their place so that they could be liberated. (Chaitanya Charitamrita 1.10.42)

When Mahaprabhu heard this emotional plea on behalf of the living beings of the world, he said to Vasudeva:

"You have desired the liberation of all the living beings in the entire universe, so it will happen. They will be saved without having to suffer the consequences of their sins. Krishna is not incapable of it. He has all powers, so why should He make you suffer for their sins? Those whose welfare you desire will all become Vaishnavas, and Krishna removes the sins of the Vaishnavas."

(Chaitanya Charitamrita 2.15.167-169)

Srila Bhaktisiddhanta Saraswati Goswami Thakur writes in his *Anubhāṣya* to the Chaitanya Charitamrita: "In the Western world, Christians believe that only their guru, Jesus Christ, appeared in this world out of a desire to suffer on behalf of the people of the world by accepting their sins. But here we see that amongst Mahaprabhu's associates, Vasudeva Datta Thakur, like Hari Das Thakur, showed a compassion millions of times greater and more generous, as he was willing to suffer in the place of all creatures in the universe. By so doing, he taught the world the unlimited nature of the Vaishnava's selfless love."

Raghunath Das Goswami's diksha guru, Yadunandan Acharya, was blessed by Vasudeva Datta. The author of Chaitanya Bhagavata, Vrindavan Das Thakur, was born in Mamgachi in Modadrumdwip, one mile from the Purvasthali station on the Howrah-Katwa line of the Eastern Railway. Vasudeva Datta consecrated the worship of the Madana Gopal deity that is still being worshiped at this site.

We can see how dear Vasudeva Datta was to Mahaprabhu by the Lord's statements made when he was visiting Srivas Pandit's house in Kumarahatta:

Gaurachandra repeated again and again, "This body of Mine belongs to Vasudeva. If he wants to sell Me, I allow Myself to be sold; I will not act against his wish. This is the truth I announce to you all. If someone has even come into the briefest contact with Vasudeva Datta, he will be protected by Krishna. Listen all you Vaishnavas! I tell you the truth: this body of Mine belongs to Vasudeva alone."

(Chaitanya Bhagavata 3.5.27-30)

Srila Mahesh Pandit

maheśa-paṇḍitaḥ śrīman-mahābāhur vraje sakhā

In Vraja, Mahesh Pandit was Krishna's cowherd friend, Mahabahu. (*Gaura-gaṇoddeśa-dīpikā* 129)

Mahesh Pandit was one of the *Dvādaśa-gopala*, or twelve cowherd boys. His home (Sripat) was first situated in Masipur across the river from Jirat on the eastern bank of the Ganges. When Masipur fell into the river, the Sripat was moved to Beledanga near Sukhasagar. Here too, the banks of the Ganges fell into the river causing the destruction of the village. Once again the Sripat was moved, this time to its present location in Pal Para near Chakdaha. This last move took place in the Bengali year 1334, or 1927 AD. Pal Para is situated within the Panchnagar administrative block. Srila Bhaktisiddhanta Saraswati Goswami Thakur mentions in his commentary to Chaitanya Charitamrita 1.10.32 that this final resting place for Mahesh Pandit's Sripat is in Kanthal Puli.

Mahesh Pandit is also considered to be a branch of both Nityananda and Chaitanya Mahaprabhu. Some people say that he was the youngest brother of Jagadish Pandit (see page 14), whose Sripat is in nearby Jashra. According to this opinion, there were three brothers in the family, Jagadish, Hiranya and Mahesh.

Mahesh Pandit's Sripat is a small construction in the style of an ordinary residential building. It houses Gaura-Nityananda deities, as well as Sri Gopinath, Madanamohana, Radha-Govinda and a Shalagram Shila. In front of the temple building is a memorial to Mahesh Pandit, his *puṣpa-samādhi*.

Sri Mahesh Pandit participated in the Chira-dadhi Mahotsava ("the festival of chipped rice and yogurt") in Panihati, after which he followed Nityananda Prabhu to Saptagram. He was present in Khardaha when Narottam Das Thakur came there to pay a visit (*Bhakti-ratnākara* 8.220). Mahesh Pandit, like all of Nityananda Prabhu's associates, resembled him in being extremely magnanimous and devoted to the salvation of all the fallen living beings. In his ecstasies of devotional love, he would dance madly.

Mahesh Pandit was a magnanimous cowherd boy. In his love for Krishna, he would dance to the sound of kettledrums like a madman.

(Chaitanya Charitamrita 1.11.32)

His name is also mentioned in Chaitanya Bhagavata; Vrindavan Das Thakur calls him a great soul, *parama-mahanta.* (Chaitanya Bhagavata 3.6).

His disappearance day is celebrated on the thirteenth day of the dark moon (*kṛṣṇā trayodaśī*) in Paush.

Sri Gauri Das Pandit

subalo yaḥ priya-śreṣṭhaḥ sa gaurīdāsa-paṇḍitaḥ |

In Vraja, Gauri Das Pandit was Subala, one of the twelve Gopals. He is one of Nityananda Prabhu's dearest associates. (*Gaura-gaṇoddeśa-dīpikā* 128)

Gauri Das Pandit was most fortunate. His body, mind and soul were all devoted to Nityananda Prabhu.

(Chaitanya Bhagavata 3.5.730)

GAURI DAS' TEMPLE IN AMBIKA

Gauri Das' first residence was in the village known as Shaligram, not far from Muragacha, just a few kilometers north of Mayapur. Later he moved to Ambika Kalna in Burdwan district, where his Sripat is extremely well known. His father's name was Kamsari Mishra and his mother was Kamala Devi. Kamsari Mishra belonged to the Vatsa gotra, and their family name was Ghoshal. Gauri Das was the fourth of six sons. His three older brothers were named Damodar, Jagannath and Surya Das. Surya Das, whose title was Sarkhel, gave his two daughters, Vasudha and Jahnava, in marriage to Nityananda Prabhu. Gauri Das Pandit's younger brothers were named Krishna Das Sarkhel and Nrisingha Chaitanya.

Pandit Surya Das Sarkhel was a very magnanimous person. His younger brother was named Gauri Das. Gauri Das Pandit took permission from his older brother before moving from Shaligram to Ambika.
(*Bhakti-ratnākara* 7.330-1)

Gauri Das and his disciple Hriday Chaitanya left only a line of initiated disciples and not one of family descendants. The *Gauḍīya Vaiṣṇava Abhidhāna* states that Gauri Das Pandit and his wife Bimala Devi had two sons, Balaram and Raghunath. Srila Bhaktisiddhanta Saraswati Goswami Thakur, however, did not accept the validity of this family connection. He has written as follows in his *Anubhāṣya:* "Gauri Das Pandit's disciple was named Hriday Chaitanya Das. His disciple was the son of Gauri Das Pandit's daughter Annapurna Devi, Gopiraman. It is the family descendants of this Gopiraman who are the current owners of the Ambika Sripat."
(*Anubhāṣya* to Chaitanya Charitamrita 1.11.26)

The current temple at Ambika houses deities of Gauri Das, Radha-Krishna, Gaura-Nityananda, Jagannath, Balaram, and Sita-Rama. As one enters the temple grounds, there is a large tamarind tree. It is said that Mahaprabhu and Gauri Das met under this very tree. Other valuable items held in the temple are a paddle used by Mahaprabhu Himself and a Bhagavad-Gita said to have been handcopied by the Lord.

One day Gauranga crossed the Ganges from Shantipur to visit Ambika. He told Gauri Das Pandit, "I was in Shantipur and from there I went to Harinadi village and took a boat to come here. I have brought one of the paddles with me—here, take it. Use it to take the fallen living beings across the river of material suffering." So saying, the Lord embraced him.
(*Bhakti-ratnākara* 7.333-6)

Fortunate souls can still see the Gita that the Lord gave to Gauri Das as well as the paddle when they visit the deities in Ambika. (*Bhakti-ratnākara* 7.341)

Nityananda Prabhu made no distinctions between those who were qualified or unqualified, but simply gave Krishna prema to everyone as though intoxicated. His intimate associate, Gauri Das Pandit, similarly displayed a great power in preaching.

Gauri Das was possessed of great spiritual power. He was able to give or take Krishna prema to anyone. He surrendered everything he had to Nityananda and made Chaitanya and Nityananda the masters of his life and soul.
(Chaitanya Charitamrita 1.11.26-7)

Surya Das Sarkhel's house and temple are also in Ambika, a little to the west of Gauri Das Pandit's Sripat. Bhagavan Das Babaji's ashram is also a little further west of there.

MAHAPRABHU VISITS KALNA

A wonderful story is told about Mahaprabhu and Gauri Das Pandit in Ambika Kalna. It is said that on the day that Mahaprabhu paddled across the Ganges to come to visit Gauri Das, He sat under the tamarind tree in the courtyard. Gauri Das asked Mahaprabhu to stay permanently with him in Ambika. In order to fulfill His devotee's desire, Mahaprabhu revealed that His form and that of Nityananda Prabhu were hidden in a nearby neem tree. Gauri Das took this as a hint to have images of Gaura-Nitai carved from its wood. It is also said that Nityananda was physically present when these deities were being carved.

When Mahaprabhu and Nityananda Prabhu were about to leave, Gauri Das did everything in his power to hold them back. Mahaprabhu calmed him by saying, "Nityananda and I are directly present in these forms. You can tell either the deities to go, or we can leave. You choose." Naturally, Gauri Das chose the real Gaura-Nitai to stay and said that the deities could leave. So this is what happened, demonstrating the truth of the Chaitanya Charitamrita's statement:

nāma vigraha svarupa, ei tina eka-rūpa
tine bheda nāhi tina cidānanda-rūpa

These three, the name, the deity form and the original form of the Lord, are all one. No distinction should be made between them, for all three are of transcendental, spiritual substance.
(Chaitanya Charitamrita 2.17.131)

Subsequently, conquered by Gauri Das' love for Them, the deities would physically eat everything that he offered to them.

Gauri Das' samadhi is in Vrindavan, indicating that he finished his life there. According to *Bhakti-ratnākara,* Jahnava Devi visited her uncle's samadhi tomb when she came to Vraja.

When she saw Gauri Das Pandit's samadhi, torrents of tears fell from her eyes and she could do nothing to stop them. (*Bhakti-ratnākara* 11.259)

Gauri Das Pandit Goswami disappeared in the month of Shravan on the *śuklā dvādaśī,* the twelfth day of the waxing moon.

Sri Abhiram Thakur (Sri Rama Das)

purā śrīdāma-nāmāsīd abhirāmo'dhunā mahān
dvātriṁśatā janair eva vāhyaṁ kāṣṭham uvāha saḥ

He who was previously known as Sridama is today Abhiram Thakur. He picked up a piece of wood that took 32 men to lift. (*Gaura-gaṇoddeśa-dīpikā* 126)

Abhiram Thakur lived with his wife Malini in the village of Khanakul Krishnagar in the Hooghly district. Khana refers to the Dvarakeshwar River, *kūla* means banks; thus, the village of Krishnagar on the banks of the Dvarakeshwar River is also known as Khanakula Krishnagar. At the doors of his temple stands a large bakula tree known as the Siddha Bakula, and the place is popularly called Siddha Bakula Kunj. This is the place where Abhiram Thakur first sat down when he arrived in the village. The Gopinath deity was found when the digging for an artificial pond first began. This pond goes by the name of Sri Abhiram Kund. The temple also houses the deities of Vrajavallabha, Gopal and a Shalagram Shila.

Sri Abhiram Thakur was a very vigorous and powerful acharya. He engaged in preaching on the orders of Lord Nityananda and saved many atheists and people opposed to the Vaishnava religion.

Abhiram Goswami possessed a fiery temper and great spiritual power. The atheists trembled whenever they saw him. He was intoxicated, as if he had been possessed by Nityananda, and his enchanting mercies are famed throughout the world. (*Bhakti-ratnākara* 4.103-4)

Abhiram Das was fully absorbed in the mood of friendship. He lifted a flute that contained sixteen knots. (Chaitanya Charitamrita 1.10.116)

This Chaitanya Charitamrita verse is making reference to the same piece of wood that according to the *Gaura-gaṇoddeśa-dīpikā* would have taken 32 people to lift. The *Bhakti-ratnākara* states that it would have taken hundreds of people to pick it up. After Abhiram Das lifted it, he held it like a flute.

He held in his hands a piece of wood that a hundred men could not move, in the way one holds a flute. (*Bhakti-ratnākara* 4.123)

The devotees were greatly astonished when they saw him perform such superhuman feats. According to one legend, whenever Abhiram Thakur paid his obeisances to a stone or statue, if it was not a Vishnu Shila or a consecrated deity, it would crack or be reduced to powder. Non-devotees were also unable to tolerate his *praṇāmas*. Nityananda's son Virachandra Goswami and his daughter Ganga Devi survived his obeisances, and this confirmed their divine status. These things are written in the *aṣṭakas* (eight-verse Sanskrit hymns) composed by Abhiram Thakur in their name.

Srila Abhiram Thakur possessed an amazing whip that he named Jaya-maṅgala. Anyone touched by this whip would immediately experience the transcendental ecstasies of prema. One day Srinivas Acharya visited Abhiram Thakur who gave him three lashes with that whip. Abhiram's wife Malini stopped her husband from hitting him again, saying that Srinivas was just a young lad who wouldn't be able to tolerate the effects of divine love. Nevertheless, Srinivas Acharya was very dear to Abhiram and received many blessings from him. Though not his initiated disciple, he was like a disciple to him. The Jaya-maṅgala whip is still held in the Krishnagar temple.

In the *Bhakti-ratnākara*, the following statement is also made:

O Srinivas! How much more can I say? Abhiram descended into this world in order to deliver it. Taking birth in a Brahmin family, he became a scholar in all the scriptures and an unequalled musician, not only in song and playing musical instruments, but in dance also. He married at Nityananda Balaram's request. His wife Malini is also indescribably powerful. (*Bhakti-ratnākara* 4.105-8)

Many people say that the Bali Math in Puri was also established by Abhiram Thakur. An annual festival is held in Khanakula Krishnagar on his disappearance day, the Chaitra *kṛṣṇā saptamī*. Our parama-guru, Jagad-guru Srila Bhaktisiddhanta Saraswati Goswami Thakur visited this site when travelling on the parikrama of Sri Gaura Mandala. At that time, the devotees in charge of the temple greeted him with great hospitality and honored him and his followers with special treatment.

Sri Paramesvara Das Thakur (Sri Parameshvari Das)

nāmnārjunaḥ sakhā prāg yo dāsa sa parameśvaraḥ |

Paramesvara Das Thakur was previously Arjuna, one of Krishna's twelve cowherd boyfriends. (*Gaura-gaṇoddeśa-dīpikā* 132)

Srila Parameshvari Thakur appeared in a Vaidya family. He made his home in Antpur, a village that was previously known as Bishakhali. The Antpur station is on the Champadanga branch of the Howrah-Amta rail line. Parameshvari Thakur's Sripat is not far from the train station and near the old Radha-Govinda temple established by the diwan (chief minister) of Burdwan's king, Tej Bahadur.

After the Lord took sannyas in Katwa, he headed for

Vrindavan in a state of divine intoxication before being diverted to Advaita Acharya's house in Shantipur by Nityananda Prabhu. Sachi Mata and the other devotees from Nabadwip all came to see the Lord there. At His mother's request, Mahaprabhu agreed to stay in Puri and took the path through Chatrabhoga to Nilachala in the company of Nityananda, Mukunda, Jagadananda and Damodar.

The first time that the Lord wished to go to Vrindavan from Nilachala, He came through Bengal, though He was eventually unsuccessful, he passed through Panihati, Kumarahatta, Kuliya, Ramakeli, Kanair Natshala, and Shantipur before returning to Puri. When Nrisinghananda Brahmachari heard that Mahaprabhu was going to Vrindavan, he meditated on the Lord's route, imagining a road of jewels as far as Kanair Natshala, when he realized that this was as far as the Lord would go, and that he would not make it to Vrindavan this time. Thousands of people were accompanying the Lord at this time. When he arrived at Kanair Natshala, he remembered Sanatan Goswami's advice:

"To go on pilgrimage with such a large company of devotees is not recommended. You are going to Vrindavan with an entourage of hundreds and thousands of people, and this is not a fitting way to go on a pilgrimage."
(Chaitanya Charitamrita 2.1.222-4)

On His way back to Nilachala, Mahaprabhu stopped at Advaita's house in Shantipur. This time He was accompanied by Balabhadra Bhattacharya and Damodar Pandit. When the Lord returned from Gaya, He also went as far as Kanair Natshala where He had a vision of Muralidhar Sri Krishna, who embraced Him before He disappeared (Chaitanya Bhagavata 2.2.179-85). Once He returned to Nilachala, Mahaprabhu told Nityananda Prabhu to go with his own associates to Bengal to deliver the lowborn, foolish and fallen people. Amongst his associates at that time were Sri Rama Das, Gadadhar Das, Raghunath Vaidya, Krishna Das Pandit, Parameshvari Das and Purandara Pandit. While travelling with Nityananda, these devotees displayed various ecstatic moods. These are described in the Chaitanya Bhagavata:

Krishna Das Pandit, Parameshvari Das and Purandara Pandit were all enthusiastic to join Nityananda. So all of his personal associates accompanied him on this journey back to Bengal. Before starting off, Nityananda first empowered them by saturating them with Krishna prema. They all completely forgot their external identities. There was no end to the variety of ecstatic moods that manifested in each one of their bodies.
(Chaitanya Bhagavata 3.5.232-235)

Parameshvari Das and Krishna Das both shouted "*Hoi! Hoi!*" in the spirit of cowherd boys.
(Chaitanya Bhagavata 3.5.240)

Parameshvari Das was one of the most important of Nityananda Prabhu's companions, who appeared specifically to enrich his pastimes. Nityananda Prabhu considered him to be his very own life. This too is stated in the Chaitanya Bhagavata:

Parameshvari Das is Nityananda's life. Nityananda used his body as an extension of his own.
(Chaitanya Bhagavata 3.5.732)

It is also stated in the Chaitanya Bhagavata that Mahaprabhu manifested Himself in the Gauranga deity Parameshvari Das worshiped in Antpur.

Purandara Pandit and Parameshvari Das both saw the manifestation of Gaurachandra in the deity. As soon as they saw Him, they ran towards Him and fell down, crying in the ecstasy of love. (Chaitanya Bhagavata 3.5.95-6)

It is said in the *Bhakti-ratnākara* that Parameshvari Das was in the entourage of Nityananda's shakti, Jahnava Mata, when she went to the Kheturi festival.

Jahnava Ishvari happily walked in the company of Gauranga, Nakari Krishna Das, Damodar, Parameshvari, the learned Balaram, Mukunda, Vrindavan Das, etc.
(*Bhakti-ratnākara* 10.376-7)

Sri Parameshvari Das Thakur also accompanied Jahnava Mata on her last trip to Vraja Dham and witnessed her merging into the body of Srimati Radhika in the Gopinath temple. On Jahnava's order he established the worship of Radha-Gopinath deities in Antpur.

Once back from Vraja, Parameshvari Das stayed for some time in Khardaha and Garalagacha village in Puri district. When Narottam Das came to Khardaha, Parameshvari gave him directions to Puri.

In Chaitanya Charitamrita, it is written that just by remembering Parameshvari Das one can attain love for Krishna.

Parameshvari Das took exclusive shelter of Nityananda Prabhu. Whoever remembers him attains devotion to Krishna. (Chaitanya Charitamrita 1.11.29)

Sri Parameshvari Das had miraculous powers. On one occasion, he was dancing in ecstasy during Harinam sankirtan at the house of Kamalakar Pippalai in the town of Akna Mahesh, which is situated near Serampore. Hearing the sounds of the kirtan and seeing the ecstatic dancing caused some of the local atheists to become very envious. They decided to pollute the kirtan area and teach the devotees a lesson, so they threw a dead jackal in the midst of the kirtan group. But Parameshvari did not stop dancing for a moment. By the force of his kirtan, the jackal came back to life and started to howl along with the kirtan. The other devotees were astonished by this display of power and were overcome by transcendental joy. This incident has been mentioned in the *Vaiṣṇava-vandanā*:

I very attentively worship Parameshvari Das, who made a jackal come back to life during sankirtan.

In front of the temple in Antpur are two huge bakula trees and a kadamba tree. Between them is the samadhi tomb of Parameshvari Das, over which is a tulasi altar. It is said that bakula trees grew from the branch of a tree that grew there during the time of Parameshvari Thakur. Every year, the kadamba tree produces a flower that is used for the worship of the deities. Parameshvari Thakur's *tirobhāva (disappearance)* festival is held every year on the *vaiśākhī pūrṇimā*.

Sri Uddharan Datta Thakur

Uddharan Datta was the best of the Bhagavatas, who served Nityananda's lotus feet in every way possible.
(Chaitanya Charitamrita 1.11.41)

Whenever the Supreme Divinity, Nandanandan Sri Krishna, adopts the devotional mood and bodily luster of Srimati Radharani in order to become Sri Krishna Chaitanya, He is always accompanied by His eternal associates, who join Him in order to enrich His pastimes. Thus, Krishna's primary expansion or *prakāśa*, Baladeva, accepts the attitude of a devotee as Sri Nityananda Prabhu, appearing in Ekachakra village in order to embellish Mahaprabhu's lila. He too has his entourage of personal confidantes who descend to this earth to assist him in playing his role. Nityananda is Baladeva Tattva: he is none other than Lord Sesa, the source of three *puruṣāvatāras*, Maha Sankarshan's causal form or *mūla* Sankarshan. His chief companions are known as the *Dvādaśa-gopālas* or twelve cowherds. Thus it is stated in the *Gaura-gaṇoddeśa-dīpikā* (129):

subāhur yo vraje gopo datta uddhāraṇākhyakaḥ |

THE COWHERD NAMED SUBAHU BECAME UDDHARAN.

Uddharan Datta Thakur is thus one of the Twelve Gopals. In order to assist Nityananda in his incarnation, he took birth in the town of Saptagram in the year 1481 AD. Saptagram is in Hooghly district, near the Trishbigha railway station. His parents were named Srikara and Bhadravati and they belonged to the gold merchant class. Any caste in which a Vaishnava appears is to be considered holy—the earth itself is blessed by the appearance of a Vaishnava—and his or her mother has achieved the perfection of motherhood. Vrindavan Das has thus written:

Nityananda remained a few days in Khardaha and then went on to Saptagram with his troupe of associates. They stayed at the home of the fortunate Uddharan Datta on the banks of the Triveni. Completely surrendered to the feet of Nityananda Prabhu, Uddharan Datta worshiped him without any false pretense... The entire caste of gold merchants was purified by the presence of Uddharan Datta in its midst, of this there can be no doubt.

(Chaitanya Bhagavata 3.5.443, 449-50, 453)

jāti-kula saba nirarthaka jānāite
janmāilena haridāse mleccha-kulete

In order to show that one's caste and family background are completely irrelevent, Hari Das Thakur took birth in an outcaste family.

Sri Krishna Chaitanya and Nityananda wanted to teach that a great devotee may appear in any family in any caste, and so they had some of their devotees take birth in such households.

One who takes birth in a low-class family is not disqualified from performing devotional service, nor is one who is born in a pure, high-class Brahminical family automatically qualified for such service. Whoever engages in the worship of the Lord is a great person; one who does not worship is rejected. (Chaitanya Charitamrita 3.4.66-7)

arcye śiladhīr guruṣu nara-matir vaiṣṇave jātibuddhir
viṣṇor vā vaiṣṇavānāṁ kalimala-mathane
padatīrthe "mbubuddhiḥ
śrī-viṣṇor nāmni mantre sakala-kaluṣahe
śabda-sāmānya-buddhir
viṣṇau sarveśvareśe tad-itara-samadhīr yasya vā nārakī saḥ

Anyone who considers the deity to be nothing but stone, the guru to be an ordinary human being, or the Vaishnava to be a member of a particular caste or race, who takes the holy water which has washed Vishnu or the Vaishnava's feet and can destroy all the sins of the age of Kali to be ordinary water, who thinks that the name or mantra of Vishnu, which destroys all evils, is the same as any other sound, or who takes Vishnu to be equal to anything other than him, has a hellish nature. (*Padma-purāṇa*)

Anyone who sees a Vaishnava in terms of his material birth is destined for a hellish existence. Subahu took birth in a family of gold merchants, but this does not mean that he was a gold merchant—he was an eternal associate of the Lord beyond the material qualities. One cannot understand the underlying nature or ontological aspect of the Lord and His devotees by using the gross or subtle material senses; one can only get a superficial understanding of their morphological or external aspect. The true nature of the devotee and the Supreme Lord is revealed to the surrendered heart. If Uddharan Datta Thakur is merciful, one can understand his transcendental nature and his divine glories.

Amongst deities, Vishnu is supreme. Only by uttering the name of Vishnu can all of one's sins be burned up, all inauspiciousness in one's destiny be destroyed and auspiciousness gained. A single utterance of the name of Rama equals a thousand repetitions of the name of Vishnu.

rāma rāmeti rāmeti rame rāme manorame
sahasra-nāmabhis tulyaṁ rāmanāma varānane

Oh sweet-faced Durga, I take great pleasure in chanting the names of Rama, Rama, Rama. A single utterance of the name of Rama is equivalent to a recital of the thousand names of Vishnu. (*Padma-purāṇa, Uttara-khaṇḍa,* 72.335; Chaitanya Charitamrita 2.9.32)

sahasra-nāmnāṁ puṇyānāṁ trirāvṛttyā tu yat phalam
ekāvṛttyā tu kṛṣṇasya nāmaikaṁ tat prayacchati

The fruits of three recitals of the thousand names of Lord Vishnu are attained by a single utterance of the name of Krishna. (*Brahmaṇḍa-purāṇa, Laghu-bhāgavatāmṛta.*1.631, Chaitanya Charitamrita 2.9.33)

Even though the name of Krishna and the Krishna mantra are supremely powerful, offenses are taken into consideration in its chanting. Even negligent chanting of the Holy Name (*nāmābhāsa*) can destroy all sins and give one liberation. Nevertheless, if one commits offenses, the benefits of *nāmābhāsa* are lost. Lord Krishna withholds His mercy from the offensive person. The difference between a sin (*pāpa*) and an offense (*aparādha*) is the following: an improper act committed toward a conditioned embodied being is a sin, whereas a similar improper act committed toward Vishnu or the Vaishnava is an offense. An offense has more grave consequences than a sin. Ajamila was a great sinner, but because he had committed no offenses, he was delivered by the power of *nāmābhāsa*. Lord Sri Chaitanya Mahaprabhu and Nityananda Prabhu delivered everyone, both sinners and offenders.

There are offenses to be considered while chanting the Hare Krishna mantra. Therefore simply by chanting Hare Krishna, the offender does not become ecstatic. But these considerations do not exist where Lord Chaitanya and Nityananda are concerned. So as soon as one chants the name, he feels the ecstasy of love for God.
(Chaitanya Charitamrita 1.8.24,31)

Bhaktivinoda Thakur glosses the above verse in the following way: "If one takes shelter of Lord Chaitanya and Nityananda in faith, He is very quickly cleansed of all offenses. Thus as soon as he chants the Hare Krishna Maha Mantra, he feels the ecstasy of love for God."

Krishna Das Kaviraj Goswami has glorified Nityananda Prabhu's quality of being merciful to the most fallen in the following words:

Nityananda is the incarnation of mercy; he is so intoxicated by ecstatic love that he does not discriminate between the good and the bad. He delivers anyone who falls down before him. Therefore he has delivered such a sinful and fallen person as me.
(Chaitanya Charitamrita 1.5.208-9)

Srila Vrindavan Das Thakur has particularly given extensive glorifications of Nityananda Prabhu. The sinful and offensive living beings of this world have no alternative but the mercy of Nityananda Prabhu if they want to be delivered. Even though Nityananda is *Bhagavat-tattva*, he behaves as a devotee. All of his associates are expansions of his mercy. Nityananda Prabhu is said to be the deliverer of the most fallen; his companions seek out even more fallen souls to deliver. In fact, Nityananda distributes his mercy to the conditioned souls through his devotees.

As one of Nityananda's closest confidantes, Uddharan Datta Thakur is called *parama-parama-patita-pāvana*, "the deliverer of the most fallen amongst the most fallen". Thus any jiva who takes shelter of Uddharan Datta Thakur is quickly delivered from his material entanglements and attains the service of Nityananda Prabhu and Gauranga Prabhu's lotus feet. Therefore Krishna Das Kaviraj Goswami describes him as the best of the *mahā-bhāgavatas* and Vrindavan Das Thakur writes in the Chaitanya Bhagavata: "Uddharan Datta is a great and magnanimous Vaishnava, who has a title to the service of Nityananda Prabhu."

From a superficial point of view, Uddharan Datta worked as the manager of a big zamindar (Nairaja) of Naihati, about one and a half miles north of Katwa. The relics of this wealthy family are still visible not far from the Dain Hat station. The village where Uddharan Datta Thakur lived while acting as the manager of the estate was named Uddharanpur.

Though he possessed a vast fortune, Uddharan Datta renounced all sense gratifications, dedicating his sense activities to the service of Nityananda Prabhu. Being controlled by the love of his devotee, Nityananda enjoyed the foodstuffs that Uddharan had cooked.

bhaktera dravya prabhu kāṛi kāṛi khāya
abhaktera dravya-pāne ulaṭi nā cāya

The Lord grabs the offerings given him by his devotee. That which is given him by a non-devotee is of no interest to him.

Saptagram stands on the banks of the Saraswati River. At Uddharan Datta's Sripat, one can still see the six-armed figure of Mahaprabhu that he personally worshiped. On the right side of Sri Chaitanya Mahaprabhu is a deity of Sri Nityananda. On another altar are the figures of Radha Govinda and a Shalagram Shila, and below the throne is a picture of Sri Uddharan Datta Thakur. After Uddharan Datta disappeared, Jahnava Devi made an auspicious visit to his home.

Krishna Das Kaviraj Goswami writes in the Chaitanya Charitamrita that his brother did not have as much faith in Nityananda Prabhu as he had in Chaitanya Mahaprabhu. This was the cause of an argument between his brother and Nityananda's follower Minaketana Rama Das. Krishna Das took Rama Das' side in this argument and rebuked his brother. Nityananda Prabhu was pleased with Krishna Das for having supported his devotee, even though this was a fairly ordinary qualification. Nityananda gave Krishna Das a vision of himself, the right to live in Vrindavan and service to the lotus feet of Radha and Krishna. The conclusion is this that if we worship Uddharan Datta Thakur, serve him and try to please him, we will quickly be able to get the mercy of Lord Nityananda Prabhu, through which we will become eligible to attain love for Krishna and thus perfect our lives. In order to attract people to Uddharan Datta's Sripat it is necessary to make repairs to the buildings on the site. Through this, people will become aware of his glories and will seek his mercy and become blessed. If one makes an effort to serve the devotee, then he will give the commensurate power to serve.

In front of the Saptagram temple, a large hall has been constructed, in front of which is a shady, cool terrace covered by a madhavi creeper.

Srinivas Datta Thakur was Uddharan Datta's only son. Their descendants have spread into many branches and today live in Calcutta, Hooghly and many other places. Those who have taken birth in this family are doubtlessly very fortunate individuals. We pray that they abandon the superficial illusory family connection and establish their transcendental relation with him.[10]

Uddharan Datta Thakur left this world in the Shaka year 1463 (1552), on the *kṛṣṇā trayodaśī* of the month of Paush.

[10] The following comments are added in A. C. Bhaktivedānta Swami's commentary on Chaitanya *Charitāmṛta* 1.11.41: "When we returned from America in 1967, the executive committee members of this temple invited us to visit it, and thus we had the opportunity to visit this temple with some American students. Formerly, in our childhood, we visited this temple with our parents because all the members of the *suvarṇa-vaṇik* community enthusiastically take interest in this temple of Uddharan Datta Thakur. In the Bengali year 1283 (AD 1876) a babaji named Nitai Das arranged for a donation of twelve bighas of land for this temple. The management of the temple later deteriorated, but then in 1306 (AD 1899), through the cooperation of the famous Balaram Mullik of Hooghly, who was an assistant magistrate, and many rich *suvarṇa-vaṇik* (gold merchant) community members, the management of the temple improved greatly. Not more than fifty years ago, one of the family members of Uddharan Datta Thakur named Jagamohana Datta established a wooden *mūrti* (statue) of Uddharan Datta Thakur in the temple, but that mūrti is no longer there; at present, a picture of Uddharan Datta Thakur is worshiped. It is understood, however, that the wooden *mūrti* of Uddharan Thakur was taken away by Sri Madana-mohana Datta and is now being worshiped with a Shalagram Shila by Srinath Datta."

Sri Purushottam Das

sadāśivasuto nāmnā nāgaraḥ puruṣottamaḥ
vaidya-vaṁśodbhavo nāmnā dāma yo vallavo vraje

Nagar Purushottam was previously the cowherd named Daman in Vraja. He is now born in a Vaidya family as the son of Sadashiva. (*Gaura-gaṇoddeśa-dīpikā* 131)

Daman was one of the twelve Gopals and a companion of Krishna in his childhood pastimes in Vraja. In the eleventh chapter of the *Ādi-līlā* of Chaitanya Charitamrita, Krishna Das Kaviraj Goswami has listed Purushottam Das amongst the devotees of Lord Nityananda.

Sadashiva Kaviraj was a great personality. Purushottam Das was his son. From birth, Purushottam Das was absorbed in the service of the lotus feet of Lord Nityananda Prabhu, and he always engaged in childish play with Lord Krishna. His son was named Sri Kanu Thakur, a very respectable gentleman. His body was saturated with the nectar of love for Lord Krishna.

(Chaitanya Charitamrita 1.11.38-40)

Vrindavan Das Thakur has also named Purushottam Das as one of Nityananda Prabhu's chief associates:

Sadashiva Kaviraj was very fortunate to have a son like Purushottam Das. Purushottam Das had no external consciousness of his body, for Nityananda Prabhu is constantly acting through him.

(Chaitanya Bhagavata 3.5.741-2)

For four generations, the family of Purushottam Thakur consisted of eternally perfect direct associates of Mahaprabhu: Kamsari Sen, Sadashiva Kaviraj, Purushottam Thakur, and Kanu Thakur. *The Gaura-gaṇoddeśa-dīpikā* identifies Kamsari Sen as Ratnavali Sakhi and Sadashiva Kaviraj as Chandravali (156).

Purushottam Thakur's wife was named Jahnava Devi. She died while her son, Kanu Thakur, was just a young child. Nityananda Prabhu named the boy Sisu Krishna Das. It is said that Nityananda Prabhu's wife Jahnava Devi adopted Kanu and took him with her to Vrindavan. Some say that he was also one of the twelve Gopals. One legend about Kanu Thakur holds that when in Vrindavan, while he was dancing in kirtan, his ankle bell flew off. He vowed that he would make his residence wherever the ankle bell was recovered. When it was found in the town of Bodhkhana in Jessore district, he established his Sripat there. In the opinion of some, Madhavacharya (Madhava Chattopadhyaya) of Jirat in Hooghly district, the husband of Nityananda Prabhu's daughter Ganga Devi, was Purushottam Thakur's disciple.

Srila Bhaktisiddhanta Saraswati Goswami Thakur has the following to say about Purushottam Thakur's Sripat: "Purushottam Das Thakur lived at Sukhasāgara, midway between the Chakdaha and Simurali railway stations. The deities he installed were formerly served in Beledanga village, but when the temple fell into the river, the deities were taken to Sukhasāgara. That temple was also swallowed by the Ganges and so the deities were brought with Jahnava Mata's deity to Sahebdanga Berigram. Since that place was also destroyed, all the deities were again moved about three or four miles to the village named Chanduregram, on the banks of the Ganges about one mile up from Pal Para." (*Anubhāṣya* 1.11.39)

Devakīnandana Das, the author of the *Vaiṣṇava-vandanā,* was Purushottam Thakur's disciple. There he writes,

I worship Sadashiva Kaviraj with great attentiveness. He was constantly intoxicated with love and had no external consciousness.... I bow down to my worshipable Lord, Purushottam Thakur. Who can list his incomparable qualities? He was merciful to those who were devoid of virtue, displaying the natural power of his compassion. When only seven years old, he was so intoxicated with love for Krishna that he danced in a way that enchanted the entire world.

The following supplementary information is given in the *Gauḍīya Vaiṣṇava Abhidhāna*:

"Some people say that Purushottam's surname was Nagar, while others say that the name Nagar comes from the name of the area where he lived. Since the five villages (Beledanga, Berigram, Sukhasagar, Manasapota and Pal Para) are so close together, this area is sometimes called Nagaradesh. Purushottam once ate snake poison when in a trance state without experiencing any ill effects. This was a source of great astonishment to all who witnessed it. Many of Nityananda Prabhu's associates often displayed such miraculous powers."

SRI KAMALAKAR PIPPALAI

kamalākaraḥ pippalāi-nāmnāsīd yo mahābalaḥ

Nityananda's associate Kamalakar Pippalai was one of the twelve Gopals, formerly known as Mahabala.
(*Gaura-gaṇoddeśa-dīpikā* 128)

Kamalakar Pippalai's behavior and his love of God were uncommon. Thus his fame spread around the world.
(CC 1.11.24)

The cowherd boy who was known as Mahabala in Vrindavan is now known as Kamalakar Pippalai. Day and night he sang the glories of Radha and Krishna and is counted as one of Nityananda's branches. He lived in Mahesh on the west bank of the Ganges where he served a deity of Jagannath. (*Vaiṣṇavācāra-darpaṇa*)

In the *Gauḍīya Vaiṣṇava Abhidhāna*, Kamalakar Pippalai's birth year is given as 1492 AD. According to *Sripat-paryaṭana*, he was born in Akna Mahesh and lived in Jageshwar, but according to other sources he was born in the village known as Khalijhuli in the Sundarbon area. His father was a rich landlord who belonged to a Brahmin family of the Rarha branch. He had a younger brother named Sri Nidhipati Pippalai.

Though born in Khalijhuli, Kamalakar moved to the village of Mahesh, which is about 2 miles from the Serampore railway station in Hooghly. The famous Jagannath deity in Mahesh was consecrated by him. Prior to Kamalakar's arrival, the area around Mahesh was nothing but jungle, but he had the land cleared and made into a model village whose fame spread everywhere.

Srila Bhaktisiddhanta Saraswati Goswami Thakur has told two stories about Kamalakar Pippalai in his *Anubhāṣya* to the Chaitanya Charitamrita:

(1) When Kamalakar Pippalai left home, his younger brother Nidhipati Pippalai searched for him and in due course of time found him in the village of Mahesh. When his brother refused to return despite his remonstrances, Nidhipati Pippalai came to live in Mahesh with all his family members. His descendants still reside in the Mahesh area, numbering some twenty households.

(2) There was once a vairagi named Dhruvananda who went on pilgrimage to Puri. It was his strong desire to offer Lord Jagannath food he had cooked with his own hands. Jagannath appeared to him in a dream one night and told him to go to Mahesh on the Ganges and when Jagannath was installed there, his wish to cook and make an offering to him would be fulfilled. When Dhruvananda came to Mahesh, he saw Jagannath, Balaram and Subhadra floating in the river. He picked them out of the water and had a small hut built where he could shelter and worship them. As he neared his death and was searching about for someone suitable to replace him in caring for the deities, Lord Jagannath once again appeared to him in a dream and said, "My devotee, a great Vaishnava named Kamalakar Pippalai lives in the village of Khalijuli in the Sundarban. I have ordered him in a dream to come here and take over My service. When he comes, you should turn the responsability for caring for Me over to him."

The next morning, Kamalakar Pippalai, who had indeed had such a dream, arrived there and Dhruvananda immediately gave him charge of the worship of Jagannath, Baladeva and Subhadra. Having been empowered in this way to serve the Lord, Kamalakar Pippalai took the title Adhikari, and this title has been used as the family name ever since. The Pippalai name belongs to one of the fifty-five branches of the Rarha Brahmins.

A devotee is always anxious to serve the Lord, so the Lord gives him directions for service. He never does this for a non-devotee. Kamalakar was gratified to have received Lord Jagannath's order, and immediately abandoned his home and family to go to Mahesh. The conditioned souls are normally so attached to the pleasures of their gross and subtle senses that the mere mention of service to Krishna and the Vaishnavas fills their hearts with trepidation. They consider such service to be a burden and look for any excuse to avoid it. Because it does not contribute to the gratification of the senses, they do not consider service to Vishnu and the Vaishnavas to be a wealth or a source of profit in the way that a Vaishnava does. To the eyes of the world, a Vaishnava may be playing the role of a family man, but he is not of the same order as a worldly householder. Sometimes it is the Lord's wish that someone take a wife and have a family, but even though he is externally subject to the same conditions that an ordinary materialists faces, his mind is absorbed in feelings of separation from the Lord. Thus, as soon as he receives direction from the Lord, he enthusiastically abandons his material connections and becomes fully engaged in the Lord's service. This renunciation of family life is not painful as it is for one on the *jñāna-yoga* path, but is natural and spontaneous.

The *Vijaya-khaṇḍa* says that Nityananda gave Panihati over to Kamalakar.

Srila Bhaktisiddhanta Saraswati Goswami Thakur has noted a few of the generations that descended from Kamalakar. Kamalakar had a son named Caturbhuja, who in turn had two sons, Narayan and Jagannath. Narayan's son was named Jagadananda whose son was Rajivalochan. During Rajivalochan's lifetime, service to the Jagannath deity was at first hampered by a shortage of finances. The Nawab of Dhaka, Wali Shah Shuja, donated 1185 bighas of land to Jagannath in the Bengali year 1060 (1653 AD). This land is found in the area of Jagannathpur, about 2.5 krosas from the Mahesh temple. The village was named Jagannathpur after the deity.

The *Gauḍīya Vaiṣṇava Abhidhāna* cites the following verses from *Nityānanda-vaṁśa-vistāra*:

> A pure-hearted Brahmin who regularly worshiped Vishnu and the Vaishnavas lived in the town of Mahesh. He was Pippalai's son-in-law named Sudhamaya. His wife was Vidyunmala.

Thus, Vidyunmala, Kamalakar Pippalai's daughter, married Sudhamaya Chattopadhyaya. They had a daughter named Narayani Devi. Virabhadra Prabhu later married this Narayani Devi. The descendants of the Pippalai family in Mahesh say that this girl's name was Radharani. On the other hand, Srila Bhaktisiddhanta Saraswati Goswami Thakur has said that Virabhadra Prabhu married Srimati, who was the daughter of Yadunātha Acharya and his wife Vidyunmala, as well as their adopted daughter, Narayani.

The *Vaiṣṇavācāra-darpaṇa*, however, gives contradictory information. It says that Vidyunmala married a highly qualified Brahmin named Yadunandan, "who thus had a great devotee of Jagannath, who knew nothing but the desire to serve Jagannath, as his father-in-law."

Kamalakar was present in Panihati at the *Danda-mahotsava* of Raghunath Das. He also came to the renowned festivals at Kheturi and Katwa. He joined Jahnava Devi for the journey, as his name is mentioned in this connection in *Bhakti-ratnākara* (10.375).

According to the *Vaiṣṇavācāra-darpaṇa*, Kamalakar left for Vrindavan after giving his daughter away in marriage and lived there until the end of his days. According to the tradition maintained by his descendants, the disappearance day of the founder of their line was the Chaitra *śuklā trayodaśī* of the year 1563 AD.

Sri Saranga Thakur

vraje nāndīmukhī yāsīt sādya sāraṅga-ṭhakkuraḥ
prahlādo manyate kaiścin matpitrā sa na manyate

Vraja's Nandamukhi became Saranga Thakur in Gaura lila. Some people say that he is Prahlad, but that is not the opinion held by my father.

(*Gaura-gaṇoddeśa-dīpikā* 172)

Sri Saranga Thakur is mentioned in the listing of branches of the Chaitanya trunk of the tree of devotional service along with Rama Das, Kavidatta, Gopal Das and Bhagavata Acharya (Chaitanya Charitamrita 1.10.113). He is also known as Sarngadhar and Sarngapani. He used to live in Modadrumdwip, which is the island in Nabadwip that represents, of the nine types of devotional service, the service attitude. The name of the town is Mamgachi. He would sit in a secluded place by the banks of the Ganges to meditate and chant the Holy Names. Through these practices he obtained many miraculous powers.

At first, Saranga Thakur did not want to make any disciples for fear of disturbances to his bhajan, but Mahaprabhu repeatedly encouraged him to do so. The following account is given in the *Gauḍīya Vaiṣṇava Abhidhāna*, "When the Lord was criticizing Devananda Pandit for having offended Srivas Pandit, Saranga Thakur met him on the streets of Nabadwip. Mahaprabhu ordered him to give up his determination to never take disciples."

Srila Bhaktisiddhanta Saraswati Goswami Thakur writes in his *Anubhāṣya*: "Having been ordered by Mahaprabhu to take disciples, Saranga Thakur decided that he would make a disciple of the first person that he met the following morning. As fate would have it, the next morning, a dead body washed up against him while he was taking bath in the Ganges. He revived the corpse and made him his disciple. This disciple was known as Thakur Murari, or sometimes as Saranga Murari.

In the *Gauḍīya Vaiṣṇava Abhidhāna*, it is further said that Murari was a boy who had been killed by snakebite and his parents had set his uncremated body afloat on a raft in the Ganges, as was the custom in that time. Saranga Thakur himself became an empowered preacher of Mahaprabhu's dharma. Descendents of his disciples still live in a village named Shava ("corpse").

Saranga Thakur's deities were served in the town of Mamgachi. The original temple was built in front of a bakula tree. The deities of Radha-Gopinath can be seen in this temple, as can the deity of Mahaprabhu's other parshad, Vasudeva Datta Thakur, Sri Madana Gopal. The devotees who do parikrama of Nabadwip Dham visit this temple for darshan. Srila Bhaktisiddhanta Saraswati Goswami Thakur established a temple not far from the above-mentioned home of Sharnga Murari at the birthplace of Vrindavan Das Thakur.

Saranga Thakur disappeared on the thirteenth day of the waning moon (*kṛṣṇā trayodaśī*) in the month of Agrahayan. An alternative opinion is that he disappeared on the Asharh *kṛṣṇā caturdaśī*.

Sri Kaliya Krishna Das (Kala Krishna Das)

kālaḥ śrī-kṛṣṇadāsa sa yo lavaṅgaḥ sakhā vraje

In Vraja, Kala Krishna Das was Krishna's cowherd friend named Lavanga. (*Gaura-gaṇoddeśa-dīpikā* 132)

Kaliya Krishna Das was known throughout the three worlds. One can attain Gaurachandra through remembrance of him. (Chaitanya Bhagavata 3.5.740)

Lavanga Sakha is one of the twelve Gopals. His Sripat is in the town of Akai Hat, within the jurisdiction of Katwa just off the road that leads to Nabadwip. It is about two miles south of the Katwa train station and one mile north of Dain Hat station. Near the Sripat is a pond called Nupur Kund. It is said that the ankle bell of Raghunandan Thakur, the son of the Khandavasi Mukunda, fell here. Others say that it was Nityananda Prabhu's ankle bell.

In his *Anubhāṣya* commentary to the Chaitanya Charitamrita, Srila Bhaktisiddhanta Saraswati Goswami Thakur has written: "In the opinion of the Goswamis of the Sonatala village on the north bank of the Icchamati River about three miles west of Bera Bandar in Pabna district, Kala Krishna Das was a Brahmin of the Varendra group, of the Bharadwaj gotra in Bhadara Gram. Kala Krishna Das went to Pabna to preach the chanting of the Holy Names. There are still the ruins of the buildings where he built his ashram. Later, members of his family came to live there. Since there were no other Brahmins of the Varendra group in Akai Hat, he came there to marry. Afterwards he returned to Akai Hat and finished his days in Vrindavan."

He had two sons named Sri Mohana Das and Sri Gauranga Das, or Vrindavan Das. Their descendants still live in the Sonatala village. There they celebrate Kala Krishna Das' disappearance day on the twelfth day of the waning moon in the month of Agrahayan. The deity he worshiped was named Kala Chand.

Kala Krishna Das was the best of the Vaishnavas. He knew nothing other than Nityananda Prabhu's lotus feet. (Chaitanya Charitamrita 1.11.37)

When Jahnava Devi came to Katwa, Kala Krishna Das was in her entourage.

They all arrived in Kaṇṭaka Nagara (Katwa) with company of many devotees, including Kala Krishna Das from Akai Hat. (*Bhakti-ratnākara* 10.409)

The Kala Krishna Das who accompanied Sri Chaitanya Mahaprabhu to southern India was not the same personality. (Cf. *Anubhāṣya*, 2.7.39)

Srila Dhananjaya Pandit

vasudāmā sakhā yaś ca paṇḍitaḥ śrī-dhanañjayaḥ

Krishna's friend Vasudama became Dhananjaya Pandit in Gaura lila. (*Gaura-gaṇoddeśa-dīpikā* 127)

Dhananjaya Pandit was Nityananda Prabhu's dear servant; he was very renounced and full of love for Krishna. (Chaitanya Charitamrita 1.11.31)

Opinions vary about Dhananjaya Pandit's birthplace and his parentage. In the *Gauḍīya Vaiṣṇava Abhidhāna*, it is said that he was born in the village of Jargram in Chittagong district on the fifth day of the waxing moon in the month of Chaitra, 1485. His father's name was Sripati Bandyopadhyaya, his mother's was Kalindi Devi. His wife was Haripriya.

In the book *Gauranga-mādhurī*, another version is given: He was born in the village of Siyan Muluk, near Bolpur in the Birbhum district. His father's name was Adideva Vachaspati and his mother's was Dayamayi. Srila Bhaktisiddhanta Saraswati Goswami Thakur subscribes to the former view in his *Anubhāṣya.*

Dhananjaya Pandit's primary home was in the village of Shitala Gram, which is served by the Kaichara post office in the precinct of Mangalkot in Burdwan district. Shitala Gram is about one mile north of the Kaicara railway station, nine miles west of Katwa on the narrow gauge line to Burdwan city. He is also said to have had homes in the village of Sanchara, Panchara and Jalandi. The first of these villages lies two miles south of Satdeula Tajapur, which is four miles from the Memari train station. Jalandi is about ten miles east of city of Burdwan and is served by Lokanagar post office. Also found in this village is the home of Sanjaya Pandit, who is said by some to have been Dhananjaya's brother and by others his disciple. Dhananjaya had no offspring. Those who supervise the Shitala Gram temple are descendants of his disciples.

Both the *Gauḍīya Vaiṣṇava Abhidhāna* and *Gauranga-mādhurī* agree that Dhananjaya Pandit was married and that his wife's name was Haripriya. It is also mentioned that he would prostrate himself in obeisances before Tulasi Devi three times a day. He was married when very young, but this did not stop him from leaving on a pilgrimage shortly after his wedding. His wealthy father gave him money for travelling expenses, but Dhananjaya gave it all to Mahaprabhu and carried only a begging bowl. This particular action has been recalled by the author of *Vaiṣṇava-vandanā*:

vilāsī vairāgī vandoṅ paṇḍita dhanañjaya
sarvasva prabhure diyā bhāṇḍa hāte laya

Dhananjaya's main home, or Sripat, was in Shitala Gram. The deities of Gopinath, Nitai-Gauranga and Damodar worshiped by him are still being served there.

These deities are brought into a field not far from the temple where the disappearance day festival is held annually in the middle of Magh.

Dhananjaya Pandit participated for a few days with Mahaprabhu in his sankirtan pastimes in Nabadwip. From there he returned to Shitala Gram whence he went on a pilgrimage to Vrindavan. Before travelling to Vrindavan, he stayed for a few days in Sanchara Panchara, leaving a disciple who was travelling with him in charge of the deity service. At present, there is no further sign of this temple in Sanchara Panchara.

Nityananda Prabhu delivered the most fallen and crushed the atheistic. These powers were manifest in his dear devotee, Dhananjaya. Dhananjaya Pandit converted many robbers and atheists in the Shitala Gram area.

Dhananjaya Pandit was an extraordinarily great Vaishnava. Nityananda took up permanent residence in his heart. (Chaitanya Bhagavata 3.5.773)

As one enters the Shitala Gram temple, a small Tulasi altar stands on the left. This is the site of Dhananjaya Pandit's samadhi tomb. His disappearance day is the *śuklā aṣṭamī* of Karttik month.

Sundarananda Thakur

purā sudāma-nāmāsīd adya sundara-ṭhakkuraḥ

Sundarananda Thakur was previously one of the twelve Gopals known as Sudama.
(*Gaura-gaṇoddeśa-dīpikā* 127)

Sundarananda, a true servant, is counted amongst the branches of Nityananda Prabhu. Nityananda joked with him in the Vrindavan mood.
(Chaitanya Charitamrita 1.11.23)

Sundarananda is an ocean of sacred rapture. He is chief amongst the associates of Nityananda Prabhu.
(Chaitanya Bhagavata 3.5.728)

His home was in the village of Maheshpur in Jessore district. Maheshpur stands on the Betravati River, fourteen miles east of the Mazdia railway station. Only his place of birth remains there at present.

His deities were named Radha-Vallabha and Radha-Raman. Their priests later moved these deities to Sayyidabad and installed a wooden deity in Maheshpur.

Sundarananda never married and thus has no descendants. Descendants of his disciples continue to maintain the site in Maheshpur. Some relatives of his established a temple in Mangaldihi in Birbhum district.

Sundarananda possessed great mystic powers. He made kadamba flowers bloom on a lime tree, which he later used in the service of Radha-Raman, as is stated in the *Vaiṣṇava-vandanā:*

sundarānanda ṭhākura vandibo baṛa āśe
phuṭālo kadamba-phula jabīrera gāche

In great hope, I worship Sundarananda Thakur who made a kadamba flower bloom on a lime tree.

On another occasion he dove into a river and pulled a crocodile out. He resembled Nityananda Prabhu in being a savior of the most fallen. His disappearance took place on the full moon day of Karttik month.

Sri Minaketan Rama Das

amuṁ praviśatāṁ kāryāt sahajau niśaṭholmukau
mīnaketana-rāmādir vyūhaḥ saṅkarṣaṇo'paraḥ

The two brothers Nishath and Ulmuka entered into the expansions of Nityananda as Minaketan and Rama.
(*Gaura-gaṇoddeśa-dīpikā* 68)

RAMA DAS, A DEVOTEE OF NITYANANDA

Though the *Gaura-gaṇoddeśa-dīpikā* here indicates that Minaketan and Rama Das are two different people, it is clear from the Chaitanya Charitamrita and the *Bhakti-ratnākara* that Minaketan Rama Das is a single individual. Perhaps both Nishath and Ulmuka, participants in Baladeva-lila, entered into the body of Minaketan Rama Das during Gaura lila.

No details are known about Minaketan Rama Das' birthplace or his parents. From the account of Krishna Das Kaviraj Goswami, it would appear that his residence was somewhere in the vicinity of his home in Jhamatpur.

He was one of the associates of Nityananda who went to Kheturi with Jahnava Devi. Narahari Chakravarti writes that the three worlds are purified by the sight of Vaishnavas like Minaketan Rama Das:

All the great devotees gathered to go to Kheturi. Seeing them, the entire universe is sanctified. Amongst them were Minaketan Rama Das, Abhiram Thakur, Murari Chaitanya, Jnana Das, Mahidhara, Shankar, Kamalakara Pippalai, Nrisingha Chaitanya, Jiva and Kanai Pandit.
(*Bhakti-ratnākara* 10.372-5)

Krishna Das Kaviraj Goswami recounts some details about Minaketan Rama Das in his Chaitanya Charitamrita in the course of glorifying Nityananda Prabhu. Just as Nityananda Prabhu was an *avadhūta*, his follower Minaketan also behaved in the manner of an *avadhūta*. Srila Bhaktisiddhanta Saraswati Goswami Thakur discusses the word in his commentary: "The word *avadhūta* is defined by Sridhar Swami in his commentary to Srimad Bhagavatam 3.1.19 by the words *asaṁskṛta-deha*, or "one who does not take care of his body." Nityananda Prabhu was an *avadhūta*, and his disciple was also an eternally perfect, Mahabhagavata paramahamsa like him—beyond the varṇashram system. As a result, none of the characteristics of any of the castes or states of life were manifest in his body. He was completely absorbed in the mood of Vraja and had no consideration whatsoever for the duties of the body." (*Anubhāṣya*, 1.5.161).

RAMA DAS AT JHAMATPUR

On one occasion, Minaketan Rama Das was invited to attend an all-night kirtan at Krishna Das Kaviraj's home in Jhamatpur. The other guests were impressed by his appearance and his display of transcendental emotions and came to pay their obeisances to his feet. In his ecstatic mood, he would sometimes hit the person prostrated before him with his flute, sometimes slap him. Occasionally, he would even climb onto some other devotees' shoulders. Tears poured from his eyes like the uninterrupted flow of a river. Seeing this, other devotees' also felt their eyes fill with tears. All the eight amazing manifestations of ecstatic love appeared in his body. When he shouted the name of Nityananda in this state, all the devotees felt their hearts fill with a divine ecstasy.

Gunarnava Mishra was engaged as a pujari in Krishna Das' house. This Brahmin was a kaniṣṭha adhikārī and had faith in the deity but was unable to recognize the devotee and did not have much enthusiasm to pay him proper respect. Minaketan Rama Das was able to understand that this Gunarnava Mishra had no faith in Nityananda Prabhu and that for this reason he was deliberately ignoring him because he was Nityananda's disciple. In order to teach the world, Rama Das said,

"Just look! A second Romaharshan Suta who did not come forward to show respect when he saw Balaram!"
(Chaitanya Charitamrita 1.5.170)

Romaharshan was seated on the Vyasasana and engaged in reciting the Bhagavata at the request of the assembled sages in Naimisharanya when Baladeva himself appeared there. All the other sages stood up to show Lord Balaram the appropriate respect, with the exception of Romaharshan. For this, he was punished. Someone who is proud has no authority to speak on the Bhagavata, nor, for that matter, is he authorized to worship the deity. The Bhagavata is identical to Krishna Himself. However, in this case, the pujari Gunarnava Mishra did not object to Rama Das' chastisement and simply continued in the performance of his service to the deity.

At the end of the kirtan festival, however, Minaketan Rama Das got into an argument with Krishna Das Kaviraj's brother. Krishna Das' brother had strong faith in Chaitanya Mahaprabhu, but lacked such faith in Nityananda Prabhu. When Rama Das discovered this, he broke his flute in anger and left the place. The result of this curse was that Krishna Das' brother was doomed to destruction. Krishna Das Kaviraj himself rebuked his brother, an act which pleased Lord Nityananda who came to him in a dream and told him to go to live in Vrindavan.

The above account reveals how dear Minaketan Rama Das was to Nityananda Prabhu. Nityananda's followers are like him: they are deliverers of the most fallen and capable of fulfilling all desires.

Sri Uddhava Das

śrīmān uddhava-dāso'pi candrāveśāvatārakaḥ

Uddhava Das is an *āveśa* incarnation of the Moongod. (*Gaura-gaṇoddeśa-dīpikā* 192)

In the Chaitanya Charitamrita (1.12.83), it is said that Uddhava Das is a branch of Gadadhar Pandit Goswami. As such, he is mentioned by Yadunath Das in the *Śākhā-nirṇayāmṛta* (35):

ati-dīnajane pūrṇa-prema-vitta-pradāyakam
śrīmad-uddhava-dāsākhyaṁ vande'haṁ guṇa-śālinam

I venerate the highly virtuous Uddhava Das, who gave the wealth of love to those who were most fallen.

When Rupa Goswami was old and living in Vrindavan, he was desperate to see Madhavendra Puri's Gopal deity, but unable to go to Govardhan because of his advanced years. Fortunately, Gopal came to stay in Mathura at the house of Bitthalnath, the youngest son of Vallabhacharya, ostensibly out of fear of possible attacks by the Muslim iconoclasts. Rupa Goswami thus had the opportunity to see Madhavendra Puri's deity. Uddhava Das was amongst the devotees who stayed with Rupa at Bitthalnath's house for an entire month on this occasion. (Chaitanya Charitamrita 2.18.51, *Bhakti-ratnākara* 5.1333)

Uddhava Das lived in Vrindavan. When Srinivas Acharya and Raghava Goswami were touring Vraja Dham, they came to his cottage. He greeted them with enthusiastic hospitality. Uddhava Das was amongst those who gathered to bless Srinivas Acharya, Narottam Das Thakur and Shyamananda Prabhu as they set off to Bengal with the books that had been given to them by Jiva Goswami.
(*Bhakti-ratnākara* 6.514)

According to the *Gauḍīya Vaiṣṇava Abhidhāna*, there are at least two devotees named Uddhava Das. One was a follower of Sanatan Goswami who worshiped in Vraja on the banks of Pavan Sarovar, another was an initiated disciple of Radha Mohan Thakur who wrote many songs about Radha-Krishna lila. He lived in Murshidabad district in the village of Teyagram. His real name was Krishna Kanta Majumdar.

KURMA VIPRA

When Mahaprabhu decided to deliver the people of the South, he left Puri on the pretext of going on pilgrimage in the month of Vaishakh. At Nityananda Prabhu's request, he accepted Krishna Das Vipra as a servant. Distributing prema to all as he passed, he arrived in the place known as Kurmasthan (or Kurma Kshetra) where he bestowed his blessings on the Vedic Brahmin also named Kurma.

Krishna Das Kaviraj Goswami has not given anything more than this Brahmin's name in his account of this event in his Chaitanya Charitamrita. Though many devotees descended to this world to participate in the Lord's pastimes, the worldly identities of many of them unfortunately remain unknown. There is not much possibility that historians will ever be able to unearth any more informtion about this Kurma Vipra's background. Detailed knowledge about the Lord's associates' worldly identities is far less important, however, than the lessons we are taught through their saintly lives.

Mahaprabhu was influenced by the intense devotion of Kurma Vipra to accept his service. He was fortunate enough to be able to take the Lord to his house, where he washed his feet and gave the holy water to all his family members to drink. He gave the Lord food to eat and took His remnants as maha prasad.

> In that village there was a Vedic Brahmin named Kurma. He respectfully invited Lord Chaitanya Mahaprabhu to his home. He washed the Lord's lotus feet and drank the water with his family members. With great affection and respect, he gave Mahaprabhu all kinds of food to eat. After that, all the members of the family shared his remnants. (Chaitanya Charitamrita 2.7.121-3)

The Brahmin glorified Mahaprabhu, pleasing him, but as the Lord left he was unable to bear the thought of being separated from him. He asked the Lord for permission to accompany him, but the Lord denied it, telling him to stay at home and chant the names of Krishna and then to take the role of an acharya and preach the Holy Names to others.

prabhu kahe aiche bāta kabhu nā kahibā
gṛhe rahi kṛṣṇa-nāma nirantara laibā
jāre dekha tāre kaha kṛṣṇa upadeśa
āmāra ājñāya guru hañā tāra ei deśa
kabhu nā bādhibe tomāya viṣaya taraṅga
punar api ei ṭhāi pābe mora saṅga

> The Lord said, "Never make this suggestion again. You should rather remain at home and constantly chant the holy name of Krishna. Instruct whomever you see in the religion of Krishna. Become a spiritual master on my order and deliver everyone in this land. Do this and you will never again be entangled in the waves of materialistic life. Indeed, you will have my company again, here in this very place." (Chaitanya Charitamrita 2.7.127-9)

Srila Bhaktisiddhanta Saraswati Goswami Thakur has elaborated on this instruction to Kurma Vipra in his *Anubhāṣya* as follows: "For those who are determined to abandon everything to take shelter of the Supreme Lord Sri Chaitanya Mahaprabhu and serve Him exclusively, the Lord here gives the instruction to remain in the home, that is, to give up the pride of being a heroic performer of bhajan and adopt the regular practice of chanting the holy name of Krishna in the home and, with the humility that is characterized by remaining in the householder life, instruct others in chanting the Holy Names. If one takes up the duties of a spiritual master in this way, he will never become entangled in the 'waves of materialistic life' in the form of the desire for self-aggrandizement.

"Many foolish people think that to teach through writing books as Rupa Goswami, Sanatan Goswami, Jiva Goswami or Raghunath Das Goswami have done, or to take on large numbers of disciples like Madhvacharya, Ramanujacharya or Narottam Das Thakur, is an impediment to spiritual practice. Indeed, these less intelligent persons even claim that such activities are material entanglements. By adhering to such erroneous ideas, they become offenders to the many unalloyed devotees who have nothing to do with the material world and yet preach. This teaching of the Lord is intended for these people, who, if they analyze it carefully, will eventually give up false pride and the show of humility and, rather than demonstrating an inimical attitude towards those who are devoid of devotion to the Lord, will advance the cause of genuine bhajan."

FRIENDSHIP WITH VASUDEVA VIPRA

While in Kurmasthan, Mahaprabhu was also attracted by the heartfelt devotion of the leper Vasudeva Vipra (see the next chapter). He delivered him and embraced him, transforming him into a handsome man. Vasudeva said:

> "Listen, O merciful one! The qualities You possess could not possibly manifest in an ordinary living being. The lowest of the low run away at the sight and smell of my body, yet You touched and embraced me! You are the supremely independent Lord. But I was well off in my humble state. By transforming me, You have put me at risk of becoming proud." (Chaitanya Charitamrita 2.7.144-6)

The Lord then gave him assurances that even though his body had been made handsome, he would not become entangled in the egoism that physical beauty usual brings. He also told him to help others by teaching them to chant the holy names of Krishna.

The mercy of the Lord and His devotees upon seeing the distress of the conditioned souls is demonstrated by these words of the Lord and the above quotation from the writings of Srila Bhaktisiddhanta Saraswati Goswami Thakur. As Mahaprabhu left the pilgrimage town of Kurma Kshetra, Kurma Vipra and Vasudeva embraced each other and sang His glories, their eyes filled with tears of sadness at His departure.

Sri Vasudeva Vipra

Then Mahaprabhu set off for South India. In Kurma Kshetra, he liberated Vasudeva Vipra.

(Chaitanya Charitamrita 2.1.103)

Srila Bhaktisiddhanta Saraswati Goswami Prabhupada has written the following comments on Kurma Kshetra or Kurmasthan: "On the BNR railroad line there is a station named Chikakola Road in the district of Ganjam. Eight miles east of this station is a place known as Kurmachala (Kurma's mountain) or Sri Kurmam. This is the most popular pilgrimage site for those who speak the Telugu language. When Ramanuja was flung there by Jagannath Deva in the 11th century of the Shaka era, he thought that the Kurma deity was a Shiva-linga and so started a fast. Later, when he learned that it was in fact an image of the tortoise avatar of Vishnu, he arranged for it to be worshiped."

Ganjam is a district of Orissa. Today, the Chikakola Road station is found in the state of Andhra Pradesh and has been renamed as Sri Kakulam Road. The BNR railway line is now India's South Eastern Railway.

THE LORD'S MERCY TO VASUDEVA

Vasudeva Vipra was one of Mahaprabhu's great devotees in the Deccan. It is very difficult to recognize a devotee. When a devotee is very poor and materially undistinguished, it is very hard for an ordinary mundane person to recognize him. Mahaprabhu revealed Vasudeva Vipra's glories to the world. While wandering through South India, Mahaprabhu blessed a Brahmin named Kurma Vipra. Vasudeva Vipra was a leper, who upon learning that Mahaprabhu was at Kurma's house, went there in the hope of getting a glance of Him. He learned from Kurma, however, that the Lord had already departed. Vasudeva was so disappointed at this news that he fell down on the ground and fainted.

The Lord is so affectionate to His devotees that even though he had already walked a good distance from there, He returned to grant Vasudeva the opportunity to see and embrace him. Mahaprabhu's touch immediately cured him of his leprosy and turned him into a healthy and handsome young man. The Lord is everywhere. If one is eager to have Him, one can have Him. The Lord can only be influenced by devotion. He takes no notice of any mundane qualification or virtue. He took no notice of Vasudeva's advanced case of leprosy, but embraced him out of His affection for him as a devotee.

Vasudeva was an incredible individual. The open sores of his body were home to maggots that fed off the pus and blood oozing from them. If one of them should fall from the wound, Vasudeva would pick it up off the ground and put it back. Krishna Das Kaviraj Goswami has written as follows:

When Vasudeva Vipra saw the limitless mercy of the Supreme Lord, he responded in his amazement with a verse spoken by Sudama Vipra from the Bhagavatam:

kvāhaṁ daridraḥ pāpīyān
kva kṛṣṇaḥ śrī-niketanaḥ
brahma-bandhur iti smāhaṁ
bāhubhyāṁ parirambhitaḥ

Just see the difference between a miserable sinner like myself and the abode of the Goddess of Fortune, Sri Krishna. Though I am an unqualified Brahmin, He has embraced me in His arms. (Srimad Bhagavatam 10.89.16)

Such mercy could never be found in an ordinary human being. Ordinary people would stay far away from Vasudeva, being disgusted by the foul odor of his disease, but Mahaprabhu, the independent Lord, not only touched him, but embraced him.

A VAISHNAVA'S BODY IS NEVER MATERIAL

It should be remembered that a Vaishnava's body is never material. It is transcendental and completely pure. Mahaprabhu's affection for His devotees was displayed to Hari Das Thakur, which has been described in the Chaitanya Charitamrita as follows:

Hari Das said, "You are the merciful Supreme Lord; no one can understand the depths of Your heart. Vasudeva had such terrible leprosy that his gaping wounds were full of maggots, you are so merciful that You embraced him in spite of it. Your embrace turned him into a young man as beautiful as Cupid. No one can understand the waves of Your mercy."

prabhu kahe—vaiśnava deha prākṛta kabhu naya
aprākṛta deha bhaktera cid-ānanda-maya

The Lord answered, "A devotee's body is never material. The devotee's transcendental body is made of divine and ecstatic spiritual substance."

(Chaitanya Charitamrita 3.4.191)

A person who is without introspection or awareness of Krishna sees a Vaishnava's body only externally and thus is deprived of the vision of his spiritual form.

THE LORD'S INSTRUCTION TO VASUDEVA

When Vasudeva became a beautiful young man by the Lord's miraculous touch, he became afraid that he would become vain and that would be his downfall. Those who are proud and vain are deprived of the Lord's mercy and are not even qualified to chant the names of the Lord. Mahaprabhu considered Vasudeva Vipra to be most qualified and instructed him to act as an acharya:

prabhu kahe kabhu tomāya nā habe abhimāna
nirantara kaha tumi kṛṣṇa kṛṣṇa nāma

kṛṣṇa upadeśi kara jīvera nistāra
acirāte kṛṣṇa tomā karibena pāra

The Lord said, "You will never become vain if you constantly chant Krishna's name. Deliver the fallen souls by instructing them about Krishna and Krishna will very quickly accept you." (Chaitanya Charitamrita 2.7.147-8)

SRI RAGHUPATI UPADHYAYA

Sri Raghupati Upadhyaya was a Brahmin who originated from the region of Mithila. He was born in Tirhut, in the Sitamari subdivision of Darbhanga district in Bihar state. Tirhut or Tiruhita, was also the name for a kingdom which included the four modern districts of Darbhanga, Sitamarhi, Muzaffarpur and Champaran in northwestern Bihar. Paramananda Puri also came from Tirhut.

When Mahaprabhu heard Raghupati Upadhyaya's verses, he became overwhelmed with feelings of ecstatic love. Srila Rupa Goswami later included several of these verses in his *Padyāvalī*. Krishna Das Kaviraj Goswami has recounted the meeting of Raghupati with the Lord in his Chaitanya Charitamrita, *Madhya-līlā*, Chapter 19. This meeting took place when Mahaprabhu was in Prayag and had gone to visit Vallabhacharya in Arail. [See Chapter 69 on Rupa Goswami.]

At that time Raghupati Upadhyaya arrived there. He was from Tiruhitā district, a learned scholar, a Vaishnava and a gentleman. He offered his respects to Sri Chaitanya Mahaprabhu and the Lord blessed him, saying, "May you always remember Krishna."

(Chaitanya Charitamrita 2.19.92-3)

When Mahaprabhu asked Raghupati to speak to him about Krishna, Raghupati recited a verse of his own composition:

śrutim apare smṛtim itare
bhāratam anye bhajantu bhava-bhītāḥ
aham iha nandaṁ vande
yasyālinde paraṁ brahma

Let those afraid of material existence worship the Vedas and Upaniṣads, the smṛtis and purāṇas, or the Mahābhārata, as they wish. I, on the other hand, shall simply worship Maharaj Nanda, in whose courtyard plays the Supreme Divinity. (*Padyāvalī*, 126)

Mahaprabhu was ecstatic upon hearing this beautiful verse and asked to hear more. Raghupati acquiesced by reciting another verse he had written:

kaṁ prati kathayitum īśe
samprati ko vā pratītim āyātu
go-pati-tanayā-kuñje
gopa-vadhūṭī-viṭaṁ brahma

Whom dare I tell that the Supreme Truth is lusting after the cowherds' brides in the bushes by the banks of the River Yamuna? And who will believe me when I say it?

(*Padyāvalī*, 98)

As the Lord heard more and more of Raghupati's compositions, He went deeper and deeper into a trance of prema, demonstrating powerful ecstatic symptoms that made a great impression on the scholar, leading him to believe that Mahaprabhu was Krishna Himself.

Mahaprabhu then asked Raghupati which of Krishna's many forms was the best. The scholar replied: "The Lord's blackish form is supreme." Mahaprabhu then asked, "Which abode of the Lord is the best?" Raghupati answered, "Mathura is the best city." In response to Mahaprabhu's question about Krishna's best age, he answered that it was His adolescence. And then to the question about the best amongst the rasas, Raghupati stated that the primary rasa, or the erotic mood, was supreme. The complete verse is found in the *Padyāvalī* (82):

śyāmam eva paraṁ rūpaṁ
purī madhu-purī varā
vayaḥ kaiśorakaṁ dhyeyam
ādya eva paro rasaḥ

Mahaprabhu embraced Raghupati in His ecstasy and then began to dance. Vallabha Bhatta and all the members of his householders were astounded by Raghupati Upadhyaya's great fortune.

THE SANORIYA VIPRA

Krishna Das Kaviraj Goswami tells about Mahaprabhu's meetings with the Sanoriya Brahmin in the seventeenth and eighteenth chapters of the *Madhya-līlā*. Nothing is known about this Brahmin's family background—even his name is unknown. What we are concerned with here are the teachings which are to be found through his example.

MAHAPRABHU MEETS THE SANORIYA BRAHMIN

When Mahaprabhu arrived in Mathura after passing through Kashi and Prayag, He first came to the Viśrāma Ghat in Mathura where He bathed. Then He visited Krishna's birthplace and the deity of Ādi Keshava, dancing before him in ecstatic love. Other visitors to the temple were amazed and charmed by the Lord's ecstatic dancing. At the same time, a certain Brahmin fell at the Lord's feet and then started to dance with Him, joining the Lord in His trance of divine love. They embraced each other and then raised their arms and told everyone to sing the holy names of Hari and Krishna, and a great tumult arose within the Ādi Keshava temple. When the kirtan finished, Mahaprabhu took the Brahmin aside and asked him,

"You are a sincere and respectable elderly Brahmin. Tell me where you got this wealth of love for Krishna."
(Chaitanya Charitamrita 2.17.155)

In reply, the Brahmin said, "While travelling throughout India, Madhavendra Puripada came to Mathura. He blessed me by setting foot in my humble abode. He initiated me by giving me the mantra and further blessed me by accepting food which I had cooked. He discovered the Gopal deity which is still being worshiped to this day in Govardhan."

As soon as he learned of the elderly Brahmin's relationship to Madhavendra Puri, the Lord fell at his feet. The Brahmin became afraid at this action of the Lord and himself touched the Lord's feet. To teach that the spiritual master's godbrothers are worshipable by the disciple, the Lord said, "You are my guru, and I am practically your disciple. It is not fitting for a guru to pay obeisances to a disciple."
(Chaitanya Charitamrita 2.17.170)

The Brahmin was astonished by the Lord's humility and said, "You are a sannyasi; it is not proper for a sannyasi to pay obeisances to a fallen person like myself." But the Brahmin had also determined from the Lord's ecstatic symptoms that he too had some relationship to Madhavendra Puri. He asked the Lord's travelling companion, Balabhadra Bhattacharya the name of the Lord's guru. Upon learning that his guess had been correct, he was overjoyed.

The Brahmin then invited the Lord to his house and the Lord accepted, giving him the opportunity to personally render him various kinds of service.

THE LORD ACCEPTS THE BRAHMIN'S INVITATION

When it was time, the Brahmin asked Balabhadra Bhattacharya to cook the Lord's lunch, but Mahaprabhu intervened. He said, "Puri Gosai ate your cooking, so you should cook for Me too. This is what I have learned from his example."

The Lord's host belonged to the Sanoriya community of Brahmins. According to Srila Bhaktivinoda Thakur, members of the business community (*vaiśyas*) in the west of India are divided into several castes: Agrawalas, Kanwars, Sanwars, etc. Of these, the Agrawalas are considered to be very pure, while the two other groups are considered fallen as a result of their own karma. Those Brahmins who perform the ritual activities for the gold and jewellery merchants (Kanwars and Sanwars) are known as Sanoriya Brahmins. Normally, because of these low caste associations, they are considered to be fallen as a caste. Sannyasis thus refuse to accept food in their homes.

Srila Bhaktisiddhanta Saraswati Goswami Thakur adds to this the following analysis based on pure devotion. "The Sanoriya Brahmin was a pure devotee, and although even drinking water from his hand was prohibited due to his caste status, he nevertheless was fixed in the *daiva-varṇāśrama* system and the Absolute Truth, both of which favor pure devotion. Those who judged devotees in terms of their mundane caste status (the *adaiva-varṇāśrama*) or who cast aspersions on *maha prasad* were unhesitatingly identified as wicked fools by the Lord."

Though sannyasis generally do not accept food from members of the Sanoriya caste, Madhavendra Puri did not hesitate to do so. Judging this Brahmin to have the qualities of a Vaishnava, Puripada gave him initiation and then ate in his house. The Sanoriya Brahmin himself was simply taking consideration of the Lord's reputation, which would be subject to criticism if He ignored caste rules. The Lord explained that since there may be some difference of opinion between the various scriptures and the seers, the best course of action was to follow the example set by saintly persons who establish the principles of religion. Finally, the Brahmin could understand the desire of the Lord and he cooked for Him himself.

SAVING THE LORD'S COMPANIONS FROM DANGER

As the Lord travelled from Puri to Mathura, His absorption in ecstatic love increased a hundredfold over that which He experienced in Puri. Upon arriving in Mathura, it increased a thousandfold, and when He went through the twelve forests of Vraja, it increased a hundred-thousandfold. Before leaving Nilachala, Ramananda Raya and Svarupa Damodar Goswami had arranged for two people to accompany Him, Balabhadra Bhattacharya and another Brahmin servant.

While He was wandering through the twelve forests, a Rajput, Krishna Das, was attracted by the Lord and joined Him and His companions. When the Lord came to Akrura Ghat, He jumped into the Yamuna in a transport of ecstasy and remained submerged for a long period of time. Krishna Das became afraid that the Lord had drowned and started to cry out for help. Balabhadra Bhattacharya heard His shouts and immediately went into the water to pull the Lord out.

Balabhadra was anxious about the Lord's great distraction in divine ecstasy and so he discussed with Madhavendra Puri's disciple, the Sanoriya Brahmin, about what could be done to protect Him. After some discussion, they decided that it was not wise to allow the Lord to stay any longer in Vrindavan. Rather, by telling Him of the full-moon bath at the end of the month of Magh, known also as Makara-sankranti, they should incite Him to go to Soro Kshetra on the banks of the Ganges, whence they could go on to Prayag. Since the Sanoriya Brahmin was the worshipable godbrother of His guru, the Lord was not able to refuse him when he made the suggestion to leave Vraja.

Though the Lord's body left the boundaries of Vrindavan, His consciousness remained fixed in love for Krishna, and His ecstatic trance remained unbroken. As He became tired from walking, the Lord sat down underneath a tree. Nearby, a herd of cows was grazing which reminded him of Krishna's Vrindavan lila. All of a sudden, a cowherd began to play his flute causing Mahaprabhu to faint in an ecstasy of love. The Lord fell to the ground, His breathing stopped and foam accumulated around His mouth. At this very moment, the Muslim soldier Bijli Khan was passing by with a troop of ten cavalrymen. On seeing the Lord's condition, Bijli Khan immediately became suspicious that foul play was afoot. He thought that the four men accompanying the Lord had poisoned Him with datura in order to steal gold He had in His possession.

The Pathan immediately made prisoners of the Lord's four companions with the intention of killing them. The two Bengali Brahmins began to tremble in fear; the two others, however, were fearless and able to think on their feet. The Sanoriya Brahmin tried to explain to the Pathan by saying: "I am a Brahmin from Mathura and I know hundreds of people in the Emperor's court. This sannyasi is my guru and he happens to have an illness that makes Him faint from time to time. Go ahead and tie us up and wait for a few minutes. My guru will soon regain consciousness and you will be able to hear the truth from Him."

Bijli Khan listened to the Sanoriya Brahmin speak fearlessly and began to doubt his understanding of the situation. He replied, "I can recognize from your speech that you are from Mathura, but these two people are foreigners. They are also trembling, so they must be guilty of something."

The Rajput Krishna Das sensed that the situation was becoming more dangerous and said brazenly, trying to frighten the Pathan, "I live in the neighboring village. I have two hundred soldiers with a hundred cannons. I only have to shout and they will come here and take your horses and equipment. I think that you must be the real highwaymen and not these two Bengalis."

The Muslim cavalrymen were cast into doubt by the Rajput's fearless words. Meanwhile, the Lord came back to consciousness and in a transport of ecstasy, loudly cried out the names "Hari! Hari!" and began to dance. The Pathan soldiers were overcome with fear when they heard the Lord bellow and saw His ecstatic dancing. They immediately liberated their four prisoners so that the Lord did not see His devotees tied up. The Muslims were attracted by the Lord's physical beauty and spiritual mood and they asked Him the question which had been troubling them: were these four people robbers who had drugged Him in order to steal His possessions?

The Lord answered, "I am a sannyasi and I live by begging. I have no wealth. These four men are My followers. I sometimes suffer from epilepsy and fall unconscious as a result. These four companions mercifully stay with Me when this happens to protect Me and take care of Me."

ONWARD TO PRAYAG

Upon his arrival at Soro Kshetra, Mahaprabhu took his bath in the Ganges and then desired to set off for Prayag along the banks of the holy river. He turned to the Sanoriya Brahmin and the Rajput Krishna Das, "You have taken such trouble to come all this way from Mathura just to show us the way. I do not wish you to trouble yourselves any further. Please go back now."

The two Vrajavasis answered, "We don't know when we will have the good fortune of Your company again. There is a great likelihood of danger on the highways of this land, which is dominated by non-Hindus. Balabhadra Bhattacharya does not know the local language. We think that these are good reasons for us to accompany You as far as Prayag."

The Lord laughed slightly and agreed.

THE PATHAN VAISHNAVA, SRI BIJLI KHAN

Sri Bijli Khan was a Pathan Muslim. Even so, after receiving Mahaprabhu's mercy, he became well known as a Vaishnava. His father was a rich man. Krishna Das Kaviraj Goswami has described how he met the Lord and received his mercy in the eighteenth chapter of the *Madhya-līlā*.

MAHAPRABHU LEAVES VRAJA

That year, Mahaprabhu took the Jharikhanda route to Vrindavan after the Rathayatra festival. Ramananda Raya and Svarupa Damodar Goswami arranged for two people to accompany Him, Balabhadra Bhattacharya and another Brahmin servant. As he travelled, his absorption in ecstatic love increased a hundredfold over that which he experienced in Puri. Upon arriving in Mathura, it increased a thousandfold, and when he went through the twelve forests of Vraja, it increased a hundred-thousandfold.

As he was wandering through the twelve forests, the Lord came to the place known as Akrura Ghat on the Yamuna. The Lord jumped into the water and remained immersed for a long time. Krishna Das, a Rajput who had been attracted by the Lord and was accompanying Him, became afraid that the Lord had drowned and started to cry out for help. Balabhadra Bhattacharya heard His shouts and quickly dove into the water to pull Him out.

Balabhadra was anxious about the Lord's great distraction due to his divine ecstasies and so he discussed with Madhavendra Puri's disciple, the Sanoriya Brahmin, about what could be done to protect him. After some discussion, they decided that the best thing to do was to propose to Mahaprabhu that he go to Soro Kshetra on the banks of the Ganges for the full-moon bath at the end of the month of Magh, known also as Makara-sankranti. From there, they could take him on to Prayag. The Rajput Krishna Das and the Mathura Brahmin were well acquainted with the route along the Ganges and so they remained with the Lord and the two Brahmins as guides.

As they tired from walking, the Lord sat down underneath a tree. Nearby, a herd of cows was grazing which reminded the Lord of Krishna's Vrindavan lila. Suddenly, the cowherd began to play his flute causing Mahaprabhu to faint in ecstasy. He fell to the ground, His breathing stopped and foam accumulated around His mouth.

BIJLI KHAN TIES UP THE LORD'S COMPANIONS

At this very moment, the Muslim soldier, Bijli Khan was passing by with a troop of ten cavalrymen. His immediate suspicion on seeing the Lord's condition was that the four men accompanying Him had poisoned Him with datura in order to steal His money.

The Pathan immediately bound the Lord's four companions, intending to kill them, causing the two Bengali Brahmins to tremble in fear. The two others, however, were fearless and quickly thought of a way out of the situation. The Sanoriya Brahmin explained to the Pathan as follows: "I am a Brahmin from Mathura and I know hundreds of people in the Emperor's court. This sannyasi is my guru and he happens to be ill, which makes Him faint from time to time. Tie us up and wait for a few minutes. He will regain consciousness and you will hear the truth from Him."

The Pathan listened and said, "I can understand what you two are saying. You are from Mathura, but these two Bengalis are trembling with guilt. They must have done something wrong."

The Rajput Krishna Das was acutely aware of the danger of the situation and said, "I live in the neighboring village. I have two hundred Turkish mercenaries with a hundred cannons at my command. I only have to shout and they will come here and take your horses and equipment. I think that you must be highwaymen, not these two Bengalis. You are only interested in robbing pilgrims like us."

The Muslim cavalrymen were cast into doubt by these fearless words. Meanwhile, the Lord came back to consciousness and in a transport of ecstasy, shouted out the names "Hari! Hari!" and began to dance. The Pathan soldiers were overcome by fear when they heard the Lord bellow and saw his ecstatic dancing. They immediately liberated their four prisoners and the Lord never saw his devotees tied up. They were attracted by the Lord's physical beauty and by His spiritual mood and they asked Him the question that had been troubling them: "Were these four people robbers who had drugged Him in order to steal His possessions?"

The Lord answered, "I am a sannyasi and I live by begging. I have no wealth. These four men are My followers. I sometimes suffer from epilepsy and fall unconscious as a result. These four companions mercifully stay with Me when this happens to protect Me and take care of Me."

THE LORD DISCUSSES RELIGION WITH A SUFI

In the group of cavalrymen, one Muslim dressed all in black introduced himself as a Sufi practitioner. He was pleased by the Lord's appearance and wished to discuss scriptures with Him. He established that the Supreme Truth was impersonal on the basis of the Islamic scriptures. The Lord, however, displayed His own knowledge of the Koran and demonstrated the invalidity of the Sufi's arguments, establishing the personal nature of the Supreme Truth and the Supreme Lord's transcendental qualities. Then the Lord went on to show that the philosophies of karma, jnana and yoga did not hold the answers to the supreme goal of life, which is nothing other than pure love of God.

All the Pathans were enchanted by the Lord's physical appearance and were even more attracted when they heard Him speak on spiritual life and its goal. The Sufi Pathan spontaneously began to chant the names of Krishna. When Mahaprabhu heard the saintly Muslim chant the Lord's names, He was pleased, thinking that all the sins that he had accumulated over millions of births had all been destroyed and that he had been purified. The Lord told them all to chant, which they did. He initiated the Sufi Pathan in the Holy Name and gave him the name Rama Das. When the prince Bijli Khan saw the good fortune of his own servant, he fell down at the Lord's feet and repeated the name, "Krishna, Krishna." The Lord also blessed him.

After bestowing His mercy upon them in this way, Mahaprabhu continued on His way. All the Muslim soldiers then became mendicants and were celebrated as the "Pathan Vaishnavas." They toured all over the country, glorifying Mahaprabhu's activities. Bijli Khan became a greatly advanced devotee, and his fame was sung at every holy place of pilgrimage. (Chaitanya Charitamrita 2.18.210-2)

DAMODAR PANDIT

śaivyo yāsīd vraje caṇḍī sa damodar-paṇḍitaḥ
kutaścit kāryato devī prāviśat taṁ sarasvatī

The terrible-tempered gopi named Shaivya became Damodar Pandit in Gaura lila, though occasionally the goddess Saraswati also entered into him for some special purpose. (*Gaura-gaṇoddeśa-dīpikā* 159)

Damodar Pandit is considered to be one of Chaitanya Mahaprabhu's branches.

Damodar Pandit is another branch of the Chaitanya trunk. His love for the Lord was so intense that he even chastised Him on occasion. This verbal punishment so satisfied the Lord that He sent him to Nadīyā. I will tell this story later. (Chaitanya Charitamrita 1.10.31-2)

DAMODAR ACCOMPANIES THE LORD TO PURI

After the Lord took sannyas in Katwa, Nityananda Prabhu tricked Him into coming to Advaita Prabhu's house in Shantipur. Many people came from Nabadwip to see Him there, one of whom was Damodar Pandit. Mahaprabhu stayed ten days in Shantipur, after which He was asked by His mother to make His home in Puri where she could always have news of Him. Damodar Pandit was one of the devotees who accompanied the Lord on His trip to Jagannath Puri. The others were Nityananda Prabhu, Mukunda Datta and Jagadananda Pandit.

When Mahaprabhu arrived in Puri, He immediately went to the Jagannath temple where He fainted in ecstasy upon seeing Lord Jagannath. Vasudeva Sarvabhauma then took Him to his own house to take care of Him. At that time, Sarvabhauma was convinced of the mayavada philosophy, but by Chaitanya Mahaprabhu's mercy, he gave up his predilection for these doctrines and took up the path of devotion. He then had a vision of Mahaprabhu in a six-armed form which inspired him to compose a Sanskrit hymn to the Lord in a hundred verses. He wrote the first two verses glorifying Mahaprabhu on a palm leaf and gave it to Jagadananda Pandit and Damodar Pandit to show to the Lord. Mukunda Datta was there when they came from Sarvabhauma's house, and he took the precaution of copying the two verses down on the wall in front of the Lord's residence before Jagadananda carried it in to show Him. As soon as Mahaprabhu saw the verses, which glorified Him as an incarnation of the Supreme Lord, He tore up the palm leaf, but because Mukunda had preserved them, the devotees were able to memorize them.[11]

Mahaprabhu took sannyas during the fortnight of the waxing moon of Magh. He arrived in Puri in the month of Phalgun and delivered Sarvabhauma Bhattacharya in the following month of Chaitra. He departed alone on His pilgrimage to Southern India in the month of Vaishakh. Nityananda Prabhu and the other devotees He left behind in Puri suffered greatly in His separation. Nitai had tried to persuade the Lord to take one of them as a companion, but He refused. He then apparently criticized them, while in fact praising them. Of Damodar Pandit He said:

> Even though I am a sannyasi and Damodar just a brahmachari, he is always telling Me what to do, holding the rod of chastisement over Me. He does not like Me to act independently and so I do not know how to behave in front of him. By Krishna's mercy, he does not care for public opinion whereas I cannot be indifferent to what people think. (Chaitanya Charitamrita 2.7.25-7)

When Mahaprabhu returned from South India, getting as far as Alalanath, He sent His servant companion Krishna Das to inform Nityananda and the other devotees that he had arrived. Damodar Pandit joined Jagadananda, Nityananda and Mukunda and joyfully rushed onto the main road where they met Him.

> As soon as he heard that the Lord had arrived, Nityananda got up and started off to meet him, as nothing could hold back his love. Jagadananda, Damodar Pandit and Mukunda all danced down the road, bursting with joy. (Chaitanya Charitamrita 2.9.339-40)

Once He had settled back in Puri, Mahaprabhu told Sarvabhauma Bhattacharya about the behavior of Kala Krishna Das. While in the South, Kala Krishna Das had been seduced away from his service to the Lord by a group of Bhattathari women. Mahaprabhu somehow managed to free him from their clutches and brought him back to Puri. He then told him that he was free to go wherever he liked as he was no longer welcome to stay in His company. Kala Krishna Das started to cry at this rejection, and out of sympathy for him, Nityananda, Damodar Pandit, Jagadananda and Mukunda discussed what to do with him. Finally, they recommended to the Lord that he be sent to Nabadwip with news of the Lord's return from His pilgrimage. The Lord approved the proposal and Kala Krishna Das set off, delighting everyone in Bengal with the good news. Later, when Damodar Pandit went back to Bengal himself, he met Kala Krishna Das.

DAMODAR'S BROTHER SHANKAR PANDIT

Mahaprabhu had a mixture of respect and affection for Damodar Pandit. Towards Damodar's younger brother Shankar Pandit, however, he had pure affection unseparated by any distance. However, for his own good, he put Shankar in the care of his older brother because he knew that Damodar would keep him under strict discipline.

> Seeing Shankar, the Lord turned to Damodar Pandit and said, "My love for you is mixed with reverence, whereas I love Shankar with all my heart. For this reason I am putting him under your care." (Chaitanya Charitamrita 2.11.146-7)
>
> Damodar answered, "Shankar is younger than me, but from this day on, by your grace, I will treat him as my elder."

During Mahaprabhu's later pastimes, Shankar stayed in His direct association, sleeping in the same room. The Lord would even sleep sometimes with his feet resting on Shankar's body, as a result of which he received the nickname *prabhu-pādopādhāna*—"Mahaprabhu's foot pillow."

DAMODAR'S TENDENCY TO CRITICIZE THE LORD'S BEHAVIOR

One day, the Lord Himself began serving prasad to His devotees. Since He was engaged in serving, He was not eating. The other devotees raised their hands and sat silently, refusing to eat until the Lord did so. Finally, Svarupa Damodar asked the Lord to sit down with Nityananda and take prasad. Svarupa Damodar, Jagadananda, Damodar Pandit and others then served. Only then did the devotees feel capable of eating.

When the Lord returned from the South, Maharaj Prataparudra asked several times for permission to meet Him. When Mahaprabhu refused, the King became so distraught that he threatened to give up his kingdom and become a beggar. The Lord's devotees were all impressed by the King's show of devotion and wished to intervene on his behalf. Sarvabhauma Bhattacharya suggested that instead of directly asking the Lord to meet with the King, they should simply praise his faith and devotion in the hope that this would change the Lord's attitude. Following this policy, Nityananda told the Lord of the King's intention to become a yogi beggar if he could not have a personal audience with Him. Mahaprabhu was somewhat mollified upon hearing this, but nevertheless maintained a hardline attitude. He named Damodar Pandit as a reason for such strict behavior:

"It is your wish to take Me to Cuttack to meet with the King. Not only will my spiritual practice be affected by such an action, but people will criticize Me. If they do, that does not bother Me so much, but I am afraid that Damodar Pandit will chastize Me. I will not go to meet the King on your order alone. I will only go if Damodar tells Me to."

(Chaitanya Charitamrita 2.12.23-5)

Srila Bhaktivinoda Thakur comments on these verses in the following way: "Mahaprabhu said, 'I will not grant an audience to the King on your order alone. Only if Damodar Pandit commands Me shall I consider it.' These words had a particular significance: though the Lord appreciated Damodar's devotion, his criticisms of the Lord's behavior were often unnecessary. The Lord was thus hinting that Damodar should stop this tendency to unnecessary criticism." (*Amṛta-pravāha-bhāṣya,* 2.12.25)

When Damodar Pandit heard the Lord's words, he muttered in response, "Mahaprabhu is the supremely independent Lord. He knows what should or should not be done. No insignificant jiva is going to dictate to Him what to do. The Lord is subject to devotion and the King is devoted to Him, so He will surely meet with him some day. He may be supremely independent, but He is controlled by His devotee's love."

OTHER PASTIMES IN PURI

Damodar Pandit was also the Lord's companion during the Rathayatra festival. He was a chorus singers in one of the seven kirtan groups where Svarupa Damodar was the lead singer. Advaita Acharya danced in the same group. Mahaprabhu set off for Vrindavan through Bengal with many of His associates, including Damodar Pandit. On this occasion, the Lord did not make it all the way to Vraja, as He changed His mind on the advice He received from Sanatan Goswami in Ramkeli. The following year, Mahaprabhu travelled through northern India, going as far as Vrindavan. He then returned to Puri with Balabhadra on the path through Jharikhanda. When they received the news of the Lord's arrival at Atharo Nala, all the Lord's devotees rushed there to welcome Him back. Mahaprabhu paid obeisances to all those who were His elders. At that time, Damodar Pandit received His embrace.

MAHAPRABHU AND THE WIDOW'S SON

A certain Orissan widow was living in Puri while Mahaprabhu was there. She had a handsome young son who would come to visit the Lord daily. He would pay his obeisances to the Lord and then engage Him in a lengthy, affectionate conversation. The boy came to love the Lord as he loved himself and was not able to go through a day without seeing Him. The Lord also treated the boy with great warmth. Damodar Pandit, however, could not tolerate seeing the affectionate relationship between the Lord and this boy. Though he repeatedly forbade him, the boy continued to come to see the Lord. A child will naturally go where he receives affection and the Lord was indeed very affectionate to him.

One day, Damodar Pandit finally exploded and said sarcastically to the Lord:

"Everyone says You are very learned because of the instructions You so generously give to others. I shall see what kind of master You really are. Now people will glorify You for being a great master and You will truly be famous as a master throughout Puri."

(Chaitanya Charitamrita 3.3.11-12)

The Lord did not understand at first what Damodar was getting at and made him explain himself. The Pandit made himself more explicit, "Lord, You do as you like. No one has the authority to dictate to You. Even so, this is a world full of gossipers whose speech no one can stifle. You are learned, so why don't You see the implications of Your acts? Why do You behave so affectionately towards a widow's child? She may be an austere and chaste Brahmin woman, but she has the fault of being young and beautiful. You too are a young and handsome man. Such a close relationship with her son gives the world occasion to whisper. Do you think that this is intelligent behavior?"

With that, Damodar fell silent. Mahaprabhu was satisfied with his sentiments and said,

"This is what I call a wave of pure love! None of my associates is as uninhibited as Damodar."

(Chaitanya Charitamrita 3.3.19)

MAHAPRABHU SENDS DAMODAR TO NADIA

One day Mahaprabhu called Damodar Pandit and asked him to go to Sachi Mata in Nabadwip and to help supervise her material affairs.

"No one is more suited than you to act for her protection, for you have put even Me on My guard. Amongst My associates, no one is as impartial as you. Religious principles can only be defended by someone who is free from bias or prejudice." (Chaitanya Charitamrita 3.3.22-3)

After telling Damodar to return to Nabadwip, He then consoled him by telling him to return to Puri from time to time. He also told him to pay repeated obeisances to His mother and gave him a confidential message to deliver to her:

"Tell her that I am happy, as this will give her happiness. Tell her that I have sent you to tell her of My personal activities. After you have warmed her heart in this way, remind her of one most secret event: I come to her home repeatedly to eat all the sweetmeats and vegetables she offers. She experiences my coming and eating of the offerings to be real, but because of external separation, she thinks that it is nothing but a dream. During the last Magh sankranti festival, she cooked a variety of vegetables, condensed milk, cakes and sweet rice for Me. She then offered the food to Lord Krishna, and while in meditation, I suddenly appeared and her eyes filled with tears. When she saw Me come there in great haste and eat everything, she felt great happiness. But a moment later, after she had wiped her eyes, she saw that the plate she had offered me was empty and thought, 'I only dreamt that Nimai was eating everything.'

"In the condition of external separation, she again became bewildered, thinking that she had not offered any food to Lord Vishnu. She went back to the kitchen to look at the cooking pots and found that every one of them was still filled with food. So she cleansed the altar and made the offering once again. This is how I come again and again to eat everything she offers Me, for I am attracted by her pure love. I reside in Nilachala only because she told Me to. Even still, she repeatedly pulls Me back to her out of her great love for Me." (Chaitanya Charitamrita 3.3.19-39)

Mahaprabhu then gave some Jagannath prasad to Damodar Pandit and told him to give it to Sachi Mata and the other Nabadwip devotees. Damodar set off and carried out the Lord's instructions to the letter. With the Pandit there in Nabadwip, the devotees became very careful about their behavior. No one dared to act in an independent manner. If any one of Mahaprabhu's followers made even the slightest transgression in etiquette, Damodar Pandit would establish the standards of behavior by verbally punishing the offender.

The ignorance of atheism will flee from anyone who hears this history of Damodar Pandit's chastisement of the Lord which has just been described.

(Chaitanya Charitamrita 3.3.46)

Damodar Pandit is thus one of the great devotees through whose preaching the glories of the Holy Name have spread throughout the universe. Mahaprabhu glorified these great souls when He said,

"I have come to possess devotion to Krishna through the grace of all these great devotees who have preached love for the Holy Name throughout the world."

(Chaitanya Charitamrita 3.7.50)

In the *Bhakti-ratnākara*, Narahari Chakravarti says that Narottam Das Thakur met Damodar Pandit in Nabadwip. Narottam paid his obeisances to his feet in excitement at meeting a direct associate of the Lord.

(*Bhakti-ratnākara* 8.93)

[11] The verses can be found in the chapters on Jagadananda Pandit and Sarvabhauma Bhattacharya.

Sri Jagadananda Pandit

kenāvāntara-bhedena bhedaṁ kurvanti sātvatāḥ
satyabhāmā-prakāśo'pi jagadānanda-paṇḍitaḥ

Devotees make no inner distinction between Satyabhama and Jagadananda Pandit.

(*Gaura-gaṇoddeśa-dīpikā* 51)

Jagadananda Pandit is the very life of the Lord. He is known everywhere as being a manifestation of Satyabhama. (Chaitanya Charitamrita 1.10.21)

All glories to Gauranga, the life of Jagadananda and Sri Garbha! All glories to the wealth of Vakresvara Pandit! (Chaitanya Bhagavata 2.7.3)

The date and place of Jagadananda Pandit's birth are unknown. Devotees who are seeking devotion as the goal of their lives do not consider detailed information about a spiritual master's material identity to be essential. From Chaitanya Bhagavata we learn that Jagadananda Pandit was present at Srivas Angan and at Chandrasekhar's house after Mahaprabhu returned from Gaya and so participated in the sankirtan movement from its very beginnings.

All the Vaishnavas felt great enthusiasm when they heard that Mahaprabhu had begun his sankirtan movement. Every night, these kirtans took place in the house of Srivas Pandit, and on certain occasions, in the house of Chandrasekhar Acharya. Nityananda, Gadadhar, Advaita, Srivas, Vidyanidhi, Murari, Hiranya, Hari Das, Ganga Das, Vanamālī, Vijaya, Nandan, Jagadananda, Buddhimanta

Khan, Narayan—these were some of the personalities who accompanied the Lord as He danced. Other than such intimate associates, no one was allowed entrance into the sankirtan. (Chaitanya Bhagavata 2.8.110-113, 117)

Thus from Vrindavan Das' account, we know that Jagadananda Pandit is an eternal associate of the Lord and participated with Him in His Nabadwip sankirtan pastimes. From this we can surmise that he was born somewhere in Bengal.

JAGADANANDA ACCOMPANIES THE LORD TO PURI

According to the Chaitanya Bhagavata, Jagadananda Pandit was in the group of devotees who accompanied Mahaprabhu from Shantipur to Puri after He took sannyas, the others being Nityananda Prabhu, Gadadhar Pandit, Mukunda Datta, Govinda and Brahmananda. The Chaitanya Charitamrita version has the Lord being accompanied by Nityananda, Jagadananda, Damodar and Mukunda.

On their way to Puri, as they travelled through Atisara, Chatrabhog, Northern Orissa, Suvarnarekha, Jaleshwar, Remuna, Jajpur, Vaitarani, Cuttack, Sakshi Gopal, Bhubaneshwar, Kamalpur, and Atharo Nala, Mahaprabhu gave His companions many lessons in being impartial and desireless, depending absolutely on the Lord and other such matters. In one place named Ganga Ghat, just across the frontier into Orissa, Mahaprabhu Himself told His companions to wait in a temple while He went to the village to beg. He came back with rice and vegetables in His cloth and gave them to Jagadananda to cook. When the Pandit had finished preparing the meal, Mahaprabhu and His other companions ate his cooking with great relish.

According to the Chaitanya Bhagavata, Mahaprabhu gave his danda (staff) to Jagadananda to carry as they walked. One day, Jagadananda gave the danda to Nityananda Prabhu to hold as he went to collect foodstuffs. Nityananda Prabhu is non-different from Balaram and he took this opportunity to break Mahaprabhu's staff into three pieces, so teaching his followers to take the tridanda, a staff of three branches signifying the acceptance of Vaishnava tridandi sannyas. According to the Chaitanya Bhagavata, Jagadananda took the broken staff to Mahaprabhu, who was extremely unhappy to have lost His one and only possession. Mahaprabhu told His companions that He wished to travel alone, giving them the choice of whether they would walk in front or behind Him. The devotees answered that they would walk behind Him, not in front.

Leaving Nityananda and Svarupa in one place, Jagadananda went to look for food. Jagadananda carried the Lord's danda, and he left it with Nityananda when he went. He said, "Take care of the Lord's danda. I will be right back after begging foodstuffs."

(Chaitanya Bhagavata 3.2.202-4)

Still walking in front of the other devotees, when He arrived at Atharo Nala Mahaprabhu saw a vision of Krishna playing His flute on the pinnacle of the Jagannath Puri temple. He ran toward the temple and entered to behold the form of Jagannath, whereupon He fell into a swoon. Sarvabhauma Bhattacharya noticed Him and took Him to his own house where he saw to His care. Nityananda, Jagadananda, Mukunda and Damodar arrived at the Jagannath temple not long afterwards. There they heard that the Lord was at Sarvabhauma's residence and immediately went there. This was Jagadananda's first meeting with Sarvabhauma Bhattacharya.

A PERMANENT ASSOCIATE OF THE LORD AT PURI

The first time that Mahaprabhu wished to go to Vrindavan, he came to Gauda Mandala from Puri. He stayed in Vidyanagar for five days; from there he went on to Kuliya, and then through Maldah district to the village of Ramakeli where He met with Rupa and Sanatan. Jagadananda was amongst the associates of Mahaprabhu present on that occasion along with Nityananda, Hari Das, Srivas, Gadadhar, Mukunda, Murari and Vakresvara.

Jagadananda Pandit was a permanent associate of the Lord at Puri:

Gadadhar Pandit, Vakresvara, Damodar, Shankar, Hari Das, Jagadananda, Bhavananda, Govinda, Kashisvara, Paramananda Puri and Svarupa Damodar, all came and made their residence in Puri. They, along with Ramananda Raya and other long-time residents of Sri Kṣetra, were Mahaprabhu's permanent companions.

(Chaitanya Charitamrita 2.1.252-4)

Jagadananda Pandit's mood was primarily that of madhura rasa, which was very pleasing to Mahaprabhu and won His heart. In the Chaitanya Charitamrita, this is described as follows:

Paramananda Puri had parental affection for Mahaprabhu; Ramananda Raya had love for him in pure friendship; Govinda Das' love for him was as a servant. Gadadhar, Jagadananda and Svarupa Damodar worshiped in the ecstasy of the chief rasa. Mahaprabhu's heart was won by these four different loving attitudes.

(Chaitanya Charitamrita 2.2.78)

By Mahaprabhu's mercy, Sarvabhauma Bhattacharya gave up his predilection for the impersonal philosophy of mayavada and took up the path of devotion. He then had a vision of Mahaprabhu in a six-armed form that inspired him to compose a Sanskrit hymn to the Lord in a hundred verses. He wrote the first two verses glorifying Mahaprabhu on a palm leaf and gave it to Jagadananda to show the Lord. Mukunda Datta was there when Jagadananda came from Sarvabhauma's house, carrying Jagannath prasad and the palm leaf. He took the precaution of copying the two verses down on the wall in front of the Lord's residence before Jagadananda carried it in to show Him. As soon as Mahaprabhu saw the verses, which glorified Him as an incarnation of the Supreme Lord, He tore up the palm leaf. Fortunately, as a result of Mukunda's foresight, the devotees were able to relish the joy from reading the verses. They are as follows:

vairāgya-vidyā-nija-bhakti-yoga-
śikṣārtham ekaḥ puruṣaḥ purāṇaḥ
śrī-kṛṣṇa-caitanya-śarīra-dhārī
kṛpāmbudhir yas tam ahaṁ prapadye

kālān naṣṭaṁ bhakti-yogaṁ nijaṁ yaḥ
prāduṣkartuṁ kṛṣṇa-caitanya-nāmā
āvirbhūtas tasya padāravinde
gāḍhaṁ gāḍhaṁ līyate citta-bhṛṅgaḥ

Let me take shelter of the Supreme Personality of Godhead, the ocean of transcendental mercy, Sri Krishna, who has descended in the form of Lord Chaitanya Mahaprabhu to teach us detachment, real knowledge and His own devotional service.

The Supreme Personality of Godhead, who has taken the name of Sri Krishna Chaitanya, has appeared to reveal the ancient system of devotional service to Himself which had almost been lost due to the influence of time. I pray that the honeybee of my mind will drink deeply of the honey of His lotus feet. (Chaitanya Charitamrita 2.6.253-4; *Chaitanya-candrodaya-nāṭaka* 6.74)

Mahaprabhu took sannyas during the fortnight of the waxing moon of the month of Magh (January-February). He arrived in Nilachala in the month of Phalgun (February-March). In the month of Chaitra (March-April), He converted Sarvabhauma Bhattacharya to Vaishnavism. In the month of Vaishakh (April-May), He left on pilgrimage to the south of India. When Mahaprabhu said that He wanted to go on this pilgrimage alone, Nityananda Prabhu tried to convince Him that He should take a companion and suggested that he would accompany Him. At this time, Mahaprabhu showed his great affection for His companions (Nityananda Prabhu, Damodar Brahmachari, and Jagadananda Pandit) by remonstrating with them and refusing their company. Of Jagadananda, He said:

"Jagadananda wants me to enjoy sense gratification. I try to do whatever he tells me because I am afraid of him. Whenever I act contrary to his wishes, he gets angry and stops talking to Me for three days at a time."
(Chaitanya Charitamrita 2.7.21-2)

While Mahaprabhu was travelling in the South, the devotees waited for Him, feeling great distress on account of His absence. The deeper one's love, the more one feels the pain of separation. The sign of real love is in the intensity of the joy one feels at being united with someone from whom one has been separated. After travelling for several months, the Lord arrived in Alalanath, near Puri, and sent His servant Kala Krishna Das to tell Nityananda and the other devotees that He had returned. The enthusiasm that they all felt in seeing Him again knew no bounds and they all rushed to Alalanath. Krishna Das Kaviraj Goswami describes their reaction to the news of His arrival in his Chaitanya Charitamrita as follows:

As soon as Nityananda heard of Mahaprabhu's arrival, he immediately set off to see Him. Indeed, his love for the Lord made him very impatient. Jagadananda, Damodar Pandit and Mukunda danced as they went to greet the Lord, their bodies unable to hold back their ecstasy.
(Chaitanya Charitamrita 2.9.339-40)

Nityananda Prabhu, Jagadananda and the others advised Mahaprabhu to send Kala Krishna Das to Bengal to tell Sachi that He had returned from the pilgrimage to South India. Desiring to please His devotees, Mahaprabhu approved of the idea. While in Puri, Jagadananda gradually met with all of Mahaprabhu's devotees, including Svarupa Damodar, Raya Ramananda, and Hari Das Thakur. One of Jagadananda's most enjoyable services to the Lord and his devotees was to satisfy them with the foodstuffs that he had himself cooked.

The Bengal devotees came annually during the Chaturmasya period to be with the Lord in Nilachala. They did this three years in a row before Mahaprabhu announced His determination to go to Vrindavan. This time, Jagadananda was amongst the Lord's companions as He travelled through Orissa and Gaudadesh. They went to Panihati, Kumarahatta, Kuliya village, and Ramakeli, before finally turning back from the village of Kanair Natshala to return to Puri, abandoning the pilgrimage to Vrindavan because of the large crowd of devotees that had gathered around Him. The Lord vowed that the next time He would travel to Vrindavan alone. Indeed, the next time He went, He took the path through the Jharikhanda jungles accompanied only by a servant named Balabhadra Bhattacharya. When Mahaprabhu returned by the same path, He was once again reunited with His loving devotees including Jagadananda, who had once again been suffering greatly in His absence. This reunion was so joyful that it is beyond description.

SANATAN COMES TO PURI

On one occasion, Sanatan Goswami took the Jharikhanda route to Nilachala from Vraja. On the way, he developed blistering sores all over his body due to drinking bad water and fasting. Sanatan became extremely troubled by the disease because his physical impurity would make him an obstacle to the servants of Jagannath. In view of this potential offense, he decided that he would throw himself under the wheels of Jagannath's chariot during the Rathayatra festival. Mahaprabhu, the indweller of all beings, knew that Sanatan had made this decision and said to him, "You cannot attain Krishna through suicide. You can only attain Him through bhajan. You have no right to destroy the body which has been given to you so that you can render service."

These instructions had an effect on Sanatan and he changed his mind. The Lord does not concern Himself with the purity or impurity of a devotee's external body; He is attracted by the inner purity of one's desire for service. Therefore Mahaprabhu did not hesitate to embrace Sanatan, again and again. When He did so, the pus leaking from Sanatan's sores touched the Lord's body, which embarrassed and shamed him. Sanatan turned to Jagadananda Pandit for advice and Jagadananda told him that he should leave for Vrindavan immediately after the Rathayatra. Sanatan thought that this was the best solution and went to Mahaprabhu to ask Him permission to depart. When Mahaprabhu heard this, He became angry and chastised Jagadananda, saying:

"Jagadananda is just a newcomer, a boy. Yet, he has become so proud that he thinks he can give even you advice. You are his guru in every respect, both in material and spiritual terms. And yet he gives you counsel? Doesn't he know his own worth? You are My teacher; you are an authority to even Me. And yet, like an impudent child, he is giving instruction to one as qualified as you."

(Chaitanya Charitamrita 3.4.158-60)

The devotee and the Lord occasionally chastise their intimates. If a devotee is chastised by the Lord, he should consider it a great good fortune. Sanatan reacted to Mahaprabhu's criticism of Jagadananda as a sign of his great fortune and his own misfortune. He said,

"You have accept Jagadananda into your inner circle of intimates, while you treat me with veneration. It is as though you were giving him ambrosia to drink and me the bitter juice of neem and tobacco leaves."

(Chaitanya Charitamrita 3.4.163)

Even though Mahaprabhu had long been won over by Jagadananda's devotion to Him, He made a point of teaching all His followers Vaishnava etiquette and the importance of offering the proper respect to senior Vaishnavas such as Sanatan Goswami Prabhu through him. He said,

"Jagadananda is not more dear to Me than you are, but I cannot tolerate transgressions of etiquette."

(Chaitanya Charitamrita 3.4.166)

Later, when Mahaprabhu was telling Vallabha Bhatta about the greatness of devotees, he said that one could attain devotion to Krishna through the association of preachers of the Holy Name like Jagadananda Pandit.

Acharyaratna, Acharyanidhi, Gadadhar Pandit, Jagadananda, Damodar, Shankar, Vakresvara, Kashisvara, Mukunda, Vasudeva, Murari and so many other great devotees have appeared in Bengal. They have preached the glories of the Holy Name throughout the world. It is through their association that I have whatever little devotion to Krishna I do. (Chaitanya Charitamrita 3.7.48-50)

Krishna Das Kaviraj Goswami contrasts the sincere loving attitude of Jagadananda Pandit with the hypocrisy of Ramachandra Puri. Even though Ramachandra Puri was officially a disciple of Madhavendra Puri, he had no proclivity for service. Because of his lack of sincerity and his false piety, he was ultimately deprived of his guru's mercy. Jagadananda was also present at Hari Das Thakur's funeral celebration, serving prasad to the senior associates of the Lord. By his behavior, he showed that giving prasad to the devotees is an important element of devotional service.

JAGADANANDA AS SATYABHAMA

Jagadananda is the incarnation of Satyabhama. Thus, because of his refractory nature, he would often quarrel with Mahaprabhu.

Jagadananda Pandit had a deep and pure love for the Lord, like that of Satyabhama for Krishna. He was moody, being possessed of the *vāmā* nature. He would repeatedly provoke loving arguments with the Lord and there always seemed to be some misunderstanding between them.

(Chaitanya Charitamrita 3.7.142-3)

During the Chaturmasya, all the devotees would come to meet the Lord in Nilachala and only return home at the end of the four-month period. In the same year that Mahaprabhu told Nityananda not to come to Puri, He also sent Jagadananda to Nabadwip with a message for His mother. Jagadananda related all that Mahaprabhu had told him about the exact times when Sachi Mata thought that she had dreamt or hallucinated His coming and eating her food offerings. When she heard this from Jagadananda, Sachi came to believe that these secret visits had not been hallucinations, but in fact real—the Lord really had come to Nabadwip. When the other devotees in Mahaprabhu's hometown met His intimate associate, Jagadananda, they all were immersed in an ocean of happiness.

From Nabadwip, Jagadananda went to Shivananda Sen's house where he collected a fragrant sandalwood oil for rubbing on Mahaprabhu's head. He filled an earthen jug with the oil and brought it back to Puri where he gave it to Govinda, the Lord's servant. Govinda told Mahaprabhu, "Jagadananda Pandit has brought aromatic sandalwood oil back from Gaudadesh with him. If you rub it on your head, it will relieve the symptoms of disturbed bile and wind."

In order to set a proper example for those in the renounced order of life, Mahaprabhu answered, "Sannyasis are forbidden the use of body oils. It is even more reprehensible for them to use aromatic oils. Since Jagadananda has gone to the trouble of bringing the oil all the way here, you can give it to the Jagannath temple. They can use the oil to light lamps for the Deity. That will make all his troubles worthwhile."

Govinda told Jagadananda of Mahaprabhu's decision. Jagadananda began to sulk and stopped talking. After ten days, Govinda told Mahaprabhu that Jagadananda still wished him to use the oil. Mahaprabhu became angry and, in order to teach the world, said,

"Why don't we hire a masseur to give me massage?

Are these the pleasures for which I have taken the renounced order? It will no doubt amuse you all to see My downfall. As I walk along the road, people will get a whiff of my perfumes and say, 'There goes that womanizing monk.'" (Chaitanya Charitamrita 3.12.112-4)

Govinda was speechless at Mahaprabhu's tirade. When Jagadananda Pandit came to vist Mahaprabhu the next morning, the Lord said, "A sannyasi should not use fragrant oils. The best thing to do is to offer it to Lord Jagannath for His service." Jagadananda became angry and proudly retorted, "Who told you I brought this oil all the way from Gaudadesh? It's a lie." With that he threw down the earthen jug in the courtyard and broke it. Then he went to his own room, locked the door and lay down.

After he had fasted for three days, Mahaprabhu finally went to assuage him, knocking on his door and saying gently, "Jagadananda! Open the door. I am going now to bathe and then to the temple for darshan of Jagannath. When I come back I will take whatever food you have prepared for Me. So start cooking."

Out of his love for the Lord, Jagadananda immediately got up, bathed and started preparing the Lord's lunch. After performing His noonday rituals, the Lord returned, let Jagadananda wash His feet and then sat down to eat. Jagadananda set a banana leaf before Him and then covered it with fine rice soaked in clarified butter, numerous vegetable preparations and then cakes and sweet rice. Mahaprabhu told Jagadananda to set out another banana leaf and fill it with food as he had done so that he could eat beside Him. He lifted his hands in the air and refused to eat a bite until Jagadananda sat down and ate with Him. Finally, Jagadananda's pride melted and he agreed to take the Lord's prasad once He had finished. As He ate, Mahaprabhu repeatedly praised the food that Jagadananda had cooked in his loving anger.

"This is the kind of nectar that you offer to Krishna. Who can estimate the extent of your good fortune?"
(Chaitanya Charitamrita 3.12.133)

Jagadananda kept serving more and more vegetables to the Lord, who out of fear refused nothing, eating everything that He was given. The Lord was afraid that if He refused even a single preparation Jagadananda would again start fasting. So on that day He ate ten times as much as He did normally. After the meal, Jagadananda gave Him some aromatic spices, sandalwood and a garland. Mahaprabhu then insisted that he sit down and take his meal in front of Him. Jagadananda pleaded with Mahaprabhu to go and rest, as he was well aware of the demands of etiquette. Ramai and Raghunath Bhatta had also helped with the cooking, so he wanted them to eat before sitting down himself, but he assured the Lord that he would. Mahaprabhu was still not convinced and told Govinda to remain there and report to Him whether or not Jagadananda had eaten. But Jagadananda immediately told Govinda to go and massage the Lord's feet. After he had served Ramai, Nandai, Govinda and Raghunath Bhatta prasadam, Jagadananda himself took the remnants of Mahaprabhu's plate. When Mahaprabhu heard that Jagadananda had finally eaten, He was able to rest peacefully.

"Jagadananda's love for the Lord was just like the descriptions of Satyabhama's love for Krishna in the Bhagavata. Who can describe the extent of Jagadananda's good fortune? His love is the standard by which that of others is to be compared. Anyone who hears about the loving exchanges (*prema-vivarta*) between Jagadananda Pandit and Sri Chaitanya Mahaprabhu will know the characteristics of prema and will attain the wealth of pure love.
(Chaitanya Charitamrita 3.12.152-4)

Srila Bhaktisiddhanta Saraswati Goswami Thakur writes that the words *prema-vivarta* in this verse can mean both the kind of confused transformations of love that Jagadananda underwent with the Lord, or the book of that name which he authored.

THE LORD SLEEPS ON PLANTAIN BARK

Due to his intense feelings of separation from Krishna, Mahaprabhu started to increase His penances. He decided to sleep on a bed of dried plantain bark, which caused pain by rubbing against His bones. The devotees were greatly distressed to see the Lord's suffering. Jagadananda decided to take steps to alleviate the Lord's pain by getting some cloth and dying it saffron, and then filling it with cotton from the silk cotton tree. In this way he made both a mattress and a pillow for the Lord's comfort. Jagadananda then asked Govinda Das to give the mattress and pillow to the Lord and Svarupa Damodar to convince Him to use them. When it was time for the Lord to go to bed and He saw the cotton pillow, He became angry. When he heard that Jagadananda Pandit had given it, however, He hesitated. He made a pretense of anger, "A mattress and pillow? Why don't you just go and get me a bed? A sannyasi is supposed to sleep on the ground. Jagadananda wants Me to become a sense enjoyer. This is shameful."

Jagadananda was saddened when he heard from Svarupa Damodar that Mahaprabhu had refused the bedding. However, Svarupa Damodar cleverly made some bedding out of dried banana leaves that the Lord accepted. This satisfied all the devotees with the exception of Jagadananda.

Though he said nothing about it, Jagadananda was angry and asked Mahaprabhu for permission to go to Vrindavan. The Lord was able to understand the real reason for his dissatisfaction and said to him in a consoling voice, "You are angry and blame me for it. And so you want to go to Mathura and become a beggar?" The petulant Jagadananda hid his true feelings and simply said, "I have wanted to go to Vrindavan for a long time. Previously you would not give me permission, so I could not."

Mahaprabhu out of His affection for Jagadananda would not allow him to leave, even though he asked Him repeatedly. Finally, Jagadananda asked Svarupa Damodar to intercede on his behalf and get the Lord's permission to go. Svarupa Damodar went to Mahaprabhu and said, "Jagadananda's desire to see Vrindavan is very strong. I think it would be a good idea if you sent him to Vrindavan just as you previously sent him to Nabadwip with a message for Sachi Mata." Mahaprabhu finally allowed Himself to be persuaded and gave Jagadananda permission to go to Vraja. Out of his affection for him, however, He gave him elaborate instructions for his voyage. "The road up to Benares is free from any problems. After Benares, however, the road is full of robbers, so be careful. You should take some soldiers with you for protection. If the highwaymen see a single Bengali on the road, they will be sure to attack and loot him. When you get to Mathura, first go and see Sanatan. Offer your respects to the Chobey Brahmins of Mathura, but don't associate with them. You will not be able to understand their behavior, so respect them at a distance. Perform parikrama of Vraja-mandala with Sanatan, do not leave his side for even a moment. Don't climb Govardhan to see Gopal. Don't stay in Vraja for a long time. Hurry back." (Chaitanya Charitamrita 3.13.39)

JAGADANANDA CHASTISES SANATAN

Jagadananda paid his obeisance to the Lord and left on foot for Benares where he met with Tapan Mishra and Chandrasekhar. From there he went on to Mathura where he met Sanatan Goswami. Sanatan took him around the twelve forests of Vraja and then they stayed together for some time in Gokula Mahavan. Sanatan Goswami used to live on madhukari (begging for pieces of bread from the local people), but since Jagadananda was not habituated to a wheat-based diet, he went to a local temple and cooked rice. One day, Jagadananda invited Sanatan Goswami to eat. A certain sannyasi named Mukunda Saraswati had given a saffron cloth to Sanatan, which he wore wrapped around his head. When Jagadananda saw this, he thought that the cloth must have been given to Sanatan by Mahaprabhu and was overwhelmed with love. When he learned, however, that it had been given by someone else, he became so angry that he was ready to hit Sanatan with the rice pot. He criticized Sanatan:

> "You are Mahaprabhu's most important associate. No one is dearer to Him than you. How could anyone tolerate you wearing another sannyasi's cloth around your head?" Sanatan answered, "Well said! It is clear, Pandit Mahashaya, that you are unequalled in your love for the Lord. I could not have learned this lesson from anyone but you, for you alone have such solid faith in the Lord. My purpose in binding the cloth around my head has been realized, for as soon as you saw it, I was able to witness the manifestations of your love for the Lord. A Vaishnava should not wear red cloth. I will give it to someone else, for I have no further need for it."
>
> (Chaitanya Charitamrita 3.13.56-61)

Jagadananda offered the food he had cooked to Mahaprabhu and then took prasad with Sanatan. After staying with him for two months, he started to feel his absence from Mahaprabhu too intensely and asked Sanatan for permission to return to Puri. Sanatan bid him goodbye, giving him sand from the place where Krishna held the rāsa dance, a stone from Govardhan, a garland of guñja berries and some dried ripe pīlu fruits for Mahaprabhu. Jagadananda was delighted to return to Puri and see Mahaprabhu and the other devotees again. Mahaprabhu embraced him tightly and was extremely pleased with the gifts sent by Sanatan. Most of the devotees did not know how to eat pīlu fruits, but because they were from Vrindavan, they enjoyed them anyway.

ADVAITA'S MESSAGE

Mahaprabhu never forgot Sachi Maha's pure parental affection for Him, and would send Jagadananda every year to Nabadwip with a piece of His used cloth. Jagadananda would come and talk to her about the Lord and alleviate somewhat the suffering she felt in separation from her son. The last time that he went, he went to Advaita Acharya's house to ask for permission to return to Puri. Advaita gave Jagadananda a cryptic message to deliver to Mahaprabhu. The riddle went as follows:

> Tell the Lord that I pay him a million obeisances and that I humbly submit to him the following: Tell the madman that everyone has gone mad. Tell the madman that they are no longer selling rice in the market. Tell the madman that the crazies are no longer good for anything. Tell the madman that this is what the madman said.
>
> (Chaitanya Charitamrita 3.19.19-21)

Bhaktivinoda Thakur explains this riddle in this way: "Tell Mahaprabhu that everyone has become intoxicated with love for Krishna and so in the marketplace of love, no one is buying the rice of Krishna prema any longer. Tell Mahaprabhu that the saintly madmen (*āul*) are so intoxicated with love that they are no longer involved in their material duties. Tell Mahaprabhu that Advaita said this in a state of complete intoxication of prema. In short, the message was that the purpose for which Advaita had been called Mahaprabhu to earth had been achieved. The Lord may now do as He pleases."

The date and place of Jagadananda Pandit's departure from this world are unknown.

VASUDEVA SARVABHAUMA BHATTACHARYA

bhaṭṭācāryaḥ sārvabhaumaḥ purāsīd gīṣpatir divi

Sarvabhauma Bhattacharya was formerly Brihaspati, the guru of the gods. (*Gaura-gaṇoddeśa-dīpikā* 119)

SARVABHAUMA'S SCHOLARSHIP

When Krishna Das Kaviraj Goswami lists Sri Chaitanya's branches, he first names devotees like Paramananda Puri and Svarupa Damodar, who came to join the Lord in Jagannath Puri. After them, he enumerates the Bengali devotees who were already living in Puri when the Lord arrived there and who then met Him for the very first time. Sarvabhauma Bhattacharya is considered to be the most important of these devotees.

> One of the Lord's biggest branches was Sarvabhauma Bhattacharya. Another was Sarvabhauma's brother-in-law, Gopinath Acharya.
> (Chaitanya Charitamrita 1.10.130)

Srila Bhaktisiddhanta Saraswati Goswami Thakur's has commented on this Bengali verse as follows: "Sarvabhauma Bhattacharya's given name was Vasudeva. He was the son of Maheshvara Visharad, a celebrated resident of Vidyanagar, a village that lies about two and a half miles away from both Nabadwip and Champahati. Sarvabhauma Bhattacharya was a student of Pakshadhar Mishra, the head professor of what was at that time India's leading school of logic (Nyaya), in Mithila, Bihar. Sarvabhauma Bhattacharya memorized the entire body of learning available there and then returned to Nabadwip to establish his own school for the study of logic. This caused a revolution in the history of this branch of learning, as the importance of Mithila was diminished to the profit of Nabadwip, which to this day still has the reputation of being the leading centre of Nyaya studies. According to some, the celebrated logician Raghunath Shiromani, author of the work *Dīdhiti*, studied under Sarvabhauma Bhattacharya. Whatever the truth of such statements, it is clear that Sarvabhauma Bhattacharya had tremendous learning in both Nyaya and Vedanta. Although he was a gṛhastha, he took the *kṣetra-sannyāsa,* vowing never to set foot outside of Jagannath Puri, and taught Vedanta to students there. He gave discourses on Shankaracharya's commentary on the Vedanta to Mahaprabhu Himself until he came to understand its real meaning by the Lord's grace."

Sarvabhauma Bhattacharya was an aristocratic Brahmin of the Rarha class. From the *Gauḍīya Vaiṣṇava Abhidhāna*, we learn that he took birth in the first half of the 14th century of the Shaka era. We also learn there that when he studied in Mithila, the Nyaya scholars of that city attempted to maintain their monopoly on teaching this branch of philosophy by prohibiting their foreign students from copying the textbooks. For this reason it was impossible to either teach or study logic in Bengal at that time. Vasudeva Bhattacharya was endowed with marvellous powers of retention and was thus able to memorize all the texts that he had studied in Mithila. When he returned to Bengal, he was thus able to transcribe these texts and make them readily available to his students. The scholar Dr. Dinesh Chandra Bhattacharya has argued that this is only a legend, however. He says that in fact Vasudeva Sarvabhauma learned the Navya-nyāya ("new logical method") from his father, Visharad, and never went to Mithila. When Maharaj Prataparudra heard of his tremendous learning, he invited him to come to Puri to become the chief scholar of his court.

SARVABHAUMA, THE TEACHER OF MAYAVADA

Even though he was a householder, Sarvabhauma Bhattacharya was so highly qualified that he became the teacher even of many sannyasis of the impersonalist school. In fact, the guru of the gods, Brihaspati, took birth as Sarvabhauma Bhattacharya in order to support Mahaprabhu's pastime of delivering the mayavadis. Little wonder that he was an incomparable scholar!

Sri Chaitanya Mahaprabhu and all the Vaishnava acharyas have accepted as dogmatic truth that the object of worship (*bhajanīya*), the worshiper (*bhajana-kārī*) and the act of worship (*bhajana*) are all eternal principles. Pure devotional service cannot be present if the eternal existence of any one of these three principles is denied. According to the pure and true doctrines of Vaishnavism, the Supreme Lord, who is the object of worship, possesses an eternal identity and His name, form, qualities and pastimes are all eternal and spiritual in nature. The mayavadis who follow the path of knowledge deny the eternal spiritual character of the Lord's essence, name, form, qualities and pastimes. They hold that these are a product of the illusory energy. This is the source of the word "mayavada," which means "illusory" (*māyā*), "form" (*rūpa*), and "doctrine" (*vāda*). The mayavadis hold that the form of the Lord is a fabrication that is only useful as a meditation aid for less advanced spiritual practitioners. They hold that Brahman, the formless, undifferentiated and potency-less form is the supreme truth. Nothing exists outside of this Brahman and thus the individual living being is identical with it.

The mayavadis also hold that devotional practice has a momentary value for less advanced spiritual practitioners. They say it helps them to attain the state of identification with Brahman, after which it can be discarded as it has no status in the eternal truth. It is clear, then, that such a doctrine interferes with the attainment of the fifth and ultimate goal of life, love of God. The founders of the four schools of Vaishnava thought,

Madhvacharya, Ramanujacharya, Vishnu Swami and Nimbārka, as well as the Supreme Lord, Sri Chaitanya Mahaprabhu, have thus fought against the mayavadi teachings of Sankaracharya characterized by the *vivarta-vāda* (the doctrine of the apparent transformation of Brahman). Those who seek their ultimate benefit accept the teaching given by Vedavyasa himself, known as *śakti-pariṇāma-vāda* ("the doctrine of the transformation of the energies of Brahman").

Sri Chaitanya Mahaprabhu appeared in this most fortunate age of Kali in order to bestow the most elevated service to Krishna in the conjugal mood upon everyone, whether low or highborn. He gave the supreme gift of love for God without judging the qualifications of the recipient. Furthermore, He descended with the intention of destroying the desires that lead the living being away from the Lord and interfere with his attainment of love; He also bestowed upon them the desire for this love and the power through which it can be established in their hearts. Even with all this mercy, the mayavada doctrine remains the biggest obstacle to attaining love for Krishna.

Mahaprabhu delivered the mayavadi Sarvabhauma Bhattacharya. Both Vrindavan Das Thakur, who is not different from Vedavyasa, and Krishna Das Kaviraj Goswami have described how this took place in their biographies of the Lord. The essence of the accounts of the Chaitanya Bhagavata and Chaitanya Charitamrita are given below.

SARVABHAUMA TAKES THE LORD TO HIS HOUSE

At the age of 24, Mahaprabhu left Nabadwip to take sannyas from Keshava Bharati in Katwa. From there He went to Shantipur and then on to Puri. When He arrived at Atharo Nala, the bridge with eighteen arches that marks the entrance to the town of Jagannath Puri, the Lord saw the temple spire and had a vision of Krishna. He ran toward the temple in a trance of love and when He entered it, ran towards the deity of Jagannath in order to embrace Him. As He came close to the altar, He fell down in a faint. The temple watchmen and sevakas saw Him lying unconscious in the temple, and thinking Him to be a vagrant, prepared to beat and evict Him from the grounds.

Vasudeva Sarvabhauma happened to be present and he stopped them from so doing. He had been impressed by the beauty of the Lord as well as by His manifestations of spiritual ecstasy at the sight of Lord Jagannath. He could understand that this was no ordinary person. With the help of his disciples and the temple guards, Vasudeva Sarvabhauma had the unconscious Lord transported to his own home. He was quite anxious about the Lord's condition and placed a tuft of cotton in front of His nose to see if He was still breathing. He was relieved when he saw the cotton move slightly.

In the meantime, Nityananda Prabhu, Mukunda Datta, Jagadananda Pandit and Damodar Pandit arrived at the Lion's Gate entrance to the temple. They heard from other visitors to the temple that Mahaprabhu had been removed and taken to Sarvabhauma Bhattacharya's house. At that very moment, Sarvabhauma's brother-in-law Gopinath Acharya passed by. Since he too was from Nabadwip, the Lord's devotees instantly recognized him. Mukunda told Gopinath everything about Mahaprabhu's sannyas and His coming to Puri, as well as about His being taken to Ṣarvabhauma's house. Gopinath was thrilled to hear all this news and immediately took them to his brother-in-law's house.

The devotees were relieved and overjoyed to see the Lord there. Sarvabhauma paid his obeisances to Nityananda Prabhu and then told them to go and take darshan of Jagannath Deva, sending his son Chandaneshwar to accompany them as their guide. When they had returned, they began to sing the Holy Names aloud and this brought Mahaprabhu back to consciousness. Feeling protective toward the Lord, Sarvabhauma prohibited Him from going to the temple alone. He invited the Lord and His companions for lunch and sent them to take bath in the ocean. When they returned, he fed them to their full satisfaction with a feast of Jagannath's maha prasad.

When Sarvabhauma learned of Mahaprabhu's family background, he was very happy, for his father Mahesvara Visharad had been a good friend of Mahaprabhu's maternal grandfather, Nilambar Chakravarti. Sarvabhauma was much older than the Lord and so he felt protective toward Him. He said, "The name Krishna Chaitanya you have been given is a very good name. But you have been initiated into the Bharati line of sannyasis, which has only a moderately good reputation. I can get you reinitiated into a more prestigious line if you wish."

Gopinath and the other devotees were disappointed to hear Sarvabhauma make this suggestion. Gopinath objected, "Sri Chaitanya Mahaprabhu is the Supreme Lord himself. He does not depend on any sampradaya." Sarvabhauma and his disciples debated these points with Gopinath at some length, all of which has been described by Krishna Das Kaviraj Goswami in the sixth chapter of the Chaitanya Charitamrita's *Madhya-līlā*.

Mahaprabhu asked the devotees not to argue with Sarvabhauma Bhattacharya because he was the Lord's senior and was only advising Him out of affection for Him. How could they object to this? The Lord, setting the example of one who is free from any hankering after prestige and who is ready to offer all respect to others, indicated that He was willing to hear Sarvabhauma's advice.

Sarvabhauma Bhattacharya then said to the Lord that he was a handsome young man and that if He wished to maintain His sannyas vows, He should study Vedanta diligently. This would awaken the required attitude of renunciation from the world in Him. The Lord accepted Sarvabhauma's invitation to learn from him and, for the next seven days, took lesson in Vedanta at his house.

When Sarvabhauma saw that Mahaprabhu was not asking any questions, but simply listening silently, he said, "The study of Vedanta is demanding. A student who wishes to understand the material properly is generally obliged to ask questions to clarify troublesome areas."

The Lord answered, "You told me to listen, not to ask questions. So I have been listening. I find no difficulty understanding the meaning of the sutras for they are as self-evident as the sun. On the other hand, your explanations are confusing. I find them to hide the clear meaning of the sutras just like clouds covering the sun."

Sarvabhauma Bhattacharya felt slighted by the Lord's comments and indeed, somewhat angry. He started to debate the meaning of the word *brahman* with the Lord. Sarvabhauma argued that Brahman was without form or qualities, having recourse to various scriptures as evidence. The Lord rebutted his arguments with logic and scriptural references, showing that Brahman possessed form and qualites. The Lord cited the *ātmārāma* verse from the Bhagavata and asked Sarvabhauma to explain it.

ātmārāmāś ca munayo
nirgranthā apy urukrame
kurvanty ahaitukīṁ bhaktim
itthambhūta-guṇo hariḥ

Even those silent sages who are fully self-satisfied and freed from bondage perform causeless devotional service to Lord Hari, whose pastimes are wonderful, for such is the glorious nature of His qualities.

(Srimad Bhagavatam 1.7.10)

After Vasudeva Sarvabhauma had given nine different explanations of the verse, Mahaprabhu put on a display of superhuman scholarship by explaining the same verse in eighteen ways without even touching on the meanings given by Sarvabhauma. The scholar was astounded and speechless. He began slowly to understand that Mahaprabhu was not an ordinary human being, but the Supreme Lord Himself. He started to regret his arrogance and finally fell down at the feet of the Lord and begged Him for forgiveness.

SARVABHAUMA BECOMES THE LORD'S DEVOTEE

In his kindness, the Lord displayed a number of different divine forms to Sarvabhauma, starting with a four-armed Narayan form, then a two-armed Krishna form, holding a flute, and finally a six-armed form.

When Sarvabhauma saw the six-armed form of the Lord, as brilliant as a million suns, he fell down in a faint.

(Chaitanya Bhagavata 3.3.107)

After seeing these divine manifestations, Sarvabhauma Bhattacharya wrote a panegyric of the Lord in a hundred Sanskrit verses. He inscribed two of these verses down on a palm leaf and sent them to Mahaprabhu through Jagadananda Pandit. Jagadananda took the precaution of writing the verses down on the wall before showing them to the Lord, and as a result of this foresight the verses were preserved, for Mahaprabhu tore the palm leaves up as soon as He saw them. The devotees saw the verses written on the wall by the doorframe and memorized them:

vairāgya-vidyā-nija-bhakti-yoga-
śikṣārtham ekaḥ puruṣaḥ purāṇaḥ
śrī-kṛṣṇa-caitanya-śarīra-dhārī
kṛpāmbudhir yas tam ahaṁ prapadye

Let me take shelter of the Supreme Personality of Godhead, the ocean of transcendental mercy, Sri Krishna, who has descended in the form of Lord Chaitanya Mahaprabhu to teach us detachment, real knowledge and His own devotional service.

kālān naṣṭaṁ bhakti-yogaṁ nijaṁ yaḥ
prāduṣkartuṁ kṛṣṇa-caitanya-nāmā
āvirbhūtas tasya padāravinde
gāḍhaṁ gāḍhaṁ līyate citta-bhṛṅgaḥ

The Supreme Personality of Godhead, who has taken the name of Sri Krishna Chaitanya, has appeared to reveal the ancient system of devotional service to himself, which had almost been lost due to the influence of time. I pray that the honeybee of my mind will drink deeply of the nectar of His lotus feet. (Chaitanya Charitamrita 2.6.253-4; *Chaitanya-candrodaya-nāṭaka* 6.74)

A deity of Mahaprabhu's six-armed form is still worshiped today in the Jagannath temple at Puri.

SARVABHAUMA'S FAITH IN MAHA PRASAD

One day not long afterward, Mahaprabhu came to Sarvabhauma's house with Jagannath's maha prasad and offered it to him. Sarvabhauma had not yet bathed, cleaned his teeth or performed his morning rituals. Despite his ritually impure state, he joyfully honored the prasad, quoting a verse from the *Padma-purāṇa*:

śuṣkaṁ paryuṣitaṁ vāpi
nītaṁ vā dūra-deśataḥ
prāpti-mātreṇa bhoktavyaṁ
nātra kāla-vicāraṇā

One should honor prasad as soon as one receives it, whether it is dried up, stale or brought from afar. In this, there should be no consideration of time or circumstances.

(Chaitanya Charitamrita 2.6.225)

Mahaprabhu was delighted to see that Sarvabhauma had developed faith in maha prasad and immediately started to dance in ecstasy. Sarvabhauma joined him and the two danced madly, shedding tears and trembling in their divine joy. Mahaprabhu said,

Today I have been transported beyond the three worlds and have been taken to Vaikuntha. All my desires have been fulfilled simply because Sarvabhauma Bhattacharya has developed faith in maha prasad.

(Chaitanya Charitamrita 2.6.230-1)

SARVABHAUMA CHANGES THE WORDS OF THE BHAGAVATA

Sarvabhauma's attitude was so changed as a result of his conversion that one day, he recited a verse of the Srimad Bhagavatam, in which he had altered a word.

tat te 'nukampāṁ su-samīkṣamāṇo
bhuñjāna evātma-kṛtaṁ vipākam
hṛd-vāg-vapurbhir vidadhan namas te
jīveta yo bhakti-pade sa dāya-bhāk

One who lives his life while joyfully seeing everything as your compassion even as he experiences the adverse conditions arising from his past deeds, and constantly pays obeisances to You with his mind, words and body, is certain to inherit a place at Your lotus feet, the object of all devotion. (Srimad Bhagavatam 10.14.8)

Sarvabhauma had changed the word *mukti-pade* found in the original verse to *bhakti-pade*. Mahaprabhu explained that there was no need to change the words, inasmuch as *mukti-pada* ("the source of liberation") is an epithet of Krishna. Vasudeva answered, "You are quite correct to say that the words *mukti-pade* refer to Krishna, but the word *mukti* is used customarily in its sense of impersonal liberation and thus does not bring as much pleasure as the word *bhakti*.

When the other scholars in Puri heard that Sarvabhauma Bhattacharya had been converted to devotion to Krishna, they all took shelter of Chaitanya Mahaprabhu.

MAHAPRABHU LEAVES FOR THE SOUTH

Mahaprabhu took sannyas in the month of Magh and arrived in Puri in the month of Phalgun. He delivered Sarvabhauma Bhattacharya in the month of Chaitra and left for southern India in the month of Vaishakh. Nityananda Prabhu arranged for a certain Krishna Das Vipra to accompany Mahaprabhu as a servant. Before he left, Sarvabhauma gave the Lord a *kaupin* and *bahirvāsa* and made a special request to the Lord to visit Ramananda Raya on the banks of the Godavari. At one time, Sarvabhauma had mocked Ramananda when conversing with him about devotional sentiment. Now, by the mercy of the Lord, he was able to recognize him for what he was, a highly advanced devotee of Krishna. His words to the Lord were:

Ramananda Raya is the governor of Vidyanagar on the bank of the Godavari. It is my request that you meet him without fail. Please do not avoid him, thinking that he is a shudra who is only interested in material activities. If anyone is fit to associate with You, it is Ramananda Raya. No one in this world is equal to him in the knowledge of the divine sentiments. He is not only a most learned scholar, but very knowledgeable in the science of sacred rapture. You will learn the extent of his glories by talking with him. When I first met Ramananda Raya, I could not understand what he was talking about, nor his activities, all of which are transcendental. I made fun of him because he is a Vaishnava. Now, by Your mercy, I am able to understand his greatness. So too will You, once You converse with him.
(Chaitanya Charitamrita 2.7.63-7)

KASHISVARA AND GOVINDA COME TO PURI

After Ishvara Puripada's disappearance, his two disciples and personal servants, Kashisvara and Govinda, came to Puri in order to serve Mahaprabhu as they had been told to do by their guru. When Sarvabhauma learned that Govinda was a shudra, he asked Mahaprabhu why his guru had taken a person of a lower caste as a personal servant. Mahaprabhu answered, "The Supreme Lord is completely autonomous and His mercy does not take anyone's caste or creed into consideration. Service performed out of affection is thousands of times better than that which is performed out of a sense of duty or reverence. Krishna joyfully took His meal in the home of Vidura. However, as My guru's personal servant, Govinda is an object of reverence and therefore it is improper for Me to accept his service. On the other hand, My guru has ordered him to serve Me and I cannot ignore My spiritual master's order. What do you think should I do?"

Sarvabhauma responded to the Lord's request for advice by saying, "One should never ignore the orders of the spiritual master. Scripture says that this is the supreme guiding principle."

SARVABHAUMA SEEKS AN AUDIENCE FOR THE KING

While Mahaprabhu was travelling through the South, Maharaj Prataparudra heard a great deal about His glories from Sarvabhauma Bhattacharya. As a result, the King developed a desire to have an audience with the Lord, but Sarvabhauma warned him that the Lord was a monk who had taken strict vows of renunciation, one of which was that he would not grant audiences to kings. Nevertheless, he promised the King that when the Lord returned, he would arrange a meeting with Him by whatever means possible.

Later, after the Lord's return, all of Sarvabhauma's efforts to bring the King into the Lord's presence failed. Subsequently, Nityananda Prabhu and other devotees glorified the King's qualities to the Lord, which caused Him to change his attitude somewhat. Even so, He continued to refuse to give the King an audience. He agreed, however, to give him one of His outer garments. Nityananda gave the Lord's cloth to Sarvabhauma to bring to the King. As soon as Prataparudra touched the cloth, he experienced the symptoms of love of God.

THE LORD CURES SARVABHAUMA'S SON-IN-LAW

When the Lord's Bengali associates had returned home after the Chaturmasya period, Sarvabhauma Bhattacharya invited the Lord to eat at his house for an entire month. The Lord refused, saying that it was against the principles of a sannyasi to take regular invitations in that way. Sarvabhauma reduced his invitation to twenty days, then to fifteen days, but the Lord continued to turn him down, agreeing to go only once. Sarvabhauma Bhattacharya continued to press Him to accept more than one invitation and the Lord finally agreed to go for five days a month. Sarvabhauma then asked Paramananda Puri to also come for five days, Svarupa Damodar for four, and each of the Lord's eight other sannyasi associates for two days each. He told the Lord that it was difficult to offer proper service when there were many guests, so he asked Him to please come alone or with Svarupa Damodar.

Sarvabhauma Bhattacharya's wife, who was known as "Sathi's mother," was very devoted to the Lord and extremely excited to hear that He was going to be coming to their house to eat. She was a very good cook and had prepared a large number of vegetable preparations as well as cakes and sweets. Sarvabhauma set the Lord a place in a quiet room, putting out an uncut banana leaf from a mature tree (which produces a giant banana cluster of thirty two hands) upon which he placed all the different preparations.

Mahaprabhu saw the elaborate preparations made for offering food to Radha and Govinda and to serve Him, and praised Sarvabhauma for his efforts. When He sat down to eat, however, Sarvabhauma's son-in-law, Amogha, came to watch. Sarvabhauma knew Amogha's faultfinding character and so had kept a stick at hand to chase him away if he came to disturb the Lord. Unfortunately, he was so absorbed in serving the Lord that Amogha managed to sneak in without him noticing. Amogha saw the lavish feast and immediately began to criticize Mahaprabhu as a glutton:

> "There is enough food here to satisfy a dozen people and yet this so-called sannyasi is going to eat it all by himself?" (Chaitanya Charitamrita 2.15.248)

Sarvabhauma Bhattacharya flared up in anger, took the stick lying by his side and went after Amogha, who fled as fast as he could. Sarvabhauma's wife, shocked on hearing her son-in-law insult the Lord, began to flail herself on the head and chest and repeatedly said, "May my Sathi become a widow!"

As for the Lord, He laughed off Amogha's trivial criticisms and tried to pacify His hosts. The next day, however, Amogha came down with cholera. Sarvabhauma thought that justice was being done, that it was a suitable punishment for the offensive words his son-in-law had spoken. When Gopinath Acharya informed Mahaprabhu that Sarvabhauma and his wife were both fasting as a penance for the offense that had taken place in their house and that Amogha was on his deathbed with cholera, the merciful Lord immediately went to Amogha's bedside, placed His hand on his chest and said,

> "This brahmin's heart is naturally holy and is therefore a proper place for Krishna to sit. Why have you given brutish envy a place in it, allowing it to become contamined? Fortunately, all your sins have been destroyed by your relationship with Sarvabhauma Bhattacharya. When the heart is cleansed of all contamination, one is able to chant the name of Krishna. So, get up, Amogha, and chant Krishna's names! The Supreme Lord will bestow His mercy upon you before long."
>
> (Chaitanya Charitamrita 2.15.274-7)

The Lord's touch and His compassionate words had an immediate effect. Amogha rose up and started chanting, "Krishna! Krishna!" The eight symptoms of ecstatic love manifested on his body. He remembered his offensive words to the Lord and remorsefully began to slap himself repeatedly on the cheeks until his face was swollen and Gopinath Acharya stopped him. The Lord again said to Amogha that he was dear to Him because of his relationship with Sarvabhauma.

> "I love everyone in Sarvabhauma's house, even his servants. If even his household dog is dear to Me, will I not have affection for his relatives?
>
> (Chaitanya Charitamrita 2.15.284)

The Lord then went to Sarvabhauma's house and asked him and his wife to forgive their son-in-law, whose offensive behavior was only the result of immaturity. After convincing them that He was not angry, He had them break their fast.

THE LORD PRAISES SARVABHAUMA

Sarvabhauma participated in many other activities with the Lord in Puri, such as the water sports and the feasts of prasad. When Vallabha Bhatta came to Puri, the Lord glorified Sarvabhauma Bhattacharya to him as follows:

> "Sarvabhauma Bhattacharya is not only such a great scholar in the six philosophical systems that he is a world teacher in these doctrines, but is also a foremost devotee of the Lord. He has taught Me the science of bhakti yoga. Through His mercy I have learned that devotion to Krishna is the essence of all mystical systems."
>
> (Chaitanya Charitamrita 3.7.21-2)

King Sri Prataparudra Deva

indradyumno mahārājo jagannāthārcakaḥ purā
jātaḥ pratāparudraḥ san sama indreṇa so'dhunā

Indradyumna, who previously worshiped Lord Jagannath, was born as Prataparudra, with the same opulences as Indra himself. (*Gaura-gaṇoddeśa-dīpikā* 118)[12]

PRATAPARUDRA'S ANCESTORS

King Prataparudra's was an independent king of considerable power whose capital city was Cuttack. His ancestors are listed in the Orissan history, *Mādalā-pañjī*. There it is said that when King Kajjalabhanu, the last ruler of the Ganga dynasty, was overthrown by his minister Kapilendra Deva while absent from the kingdom in wartime. Also known as Kapilesvara, this king founded Orissa's Gajapati dynasty. Kapilendra's queen was Parvati, to whom was born their son and successor, Purushottam Deva. Purushottam Deva was Prataparudra's father and Padmavati, or Rupambika, his mother.

Prataparudra was an important associate of Lord Chaitanya Mahaprabhu and is named as a branch of Gadadhar Pandit Goswami. He, his wives and his sons, were all devotees of Mahaprabhu. His chief wife (or *paṭṭa-mahiṣī*) was named Gauri. She had five sons, the eldest of whom was named Purushottam Jana. This information is given in *Bhakti-ratnākara* (6.65).

We also learn from Ramananda Raya's *Jagannath-vallabha Nāṭaka* that Prataparudra was a mighty and heroic military leader, despite which he maintained a humble demeanor. It is also said there that he was a generous and liberal Vaishnava, devoted to the promotion of learning. Kavi Karnapur also writes about Prataparudra's military qualities in his *Chaitanya-candrodaya Nāṭaka*. He protected Brahminical culture and was especially benevolent towards the Vaishnava religion. Many books have been attributed to Prataparudra, such as *Sarasvatī-vilāsa*, *Pratāpa-mārtaṇḍa*, *Kautuka-cintāmaṇi*, and *Nirṇaya-saṅgraha*. In fact, the first two of these books were written by two of his court scholars, Lolla Lakshmidhara and Ramakrishna, respectively.

PRATAPARUDRA, KASHI MISHRA'S DISCIPLE

King Prataparudra accepted Kashi Mishra as his spiritual master and served him with great dedication. When in Puri, he would go daily to Kashi Mishra's house and massage his feet after he had taken his midday meal. While doing so, he would inquire about the state of Jagannath's service.

Prataparudra had a regular duty that he performed whenever he was at Nilachala. He would daily massage Kashi Mishra's feet and would hear a report on Jagannath's service. (Chaitanya Charitamrita 2.9.81-2)

Mahaprabhu stayed at Kashi Mishra's house in a one-roomed cottage on the veranda. In Orissan, such a small cottage is called a *gambhīrā*.

Many works of Vaishnava history dating to that period have given testimony that Mahaprabhu, Ramananda Raya, Kashi Mishra and Sarvabhauma Bhattacharya felt affection for Prataparudra. Every one of Mahaprabhu's biographies states that Prataparudra received the Lord's mercy.

There is a legend that when Mahaprabhu left Puri for Vrindavan, Prataparudra felt such separation that he had a murti of the Lord made. He assigned 54 brahmins to the service of the deity, as well as giving a large tract of land for its maintenance. In the royal palace at Puri, deities of Gaura-Nityananda and Gaura-Gadadhar are worshiped alongside numerous other images.

PURUSHOTTAM FIGHTS FOR JAGANNATH'S HONOR

During Prataparudra's reign, his kingdom stretched as far as Rajahmundry in modern Andhra Pradesh. It is not necessary to go into detail here, but the following is a brief summary of some of the historical background. Prataparudra's father, Purushottam Deva, retrieved lands that had been lost to his kingdom and expanded it further through his own might. Being entirely surrendered to Jagannath, he was successful in extending Orissan lands as far as Rajahmundry. It was said that Jagannath himself would appear on the battlefield to help the king.

On one occasion, marriage was contracted between Purushottam and the king of Kanchi's daughter Padmavati. The king of Kanchi came to Puri to have a look at the groom. He arrived there during the time of the Rathayatra and saw his prospective son-in-law sweeping the parade ground before the chariot of the Lord, as was the custom. Though Purushottam was sweeping the ground with a golden broom, the king of Kanchi thought that it was an insult to his daughter to marry her to someone who took the tasks of a sweeper, the lowest outcaste of Hindu society. He thus cancelled the marriage between them. The king of Kanchi was a devotee of Ganesh, and had no great faith in Jagannath.

When Purushottam heard of the sovereign of Kanchi's faithlessness, he became angry and attacked his territories with a large force. At first he was unable to secure a victory, so he prostrated himself before Jagannath and surrendered to him. This time Jagannath assured him that he would aid his war effort and so Purushottam took up arms again.

As Purushottam passed through the village of Anandpur, about 12 miles from Puri, a milk maid said to him, "Two horsemen passed through here. They bought milk, yogurt and buttermilk from me and paid for it with a ring. They told me to give you the ring and ask for money in exchange." When Purushottam looked at the ring, he realized at once that the two horsemen had been none other than Jagannath and Balaram. He rewarded the milkmaid and set off to certain victory against Kanchi. He returned with the jewelled throne of that kingdom and offered it to the service of Jagannath. He also took the Ganesh deity worshiped in Kanchi back to Puri. In this way, Jagannath Deva crushed the arrogant pride of the king of Kanchi. It is said that Ganesh tried to cast obstacles in

Purushottam's way during the battle. Since he went against his customary role of eliminating obstacles, he was given the name Bhanda (deceitful) Ganesh.

Kanchi's king personally returned to Puri with his daughter Padmavati and offered her as Purushottam's bride while he was sweeping the Rathayatra route for Jagannath. Purushottam kept his promise and remained king of Puri until 1497 AD. He was followed by Prataparudra, who remained on the throne until his death in 1540. Other than the abovementioned queen Gauri, he also had four other wives, named Padma, Padmalaya, Ila and Mahila.

PRATAPARUDRA'S DESIRE TO MEET MAHAPRABHU

Prataparudra was the most fortunate member of the Gajapati dynasty of Orissan kings, as he received the mercy of Sri Chaitanya Mahaprabhu, the combined form of Radha and Krishna. Even though Mahaprabhu felt that it was not beneficial for a sannyasi to come into contact with a worldly man like a king, His disdain for him was purely for show. Inwardly, He was won over by the king's pure devotional attitude and generously showered him with His causeless mercy. Krishna Das Kaviraj Goswami has described how the Lord taught the people of this world through King Prataparudra in his Chaitanya Charitamrita. The story is told in the eleventh chapter of the *Madhya-līlā*. At first Prataparudra approached Sarvabhauma Bhattacharya to tell him of his desire to meet Chaitanya Mahaprabhu. He asked him so many times that finally Sāravabhauma asked Mahaprabhu to allow the king to see Him. As soon as He heard the request, however, the Lord covered his ears and said, "For a sannyasi like Myself, to see a king is the same as looking at a woman— it is pure poison" (2.11.7). Even though the king was a great devotee, the fact that he was a king made him an object of fear, like a cobra.

PRATAPARUDRA'S DREAM

In the fifth chapter of the *Antya-khaṇḍa* of the Chaitanya Bhagavata, Vrindavan Das Thakur has described the King's deep desire to meet with the Lord as well as a dream in which the King saw that Lord Jagannath and Lord Chaitanya Mahaprabhu are non-different. The first time the King saw Mahaprabhu dance, however, he had some doubts when he observed His body covered in dust and His mouth filled with frothing saliva from ecstatic dancing.

That very night, Prataparudra saw Jagannath in a dream. Jagannath too was covered in dust and saliva. Then he saw the same dust-covered form of Lord Chaitanya Mahaprabhu sitting on Lord Jagannath's throne along with the Deity. From this amazing dream he understood Lord Chaitanya Mahaprabhu's divine nature.

[Jagannath said,] "Just look! My body is covered with dust and spit. You are a king and the son of a king. Surely it is not proper for you to touch someone like Me." Having said this, Lord Jagannath looked at his servant and laughed. In that very moment, the King saw Chaitanya Mahaprabhu sitting on the altar alongside the Lord.

(Chaitanya Bhagavata 3.5.175-7)

RAMANANDA AND SARVABHAUMA TRY TO INTERVENE

One day, Prataparudra came to Puri with Ramananda Raya and other members of his retinue. Ramananda knew of the king's eagerness to meet Mahaprabhu, so when he went to visit the Lord, he tried to persuade Him to allow such a meeting to take place, telling Him of the king's deep affection for Him. He added that the king had given him leave from his job with full pay to allow him to stay with the Lord. When He heard how the king was filled with love for Him and how he had served His devotee, Mahaprabhu replied: "The king has shown so much love for you that the Lord is sure to accept him on the basis of this virtue alone."

ye me bhakta-janāḥ pārtha
na me bhaktāś ca te janāḥ
mad-bhaktānāṁ tu ye bhaktās
te me bhaktatamā matāḥ

Those who claim to be My devotees are in fact not so. The best of My devotees are those who are devoted to My servants.

Sarvabhauma Bhattacharya again entreated the Lord on the king's behalf to allow such a meeting to take place, but the Lord said that under no circumstances would He come face to face with a king, and that if people continued to ask Him to do so, He would leave Puri and go to live elsewhere. When the king heard this, he was devastated. He said:

"The Lord has descended just to deliver all kinds of sinful, lowborn persons. He has even delivered sinners like Jagai and Madhai. But it seems that He has made a promise to deliver the entire universe with the exception of someone named Prataparudra. He may have taken a vow to never see me, but I have sworn to give up my life if I cannot see Him. Without Sri Chaitanya Mahaprabhu's mercy, my life and kingdom are worthless."

(Chaitanya Charitamrita 2.11.45-6, 48-9)

Vasudeva Sarvabhauma thought up a way to arrange a meeting between Prataparudra and the Lord. During the Rathayatra festival, after having danced in the sankirtan with His devotees, the Lord customarily went into a flower garden to rest. Sarvabhauma Bhattacharya suggested to the king that he take this opportunity to approach the Lord dressed as a commoner and to recite the verses of the *Rāsa-pañcādhyāya* from the Bhagavata. The Lord would be in a trance-like state and allow Himself to be transported by the recital of the love of Krishna and the gopis. In this condition, He would surely embrace the king. The king was comforted by these words of advice.

When the Lord returned from His pilgrimage to the South of India, Prataparudra sent a letter to Sarvabhauma in which he once again expressed his desire to meet with the Lord. Sarvabhauma showed the letter to the other devotees and all were duly impressed by the degree of devotion exhibited by the King. Nityananda Prabhu decided that he would speak to the Lord, not about meeting the King but simply about his personal qualities and actions. He said the following to the Lord:

> We want to submit everything to You, whether or not it is fitting. The King has decided that he will become a yogi if he cannot meet You. He says, "I will pierce my ears and wear the big wooden earrings of the Nath yogi mendicant sect. I have no desire to enjoy this kingdom without the mercy of Gaura Hari. When will I be able to see the Lord's moonlike face to my full satisfaction and when will I be able to hold His lotus feet to my heart?"
>
> (Chaitanya Charitamrita 2.12.19-21)

Though the Lord listened to Nityananda's account of the King's mood, He maintained His hard line in order to set an example for renouncers of the world. He said that for the sake of spiritual advancement, a sannyasi is forbidden to set sight on a King. Furthermore, the Lord said, Damodar Pandit would criticize Him if He were to engage in such forbidden acts. Damodar Pandit answered, saying,

> "I am merely an insignificant jiva, so what power do I have to tell You what to do? I shall see You meet the King of Your own volition. The King loves You very much, and You are influenced by a devotee's feelings of love. It is the power of this love for You that will reward him with the opportunity to touch You. Although You are the Supreme Lord and are completely independent, still it is your nature to be influenced by the love and affection of Your devotees."
>
> (Chaitanya Charitamrita 2.12.27-9)

Nityananda added that people who experience unrequited love tend to commit suicide. Thus, in order to save the King's life, he asked Mahaprabhu to at least give him a used loincloth (*bahirvāsa*). The Lord could not refuse, so Nityananda asked Govinda for the loincloth and sent it to the King via Sarvabhauma Bhattacharya. Prataparudra was overjoyed to receive the cloth and began to worship it as though it were the Lord himself.

MAHAPRABHU SEES THE KING'S SON

When Ramananda Raya received the King's permission to come to live near the Lord in Puri, he also described Maharaj Prataparudra's intense desire to see the Lord and tried to persuade the Lord to fulfill that desire. Mahaprabhu continued to answer in a way that established the rules of conduct for the renounced orders: He said that just as even a slight mark on a piece of white cloth immediately becomes noticeable, the smallest character flaws of a sannyasi are noticed by the general public. A jug full of milk is contaminated by even a drop of liquor; similarly, though it may be true that King Prataparudra possesses all virtues, the very fact that he is a king makes his association undesirable.

However, the Lord was unable to completely ignore Ramananda Raya's request because of their close friendship. He himself suggested that He could see the King's son, for according to the maxim *ātmā vai jāyate putraḥ* ("one is reborn as one's own son"), there is no difference between the father and the son. When he learned of the Lord's will, Prataparudra immediately sent Him his son. When Mahaprabhu saw the teenage prince with his almond eyes and dark skin and wearing a yellow cloth, He immediately thought of Krishna. He embraced the lad, making him experience the ecstatic transformations of prema. When the prince came back to the palace, the King embraced him and felt the same ecstasies through him. From that day onward, the King's son was considered one of Mahaprabhu's associates.

THE KING'S HUMBLE SERVICE TO LORD JAGANNATH

A devotee who is free from pride, is surrendered and without any ulterior motive, is eligible to receive the Lord's mercy.

dīnere adhika dayā karen bhagavān
kulīn paṇḍit dhanīr baṛa abhimān

The Lord bestows greater blessings on the meek and humble. Those of noble birth, the learned and the wealthy, are all filled with pride. (Chaitanya Charitamrita 3.4.68)

Maharaj Prataparudra was without any pride, even though he had so much material power as well as having all good qualities. Mahaprabhu had noticed his willingness to engage in even menial service and was pleased with him and ready to give him his mercy, even though externally he made a show of being hard-hearted.

While the Lord was being carried from the throne to the car, King Prataparudra personally engaged in the Lord's service by cleansing the road with a gold-handled broom. He also sprinkled the road with sandalwood-scented water. Although he sat on the royal throne, he engaged in such menial service for the sake of Lord Jagannath. Although the King was the most exalted person in the kingdom, he still accepted to do this menial service for the Lord and thus became the recipient of the Lord's blessings. Mahaprabhu was happy to see the King's service to the Lord and it was through this service, that he finally received the mercy of the Lord.

(Chaitanya Charitamrita 2.13.15-18)

The Lord's mercy has no cause. Only He knows who will receive His blessings and when. He often does so in an indirect manner rather than doing it openly. The Lord was pleased by the King's engagement in a menial service and even though He did not make a public show of mercy to Him, He did reveal his personal form to the King and thus fulfill his deepest desire.

HARICHANDAN IS SLAPPED BY SRIVAS PANDIT

In the thirteenth chapter of the *Madhya-līlā*, these events are described. During the Rathayatra festival, the Bengali devotees were divided into seven groups for chanting the Holy Names. Each one of these groups thought that Mahaprabhu was with them alone. Prataparudra was able to witness this pastime and felt wonder and ecstatic love. All this was Mahaprabhu's indirect mercy.

When Mahaprabhu wanted to dance in front of Jagannath's chariot, he would gather the seven sampradayas together into one kirtan group. Meanwhile, the devotees formed three rings of protection around the Lord. The innermost line of defense was headed by Nityananda Prabhu, the second by Kashisvara Pandit, Mukunda and other devotees. Prataparudra and his soldiers formed the outermost circle to defend the Lord from the crowds.

Maharaj Prataparudra watched mesmerized while the Lord danced, resting his hand on the shoulder of his minister (*mahāpātra*) Harichandan. At that time, Srivas Pandit, who was also absorbed in watching the Lord's ecstatic dancing, came and stood in front of the King, blocking his vision. Harichandan repeatedly tried to push Srivas to one side, telling him to let the King see until finally Srivas lost his temper and slapped Harichandan. When Harichandan became angry and was about to respond to Srivas' aggression, the King said:

> "You are very fortunate, for you have been graced by the touch of Srivas Thakur. I have not been so fortunate. You should feel obliged to him."
>
> (Chaitanya Charitamrta 2.13.97)

PRATAPARUDRA CATCHES THE LORD

In Mahaprabhu's lila we find a delightful mixture of the highest manifestations of love, mercy and teachings for the general public. As He pulled the chariot of Lord Jagannath, Mahaprabhu was absorbed in the mood of Radha and the other gopis at their meeting with Lord Krishna who had come to Kurukshetra from Dvaraka on the occasion of the solar eclipse. Thus Mahaprabhu wished to drag Krishna (in his Jagannath form) from the site of his majestic pastimes in Kurukshetra, represented by Nilachala (the Jagannath temple) to the site of his sweet, loving pastimes in Vrindavan, represented by Suryachala or the Gundicha temple. Sometimes, Mahaprabhu would lag behind as He tried to understand the depth of the gopis' loving power; Jagannath would seem to understand the Lord's emotions and slow down the movement of the chariot. Thus, the Lord danced more frenziedly as He and Lord Jagannath went deeper and deeper into ecstatic communion. As He danced in this *divyonmāda* state, the Lord seemed about to fall down in the very spot where King Prataparudra was standing. The King immediately held the Lord to keep Him from falling. This was how the Lord blessed the King and allowed him to touch Him, but Mahaprabhu immediately began to rebuke Himself for having allowed a materialistic person to touch Him. The inconceivable activities of the Lord contain both delightful manifestation of emotion and teachings for the world, neither of which are easy to understand.

When he saw that it was the King, Mahaprabhu condemned Himself, saying, "O, how pitiful it is that I have touched a person interested in mundane affairs." Even though the Lord had already made up His mind to give the King an audience upon seeing him act as a sweeper in the service of Lord Jagannath, He still externally expressed feelings of anger in order to warn His personal associates.

THE LORD EMBRACES THE KING

There is a spot about halfway between the Jagannath temple and Gundicha, or halfway between Sraddha Balu and Ardhasani Devi, which is called Balgandi. On the Rathayatra day, Lord Jagannath's chariot stops here at midday so that He can lunch and rest. The custom is that all devotees, whether important or not, can make food offerings to Him on this occasion. Because of the large crowds that normally accumulated, Mahaprabhu would go to rest in a nearby flower garden by a coconut grove. King Prataparudra remembered Sarvabhauma's counsel and approached the Lord in a commoner's dress and began to massage His feet. He began to recite texts from the *gopī-gīta* portion of the Rasa lila, starting with the following verse:

jayati te'dhikaṁ janmanā vrajaḥ
śrayate indirā śaśvad atra hi
dayita dṛśyatāṁ dikṣu tāvakās
tvayi dhṛtāsavas tvāṁ vicinvate

The land of Vraja's glories have increased ever since You took birth here; ever since then, the goddess of fortune has taken up residence here. O beloved! We whose lives depend completely on You are searching for You, please show Yourself to us. (Srimad Bhagavatam 10.31.1).

Mahaprabhu was ecstatic and told the King to go on reciting. The King reached the the chapter's ninth verse:

tava kathāmṛtaṁ tapta-jīvanaṁ
kavibhir īḍitaṁ kalmaṣāpaham
śravaṇa-maṅgalaṁ śrīmad-ātataṁ
bhuvi gṛṇanti te bhūridā janāḥ

Nectarean discussions about You give life to those who are suffering. The philosophers have glorified them, for they destroy all of one's sins. They are auspiciousness for the ears, for they bring the fortune of love for Krishna. Those who are most munificent of benefactors distribute these wonderful words throughout the world.

(Srimad Bhagavatam 10.31.9)

As soon as Mahaprabhu heard this verse, He became ecstatic with love and embraced the king, while repeating the word *bhūridā* ("most munificent of benefactors") from the verse. Though the Lord is all-knowing, He asked the king his identity. Prataparudra answered that he was the servant of the servant of the Lord. Satisfied with the King's answer, the Lord revealed to him a glorious divine form. All the devotees were overjoyed to see that the King had finally received the Lord's mercy.

While the ratha was being pulled from Balgandi to Gundicha, it suddenly came to a stop and even the strongest men and most powerful elephants were unable to move it. Maharaj Prataparudra became anxious that the festival had been interrupted. When the Lord saw that everyone was worried, He told everyone to leave the chariots alone and told his own devotees to man the ropes. Then He Himself went behind the chariot and began to push it with His head. In a moment, the chariot began to move with a great rumbling noise. King Prataparudra and the rest of his entourage marveled at this feat of the Lord.

PRATAPARUDRA SEES OTHER WONDERFUL PASTIMES

While spending the four months in Puri, the Bengali Vaishnavas witnessed numerous pastimes of Lord Jagannath. On the Nandotsava, the day after Krishna's birth ceremony, Mahaprabhu would dress up as a cowherd and put on a play about Krishna's Vraja pastimes with His devotees. Prataparudra also participated in this lila.

When the Lord made his first attempt to go to Vrindavan, He left Puri on Vijayā-daśamī and went to Cuttack where He met Prataparudra in a garden under a bakula tree. Here too, the Lord saw the great prema of the King and embraced him, drenching him in His own tears of love. From that day on, the Lord was given the epithet *pratāparudra-santrātā*, "the savior of King Prataparudra."

At one time, the King's son placed Bhavananda Raya's son Gopinath Pattanayak on the scaffold for having misappropriated state funds. Some devotees came to Mahaprabhu to ask him to intervene in the affair in order to save Gopinath's life. The Lord was unhappy at being asked to get involved in such mundane affairs and made up His mind to go to Alalanath. The king himself was disturbed at hearing this news and prepared himself to give up everything in order to keep the Lord in Puri. These are all further proofs of the extent of the King's love for the Lord's lotus feet.

When King Prataparudra heard all these details, he felt great pain in his heart. "I shall give up everything I am owed," he said, "if Mahaprabhu will only stay here in Jagannath Puri. Even a moment's contact with the Lord is worth more to me than millions of chintamani jewels. I care nothing for this small sum of 200,000 *kāhans*.[13] I would indeed give up everything, not only this, but even my life and kingdom, for the Lord's lotus feet."

(Chaitanya Charitamrta 3.9.94-96)

A PRAYER TO RADHA BY KING PRATAPARUDRA

In the description of Bengali manuscripts in the Banga Sahitya Parishad library in Calcutta, a notice is given of a song with Prataparudra's signature. There is some doubt as to whether the song is indeed his or not. A portion of that song goes as follows:

I will become an ornament on Your body,
the ankle bells upon Your feet.
I will become the chakora who gazes
at the moons of Your fingernails,
the bee who buzzes around Your lotus feet.
I will become the mirror You look into,
and the whisk that fans You.
And I have yet another desire:
Let me become a layer of fine dust on Your feet.
If I cannot become the dust of Your feet,
then be merciful and do with me as you please,
this is Prataparudra's prayer.

When Mahaprabhu disappeared, Prataparudra felt great separation from Him. This is described in the *Bhakti-ratnākara* as follows:

When the King heard that the Lord had departed, he fell to the ground and began lamenting. Hitting his head again and again, he fell unconscious and only the association of Ramananda Raya kept him alive. The King was unable to bear the absence of the Lord and so he left Puri, remaining elsewhere for the rest of his days.

(*Bhakti-ratnākara* 3.217-19)

Maharaj Prataparudra's descendants are: (1) Kaluwa Pratapa, (2) Kakharuwa Pratapa, (3) Govinda Vidyadhara, (4) Cakra Pratapa, (5) Narasimha Deva, (6) Raghurama Deva, (7) Mukunda Deva Harichandan, (8) Ramachandra Deva, (9) Purushottam Deva, (10) Nrisimha Deva, (11) Gangadhar Deva, (12) Balabhadra Deva, (13) Mukunda Deva II, (14) Divyasimha Deva, (15) Hare Krishna Deva, (16) Gopinath Deva, (17) Ramachandra Deva II, (18) Virakesari Deva, (19) Divyasimha Deva II, (20) Mukunda Deva III, (21) Ramachandra Deva III, (22) Virakesari Deva II, (23) Divyasimha Deva III, (24) Mukunda Deva IV, (25) Ramachandra Deva IV, (26) Virakesari Deva III, (27) Divyasimha Deva IV.

[12] In a Satyayuga during the second half of Brahma's lifetime, a certain king named Indradyumna was born into the dynasty of the Sun. He ruled over the kingdom of Malwa with its capital at Avantipur. He was a great devotee of Vishnu, as was his priest Vidyapati. In the first half of Brahma's life, Jagannath had appeared in Nilachala as Nila Madhava with the purpose of delivering the conditioned souls of this world. Nila Madhava was served by a tribal king named Visvavasu. Nila Madhava manifested the deity form of Jagannath through these three persons: Indradyumna, Vidyapati and Visvavasu. The Lord appeared in three forms at the place known as Banki Mohan in order to show His mercy for King Indradyumna. These three deities are, of course, Balaram, Subhadra and Jagannath.

[13] A *kāhana* equals 1280 cowries.

Sri Ramananda Raya

priya-narma-sakhā kaścid arjunaḥ pāṇḍavo 'rjunaḥ
militvā samabhūd rāmānanda-rāyaḥ prabhoḥ priyaḥ
ato rādhā-kṛṣṇa-bhakti-prema-tattvādikaṁ kṛtī
rāmānando gauracandraṁ pratyavarṇayad anvaham
lalitety āhur eke yat tad eke nānumanyante
bhavānandaṁ prati prāha gauro yat tvaṁ pṛthāpatiḥ
gopyārjunīyayā sārdham ekībhūyāpi pāṇḍavaḥ
arjuno yad rāya-rāmānanda ity āhur uttamāḥ
arjunīyābhavat tūrṇaṁ arjuno 'pi ca pāṇḍavaḥ
iti pādmottara-khaṇḍe vyaktam eva virājate
tasmād etat trayaṁ rāmānanda-rāya-mahāśayaḥ

There are two Arjunas in Krishna lila: one is a *priya-narma-sakhā* in Vraja, the other is one of the Pandavas. These two combined to become Mahaprabhu's dear companion Ramananda Raya. Ramananda was very knowledgeable in the teachings of loving devotion to Radha and Krishna, which he described to Gaurachandra on a daily basis. Some people say that Ramananda Raya was Lalita Sakhi, while others do not. Mahaprabhu Himself told Bhavananda Raya that he was Pandu, the husband of Kunti and father of the Pandavas. The Pandava Arjuna also united with the gopi named Arjuniya. Thus the most aware say that Ramananda Raya combined all these three personalities. Proof of this is found in the *Padma-purāṇa*, where it is stated that the Pandava Arjuna became the gopi Arjuniya.

(*Gaura-gaṇoddeśa-dīpikā* 120-124)

As stated in these verses from *Gaura-gaṇoddeśa-dīpikā*, some people hold that Ramananda Raya was an incarnation of Lalita. Some others are of the opinion that he was Vishakha. In his commentary on Chaitanya Charitamrita (2.8.23), Srila Bhaktivinoda Thakur writes, "The love that awakened in Ramananda and Mahaprabhu when they met was the same as the love that Vishakha had for Radha and Krishna in Vraja, and that which Radha and Krishna had for Vishakha." Thus it is clear that Srila Bhaktivinoda Thakur saw Ramananda Raya as Vishakha. Ramananda Raya was one of the Lord's three and a half most intimate associates.

The Lord accepted that Shikhi Mahiti's sister was one of Radha's friends. In the entire world, there were only three and a half devotees who were as worthy. They were Svarupa Damodar Goswami, Ramananda Raya and Shikhi Mahiti. Shikhi Mahiti's sister was the half person.

(Chaitanya Charitamrita 3.2.105-6)

RAMANANDA'S SOCIAL STATUS

Ramananda Raya's father was named Bhavananda Raya. He was born in a family of the Orissan karana caste, an administrative clan like the kayasthas. Bhavananda was previously King Pandu. He had five sons, of whom Ramananda was the oldest. The other four brothers were Gopinath Pattanayak, Kalanidhi, Sudhanidhi and Baninath Pattanayak. The Lord states in Chaitanya Charitamrita: "You are Pandu himself, and your wife is Kunti. Your five sons are the five Pandavas."

(Chaitanya Charitamrita 2.10.53)

Manohar Raya, a descendant of Ramananda Raya, has written his family's history. Srila Bhaktisiddhanta Saraswati Goswami Thakur has summarized some details of this account in his *Anubhāṣya* and concludes: "Orissan society considers the karana community to be part of the shudra caste. Ramananda Raya was born into this community. Nevertheless, though he was considered by society to be a shudra by birth, he was a de facto Brahmin, indeed, as a Vaishnava paramahaṁsa, he was spiritual master to the Brahmins."

By Krishna's will, the creator Brahma himself appeared in an outcaste family in order to show that one's family and one's race have absolutely no importance. Born as a Muslim, Hari Das still enriched Lord Gauranga's pastimes.

Hari Das Thakur was born in a low-caste family on the Lord's desire in order to show that caste and class have no importance at all. All the scriptures say that a devotee of Vishnu, though born in a lowly family, is still worshipable by all. What will one's caste do for one born in a high-caste but who does not worship Krishna? He will go to hell in spite of his high birth. Hari Das took a low birth just to bear witness to these scriptural statements. He is comparable to Prahlad who was born in a family of demons, or Hanuman, who was born a monkey. They belong only superficially to low castes or species.

(Chaitanya Bhagavata 1.16.237-240)

A Vaishnava is beyond the qualities of the material nature. Anyone who considers a devotee in terms of his birth or race is destined for a hellish existence.

arcye śīladhīr guruṣu naramatir vaiṣṇave jātibuddhir
viṣṇor vā vaiṣṇavānāṁ kalimalamathane pādatīrthe 'mbubuddhiḥ
śrīviṣṇor nāmni mantre sakala-kaluṣahe śabda-sāmānya-buddhir
viṣṇau sarveśvareśe tad-itara-samadhīr yasya vā nārakī saḥ

Anyone who considers the deity to be nothing but stone, the guru to be an ordinary human being, or the Vaishnava to be a member of a particular caste or race, who takes the holy water which has washed Vishnu or the Vaishnava's feet and can destroy all the sins of the age of Kali to be ordinary water, who thinks that the name or mantra of Vishnu, which destroys all evils, is the same as any other sound, or who takes Vishnu to be equal to anything other than him, has a hellish nature. (*Padma-purāṇa*)

Bhavananda Raya made his home in Brahmagiri or Alalanath, about 12 miles west of Puri. Raya Ramananda was King Prataparudra's governor in Vidyanagar and later was one of his ministers. According to the *Bhajana-nirṇaya*, he was the disciple of Raghavendra Puri and grand-disciple of Madhavendra Puri.

SARVABHAUMA TELLS THE LORD ABOUT RAMANANDA

The Lord took sannyas in the month of Magh and arrived in Puri during the month of Phalgun. After celebrating the Dol Yatra in Puri, Mahaprabhu delivered Sarvabhauma Bhattacharya in the month of Chaitra. In the month of Vaishakh, he set off on his pilgrimage to South India. Though Mahaprabhu had decided to travel alone, Nityananda Prabhu convinced Him to take a servant, Krishna Das, as a travelling companion. As he was leaving, Sarvabhauma Bhattacharya gave the Lord four kaupins and loincloths, and requested Him to visit Ramananda Raya on the banks of the Godavari.

As Lord Sri Chaitanya Mahaprabhu was departing, Sarvabhauma Bhattacharya submitted the following at his lotus feet, "My Lord, you must fulfill this request of mine. In the town of Vidyanagar, on the bank of the Godavari, there is a responsible government officer named Ramananda Raya. Please do not neglect him, thinking he belongs to a shudra family engaged in materialistic activities. Please take my word for it that You should meet him without fail. If anyone is fit to associate with you, it is he. No other devotee can compare with him in knowledge of the divine sentiments. He has attained the highest limits of learning as well as being experienced in the science of devotional sentiments. If You converse with him, You will recognize his exalted character. When I first met him, I could not understand that everything he said and did was transcendental. I made fun of him simply because he was a Vaishnava. By Your mercy I can now understand the truth about Ramananda Raya. In talking with him, You also will acknowledge his greatness."

(Chaitanya Charitamrita 2.7.61-67)

Srila Prabhupada Bhaktisiddhanta Saraswati has commented as follows (2.7.63): "To superficial understanding, Ramananda Raya was not a sannyasi wearing a loincloth. In common understanding, those who are courtiers engaged in government service are materialistic, but Ramananda Raya was in fact a learned person who was a de facto sannyasi, a perfected human being. Sarvabhauma Bhattacharya had previously been able to recognize his natural qualities as a Vaishnava, even though he himself was not a Vaishnava at that time. When he took to devotional service by the grace of the Lord, he reconsidered his opinion of Ramananda and realized the extent of his qualifications, calling him an *adhikārī rasika-bhakta*—the most highly qualified authority in the matters of devotional sentiment."

Sarvabhauma Bhattacharya was the incarnation of Brihaspati and the court paṇḍita of King Prataparudra. He was so learned that even though a householder, he had sannyasis as his disciples. Nevertheless, he had been unable to recognize that Chaitanya Mahaprabhu was the Supreme Lord Himself, nor was he able to identify Ramananda Raya as his most intimate associate. If he was unable to do so, then how much more difficult it would be for others! No one is able to understand the glories of the Lord and his devotees without being blessed by their mercy.

Mental speculation has no value for understanding the nature of the Supreme Lord. Without the Lord's mercy, no person can come to know Him. One to whom the Lord gives even a tiny drop of mercy is able to understand His nature. (Chaitanya Charitamrita 2.6.82-3)

MAHAPRABHU MEETS RAMANANDA

Mahaprabhu set off to the south, blessing the inhabitants of the land by bestowing devotion to Krishna on them. He visited Kurmasthan, delivering the brahmin also named Kurma, and giving everyone the order to preach devotional service to Krishna. He saved Vasudeva Vipra and then went on the Singhachalam where He danced before the deity of Jiyar Nrisingha. Then He went on to the Godavari River, which in His vision was the Yamuna, and the woods on its banks, Vrindavan. He joyfully crossed the river and came to the place known as Kavoor, where he bathed in the river, hoping to meet Ramananda Raya. Coming out of the water, He sat down and waited for him. At the same time, Ramananda Raya passed by with fanfare. When he saw Mahaprabhu's supernatural form, he descended from his palanquin and paid his obeisances to the Lord. Though Mahaprabhu recognized him, He asked him to identify himself. Ramananda replied that he was nothing but a lowly shudra servant. When the Lord heard him speak in this humble manner, He immediately embraced him. Both the Lord and His servant felt the onset of divine emotions and both experienced the eight ecstatic transformations of prema. The brahmins who were accompanying Ramananda were astonished to see such a display. They thought:

"This sannyasi is as effulgent as the brahmajyoti. Why is He crying while embracing this shudra? The governor Ramananda is a scholar and normally very serious. Why has he suddenly become so emotional upon being touched by this sannyasi, as though intoxicated?"

(Chaitanya Charitamrita 2.8.26-7)

Seeing that there were outsiders present, the Lord controlled his emotions and told Ramananda that He had been told by Sarvabhauma Bhattacharya to seek him out. Ramananda replied with humility,

"This is the proof of Your mercy to Sarvabhauma Bhattacharya: You have touched me, an untouchable, simply due to his love for You. What a difference exists between us—You are the Supreme Lord, Narayan Himself, and I, a government servant interested in materialistic activities. Indeed, I am the lowest amongst men of the fourth caste. Even so, You were not contemptuous of my touch; neither did You fear the Vedic injunctions, which forbid one to even look upon a shudra. Your mercy makes You touch me, even though such an action is condemned both by scripture and society. You are the Supreme Lord Himself, so who can understand your intention?"
(Chaitanya Charitamrita 2.8.34-7)

Though the Brahmins had never shown the slightest interest in bhakti, they too were influenced by the sight of the Lord and began to chant the names of Krishna, their voices tremulous with divine ecstasy. Ramananda Raya said aloud that Mahaprabhu was the Supreme Lord, both in *ākṛti* (form), and in *prakṛti* (nature). The Lord immediately responded in a way that would show the greatness of His devotee:

The Lord said, "You are a great devotee, indeed you are the best amongst them. All those who behold you are immediately affected so that their hearts melt. What to speak of others—I am a mayavadi sannyasi, yet even I feel the onset of Krishna prema when I touch you."
(Chaitanya Charitamrita 2.8.44-5)

THE LORD LISTENS TO RAMANANDA SPEAK

When Mahaprabhu told him of His desire to hear Krishna katha from his lips, Ramananda suggested that He stay at his house for a week or longer so, that his own wicked mind could be pacified and purified. The two then each went their way to finish their duties, returning to the same spot in the evening. Ordinarily, it is seen that a devotee asks the questions and the Lord answers. This time, however, the roles were reversed and the Lord asked Ramananda to clarify certain spiritual truths and then empowered him to respond. Krishna Das Kaviraj Goswami makes this explicit in the verse that opens the eighth chapter of the *Madhya-līlā*:

sañcārya rāmābhidha-bhakta-meghe
svabhakti-siddhānta-cayāmṛtāni
gaurābdhir etair amunā vitīrṇais
taj-jñatva-ratnālayatāṁ prayāti

Gauranga is like the ocean of spiritual truths; He filled the cloud named Ramananda with the nectar of the purest conclusions of devotion to Himself.

Ramananda then rained down that same nectar on the very ocean from which it had come, producing the jewels of transcendental knowledge.
(Chaitanya Charitamrita 2.8.1)

A person who has not taken shelter of the Lord may try to understand the Supreme Truth by using empirical means without achieving any success. Indeed, he will fall into confusion and be unable to understand the words of the Lord.

Mahaprabhu asked Ramananda Raya to explain to Him, with evidence from the scriptures, the ultimate goal of life. Ramananda started his response by explaining that devotion to Vishnu was the ultimate aim of human achievement, or *sādhya*. He described the progressive path of different practices leading to that supreme theistic goal, starting from the practice of varnashram dharma, to offering the fruits of one's activities to Krishna (*karmārpaṇa*), the renunciation of prescribed duties (*karma-tyāga*) and then devotion mixed with knowledge (*jñāna-miśra-bhakti*), offering the scriptural basis for each step. Mahaprabhu rejected each proposal, however, saying that it was superficial or external, for none of these practices were potential means for achieving the pure devotion that He had come to give.

By starting this conversation with Ramananda Raya with varnashram dharma, Mahaprabhu showed that all activities that ignore the Vedic principles or go against them are to be completely rejected. When responding to each of Ramananda's suggestings, Mahaprabhu did not say, "Absolutely not!" Rather, He used the words, *eho bāhya*, "This too is peripheral." The idea is that one must first give up activities that are outside the scope of the Vedic standard. Once one is fixed in these principles, one can progressively gain the qualifications to proceed through each of the various steps described by Ramananda. This holds true even though bhakti itself is completely independent and may manifest in an individual through the association of saintly persons despite his having no prior qualifications or having gone through these prior steps.

When Ramananda Raya finally answered Mahaprabhu's question by saying "Pure devotional service without any tinge of speculative knowledge (*jñāna-śūnya-bhakti*) is the means to achieve the supreme perfection." Mahaprabhu finally accepted his conclusion. Mahaprabhu's original contributions actually begin from this point on. The words *jñāna-śūnya* are meant to completely eradicate any consciousness of the impersonal aspect of the supreme, and not the kind of knowledge of relationships (*sambandha-jñāna*) that is favorable to the attainment of pure devotional service.

Srila Bhaktivinoda Thakur writes in his *Amṛta-pravāha-bhāṣya*, "The purport is that sacrificing the results of one's actions is better than merely engaging in one's prescribed duties according to the varnashram dharma; the renunciation of fruitive activities is better than simply giving up the fruits; better than this is the cultivation of knowledge mixed with devotional service. However, despite this progressive improvement in spirituality through these stages, they are all superficial because these four kinds of practices have no power to achieve pure devotion, or *śuddhā bhakti*. The devotion known as *āropa-siddhā* (adding a devotional veneer as an afterthought to another action), or *saṅga-siddha*, (devotion by associating some devotional act with one's fruitive activity), are never to be considered pure devotional service. Pure devotional service is *svarupa-siddhā bhakti*, that is, it is devotion both in form and in intent. It is entirely different from these other activities that have only a superficial relationship to devotional service. The characteristics of *śuddhā bhakti* are that it is activity executed uniquely for the pleasure of Krishna, devoid of any material desires; it is not hidden by the presence of fruitive intent or identification with Brahman. This is the consciousness that is the ultimate goal of spiritual practice, for though it is practiced by an aspiring devotee, it is realized when he reaches perfection of his practice." (2.8.68)

As long as Ramananda Raya suggested anything other than following in the footsteps of the great devotees and listening to Krishna katha from their lips, Mahaprabhu kept saying, "This is irrelevant." Therefore it is to be understood that pure devotion starts from the moment one begins to hear about the activities and teachings of Lord Krishna from the lips of a pure devotee. From this point, Ramananda Raya described the various stages of pure devotion, the moods of neutrality, servitude, friendship, parenthood and conjugal love. From there, he went on to describe the supremacy of Radha's love as well as both Radha and Krishna's characteristics. Then Mahaprabhu asked questions like, "What is the essence of education?" and "What kind of fame is best for the living being?" All these things have been extensively described in the eighth chapter of Chaitanya Charitamrita's *Madhya-līlā*. In order to avoid deviating too much from the account of Ramananda's life, we will not go into these matters any further here.

RAMANANDA'S PERCEPTION OF THE LORD'S IDENTITY

The identity of the Lord cannot remain hidden to His devotee. Ramananda was able to recognize the Lord for who He was. He said:

"First I saw You as an ordinary sannyasi. Now I see that You are actually a dark-skinned cowherd boy. I see a golden puppet standing in front of You; its golden effulgence covers your entire body."

(Chaitanya Charitamrita 2.8.268-9)

Mahaprabhu made an effort to dismiss His identity when He heard this, saying that Raya Ramananda was a great devotee and thus saw Krishna everywhere. Ramananda, however, clearly stated the primary purpose of the Lord's incarnation. Mahaprabhu was pleased with His insightful realization and displayed His form as the combination of *rasa-rāja* ("the king of the devotional sentiments") Krishna and the incarnation of *mahā-bhāva* ("the supreme devotional mood"), Srimati Radharani. When he saw this amazing combined form of the Lord, Ramananda Raya fell to the ground in a faint. When the Lord touched him, he regained consciousness.

Ramananda and the Lord remained together for ten days, enjoying discussions of Krishna conscious topics. Before Mahaprabhu continued on His southern pilgrimage, He asked Ramananda to abandon his involvement with government service and join Him in Puri when He returned.

When Mahaprabhu completed His sojourn in southern India, He met with Ramananda once again on the banks of the Godavari. He showed him the two books, *Kṛṣṇa-karṇāmṛta* and *Brahma-saṁhitā*, he had found in His travels and which substantiated all that Ramananda Raya had said in their previous conversations. Ramananda Raya transcribed the two manuscripts himself. The Lord remained another week with Ramananda, enjoying the pleasure of discussions about Krishna before heading back to Nilachala. Ramananda refused to go with the Lord immediately as he was obliged to wait for the King's permission and also would need to take care of his personal affairs. He promised to join the Lord in Puri as soon as he was able.

RAMANANDA COMES TO PURI

When the Lord arrived in Puri, he made His permanent residence in the house of Kashi Mishra. King Prataparudra had heard about the Lord and was very enthusiastic about meeting Him. Sarvabhauma Bhattacharya had assured him that once the Lord had returned from his southern pilgrimage, he would somehow or other arrange for him to have His darshan. Unfortunately, no matter how hard Sarvabhauma Bhattacharya tried to convince him, the Lord insisted that He would not look upon a king. Thus all attempts to arrange a meeting met with failure.

When the King heard that Ramananda wished to return to Puri in order to be close to Mahaprabhu, he was quite happy to grant him permission. He allowed him to leave his duties in the government and continued to pay him a pension. Thus Ramananda first met with the king in Cuttack, and then in Puri, before going to Kashi Mishra's home to meet with the Lord. Ramananda knew just how eager the King was to encounter Mahaprabhu, but rather than bringing up the matter directly, he simply glorified the king, telling Mahaprabhu how much faith he had in Him, how deep was his devotion to Krishna, and how kind he had been to free Ramananda from his governmental duties so that he could serve the Lord directly. By recounting the King's virtues in this way, he was able to soften the Lord's resolve.

In the meantime, Nityananda Prabhu had sent one of the Lord's loincloths to King Prataparudra as a consolation. Though this gave the King a great deal of joy, his desire to meet the Lord simply increased and he asked Ramananda to intercede on his behalf and make some kind of arrangement. When Ramananda finally approached the Lord directly, asking him to be compassionate toward the King, the Lord was not able to refuse him directly. He agreed that the King was no ordinary materialistic person, but nevertheless, the very title *rājā* was a type of contamination that He could not overlook. So He agreed to allow the king's son to come and see him, as the son and father are one, in a sense.

Mahaprabhu said, "There may be much milk in a big pot, but if it is contaminated by a drop of liquor, it is untouchable. The King certainly possesses all good qualities, but everything has been ruined simply by his possession of the kingly title. If you are still very eager for the King to meet with Me, then you can bring Me his son in his place. The scripture states that one's self is reborn in the son, therefore if his son comes, it will be equal to his meeting with Me." Ramananda Raya then went to inform the King about his talks with the Lord, and, according to his request, brought the King's son to see Him.

(Chaitanya Charitamrita 2.12.53-7)

APPRECIATING RUPA'S PLAYS

Rupa Manjari is the follower of the sakhis Lalita and Vishakha, who are not different from Ramananda Raya. Rupa Goswami discussed the subject of his two plays, *Lalita-mādhava* and *Vidagdha-mādhava* with Ramananda. When Ramananda asked to hear a verse about the author's worshipable deity, Rupa recited the second verse of the first act, the play's *maṅgalācaraṇa.*

anarpita-carīṁ cirāt karuṇayāvatīrṇaḥ kalau
samarpayitum unnatojjvala-rasāṁ sva-bhakti-śriyam
hariḥ puraṭa-sundara-dyuti-kadamba-sandīpitaḥ
sadā hṛdaya-kandare sphuratu vaḥ śacīnandanaḥ

The elevated, effulgent taste of sacred rapture is the wealth of devotional love. The Lord never gives it at any time; yet, out of His desire, to distribute this treasure to the world, He has become incarnate in His golden form in this age of quarrel. The son of Sachi is like a lion. May He dwell in the cave of your hearts forever.

When Ramananda Raya heard this verse, he began to praise Rupa Goswami with what seemed like a thousand tongues. He said that Rupa could only have written such an accurate portrayal of these difficult concepts as a result of the Lord's mercy.

PRADYUMNA MISHRA MEETS RAMANANDA

In order to reveal the extent of his transcendental character and identity, Mahaprabhu sent Pradyumna Mishra, who was born in an upper class Brahmin family to Ramananda to be instructed, even though Ramananda was not of such high caste. Pradyumna Mishra was born in Sylhet, but later made his permanent home in Orissa. He came one day to Mahaprabhu asking to hear some Hari katha. Mahaprabhu replied with great humility that he was not qualified to speak on elevated matters of sacred rapture, and sent him to meet Ramananda Raya.

At that time, Ramananda Raya was in the Jagannath-vallabha gardens, engaged in preparing two young *deva-dāsīs* for a play that was to be given before Lord Jagannath. Not only was he training them in the songs that they would sing and in the dance they would perform, but also bathing, dressing and decorating them. The first time that Pradyumna Mishra came to see Ramananda, one of Ramananda's servants told him that he was busy doing this work and asked Mishra to sit outside and wait. None of Ramananda Raya's servants dared to interrupt him while he was busy preparing the performance that was to be given before Lord Jagannath. Only after he had finished the rehearsal and come outside did he learn that Pradyumna Mishra had come there to hear about Krishna from him.

Ramananda showed the Brahmin the appropriate respect and begged forgiveness for the long delay. Mishra realized that it was too late that day for his wish to be fulfilled and he returned home. Some days later, when Mahaprabhu saw Mishra, he asked him how the meeting with Ramananda had gone and what topics they had discussed. Pradyumna Mishra told him everything that had happened and told the Lord that some doubts had risen in his mind about Ramananda's activities. The Lord immediately took steps to erase these doubts from the Brahmin's mind. He began to glorify Ramananda's extraordinary character with great force. He said:

"I am a sannyasi and consider Myself to be renounced. But if I even hear the name of a woman, what to speak of seeing one, I feel its effect on My mind and body. So who is not moved by the sight of a woman? Listen to me, everyone. Let Me tell you about Ramananda Raya's activities, even though they are so wonderful and uncommon that they really cannot be properly described. He personally serves Jagannath's young and beautiful *deva-dāsīs* in every possible way. He personally bathes and dresses them and decorates them with ornaments. While doing so, he naturally sees and touches their bodies' private parts, but even so, his mind is never affected. He teaches the girls how to physically express all the moods of love so they can act them out before Jagannath Deva, but his mind and body are as steady as wood or stone. Indeed, it is amazing that even when he touches such young girls, his mind is not disturbed. Only Ramananda has the right to do such things, and when I see him do them, I can understand that his body is not material, but has been completely transformed into a spiritual entity."

(Chaitanya Charitamrita 3.5.35-42)

Mahaprabhu thus revealed Ramananda's amazing powers to Pradyumna Mishra, and through him, to the world. He told Pradyumna that He Himself went to Ramananda to hear about Krishna and advised him to go a second time. This time, Pradyumna was able to hear Ramananda speak about Krishna in such depth and with such insight that he was astonished, so astonished in fact, that he began to dance in ecstasy.

Bhaktivinoda Thakur has written the following comment on the above pastime: "Raya Ramananda had composed the play known as *Jagannath-vallabha-nāṭaka.* This play was performed in the Jagannath temple for the pleasure of Jagannath. The *deva-dāsīs*, or "virgins of the God," were girls who were given to the deity to be His wives and they were trained up in performing just for the deity. In Orissan, they are now called *mahārīs*. Ramananda engaged two of these girls to play in his drama, directing them in how to play the emotions appropriate to the gopis. Since the two *deva-dāsīs* were playing the roles of chief gopis, Ramananda made no distinction between them and Krishna's beloved mistresses. He considered himself to be their maidservant, and in that spiritual identity, engaged in their service by teaching them to dance and sing for their Lord. Because Ramananda Raya knew himself to be one of Srimati Radharani's handmaidens, he was able to project the identity of his worshipable mistress on the two *deva-dāsīs* and this is why he was able to serve them in this most intimate fashion without experiencing the disturbance of mundane sexual desire." (*Amṛta-pravāha-bhāṣya*, 3.5.20)

Though a householder, Ramananda is not under the control of the six deadly sins (lust, anger, greed, illusion, intoxication and envy). Though a so-called materialistic person, he is qualified to instruct those in the renounced order of life. The Lord wished to reveal these qualities of Ramananda, and so He sent Pradyumna Mishra to listen to him speak about Krishna. The Lord knows very well how to make His devotee's virtues public. He considers it to be to His personal profit to do so by using various stratagems. O devotees! Listen carefully to yet another of the Lord's characteristics: He manifests His own majestic nature, though these are usually hidden. He spreads real religious principles through a man from the lowly shudra class in order to vanquish the false pride of so-called renunciants and learned scholars. He preached about devotional service, ecstatic love and the Absolute Truth by making Ramananda Raya, a grihastha born in a low family, the speaker, while He Himself, an exalted Brahmin-sannyasi, and Pradyumna Mishra, a pure Brahmin, both listened and took lessons from him.(Chaitanya Charitamrita 3.5.80-85)

Srila Bhaktisiddhanta Saraswati Goswami Thakur comments on these words from the Chaitanya Charitamrita as follows: "To materialistic vision, Ramananda Raya is a grihastha on the *pravṛtti-mārga*, engaged in an active life in the world. He is not, it is clear, a self-controlled brahmachari, vanaprastha, or sannyasi. A materialistic householder is under the control of his senses and this is the basis of his involvement in worldly activities. A Vaishnava householder who has attained the transcendental state, however, is not at all on the same level, transcending the influences of the six deadly sins and standing aloof from the influence of the senses. Ramananda Raya accepted the householder state as his role in the pastimes of Sri Chaitanya Mahaprabhu. Ordinary materialistic persons look upon him from a perspective that is tinted by their own desire for sense gratification and thus consider him to be one of their own, but in fact his mind had been totally spiritualized through fixation on the supreme worshipable object. He was thus a *kṛṣṇa-viṣayī*, one who seeks only the pleasure of Krishna's senses and not his own. He was not an impersonalist or argumentative nihilist opposed to the Lord's transcendental activities. Indeed, he possessed the power to transform the minds of such sannyasis who had abandoned sense gratification and were absorbed in the undifferentiated Brahman without any appreciation for Krishna's form and pastimes, and turn them away from their fundamentally materialistic conception of transcendence, attracting them to the practice of devotional service through hearing and chanting about Krishna's name, form and activities."

OTHER ACTIVITIES IN PURI

When Vallabha Bhatta came to Puri and into contact with Chaitanya Mahaprabhu, the Lord kept His glories hidden from him because He knew him to be proud of his learning. He thus preferred to speak to Vallabha Bhatta about the qualifications of His entourage. At that time He said of Ramananda that he was expert both in the sambandha, or knowledge of the relationships between God, man and the universe, and the *prayojana-tattva*, or knowledge of life in the state of divine perfection. Furthermore, He indicated that Ramananda was the greatest connoisseur of the pure and sacred raptures of Vrindavan.

Ramananda Raya is the treasure house of divine sentiments. It was he who disclosed to Me that Krishna is the Supreme Personality of Godhead. No one can fully describe the extent of Ramananda's spiritual power. Through him I was able to learn about the pure moods of the devotees of Vraja. (Chaitanya Charitamrita 3.7.23, 37)

Ramananda Raya had the same type of relationship with Mahaprabhu that Subala, Krishna's friend and helper used to have in Vraja. (Chaitanya Charitamrita 3.6.9)

Ramananda Raya was also present in Nilachala when Hari Das Thakur passed away. Mahaprabhu praised Hari Das before the devotees led by Ramananda and Sarvabhauma Bhattacharya. (3.11.50)

RAMANANDA DURING THE LORD'S LAST DAYS

During His last years in this world, Mahaprabhu spent most of His time in a condition of divine ecstatic madness. He would sometimes disappear from His chambers, even though there were three barred doors through which He had to pass in order to go outside. Once He was found near the Lion's Gate, His joints loosened and taking on a giant, distended form. He was revived and returned to normal by the loud singing of the Holy Names. On another occasion, He was found in the sand dunes that in his state of trance He had taken to be Govardhan. Once again, He had to be pacified by sankirtan and returned to His home. On these occasions, Ramananda Raya was present with Svarupa Damodar. Throughout the ten transformations of the Lord's ecstatic madness (*divyonmāda*),

Ramananda Raya would recite verses that fit the Lord's emotional state. In this way, he brought Mahaprabhu pleasure.

This was Mahaprabhu's life in Nilachala, passing the days and nights absorbed in the anxiety of separation from Krishna. Svarupa and Ramananda were always with Him, bringing Him ecstasy with their recitation of songs and verses appropriate to his mood.

(Chaitanya Charitamrita 3.20.3-4)

The Lord took Svarupa Damodar and Ramananda Raya by the shoulders and said, "Listen, Svarupa and Rama Raya! Tell Me what I should do, where should I go in order to find Krishna? You can tell Me the best thing to do." In this way, Gauranga would tell his tale of woe to Svarupa and Ramananda and they would console Him in His grief. Svarupa would sing and Ramananda would recite Sanskrit verses, giving joy to the Lord with poems from *Kṛṣṇa-karṇāmṛta*, the songs of Vidyapati and *Gīta-govinda*.

(Chaitanya Charitamrita 3.15.24-7)

Remaining in the company of Svarupa and Ramananda both day and night, Mahaprabhu ecstatically relished the songs of Chandi Das, Vidyapati and Ramananda Raya's plays, as well as *Kṛṣṇa-karṇāmṛta* and *Gīta-govinda*. (Chaitanya Charitamrita 2.2.77)

Ramananda Raya performed his bhajan in the Jagannath Ballabha gardens, a place that was very dear to Mahaprabhu also. As soon as the Lord entered within this garden, He would be overwhelmed by feelings of divine love. One day, while the Lord was there, He had a vision of Krishna under an ashok tree. Then, the vision was suddenly lost to Him, and Mahaprabhu fell to the ground in a faint.

The main park in Puri is the Jagannath Ballabha garden. The Lord entered there with His devotees. The trees and flower bushes were in bloom, and it seemed as though it was Vrindavan. The parrots, mynah birds, and cuckoos were singing their songs and the bees were all buzzing.

(Chaitanya Charitamrita 3.19.79-80)

Wandering through the garden, He went from tree to tree. When He came to an ashok tree, He suddenly saw Krishna standing there. The Lord started to run towards Him, but Krishna laughed at Him and disappeared. The Lord was stunned: He had found Krishna and then lost Him again. He lost consciousness and fell to the ground.

(Chaitanya Charitamrita 3.19.85-87)

Through Ramananda Raya and Sri Svarupa Damodar Goswami, Lord Chaitanya Mahaprabhu joyfully announced to the world that Harinam sankirtan is the best means to attain love of God in this age of quarrel.

The Lord, in a wave of jubilation said, "Listen Svarupa Damodar and Ramananda Raya! In the age of Kali, Harinam sankirtan is the supreme means of deliverance. In the age of Kali, Krishna is to be worshiped by the congregational chanting of his Holy Names. This is the way that an intelligent person attains the lotus feet of Krishna. Through the chanting of the Holy Name, all of one's sinful reactions are extinguished and all auspiciousness arises until finally one experiences the joys of love for Krishna."

(Chaitanya Charitamrita 3.20.8-11)

There are two opinions about Ramananda Raya's disappearance day: some people say Jyestha *kṛṣṇā pañcamī*, others Vaishakh *kṛṣṇā pañcamī*.

Sri Paramananda Puri

purī paramānando ya āsīd uddhavaḥ purā

He who was Uddhava in Krishna lila came to enrich the pastimes of Gaura as Paramananda Puri.

(*Gaura-gaṇoddeśa-dīpikā* 118)

Nothing is known about Paramananda Puri's antecedents or his appearance and disappearance dates. It is known that he was born in Tirhut, the area that surrounds Muzaffarpur and Darbhanga in Bihar. Srila Bhaktisiddhanta Saraswati Goswami Thakur has described him as a brahmin from Tirhut.

Paramananda's diksha guru was Madhavendra Puri, which meant that Mahaprabhu treated him as a very dear superior. Krishna Das Kaviraj Goswami describes Paramananda Puri as one of the nine sannyasi roots that came out of the trunk of the desire tree of devotion. The first sprout of this desire tree was Madhavendra Puri; its well-nourished second sprout was Ishvara Puri; its trunk was Chaitanya Mahaprabhu Himself. The entire tree remained stable sitting on nine sannyasi roots: Paramananda Puri, Keshava Bharati, Brahmananda Puri, Brahmananda Bharati, Vishnu Puri, Keshava Puri, Krishnananda Puri, Nrisingha Tirtha and Sukhananda Puri. Of these nine, Paramananda Puri is the central root. The great mystery here is that Chaitanya Mahaprabhu could both be the trunk of the tree and the gardener who takes care of it. (Chaitanya Charitamrita 1.9.14)

The central root of the tree was the grave and sober Paramananda Puri. The tree stood solidly on these nine roots. (Chaitanya Charitamrita 1.9.16)

MAHAPRABHU'S MEETING WITH PARAMANANDA PURI

When Mahaprabhu left Nilachala to do His pilgrimage of Southern India in the company of Krishna Das Vipra, he travelled through Kurmasthan, Jiyar Nrisingha, Vidyanagar where he met with Raya Ramananda, Gautami Ganga, Mallikarjuna, Ahobala Nrisingha, Siddhabaṭa, Skandha Kshetra, Trimath, Vrddha Kashi, Bauddhasthan,

Tirupati, Trimalla, Pana Nrisingha, Shiva Kanchi, Vishnu Kanchi, Trikalahasti, Vriddhakola, Shiyali Bhairavi, the banks of the Kaveri River, Kumbhakarna's forehead, Srirangam (where he bestowed bhakti on Venkata Bhatta and his entire family).

When he arrived at Rishabha Mountain he met Paramananda Puri for the first time. Ṛṣabha Parvata is in the state of Tamil Nadu in Madurai district. Twelve miles north of the town of Madurai are the Anagadamalai Mountains where Rishabhadeva was burned in a forest fire in the forest surrounding Kutakachalam. The place is known today as Palni Hill, or Varāha Parvata, according to the local people. Paramananda Puri was observing the Chaturmasya vrata at this Rishabha Parvat when Mahaprabhu arrived there. The Lord paid his obeisances to Paramananda, who stood up and embraced him. The two of them spent three days discussing topics of Krishna. When Paramananda Puri told the Lord of his intention to travel north to Puri and then continue on to bathe in the Ganges, Mahaprabhu invited him to return to Puri afterwards and join Him. He said that He Himself would quickly return from Setubandha to Puri where they would meet again.

> Puri Goswami said, "I intend to go to Puri. After visiting Puri, I will go on to Bengal to bathe in the Ganges." The Lord said, "Come back again to Puri afterward. I will be there before long, after I have visited Setubandha. I would like to have your company, so please be kind and come to Puri to take up permanent residence there."
> (Chaitanya Charitamrita 2.9.171-3)

PARAMANANDA GOES TO PURI

When Mahaprabhu returned from his southern tour to Nilachala, he sent Kala Krishna Das to Nabadwip to announce to Sachi and the other devotees that He had returned. They were all overjoyed by the news, and then Advaita Acharya and the others took Sachi's permission to visit the Lord in Puri. Paramananda Puri happened to be in Nabadwip at the time, as he had been walking along the Ganges. He had been staying in Mayapur at Sachi Mata's house where she had been taking care of him with great affection. He thus also learned from Kala Krishna Das that Mahaprabhu had returned to Nilachala. Feeling an intense eagerness to see the Lord again, he and another devotee, Kamala Kanta Dvija, immediately left for Puri.

On his arrival, Mahaprabhu respectfully paid obeisances to Paramananda Puri, who was overwhelmed with feelings of ecstasy and took the Lord in his arms. They told each other how much they desired their association.

> The Lord said, "I desire very much to remain in your company. I request you to be merciful to me and take up residence in Nilachala." Puri answered, "And I too am very eager to remain in your company. It is for that reason that I left Bengal to come here to Nilachala."
> (Chaitanya Charitamrita 2.10.17-8)

Mahaprabhu gave Paramananda Puri a secluded room in Kashi Mishra's house as living quarters. Paramananda Puri was therefore always present during the Chaturmasya period, participating in all of the Lord's pastimes during that time along with his others associates. We can see from Vrindavan Das' Chaitanya Bhagavata just how dear Paramananda Puri was to Mahaprabhu:

> Mahaprabhu caught sight of Paramananda Puri from a distance and immediately got up respectfully. Filled with joy at seeing His devotee, the Lord glorified him and danced in ecstatic love. Lifting His arms, He cried out "Hari! Hari! I have finally seen Paramananda Puri with My own eyes! My eyes have been fulfilled, My life has finally been perfected! All My religious works have finally borne fruit. My sannyas has been fulfilled. It is as though I am seeing Madhavendra Puri himself." Having said this, the Lord embraced His dear devotee and bathed his body with tears from His lotus eyes. Puri also forgot himself in ecstasy as soon as he saw the Lord's moonlike face. The two paid obeisances to each other for a long time. Paramananda Puri is the abode of love for Chaitanya Mahaprabhu. (Chaitanya Bhagavata 3.3.168-175)

> Svarupa Damodar is as dear to the Lord as Puri Goswami. (Chaitanya Bhagavata 3.10.42)

> Amongst all His sannyasi associates, no one was as dear to the Lord as Puri Goswami. Svarupa Damodar and Paramananda Puri were the most qualified of the Lord's sannyasi associates. The two of them remained constantly in the Lord's company, taking the staff (*danda*) of renunciation for the sake of the Lord. Puri engaged primarily in meditation, while Svarupa Damodar was devoted to kirtan. They were like two arms of the Lord's sannyasi form.
> (Chaitanya Bhagavata 3.10.46-49)

Vrindavan Das also says that Mahaprabhu spent entire days conversing with Paramananda Puri about Krishna, just as Krishna engaged his friend Arjuna in intimate conversation (3.3.233-4).

PARAMANANDA'S ACTIVITIES WITH THE LORD IN PURI

Mahaprabhu ostracized Chota Hari Das for having talked to a woman, refusing him entrance to His house. Chota Hari Das was greatly distressed by this punishment and fasted for three days. Svarupa Damodar and the rest of Mahaprabhu's entourage repeatedly asked the Lord to soften his stance toward Hari Das, but He would not be shaken. Indeed, He rebuked the devotees for suggesting that He repeal His order. When the devotees learned that Chota Hari Das intended to commit suicide because he was no longer allowed to see the Lord, they came to Paramananda Puri as a last resort to ask the Lord to forgive him. The Lord considered Paramananda Puri to be as worshipable as His own guru, as he was Ishvara Puri's godbrother. The devotees hoped that if he were to approach the Lord on behalf of Chota Hari Das, that the Lord would accept his demand.

When Paramananda came to Mahaprabhu, the Lord said that He was willing to allow Chota Hari Das to return to the Gambhira, but that He Himself would go to Alalanath. Paramananda Puri was taken off guard by Mahaprabhu's proposal to leave Puri. He said that He was the independent Lord and that it had been incorrect of him to try to interfere with His decision. He then tried to dissuade Mahaprabhu from going to Alalanath.

> Mahaprabhu taught by His own behavior that the guru's godbrother is worshipable, like the guru. It is extremely detrimental to one's devotional life to disrespect those who are one's guru-varga. The Lord says, "I cannot tolerate breaches of Vaishnava etiquette."
> (Chaitanya Charitamrita 1.4.166)

Paramananda Puri participated in nearly all of the Lord's pastimes in Purushottam: the cleaning of the Gundicha temple, the Rathayatra festival, the water sports in the Narendra Sarovar. He was present at the festival in honor of Hari Das Thakur after his disappearance. Once the Bengali devotees returned home after the rainy season, Sarvabhauma Bhattacharya invited either Mahaprabhu or one of his ten sannyasi associates (Paramananda Puri, Damodar Svarupa, Brahmananda Puri, Brahmananda Bharati, Vishnu Puri, Keshava Puri, Krishnananda Puri, Nrisingha Tirtha, Sukhananda Puri and Satyananda Bharati) to take lunch at his house every day for a month. Five of these days were consecrated to nicely feeding Paramananda Puri with delicious maha prasad.

All the Gaudiya Vaishnavas and the residents of Puri treated Paramananda Puri as a senior spiritual leader and gave him all respect. Mahaprabhu Himself followed the etiquette of placing sandalwood paste and giving garlands to Paramananda Puri and Brahmananda Bharati before anyone else during the Rathayatra festival.

> Paramananda Puri and Brahmananda Bharati were overjoyed to receive sandalwood paste from Mahaprabhu's own hand. Advaita Acharya and Nityananda Prabhu were also ecstatic on being touched by the Lord's hand.
> (Chaitanya Charitamrita 2.13.30-1)

During the Gundicha temple cleaning, he did not engage his guru varga in any of the difficult tasks like carrying buckets of water. Rather, they worked alongside the Lord with the water the other devotees had carried in.

> All the devotees carried water except for Nityananda, Advaita, Svarupa, Brahmananda and Paramananda Puri.
> (Chaitanya Charitamrita 2.12.109)

PARAMANANDA PURI'S WELL

The Vyasadeva of Lord Chaitanya's pastimes, Vrindavan Das Thakur, describes Paramananda Puri's glories in the Chaitanya Bhagavata (*Antya-khaṇḍa*, chapter 3), making special mention of his well. Srila Bhaktisiddhanta Saraswati Goswami Thakur makes the following remarks about Paramananda Puri's well in his *Bhāṣya* on the Chaitanya Bhagavata: "This well is not far along the road leading west from the Jagannath temple, just next to the police station. Srila Bhaktivinoda Thakur identified this well was the one associated with Paramananda Puri in the Chaitanya Bhagavata."

Being omniscient, Mahaprabhu knew that the water from this well was not good; later He heard the same thing directly from Paramananda. Jagannath knew that any living being who touched or drank the water from Paramananda's well would be freed from all his sins and thus liberated, thus He Himself had made the water of this well muddy in order to discourage anyone from taking it. This was a sign of Jagannath's miserliness, as He did not seem to want anyone to have such an easy time of attaining liberation. Mahaprabhu thus stood up and prayed with arms upraised, asking Lord Jagannath to be merciful to the jivas.

> Lord Jagannath, grant me this boon: Let the Ganges enter into this well. Please order the Bhogavati Ganga, which travels underground, to flow into the well.
> (Chaitanya Bhagavata 3.3.235-6)

When the devotees heard the Lord's sweet prayer, they all shouted the names of Hari in approval. Taking the order of the Lord seriously, Ganga Devi entered into the well. The next morning, the devotees were amazed and overjoyed to see that its water had become pure and clear. Paramananda Puri glorified the well, saying that anyone who took a bath with water from it would obtain the same benefits as from bathing in the Ganges and would attain devotion to Krishna. Mahaprabhu Himself often bathed in water from this well and drank from it.

Just as the devotee glorifies the Lord, so too does the Lord sing His devotee's glories and seek to increase them. Those who are uninterested in the Supreme Lord are incapable of understanding the glories of a devotee. The compassionate Lord glorifies the devotees so everyone can learn that without the association of devotees and without their mercy, there is no such thing as auspiciousness for the jiva.

> The Lord said, "I am present on this earth only out of affection for Paramananda Puri. I belong to him alone. If he sells Me, I allow Myself to be sold. Anyone who sees Paramananda Puri, even once, will receive love for Krishna.
> (Chaitanya Bhagavata 3.3.255-7)

In the *Gauḍīya Vaiṣṇava Abhidhāna,* it is said that Paramananda Puri wrote a book named *Govinda-vijaya.*

SRI SVARUPA DAMODAR

Krishna Das Kaviraj writes that Sri Svarupa Damodar Goswami was one of Mahaprabhu's three and a half most intimate associates.

The Lord accepted that Shikhi Mahiti's sister was one

of Radha's friends. In the entire world, there were only three and a half devotees who were as worthy. They were Svarupa Damodar Goswami, Ramananda Raya and Shikhi Mahiti. Shikhi Mahiti's sister was the half person.
(Chaitanya Charitamrita 3.2.105-6)

Elsewhere Krishna Das called Svarupa Damodar the most important of the Lord's companions. "Two persons knew the Lord best: Paramananda Puri and Svarupa Damodar" (Chaitanya Charitamrita 1.10.124-5).

In His lila as the golden avatar, Mahaprabhu is Krishna Himself enveloped by the desire and bodily luster of Srimati Radharani. Sri Svarupa Damodar Goswami was the Lord's alter ego. In Vraja-lila, he was also Radharani's alter ego, Lalita Sakhi. This is the prevailing opinion in the Gaudiya sampradaya, even though Kavi Karnapur identifies him as Radha's other companion, Vishakha Devi, in the *Gaura-gaṇoddeśa-dīpikā*.

kalām aśikṣayad rādhāṁ yā viśākhā vraje purā
sādya Svarupa-gosvāmī tat-tad-bhāva-vilāsavān

That same Vishakha who previously taught Radha the arts in Vraja is today Svarupa Goswami, who rejoices in the moods of Radha and Krishna.

In either case, Svarupa Damodar had a special affinity for the madhura-rasa, in the mood of a sakhi of Radha. As Krishna Das says:

Paramananda Puri had parental affection for Mahaprabhu; Ramananda Raya loved Him in pure friendship; Govinda Das' love for the Lord was as a servant. Gadadhar, Jagadananda and Svarupa Damodar worshiped Him in the ecstasy of the chief rasa. Mahaprabhu's heart was won by these four different loving attitudes.
(Chaitanya Charitamrita 2.2.78)

Srila Bhaktisiddhanta Saraswati Goswami Thakur explains these verses in his *Anubhāṣya* as follows: "Sri Paramananda Puri, who was Uddhava in Krishna lila, loved Mahaprabhu with parental affection; Ramananda, who was either Vishakha or Arjuna, had the pure sentiment of a close friend; Govinda and others were devoted to their service to the Lord, and possessed a pure mood of service (*śuddha-dāsya*). Gadadhar, Jagadananda and Svarupa Damodar served the Lord in the primary sentiment, i.e., that of erotic love (*madhura-rasa*). The Lord became obliged to these devotees, accepting their worship, their association, their service and their joy."

In the last twelve years of His pastimes in Puri, the Lord remained constantly absorbed in the mood of Radharani. During this time, only Svarupa Damodar and Ramananda Raya were able to experience the depths of his emotion through relishing topics they alone were privileged to know.

candidāsa vidyāpati rāyera nāṭaka gīti
karṇāmṛta śrī gīta-govinda
svarupa ramananda sane mahaprabhu rātri-dine
gāya, śune parama ānanda

Day and night, Mahaprabhu ecstatically relished the songs of Chandi Das, Vidyapati and Ramananda Raya's plays, as well as *Kṛṣṇa-karṇāmṛta* and *Gīta-govinda*, in the company of Svarupa and Ramananda.
(Chaitanya Charitamrita 2.2.77)

SVARUPA DAMODAR'S KARACA

The special relationship that Svarupa Damodar had with the Lord meant that He had intimate knowledge of the Lord's final years and His mystic ecstasies. Krishna Das writes that Svarupa Damodara is the source of the most confidential knowledge of Lord Chaitanya's incarnation:

I have already shown that preaching the sankirtan movement was the external cause for the Lord's descent. There is another, primary purpose for the Lord's incarnation. This is the personal work of Krishna, the foremost enjoyer of loving exchanges. This very confidential cause is three-fold, as has been revealed by Svarupa Damodar Goswami. Sri Svarupa Damodar Goswami was extremely close to the Lord and thus was able to know all these matters.
(Chaitanya Charitamrita 1.4.103-5)

Svarupa Damodar was thus the authority through whom knowledge of the last years of Mahaprabhu's lila came into devotee society.

Murari Gupta explained all of the Lord's early pastimes in the form of an outline. Svarupa Damodar did the same for the Lord's later pastimes. The devotees describe the Lord's activities by following the order given in these two outlines. (Chaitanya Charitamrita 1.13.15-17)

Srila Bhaktivinoda Thakur has commented on these verses as follows: "Murari Gupta's outline of the Lord's early pastimes are still extant, so devotees were able to expand on them after looking at his written text. On the other hand, the Vaishnavas only heard Svarupa Damodar's *kaṛacā* through Raghunath Das Goswami."

Chaitanya lila is like the finest of jewels. Sri Svarupa Damodar Goswami guarded it in his treasure chest and afterwards placed it around Raghunath Das' neck. I have written down here what I heard from Raghunath Das. To the extent that I have been able, and now make a gift of it to the devotees. (Chaitanya Charitamrita 2.2.85)

Srila Bhaktivinoda Thakur says the following of this verse: "Svarupa Damodar described the Lord's latter pastimes in summary Sanskrit verses known as a *kaṛacā*. He made Raghunath Das memorize these verses, and later Krishna Das Kaviraj Goswami spread these accounts of the Lord's activities throughout the world. Thus, though Svarupa Damodar's *kaṛacā* was never published in book form, the Chaitanya Charitamrita itself is its essence."
(*Amṛta-pravāha-bhāṣya*)

SVARUPA DAMODAR'S KIRTAN

Sri Svarupa Damodar used to make Mahaprabhu very happy by singing the songs of Vidyapati, Chandi Das and *Gīta-govinda*. He was as expert a musician as the Gandharvas, and in knowledge of the scripure he was just like Brihaspati. No personality was his equal. Sri Svarupa Damodar was also very dear to Advaita Acharya and Nityananda Prabhu, and he was the life and soul of all the devotees, headed by Srivas Thakur.

(Chaitanya Charitamrita 2.10.115-7)

Krishna Das Kaviraj Goswami has described the extent to which Sri Svarupa Damodar Goswami and Ramananda Raya were dear to Mahaprabhu in the 15th chapter of the *Antya-līlā*:

After saying these things, the Lord took Svarupa Damodar and Ramananda Raya by the shoulders and said, "Listen, Svarupa and Rama Raya! Tell me what I should do, where should I go in order to find Krishna? You can tell me what is best for me to do." In this way Gauranga would tell His tale of woe to Svarupa and Ramananda, and they would console Him in His grief. Svarupa would sing and Ramananda would recite Sanskrit verses, giving joy to the Lord with *Karṇāmṛta*, Vidyapati and *Gīta-govinda*.

(Chaitanya Charitamrita 3.15.24-7)

A similar passage is found in the 20th chapter of the *Antya-līlā*.

This was Mahaprabhu's life in Nilachala: He went through the days and nights absorbed in anxiety of separation from Krishna. Svarupa and Ramananda were always with Him, bringing Him ecstasy with their recitations of songs and verses appropriate to His mood.

(Chaitanya Charitamrita 3.20.3-4)

Vrindavan Das Thakur has also named Sri Svarupa Damodar Goswami as one of Mahaprabhu's principal associates in his Chaitanya Bhagavata. He describes there how the Lord would lose external consciousness upon hearing Svarupa's kirtan. When Srila Gadadhar Pandit Goswami was living at the Tota Gopinath temple, he would give discourses on the Bhagavata while in an ecstatic trance, primarily speaking on the sections dealing with the lives of Prahlad and Dhruva. Mahaprabhu would be overcome by the eight ecstatic symptoms on hearing Svarupa Damodar's kirtan, just as He would at Gadadhar's Bhagavata readings.

Gadadhar Pandit was the main expert in the Bhagavata and Svarupa Damodar in kirtan. Svarupa Damodar would sing solo and Mahaprabhu would lose Himself in dance. Mahaprabhu would reveal the symptoms of ecstatic love such as tears, trembling, laughing, fainting, horripilation and roaring, all of which manifested on His body as He danced with the devotees. Whenever the Lord heard Svarupa Damodar singing kirtan aloud, He would lose external consciousness and fall down on the spot. There was no equal to Svarupa amongst all of the Lord's sannyasi associates. Svarupa was as dear to Him as Paramananda Puri. Sri Svarupa Damodar Goswami was the incarnation of the delight of transcendental song, which would make Mahaprabhu dance.

(Chaitanya Bhagavata 3.10.36-43)

EARLY LIFE AND SANNYAS

We have the following information about Sri Svarupa Damodar Goswami in terms of his bodily identity. Before taking sannyas, he was known as Purushottam Acharya or Purushottam Bhattacharya. The *Gauḍīya Vaiṣṇava Abhidhāna* gives the following account of his antecedents: His father's name was Padmagarbha Acharya. His mother's name is not known, but she was the daughter of Jayaram Chakravarti. Jayaram's original residence was in the village of Bhitadiya on the banks of the Brahmaputra River in Bangladesh, but he and his family later moved to Nabadwip. After arranging for his daughter to be married to Padmagarbha, he made his son-in-law also come to Nabadwip. After Purushottam was born, however, Padmagarbha left his wife and child at his father-in-law's house and went to Mithila and Kashi in order to study. Purushottam Acharya was thus raised in his maternal grandparents' home in Nabadwip.

Later, when Mahaprabhu took sannyas, Purushottam was unable to remain in Nabadwip due to the feelings of separation from the Lord and he departed for Benares where he also took the renounced order of life. This is described as follows in the *Prema-vilāsa*:

Purushottam became a resident of Nabadwip, staying with his mother's parents. Filled with all virtues, he became Mahaprabhu's dear devotee. When the Lord took sannyas, he went mad with separation and left for Benares where he also took sannyas. Svarupa Damodar is the name he recieved. He was an intimate devotee of the Lord, an ocean of rasa.

Krishna Das Kaviraj Goswami gives a brief account of Sri Svarupa Damodar Goswami's early life and sannyas in the Chaitanya Charitamrita (2.10.102-114) when telling of his arrival in Jagannath Puri:

Svarupa Damodar was a most intimate friend of the Lord and an ocean of transcendental mellows. Before taking sannyas, he had resided at Nabadwip in Mahaprabhu's association where he was known as Purushottam Acharya. When he saw Mahaprabhu accept the renounced order, he became like a madman and immediately went to Benares to take sannyas. His sannyas guru, Chaitanyananda Bharati, ordered him to study the Vedanta Sutra and to teach it to others. Svarupa Damodar was a great renunciate as well as a learned scholar. He took shelter of Krishna's pastimes with heart and soul.

In his eagerness to worship Sri Krishna without any disturbance, he accepted the sannyas order in a state of delirium. When taking sannyas, Purushottam Acharya followed the regulative principles by giving up his tuft of hair and sacred thread, but he did not take the saffron-colored dress. Nor did he take a sannyasi title, but rather kept the brahmachari name, Svarupa.

Svarupa Damodar then took permission from his sannyas-guru to go to Nilachala where day and night he enjoyed the ecstacies of love for Krishna. Though he had attained the peak of learning, he spoke to no one but remained in seclusion and incognito.

Srila Bhaktisiddhanta Saraswati Goswami Thakur has made the following comments on this section of the Chaitanya Charitamrita: "In the Daśanāmī sect founded by Shankaracharya, the lineages that take the sannyas names of Tirtha and Ashram follow the custom of giving postulants to the renounced order the title Brahmachari. Such a postulant is then required to vow to remain celibate for the rest of his life. In Purushottam Acharya's case, the brahmachari title was Svarupa Damodar. Brahmacharis called Svarupa normally receive the sannyas title Tirtha upon taking the saffron cloth or *yoga-paṭṭa*." (*Anubhāṣya,* 2.10.102) "In the Daśanāmī sect, certain regulative principles must be followed before taking sannyas: one must perform eight kinds of *śrāddha*, offering oblations to one's forefathers, and the *virajā* sacrifice. Then one cuts off the tuft of hair called *śikhā* and gives up the sacred thread. Svarupa Damodar accepted these preliminary processes to the acceptance of sannyas, but not the *gurvāhvāna*, or 'call of the guru,' the saffron cloth, a sannyas title or a danda, and for this reason he retained his brahmachari name."

(*Anubhāṣya,* 2.10.108)

It may be pointed out here that for those who follow the formalities of tridandi sannyas, the keeping of the *śikhā*, the sacred thread and saffron cloth are approved by the *Skanda-purāṇa*, which states:

śikhī yajñopavītī syāt tridaṇḍī sa-kamaṇḍaluḥ
sa pavitraś ca kāṣāyī gāyatrīṁ ca japet sadā

Wearing the *śikhā*, sacred thread and saffron cloth and carrying the kamandalu water pot, a tridandi sannyasi should remain pure in his habits and constantly chant the *gāyatrī* mantra.

Srila Bhaktivinoda Thakur has also commented on the same text in his *Amṛta-pravāha-bhāṣya*: "Purushottam Acharya took Mahaprabhu's example and took sannyas simply by renouncing his *śikhā* and sutra. His sannyas name was Svarupa Damodar. He did not accept the formality of the *yoga-paṭṭa* because he wished to avoid any danger of becoming falsely proud of the status that would come with taking sannyas. He only wished to worship Krishna without any worries."

In the *Anubhāṣya* commentary to *Ādi-līlā* (4.105) of Chaitanya Charitamrita, Srila Bhaktisiddhanta Saraswati Goswami Thakur writes, "Purushottam Bhattacharya was a resident of Nabadwip. Even prior to Mahaprabhu's taking sannyas, he desired to renounce the world. He left home and went to Benares, where he accepted the position of brahmacarya in a group of Daśanāmī sannyasis. When he became a brahmachari, he was given the name Damodar Svarupa. He did not bother completing the sannyas rituals and came to Nilachala, Jagannath Puri, where spent the rest of his life at the Lord's lotus feet. He became Mahaprabhu's constant companion, enhancing the Lord's pleasure by singing the songs requested by the Lord. Svarupa Damodar could understand Mahaprabhu's secret mission and it was by his grace alone that all the Lord's devotees could know his deepest purpose."

SVARUPA ARRIVES IN PURI

Mahaprabhu took sannyas on the full moon day of the month of Magh and left for Nilachala in the following month of Phalgun. After delivering Sarvabhauma Bhattacharya, he left for his pilgrimage to South India in the month of Vaishakh. Nityananda Prabhu gave him a Brahmin named Kala Krishna Das to be His servant and companion on this trip. When Mahaprabhu returned from this journey, after having brought good fortune to the inhabitants of the South through the gift of Krishna prema, Nityananda sent Krishna Das back to Nabadwip to inform the devotees that the Lord had arrived in Puri. The news brought great joy to Sachi Mata, Advaita Acharya, Srivas Pandit and the other devotees. They immediately started making preparations to visit the Lord in Puri.

Paramananda Puri had been staying at Sachi Mata's house and decided to leave ahead of the others with a Brahmin named Kamala Kanta. They were thus the first from Bengal to arrive in Puri to meet the Lord. Not long afterward, Purushottam Acharya, who had already been to Benares and taken sannyas from Chaitanyananda Bharati and received the name Svarupa Damodar, arrived and joyously entered the Lord's entourage. When he first saw the Lord, Sri Svarupa Damodar Goswami recited the following prayer:

heloddhulita-khedayā viśadayā pronmīlad-āmodayā
śāmyac chāstra-vivādayā rasa-dayā cittārpitonmādayā
śaśvad-bhakti-vinodayā sa-madayā mādhurya-maryādayā
śrī-caitanya dayā-nidhe tava dayā bhūyād amandodayā

O ocean of mercy, Sri Chaitanya Mahaprabhu! May your auspicious mercy rise like the dawn driving away all kinds of material lamentation, making everything pure, and awakening transcendental bliss, ending all quarrels and disagreements among different scriptures, giving the taste of spiritual life and the intoxicating joy of devotional service, revealing the extent of the conjugal mood's sweetness, and maddening the minds of those surrendered to You, (Chaitanya Charitamrita 2.10.119, *Caitanya-candrodaya-nāṭaka* 10.8).

Sri Svarupa Damodar Goswami first received the mercy of the Lord in the form of a heartfelt embrace. Then he paid his obeisances to Nityananda Prabhu and Paramananda Puri and was introduced to Jagadananda and the other devotees. He first met Raya Ramananda when the latter came to Puri with King Prataparudra.

FRIENDSHIP WITH PUNDARIKA VIDYANIDHI

In Puri, Sri Svarupa Damodar Goswami parcipated in the water sports in Narendra Sarovar at the time of the Chandan Yatra and in the Indradyumna Sarovar after the cleaning of the Gundicha temple. He and Pundarika Vidyanidhi enjoyed splashing each other.

The two friends, Vidyanidhi and Svarupa Damodar, joyously splashed each other and laughed.
(Chaitanya Charitamrita 3.8.124)

Jagannath has an annual festival in Puri named Oṛana Ṣaṣṭhī. On this occasion, Jagannath's pujaris dress the deity in cloth that still has the tapioca-based starch (*māṛ*) in it. Sri Pundarika Vidyanidhi did not like this behavior of the pujaris, as he considered such cloth to be unclean. He went to Svarupa Damodar and asked him for his opinion on the matter. Svarupa Damodar said, "The Lord is completely independent. He is not dependent on the rules regulating deity worship found in the smṛtis."

Vidyanidhi immediately answered him, "I accept that Jagannath is completely independent. That does not mean that the pujaris are completely independent of the rules and regulations of scripture. They are not Brahma, that they dress the Lord in unwashed cloth. Didn't you know that if you even touch cloth that has *māṛ* in it, you are supposed to wash your hands?"

That night Jagannath and Balaram appeared to Sri Pundarika Vidyanidhi in a dream and slapped him on his cheeks for having criticized their servants. By so doing, Jagannath showed that no one is allowed criticize His servants for apparent lapses in behavior. The Smartas are especially inclined to criticizing Vaishnava behavior for failing to adhere to the arcane standards of the Smritis. Sri Pundarika Vidyanidhi, though his cheeks were swollen from the slaps, was overjoyed to have been touched by their Lordships. Svarupa Damodar also congratulated Vidyanidhi for his good fortune:

As he looked Pundarika Vidyanidhi over, Svarupa Damodar felt great affection arise for his friend. Indeed, he started to float in an ocean of ecstasy. A friend always feels joy at the good fortune of a friend. The two of them began to laugh spiritedly and Svarupa Damodar said, "Listen, brother. I have never seen or heard of a punishment like this one. The Lord came personally to chastise you in a dream. I never heard of such a thing, but now I see that it has happened to you!" The two friends floated in a feeling of satisfaction. They spent day and night talking of nothing but Krishna conscious topics.
(Chaitanya Bhagavata 3.10.173-177)

GUNDICHA AND RATHAYATRA PASTIMES

Sri Svarupa Damodar Goswami was one of the chief participants in the cleaning of the Gundicha temple on the eve of the Rathayatra. "Other than Nityananda, Advaita, Svarupa, Brahmananda Bharati and Paramananda Puri, everyone carried buckets of water."
(Chaitanya Charitamrita 2.12.109)

During the washing of the Gundicha temple, a simple but intelligent Brahmin who was not aware of the nature of the Vaishnavas' devotional etiquette, took some water, suddenly poured it over the Lord's feet, and drank it. In view of Mahaprabhu's identity as the incarnation of Krishna, it was certainly no offense to drink the water that had washed His feet, even though it was done inside the temple, but here Mahaprabhu acted as an exemplar for the world and showed dissatisfaction at the Brahmin's behavior so that no other person would imitate him and become an offender at the Deity's feet. He let His anger be known to Svarupa Damodar who caught the Bengali Brahmin and

pushed him out of the temple. The next instant, however, Svarupa Damodar returned to the Lord's side and asked Him to forgive the Brahmin. Though a Vaishnava may externally appear to be hard-hearted, internally he or she is always filled with compassion and thinks of the welfare of every living being.

Every year during Balaram, Jagannath and Subhadra's Rathayatra festival, the Lord would make four kirtan groups with His devotees. Svarupa Damodar would sing in the first of these, with Advaita participating as the principal dancer. With the addition of other kirtan groups from Shantipur, Srikhanda and Kulina, there were seven sampradayas altogether. In each group, there were two drummers, meaning that there were fourteen altogether. When the kirtan started in each of the seven groups, Mahaprabhu demonstrated His divine powers by appearing simultaneously in the midst of each one of them. Srila Bhaktivinoda Thakur writes, "Just as the Lord expands into numerous forms during the Rasa dance and to marry the queens in Dvaraka, Lord Chaitanya expanded in order to be present in the midst of each sampradaya's kirtan. The members of each group were convinced that the Lord was in his group alone and in none of the others."

When Mahaprabhu wished to dance madly, He would have the seven groups come together and would dance in their midst, appointing nine singers and making Svarupa Damodar the principal singer. As the devotees became progressively intoxicated by the kirtan, Mahaprabhu danced frenziedly for many moments. After this, Mahaprabhu's mood changed. Svarupa Damodar was able to understand the Lord's intention and began to sing:

sei to parāṇanātha pāinu
jāhā lāgi madana-dahane jhuri genu

"I have finally found my life's Lord, for whom I had so long burned in the flames of desire."

Bhaktivinoda Thakur writes, "As the Lord's frenzied dancing came to an end, He became absorbed in the mood of Radharani at Kurukshetra. This song about meeting the beloved after a long separation came naturally to Svarupa Damodar's lips." As He felt the mood of union strengthening, the Lord began to loudly recite the following verse:

yaḥ kaumāra-haraḥ sa eva hi varas tā eva caitra-kṣapās
te conmīlita-mālatī-surabhayaḥ prauḍhāḥ kadambānilāḥ
sā caivāsmi tathāpi tatra surata-vyāpāra-līlā-vidhau
revā-rodhasi vetasī-taru-tale cetaḥ samutkaṇṭhate

My groom is the same person who took my maidenhead, and these are the moondrenched spring nights we knew. The very same breeze is blowing from the Vindhya hills, heavy with the scent of newly blossomed jasmine. I too am still the same, and yet I yearn with all my heart for the reedbeds by the stream where we knew our happy, graceful, unending bouts of love.

(Chaitanya Charitamrta 2.1.58)

This verse was written about a mundane lover and his mistress, but Mahaprabhu recited it with great respectful feeling. No one could understand His hidden intention other than Svarupa Damodar. When Rupa Goswami heard the Lord recite this verse, he himself composed a verse that revealed the deeper meaning the Lord had envisioned. He wrote it down on a palm leaf and hid it in the roof of his cottage. When Mahaprabhu went to the residence of Srila Rupa Goswami, He accidentally saw the palm leaf on the roof, and thus He read his verse. After reading it, He went into a ecstatic mood and while He was in that state, Srila Rupa Goswami came and immediately fell down on the floor like a stick.

The Lord got up and gave him a slap. Then, he embraced him and began to speak as follows: "No one knows the purport of my verse. How could you understand my intention?"

Saying this, Lord Chaitanya Mahaprabhu bestowed various blessings upon Rupa Goswami, and taking the verse with Him, showed it to Svarupa Goswami. With great wonder, the Lord asked him how Rupa Goswami could have understood His mind. Srila Svarupa Damodar Goswami replied, "If Rupa Goswami can understand your mind, I believe it must be the result of Your special benediction." (Chaitanya Charitamrita 2.13.66-72)

This was Rupa Goswami's verse:

priyaḥ so'yaṁ kṛṣṇaḥ sahacari kurukṣetra-militas
tathāhaṁ sā rādhā tad idam ubhayoḥ saṅgama-sukham
tathāpy antaḥ-khelan-madhura-muralī-pañcama-juṣe
mano me kālindī-pulina-vipināya spṛhayati

O companion! This is my beloved Krishna meeting Me here in Kurukshetra; I am the same Radha and both of us are feeling the joy of union. Even so, my mind wishes for the forest by the banks of the Yamuna where the fifth note of His flute reverberates sweetly within My heart.

(*Padyāvalī*, 383)

Mahaprabhu's vision was that the Jagannath temple was Kurukshetra and the Gundicha temple Vrindavan. He pulled on Jagannath's chariot in the mood of a gopi, dragging Him back to Vrindavan. Sri Svarupa Damodar Goswami was able to understand everything that Mahaprabhu experienced during the Rathayatra.

The Lord had relished these topics in his room with Svarupa Damodar for days and nights. When He was overcome with the mood of the gopis while dancing before the Lord's chariot, He would repeat this verse while gazing upon Jagannath's face. No one can describe Sri Svarupa Damodar Goswami's good fortune, for he was completely absorbed, body, mind and soul, in the Lord. His senses are the Lord's senses, and he would sing so that the Lord could more deeply relish the sentiments of love.

(Chaitanya Charitamrita 2.13.161-4)

Jagannath Deva lives in Dvaraka, but once every year He desires to go to Vrindavan. The Rathayatra festival, when He travels from the Jagannath temple (Dvaraka) to Gundicha (Vrindavan), symbolizes this desire. Jagannath does not take Lakshmi with Him to Vrindavan, because Lakshmi is not qualified to participate in the Vrindavan lila. Only the gopis have such qualifications, and Radha is the best of the gopis. Svarupa Damodar explained these things.

"Lakshmi does not have the right to participate in the games of Vrindavan. Krishna's companions in the Vrindavan lila are the gopis, and there are none but they who can enchant his mind."

(Chaitanya Charitamrita 2.14.122-3)

Radha is the best among the gopis. She is a treasure chest of jewels of love in the bright and spotless sentiment of conjugal love. (Chaitanya Charitamrita 2.14.160)

Jagannath mounted His chariot after telling Lakshmi that He would be back on the very next day. When Lakshmi saw that the Lord was late in returning, she became angry and, gathering up her forces, sallied forth to attack her beloved. Her servants captured the servants of Lord Jagannath and brought them to her. Such lovers' quarrels are not heard of anywhere in the world. Nevertheless, the *māna* (loving jealousy) of the gopis is superior to that of Lakshmi, and of all the gopis, that of Radha is the purest. When Mahaprabhu wished to hear about the gopis' *māna* from Svarupa Damodar, Svarupa gave Him great satisfaction by answering in great detail. He was always able to please the Lord because he knew His wishes so intimately.

BHAGAVAN ACHARYA AND HIS BROTHER

Sri Svarupa Damodar Goswami had a close friendship with the lame Bhagavan Acharya of Halisahar.

Bhagavan Acharya was a great devotee, a scholar and a man of refined habits. He came to Purushottam to be with the Lord. He was an incarnation of a cowherd who served Krishna in the mood of friendship. His dealings with Svarupa Damodar were also those of a close friend. He was completely surrendered to the Lord's lotus feet, and occasionally invited him to eat at his residence.
(Chaitanya Charitamrita 3.2.84-6)

Bhagavan Acharya was a generous and unpretentious Vaishnava. Even so, his father Shatananda Khan was a very materialistic person and his younger brother Gopal Bhattacharya a mayavadi. When Gopal Bhattacharya came to Puri, the simple, straightforward Bhagavan Acharya asked Svarupa Damodar to listen to his brother speak on Shankar's *Vedānta-bhāṣya*: "Gopal, my younger brother, has come here after finishing his study of Vedanta philosophy. Come, everyone, and hear him speak on the Vedanta."

Svarupa Damodar Goswami, however, somewhat angry because of his affection for Bhagavan Acharya, answered as follows: "You have lost your intelligence in the association of Gopal, and now you are eager to hear the mayavada philosophy. When a Vaishnava listens to the *Śārīraka-bhāṣya* (the mayavada commentary upon Vedanta Sutra), he gives up the attitude that the Lord is the master and the living entity His servant. Instead, he considers himself to be the Supreme Lord. The mayavada philosophy is so dangerous that even a highly elevated devotee who has accepted Krishna as his life and soul changes his attitude when he reads or hears it."

Bhagavan Acharya continued, "We are all fixed at the lotus feet of Krishna with our hearts and souls. So I don't think that the *Śārīraka-bhāṣya* could change our minds." Svarupa Damodar replied, "Maybe so, but when we hear mayavada philosophy, we hear that Brahman is the only spiritual reality and that the universe of maya is false, but we gain no real spiritual understanding. When a devotee hears the mayavadi say that the living entity is only imaginary and that the Supreme Lord is a manifestation of ignorance, it breaks his heart."
(Chaitanya Charitamrita 3.2.92-99)

SVARUPA WATCHES FOR RASABHASA

Svarupa Damodar was the personification of ecstatic love, fully cognizant of the transcendental mellows in relationship with Krishna. He was like a second manifestation of Mahaprabhu. If someone wrote a book or composed verses and songs and wanted to recite them before Sri Chaitanya Mahaprabhu, Svarupa Damodar would have to first examine them before the Lord would agree to listen. Mahaprabhu was never pleased to hear books or verses opposed to siddhanta, nor did he like hearing *rasābhāsa,* an improper mixture of devotional sentiments. It was the practice of Svarupa Damodar Goswami to examine all works of literature to find out whether their conclusions were correct. Only then would he allow them to be heard by the Lord. (Chaitanya Charitamrita 2.10.110-114)

One day a poet came from eastern Bengal who wrote according to his own whim. He had written a play and had read it to Bhagavan Acharya who then asked Svarupa Damodar to give an opinion on it. If Svarupa Damodar approved then it could be presented to Mahaprabhu for His enjoyment. Many of the other Vaishnavas had also praised the play's literary qualities and so, after repeated requests from his friend, Svarupa Damodar finally agreed to read it. But Svarupa Damodar only had to hear the invocation verse to point out numerous faults in it, demonstrating how it contradicted Vaishnava dogma. When he saw the poet's distress at being criticized, however, Svarupa Damodar became compassionate and said,

jāha bhāgavata paṛa vaiṣṇavera sthāne
ekānta āśraya kara caitanya-caraṇe
caitanya bhakta-gaṇera nitya kara saṅga
tabe ta jānibe siddhānta-samudra-taraṅga
tabe pāṇḍitya tomāra haibe saphala
kṛṣṇera svarūpa-līlā varṇibā nirmala

Go and study the *Bhāgavatam* from a Vaishnava. Take exclusive shelter of Chaitanya Mahaprabhu's lotus feet. Always associate with Chaitanya Mahaprabhu's devotees. If you do all this, you will be able to plunge into the ocean of his divine teachings. This will bring your scholarship to fruition and then you will be able to describe Krishna's nature and pastimes purely.
(Chaitanya Charitamrita 3.5.131-3)

It was in Bhagavan Acharya's house that Chota Hari Das came to beg for fine rice from Madhavi Devi and engaged in conversation with her. As a result of his conversing with a woman, Mahaprabhu ostracized Chota Hari Das. The Lord was as hard as a thunderbolt towards Hari Das, and Sri Svarupa Damodar Goswami made an attempt to intercede, persuading Hari Das to eat after he had undertaken a fast. However, Mahaprabhu remained untouched by Svarupa Damodar's efforts and a year later, Hari Das went to Prayag and gave up his life.

SVARUPA AND THE GOSWAMIS

When Sanatan Goswami came alone to Puri from Mathura, he caught scabies in the Jharikhanda jungle. In Puri, he stayed in Hari Das Thakur's cottage where Mahaprabhu came to see him daily, embracing him despite the pus-filled sores that covered his body. Ashamed at his condition, Sanatan decided to commit suicide, but was prevented from doing so by the all-knowing Lord. During his stay in Puri, Sanatan was introduced to all the devotees of the Lord including Svarupa Damodar.

Govardhan Majumdar's son, Raghunath Das tricked his guru and family priest Yadunandan Acharya into giving him permission to leave his home. He walked to Puri in only twelve days where he met Mahaprabhu. Mahaprabhu was extremely merciful to Raghunath and turned him over to Sri Svarupa Damodar Goswami for tutelage. From that day on he was known as "Svarupa's Raghu."

When he saw Raghunath's thin and dirty body, the Lord felt sympathy for him. He turned to Svarupa Damodar and said, "I am turning this Raghunath over to you. I want you to take care of him as though he were your own son and personal servant. I now have three Raghunaths in my entourage, so henceforward we will call this one 'Svarupa's Raghu'." After he had said these words, the Lord took Raghunath's hand and placed it in that of Svarupa Damodar. (Chaitanya Charitamrita 3.7.201-4)

Raghunath Das never spoke directly to Mahaprabhu. If he wished to make a submission to the Lord, he made it through either Svarupa Damodar or Govinda. He told Svarupa Damodar repeatedly that he wished to hear Mahaprabhu's personal instructions on how to practice spiritual life. After Svarupa passed this request on to the Lord, Mahaprabhu smiled and told Raghunath Das, "I have appointed Svarupa Damodar to be your instructor. You may learn from him about the spiritual practices and their goal. I myself do not know as much as he. Nevertheless, if you have faith in my orders, you may fix your direction from the following words: Do not listen to gossip nor engage in gossip yourself. You should not eat very palatable food, nor should you dress very nicely. Always chant the holy name of Lord Krishna without any expectation of honor, offering all respect to others. Mentally render service to Radha and Krishna in Vrindavan. I have briefly given you my instructions, you will learn about them in detail from Svarupa Damodar."

(Chaitanya Charitamrita 3.6.233-8)

On the day of Hari Das Thakur's disappearance, the Lord initiated sankirtan. The devotees surrounded Hari Das Thakur's body and Svarupa Damodar sang the Holy Names with the devotees while Vakresvara Pandit danced. Svarupa Damodar then went to the Jagannath temple to seek prasad for the feast that followed Hari Das' burial and he joined Jagadananda Pandit and others in serving the devotees.

Raghunath Bhatta, the son of Tapan Mishra, left his home in Benares to come to Puri via Bengal. When he met Mahaprabhu, the Lord embraced him and introduced him to Svarupa Damodar and the other devotees.

MAHAPRABHU'S INTENSE AUSTERITIES

At one time, Mahaprabhu went through a period of intense austerity. Constantly crying the names of Krishna, He lost a great deal of weight due to His feelings of separation. He began sleeping on a bed of plantain bark, taking no notice of the pain that resulted when His bones rubbed against the bark. The devotees, however, were greatly distressed to see Him suffering. Jagadananda Pandit in particular was affected and decided to do something about it. He obtained some fine cloth and dyed it saffron, and then filled it with cotton from the silk cotton tree. In this way he made both a mattress and a pillow for the Lord's comfort. Jagadananda then asked Govinda Das to give the mattress and pillow to the Lord and Svarupa Damodar to convince Him to use them. When it was time for the Lord to go to bed, however, He saw the nice bed and asked angrily, "Who has made this bed?" When He heard from Govinda that Jagadananda Pandit had given it, He hesitated because Jagadananda was an incarnation of Satyabhama and given to fits of jealous anger. Even so, the Lord had Govinda remove Jagadananda's bedding and went to sleep on the plantain bark bed. When Svarupa Damodar reminded the Lord that Jagadananda would be distressed if He did not use his bedding, He answered, "A mattress and pillow? Why don't you just go and get Me a bed? A sannyasi is supposed to sleep on the ground. Jagadananda wants Me to become a sense enjoyer. This is shameful."

Jagadananda was indeed upset when he heard from Svarupa Damodar that Mahaprabhu had refused the bedding. Svarupa Damodar cleverly made a mattress and pillow out of dried banana leaves torn into small pieces and stuffed into pieces of the Lord's used clothes. Despite His reluctance, the Lord accepted this new bedding. This satisfied all the devotees with the exception of Jagadananda, who asked the Lord permission to leave for Vrindavan. Mahaprabhu said, "Jagadananda is angry with Me, that is why he wants to go to Vrindavan." This story gives a brilliant example of Svarupa Damodar's expertise in serving the Lord.

MAHAPRABHU'S ECSTASIES

As Mahaprabhu's feelings of separation intensified to the point of seeming insanity, He was kept at night in the Gambhira, behind three locked doors. One day, Svarupa and Govinda noticed that even though the doors were still bolted, Mahaprabhu was missing. In great anxiety, the two of them started looking for Him everywhere. Finally they found the Lord near the Lion's Gate of the Jagannath temple, lying unconscious on the ground with all His joints loosened, His entire form lengthened. Svarupa Damodar started to sing the names of Krishna into the Lord's ear until suddenly He jumped up, His body returning to its normal condition, and shouted, "Haribol!" When the Lord returned to normal consciousness, Svarupa Damodar led Him back to the Gambhira.

One day, the Lord saw some sand dunes and took them to be Govardhan. He ran towards them, while Svarupa Damodar and Jagadananda ran behind Him. His body was overwhelmed by the ecstatic transformations and He fell to the ground in a faint. When the devotees saw the Lord in this state, they began to cry. He partially regained consciousness when the devotees started to chant the Holy Name aloud. In this state, the Lord started to prattle, "I was at Govardhan. I saw Krishna herding the cows and playing the flute. When they heard the flute, the gopis came running toward Him. Srimati Radharani was there and Krishna took Her into a grotto. Then suddenly you all started to call Me back here. Why did you do that? Just to bring Me pain?" The Lord began to cry and the devotees, affected by His great distress at losing His vision, joined Him in shedding tears.

A few days later, Mahaprabhu was in the Gambhira in the *divyonmāda* state, the madness of separation. Svarupa Damodar and Ramananda Raya stayed up until the middle of the night with the Lord, enjoying discussions of Krishna's pastimes. Finally, after a great deal of effort, they managed to persuade the Lord to lie down and take some rest, after which they all returned to their own quarters. Govinda also slept in the Gambhira. As He chanted the names of Krishna, Mahaprabhu suddenly heard the sound of Krishna's flute and in the ecstasy that overcame Him, He ran out of the Gambhira, even though there were three doors bolted from the outside. This time He fell down amongst a herd of Tailangi cows to the south of the Lion's Gate. When Govinda heard no answer from the Lord, despite calling for Him, he informed Svarupa Damodar of the situation.

Svarupa Damodar organized a search party of devotees with torches until finally they found the Lord lying unconscious in the midst of the cows. This time, his limbs were retracted into his body giving it the appearance of a tortoise; His mouth was covered with foam, there were eruptions on His body and His eyes were filled with tears. He looked like a pumpkin, without any limbs. Externally suffering as though poisoned, internally he was experiencing divine ecstasies. The cows had surrounded the Lord and were sniffing his body, and even when the devotees shooed them away, they would come back, attracted by the Lord. After many attempts to arouse the Lord, when the devotees failed to bring him back to consciousness, they picked him up and carried him to the Gambhira. There they started loudly singing the Holy Names in kirtan. This continued for some time until finally the Lord returned to an external state of consciousness and his body also took on its normal appearance.

Still in a trance-like state, Mahaprabhu asked Svarupa Damodar, "Where have you brought Me? I had heard the sound of Krishna's flute and I went to Vrindavan. I saw Krishna with the cattle, playing His flute. Radha and the gopis understood His signal and came to the bower trysting place. I followed them there and felt ecstasy when hearing the sound of their tinkling ornaments and their voices and laughter. You forced Me to come back here and I can no longer hear their humorous conversations, nor the sound of their ornaments and musical instruments."

Sri Svarupa Damodar Goswami recognized the Lord's state and sang a verse from the Bhagavatam in his sweet voice:

> *kā stry-aṅga te kala-padāyata-veṇu-gīta-*
> *sammohitārya-caritān na calet trilokyām*
> *trailokya-saubhagam idaṁ ca nirīkṣya rūpaṁ*
> *yad go-dvija-druma-mṛgāḥ pulakāny abibhrat*

> Dear one! What woman in these three worlds would not be captivated by the sweet rhythms of Your wonderful flute-song? What woman would not abandon her vows of chastity as a result? For upon beholding Your beauty, the most sublime in this universe even cows, birds, trees and animals horripilate in jubilation.
>
> (Srimad Bhagavatam 10.29.40)

As soon as the Lord heard this verse, He once again merged into the mood of the gopis and began to sing all the statements the gopis made in separation from Krishna, known as *citra-jalpa*.

THE LORD JUMPS INTO THE SEA

Krishna Das Kaviraj Goswami has described another extraordinary event of this type. Once, during a full-moon evening in autumn, the Lord was inspired to remember Krishna's Rāsa lila. Accompanied by his devotees, he wandered through the Ai Tota garden next to the Gundicha temple, relishing songs about the Rāsa dance. As they approached the seashore, Mahaprabhu took the sea to be the Yamuna River and jumped into it. His body floated south toward Konarak until a fisherman caught him in his nets, thinking Him to be a large fish. When he dragged the Lord on board his boat, he saw that all His limbs were distended, transformed into a giant human form. Upon touching Him, the fisherman was immediately infused with prema and started crying and calling the name of Krishna.

Meanwhile, Svarupa Damodar and the other devotees were desperately seeking the Lord. Finally they saw the fisherman standing on the shore with the Lord on his shoulders. When Svarupa saw the fisherman in a state of ecstatic transformation, he came and explained who Mahaprabhu was, but still had to slap him several times before he calmed down. Then the devotees began to sing the Holy Names aloud until the Lord jumped up with a roar. Once again, while in a state of half-absorption in trance, Mahaprabhu recounted everything that He had experienced. Mahaprabhu had been in the world of Krishna's Rāsa lila and water sports. When they heard all His ecstatic utterances, the devotees trembled in awareness of the Lord's divine loving madness. Then they led Him back to the Gambhira.

THE LORD'S FINAL DAYS

When Advaita Acharya sent the riddle message back from Bengal with Jagadananda Pandit, indicating that the Lord's pastimes would soon come to an end, Svarupa Damodar became distracted, while the Lord's divine madness became more and more intense. In his final instructions to Svarupa Damodar and Ramananda Raya, the Lord made it very clear that Harinam sankirtan is the supreme method for attaining love for Krishna.

The Lord, in a wave of jubilation said, "Listen Svarupa Damodar and Ramananda Raya! In the age of Kali,

Harinam sankirtan is the supreme means of deliverance. In the age of Kali, Krishna is to be worshiped by the congregational chanting of his Holy Names. This is the way that an intelligent person attains the lotus feet of Krishna. Through the chanting of the Holy Name, all of one's sinful reactions are extinguished and all auspiciousness arises until finally one experiences the joys of love for Krishna."
(Chaitanya Charitamrita 3.20.8-11)

After saying this, the Lord recited His own eight verses known as the *Śikṣāṣṭaka.* As He relished them, He felt more and more humble in feelings of separation from Krishna. Taking on the mood of Srimati Radharani, He became totally absorbed in love for Krishna.

Sri Svarupa Damodar Goswami and Ramananda Raya remained constantly by the Lord's side throughout His ecstasies in *divyonmāda,* calming Him and enriching His feelings of love. Sri Svarupa Damodar Goswami left the world on the day of Lord Jagannath's Rathayatra, not long after the Lord's disappearance.

Srila Kashisvara Pandit

purā vṛndāvane cetau sthitau bhṛṅgāra-bhaṅgurau
śrī-kāśīśvara-govindau tau jātau prabhu-sevakau

Srila Kashisvara Pandit (also Brahmachari or Goswami) was Krishna's servant Bhringara and Govinda was Bhangura. They became Mahaprabhu's servants in Gaura lila. Some say Kashisvara was the sakhi Shashirekha.
(*Gaura-gaṇoddeśa-dīpikā* 137)

Kashisvara Pandit's home was in the village of Chatra in the district of Hooghly, about one mile from the present day Serampore railway station. His father was Vasudeva Bhattacharya, a Brahmin of the Vatsya gotra in the line of Kanva. He also had the title Chaudhuri. He established deities of Gauranga and Sri Radha Govinda in the neighborhood of Chatra village known as Chaudhuri Para. There is an annual festival there on Dol Purnima. Rudra Pandit of Ballabhpura was his nephew. Kashisvara Pandit was especially known for his physical strength.

A DISCIPLE OF ISHVARA PURI

Kashisvara Pandit was a disciple of Ishvara Puri who had received much mercy from him. For this reason he is counted as one of Chaitanya Mahaprabhu's branches. Sri Govinda was also Ishvara Puri's disciple. Both of them devotedly served their spiritual master as long as he was present in this world. Just before he disappeared, he instructed them both to go engage in Mahaprabhu's service. Govinda was the first to come to Puri to serve the Lord after the disappearance of their guru; Kashisvara travelled throughout India on a pilgrimage before finally coming to Mahaprabhu's lotus feet.

"I am a servant of Ishvara Puripada, my name is Govinda. On his order I have come to you. At the time of his departure, my master ordered me: Go to Sri Krishna Chaitanya and serve him. Kashisvara will also come after he has seen the pilgrimage sites. I have come directly to you."
(Chaitanya Charitamrita 2.10.132-4)

On another day, Kashisvara Gosai arrived; the Lord greeted him respectfully and gave him a place to stay with Him. (Chaitanya Charitamrita 2.10.185)

Mahaprabhu felt something of a quandary about accepting the service of His godbrothers. He consulted with Sarvabhauma Bhattacharya, saying, "The servant of my spiritual master is my superior, so how can I accept his service? On the other hand, if I do not obey My guru's order, that too would be an offense. What should I do?" Sarvabhauma answered that the spiritual master's order should take priority and so the Lord followed His guru directives and accepted Govinda and Kashisvara Pandit as His personal servants.

sa śuśruvān mātari bhārgaveṇa
pitur niyogāt prahṛtaṁ dviṣadvat
pratyagrahīd agraja-śāsanaṁ tad-
ājñā gurūṇāṁ hy avicāraṇīyā

On the order of his father, Parashuram killed his own mother as though she were an enemy. When he heard this, Lakshman accepted the order of his elder brother Rama, for the orders of a guru are not to be debated.
(*Raghuvaṁśa*, 14.46)

nirvikāraṁ guror ājñā mayā kāryā mahātmanaḥ
śreyo hy evaṁ bhavatyāś ca mama caiva viśeṣataḥ

I must follow the order of my guru because he is a great soul. You will certainly benefit from this, but so will I.
(*Rāmāyaṇa Ayodhya-khaṇḍa*, 22.9)

KASHISVARA'S SERVICE TO MAHAPRABHU

Whenever Mahaprabhu went to see Jagannath, Kashisvara would use his physical strength to hold back the crowds, allowing the Lord to pass without being touched by anyone.

Ishvara Puri's disciples were Kashisvara Brahmachari and Govinda. At the time of his departure from this world, he instructed them both to come to Nilachala and to engage in Mahaprabhu's personal service. The Lord considered them both to be His superiors because they had personally served his spiritual master, but He nevertheless accepted their service because it was His guru's order. Govinda would engage in personal, bodily service, while Kashisvara would go before Him when He went to see

Jagannath. He would push people aside to make a path for the Lord so that He could go through the crowd without being touched. (Chaitanya Charitamrita 1.10.138-142)

Mahaprabhu joyfully took the devotees to the temple to see Jagannath. Kashisvara led the way, clearing the path, while Govinda followed carrying the Lord's waterpot.
(Chaitanya Charitamrita 2.12.206-7)

In Puri, the abode of the Supreme Person (Purushottam Dham), when the Lord was dancing in front of Jagannath's Rathayatra cart, three rings of people would be formed around the Lord in order to hold the people back. The innermost ring consisted of Nityananda Prabhu and other devotees, the second of Kashisvara, Mukunda and others, and the third of King Prataparudra and his bodyguards.

Kashisvara, Mukunda and many other devotees held hands to form a second protective circle.
(Chaitanya Charitamrita 2.13.89)

Kashisvara was one of the seven persons who would serve maha prasad to the devotees after the kirtan at the Rathayatra. The others were Svarupa Damodar, Jagadananda, Damodar, Gopinath, Baninath and Shankar. Kashisvara also participated in some of the Lord's lilas in Nabadwip, such as the kirtans at Srivas Angan and bathing in the Ganges. He was also present when the Lord went with kirtan to the house of Sridhar and drank from his iron pot. He, along with the other devotees present, cried to see the Lord's mercy on that occasion. Govinda, Govindananda, Srigarbha, Sriman, Jagadananda and Rama were others present on that occasion.
(Chaitanya Bhagavata 2.23.451)

Vrindavan Das Thakur tells just how dear Kashisvara was to the Lord, calling Mahaprabhu Kashisvara's heart on one occasion (Chaitanya Bhagavata 2.1.6) and the wealth of Kashisvara's life (*Kāśīśvara-prāṇa-dhana*) on another (Chaitanya Bhagavata 2.24.3).

Kashisvara was also present when Mahaprabhu went to greet Advaita and the other devotees on their arrival from Bengal. His disappearance day is on the fourteenth day of the waxing moon (*kṛṣṇā caturdaśī*) in the month of Karttik. According to another opinion, it is on the full moon day of the month of Ashwin, when Radha and Krishna's Rasa Purnima is also celebrated.

Sri Bhagavan Acharya

ācāryo bhagavān khañjaḥ kalā gaurasya kathyate

Khanja Bhagavan Acharya was said to be Gauranga Mahaprabhu's expansion.

ācāryaṁ bhagavantaṁ tu tejomaya-kalevaram
yasya smaraṇa-mātreṇa gaura-prema prajāyate

[I offer obeisances to] Bhagavan Acharya, whose powerful body is filled with effulgence. Just by remembering him, one will develop love for Gauranga Mahaprabhu (*Śākhā-nirṇayāmṛta*).

Bhagavan Acharya was originally from the town of Halisahar, which is in the twenty-fourth Pargana district. Krishna Das Kaviraj Goswami writes that he is considered to be Chaitanya's branch along with Brahmananda Bharati, Shikhi Mahiti and Murari Mahiti.
(Chaitanya Charitamrita 1.10.136)

It is written in the *Gauḍīya Vaiṣṇava Abhidhāna* that Bhagavan Acharya appeared in Sri Dham Nabadwip, but left to live in Halisahar. His father Shatananda Khan was a wealthy materialist, while he himself was a scholar and a great Vaishnava who worshiped in the mood of friendship.

Bhagavan Acharya was a householder. His son was named Raghunath Acharya. Both he and his son accompanied Jahnava Mata to Kheturi. (*Bhakti-ratnākara* 10.382)

The following further information is found in the *Gauḍīya Vaiṣṇava Abhidhāna*: "Bhagavan Acharya was particularly advanced in the study of logic, so much so that he received the title of Nyayacharya. When his father saw that he was developing the renounced spirit at a young age, he arranged for his marriage with the daughter of Nabadwip's Madhusudan Ghataka. Despite this, Bhagavan Acharya overcame the entanglements of his householder life to go to live in Puri with the Lord. Mahaprabhu enjoined him to return to his wife, however, and so he came back to Bengal. He had two sons Raghunath and Ramanath. Nevertheless, Bhagavan Acharya was unable to remain in householder life for long and he ultimately gave the responsibility for his wife and children to his brother-in-law and disciples. He then took the renounced order and returned to Puri to live with the Lord."

Bhagavan Acharya in Puri

When the devotees heard that Mahaprabhu had returned from South India, they rushed to see him. Bhagavan Acharya renounced everything and came to live there near the Lord.

Ramabhadra Acharya and Bhagavan Acharya came to live near the Lord, giving up all other duties.
(Chaitanya Charitamrita 2.10.184)

Bhagavan Acharya was a great devotee, a scholar and a man of refined habits. He came to Purushottam to be with the Lord. He was an incarnation of a cowherd who served Krishna in the mood of friendship. His dealings with Svarupa Damodar were also those of a close friend. He was completely surrendered to the Lord's lotus feet, and he occasionally invited Him to eat at his residence. He made various vegetable preparations that he personally served to the Lord. (Chaitanya Charitamrita 3.2.84-7)

Bhagavan Acharya would not brook any materialistic conversation, only listening to Krishna's name, form, qualities and pastimes (Chaitanya Bhagavata 3.3.188).

He was one of the many devotees who came to meet Mahaprabhu in Puri after the Lord delivered Sarvabhauma Bhattacharya.

The great personality Bhagavan Acharya arrived. Mundane topics never entered his ears.

(Chaitanya Bhagavata 3.3.188)

Bhagavan Acharya was also present when Mahaprabhu went to greet Advaita Acharya, along with Kashisvara Pandit, Pradyumna Mishra and others. He was there when Mahaprabhu went into an ecstatic trance and fell into the ocean, after taking the dunes on the beach to be Govardhan.

Paramananda Puri, Brahmananda Bharati and others ran to the beach while Bhagavan Acharya, being lame, followed them as quickly as he could.

(Chaitanya Charitamrita 3.14.90)

One day Bhagavan Acharya wanted to feed Mahaprabhu nicely and sent Chota Hari Das to beg for fine rice from Madhavi Devi. While eating, Mahaprabhu learned of this and became angry and ostracized Chota Hari Das. He said that for a renunciate to talk to a woman is worse than drinking poison.

prabhu kahe — vairāgī kare prakṛti sambhāṣaṇa
dekhite nā pāroṅ āmi tāhāra vadana

The Lord said, "I cannot look upon the face of someone who after taking the vows of renunciation continues to converse with women."

(Chaitanya Charitamrita 3.2.117)

BHAGAVAN ACHARYA'S BROTHER, GOPAL

Bhagavan Acharya was a generous and unpretentious Vaishnava. Because of these qualities he was particularly dear to Mahaprabhu. The following account of his simplicity is given in the Chaitanya Charitamrita:

Bhagavan Acharya's younger brother, Gopal Bhattacharya, had been to Kashi where he had studied Vedanta. After finishing his studies, he came to Puri to see his older brother who was quite pleased to hear that he had become learned in the field. With great enthusiasm, Bhagavan Acharya asked to introduce him to Mahaprabhu. The Lord, being the indweller of all beings, knew that Gopal was a mayavadi, so he was not delighted to meet him. Even so, He formally showed him polite affection. The simple, straightforward Bhagavan Acharya went to Svarupa Damodar and asked him to hear his brother speak on Shankar's *Vedānta-bhāṣya*: "Gopal, my younger brother, has come here after finishing his study of Vedanta philosophy. Please come and hear the Vedanta commentary from him."

Svarupa Damodar Goswami, however, somewhat angry due to his love for Bhagavan Acharya, chastised him as follows:

"You have lost your intelligence in Gopal's association, and now you are eager to hear the mayavada philosophy. When a Vaishnava listens to the *Śārīraka-bhāṣya,* the mayavada commentary upon Vedanta Sutra, he gives up the attitude that the Lord is the master and the living entity is His servant. Instead, he considers himself to be the Supreme Lord. The mayavada philosophy is so dangerous that even a highly elevated devotee who has accepted Krishna as his life and soul changes his attitude if he studies it." (Chaitanya Charitamrita 3.2.94-6)

Bhagavan Acharya continued, even though he had been chastised by Svarupa Damodar, "The devotees are all fixed at the lotus feet of Krishna in heart and soul. Listening to the *Śārīraka-bhāṣya* could not possibly have a negative effect on them."

Svarupa Damodar answered with a further warning about the dangerous effects of the mayavada philosophy. He said, "When we hear the mayavada philosophy, not only do we hear that Brahman is the only spiritual reality and that the universe of Maya is false, but we gain no spiritual understanding. When a devotee hears a mayavadi say that the living entity is only imaginary and that the Supreme Lord is a manifestation of ignorance, it breaks his heart and soul." (Chaitanya Charitamrita 3.2.98-99)

Svarupa Damodar's remarks made Bhagavan Acharya ashamed and a little afraid, so he sent his brother Gopal back to Bengal.

THE POET FROM EAST BENGAL

One day a poet came to Puri from eastern Bengal who wrote poetry according to his own whim. He had also written a play about Mahaprabhu. Since he knew Bhagavan Acharya personally, he read the play to him and afterwards to the other devotees, who all praised his work. They felt that Mahaprabhu should hear his play, being under the impression that He would enjoy it. Svarupa Damodar would normally censor literary works before allowing them to be read to the Lord, however; he would examine them for improper presentation of devotional sentiment and doctrine. Only if he approved could any work of poetry be presented to Mahaprabhu for His enjoyment. Since his friend Bhagavan Acharya had praised the literary qualities of the play, Svarupa Damodar finally agreed to read it after repeated requests. As soon as the poet read the invocation verse and explained it, however, and even though all the devotees were pleased, Svarupa Damodar pointed out two faults that, in his view, had an offensive character. The poet's explanation was as follows:

"Lord Jagannath is a most beautiful body, and Sri Chaitanya Mahaprabhu, who is exceptionally grave, is the owner of that body. Sri Chaitanya Mahaprabhu has appeared here in Puri to spiritualize the entire dull material world." (Chaitanya Charitamrita 3.5.114-5)

Hearing this glorification of the Lord, everyone present was delighted. Svarupa Damodar alone was not and he began to speak in great anger.

"You are a fool and have brought ill fortune upon yourself, for you have no faith in either of the two Lords, Jagannath Deva or Sri Chaitanya Mahaprabhu. Lord Jagannath is completely spiritual and full of transcendental bliss, but you have said that He is nothing but a dull, destructible body composed of the inert, external energy. At

the same time, you have said that Sri Chaitanya Mahaprabhu, who is the Supreme Personality of Godhead, full in six opulences, is an ordinary living being, a spark of spiritual energy rather than the supreme fire. You have committed offenses to both Lords. This is what happens when someone who knows no theology tries to glorify the Lord.

"Furthermore, you have made another great error. You have made a distinction between the Lord and His body. Such a distinction does not exist, for the Lord's body and His identity are one. This is a great offense. At no time is there a distinction between the body and soul of the Supreme Personality of Godhead. His personal identity and His body are made of blissful spiritual energy. There is no distinction between them."

(Chaitanya Charitamrita 3.5.117-122)

When he saw the poet's distress at being criticized, Svarupa Damodar became compassionate and told him to take shelter of a pure devotee.

jāho bhāgavata paṛo vaiṣṇavera sthāne |
ekānta āśraya karo caitanya-caraṇe
caitanyera bhakta-gaṇera nitya karo saṅga
tabe to jānibā siddhānta-samudra-taraṅga

Go and study the Bhagavata from a Vaishnava. Take exclusive shelter of Chaitanya Mahaprabhu's lotus feet. Associate constantly with the devotees of Chaitanya Mahaprabhu. Only then will you be able to understand all the waves of the ocean of Vaishnava philosophy.

(Chaitanya Charitamrita 3.5.131-2)

The Brahmin poet was amazed, ashamed and afraid, all at once. Svarupa Damodar was kind to him and showed him how his own verse could be reinterpreted to glorify Krishna. When he gave this elaborate explanation, the poet had a change of heart and surrendered to the Lord's devotees.

Sri Pradyumna Mishra

āvirbhāvo gauraharer nakula-brahmacāriṇi
āveśaś ca tathā jñeyo miśre pradyumna-saṅgake

The Lord's *āvirbhāva* (manifestation) took place in Nakula Brahmachari, and his *āveśa* ("possession") in Pradyumna Mishra. (*Gaura-gaṇoddeśa-dīpikā* 73-74)

Srila Bhaktisiddhanta Saraswati Goswami Thakur has written that Pradyumna Mishra was an Orissan (Chaitanya Charitamrita 1.10.131, *Anubhāṣya*). Vrindavan Das Thakur has stated the same in Chaitanya Bhagavata.

Many of Mahaprabhu's associates took birth in Orissa. It was not long before they came and met with the Lord. Amongst them were Pradyumna Mishra, whose body was solidified prema. The great self-controlled devotees Paramananda Mahapatra and Ramananda Raya were others.

(Chaitanya Bhagavata 3.3.183-4)

According to *Gauḍīya Vaiṣṇava Abhidhāna,* Pradyumna Mishra was originally a resident of Sylhet and only later moved to Orissa. He is counted amongst the branches of Chaitanya Mahaprabhu Himself. The extent to which he was dear to Mahaprabhu is described in both the Chaitanya Charitamrita and Chaitanya Bhagavata:

Pradyumna Mishra was an ocean of love for Krishna and Lord Gaurasundar put him on the same level as Himself. (Chaitanya Bhagavata 3.5.211)

Chief amongst the loving devotees of the Lord in Puri were Kashisvara Pandit, Bhagavan Acharya and Pradyumna Mishra. (Chaitanya Bhagavata 3.8.57)

The Lord felt joy on meeting Kashi Mishra, Pradyumna Mishra and Bhavananda Raya.

(Chaitanya Charitamrita 1.10.131)

All glories to the Lord, the life of Pradyumna Mishra, the wealth of Paramananda Puri.

(Chaitanya Bhagavata 1.14.2)

When Mahaprabhu returned from South India, Sarvabhauma Bhattacharya introduced Pradyumna Mishra to the Lord as a great Vaishnava.

Pradyumna Mishra is the best of the Vaishnavas. He

was Jagannath's chief cook and had the family title of Das. (Chaitanya Charitamrita 2.10.42)[14]

Later, Pradyumna Mishra was instructed by Mahaprabhu to go to Ramananda Raya to hear Krishna katha. This has been extensively described in the Chaitanya Charitamrita, *Antya-līlā*, chapter 5. Srila Bhaktisiddhanta Saraswati Goswami Thakur writes in his *Gaudiya-bhāṣya* to the Chaitanya Bhagavata (1.14.2): "Pradyumna Mishra took birth in a Brahmin family in central Orissa. He led an exemplary pious householder life, showing nobility of character in his adherence to social etiquette. Mahaprabhu gave meaning to this behavioral standard by sending him to the great devotee, Ramananda Raya, who though not born in a material Brahmin family was the most competent instructor in the matter of *bhakti-rasa*. Pradyumna Mishra went to this Vaishnava acharya to hear him glorify Krishna's pastimes in the attitude of a disciple and thereby received Mahaprabhu's causeless mercy."

PRADYUMNA WANTS TO HEAR HARI KATHA

Pradyumna Mishra came one day to Mahaprabhu eagerly asking to hear some Hari katha. Mahaprabhu replied with great humility that He was not qualified to speak on elevated matters of sacred rapture and sent him to meet Ramananda Raya. At the time, Ramananda Raya was living in the Jagannath Ballabha gardens. The service he was engaged in for the pleasure of Lord Jagannath was beyond the capacity of even great self-controlled sages, what to speak of ordinary human beings. He would prepare two young *deva-dāsīs* for the performance of a play which was to be given before Lord Jagannath, not only by training them in the songs that they would sing and in the dance they would perform, but also by bathing, dressing and decorating them. While Ramananda Raya was engaged in such service, no one was allowed to interrupt him.

The first time that Pradyumna Mishra came to see Ramananda, one of Ramananda's servants told him that he was busy doing this work and asked Mishra to sit outside and wait. After Pradyumna Mishra had been waiting a long time, Ramananda Raya finished his service and came outside and learned that Pradyumna Mishra had been waiting there to hear about Krishna from him. He showed the Brahmin the appropriate respect and begged forgiveness for his offense in making him wait. Mishra realized that it was too late that day for his wish to be fulfilled and he returned home.

Some days later, when Mahaprabhu saw Mishra, he asked him how the meeting with Ramananda had gone and what topics they had discussed. At first, Pradyumna Mishra remained silent because of the doubts he had about Ramananda Raya's behavior. Mahaprabhu, as the *antaryāmī* was able to understand what was going through his mind and began to glorify Ramananda's extraordinary character with great force. His words are found in the Chaitanya Charitamrita:

"I am a sannyasi and consider Myself to be renounced. But if I even hear the name of a woman, what to speak of seeing one, I feel its effect on My mind and body. So who is not moved by the sight of a woman? Listen to me, everyone. Let Me tell you about Ramananda Raya's activities, even though they are so wonderful and uncommon that they really cannot be properly described. He personally serves Jagannath's young and beautiful *deva-dāsīs* in every possible way. He personally bathes and dresses them and decorates them with ornaments. While doing so, he naturally sees and touches their bodies' private parts, but even so, his mind is never affected. He teaches the girls how to physically express all the moods of love so they can act them out before Jagannath Deva, but his mind and body are as steady as wood or stone. Indeed, it is amazing that even when he touches such young girls, his mind is not disturbed. Only Ramananda has the right to do such things, and when I see him do them, I can understand that his body is not material, but has been completely transformed into a spiritual entity." (Chaitanya Charitamrita 3.5.35-42)

Thus saying that Ramananda Raya was highly qualified to speak on matters connected to Krishna, the Lord sent Pradyumna Mishra back again. When he arrived in the Jagannath Ballabha gardens, Ramananda greeted him by paying obeisances. Pradyumna then heard Ramananda explained all the different topics on *sambandha, abhidheya* and *prayojana* that he had recounted to the Lord at Vidyanagar during his trip to South India. Both the speaker and the hearer completely forgot themselves in the ecstasies of Krishna katha. The whole day passed in this way. Pradyumna Mishra felt himself to be completely fulfilled by the hearing of all these subjects of Krishna and he went to tell Mahaprabhu about it.

Srila Bhaktisiddhanta Saraswati Goswami Thakur has made the following commentary on this anecdote in his *Anubhāṣya*: "Ordinarily, the Brahmin acts as preceptor to the three other *varṇas* and the sannyasi is the guru of all Brahmins in the three other ashrams. The Lord wished to curb the false pride arising from these notions by sending Pradyumna Mishra, even though he was a pure blood Brahmin, to take instruction from Ramananda Raya, who belonged to the lowest *varṇa*, that of the shudras, and to the lowest ashram, that of the householder. The Lord himself, though a sannyasi, also showed the same example by taking instruction personally from him, accepting the conclusions he preached."

[14] Dās is sometimes used as a family name by Brahmin families in Orissa, though it is a lower caste name in Bengal.

Shikhi Mahiti

rāgalekhā kalākelyau rādhā-dāsyau purā sthitau
te jñeye śikhi-māhātī tat-svasā mādhavī kramāt

Shikhi Mahiti and his sister Madhavi Devi were previously Ragalekha and Kalakeli, two of Srimati Radharani's servants. (*Gaura-gaṇoddeśa-dīpikā* 189)

Shikhi Mahiti was an Orissan who lived in Purushottam Kshetra. He is considered to be one of Mahaprabhu's most intimate associates and one of His personal branches. He was a servant of the Jagannath deity with the title of *likhanādhikārī* (Chaitanya Charitamrita 2.10.42). Srila Bhaktivinoda Thakur explains that this was a temple secretarial position, mainly responsible for publishing the annual ephemeris known as *Mādalā-pañjī*.

Shikhi Mahiti was a great soul, noted for his great compassion and his pure heart. Besides his highly qualified sister Madhavi, he had a brother named Murari Mahanta or Mahanti, who also had strong faith in Mahaprabhu. Their devotion to Him was spontaneous and unwavering. They never forgot Mahaprabhu for even a moment and the Lord also poured down unlimited affection on them.

Lord, this is Murari Mahiti, Shikhi's brother. He knows nothing other than Your lotus feet.
(Chaitanya Charitamrita 2.10.44)

Murari and Madhavi became Mahaprabhu's devotees before their older brother. However, as much as they tried to persuade him, they were not able to convince him that the Moon of Vrindavan had become incarnate in Sri Gaurasundar. In his *Anubhāṣya,* Srila Bhaktisiddhanta Saraswati Goswami Thakur describes how Shikhi Mahiti finally came to receive Chaitanya Mahaprabhu's mercy. The following is a summary of his account, based on Kavi Karnapur's *Caitanya-carita Mahākāvya* (13.89-109):

"One day, after his younger brother and sister had spent some time trying to convince him of Mahaprabhu's divinity, Shikhi Mahiti dozed off. Towards the end of the night, he had a dream in which he saw his brother and sister looking upon the feet of Lord Gaurasundar and telling him to wake up. Startled, Shikhi Mahiti opened his eyes and saw that his siblings were indeed before him. The wonderful dream had inspired ecstatic symptoms in him and his eyes were filled with tears. He ecstatically embraced his brother and sister who asked him what was the reason for his joy. Shikhi Mahiti saw their wonder and, to put their minds at ease, said to them: 'I have just had the most wonderful dream. Listen to me. Today, I have finally become a believer in the glories of the son of Sachi, Sri Gauranga. In my dream I saw Mahaprabhu taking darshan of Lord Jagannath in the temple, and as He was doing so, He entered into Jagannath's body and then came out again. He did this over and over and I can still see the Lord doing it. Am I still dreaming? The Lord of unlimited compassion, Gaurasundar, called me by name and then embraced me with His long arms of unblemished beauty'

As he recalled his dream, Shikhi Mahiti became overwhelmed by devotional ecstasy, whereupon Murari and Madhavi asked him to accompany them to the temple to behold Lord Jagannath. As they entered the temple, they saw Mahaprabhu standing in the Jagamohana, gazing upon the deity. They started to cry tears of joy and Shikhi Mahiti saw his dream come to life before him. Then Lord Gaurasundar embraced him, saying, 'You are Murari's brother.' At the Lord's touch, Shikhi Mahiti fell into an ocean of ecstasy and from that time on, he forgot everything else but the Lord's service."

Krishna Das Kaviraj Goswami's Chaitanya Charitamrita, Vrindavan Das Thakur's Chaitanya Bhagavata and Narahari's *Bhakti-ratnākara* all describe the extent to which Shikhi Mahiti was dear to Sri Chaitanya Mahaprabhu:

The Lord joyfully met Svarupa Damodar and then Shikhi Mahiti and Bhavananda Raya.
(Chaitanya Charitamrita 2.1.130)

All the devotees joyfully came forward to meet the Lord, and he gave an embrace of love to each one of them. Amongst the devotees who were there were Kashi Mishra, Ramananda Raya, Pradyumna Mishra, Sarvabhauma Bhattacharya, Baninath, Shikhi Mahiti and others.
(Chaitanya Charitamrita 2.16.253-4)

Shikhi Mahiti is mentioned as being present at the meeting of the Bengali devotees with those of Puri in Chaitanya Bhagavata (3.8.60).

Shikhi Mahiti and others said that it was time to go and take darshan of Jagannath Deva.
(*Bhakti-ratnākara* 8.237)

Shikhi Mahiti was one of Mahaprabhu's three and a half most intimate devotees.

The Lord accepted that Shikhi Mahiti's sister was one of Radha's friends. In the entire world, there were only three and a half devotees who were as worthy. They were Svarupa Damodar Goswami, Ramananda Raya and Shikhi Mahiti. Shikhi Mahiti's sister was the half person.
(Chaitanya Charitamrita 3.2.105-6)

Sri Gopinath Pattanayak

Gopinath Pattanayak was Bhavananda Raya's second son. According to the tenth chapter of the *Ādi-līlā* of Chaitanya Charitamrita, Mahaprabhu says that Bhavananda Raya was formerly the king Pandu and that his sons were the five Pandavas. All of these five sons were very dear to the Lord.

Your sons, Ramananda Raya, Gopinath Pattanayak, Kalanidhi, Sudhanidhi and Baninath Nayak, are all objects of My affection. Ramananda and I are different in body only; in spirit we are one.

(Chaitanya Charitamrita 1.10.133-4)

Brahmagiri or Alalanath is about 12 miles west of Jagannath Puri. Beṇṭapura is a small village not far from there. Bhavananda Raya was a landowner living in this village. His descendants, who nowadays use the surname Chaudhuri-Pattanayak, continue to reside in this village.

GOPINATH FALLS IN ARREARS

Gopinath Pattanayak was King Prataparudra's *tahsildār* in Maljathya Dandapat, which is now the district of Midnapur in West Bengal. The *tahsildār's* duty is to collect taxes. On one occasion, there was a shortfall of 200,000 *kāhans* of cowries.[15] When Gopinath Pattanayak could not come up with the tax money, King Prataparudra's son, the Boro Jana,[16] decided to punish him. At that time, capital punishment was given by throwing the prisoner down from a scaffold to be impaled on swords. This system was known in Orissan as the *cāṅga*.

When they saw Gopinath in this dangerous situation, some of Bhavananda Raya's well-wishers came to Mahaprabhu to appeal to Him to intervene. When Mahaprabhu asked what the reason for Gopinath's punishment was, one of the supplicants answered, "Gopinath owes the government treasury 200,000 *kāhans* in back taxes and is unable to make a cash payment. He offered to pay back the money by selling some of his possessions and for that reason brought a dozen fine horses to the palace. The king sent one of his princes, who was an expert in evaluating horses, to evaluate them, but this prince offered a price far below what the horses were actually worth. This prince has a physical quirk in that he repeatedly stretches his neck, looking upward and then from side to side. Gopinath was angry at the attempt to cheat him and so responded by mocking the prince, saying, 'My horses may lift their necks, but at least they don't keep looking up in the air! I don't see how they can be worth so little.' In other words, he suggested that his horses were more valuable than the prince himself.

"The prince was insulted by this comment and decided to take revenge. He went to the king and got permission to put Gopinath on the *cāṅga* in order to extract the money he owed. He has now put him on the scaffold and is preparing to throw him down on the swords."

Upon hearing this account, Sri Chaitanya Mahaprabhu took an attitude of impartiality and replied with affectionate anger, asking how the king could be at fault if Gopinath Pattanayak did not pay his dues. How could the king be at fault for punishing someone who has committed an offense? What could He do about that?

THE LORD SAVES GOPINATH

However, a few moments later, news came that Bhavananda Raya and his entire family had been imprisoned. Svarupa Damodar Goswami and other close companions of the Lord appealed to Him to do something. Mahaprabhu, who as the Supreme Lord is capable of doing anything, or changing anything that has been done, or of remaining inactive if He so wishes, instructed everyone to take shelter of Jagannath Deva's lotus feet and that He would take care of the problem.

As the Supersoul within the heart, the Lord inspired Harichandan Patra, one of King Prataparudra's ministers, to recount Gopinath's entire story to the king, asking him to repeal the death sentence. The king was suprised that he had not been informed of events and immediately had the death sentence repealed and Gopinath was released.

Gopinath Pattanayak was Ramananda Raya's brother. By the Lord's grace, he was delivered from a royal death sentence. (Chaitanya Charitamrita 3.1.265)

Mahaprabhu inquired about how Gopinath's brother, Baninath, and the other members of their family reacted when they were imprisoned. The messenger replied,

"Baninath was without fear; he was constantly chanting the Maha Mantra—Hare Krishna, Hare Krishna, Krishna Krishna, Hare Hare, Hare Rama, Hare Rama, Rama Rama, Hare Hare. He counted each mantra on the fingers of his hands, and after he had finished chanting a thousand times, he would make a mark on his body." Mahaprabhu was pleased to hear that Baninath was acting in this way. Who can understand the mysterious workings of the Lord's mercy? (Chaitanya Charitamrita 3.9.56-9)

Mahaprabhu complained to the king's priest, Kashi Mishra, however, that people were repeatedly coming to disturb Him, trying to get Him to intercede on behalf of Bhavananda Raya's family, which was misappropriating state funds. He told him that he was thinking of moving to Alalanath where he could get some peace. Kashi Mishra talked him out of going, but told Maharaj Prataparudra of how the Lord had been affected by these events. As a result, in order to please the Lord, the king not only pardoned Gopinath Pattanayak but he forgave him his debt and doubled his salary. Appreciative of the Lord's mercy, Gopinath came and placed his head, which had been honored with a silken turban personally wrapped around his head by the king, at the Lord's lotus feet and said:

"The king has pardoned my tax arrears. He has reappointed me to my post and doubled my salary, while honoring me with this silken turban. All of this is due to Your mercy. What a difference! One moment I am on the *cāṅga*, preparing myself to die, the next I am being given honors like the silk turban. When on the *cāṅga*, I began meditating on Your lotus feet, and this is the result of that meditation. People are amazed at this turn of events and they sing the glories of Your mercy. I know, however, my

Lord, that these are not the principal results of meditating upon Your lotus feet, but are simply a secondary effect. Material gains are only temporary. Your real mercy has been granted to Ramananda Raya and Baninath Raya, for you have granted them freedom from material sensual entanglements, a blessing that You have not given to me. I pray, O Lord, that You bestow Your pure mercy upon me so that I may also become renounced. I no longer wish for material enjoyment."

(Chaitanya Charitamrita 3.9.133-9)

The Lord heard Gopinath's hearfelt prayer and answered:

"Whether you remain involved in material activities or become completely renounced, you and your brothers are My eternal servants, birth after birth. But I ask you to obey one order of Mine. Do not spend money that belongs to the king. Pay the king his dues and then spend the balance for religious and fruitive activities. Don't spend a farthing on sinful activities, otherwise you will be the loser both in this life and the next."

(Chaitanya Charitamrita 3.9.141-4)

[15] A *kāhan* = 16 *paṇas*, 1 *paṇa* = 20 *gaṇḍās*, 1 *gaṇḍā* = 4 cowries.

[16] In the Orissan language, the crown prince is known as Boro Jana.

Sri Ramachandra Puri

vibhīṣaṇo yaḥ prāg āsīd rāmacandra-purī smṛtaḥ
uvācāto gaura harir naitad rāmasya kāraṇam
jaṭilā rādhikā-śvaśrūḥ kāryato 'viśad eva tam
ato mahāprabhur bhikṣā-saṅkocāditato 'karot

Ramachandra's dear devotee, Vibhishan, took birth as Ramachandra Puri. Radharani's mother-in-law, Jatila, also entered into him for certain special purposes. On account of him, Mahaprabhu reduced his food consumption.

(*Gaura-gaṇoddeśa-dīpikā* 92-3)

taṁ vande kṛṣṇa-caitanyaṁ rāmacandra-purī-bhayāt
laukikāhārataḥ svaṁ yo bhikṣānnaṁ samakocayat

I offer my prayers to Sri Krishna Chaitanya, who out of fear of Ramachandra Puri reduced his eating in the eyes of the world. (Chaitanya Charitamrita 3.8.1)

RAMACHANDRA PURI AS COUNTER-EXAMPLE

Before discussing the character of Ramachandra Puri, we must remember that the lessons of his life are taught as counter-examples. Anyone who seeks the perfection of his own life should bear in mind that the following lessons are to be learned from Ramachandra's actions:

(1) Faultfinding, especially finding fault in Vishnu and the Vaishnavas, is extremely detrimental to one's spiritual advancement. A devotional practitioner should look at his own faults rather than at others'. By correcting his own faults, he will be able to make some advancement. Anyone who sincerely seeks to achieve pure devotional service should always remember the following verse from Mahaprabhu's teachings to Rupa Goswami:

yadi vaiṣṇava aparādha uṭhe hātī mātā
upāṛe vā chiṇḍe tāra śukhi jāya pātā

If the maddened elephant of *vaiṣṇava-aparādha* enters the devotional garden, the creeper of bhakti will be uprooted and all its leaves will dry up.

(Chaitanya Charitamrita 2.19.156)

(2) All the disciples who take initiation from the same guru are not to be considered equal. Though superficially all may have taken shelter of the spiritual master and received the mantra from him, they cannot all be considered true or sincere disciples. The spiritual master rewards the disciple who dedicates himself to affectionate service of the master; such a disciple is furthermore able to recognize the mercy of his spiritual master. A disciple seeking his own perfection will bear in mind that of the sixty-four limbs of devotional service, one of the most important is *viśrambhena guroḥ sevā*, "service to the spiritual master in reverence and respect." The sincere disciple recognizes that the spiritual master's instructions are beneficial both for himself and for others.

(3) To show disrespect to one's spiritual master and to other Vaishnavas has a pernicious effect on one's spiritual life. One should remember that "the Lord cannot tolerate transgression of the rules of etiquette" (Chaitanya Charitamrita 3.4.166). Unfortunately, some conditioned souls come under the influence of the illusory energy and are so bewildered by a pride in their own knowledge or self-worth that they arrogantly try to correct or instruct the Vaishnava or the guru.

(4) Those who want to increase in devotion should associate with and serve other devotees who are affectionate and who have similar spiritual goals. The tendency to serve Vishnu and the Vaishnavas is increased by associating with those who possess this tendency in greater quantities.

(5) Because of his relation to the guru, the guru's godbrother is as worshipable as the guru himself. One must always show him the proper respect. Even if one thinks that his instructions are not correct, one should still maintain the outer decorum and not use direct critical speech with him. Mahaprabhu taught this kind of behavior by his own actions.

gorāra āmi, gorāra āmi mukhe balile nāhi cale
gorāra ācāra gorāra vicāra laile phala phale

Just repeating "I belong to Gaura, I belong to Gaura" is not in itself sufficient. One has to follow the practice and the teachings given by Gaura if one wishes to achieve the promised results. (*Prema-vivarta*).

RAMACHANDRA CRITICIZES JAGADANANDA PANDIT

Ramachandra Puri's family background and birthplace are unknown. It is well known that he took initiation from Madhavendra Puri. Krishna Das Kaviraj Goswami has related the story of his relationship to his guru and to Mahaprabhu in the *Antya-līlā* of Chaitanya Charitamrita. Because he was Madhavendra Puri's initiated disciple, both the Lord and Paramananda Puri showed him respect. Nevertheless, despite his relationship to such a distinguished master, Ramachandra Puri associated closely with others who followed the path of dry knowledge and was attracted to doctrines opposed to those of pure devotional service.

One day, Jagadananda Pandit saw the Lord, Paramananda and Ramachandra paying obeisances to each other, embracing each other and engaging in conversation. He decided to invite the three of them to eat a meal together. He arranged for copious amounts of Jagannath prasad to be brought for them and fed them very well. When they had finished, Ramachandra Puri himself told Jagadananda to sit down and take prasad. He took special care of the pandit, personally serving him with the Lord's remnants. After Jagadananda had finished eating, however, he criticized Mahaprabhu's followers saying:

"I had heard that Chaitanya's followers were big eaters. Now I have seen with my own eyes that this is true. To feed a sannyasi excessively leads to the destruction of religious principles. A renunciate who eats this much will find that his vows will dissipate."
(Chaitanya Charitamrita 3.8.15-16)

HOW RAMACHANDRA BECAME A FAULTFINDER

This propensity to find fault with others, to criticize and to give instructions in dry philosophy was the result of offenses Ramachandra Puri had committed at the feet of his spiritual master. When Madhavendra Puri was on his death bed in Remuna, he was in the depth of separation from Krishna and was crying in the mood of Radha after Krishna's departure for Mathura. He kept repeating the verse,

ayi dīnadayārdra nātha he, mathurānātha kadāvalokyase
hṛdayaṁ tvad-aloka-kātaraṁ dayita bhrāmyati kiṁ
karomy aham

"O Lord, whose heart softens at seeing the condition of the unfortunate! Oh Lord of Mathura, when will I see you? My heart is filled with pain from not seeing you, oh my love, and is confused. What can I do?"

Both Ishvara Puri and Ramachandra Puri were present at this time. Ramachandra had no understanding of his spiritual master's mood and treating him like an ordinary human being, arrogantly began to give him instruction. He said, "Remember that you are completely full of the bliss of Brahman. Why are you crying like this despite being knowledgeable of your own Brahma-nature?"

When Madhavendra Puri heard these words so full of ignorance and effrontery, he became angry and began to rebuke Ramachandra, saying,

"Get away from me, you most sinful rascal! I am dying from the distress of not having received Krishna's mercy, of not having attained Mathura, and you come to simply add to my misery! Don't show me your face again. Go wherever you like! If I see you while I am dying I will take a lower birth. I am dying from the distress of not having attained Krishna and this lowly fool is teaching me about Brahman." (Chaitanya Charitamrita 3.8.22-5)

As a result of his offenses, Madhavendra Puri withdrew his blessings from Ramachandra Puri who thenceforth started to develop material desires. He became a dry philosopher without any interest in Krishna. Not only that but he became critical of everyone, exclusively devoting himself to faultfinding.

In this connection, Srila Bhaktisiddhanta Saraswati Goswami Thakur has written: "Even though Ramachandra Puri saw his own guru suffering of separation from Krishna, he was incapable of recognizing the transcendental nature of this transport of emotions. He judged his guru to be an ordinary man and took his mood to be material, the result of some material insufficiency. As a result he tried to explain to him the value of experiencing the oneness of Brahman. Madhavendra Puri reacted to his disciple's stupidity and disregard for his instructions and thus stopped wishing for his well-being. He abandoned him and drove him away."

On the other hand, Ishvara Puri not only adhered to his guru's teaching but served him physically and thus received his mercy, thus becoming immersed in love of Krishna.

Ishvara Puri received his spiritual master's mercy, while Ramachandra Puri received his enmity. For the edification of the world, these two served as examples of the guru's blessings and his punishment.
(Chaitanya Charitamrita 3.8.32)

RAMACHANDRA PURI FINDS FAULT WITH THE LORD HIMSELF

Deprived of his spiritual master's blessings, Ramachandra Puri sought out sannyasis to find out what their activities were, like how much they ate, all for the sake of discovering their faults. He criticized those in the renounced order for eating sweetmeats, saying that it made it difficult to control the senses.

Unable to appreciate the Lord's glories and thinking of Him as an ordinary man, Ramachandra Puri concerned himself with gathering all sorts of information about His lodgings, His habits, how much He ate and slept and His comings and goings. He was interested only in finding faults and finally he found one. Though his only goal was to find fault with the Lord, Ramachandra Puri nevertheless came regularly to see Him. When they met, the Lord would always offer him respectful obeisances, in virtue of his position as His spiritual master's godbrother

One day Ramachandra Puri came to Mahaprabhu's residence in the morning. On seeing many ants in the Lord's room, he began to criticize Him, saying, "Last night there was surely molasses in here. This is why there are so many ants. Alas, how sad to see such an attachment to sense gratification amongst those in the renounced order of life!" After saying this, he got up and left.

Though ants quite naturally roam about everywhere, Mahaprabhu became apprehensive as a result of

Ramachandra Puri's accusations. He called Govinda and instructed him to reduce His daily regimen to one-fourth of a pot of rice prasad and five *gaṇḍās* worth of vegetables. He warned him that if Govinda brought him more than this amount, he would leave Puri.

When the devotees heard about Mahaprabhu's reduction in prasad consumption, they were thunderstruck. They condemned Ramachandra Puri and themselves stopped eating. When Ramachandra Puri heard that Mahaprabhu and His devotees had all reduced the amount of food they were taking, he went to see him and impudently said:

A sannyasi is not supposed to gratify his senses. He should fill his belly with the bare minimum. I see that you have become thin. Indeed, I have heard that you have cut your eating in half. But this kind of dry renunciation is not the religion of a sannyasi, either. A sannyasi eats as much as is necessary to maintain his body, but without engaging in sense gratification. By so doing, he becomes perfect in the discipline of knowledge."

nātyaśnato 'pi yogo 'sti na caikāntam anaśnataḥ
na cāti-svapna-śīlasya jāgrato naiva cārjuna
yuktāhāra-vihārasya yukta-ceṣṭasya karmasu
yukta-svapnāvabodhasya yogo bhavati duḥkha-hā

O Arjuna, yoga practice is impossible for anyone who overeats, undereats, oversleeps, or undersleeps. For a person who eats, relaxes and exerts himself in all duties in a regulated way, and who keeps regular hours in proper measure, the practice of yoga brings about the end of all worldly suffering. (Bhagavad Gita 6.16-17)

Mahaprabhu continued to show Ramachandra Puri the same respect as before, however, and humbly submitted, "I am just like an ignorant boy and it is my great fortune that you treat me like your disciple and instruct me. I will do my best to follow your instructions." Hearing this, Ramachandra Puri got up and left.

PARAMANANDA PURI TRIES TO INTERCEDE

In the meantime, Paramananda Puri heard that all the devotees of Sri Chaitanya Mahaprabhu were eating only half as much as usual. He and some other devotees approached the Lord with great humility and submission and said, "Ramachandra Puri is by nature a slanderer. It is not wise to give up eating on his say-so. It is his wont to make someone eat far more than he wants. Then he reproaches that person for overeating. Two kinds of activity, though rejected in the revealed scriptures, constitute the substance of his daily affairs:

para-svabhāva-karmāṇi na praśaṁsen na garhayet
viśvam ekātmakaṁ paśyan prakṛtyā puruṣeṇa ca

One should neither praise nor criticize the activities of others which result from their nature, because everything in the universe is a combination of the material nature and the living souls, and is thus one sole entity. (Srimad Bhagavatam 11.28.1)

"Of the two rules, Ramachandra Puri obeys the

first by abandoning praise, but although he knows that the second is more prominent, he neglects it by criticizing others."

Srila Bhaktisiddhanta Saraswati Goswami Thakur comments on this verse by saying, "The above-mentioned verse from Srimad Bhagavatam gives two injunctions. The first, called *pūrva-vidhi*, is that one should not praise, and the second, *para-vidhi*, is that one should not criticize. It is generally said that the rule which is given later takes precedence over previously given injunctions. From this we can understand that to praise someone is not so dangerous, while one should avoid calumny. Here, however, Ramachandra Puri observed the injunction to avoid praising others, but did not observe the prohibition against criticism. Thus he neglected the *para-vidhi* but strictly observed the *pūrva-vidhi*. This verse thus has an ironical meaning."

Paramananda Puri continued: "Ramachandra Puri does not praise even a person who has hundreds of good qualities; he rather finds some way of calling these qualities faults. You should not give up eating properly because of his criticism; you should rather accept invitations as before."

Mahaprabhu replied, "There is no reason to get angry at Ramachandra Puri. A sannyasi should not be lusty after the pleasures of the tongue, but only eat in order to keep body and soul together."

When the devotees continued to press the Lord to abandon his new principle, he would not do so. Finally, he responded to their request by accepting half of the original amount of prasad (rather than a quarter as he was then doing). Mahaprabhu's custom had been to take lunch on the invitation of His various devotees. If anyone was unable to invite the Lord to his house for a meal for whatever reason, he would make a donation of money to buy Jagannath prasad for the Lord. The customary amount at that time was four *paṇas* or strings of cowries. After this reduction, the cost for the food needed to invite Him was fixed at two paṇas of cowries (160 conchshells); which would be taken by two men, and sometimes three.

Krishna Das Kaviraj Goswami writes:

> When a Brahmin at whose home an invitation could not be accepted invited the Lord, he would pay two *paṇas* of conchshells to purchase the prasad. When a Brahmin at whose home an invitation could be accepted invited him, the Brahmin would purchase part of the prasad and cook the rest at home.
>
> (Chaitanya Charitamrita 3.8.89-90)

RAMACHANDRA LEAVES PURI

If Gadadhar Pandit, Bhagavan Acharya or Sarvabhauma Bhattacharya invited the Lord on a day when He had already been invited to dine by someone else, He would break His previous engagement. Then He would eat as much as they served him.

> Mahaprabhu sometimes treated Ramachandra Puri according to worldly etiquette, and sometimes He would ignore him as though he were of no more significance than straw. All the Lord's activities are auspicious and beautiful, in all times and circumstances.
>
> Sometimes the Lord acted almost like a servant to Ramachandra Puri. At other times, he treated him like straw. The Lord's activities are beyond human comprehension. Whatever he does, to whomever, is always enchanting. (Chaitanya Charitamrita 3.8.94-5)

Ramachandra Puri stayed in Jagannath Puri for a short while longer before departing on pilgrimage. When he left, the devotees felt extremely happy, as if a great burden of stones had suddenly been taken from their heads and fallen to the ground. Mahaprabhu once again began to accept invitations as before and the devotees were able to serve Him without hindrance.

> This is the result of being rejected by one's spiritual master. Eventually, the offense reaches as far as the Supreme Personality of Godhead. Even though the Lord did not take account of Ramachandra Puri's offenses, considering him to be a senior, through His behavior He instructed everyone about the result of offending the spiritual master. (Chaitanya Charitamrita 3.8.99-100)

MAHAPRABHU STAYS WITH RAMACHANDRA PURI IN BENARES

Vrindavan Das Thakur has also mentioned that while in Benares Mahaprabhu hid in Ramachandra Puri's house.

> Mahaprabhu remained hidden for two months in Ramachandra Puri's math.
>
> (Chaitanya Bhagavata 2.19.105)

Srila Bhaktisiddhanta Saraswati Goswami Thakur writes in his *Gauḍīya-bhāṣya*, "Gaurasundar stayed in the house of Chandrasekhar while in Benares. Chandrasekhar was a shudra of the *vaidya* caste. Vrindavan Das Thakur says that He stayed with Ramachandra Puri, who is known as a pretentious disciple of Madhavendra Puri who had a strong preference for the mayavada philosophy. In fact, Mahaprabhu simply told people in Benares that He was staying with Ramachandra Puri while in fact He prefered to spend His time with devotees. Ramachandra Puri was a sannyasi in one of the ten Shankarite orders, therefore Mahaprabhu stayed with Him to avoid criticism from the non-devotees."

Srila Lokanath Goswami & Bhugarbha Goswami

lokanāthākhya-gosvāmī śrī-līlā-mañjarī purā

Lokanath Goswami was known as Lila Manjari in Krishna lila. (*Gaura-gaṇoddeśa-dīpikā* 187)

Lokanath is considered to be Mahaprabhu's direct disciple and associate. Prior to coming to Nabadwip, he lived in the village of Talkhori in Jessore district of present day Bangladesh. Prior to that, he resided in Kanchra Para. His father's name was Padmanabha Chakravarti and his mother was Sita Devi. This is confirmed by the *Bhakti-ratnākara*:

śrīmad-rādhā-vinodaika-
sevā-sampat-samanvitam
padmanābhātmajaṁ śrīmal-
lokanātha-prabhuṁ bhaje

I worship Lokanath Prabhu, the son of Padmanabha, whose life revolved around the wealth of service he possessed to his deity Radhavinoda. (*Bhakti-ratnākara* 1.297)

The descendants of Lokanath's brother, Pragalbha Bhattacharya are still living in Talkhori. Bhugarbha Goswami was Lokanath's closest friend and constant companion. He was Prema Manjari in Vraja (*Gaura-gaṇoddeśa-dīpikā* 187).

bhūgarbha-ṭhakkurasyāsīt
pūrvākhyā prema-mañjarī.

According to the *Sādhana-dīpikā*, Bhugarbha was Lokanath's paternal uncle. The *Śākhā-nirṇayāmṛta* adds the following comments on Bhugarbha Goswami:

gosvāminaṁ ca bhūgarbhaṁ
bhūgarbhotthaṁ suviśrutam
sadā mahāśayaṁ vande
kṛṣṇa-prema-pradaṁ prabhum

śrīla-govinda-devasya
sevā-sukha-vilāsinam
dayāluṁ premadaṁ svacchaṁ
nityam ānanda-vigraham

I offer my reverence to the illustrious Bhugarbha Prabhu who was born, it is said, from the bowels of the earth. He bestows love of Krishna; he takes pleasure in the service of Govinda Deva, is compassionate, simple and always joyful.

Bhugarbha Goswami's initiating guru was Gadadhar Pandit Goswami. He is therefore considered to be part of Gadadhar's branch of the Chaitanya tree. Sri Bhagavata Das, a fellow disciple of Srila Gadadhar Pandit Goswami, was also a close friend.

Bhugarbha and Bhagavata Das are branches of Gadadhar Pandit, both of whom went to live in Vrindavan. (Chaitanya Charitamrita 2.12.81)

LOKANATH AND BHUGARBHA GO TO VRAJA

Lokanath Goswami renounced the householder ashram in 1510 (1431 of the Śaka era) and came to meet Sriman Mahaprabhu in Nabadwip. Mahaprabhu immediately told him to go and live in Vrindavan, saying to him that it was His own intention to take sannyas very shortly and go there Himself. Lokanath started to cry when he imagined the Lord with His beautiful curls shorn and the distress the devotees would feel at His departure. When the Lord saw Lokanath's anxiety, He embraced him and consoled him with various spiritual instructions and Lokanath surrendered completely to Him. When Bhugarbha saw how unhappy Lokanath was, he decided to accompany him to Vrindavan. The two companions walked through Rajmahal, Tajpur, Purnia, Lucknow and many holy places before finally arriving in Vraja.

Though he had come to Vrindavan on Mahaprabhu's order, Lokanath constantly felt intense separation from the Lord and shed copious tears in his desire to see Him again. When he received the news that Mahaprabhu had taken sannyas and gone to Puri and from there to the South on pilgrimage, Lokanath hurried to Southern India in order to join Him. When he arrived in the South, he heard that Mahaprabhu was no longer there, but had gone to Vrindavan. Lokanath immediately set off for Vrindavan, hoping to see the Lord there, but by the time he arrived, he heard that the Lord had gone on to Prayag. Disappointed, but still determined to see the Lord, Lokanath decided to set off once again for Prayag.

This time, however, Mahaprabhu appeared to him in a dream and told Lokanath to stop moving about and remain in Vrindavan to perform his bhajan. Not long afterwards, Rupa, Sanatan and Gopal Bhatta Goswamis, and other associates of the Lord started coming to live in Vraja. Their association brought Lokanath immense joy.

When Rupa was getting old, he found it difficult to walk all the way to Govardhan to take darshan of Gopal. Out of his intense desire, Gopal came to stay at the house of Bitthalesvara in Mathura, ostensibly out of fear of Muslim iconoclasts, but actually to show his mercy to Rupa Goswami. The deity stayed there for a month, during which time Rupa came for his darshan, along with Lokanath and other Gaudiya Vaishnavas.

The extent to which Bhugarbha Goswami was dear to Lokanath is described in *Bhakti-ratnākara:*

Lokanath's affection for Bhugarbha was well known everywhere. They had different bodies, but in spirit they were one. (*Bhakti-ratnākara* 1.317)

Gopal Bhatta Goswami was extremely compassionate.
Bhugarbha and Lokanath are a goldmine of virtues.
(*Bhakti-ratnākara* 6.510)

Lokanath Goswami worshiped Radha and Krishna in deep separation, which increased the intensity of his renunciation. He was always afraid of the slightest amount of fame. Thus, he forbade Krishna Das Kaviraj Goswami to write anything about him in the Chaitanya Charitamrita, with the result that nothing was written about him there other than his name. Sanatan Goswami also mentioned his name in the *maṅgalācaraṇa* to the *Hari-bhakti-vilāsa*, as well as in his *Vaiṣṇava-toṣaṇī* commentary to the tenth canto of the Srimad Bhagavatam.

vṛndāvana-priyān vande
śrī-govinda-padāśritān
śrīmat-kāśīśvaraṁ loka-
nāthaṁ śrī-kṛṣṇadāsakam

I pay obeisances to Kashisvara, Lokanath and Krishna Das, who have taken shelter of Govinda's lotus feet and to whom residence in Vrindavan is very dear.

LOKANATH AND RADHAVINODA

Lokanath Goswami constantly travelled throughout Vraja, ecstatically visiting the various holy places where Krishna had engaged in His pastimes. Once, he went to Khadiravan. Then he visited Kishor Kund near the village of Umarao by Chatravan. He was so impressed by the beauty of the site that he stayed there for some time to do his bhajan in isolation. After being absorbed in Nam bhajan for some time, Lokanath developed a deep desire to worship Radha and Krishna in their deity form.

The Lord knows the desires of his devotees and feels Himself obliged to fulfill them. He thus came personally to give Lokanath a deity, telling him before disappearing that its name was Radha-Vinoda.

Lokanath's first reaction was astonishment at seeing the deity, then he became filled with anxiety at the thought that the Lord Himself had just come and gone. But Radhavinoda cast his sweet glance on Lokanath and said to him, "I have been living here in this village of Umarao on the banks of Kishor Kund. I saw your eagerness to serve Me and so came here on My own. Who else but Me could have brought Me to you? Now I am very hungry, so quickly prepare something for Me to eat."

When Lokanath heard these words, tears began to flow from his eyes. He quickly started cooking for Radhavinoda and then made an offering that the deity ate with great satisfaction. Lokanath then made Radha-Vinoda a bed of flowers upon which he placed Him, fanned him with branches and joyfully massaged His feet. Thenceforward, Lokanath devoted himself to Radha-Vinoda in body, mind and soul.

Lokanath wondered where he would keep his deity, as he was constantly wandering through the land of Vraja. Finally he decided to make a large bag, which he made into Radhavinoda's temple. Wearing the bag around his neck, he was able to keep his worshipable deity close to his heart like a necklace. When they saw the affectionate relationship between Lokanath and his Lord, the people of Vraja were attracted to him and asked if they could build a house for him and Radhavinoda, but Lokanath refused. His spirit of renunciation was so strong that he declined to accept anything but what he absolutely needed for the deity's service.

NAROTTAM DAS BECOMES LOKANATH'S DISCIPLE

After spending some time at Kishore Kund, Lokanath came to Vrindavan. He learned that Rupa and Sanatan had ended their pastimes in this world and lamented their departure in great sadness. At around this time, Narottam Das, who was the son of the Raja Krishnananda Datta of Gopalpur in Rajshahi (now in Bangladesh), came to Vrindavan and met him there.

Many years earlier, when Mahaprabhu was traveling through Bengal, He cried in ecstasy after telling Nityananda to go to Puri. This took place at a spot on the banks of the Padmavati River that is now known as Prematali. In fact, Mahaprabhu was storing His divine love there for Narottam's later benefit. Years later, when Narottam took his bath in the river at Prematali, he was immediately overcome with prema, and was inspired to cut off all family ties and go to Vrindavan.

Upon his arrival in Vraja, Narottam met Rupa, Sanatan and Lokanath. He received Lokanath's special mercy, for he became his one and only disciple. Lokanath was extremely renounced and had made a vow not to accept any disciples. But Narottam Das also made a vow—to take initiation from no one other than Lokanath. Narottam repeatedly asked Lokanath to give him initiation, but Lokanath was firm in his refusal. In order to win his favor, Narottam went in the middle of the night to clean the area he used as a toilet. Lokanath was so surprised to see that the place was being kept clean that he became curious to to find out who was doing this service. One evening, he went and hid there in some bushes, chanting japa the entire night while waiting for his anonymous benefactor to come.

At midnight, Lokanath saw someone come and begin cleaning the place. When he saw who it was, Lokanath was astonished that Narottam, the son of a raja, was engaged in doing such a filthy task. He felt embarrassed and asked him what his purpose was in doing it. Narottam immediately began to cry. He fell at Lokanath's feet and said, "My life is useless unless I obtain your mercy." When Lokanath saw Narottam's humility and pain, his resolve to never give anyone initiation softened and he imparted mantras to him.

This is a perfect example of how one can win over the worshipable deity through honest and selfless service. Narottam Das took initiation from Lokanath on the full moon day of the month of Shravan. Lokanath and Narottam engaged in this pastime to show the value of selfless and sincere service to the whole world, and especially to the people of Northern Bengal.

Lokanath was a very renounced Vaishnava, but he saw in Narottam someone who not only had a cultured background, but an enthusiasm and taste for dealing with people. As a result, he asked him to go back to his homeland to preach Krishna consciousness.

When one has taken full shelter of the Supreme Lord and is situated on the transcendental platform in full service to the Lord, then he usually has no enthusiasm for engaging in activities for the welfare of people on the bodily platform. When a devotee of Narottam Das' caliber goes against this principle, then such welfare activities themselves are honored and they increase in prestige. So Narottam returned to Northern Bengal on the order of his spiritual master and began to preach pure devotional service and thus deliver the people of his homeland.

In his collection of songs known as *Prārthanā*, Narottam Das Thakur has written:

aneka-duḥkhera pare, layechile vraja-pure
kṛpā-ḍore galāya bāndhiyā
daiva-māyā balāt-kare, khasāiyā sei ḍore
bhava-kūpe kileka ḍāriyā

After suffering much sadness, O Lord, you brought me to Vraja, pulling me by the rope of mercy you had tied around my neck. Maya and fate forced me back into the well of material existence by cutting loose that rope of mercy.

Lokanath Goswami left this world somewhere around 1510 Śaka (1588-9 AD), on the eighth day of the dark moon in the month of Asharh. His samadhi tomb is found in the Radha Gokulananda temple in Vrindavan. His beloved Radhavinoda deity continues to be served in that same temple.

Sri Subuddhi Ray

Nothing is known about Subuddhi Ray's birthplace or his parents other than that he was born in a Brahmin family and was well known for his scholarship. His life is memorable because he received Mahaprabhu's association and special blessings. In the first part of his life, he briefly took the position as the king of Gaudadesh.[17]

While Subuddhi was king of Gauda, Husain Khan Sayyid, who later became the Shah, was his protogī and worked for him. (Chaitanya Charitamrita 2.25.180)

Subuddhi put Husain Khan in charge of digging a big pond, but when Husain made some mistakes, he had him whipped as a punishment. By the twists and turns of fate, Husain Khan himself became king of Gauda not long thereafter and was known as Alauddin Husain Shah (1493-1519). Nevertheless, even after becoming king, he continued to treat Subuddhi Ray with a great deal of respect because of the help he had received from him in the past. The Shah never resented the flogging he had received from Subuddhi, but even so the scars remained on his body.

One day Husain Shah's queen saw them and asked where they had come from. When the King told his wife the story, she became angry and urged her husband to punish Subuddhi by putting him to death. Husain Shah refused to go to such extremes, and so his wife suggested that he punish him by bringing about his caste destitution. The King refused to do this because he knew that doing so would be tantamount to having him killed. His wife insisted, however, even threatening to kill herself if he did not do something. Finally, the Shah was obliged to give in to his wife and he gave Subuddhi water to drink, which according to the Hindu rules of the time meant that he lost his caste status.

Even prior to these events Subuddhi had become completely detached from material life. He took this opportunity to leave family and home and to live in Benares. There he inquired from the Smarta Brahmins how to go about atoning for the loss of caste status. They told him that he should commit suicide by drinking boiling ghee. In the *Gauḍīya Vaiṣṇava Abhidhāna*, it is said that it was common to be told to atone by jumping into a fire of chaff, (a fire not easily extinguished). Others, however, objected saying that such a heavy punishment did not fit the minor nature of the offense. This difference of opinion amongst the Brahmins caused Subuddhi Ray to hesitate.

Some time later, when Mahaprabhu came to Benares, Subuddhi came to see Him and recounted the whole story from beginning to end. The Lord recommended that he go to Vrindavan and chant the names of Krishna.The Lord said, "Leave this place and go to Vrindavan. Chant the holy names of Krishna constantly. The mere reflection of the Name will destroy any sins you may have committed. And if you go on chanting, you will attain Krishna's lotus feet."
(Chaitanya Charitamrita 2.25.191-3)

On the Lord's order, Subuddhi Ray set off for Vrindavan, stopping in Prayag, Ayodhya and

Naimisharanya, where he stayed for some time. When he finally arrived in Mathura, he learned that the Lord had already left for Prayag and that he had missed him. Out of distress and deep separation, Subuddhi took up a life of intense renunciation. He made his living by gathering dry wood from the jungle and selling it in Mathura. He subsisted on the little money that he made from this work, eating only dried chickpeas to keep body and soul together. Even so, he was able to put some money aside, which he used for serving the Bengali Vaishnavas, feeding them with rice and yogurt.

Subuddhi Ray gathered dry wood and sold it in Mathura, receiving five or six paisa for each load. By eating dried chickpeas, he spent only one paisa for food. The rest of the money was kept with a businessman. Whenever he saw Vaishnavas in distress, he would feed them and when Gaudiya Vaishnavas arrived in town, he would provide them with rice, yogurt and mustard oil for rubbing on the body. (Chaitanya Charitamrita 2.25.197-9)

Rupa Goswami was extremely happy when he saw Subuddhi Ray's renunciation and service to the Vaishnavas. Subuddhi took Rupa with him to visit all the holy sites in Vraja Mandala (Chaitanya Charitamrita 2.25.200). It is clear from this that service to the Vaishnavas is not restricted to the very rich. Even a poor person will find the means to serve Vishnu and the Vaishnavas if he has a sincere desire to do so. By the will of the Lord, he will never have any shortage of means to do so. This is the example set by Subuddhi Ray's holy life.

When Sanatan Goswami walked from Benares to Mathura, he took the main road from Prayag on the Lord's order. In the meantime, Rupa and Anupam had taken the road along the banks of the Ganges in order to meet Mahaprabhu in Prayag. When Sanatan arrived in Mathura, he learned from Subuddhi Ray that he had missed Rupa and Anupam. Subuddhi showed a great deal of affection for Sanatan, as he had known him in his previous life as a government minister. Subuddhi wanted to serve him, but Sanatan was too humble to accept his service.

Subuddhi Ray spent the rest of his life in Vrindavan worshiping the Lord by chanting the Holy Names and living a life of great renunciation. In this way he followed the order of Sri Chaitanya Mahaprabhu. The date of his passing is unknown.

[17] According to Ashutosh Deb's Bengali dictionary, Gauda was the name of the ancient capital of Bengal in Malda district, from which the entire Bengali kingdom took its name. On the other hand, Haridas Das writes in his *Gauḍiya Vaiṣṇava Abhidhāna* that, according to the *Skanda-purāṇa*, there were five Gaudas (*pañca-gauḍa*), by which were meant the kingdoms of Saraswata, Kanyakubja (Kanauj), Utkala (Orissa), Maithila, and Bengal, but that the name was primarily used for the region lying between East Bengal (Banga) and Mithila. Vijaya Sen of Karnatak became king of Gauda and his descendents were known as *gauḍeśvara*. Vijaya Sen's son Ballal Sen established the city of Gauda on the banks of the Ganges. The course of the Ganges has since moved. At one time, all Western Bengalis were known as Gaudiyas, but the name has become synonymous with the Vaishnavas who follow Chaitanya Mahaprabhu.

Sri Rupa Goswami

śrī-rūpa-mañjarī khyātā yāsīd vṛndāvane purā
sādya rūpākhya-gosvāmī bhūtvā prakaṭatām iyāt

She who was known in Vrindavan as Rupa Manjari has now appeared as Rupa Goswami.
(*Gaura-gaṇoddeśa-dīpikā* 180)

Lalita is chief amongst the sakhis who make up Radharani's entourage, and Rupa Manjari is the foremost amongst those sakhis who follow Lalita. It is for this reason that Rupa Goswami was chief amongst the six Goswamis in Gaura lila.

RUPA GOSWAMI'S FAMILY TREE

In the new Bengali dictionary edited by Ashutosh Deb, Rupa Goswami's dates are given as 1489 to 1558 AD, or 1410-1479 of the Śaka era. In his earthly pastimes, Rupa was born in a Brahmin family of the Bharadwaj gotra which hailed from Karnatak, where they had been rajas. His father's name was Kumara Deva. His mother's name is not known. Narahari Chakravarti Thakur has given the names of seven generations of his family in *Bhakti-ratnākara* (1.540-568).

Srila Bhaktisiddhanta Saraswati Goswami Thakur has summarized this family history in his *Anubhāṣya*: "Jagadguru Sarvajna was a great soul who was born in a Brahmin raja family of the Bharadwaj gotra in the 12th century of the Śaka era. His son Aniruddha had two sons named Rupesvara and Harihara, neither of whom inherited the land holdings. The older brother Rupesvara went to live in the mountains and his son Padmanabha moved to Bengal, taking up residence in the village of Naihati on the banks of the Ganges. Padmanabha had five sons, the youngest of whom was named Mukunda. Mukunda fathered the pious Kumaradeva, who had several sons, amongst whom were Sanatan, Rupa and Anupam. Kumaradeva's house was in the village of Bakla in Chandradwip[18]. His house was in the village of Fateyabad in the Jessore district of that time. Three of his sons became Vaishnavas. These three brothers left the Fateyabad home to live in Ramakeli for their work. Jiva Goswami was born there. As a result of their service to the Nawab, all three of them were awarded the Mallik title. Mahaprabhu met Anupam for the first time when he came to Ramakeli. When Rupa Goswami abandoned his government duties to go to Vrindavan, he was accompanied by Anupam, who was also known as Vallabha."
(Chaitanya Charitamrita 1.10.84 *Anubhāṣya*)

RUPA'S FIRST MEETING WITH THE LORD

Mahaprabhu met Rupa and Sanatan Goswami for the first time beneath kadamba and tamal trees in Ramakeli village. Rupa Goswami had had a large pond excavated that still exists, named Rūpa-sāgara. The three brothers were engaged in the service of the contemporary king of Gauda, Husain Shah. Sanatan Goswami was his chief minister with the title Sakar Mallik, while Rupa Goswami was also an important minister with the title Dabir Khas. We have indication of this from the Chaitanya Charitamrita, where the Shah addresses him with this title.

When Mahaprabhu was travelling through Gauda on his way to Vrindavan, He arrived at Ramakeli surrounded by countless Hindus. With some concern, the Shah summoned Rupa Goswami to ask him who Mahaprabhu was. Rupa Goswami glorified Mahaprabhu in such a diplomatic way that the Shah's mind was put at ease.

> The king made private inquiries from Dabir Khas, who told him of Mahaprabhu's glories.
> (Chaitanya Charitamrita 2.1.175)

Vrindavan Das Thakur also confirms definitively in the Chaitanya Bhagavata that Rupa and Sanatan were named Dabir Khas and Sakar Mallik respectively:

> In the *Śeṣa-khaṇḍa* (of the Chaitanya Bhagavata), the Lord revealed His divinity to Dabir Khas and Sakar Mallik and recognizing their greatness, released them from their bondage. He then named them Rupa and Sanatan.
> (Chaitanya Bhagavata 1.2.171-2)

> Then, two great fortunate souls came to the spot where the Lord was. The two brothers were named Sakar Mallik and Rupa. The Lord looked upon them with compassionate eyes. (Chaitanya Bhagavata 3.9.238-9)

Rupa and Sanatan are eternal participants in Krishna lila. When the time came for them to make their contribution to Gaura lila, Mahaprabhu and His associates arrived in their home village. While performing their earthly pastimes, the Lord and His devotees make an effort to keep their transcendental natures concealed to facilitate the spreading of their teachings to the people in this world; however, when they come close to one they cannot help but reveal this nature. Thus, as soon as Rupa and Sanatan saw Mahaprabhu, though they were naturally attracted to Him, they behaved in the manner of conditioned souls in order to show the people of this world how to act.

When the Badshah heard that Mahaprabhu had come to Ramakeli with a company of thousands of Hindus, he was frightened and suspected Mahaprabhu of having some political purpose. A certain Keshava Khatri who knew about the Lord explained to the Shah, "He is just a sannyasi, a beggar who is out on pilgrimage. A few people are accompanying him, but there is no need to be alarmed." The Shah also consulted Rupa Goswami, who told him of Mahaprabhu's glories and succeeded in calming his fears.

Being desirous of meeting the Lord themselves, Rupa and Sanatan left the palace in the middle of the night and came to Ramakeli. They first encountered Nityananda Prabhu and Hari Das Thakur, who brought the two brothers into the presence of the Lord. Rupa and Sanatan placed some grass in their mouths and wrapped their cloths around their necks as a sign of humility. They fell down at the Lord's lotus feet and, with tears in their eyes, made the following humble submission:

> "We are millions of times more degraded, fallen and sinful than Jagai and Madhai. We have taken a wicked birth because we have become the servants of Muslims and our activities are exactly like those of the Muslims. We constantly associate with people who are inimical toward the cows and Brahmins. Due to our abominable activities we are now bound by the neck and hands and have been thrown into a ditch filled with the excrement of evil sense enjoyment." (Chaitanya Charitamrita 2.1.196-199)

When the Lord heard the extreme humility of the two brothers, He became compassionate. Even so, it is clear from his response to their statement that they were not ordinary conditioned souls, but His eternal associates.

> "I really had no need to come to Bengal, but I came anyway just to see the two of you. No one knows My purpose and so people ask Me why I have come to this village of Ramakeli. I am very glad that you have come to see Me. Now you can go home; do not fear anything. You have been My servants life after life, so Krishna will deliver you very soon." After saying this, the Lord placed His hands on the heads of Rupa and Sanatan, and they immediately took the Lord's lotus feet and placed them on their heads.
> (Chaitanya Charitamrita 2.1.212-6)

The Lord wished to teach that the conditioned soul is delivered by the mercy of the devotees, so he asked Nityananda, Hari Das, Srivasa, Gadadhar, Mukunda, Jagadananda, Murari, Vakresvara and His other associates to bless the two brothers.

Sanatan Prabhu then advised Mahaprabhu, "Dear Lord, You are going to Vrindavan with an entourage of hundreds and thousands of people, and this is not a fitting way to go on a pilgrimage." (Chaitanya Charitamrita 2.1.224) As a result of this advice, Mahaprabhu put off going to Vrindavan and turned back after going a little further, as far as Kanair Natshala.

RUPA RESIGNS FROM THE SHAH'S SERVICE

From this meeting at Ramakeli, it is evident that Mahaprabhu intended to teach the people of this world through Rupa and Sanatan. Not long afterward, an intense spirit of renunciation awakened in the two brothers and they started looking for a way to extricate themselves from their entanglement in the service of the Shah. They paid two Brahmins a large sum of money to perform a *puraś-caraṇa* of the Krishna mantra on their behalf.[19]

Srila Rupa Goswami finally resigned from his government service and he deposited 10,000 gold coins with a grocer in the capital, Gauda, on behalf of his elder brother. Then he took the rest of their accumulated wealth with him in two boats to Bakla Chandradwip where he divided it up, giving half to the Vaishnavas and a quarter for the maintenance of his family, while keeping the rest with a trustworthy Brahmin for safekeeping against any future necessity. He then sent two messengers to Puri to find out when Mahaprabhu intended to travel to Vrindavan by the jungle route through Jharikhanda.

In the meantime, Sanatan Goswami had stopped his duties in the court of the Shah. Though he claimed to be ill, he was in fact engaged in an intense study of the Bhagavata with a group of Sanskrit scholars. The Shah first sent a doctor to examine Sanatan and then, upon learning the truth of the matter, came himself to exhort him to return to work. When Sanatan showed a continued reluctance to engage in his duties, the Shah had him put in prison. He then departed to invade Orissa.

RUPA MEETS MAHAPRABHU IN PRAYAG

When Rupa received the news from his two messengers that Mahaprabhu had left for Vrindavan, he and Anupam left Bakla to attempt to join him. He sent a letter to Sanatan to inform him of their intentions, invoking him to take any necessary steps to free himself and then to come and join them. When Rupa arrived in Prayag, he learned that Mahaprabhu was there at the house of a South Indian Brahmin. When Rupa found Him there, he was overwhelmed with feelings of love for the Lord. He and Anupam placed straw between their teeth and repeatedly paid their prostrated obeisances to the Lord, chanting various verses of praise and humility. The Lord felt great affection for the two brothers and said, "Krishna's mercy is beyond description, for He has delivered you from the blind well of sensual existence."

Mahaprabhu recited verses which stated that a devotee from a family of dog-eaters is dearer to the Lord than even a Brahmin who knows the four Vedas, and that a devotee of the Lord is as worshipable as the Lord Himself. He then showed His mercy by embracing them and placing his lotus feet on their heads. The two brothers folded their hands and chanted the following verse to show their gratitude to the Lord for His mercy toward them:

namo mahāvadānyāya
kṛṣṇa-prema-pradāya te
kṛṣṇāya kṛṣṇa-caitanya-
nāmne gaura-tviṣe namaḥ

I offer salutations to You who are the most merciful incarnation; You who give love for Krishna, You who are Krishna, named Krishna Chaitanya, with skin the color of gold.

Mahaprabhu heard from Rupa Goswami that his brother Sanatan had been imprisoned by the Shah, but predicted that it would not be long before Sanatan escaped and met him. The South Indian Brahmin invited the two brothers to stay with him that day and they all honoured Mahaprabhu's prasad remnants.

MEETING WITH VALLABHA BHATTA

Meanwhile, news of Mahaprabhu's arrival in Prayag crossed the Ganges to the village of Arail where Vallabha Bhatta made his residence. When Vallabha heard that the Lord had come, he immediately rushed to Prayag to meet Him and fell to the ground in obeisance to Him. Mahaprabhu embraced him and then the two engaged in conversation about Krishna. Vallabha Bhatta was astonished to see the ecstatic reactions of the Lord in the course of their discussions.

As soon as Rupa and Anupam saw Vallabha Bhatta, they paid obeisances to him from a distance out of humility. When he came forward to touch them, they both reacted by saying, "We are lowly untouchables. You should not contaminate yourself by touching us." They then sat down at a certain distance from them.

Mahaprabhu was pleased by their display of humility, while Vallabha Bhatta was impressed. The Lord said to Bhatta, "You are an older, aristocratic Brahmin, while these two belong to a low caste. You should certainly not touch them." Vallabha Bhatta was able to divine that there was some hidden meaning to the Lord's utterance and he asked how they could be considered of a low caste when they chanted the name of Krishna.

Vallabha then invited the Lord and His entourage to come to his house to take prasad and Mahaprabhu was happy to accept. They embarked on a boat, but as they crossed the confluence of the Yamuna and the Ganga, Mahaprabhu was affected by the sight of the black waters of the Yamuna and began to dance ecstatically in the boat, causing everyone on board a great deal of anxiety and fear. Finally, Mahaprabhu jumped into the Yamuna's waters and had to be helped on board again by all the devotees.

Vallabha Bhatta took the Lord to his house, washed His feet and sprinkled this water on his own head. Then he performed an elaborate puja of the Lord with a variety of ingredients. Next, he fed Him with a great feast of numerous preparations, satisfying Rupa and Anupam with the Lord's remnants. After the Lord had eaten, he gave Him a mouth purifier and then a place to rest. When the Lord lay down, he sat beside Him and served Him by massaging His feet. In this way, Vallabha Bhatta considered himself to have attained the highest good fortune. The Lord told Vallabha to take something to eat himself.

During this time, Raghupati Upadhyaya, a Brahmin from Tirhut arrived there. The Lord was ecstatic to hear the devotional verses that this Raghupati had composed. Mahaprabhu asked him to say what was the Supreme Lord's superlative form, abode, age and last of all, what was the supreme object of worship? Raghupati answered:

śyāmam eva paraṁ rūpaṁ
purī madhu-purī varā
vayaḥ kaiśorakaṁ dhyeyam
ādya eva paro rasaḥ

The form of Shyamasundar is the supreme form, the city of Mathura is the supreme abode, Lord Krishna's adolescence should always be meditated upon, and love for

Krishna in the mood of the Gopis is thhe supreme sentiment.
(*Padvāvalī*, 82)

Mahaprabhu was very pleased with this answer and embraced Raghupati Upadhyaya. All the inhabitants of the village became devotees of Krishna upon seeing Mahaprabhu. Finally, Vallabha Bhatta again took the Lord back to Prayag by boat.

MAHAPRABHU INSTRUCTS RUPA

Afraid of attracting crowds, Mahaprabhu stayed only ten days in Prayag, remaining incognito at the Dasasvamedha Ghat. He instructed Rupa Goswami in Vaishnava dogma and explained to him about the nature of Lord Krishna, devotion to Him, and rasa theology.

The Lord taught Rupa the truths about Krishna, devotion to Him, and sacred aesthetics, as well as the conclusions of the Bhagavat. He compassionately infused all the teachings he had heard from Ramananda Ray into Rupa Goswami. The Lord transferred His power into the heart of Sri Rupa and made him expert in explaining all these teachings.
(Chaitanya Charitamrta 2.19.105-7)

The teachings Mahaprabhu gave Rupa Goswami are known as *Sri-rūpa-śikṣā*. Shivananda Sen's son, Kavi Karnapur, has described this event extensively in his *Chaitanya-candrodaya-nāṭaka*:

kālena vṛndāvana-keli-vārtā
lupteti tāṁ khyāpayituṁ viśiṣya
kṛpāmṛtenābhiṣiṣeca devas
tatraiva rūpaṁ ca sanātanaṁ ca

In the course of time, tidings of Krishna's divine sports in Vrindavan had been lost. To make them known again in detail the Lord drenched Rupa and Sanatan with His mercy in the very land of Vrindavan.
(Chaitanya Candrodaya Nataka 9.38)

priya-svarūpe dayita-svarūpe
prema-svarūpe sahajābhirūpe
nijānurūpe prabhur eka-rūpe
tatāna rūpe svavilāsarūpe

The Lord explained the *rasa-śāstra* to Rupa Goswami, in a way He did to no other person, for Rupa was the dear friend of Svarupa Damodar, his true identity was that of the Lord's beloved, his nature was that of divine love itself, and he was also possessed of natural physical beauty. Mahaprabhu knew him to be like unto Himself, and indeed, he was verily the expansion of the Lord. (Chaitanya Candrodaya Nataka 9.39)

SRI-RUPA-SIKSA

Through Rupa Goswami, Mahaprabhu taught the world about Krishna's Vrindavan pastimes and the process for attaining Krishna in Vrindavan. Krishna Das Kaviraj Goswami writes: "Through the mercy of Sanatan I have learned the devotional doctrines, while by the grace of Rupa I have been able to discover the extensiveness of the divine aesthetics of devotion."
(Chaitanya Charitamrita 1.5.203)

The Lord taught about sacred rapture and Vraja's pastimes of love through Rupa Goswami. Who can effectively describe the subtleties of Sri Chaitanya Mahaprabhu's lila?
(Chaitanya Charitamrita 3.5.87)

vṛndāvanīyāṁ rasa-kelivārtāṁ
kālena luptāṁ nija-śaktim utkaḥ
sañcārya rūpe vyatanot punaḥ sa
prabhor vidhau prāg iva loka-sṛṣṭim

Just as the Lord enlightened the heart of Lord Brahma with the details of the creation and thus made the manifestation of the cosmos possible, so did Sri Chaitanya Mahaprabhu eagerly impregnate the heart of Rupa Goswami with spiritual potency so that he could revive Krishna's Vrindavan pastimes, which had almost been lost to memory. (Chaitanya Charitamrita 2.19.1)

While in Prayag, Mahaprabhu gave Rupa the direct order to write *Bhakti-rasāmṛta-sindhu*. This has been stated by Rupa himself in the introductory verses to that book:

hṛdi yasya preraṇayā
pravartito'haṁ varāka-rūpo' pi
tasya hareḥ pada-kamalaṁ
vande caitanya-devasya

I worship the lotus feet of the Supreme Personality of Godhead known as Lord Chaitanya Deva, for though I am nothing but an ignorant wretch, I have set out to write this book by His inspiration. (*Bhakti-rasāmṛta-sindhu* 1.1.2)

Particularly relevant in this connection is Srila Bhaktisiddhanta Saraswati Goswami Thakur's commentary on the importance of studying and writing books as an element of devotional practice: "The lives of the Goswamis were exemplary in their renunciation. Sometimes they would engage in chanting the holy names of the Lord, sometimes they would worship him by writing books on divine aesthetics (*bhakti-rasa-śāstra*), and sometimes they would remember or glorify Lord Chaitanya Mahaprabhu. There is an idea that has some currency among Prakrita Sahajiyas that devotional practice entails the renunciation of studying and writing devotional scriptures, indeed that any kind of scriptural study should be stopped so that one can attain to a state of ignorance. Those who follow in the footsteps of Rupa Goswami have no patience with such ideas. However, if a devotional practitioner studies or writes devotional scriptures for the sake of making money through which to satisfy his material senses or attain material fame, respect or any of the other insignificant and superficial goals which are classified as distractions or weeds in the garden of devotional service, then he will not attain the auspicious results which are the real fruit of such activity. A real Rupanuga has no fruitive ambition for such petty results." (*Anubhāṣya*, 2.19.131)

When Mahaprabhu was giving Rupa the outline for his book on sacred rapture, He described the characteristics of the different mellows, showed him how to get a taste of the fathomless ocean of sacred rapture, and pointed out how difficult it was to attain devotional service to Krishna.

The jiva or living entity is an atomic spark of conscious energy. There are countless jivas who are divided into two categories—those that are mobile and those that are stationary. Those that have mobility are again divided into three: those which move on the land, in the air, or in the water. Amongst those who live on the land, a small number are human beings, of which only a minority accept the Vedic principles. Outcastes such as Pulindas, Mlecchas, Shabaras and Buddhists are in the majority. Of those who accept the Vedas, some do so in name only while engaging in sinful activity. Out of them, the portion who practice the Vedic principles are in the minority. Those who are engaged in religious practices toward some fruitive end form the majority in this group.

Amongst millions of such *karma-niṣṭha* followers of the Veda, one person may perhaps attain the platform of spiritual knowledge; yet only one of many millions of such *jñānīs* will be an actual liberated soul. Out of millions of liberated souls, it will still be difficult to find a devotee of Krishna. Devotion to Krishna, which is so rare, can take birth when a certain merit is attained through great good fortune.

The seed of the devotional creeper comes through the mercy of the Lord and His devotee. The creeper of spontaneous ecstatic devotion does not flower anywhere within this world, not even in Vaikuntha in the spiritual world, but only in Vrindavan at Krishna's lotus feet. Krishna's feet are like the wish-fulfilling tree around which the vine of devotion wraps itself and bears fruit. This is described in a most clear and wonderful manner by Krishna Das Kaviraj Goswami in Chaitanya Charitamrita:

After wandering through this entire universe, birth after birth, some fortunate souls receive the seed of devotion (*bhakti-latā-bīja*) by the mercy of Krishna and the guru. Upon receiving the seed of devotional service, one should take care of it by becoming a gardener and sowing it in his heart. If he waters the seed regularly by the process of śravaṇa and kirtan [hearing and chanting], the seed will begin to sprout. As one waters the *bhakti-latā-bīja*, the seed sprouts, and the creeper gradually increases to the point where it penetrates the walls of this universe and goes beyond the Viraja River between the spiritual and material worlds. It passes through Brahma-loka, the Brahman effulgence, until it finally reaches the spiritual sky and the spiritual planet Goloka Vrindavan where it takes shelter of the desire tree of the lotus feet of Krishna. There the creeper expands greatly and produces the fruit of love for Krishna, while the gardener continues to regularly sprinkle the creeper with the water of hearing and chanting here in the material world.

An offense to the Vaishnavas is like a mad elephant that uproots or breaks the creeper, causing its leaves to dry up. The gardener must therefore take care to protect the creeper by making a fence around it so that the elephant of offenses may not enter. Even so, unwanted creepers, such as the weeds of desire for material enjoyment or liberation from the world, may grow along with the creeper of devotional service. Such weeds are countless in their variety. Some examples are forbidden activity, faultfinding and duplicity, causing suffering to other creatures, seeking wealth, adulation or mundane importance. All these weeds grow alongside the main creeper as one waters it, causing its growth to be curtailed. As soon the devotee sees one of these weeds growing beside the original creeper, he must cut it down instantly. Then the real *bhakti-latā* can grow nicely all the way to Vrindavan where it will find shelter under the lotus feet of Krishna.

(Chaitanya Charitamrita 2.19.151-61)

Srila Bhaktisiddhanta Saraswati Goswami Thakur has commented on this passage in his *Anubhāṣya*: "Through the act of watering the creeper of devotional service by hearing and chanting, weeds may also grow which results in the growth of the *bhakti-latā* being stifled. If one does not avoid bad association, which is the only way to be free of offenses while hearing and chanting, then one becomes attached to sense gratification, the idea of liberation from material bondage, various mystic achievements, or the practice of deception.

One may also become addicted to the illicit association of women, practice other manifestations of false devotion like the Prakrita Sahajiyas, or become a dweller of the five places given by Parikshit to Kali, namely wherever there is gambling, intoxication, prostitution, animal slaughter or the accumulation of gold. He starts to take the Vaishnavas to be members of a particular race or caste; he finds dishonest ways of collecting money or makes a show of practicing spiritual life in seclusion while secretly harboring desires for fame and adulation. Desire for mundane reputation may also result in his making compromises with nondevotees, compromising his philosophy or spiritual life, or becoming a supporter of the hereditary caste system by professing discipleship to a so-called guru who opposes Vishnu and the Vaishnavas. The result of these aberrant paths is that one becomes intoxicated in gratifying one's own senses in pursuit of these superficial and destructive ends. One may pretend to be a great saintly or religious person but anything less than pure devotion is a hindrance in attaining service to Krishna.

"If one uproots the various weeds as soon as one sees them beginning to sprout, then the creeper of devotional service will be able to grow as far as Goloka Vrindavan where it will bear fruits of divine love. If not, one will end up being cut off from the devotional life and, remaining in the material world, whether in the higher or lower planets, will have to suffer its vagaries." (*Anubhāṣya*, 2.19.160-1)

There are twelve devotional sentiments. The five primary sentiments are those of passivity, servitude, friendship, parenthood, and consorthood. The seven secondary sentiments are humor, astonishment, heroism, compassion, anger, disgust and fear.

The five primary sentiments remain permanently within the devotee's heart, while the secondary sentiments are adventitious, appearing only when there is a cause.
(Chaitanya Charitamrita 2.19.188)

The secondary rasas act as supporting elements for the primary sentiments, coming and going under propitious circumstances. After serving their function, they again disappear, whereas the primary sentiments are permanently established in the devotee's heart. In his teachings to Rupa Goswami, Mahaprabhu established that among the five primary rasas, the divine sentiment of conjugal love is foremost. The characteristics of *śānta-rasa* are the abandonment of extraneous desires and steady attachment to Krishna. Over and above these characteristics, the possessor of the serving mood has his service, the friend has an intimacy, while the parent has a sense of being the protector. The devotee in madhura-rasa has all these qualities with the addition of serving with her own body. Just as all the qualities of the other principle elements of matter starting with the ether are added together to be united in earth, so are all the qualities of the other devotional moods united in the mood of conjugal love. Since all the sentiments are present in madhura-rasa, it is the foremost.

RUPA STARTS WRITING HIS PLAYS

After the Lord had instructed Rupa for ten days at Prayag, He prepared to leave for Benares. Rupa was eager to accompany him, but the Lord instructed him to go on to Vrindavan and that he could take the road through Bengal at some later date to see Him in Puri. In keeping with the Lord's order, Rupa Goswami continued on to Vrindavan and stayed there for one month. Then, he and Anupam set off in search of Sanatan, hoping to meet Him somewhere along the Ganges. However, by the time they reached Prayag, Sanatan had already left for Mathura by the main highway, so their paths did not cross. When he arrived in Mathura, Sanatan was able to learn of Rupa's adventures from Subuddhi Ray.

As the two brothers were travelling along the banks of the Ganges toward Bengal, Anupam departed for the eternal abode of Ramachandra. Because of Anupam's passing, Rupa Goswami was not able to join the other Bengali Vaishnavas in their annual pilgrimage to Puri, arriving there much later.

While in Vrindavan, Rupa had commenced writing a play on Krishna lila and had composed several verses of the introductory portion, known as the *nāndī*. The *nāndī* includes the obeisances, the blessing and the indication of the play's subject matter. Travelling through Orissa on his way to Puri, he stopped overnight in a village named Satyabhamapur. There he had a dream in which Satyabhama appeared to him and told him to write a separate play in her honor.

The morning after, Rupa Goswami said to himself, "Satyabhama has ordered me to write a play for her. I had started to write a play that described events from both Vraja and Dvaraka, but now I shall do them separately.
(Chaitanya Charitamrita 3.1.43-4)

When in Puri, Rupa would not go into the Jagannath temple to take darshan of Lord Jagannath. This was because of his great humility. In fact, though there was no impediment to his going there, he would not even enter Kashi Mishra's house to visit Mahaprabhu out of the same sense of being fallen. Though he had been born into a very respectable Brahmin family, he considered himself to be a Mleccha due to his long association with the Muslim rulers of Bengal. Therefore, he preferred to stay with Hari Das Thakur at Siddha Bakul. Mahaprabhu Himself respected Rupa's decision and never told him to go to see Jagannath, for He wished to teach the world humility through Rupa Goswami's example.

Through Hari Das Thakur the Lord taught forbearance. Through Rupa and Sanatan He taught humility.
(*Bhakti-ratnākara* 1.631)

When Mahaprabhu suddenly came one day to visit Hari Das, he was attracted by Rupa's humble, pure devotional attitude and embraced him. The Lord then sat down with him and asked him for the latest news about him and Sanatan and they talked about these and other things. On another day, Mahaprabhu came there with all of His entourage and Rupa paid obeisances to all of them. Mahaprabhu, out of affection for Rupa, had Advaita and Nityananda Prabhus give him their blessings. Every single day, Mahaprabhu had Govinda bring Rupa and Hari Das the remnants of His prasad.

One day, the Lord suddenly said to Rupa, "Never make Krishna leave Vraja. Krishna never abandons Vrindavan to go elsewhere." (Chaitanya Charitamrita 3.1.66) As a result of this hint from the Lord, Rupa understood that both Satyabhama and Mahaprabhu wanted two different dramas, so he composed *Vidagdha-mādhava* exclusively about Krishna's pastimes in Vraja and *Lalita-mādhava* about the Dvaraka lila.

THE LORD APPRECIATES RUPA'S POETRY

By Mahaprabhu's mercy, Rupa Goswami was able to understand His internal devotional states. While he was in Puri for the Rathayatra, Rupa observed Mahaprabhu standing before the chariot gazing upon Lord Jagannath. As He stood there, the Lord began to recite a verse from the *Kāvya-prakāśa* in the mood of Radha. The verse, though seemingly having nothing to do with Krishna, put the Lord in an ecstatic mood and He began to dance. Other than Sri

Svarupa Damodar Goswami, no one was able to understand the meaning of the verse. Rupa Goswami, however, also had an insight into the Lord's mood and he composed an original verse that expressed this sentiment. He wrote the verse down on a palm leaf and tucked it into the thatched roof of Hari Das's cottage. Then he went to take his bath in the ocean.

While he was gone, Mahaprabhu came by and found the palm leaf. When He read the verse written upon it, he was astonished to see that Rupa had had such a clear intuition into His innermost feelings.

priyaḥ so'yaṁ kṛṣṇaḥ sahacari kurukṣetra-militas
tathāhaṁ sā rādhā tad idam ubhayoḥ saṅgama-sukham
tathāpy antaḥ-khelan-madhura-muralī-pañcama-juṣe
mano me kālindī-pulina-vipināya spṛhayati

O companion! This is the same beloved Krishna meeting Me here in Kurukshetra; and I am the same Radha, and both of Us are feeling the joy of union. Even so, My mind wishes for the forest by the banks of the Yamuna where the fifth note of His flute reverberated sweetly within My heart. (*Padyāvalī*, 383)

When Rupa returned from bathing, Mahaprabhu gave him an affectionate slap, saying, "How did you know what was in My mind?" Then He embraced him tightly.

The Lord took the verse and showed it to Svarupa Damodar, asking him to examine it for any possible faults. He asked him, "How was Rupa able to know My mind?" Svarupa answered, "I believe it must be the result of Your special benediction." (Chaitanya Charitamrita 3.1.85-6)

One day, Rupa Goswami was busy writing *Vidagdha-mādhava*. Mahaprabhu arrived unexpectedly and was impressed by his beautiful handwriting, comparing it to a string of pearls. He read the verse that Rupa had just finished composing, which was a glorification of the Holy Name:

tuṇḍe tāṇḍavinī ratiṁ vitanute tuṇḍāvalī-labdhaye
karṇa-kroḍa-kaḍambinī ghaṭayate karṇārbudebhyaḥ spṛhām
cetaḥ-prāṅgaṇa-saṅginī vijayate sarvendriyāṇāṁ kṛtiṁ
no jāne janito kiyadbhir amṛtaiḥ kṛṣṇeti varṇa-dvayī

"I do not know out of how much nectar the two syllables of Krishna's name have been composed; dancing madly on my tongue, they awaken in me the desire to possess many mouths. As they sprout in my ears, they give me the hope that I may one day have millions of ears, and as they enter into the garden of my heart they overcome the activities of every one of my senses, leaving me inert!"

(*Vidagdha-mādhava* 1.15)

Hari Das Thakur, the acharya of the Holy Name, was amazed to hear such an extraordinary glorification of Krishna's name and he started to dance. He said, "I have heard the glories of the Holy Name from many scriptures and sadhus, but never have I heard a description like this of the sweetness of the Name!"

(Chaitanya Charitamrita 3.1.101)

On another day, after visiting Jagannath Deva, Mahaprabhu came to Siddha Bakul with His entire entourage, including Sri Svarupa Damodar Goswami, Ramananda Ray and Sarvabhauma Bhattacharya. Svarupa Damodar read the *priyaḥ so'yaṁ* verse quoted above to all the devotees and explained to everyone how, as a result of Mahaprabhu's special mercy, Rupa had been able to understand something that even Brahma and the demigods were unable to comprehend. Then the Lord asked Rupa to read the *tuṇḍe tāṇḍavinī* verse glorifying the Holy Name. All the devotees were delighted and said, "How often we have heard about the greatness of the Holy Name, but no one has ever written such a description of its sweetness!"

(Chaitanya Charitamrita 3.1.122)

Then Ramananda Ray began discussing the subject matter of Rupa's plays with him. He asked to hear the verse glorifying the object of his devotion that would appear at the beginning of the play. At first, Rupa was reluctant to recite his composition in front of the Lord, as it was indeed He who was the object of the *maṅgala* verse. However, when the Lord insisted that he recite, Rupa read his verse aloud. Mahaprabhu externally expressed displeasure, saying, "Your praises are overdone. It is an exaggeration," but the rest of the devotees were overcome with ecstatic love. This is the second verse in the first act of *Vidagdha-mādhava*:

anarpita-carīṁ cirāt karuṇayāvatīrṇaḥ kalau
samarpayitum unnatojjvala-rasāṁ sva-bhakti-śriyam
hariḥ purṭa-sundara-dyuti-kadamba-sandīpitaḥ
sadā hṛdaya-kandare sphuratu vaḥ śacīnandanaḥ

The elevated, effulgent taste of sacred rapture is the wealth of devotional love. The Lord never gives it at any time, yet, out of His mercy in this age of quarrel, to distribute this treasure to the world, He has incarnated in His golden form. The son of Sachi is like a lion; may He dwell in the cave of your heart forever.

When Ramananda Ray heard this extraordinary verse, drenched in love for the Lord, he began to praise Rupa Goswami with what seemed like a thousand tongues. He said that Rupa could only have written such an accurate portrayal of such difficult concepts as a result of the Lord's mercy. Ramananda said to the Lord:

"I wish I had a thousand tongues to glorify Rupa's poetic ability. This is not poetry, it is a fountain of ambrosia. He has exactly followed the classical tradition in composing his play and his description of Radha and Krishna's love affairs is truly wonderful. My ears and mind are spinning with delight upon hearing them."

(Chaitanya Charitamrita 3.1.192-4)

Once, Kali Das was considered the greatest Sanskrit poet; that is, until Rupa Goswami began to write his transcendental poetry, deeply imbued with the divine sentiments.

RUPA IN VRINDAVAN

From Puri, Rupa returned to Gaudadesh to make arrangements for the equitable distribution of his accumulated wealth amongst his family, Brahmins and temples, and stayed there for nearly a year before going to Vrindavan for good. In the meantime, Sanatan Goswami came to Puri via the Jharikhanda path and then returned by the same route to Vraja. When the two brothers met again, it had been more than a year since they had seen each other.

Rupa and Sanatan set an unequalled standard of devotional discipline and exemplary method of worship:

"These two brothers have no fixed residence, but lie down each night beneath one or the other trees in the forest. They sometimes take a meal at a Brahmin's house, or merely go door-to-door taking a handful of cooked food from each home. This way their meals consisted of only some dry bread and fried chickpeas, which they ate without any spirit of enjoyment. Their only possessions are their waterpots, and the quilts and torn loincloths they wear. Even so, they constantly chant Krishna's holy names, discuss His pastimes and dance jubilantly. They engage in Krishna bhajan for almost twenty-four hours a day, sleeping only an hour and a half. Some days, when they are absorbed in chanting the Holy Names they do not sleep at all. Sometimes they write books on the divine raptures of devotional service, and other times they spend their time talking or thinking about Chaitanya Mahaprabhu."

(Chaitanya Charitamrita 2.19.127-31)

Rupa Goswami is credited with the authorship of 16 books:

(1) *Haṁsadūta,*
(2) *Uddhava-sandeśa,*
(3) *Kṛṣṇa-janma-tithi-vidhi,*
(4) *Laghu-radha-kṛṣṇa-gaṇoddeśa- dīpikā,*
(5) *Bṛhad-rādhā-kṛṣṇa-gaṇoddeśa-dīpikā,*
(6) *Stava-mālā,*
(7) *Vidagdha-mādhava,*
(8) *Lalita-mādhava,*
(9) *Dāna-keli-kaumudī,*
(10) *Bhakti-rasāmṛta-sindhu*
(11) *Ujjvala-nīlamaṇi,*
(12) *Prayuktākhyāta-candrikā,*
(13) *Mathurā-mahimā,*
(14) *Padyāvalī,*
(15) *Nāṭaka-candrikā* and
(16) *Laghu-bhāgavatāmṛta.*

Other than these sixteen titles, *Upadeśāmṛta*, *Nāmāṣṭaka*, *Siddhānta-ratna* and *Kāvya-kaustubha*, etc., are sometimes attributed to Rupa Goswami.[20]

Raghunath Das Goswami stayed in Mahaprabhu's association in Puri for sixteen years under the tutelage of Svarupa Damodar Goswami. When the Lord and Svarupa Damodar both ended their pastimes within this world, Raghunath became so saddened by their departure that he decided to go to Vrindavan to commit suicide by jumping off Govardhan after seeing Rupa and Sanatan one last time. The two brothers were very affectionate to Raghunath, however, and would not allow him to kill himself. Rather, they adopted him as a third brother and kept him constantly by their side.

Another of the six Goswamis was Raghunath Bhatta Goswami, whose father was Tapan Mishra. When Mahaprabhu was in Benares, He stayed and ate at the home of Tapan Mishra, giving the young Raghunath the opportunity to render him service by taking His remnants and massaging His feet, etc. When he grew older, he went to see the Lord in Puri and stayed there for eight months. During this time he served Mahaprabhu by cooking various vegetable preparations which gave the Lord great satisfaction. After this, the Lord ordered him to return to Benares to serve his aging parents, which Raghunath did for four years. When his parents died, Raghunath returned to Puri where the Lord told him to follow in Rupa's footsteps and to go to Vrindavan. Raghunath followed the Lord's directions and came to Vraja where, by Rupa's mercy, he became infused with love for Krishna. He would recite Srimad Bhagavatam for Rupa's pleasure.

RUPA GOSWAMI AND GOVINDAJI

In Vrindavan, Rupa Goswami established a temple for Govindaji while Sanatan established one for Madan Mohan. Narahari describes the way that Govindaji appeared to Rupa in his *Bhakti-ratnākara*: Mahaprabhu had given four instructions to Rupa Goswami—he was to find the lost holy places in the dham, establish the service of a deity, publish scriptures on pure devotional service, and preach the love of the Holy Name. Rupa Goswami had carried out each of these desires of the Lord to perfection but one. He was worried about how he could establish deity worship and thus started wandering through the villages and forests in the Vraja area in search of Govindaji, but without success.

After the failure of these efforts, Rupa was sitting one day by the banks of the Yamuna, upset and burning with intense feelings of separation from Krishna. At that time, a divine personality taking the form of a handsome Vrajavasi came up to him and asked him in a sweet voice what was the cause of his distress. Rupa Goswami was attracted by the charming voice and appearance of the Vrajavasi and told him everything that had been troubling him. The man consoled Rupa, saying, "There is no cause for worry. You will find Govinda on the hill named Goma Tila, which is the Yoga Pith here in Vrindavan. Every morning a cow goes there and joyfully gives him milk." Having told him this, the Vrajavasi disappeared.

Rupa Goswami thought, "Krishna came here and spoke to me and I could not recognize Him," and he fainted. Even so, he was somehow or other able to overcome his feelings of loss at having been unable to recognize Krishna and proceeded to the place that the Vrajavasi had indicated. Other residents of the village helped him dig at Goma Tila until they found the deity of Govindaji, more beautiful than a million Cupids. It is said that this Govinda deity had originally been worshiped by Krishna's own grandson, Vajranabha.

After revealing his presence on Goma Tila, Govindaji was first served in a simple thatched hut, but later, a disciple of Raghunath Bhatta built a beautiful temple and *jagamohana*, etc., to house the Lord.

(*Bhakti-ratnākara* 2.404-37).

In 1590, the king of Amber, Man Singh, repaired the existing structure and built additions to it, with the result that there stood an exquisite sandstone temple. In his *Mathura Memoir*, Growse has described this temple in the following words: "The temple of Gobinda Dev is not only the finest of this particular series, but is the most impressive religious edifice that Hindu art has ever produced, at least in upper India."

It is said that the seven-story building was so high that the emperor Aurangzeb could see its pinnacle from his palace in Agra. Out of envy, he destroyed the upper portion of the building. At around this time, Govindaji was moved first to Bharatpur and then later to Jaipur out of fear of Muslim iconoclasm, and he remains in Jaipur to this day.

SRI RUPA MANJARI PADA

Narottam Das Thakur has described Rupa Manjari or Rupa Goswami as his all-in-all in the following song from *Prārthanā*:

śrī rūpa mañjarī pada sei mora sampada
sei mora bhajana-pūjana
sei mora prāṇa-dhana sei more ābharaṇa
sei mora jīvanera jīvana

sei mora rasa-nidhi sei mora vāñchā-siddhi
sei mora vedera dharama
sei vrata, sei tapa sei mora mantra japa
sei mora dharama karama

anukūla habe vidhi se pade hañbe siddhi
nirakhibo ei dui nayane
se rūpa mādhurī rāśī prāṇa kuvalaya-śaśi
praphullita habe niśi-dine

tuwā adarśana ahi garale jārala dehi
ciradina tāpita jīvana
hā hā prabhu koro dayā deha more pada chāyā
narottama lañla śaraṇa

Sri Rupa Manjari's feet are my only possession. They are my religious practice, my worship. They are my wealth, they are my ornament, the life of my life.

They are my treasurehouse of sacred rapture, they are the fulfilment of my deepest wishes, they are my prescribed duty. They are my religious vow, they are my austerities, my meditation and my mantra. They are my religious obligation.

One day, fate will smile upon me and I will be perfected in a position of service to her. I will see that form which is an ocean of sweetness, which will cause the lotus moon of my heart to bloom night and day.

The snake of separation from you spits a venom which burns my body. I have long suffered in this life. O my Lord! Please be merciful and give me the shade of your lotus feet. Narottam has taken shelter of you.

Srila Bhaktisiddhanta Saraswati Goswami Thakur also considered the dust from Rupa Goswami's feet to be the most important thing in his life. He often said that he desired nothing other than this.

ādadānas tṛṇaṁ dantair
idaṁ yāce punaḥ punaḥ
śrīmad-rūpa-padāmbhoja-
dhūliḥ syāṁ janma-janmani

With bunches of straw between my teeth, I pray repeatedly that I may take birth again and again as a particle of dust at the lotus feet of Srila Rupa Goswami.

(Raghunath Das, *Muktā-caritra*)

Rupa Goswami's samadhi temple can be found in the courtyard of the Radha-Damodar temple in Vrindavan. This is also where he performed his bhajan at the end of his life. Other places consecrated to Rupa's memory in the Vraja area include his place of worship near Nandagram, called Teri Kadamba. In this place, Radha came in disguise to give Rupa milk, rice and sugar so that he could cook a sweet-rice preparation for Sanatan Goswami. When Sanatan tasted the sweet rice, he felt divine ecstasies invade his body. Upon learning how he had received the ingredients, however, Sanatan forbade Rupa to ever cook sweet rice again, so that Radharani would not have to go to any trouble on his behalf.

Rupa Goswami's pastimes in this world came to an end in the month of Bhadra, on the twelfth day of the waxing moon, the day after Jhulan Ekadasi.

[18] Chandradwip was the ancient name of a kingdom which now lies in Bangladesh. It contained Faridpur, Bakhar Ganj and the southern parts of Dhaka and Pabna districts.

[19] According to the *Hari-bhakti-vilāsa* (17.11), a *puraścaraṇa* is a ritual performance which consists of worshiping the deity, chanting the mantra, offering oblations, performing a fire sacrifice, and feeding the Brahmins every morning, noon and evening for a fixed period of time. Such performances are not necessary for the Maha Mantra, for by even uttering the Holy Name once one obtains all the results to be obtained from *puraścaraṇa*.

[20] *Siddhānta-ratna* and *Kāvya-kaustubha* are in fact the works of Baladeva Vidyabhushan.

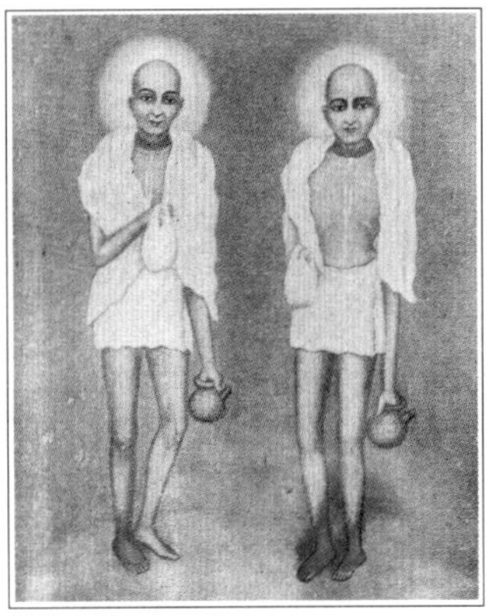

Srila Sanatan Goswami

yā rūpa-mañjarī-preṣṭhā purāsīād rati-mañjarī
socyate nāma-bhedena lavaṅga-mañjarī budhaiḥ
sādya gaurābhinna-tanuḥ sarvārādhyaḥ sanātanaḥ
tam eva prāviśat kāryān muni-ratnaḥ sanātanaḥ

Rati Manjari, who was previously very dear to Rupa Manjari and was also known by some wise persons as Lavanga Manjari, has become the worshipable Sanatan, who is non-different from Gaura Himself. The jewel amongst sages, Sanatan Kumar, has also entered into him to fulfill a certain mission. (*Gaura-gaṇoddeśa-dīpikā* 181)

SANATAN'S LIFE BEFORE MEETING MAHAPRABHU

According to the *Gauḍīya Vaiṣṇava Abhidhāna*, Sanatan was born in around 1410 of the Śaka era (1488 AD). Narahari Chakravarti Thakur has described his ancestors in *Bhakti-ratnākara* (1.541) and Srila Bhaktisiddhanta Saraswati Goswami Thakur has given a summary of this information in his *Anubhāṣya* to Chaitanya Charitamrita (1.10.84), which we have quoted in this book on page 153 in our discussion of the life of Rupa Goswami. Other than this, no reliable information about their descendents has been found. Perhaps researchers in Indian history will be able to shed more light on this.

According to the *Gauḍīya Vaiṣṇava Abhidhāna*, the following brief account is given of how Sanatan's grandfather came to be engaged in the Muslim Shah's service: "During the reign of Barbak Shah (1460-1470 AD), Sanatan's grandfather Mukunda entered the court at the capital city of Gauda. Barbak Shah engaged many Abyssinian slaves and eunuchs in both his court and harem; they were known as *hābsī* (which is now the common Bengali word for any black African). After the death of Barbak Shah, his son Yusuf became king, and he was followed by his son Fateh Shah. During the reign of Fateh Shah, the Abyssinians led a coup in which Fateh Shah himself was assassinated. They ruled for five or six years. Husain Shah was the vizir or prime minister of the last of the Abyssinian rulers and he later became himself ruler of Bengal. Mukunda left this world during the rule of Fateh Shah and Sanatan was engaged in his place. Sanatan managed to survive the Abyssinian period and during Husain Shah's reign managed to take a higher position on the strength of his personal talents, eventually becoming prime minister. Rupa Goswami held another ministerial post, possibly as finance minister." Sanatan's title was Sakar Mallik and Rupa's was Dabir Khas.

While Sri Sanatan Goswami was still young, he studied under the country's leading scholar named Vidya Vachaspati, learning many scriptures from him. He was especially attached to the study of the Srimad Bhagavatam. Although he had taken birth in a high-class Brahmin family, because he had worked for the Muslim government he considered himself to be fallen and always behaved in a most humble manner, as is appropriate for a Vaishnava.

Sanatan's teacher, Vidya Vachaspati, would come to stay in Ramakeli from time to time. Sanatan studied all the scriptures from him. No one can achieve the depth of devotion that he had for his guru.
(*Bhakti-ratnākara* 1.598-9)

Sanatan's father would perform atonement rituals even after seeing a Muslim, yet Sanatan himself would associate constantly with Muslims. Being dependent on them for his livelihood, he would even go into their homes. For this reason, he considered himself to be on the same level as the Muslims and behaved very humbly. Sometimes, when he had fallen into the ocean of humility, he would think of himself as even lower than a Mleccha. Because he had associated with Muslims and behaved in a lowly manner like them, he would speak of himself in that way. Though born in the highest class family of Brahmins, he never thought of himself as a Brahmin.
(*Bhakti-ratnākara* 1.609-14)

Through Ramananda [the Lord] destroyed Cupid's pride, and through Svarupa Damodar He demonstrated detachment. Through Hari Das Thakur, he demonstrated forbearance and through Rupa and Sanatan Goswami, He taught humility. (*Bhakti-ratnākara* 1.630-1)

All the participants in Krishna's lila also made their appearance in Gaura's incarnation in order to enrich his pastimes. Through them, the Lord gives various teachings to the people of this world.

Through Hari Das, Mahaprabhu revealed the glories of the Holy Name; through Sanatan, the current of devotional conclusions. Through Rupa He taught Radha and Krishna's pastimes of love. Who can understand the mysterious workings of the Lord?
(Chaitanya Charitamrita 3.5.86-7)

Through Sanatan's mercy, I learned the foundation of devotional doctrine, while through Rupa's mercy, I learned about the divine devotional sentiments.
(Chaitanya Charitamrita 1.5.203)

Thus Sanatan has been called the *bhakti-siddhāntācārya*, or the teacher of devotional doctrine, by which is meant the teacher of *sambandha-jñāna*, or of the basic relations between God, man and the world. The founder of the Chaitanya Math, Srila Bhaktisiddhanta Saraswati Goswami Thakur, whose various branches have spread throughout the world, mercifully gave his disciples a poem entitled "Who is a Vaishnava?" The nectarean instructions found in this poem make mention the teachings of Mahaprabhu to Sanatan Goswami from the Chaitanya Charitamrita.

tai duṣṭa mana nirjana bhajana
pracāricha chale kuyogī-vaibhava
prabhu sanātane parama yatane
śikṣā dila yāhā, cinta sei saba

"So, wicked mind, you have deceptively been preaching nirjana-bhajana, or solitary practice life, which is nothing more than a display like that of a misleading yoga practitioner interested in the mystic powers. Study the teachings of the Lord to Sanatan very carefully and meditate upon them."

Srila Bhaktisiddhanta Saraswati Goswami Thakur thus instructs us all to give great attention to the Lord's teachings to Sanatan, or those teachings He gave to the world through Sanatan Goswami.

FIRST MEETING IN RAMAKELI

After He took sannyas, Mahaprabhu first went to Shantipur, then to Puri, and then on pilgrimage to South India. After completing His pilgrimage and returning to Puri, Mahaprabhu decided to go to Vrindavan via the route which follows the Ganges through Bengal. Great crowds of people accompanied Him and He eventually decided to turn back from Kanair Natshala. He met Rupa and Sanatan for the first time while passing through the village of Ramakeli on this journey.

Ramakeli is in the district of Maldah in West Bengal, located about eight miles south of English Bazaar, and about five or six miles from the Maldah train station. Ramakeli was made district headquarters during British rule and is also known as Gupta ("hidden") Vrindavan. There are a number of sites which are worth visiting as reminders of Rupa and Sanatan: (1) The tamal and a kadamba trees under which Mahaprabhu is said to have been sitting when he met Rupa and Sanatan; a shrine containing the footprints of the Lord has been constructed there as a memorial of that meeting. In this location, the Lord distributed love of Krishna to all the devotees. (2) The temple of Madana Mohan. This Madana Mohan deity was personally worshiped by Sanatan Goswami. There are also deities of Nitai-Gauranga and Advaita Prabhus. (3) There are several ponds which are named Radha Kund, Shyama Kund, Surabhi Kund, Lalita Kund, and Vishakha Kund. (4) A large man-made lake named Rupa Sagara, which is said to have been excavated by Rupa Goswami himself, and (5) another named Sanatan Sagara. Rupa and Sanatan built large mansions both in Ramakeli and Fateyabad.

At first, the Muslim king became concerned when he heard that such great crowds of Hindus had assembled in the nearby village. One of the Hindu members of the Shah's court was Keshava Kshatriya, who explained to him that there was no reason to fear Mahaprabhu. Rupa Goswami (Dabir Khas) also glorified Mahaprabhu to the king, telling him of his fortune in having the Lord bless the country by his presence. Keshava Kshatriya, meanwhile, sent a secret message to the Lord telling Him to go elsewhere because the King could not be trusted.

The King said, "Listen, I am also beginning to think that this person must be God Himself. There is no doubt about it." After having this conversation, the king entered his private quarters and Dabir Khas also returned to his residence. After returning there, however, he and his brother decided after much consideration to go incognito to see the Lord. Thus, in the dead of night the two brothers, Dabir Khas and Sakar Mallik, went to see Mahaprabhu. First they met Nityananda Prabhu and Hari Das Thakur. Nityananda Prabhu and Hari Das then went and told the Lord that Dabir Khas and Sakar Mallik had come to see him.

(Chaitanya Charitamrita 2.1.180-4)

When Rupa and Sanatan met the Lord, they spoke to Him with extreme humility:

"We two are millions of times more degraded, fallen and sinful than Jagai and Madhai. We are of wicked birth because we are the servants of Muslims and our activities are exactly like those of the Muslims. We constantly associate with people who are inimical toward the cows and Brahmins. Due to our abominable activities we are now bound by the neck and hands and have been thrown into the ditch filled with the excrement of evil sense enjoyment."

(Chaitanya Charitamrita 2.1.196-199)

It is very distressful to us that we are so unworthy, yet when we see Your merciful qualities, we become desirous of attaining Your blessings. This powerful desire rises up in us as that of a dwarf who wants to touch the moon.

(Chaitanya Charitamrita 2.1.204-5)

When the Lord heard the extreme humility of the two brothers, He became compassionate and said to them, "You are My eternal servants. From now on you shall be known as Rupa and Sanatan. I came to Bengal just so that I could meet you here in Ramakeli village. Krishna will deliver you from your entanglements very shortly."

Srila Bhaktisiddhanta Saraswati Goswami Thakur has written the following comment in his *Anubhāṣya*: "Mahaprabhu showed his mercy to Dabir Khas and Sakar Mallik by giving them the spiritual names of Rupa and Sanatan, respectively. *Nāma-karaṇa* is a type of *saṁskāra* on the lowest level of qualification. However, those who ignore the mercy that is manifest in the spiritual name have no chance of attaining devotion to Krishna, but remain intoxicated with material prestige. Prakrita Sahajiyas pay no heed to the injunctions of the scripture that state that the minimum characteristic of a Vaishnava is that he wears the symbols of the discus and conchshell and *ūrdhva-pūṇḍra* (tilak) and takes one of the names of Krishna. As such, they cannot be qualified as Gaudiya Vaishnavas. Non-Vaishnavas have not been given a name by the Vaishnava guru and so they continue in the bodily conception of life without any awareness of their relationship with the Lord. They continue to identify themselves with their previous caste according to the name which ties them to their body." (*Anubhāṣya* 2.1.208)

Amongst the Lord's companions present on this occasion were Nityananda Prabhu, Hari Das Thakur, Srivasa Pandit, Srila Gadadhar Pandit Goswami, Mukunda Datta, Jagadananda Pandit, Murari Gupta, Vakresvara Pandit and many others. The Lord had them all give their blessings to Rupa and Sanatan. As the Lord was departing, the worldly-wise Sanatan said to Him:

"You should leave this place, Lord. You have no business here. Even though the Shah has faith in you, he is a Muslim and cannot be trusted. To go on pilgrimage with such a large company of devotees is not recommended. You are going to Vrindavan with an entourage of hundreds and thousands of people, and this is not a fitting way to go on a pilgrimage." (Chaitanya Charitamrita 2.1.222-4)

Mahaprabhu continued on as far as Kanair Natshala, but as He considered the wisdom of Sanatan's advice, He decided to turn back, first going to Shantipur and then to Puri.

After He and His entourage had given their mercy to Rupa and Sanatan, they left Ramakeli village.
(*Bhakti-ratnākara* 1.635)

SANATAN ESCAPES FROM PRISON

Rupa and Sanatan are the eternal associates of Krishna in Vrindavan. They appeared in this world in order to enrich Lord Gauranga's lila by playing the role of aspirants for spiritual perfection (*sādhakas*). After meeting Mahaprabhu, they began to feel very impatient to change their lifestyle. They became very renounced and austere. In order to quickly be united with Mahaprabhu, they engaged two Brahmins in the performance of a *puraścaraṇa*.

Srila Rupa Goswami finally resigned from his government service and he deposited 10,000 coins on behalf of his older brother with a grocer in the capital Gauda. Then he took the rest of their accumulated wealth with him to Bakla Chandradwip where he divided it up amongst the Vaishnavas, Brahmins and his family. He also kept a quarter of it with a trustworthy Brahmin against future necessity. He then sent two people to Puri to find out when Mahaprabhu intended to travel to Vrindavan.

Husain Shah used to treat Sanatan Goswami as his younger brother and had great affection for him. Sanatan thought that the affection of the king, or indeed of any materialistic person, was a source of material bondage. If the king became angry with him, it would make it easier for him to break away from his entanglements. For this reason, he stopped performing his duties in the Shah's court, pretending to be ill. Though he claimed to be seriously ill, he was in fact engaged in an intense study of the Bhagavatam with a group of Sanskrit scholars.

The Shah was disquieted by Sanatan's illness and he sent a doctor to examine him. The doctor came back and reported to the king that Sanatan was in good health and that he was studying the Bhagavata with a group of pandits. When he heard this, the Shah went to Sanatan himself and spoke to him very affectionately, trying to convince him to come back to work. Sanatan refused, however, to return to his ministerial duties and furthermore refused to accompany the Shah in the war he was preparing with Orissa. The Shah became suspicious of Sanatan and had him imprisoned.

In the meantime, Rupa had received the news that Mahaprabhu had taken the jungle route through Jharikhanda for Vrindavan. He immediately departed for Vraja with his younger brother Anupam Mallik. He sent Sanatan a letter letting him know of his intentions, telling him to take any necessary action to free himself and then to come and join them. According to Bhaktivinode Thakur, the letter consisted of the following Sanskrit verse:

yadu-pateḥ kva gatā mathurā puri
raghu-pateḥ kva gatottara-kośalā
iti vicintya kuruṣva manaḥ sthiraṁ
na sad idaṁ jagad ity avadhāraya

Where has the Mathura of the Lord of the Yadus gone? And where is the kingdom of Kosala of the Lord of the Raghus? Contemplate this and make your mind steady: Beware, this world will not last forever.(*Amṛta-pravāha-bhāṣya*, 2.20.3)

Sanatan was able to understand the secret meaning of the verse, which indicated that the Lord had gone to Mathura, and was overjoyed. He began to consider how to escape from prison.

Sanatan knew the Muslim jailkeeper for he was the one who had hired him. He began trying to persuade him to let him go saying that the Almighty would surely bless and give him salvation for setting free someone who had been unjustly imprisoned. The jailor remained unconvinced, so Sanatan tried to win him over by reminding him that he owed him a favor for having given him the job.

When the jail keeper still refused to let him go, Sanatan offered him a bribe of 5,000 rupees. At this, the jailkeeper's resolve began to waver but he was still afraid of being caught by the Badshah. Sanatan told him, "The Shah has gone to war. When he comes back, just tell him that I went to the toilet. Then when I went to the Ganges to wash myself, I jumped into the water and disappeared. Say that you looked everywhere but couldn't find me."

Sanatan further assured him that he would not remain in the area, as it was his intention to become a Sufi and go on the Haj to Mecca. Therefore, he need not worry on that account. The jailor remained reticent, however, and finally

Sanatan had the grocer bring 7,000 rupees of the money Rupa had left in his safekeeping and placed it directly in front of him. When he saw the money before him, the jailor became greedy and surrendered to his proposal. He cut Sanatan's chains and helped him to cross the Ganges.

In general, we consider flattery, asking return for a favor, putting temptation before someone, telling someone to lie, and bribery all to be unethical acts. Sanatan, however, used all the means at his disposal to escape bondage so that he could join the Lord and engage in His service. To achieve an auspicious end, any means may be permissible. The purity or impurity of a particular means depends on the purity or impurity of the objectives to be achieved. In order to serve his master Rama, the Supreme Brahman, Hanuman burned down Lanka, killing many living beings, but because he was acting for the pleasure of the all-auspicious Supreme Lord, everyone was ultimately benefited by his action, and Hanuman is still considered worshipable to this very day. On the other hand, one can bathe in a holy river three times a day and worship the deity of the Lord and be completely in the mode of ignorance if his objective is to do harm to other beings.

Even from the worldly point of view we see that one who commits murder is considered a criminal and is punished by the death penalty; but if one fights on the battlefield to save the nation and kills many members of a rival army, he is not punished but rather decorated with medals. This is because he is not acting for personal ends but rather for those of the collectivity. This is easy enough to understand; yet when one acts not for the limited purposes of serving the country or even the entire world, but for the supremely auspicious owner of unlimited millions of universes, then that is the most justifiable of purposes and the highest benefits are attained by everyone through such actions. In the *Padma-purāṇa*, it is written:

man-nimittaṁ kṛtaṁ pāpam
api dharmāya kalpate
māṁ anādṛtya dharmo 'pi
pāpaṁ syān mat-prabhāvataḥ

"Even sinful activities done for My sake are to be considered religious acts. On the other hand, pious activities done while disdaining Me are considered to be sin. Such is the extent of my power."

Those who chant the Holy Names or make a show of devotion, but in fact are seeking to achieve mundane, egoistic goals, are factually engaged in sin and are destined for a hellish fate. Krishna also states in the Bhagavad Gita:

yasya nāhaṅkṛto bhāvo
buddhir yasya na lipyate
hatvāpi sa imāl lokān
na hanti na nibadhyate

He who is free from egotism (arising from aversion to the Absolute), and whose intelligence is not implicated in worldly activities does not kill at all—even if he kills every living being in the whole world—nor does he suffer the consequences of murder. (Bhagavad Gita 18.17)

When causeless devotion is manifest in the soul and one's heart has an honest eagerness to find service to the Lord, then one gives up all consideration for happiness in this world, for renunciation is a side effect of unmotivated devotion.

ISHAN NEARLY GETS SANATAN KILLED

Sanatan had been prime minister, yet he escaped from jail with practically not a penny to his name. He did not take the main highway but travelled as quickly as he could through fields and villages until he reached Patra Mountain, which is part of the Raj Mahal Hills in the Chota Nagpur area of the modern state of Bihar. He did not know how to get across this mountain and so requested the aid of a landowner who was also a robber chieftain.

Accompanying Sanatan was a longtime personal servant named Ishan. Through the help of a palmist, the landowner was able to know that this Ishan had eight gold coins in his possession so he welcomed Sanatan into his home and treated him with great hospitality.

Sanatan was sufficiently experienced from his years in politics to be suspicious of the warm treatment he was receiving from his host and so he asked Ishan whether he was carrying anything of value. Ishan answered that he had seven gold coins, keeping his other coin a secret from him. Sanatan gently rebuked Ishan, saying, "Why have you brought this ruination upon us?" He then took the coins from him and gave them to his host, asking him to help him get across the mountain.

The landowner then revealed to Sanatan that he had known all along about the eight gold coins and that it had been his intention to murder them both that night somewhere on the mountain in order to take the money. He was very pleased that Sanatan had given him the gold and was even ready to return it to him, but Sanatan refused. He was intelligent enough to understand the adage: *avyvasthita-cittasya prasādo'pi bhayaṅkaraḥ*, "Even the kindness of an undependable person is dangerous."

dhūrtasya vacane kvāsthā
kvacit satyaṁ kvacin mṛṣā
kvacid raudraṁ kvacid vṛṣṭiḥ
śrāvaṇasya ghano yathā

"How can one have faith in the words of a rascal? Sometimes he tells the truth and sometimes falsehoods. It is just as with the clouds of Shravan—sometimes there is sunshine and sometimes rain."

After they had crossed the mountain, Sanatan told Ishan to take the remaining gold coin and return home. Ishan had shown by his attachment to this gold coin that he was not yet ready to accept a life of renunciation and that he was too dependent on material conditions. When unqualified people take to the renounced orders, then these orders themselves become contaminated. This is the lesson that Sanatan gave through his servant Ishan.

SANATAN MEETS THE LORD IN BENARES

After bidding goodbye to his servant, Sanatan continued on his way until he arrived at Hajipur on the northern bank of the Ganges near Patna. Sanatan's brother-in-law, Srikanta, made his home there. Though Srikanta invited him to stay in his home for a few days to recuperate from the voyage, Sanatan declined his invitation because of his desire to see the Lord. Srikanta gave him a valuable blanket of Bhutanese wool.

Sanatan then continued on to Benares where he was overjoyed to learn that Mahaprabhu was staying at the house of the physician, Chandrasekhara. Sanatan did not go straight into Chandrasekhara's house but waited on his front porch. The Lord, the indweller of all souls, knew of His devotee's arrival and sent Chandrasekhara to the door to invite him in. As soon as Sanatan entered, Mahaprabhu immediately rushed to embrace him. This meeting affected them both so intensely that they were overcome by the transformations of ecstatic love. In his affection for Sanatan, the Lord started to brush off the dust accumulated on his body from his travels, but this caused Sanatan to feel uncomfortable. He told the Lord not to touch him, but the Lord answered:

> "I touch you in order to purify Myself. Your devotional force is so great that you can purify the entire universe. I look at you, I touch you and I sing your glories. By so doing, all My senses attain their most perfect use."
> (Chaitanya Charitamrita 2.20.56,60)

The Lord repeated again and again that he was touching Sanatan for His own purification and for the purification of the entire universe. Then He immediately added, "Listen Sanatan. Krishna is the ocean of mercy; He saves the most fallen. He has delivered you from the hell known as Raurava."

Sanatan is, of course, an eternal associate of the Lord, so there is no question of his being truly fallen, but Mahaprabhu wished to make a point for the benefit of the people of the world. He wanted to teach that worldly honor measured in terms of one's fortune and accumulation of sense objects is in truth misfortune, since the accumulation of material possessions for the sake of gross or subtle sense gratification ultimately leads to a hellish existence.

Conditioned souls who are bewildered by the illusory energy are constantly busy working hard in order to accumulate wealth, position, and influence whether by fair means or foul. Seldom does one come across an exemplary householder who knows that Krishna is the only true enjoyer and engages all his worldly possessions in the Lord's service rather than considering them to be the objects of his own enjoyment.

While Mahaprabhu was in Benares, He stayed with Chandrasekhara and took His meals at the house of Tapan Mishra. Mahaprabhu introduced Sanatan to these two devotees, and Tapan Mishra invited Sanatan to come to his house and take Mahaprabhu's prasad remnants. After many days in prison and travelling, Sanatan's hair and beard had grown long. The Lord told him to get shaved so that he would look "respectable." Vaishnavas in general are clean shaven, growing neither beard nor moustache. With the exception of the Chaturmasya period when one does not shave nor cut the fingernails, this is the accepted practice for Vaishnava men. Vaishnava sannyasis, however, usually shave only once a month on the full moon day, as for them to shave daily would be considered unnecessary preoccupation with the body.

After being shaved, Sanatan took his bath in the Ganges. When he came back to the house, Chandrasekhara wanted to give him a new cloth, but Sanatan refused it, taking back his old one. Though he had been rich enough to give clothes to thousands of mendicants, on this day he was reluctant to accept a new cloth for himself. When one's desire to worship the Lord is real, one becomes indifferent to nice clothes or good food. Accepting gifts from Vaishnavas or taking their remnants is an exception to this rule, however, as these do not have the poisonous character that other sense objects have. Every single one of Sanatan's actions contains a lesson for the conscientious sadhaka.

Mahaprabhu was extremely pleased to see Sanatan's renunciation. Thus it is said:

> *mahāprabhura bhakta jata vairāgya pradhāna*
> *jāhā dekhi' tuṣṭa han gaura bhagavān*

> Renunciation is the predominating characteristic of every one of Mahaprabhu's devotees. When Lord Gauranga sees their renunciation, He is very pleased.
> (Chaitanya Charitamrita 2.6.220)

When one is intoxicated by material sensuality and enjoyments and engaged in competition to attain them, one is destined for a falldown from any spiritual attainment.

There was in Benares a Maharashtrian Brahmin who invited Sanatan to come daily to his house to eat for as long as he stayed there. Sanatan refused, however, saying that he prefered to keep body and soul together by eating only *madhukarī*, that is to say, by begging a handful of food from several houses each day. A pure devotee has no desire for bodily comfort.

Sanatan Goswami had torn his old cloth into two to make a loincloth (*bahirvāsa*) and a shawl (*uttarīya*), but even so, he continued to wrap himself in the Bhutanese wool blanket. Mahaprabhu looked repeatedly at this blanket, and Sanatan realized that Mahaprabhu did not approve of it. That day, when he went to the Ganges ghat, he saw a Bengali mendicant washing a quilt in the river. He offered this mendicant his expensive blanket in exchange for the quilt. When Sanatan came back wearing the threadbare quilt, the Lord was pleased.

The Lord said, "I had been thinking about this. It seems that since Lord Krishna is very merciful, He has cured you of your disease of attachment to sense enjoyment. Why then would He allow you to hold fast to a last bit of material attachment? After restoring someone to health, a good physician does not allow any trace of the disease to remain. It is contradictory to practice *mādhukarī* while wearing a blanket worth three gold coins. By so doing, you would have lost your spiritual strength and become a laughing stock."

(Chaitanya Charitamrita 2.20.90-2)

Sri Chaitanya Mahaprabhu is the Supreme Personality of Godhead Himself. Even so, He played the role of the supreme teacher. He insisted that His personal associates maintain the standards of behavior that He set and Himself followed.

"I shall accept the role of a devotee and shall teach devotional service by practicing it Myself. It is explained in the Bhagavata and the Bhagavad Gita that if one does not oneself practice a religious principle, it cannot be taught.

(Chaitanya Charitamrita 1.3.20-1)

yad yad ācarati śreṣṭhas
tat tad evetaro janaḥ
sa yat pramāṇaṁ kurute
lokas tad anuvartate

The general masses imitate the ways of great men. They follow whatever the great personality accepts as the right conclusion. (Bhagavad Gita 3.21)

THE LORD'S TEACHINGS TO SANATAN

Being pleased with Sanatan, Mahaprabhu infused him with spiritual power, giving him the capacity to ask appropriate questions about the practice of true spiritual life. Without the mercy of the Supreme Lord, genuine, honest questions on such matters cannot arise in someone's mind. Most people ask questions thinking that they already know the right answer, simply as a sort of debating technique. No spiritual benefit arises from such types of questions. Honest questions meant to find out doctrinal truths leading to surrender are called *paripraśna,* relevant inquiry, in the Bhagavad Gita:

tad viddhi praṇipātena
paripraśnena sevayā
upadekṣyanti te jñānaṁ
jñāninas tattva-darśinaḥ

You will be able to attain all this knowledge by satisfying the enlightened spiritual master with prostrate obeisances, relevant inquiry, and sincere service. Great souls who are most expert in scriptural knowledge and endowed with direct realization of the Absolute will teach you that divine knowledge. (Bhagavad Gita 4.34)

On the day a person undertakes his journey on the road to liberation and his material entanglement is about to start the process of termination, he meets a spiritual master. Sanatan Goswami was himself an ever-liberated soul and a permanent companion of the Lord, but he showed what questions the aspiring practitioner of devotional service should ask his spiritual master on that day. He said to the Lord:

"I was born in a low family and have always associated with low-class men. I am fallen and the lowest of men. Indeed, I have fallen into the well of sinful materialism and passed my whole life there. I have no idea of what is beneficial for me and what is not. In ordinary dealings, people consider me wise, and I have also come to think of myself as such. You have mercifully delivered me from the materialistic path. Now, by the same causeless mercy, please explain to me my duty. I don't know who I am or why the threefold miseries constantly wear me down, so how can I attain the highest good? Actually, I do not even know how to inquire about the goal of life and the process for obtaining it. Please bestow Your mercy on me and explain all these things." (Chaitanya Charitamrita 2.20.99-103)

Sanatan's first question was *āmi ke*? "Who am I?" This is the first question which arises in the heart of a person seeking the highest good. If one makes a mistake in assessing his true identity, then he will make errors when it comes to determining the ultimate goal of life. If one makes an error in determining the ultimate goal of life, then everything he does, every effort he makes, will be wasted. All of one's duties, religious observations and self-interest rest upon the proper knowledge of oneself. If one takes the body to be the self, then He considers the maintenance of the body itself to be the goal of life or *prayojana-tattva*, and one's self-interest will be the fulfilment of goals related to the body; duties will also be considered in terms of these ends, and all morality, or the ability to discriminate between good and bad, will be determined purely on the basis of what is good or bad for the body.

On the other hand, if someone takes the subtle body to be the self, then he will consider his personal interests in terms of its development and he will feel it his religious duty to help others develop in this way. Finally, those who consider the self to be a soul existing beyond the gross and subtle bodies will consider the soul's development to be their true self-interest and will understand religious duty in terms of helping other people develop their spiritual consciousness. Those whose vision is clear enough to recognize their identity as spirit soul, but find themselves in the undesirable situation of bondage to the gross and subtle material bodies, can still make favorable use of these coverings in an understanding of their true self-interest, that of the soul. They avoid the unfavorable use of the gross and subtle bodies.

In His teachings to Sanatan Goswami, Sri Chaitanya Mahaprabhu taught that the living being's true identity is to be Krishna's eternal servant. The jiva is the Lord's *taṭastha-śakti* or marginal energy, his separated expansion, who is simultaneously one and different from Him. The Lord taught Sanatan the *sādhya* and the *sādhana*, the goal of the seeker and the methods by which the seeker achieves his goal. Mahaprabhu summarized the three elements of His teaching as sambandha, knowledge of one's relationship with Krishna, abhidheya, the practice which leads to perfection or devotion to Krishna, and the prayojana, the supreme goal of spiritual life or love for Krishna, prema.

The sum total of the Vedic literatures explains three things: sambandha, abhidheya and prayojana. The living entity's eternal relationship with Krishna is called sambandha. Devotional service is the process by which one attains the supreme objective, Krishna. Devotional service, or sense activity for the satisfaction of the Lord is called abhidheya because it can develop one's original love of Godhead— which is the ultimate goal of life—the prayojana. This goal is the living entity's topmost interest and greatest treasure. (Chaitanya Charitamrita 2.20.124-5)

Krishna Das Kaviraj Goswami has explained all these matters at great length in his Chaitanya Charitamrita, from the 20th to the 23rd chapters of the *Madhya-līlā*, with copious quotations from scripture. Rather than repeat these teachings in detail here, which would lead to this account of Sanatan Goswami's life becoming overly extensive, we will limit ourselves to a brief summary.

Mahaprabhu told Sanatan that the various scriptures, in particular the Sruti, contain statements which indicate that the living being is both one with and different from the Supreme Lord. Different acharyas have put forth a variety of doctrines explaining the relation between this oneness and distinction, named *advaita-vāda, dvaita-vāda, viśiṣṭādvaita-vāda, śuddhādvaita-vāda, dvaitādvaita-vāda*, etc. If one accepts the scripture, one must accept it in its entirety. This includes both types of affirmation, and involves finding a way to harmonize apparent contradictions. Sri Chaitanya Mahaprabhu's solution to the problem was to establish the doctrine named *acintya-bhedābheda*, "inconceivable oneness and difference." This doctrine has been favorably accepted around the world and created a revolution in theistic thinking.

Mahaprabhu concluded his teachings with a discourse on the *ātmārāma* verse:

ātmārāmāś ca munayo
nirgranthā apy urukrame
kurvanty ahaitukīṁ bhaktim
ittham-bhūta-guṇo hariḥ

Self-satisfied sages who are freed from any bondage also engage in the unmotivated service of Sri Krishna, whose activities are all wonderful. Such are the transcendentally attractive features of Hari!

(Srimad Bhagavatam 1.7.11)

Mahaprabhu gave eighteen different explanations of this verse from the Srimad Bhagavatam to Sarvabhauma Bhattacharya. When Sanatan asked the Lord to allow Him to hear them, Mahaprabhu treated him to 61 different interpretations.

SANATAN GOES TO VRAJA

After this, Mahaprabhu converted Prakashananda Saraswati and the other sannyasis of Benares to Vaishnavism. When He had completed instructing Sanatan in a most thorough fashion, He sent him to Vrindavan while He Himself took the less frequented road to Puri. Sanatan took the main highway to Vrindavan where he met Subuddhi Ray who was following Mahaprabhu's instructions to atone for his past sins by chanting Hare Krishna. Though he was barely able to make a living selling dry wood, Subuddhi would provide for the Vaishnavas who came to Vraja from Bengal.

Sanatan took the pilgrimage circuit through the twelve forests of Vraja in the company of Subuddhi and the Sanoriya Brahmin. From them he learned that Rupa and Anupam had also completed the circuit not long before and had then taken the road along the banks of the Ganges to return to Bengal.

When Mahaprabhu performed Vraja parikrama, He discovered Radha Kund and Shyama Kund near Arit village. He took darshan of Harideva at Govardhan, after which he desired to see Giridhari Gopal. The Gopal deity of Madhavendra Puri had his temple on top of the hill, but Mahaprabhu had vowed not to walk on Govardhan. How would he be able to fulfill His desire to take darshan of Gopal? While the Lord was wondering how to solve this problem, there was a panic in the area that the Muslims were planning to destroy images throughout Vraja. This led Gopal's pujaris to take him out of his temple and hide him in the village of Gatholi, thus enabling Mahaprabhu to receive his darshan. From time to time, Gopal would perform this pastime of being moved to Gatholi in this way. Sanatan also had the good fortune to be able to visit Gopal while he was there.

SANATAN VISITS THE LORD IN PURI

It took Rupa Goswami longer to get to Bengal than he had expected and so he was unable to join the other devotees on their annual trip to Puri to see the Lord. As a result, he arrived some time after the main group and went to stay with Hari Das Thakur. When Mahaprabhu met Rupa, he inquired after Sanatan and heard from him that the brothers had taken different roads and thus missed each other.

In the meantime, Sanatan Goswami was on his way to Puri after touring Vrindavan, taking the Jharikhanda route through the jungle. There he drank some bad water and came down with scabies. Sanatan became depressed as a result of the running sores on his body and began to plan suicide in his despondency, thinking that due to his low birth and his now disgusting physical condition he would not only be unable to go near the temple and see Jagannath, but would also be deprived of Mahaprabhu's darshan. He would not even be able to stay close enough to the temple to see it, and if Lord Jagannath's servants should accidentally touch him, he would commit a great offense by rendering them impure. All in all, he thought it would be better to throw himself under the wheels of Jagannath's chariot and be crushed to death while watching Mahaprabhu dance.

When Sanatan finally arrived in Puri, he went directly to Siddha Bakul to see Hari Das Thakur and paid his respectful obeisances to him. Hari Das affectionately embraced him and invited him to stay there with him.

This way, whenever Mahaprabhu came to see Hari Das, as He was accustomed to do, Sanatan would have the opportunity to see him.

The first time the Lord saw Sanatan, He was so overcome by divine love that He approached him with the intention of embracing him. Sanatan retreated, however, thinking himself too impure to be touched by the Lord. Nevertheless, Mahaprabhu would not let him escape and took him in His arms by force, holding him so tightly that the fluid oozing from Sanatan's sores was smeared on His holy body, the sight of which broke Sanatan's heart. Mahaprabhu then gave Sanatan the news of Rupa's visit. He also spoke of Anupam's devotion to Rama and his departure for Rama's eternal abode.

On another day, the all-knowing Mahaprabhu came to Siddha Bakul and suddenly confronted Sanatan about his intention to commit suicide during the Rathayatra festival. He said:

"My dear Sanatan, if I could attain Krishna by committing suicide, then I would give up millions of bodies without a moment's hesitation. However, I cannot attain Krishna simply by giving up the body, but only through bhajan. There is no means by which to attain Krishna other than devotional service."

(Chaitanya Charitamrita 3.4.55-6)

In this way, Mahaprabhu taught the world through Sanatan that suicide is an act of the mode of ignorance which cannot be used to attain Krishna. It is only through the cultivation of pure devotion in practice that one can attain the Supreme Lord. The best forms of bhajan, or worship, are known as the nine kinds of devotional service, or *nava-vidhā bhakti*. The best of these is the congregational chanting of the Holy Names of Krishna, Harinam sankirtan.

Finally, Mahaprabhu revealed how dear Sanatan was to Him when He said:

"You have already surrendered yourself to Me, so your body is now My personal property. Why do you want to destroy another's property? Are you unable to distinguish right from wrong? Your body is an important instrument through which I shall accomplish many things."

(Chaitanya Charitamrita 3.4.76-8)

During the Chaturmasya period, many Bengali and Orissan devotees would come to Puri to be with the Lord, and that year they also met Sanatan. Sanatan was struck with wonder by the Lord's dancing before Jagannath's chariot. When the Bengali Vaishnavas returned to their homes after the four month period, Sanatan remained in Puri.

During the hot season, in the month of Jyestha, the Lord stayed with Gadadhar Pandit at Yameshwar Tota. One day, He called Sanatan to come and see Him at noontime. Rather than taking the main road leading from the Singha Dwar to the seashore, Sanatan took another path that led across the hot sands of the beach. Though Sanatan had no consciousness of the burning heat of the sand, his feet were covered in blisters when he arrived.

The Lord asked Sanatan why he had not taken the road that led directly from the Singha Dwar. Sanatan replied:

"I have no right to pass by the Singha Dwar, for the servants of Jagannath are always coming and going there. Since they are always using that road, I would not be able to pass without touching them. If that should happen, I would be ruined." (Chaitanya Charitamrita 3.4.126-7)

Mahaprabhu was very pleased with Sanatan's by his humility and respect for Lord Jagannath's pujaris. He answered him as follows:

"My dear Sanatan, you can save the entire universe; even the demigods and great saints are purified by touching you. Nevertheless, it is in a devotee's nature to observe Vaishnava etiquette. Maintenance of Vaishnava etiquette is the ornament of the devotee. One who transgresses the rules of behavior becomes a laughing stock and is ultimately lost, both in this world and the next. You have brought Me great satisfaction by observing this etiquette. If you did not act in this way, who else would?"

(Chaitanya Charitamrita 3.4.129-32)

In his pleasure, Mahaprabhu embraced Sanatan again and again. Once again, the fluids from Sanatan's blisters oozed all over the Lord's body. The situation so troubled Sanatan that he went to discuss the matter with Jagadananda Pandit, asking him for advice on how to free himself from the offenses that he was unwillingly committing. Jagadananda's suggestion was that Sanatan leave Puri and return to Vrindavan.

The next time that Mahaprabhu came to Siddha Bakul and embraced him, Sanatan blurted out his distress, saying that he should never have come to Puri as his coming had only resulted in the committing of countless offenses. The contaminating impurities from his scabies daily touched the Lord's body, and this was plunging him deeper and deeper into misery. He begged Mahaprabhu for permission to leave for Vrindavan, letting him know that it was Jagadananda who had thus advised him. When Mahaprabhu heard this, He became angry and said:

"Jagadananda is just a newcomer, a boy. Yet, he has become so proud that he thinks he can give even you advice. You are his guru in every respect, both in material and spiritual terms, and yet he dares to give you counsel? Does he not know his own standing? You are My teacher; you are a great authority. And yet, Jagadananda is giving instructions to you like an impudent child, as though he were unaware of your qualifications."

(Chaitanya Charitamrita 3.4.158-60)

When Sanatan heard Mahaprabhu criticize Jagadananda in this way, He took it as another sign of the Pandit's great fortune on the one hand and his own misfortune on the other.

"You accept Jagadananda into Your inner circle while You venerate me. It is as though you were giving him ambrosia to drink and me the bitter juice of neem and tobacco leaves." (Chaitanya Charitamrita 3.4.163)

Even after hearing these words, Mahaprabhu continued to take Jagadananda's actions as a sign of impudence. Srila Bhaktisiddhanta Saraswati Goswami Thakur has written in this connection, "Everyone has a certain status. If someone thinks that he is more important than he really is, he transgresses the prescribed lines of etiquette that are accorded to those with spiritual seniority, etc. He then gives advice to someone to whom he should rather offer deference. Mahaprabhu did not encourage such transgressions, but rather sought to discourage younger devotees like Jagadananda from behaving in this way."

The Lord further prohibited anyone from looking upon Sanatan's body as material.

> "You take your body to be disgusting, whereas I think that your body is like nectar. Your body is transcendental, never material, but you conceive of it in material terms."
>
> (Chaitanya Charitamrita 3.4.172-3)

When Hari Das Thakur objected that the Lord was exaggerating out of his own mercy, the Lord laughed and explained to him and Sanatan as follows:

> "My dear Hari Das and Sanatan, I think of you as My adopted children and of Myself as your maintainer. The maintainer never takes the faults of the maintained seriously. I never think of Myself as deserving of respect, but because of affection I always consider you to be like My little boys. A mother never hates her child even when it passes stool and urine on her body. On the contrary, she takes much pleasure in cleansing him and takes his filth to be like sandalwood pulp. Similarly, I felt no disgust at being touched by the fluids oozing from Sanatan's sores."
>
> (Chaitanya Charitamrita 3.4.184-7)

Sri Chaitanya Mahaprabhu went on to say:

> "The body of a devotee is never material. It is considered to be transcendental, full of spiritual bliss. At the time of initiation, when a devotee fully commits himself to the service of the Lord, Krishna accepts him to be as good as Himself. When the devotee's body is thus transformed into ecstatic spiritual existence, he is able to render service to the lotus feet of the Lord... Krishna produced scabies on Sanatan's body and sent him here to test Me. Had I refused to embrace him out of disgust, I would certainly have committed an offense to Krishna Himself. This is the body of an associate of Krishna. It has no foul odor coming from it. On the first day that I embraced him, I smelled the aroma of catuḥsama (a mixture of sandalwood pulp, camphor, aguru and musk)."
>
> (Chaitanya Charitamrita 3.4.191-7)

This time, when the Lord embraced Sanatan, the foul itches which covered his body immediately disappeared and his skin took on an effulgent golden glow.

Jagadananda and Sanatan in Vraja

Sanatan stayed a full year in Puri, after which Mahaprabhu told him to return to Vrindavan. He bid the Lord goodbye after the Dola Yatra and set off on the jungle path through Jharikhanda. Rupa Goswami joined Him in Vrindavan not long afterward. When Raghunath Bhatta Goswami came to Vrindavan on Mahaprabhu's order, he stayed with Rupa and Sanatan and daily recited the Bhagavatam for them in a sweet voice.

Some time later, Jagadananda Pandit took permission from Mahaprabhu to come to Vrindavan. When he came there, he met Sanatan who was overjoyed to see him. The two of them went together on a tour of the twelve forests of Vraja. Sanatan encouraged Jagadananda to stay with him in Gokula where he was settled at that time. Even though they dwelt together, they ate separately. Srila Bhaktivinode Thakur writes in his *Amṛta-pravāha-bhāṣya*, "Sanatan had become habituated to the *madhukarī* system and lived on a few pieces of bread each day. Jagadananda, however, could not live without eating rice, and so he went every day to a nearby temple to cook. In those days, rice and dahl were not regularly offered to the deities in the temples of Vraja."

One day, Jagadananda invited Sanatan to eat with him. Sanatan desired to show the world the extent of Jagadananda's devotion to Mahaprabhu so when he came to eat Jagadananda's offering, he wore around his head a saffron cloth that had been given to him by a certain Mukunda Saraswati. When Jagadananda learned that the cloth was not a gift from Mahaprabhu, he was so angry with Sanatan that he took the pot in which the rice had been cooking and threatened to hit him with it. He said,

> "You are Mahaprabhu's most important associate. No one is dearer to Him than you. How could anyone tolerate you wearing another sannyasi's cloth around your head?"
>
> (Chaitanya Charitamrita 3.13.56-7)

Sanatan answered by praising Jagadananda's exclusive dedication to Gauranga Mahaprabhu:

> "Well said! It is clear, Pandit Mahashaya, that you are unequalled in your love for the Lord. Only from you could I have learned this lesson, for you alone have such solid faith in the Lord. My purpose in binding the cloth around my head has been fulfilled, for as soon as you saw it, I was able to witness the manifestations of your love for the Lord. A Vaishnava should not wear a red-colored cloth. I will give it to someone else, for I have no further need for it."
>
> (Chaitanya Charitamrita 3.13.56-61)

Jagadananda stayed in Vraja for two months, after which he was no longer able to tolerate being separated from Mahaprabhu. He took leave of Sanatan and headed off in the direction of Jagannath Puri. As they bid each other goodbye, Sanatan gave him sand from the place where Krishna held the Rasa dance, a stone from Govardhan, a garland of gunja berries and some dried ripe pilu fruits as gifts for Mahaprabhu. Jagadananda gave all these gifts to Mahaprabhu upon his arrival in Puri; He and

His devotees especially enjoyed the pilu fruits.

SANATAN'S SERVICE TO THE LORD

Mahaprabhu gave Sanatan four responsibilities: (1) to preach pure devotional service by establishing the doctrines of pure devotion; (2) to discover and make known the various places where Krishna had His pastimes; (3) to establish the service of the deity of Krishna in Vrindavan; and (4), to establish proper Vaishnava behavior through compiling a Vaishnava rule book or Smriti, and in this way create the foundations of a Vaishnava society.

"O Sanatan, you should broadcast the revealed scriptures on devotional service and excavate the lost places of pilgrimage in the district of Mathura. Establish the deity service of Lord Krishna in Vrindavan. You should also compile a scripture containing the rules of devotional practice and preach these practices."
(Chaitanya Charitamrita 2.23.97-8)

In following the instructions to broadcast the revealed scriptures on pure devotional service and to establish the foundations of proper Vaishnava practice and etiquette, Sanatan wrote four books, all of which are considered to be jewels by the devotees. He wrote (1) a commentary on the *Hari-bhakti-vilāsa* known as *Dig-darśanī*, (2) a commentary on the tenth canto of the Srimad Bhagavatam known as the *Bṛhad-Vaiṣṇava-Toṣaṇī*, (3) *Līlā-stava* or *Daśama-carita,* and (4) *Bṛhad-Bhāgavatāmṛta*, to which he added a commentary. Mahaprabhu Himself personally gave directions to Sanatan about the contents of the *Hari-bhakti-vilāsa*, which is the Smriti scripture, or rulebook for the external practices to be followed by the devotees.

Sanatan spent a great deal of time searching out the various holy spots in the land of Vraja. He also established the service of the Madana Mohan deity. Srila Sanatan Goswami founded a Math in Vrindavan at the place known as Dvadasaditya Tila. He first had a temple built there for Radha Madana Mohan. It is said that a rich officer in the Sultan's army named Krishna Das Kapoor built the temple and a kitchen. He also financed an opulent standard of worship for the deity. Later he became Sanatan Goswami's disciple.

When Sanatan Goswami was staying in Gokula Mahavan, he saw Madana Gopal playing with a group of cowherd boys at Raman Reti. Narahari Chakravarti has given a beautiful description of this vision in his *Bhakti-ratnākara* :

O Srinivas, just look at this place. Sanatan Goswami used to live here. All the fortunate residents of Mahavan would be revitalized by seeing him. He lived in Mahavan joyously, looking upon his Madana Gopal deity. Madana Gopal enjoyed playing on the sandy beaches that line the Yamuna, known as Raman Reti. One day he came to that divine riverbank with the children of Mahavan, himself taking the form of a cowherd boy. Sanatan watched him as he played various childhood games with the other children and thought, "This is no ordinary child." When the children had finished playing and were leaving, Sanatan followed them. The child entered into the temple and when Sanatan followed Him inside, he saw no one but the deity of Madana Mohan. He paid his obeisances to the deity and then returned to his own dwelling without saying anything to anyone. So this is how Madana Mohan showed Himself to be under the control of Sanatan's love. Sanatan's wondrous character has thus filled the three worlds.
(*Bhakti-ratnākara* 5.1777-1786)

SANATAN'S GLORIOUS PASTIMES IN VRAJA

In his Chaitanya Charitamrita, Krishna Das Kaviraj Goswami has described how Rupa and Sanatan Goswami worshiped Krishna in the land of Vraja:

These brothers have no fixed residence. They spend each night beneath a different tree in the forest, one night under one tree and the next under another. Sometimes, they begged dry food from a Brahmin's house and other times it would be cooked, such as dry bread and fried chickpeas. This is how they have given up all kinds of material enjoyments. They wrap themselves in a quilt and wear nothing but a piece of torn cloth, claiming nothing but a waterpot as a possession. They engage almost twenty-four hours daily in rendering service to the Lord by chanting his holy names, discussing his pastimes, or dancing in great jubilation. They spend only an hour and a half in sleep, and some days, when overcome by the love of chanting the Lord's holy name, they do not sleep at all. Sometimes they write transcendental works about divine aesthetics, and sometimes they listen to talks about Sri Chaitanya Mahaprabhu or spend their time thinking about the Lord. (Chaitanya Charitamrita 2.19.127-31)

Sanatan Goswami had another vision of the Lord later in his life. While staying at Chakra Tirtha near Govardhan, he would regularly circumambulate the mountain. As he grew older, he became too weak to walk these 14 miles on a daily basis without becoming excessively fatigued. One day, Gopinath Himself came in the form of a cowherd boy to fan him when he became too tired from walking. After refreshing Sanatan in this way, the boy climbed onto the hill and brought down a stone marked with Krishna's footprint. He gave the stone to Sanatan and said, "You have grown old. There is no longer any need for you to trouble yourself to such an extent. I am giving you this stone from Govardhan. If you circumambulate this stone, you can consider yourself to have circumambulated Govardhan itself." Then he disappeared. Sanatan was overwhelmed with pain and began to cry upon losing sight of the cowherd boy's charming form. (*Bhakti-ratnākara* 5.728-741).

Chakra Tirtha is on the northern shore of Manasi Ganga. A temple dedicated to Chakresvara Shiva, or as he is popularly known, Chaklesvara Mahadeva, stands on the bank. Sanatan's bhajan kutir was under a neem tree that stood in front of this temple. Just north of this place is another temple housing Gaura-Nityananda. Sanatan

Prabhu's Govardhan Shila is currently kept in the Radha-Damodar temple at Radha Kund.

There are more stories about the glories of Chakra Tirtha. When Sanatan first came to this place, there were so many mosquitoes that he was unable to concentrate while meditating on the Holy Name or writing transcendental literature, so much so that he decided to move. That night, Chakresvara appeared to Sanatan in a dream and told him not to worry about the problem; He would be able to engage in his worship without disturbance. From that night on, there have been no mosquitoes at Chakra Tirtha.

Srila Sanatan Goswami also spent some time living in a cottage on the banks of Pavana Sarovar near Nandagram. Here also he was granted a vision of Krishna as a cowherd boy, who gave him milk and told him to build a hut and engage in His worship there. One day, Rupa invited Sanatan to come and eat with him. For this occasion, he wished to prepare sweet rice, but he did not have the necessary ingredients. Srimati Radharani took the form of a young cowherd girl and came to Rupa with milk, sugar, rice and ghee, in short, giving him everything he needed to make the preparation for Sanatan's pleasure. Rupa Goswami cooked the sweet rice and after offering it to the deity, gave the prasad to Sanatan.

Sanatan found that after relishing the delicious sweet rice, he was overcome by uncontrollable waves of ecstasy. Suspecting that something unusual had taken place, he asked Rupa where the ingredients had come from. When Rupa told him about the little cowherd girl, Sanatan immediately realized that it had been Radha. Because Radha was their Goddess and they were Her servants, the proper relation of served and servant had been reversed. He therefore strictly forbade Rupa from accepting such gifts in the future.

(*Bhakti-ratnākara* 5.1311-30)

Another anecdote told about Sanatan is the following. Once there was a very poor devotee of Shiva, whose name, according to the *Bhakta-māla* and *Gauḍīya Vaiṣṇava Abhidhāna*, was Sri Jivana Chakravarti. Originally from the village of Mankar in Burdwan district in Bengal, he had spent many years worshiping Shiva in Benares, praying to him for wealth. Finally, one night Shiva appeared to him in a dream and told him to go to Sanatan in Vrindavan, for he was in possession of a great wealth he would share with him.

The poor Brahmin immediately set off for Vrindavan where he found Sanatan deep in meditation. However, when he saw the Goswami, thin and dressed in a dirty loincloth, he began to doubt that he could give him the desired riches. Even so, he told Sanatan about the dream. Sanatan heard the Brahmin and came back to external consciousness. He answered, saying that he lived by begging a few crumbs from a number of different houses, so how could he possibly give him the riches he desired?

The poor Brahmin was disappointed and turned away, thinking that perhaps the message Lord Shiva had given him in the dream had been just an illusion. Meanwhile, Sanatan pondered why Shiva had sent the Brahmin to him. As he ruminated, he remembered a philosopher's stone that was lying in a pile of rubbish and had long since been covered in dust. As soon as he remembered the existence of this valuable jewel, he sent someone to fetch the Brahmin and told him to take the jewel from the rubbish heap. When the Brahmin saw the stone, he was overjoyed and thought, "Now I will be the richest person in the entire world!" After walking some distance away, however, he began to wonder why Sanatan had completely forgotten about such a valuable possession. Indeed, if he cared so little for the philosopher's stone he must have had something even more valuable. Perhaps he had been cheated! He wanted to know what riches Sanatan possessed that he cared so little for the valuable stone.

The Brahmin quickly ran back to Sanatan and expressed his doubts, asking him if he had anything more valuable in his possession. Then Sanatan told him that there was no greater wealth than love for Krishna and that material goods were insignificant and simply a cause of greater distress. The Brahmin then bowed his head and prayed to Sanatan to please give him the wealth that made him consider even a philosopher's stone insignificant. Sanatan was moved by his prayer and mercifully bestowed upon him the wealth of Krishna prema.

Sanatan Goswami's samadhi tomb is found next to the old Radha Madana Mohan temple in Vrindavan. He left this world on the full moon day of Asharh in the Śaka year 1480 (1558 AD).

Sri Raghunath Bhatta Goswami

raghunāthākhyako bhaṭṭaḥ
purā yā rāga-mañjarī
kṛta-śrī-rādhikā-kuṇḍa-
kuṭīra-vasatiḥ sa tu

In Krishna lila, Raghunath Bhatta, who made his home in a cottage by Radha Kund, was Raga Manjari.

(*Gaura-gaṇoddeśa-dīpikā* 185)

SERVING THE LORD IN BENARES

In around 1503 AD, Raghunath Bhattacharya appeared in this world as the son of Tapan Mishra, a dear devotee of Sri Chaitanya Mahaprabhu who hailed from the village of Rampur on the banks of the Padma River in East Bengal. Mahaprabhu first met Tapan Mishra when he went to East Bengal during his career as a teacher of Sanskrit. Tapan Mishra had studied many scriptures but was still bewildered about the purpose of life and how to attain it. Then one day, he had a dream in which he was instructed by a Brahmin to go to Nimai Pandit who would clarify these matters for him. When Tapan Mishra went to the Lord and told Him of his dream, Nimai answered that Harinam sankirtan was both the purpose of life and the means for attaining it. Tapan Mishra expressed his desire to come and live in Nabadwip near the Lord, but Mahaprabhu told him to go to Benares instead, assuring him that He would see him there one day. Thus, several years later, when passing through Benares on his way back from Vrindavan, Mahaprabhu stayed at Chandrasekhara Vaidya's house and took his meals with Tapan Mishra.

The Lord had three devotees in Benares. One was Chandrasekhara Vaidya, another Tapan Mishra. The third was Tapan Mishra's son Raghunath Bhattacharya. The Lord met with them when He stopped in Kashi after visiting Vrindavan. (Chaitanya Charitamrita 1.11.152-3)

Sri Raghunath Bhatta Goswami lived at home for about 28 years. During the two months that the Lord spent in Benares, Raghunath had many opportunities to personally serve Him and to receive His mercy.

Mahaprabhu stayed in the house of Chandrasekhara for two months' time, daily taking His meals at Tapan Mishra's residence. Raghunath was just a boy at the time, but he served the Lord by cleaning His place after He ate and by massaging His feet. When he grew up, he went to Puri to see the Lord. He stayed there for eight months, occasionally cooking for the Lord. (Chaitanya Charitamrita 1.11.154-6)

RAGHUNATH COMES TO PURI

Out of eagerness to see the Lord, Raghunath Bhatta hurried to Puri after visiting Bengal. He was accompanied by a servant who carried his baggage for him. While travelling, he met a certain Rama Das Bishwas, a devotee of Lord Rama initiated in the Ramanandi disciplic succession and very learned in Sanskrit poetics and other scriptures. He was a well-to-do member of the Kayastha caste who was trusted by the Shah and had been given an important position in the government treasury. Rama Das was travelling to Puri as he wanted to renounce his material entanglements and visit Jagannath Deva. He was constantly chanting the Rama mantra. Knowing Raghunath to be a Brahmin, he took many pains to render service to him, sometimes massaging his feet and sometimes carrying his baggage on his head. Raghunath was somewhat embarrassed that such a rich and important man should render him such menial service, but Rama Das tried to allay his doubts by saying, "I am a lowly Shudra and you are a Brahmin. It is my duty to serve you. I feel the greatest joy in taking this opportunity to serve you."

When Raghunath arrived in Puri, he prostrated himself on the ground before the feet of the Lord. The Lord recognized Raghunath and lifted him up with great emotion and embraced him. He asked for news of Tapan Mishra and Candrasekhara Vaidya, then sent him to see Jagannath, telling him to come and eat with Him afterward. Mahaprabhu had Govinda make housing arrangements for Raghunath and introduced him to Svarupa Damodar and His other associates.

During the eight months that Sri Raghunath Bhatta Goswami remained in Nilachal, he sometimes had the chance to invite Mahaprabhu for meals. He would take the opportunity to prepare delicious vegetable platters for the Lord's pleasure. He was an expert cook and the Lord was especially satisfied by the devotional mood in which he prepared these meals. Raghunath was then fortunate enough to be able to take the Lord's remnants. Rama Das Bishwas also came to meet Mahaprabhu during this time, but the Lord could see through him. He saw that Rama Das harbored desires for liberation and that he was proud of his learning, and so He did not show him as much mercy as He did to Raghunath.

After Raghunath had been in Puri for eight months, the Lord told him to go back to Kashi to serve his Vaishnava parents, who were now aged and infirm. He also told him not to get married. The Lord then made him a gift of His own neckbeads, which He placed around Raghunath's neck, telling him to come to Puri again.

RAGHUNATH GOES TO VRINDAVAN

Raghunath took care of his parents for the remainder of their lives, which was another four years. During this time, he also studied the Bhagavata from a Vaishnava. Raghunath had a beautiful singing voice. When he recited the Bhagavata, he would read the same verse aloud over and over again, chanting each time in a different tune. This made his readings very attractive to the devotees.

When his parents died, he returned to Puri and stayed with Mahaprabhu. After remaining with the Lord for eight months, Mahaprabhu told him to go to Vrindavan and to stay with Rupa and Sanatan. He told him to continue studying and giving discourses on the Bhagavata, as well as to chant the Holy Names. The Lord then gave him a ten-foot long tulasi garland that had been worn by Lord Jagannath as well as some pan that had none of the intoxicating spices in it. Raghunath was intoxicated with love upon receiving all this kindness from the Lord. Krishna

Das describes Raghunath's voyage to Vrindavan and his life there in the Chaitanya Charitamrita:

"Recite the Srimad Bhagavatam and chant the names of Krishna continuously. The Supreme Lord Krishna will very soon bestow His mercy upon you." After saying this, the Lord embraced Raghunath who became enlivened with ecstatic love for Krishna by His mercy. At a feast, the Lord had been given some unspiced betel and a ten-foot long garland of tulasi leaves which had been worn by Lord Jagannath. He gave the garland and betel to Raghunath Bhatta, who accepted them as his worshipable deities, taking care to preserve them. Then Raghunath took the Lord's permission and departed for Vrindavan.

When he arrived in the Dham, he put himself under the care of Rupa and Sanatan Goswamis. Whenever he recited the Bhagavata before Rupa and Sanatan, Raghunath Bhatta would be overwhelmed with ecstatic love for Krishna. By Mahaprabhu's mercy, he experienced the symptoms of ecstatic love—tears, trembling, and faltering of the voice. His eyes filled with tears and his throat became so choked that he would have to stop his recital.

Raghunath's voice was as sweet as a cuckoo's, and he would recite each verse of the Bhagavata in three or four different tunes. Whenever he recited or heard about Krishna's beauty and sweetness, he would be overwhelmed with ecstatic love and become oblivious to the world around him.

Raghunath Bhatta surrendered himself to Govinda's lotus feet and those lotus feet were the only thing that gave his life meaning. In time, Raghunath Bhatta ordered his disciples to construct a temple for Govinda. He himself made various ornaments for the deity, including a flute and dolphin-shaped earrings.

Raghunath Bhatta would never speak or listen to gossip. He would simply discuss about Krishna and worship Him day and night. He wouldn't listen to criticism of a Vaishnava's misbehavior. He knew only that everyone was engaged in Krishna's service. When Raghunath Bhatta Goswami was absorbed in remembrance of Lord Krishna, he would take the prasadi tulasi garland and neckbeads given him by the Lord, and wear them around his neck. Thus I have described the power of Sri Chaitanya Mahaprabhu's mercy by which Raghunath Bhatta Goswami experienced unlimited ecstatic love for Krishna."

(Chaitanya Charitamrita 3.13.121-135)

A further description of Sri Raghunath Bhatta Goswami is also given in *Bhakti-ratnākara* :

"As I look upon the samadhi tomb of Raghunath Bhatta, my heart breaks and my eyes are awash with tears. But who is not overjoyed as soon as he hears Raghunath Bhatta Goswami's glories? He was such an expert teacher of all the scriptures that even Brihaspati would cheer joyfully upon hearing Raghunath's explanations of Vaishnava doctrine. There is nothing to which his discourses on the Bhagavata can be compared. Even Vyasa himself wishes to sit and listen to him speak, knowing that this will bring him happiness. Even the gods were astonished when they observed Raghunath Bhatta's devotional practices." When Srinivas Acharya and the devotees heard Sri Raghunath Bhatta Goswami glorified in this way, they fell to the ground and offered their respects. Then they continued on to the Govindaji temple.

Sri Raghunath Bhatta Goswami disappeared in either 1579 or 1580 AD.

Srila Gopal Bhatta Goswami

anaṅga-mañjarī yāsīt
sādya gopāla-bhaṭṭakaḥ
bhaṭṭa-gosvāminaṁ kecid
āhuḥ śrī-guṇa-mañjarī

She who was formerly Ananga Manjari has appeared to enrich Mahaprabhu's pastimes as Srila Gopal Bhatta Goswami. Some say that Gopal Bhatta is actually Guna Manjari. (*Gaura-gaṇoddeśa-dīpikā* 184)

Srila Gopal Bhatta Goswami appeared in 1500 AD (though, according to some authorities, he was born in 1503) as the son of Venkata Bhatta in the town of Srirangam in South India.[21] Their residence was in a village not far from Srirangam called Belgundi.

According to Narahari in the *Bhakti-ratnākara*, Mahaprabhu gave Gopal Bhatta a dream vision through which he could witness all of His Nabadwip pastimes. Though Gopal was an eternal associate of Krishna, he appeared in a faraway place in order to make a special contribution to Lord Gauranga's pastimes. Thus even though he was living too far away to know anything about the Lord directly, he was still able to know long before he met the Lord in person that He had appeared and taken sannyas.

As a member of His Vrindavan entourage, Gopal Bhatta did not particularly like the Lord's appearance as a sannyasi. This austere form distressed Gopal, who was thus crying alone when the Lord appeared to him and gave him this vision of His form as a householder in Nabadwip. Gopal was overwhelmed with astonishment at seeing the Lord's beauty and he fell down at His feet. When he looked up, the Lord had transformed into His sannyasi form again. Calming Gopal, He gave him some instructions and then foretold that he would go to Vrindavan before long and there make disciples who would spread his teachings throughout the world.

The Lord then embraced Gopal and drenched him in His tears. He then told Gopal to keep all these revelations a secret. He then disappeared, leaving Gopal in a state of intense joy. (*Bhakti-ratnākara* 1.123-4)

THE LORD'S TEACHINGS TO GOPAL'S FATHER

Not long thereafter, in 1510, Mahaprabhu made His auspicious entrance to the pilgrimage city of Srirangam. He was invited by Venkata Bhatta, a Vaishnava of the Sri Sampradaya, to spend the four months of the Chaturmasya in his house. Knowing him to be a strict Vaishnava, Mahaprabhu accepted his invitation. In fact, the Lord's pastime of coming to Srirangam and staying at Venkata Bhatta's home was to give His mercy to Gopal Bhatta and his family, for the Lord knew that Gopal, his eternal com panion, had appeared there.

At this time, Gopal Bhatta was still a young boy. He was fortunate enough to be able to serve the Lord by massaging his feet. Even though he was satisfied with Venkata Bhatta and his family's service, the Lord observed that Venkata had an element of pride in his object of worship. He believed that his worshipable deity, Lakshmi-Narayan, was the supreme worshipable object and that Narayan was the source of all other incarnations, including Krishna, Rama and Nrisingha. His reasoning was that Narayan is never born, he is aja, while Krishna and Rama take birth in the world. He thus thought, "Mahaprabhu worships Krishna, the incarnation of Narayan, while we worship Narayan, the source of all incarnations."

As Madhusudan is the destroyer of false pride, Mahaprabhu finally decided one day that He would do so for Venkata. He asked him in a mild-humoured, witty tone, "Venkata, I hear that no one is equal in opulence to your Lord Narayan; the same is true for your worshipable Goddess Lakshmi Devi. On the other hand, the object of My worship, Krishna, has no opulences of any kind. He wears garlands of wild forest flowers and uses peacock feathers for decoration. He is the son of Nanda Gopa, and spends His day grazing the cows with the other cowherd boys. My worshipable goddesses, the gopis, are also nothing but poor cowherd girls. I wonder, therefore, why your worshipable Lakshmi Devi came to Vrindavan to perform austerities in the hope of gaining Krishna's company in the Rasa dance."

Venkata immediately answered, "What's wrong with that? Radha's beloved Krishna is non-different from Lakshmi Devi's husband Narayan."

siddhāntatas tv abhede 'pi
śrīśa-kṛṣṇa-svarupayoḥ
rasenotkṛṣyate kṛṣṇaḥ
kṛṣṇa-rūpam eṣā rasa-sthitiḥ

"Though according to theological doctrine, Krishna and the husband of Lakshmi are identical in essence, the form of Krishna is superior when analyzed from the point of view of divine sentiment. This is the conclusion based on the analysis of divine sentiment. (BRS 1.2.59)

"Since the divine sentiment in Krishna is superior, there is no fault if Lakshmi Devi chooses to seek His association and performs austerities to that end."

Mahaprabhu answered, "I am not saying that there is any fault. I agree that from the transcendental point of view, Krishna and Narayan are identical. The difference between them is based on the variety of rasa (transcendental taste or mood). When the Lord performs pastimes of opulence, He is Narayan. When He performs pastimes of sweetness, He is Krishna. She who is Radha in Krishna's pastimes is Lakshmi in the pastimes of Narayan. Thus, when Lakshmi performs austerities to have the association of Krishna there is no question of Her breaking Her vows of fidelity to Her husband. Thus, She went to perform these austerities in Vrindavan. But I have another question for you: Why, even after trying so hard through such penances, etc., to enter Krishna's rasa lila, was Lakshmi still unable to do so?"

Venkata Bhatta was terribly distressed at being unable to give the Lord an answer. Mahaprabhu observed his distress and tried to pacify him by saying, "You yourself said that Narayan and Krishna are identical from the theological point of view, but that the superiority of Krishna is determined by an analysis of the divine sentiments. Narayan is involved in two and a half of the five principle rasas, whereas Krishna is experienced through the complete manifestation of all twelve rasas, the five principle and seven secondary sentiments. Since Narayan's lila is primarily one of opulence and majesty, His principle devotee is Lakshmi, who also worships Him in the appropriate mood of awe and reverence. The same Lakshmi Devi is Radhika in order to heighten the experience of romantic love. Unless one follows in the footsteps of Radha and Her expansions, the gopis, who are the repositories of the erotic sentiment, then it is impossible to relish Krishna's sweet qualities, such as those virtues which are particularly inspiring for the romantic mood of love. The reason for Lakshmi Devi's failure is that She did not follow in the gopis' footsteps, but continued to perform Her austerities in the mood of awe and reverence. As a result, She repeatedly found Herself in the company of Narayan and never in that of Krishna. By way of contrast, the Srutis followed the gopis in the *rāga-mārga* and so were ultimately able to achieve Krishna's service in the erotic mood. As long as one continues to think of Krishna in majestic terms as lord and creator of the universe, one cannot possibly worship in the spirit of *rāgānugā bhakti*.

"Krishna has one extraordinary characteristic: by His sweetness He attracts the minds of the entire world. By taking on the mood of the Vraja gopis one can attain to His lotus feet—the people of Vraja have no idea that Krishna is the lord and creator of the universe. Some think of Him as their son and even tie Him to a mortar, while others take Him to be their friend and climb on His shoulders. The people of Vraja only know Him as the son of Nanda, whereas in the attitude of awe and reverence, the devotee does not have a concept of such a relationship to Him. One who takes the attitude of a resident of Vraja will attain Krishna as the son of the king of Vraja in Vrindavan.

(Chaitanya Charitamrita 2.9.127-31)

"When the gopis, the objects of my worship, were abandoned by Krishna in the Rasa dance they began to cry in the intensity of their distress at not seeing Him. Krishna came to them in the form of Narayan, but the gopis simply paid their obeisances and moved on in search of Krishna, showing absolutely no interest in Him as a lover. When Radharani stood before the disguised Krishna, however, He could not maintain the four-armed form but once again appeared in His form as the holder of the flute. Such is the power of Radharani's love!"[22]

(Bhakti Ratnakara 5.624-629)

"Nandanandan Krishna is the *avatārī*, or source of all incarnations. Narayan, Rama, Nrisingha, etc., are all His incarnations and expansions. Krishna is *svayaṁ bhagavān*, the Supreme Personality of Godhead.

"As He is the Supreme Personality of Godhead, His other divine forms are also given the appellation of *bhagavān*. He alone however can be called the *svayaṁ bhagavān*, or primeval supreme lord.

(Chaitanya Charitamrita 1.2.88)

ete cāṁśakalāḥ puṁsaḥ
kṛṣṇas tu bhagavān svayam
indrāri-vyākulaṁ lokaṁ
mṛḍayanti yuge yuge

All of the previously mentioned forms of the Lord are either plenary or partial expansions. Krishna alone is the original personality of the Godhead. He and His expansions appear in every age to bring joy to this world when tormented by the enemies of the gods.

(Srimad Bhagavatam 1.3.28)

GOPAL'S GURU

Through the power of Sri Krishna Chaitanya Mahaprabhu's merciful association, Venkata Bhatta, his brother Prabodhananda Saraswati, his son Gopal Bhatta Goswami, and all the other members of his family, were inspired to give up the worship of Lakshmi-Narayan and became engaged in the exclusive devotional service of Radha and Krishna. Srila Gopal Bhatta Goswami took initiation from his uncle, Tridandi Yati Srimat Prabodhananda Saraswati. Proof of this is found in the *Hari-bhakti-vilāsa*:

bhakter vilāsāṁś cinute prabodhā-
nandasya śiṣyo bhagavat-priyasya
gopāla-bhaṭṭo raghunātha-dāsaṁ
santoṣayan rūpa-sanātanau ca

Gopal Bhatta, the disciple of Prabodhananda who is dear to the Lord, has collected these devotional activities to satisfy Raghunath Das, Rupa and Sanatan Goswamis.

(Hari Bhakti Vilasa 1.2)

Gopal's parents were very fortunate, for they surrendered themselves, life and soul, to the feet of Lord Chaitanya. They ordered their son to go to Vrindavan before they left this world, absorbed in meditating on the Lord. Gopal travelled directly to Vrindavan where he met with Rupa and Sanatan. (*Bhakti-ratnākara* 1.163-5)

GOPAL BHATTA COMES TO VRINDAVAN

When Gopal arrived in Vrindavan, Rupa and Sanatan wrote to Mahaprabhu to tell him. The Lord was overjoyed and immediately wrote back telling them to affectionately take care of him as though he were their own younger brother. Srila Sanatan Goswami compiled the *Hari-bhakti-vilāsa* and published it in Srila Gopal Bhatta Goswami's name. Rupa Goswami considered Gopal to be as dear to him as his own life and engaged him in the deity worship of Radha Raman.

Srila Gopal Bhatta Goswami became one of the six Goswamis, but he always kept an attitude of meekness and humility. Thus, when Krishna Das Kaviraj approached him for permission to write the Chaitanya Charitamrita, he granted it, but under the condition that he not write about him. Krishna Das Kaviraj Goswami could not go against the order of Gopal Bhatta and thus did nothing more than mention his name. Sri Jiva Goswami writes in the introduction to the *Ṣaṭ-sandarbha* that he wrote it on the basis of an earlier text by Gopal Bhatta. Srila Gopal Bhatta Goswami also wrote a book called the *Sat-kriyā-sāra-dīpikā* ("Light on the essential sacraments for the Vaishnavas"). Thus his contribution to Gaudiya Vaishnava literature was in editing the *Hari-bhakti-vilāsa*, preparing the notes for Jiva's *Ṣaṭ-sandarbha* and in compiling the *Sat-kriyā-sāra-dīpikā*. He also gave great joy to the community of devotees by writing a commentary on Bilvamangala's *Kṛṣṇa-karṇāmṛta*.

Amongst his disciples were Srinivas Acharya and Sri Gopinath Pujari. The following story is told about Gopinath Pujari becoming Gopal Bhatta's disciple. One day, Gopal Bhatta went to visit the town of Saharanpur, not far from Hardwar. On that occasion, a simple, devoted Brahmin engaged in his service in a most unpretentious manner. He had no children, but desired to have a son. Srila Gopal Bhatta Goswami knew the desire of the Brahmin and blessed him that he would have a devotionally-minded male child. The Brahmin promised Gopal Bhatta that he would give him his first son to be his servant and disciple. This son was Gopinath Pujari.

It is said that Mahaprabhu had such affection for Gopal Bhatta that he sent him his own belt and kaupin as well as a wooden seat he had used. These items are still worshiped in the Radha Raman temple by the current sevakas.

SRI SRI RADHA RAMAN

When Srila Gopal Bhatta Goswami was visiting the pilgrimage centres of northern India, he found a Shalagram Sila on the banks of the Gandaki River. He took the worshipable stone form and carried it with him wherever he went, attending to it as Vrajendranandan Krishna Himself. One day he thought that he would like to worship the Lord in a deity form so that he could expand his service. On the very next day, he found that the Shalagram Sila had transformed itself into Radha Raman to fulfill the wish of his devotee. This deity stands alone without any form of Radha standing by His side. Instead, as a symbol of Radharani, a silver crown is placed on his left side.

The story is also told in the following way. It is said that Srila Gopal Bhatta Goswami used to daily worship twelve Shalagrams. He developed a desire to serve the Lord in the form of a deity, thinking that in this way he would be able to worship him in a much better way. The Lord within his heart knew his feelings. Through a rich merchant, he was provided with many beautiful items used in the worship of the deity, such as ornaments and clothes, sent to him. Gopal began to worry that all these beautiful objects would be wasted because there was no way that he could use them unless he had a deity in human form. That night, he put the Shalagrams to rest and in the morning he saw that one of them had been transformed into the Radha Raman deity.

When Rupa and Sanatan heard that Krishna had so mercifully appeared to Gopal Bhatta, they immediately came with the other devotees for darshan, and when they saw him, they were ecstatic with love. The annual festival commemorating Radha Raman's appearance, when He is bathed publicly, takes place on the full moon day of Vaishakh. The Radha Raman temple is considered one of the most important in Vrindavan.

Srila Gopal Bhatta Goswami ended his earthly pastimes on the *kṛṣṇā pañcamī* of Asharh of 1507 of the Śaka era (1585 AD). His samadhi temple is behind the current Radha Raman temple. By reading Srinivas Acharya's hymn to the six Goswamis, *Ṣaḍ-gosvāmy-aṣṭaka*, we can understand their glories.

---

[21] Srirangam is situated on the Kaveri River near Trichinopoly. It is about ten miles from Kumbhakonam in the Tanjor district of Tamil Nadu. The temple of Sri Ranganath is the largest temple in India.

[22] The place where this happened is near Govardhan and is called Paitha Dham or Paisa Dham, which means "the place of entering" because Krishna's two extra arms merged back into his body here.

❁ Srila ❁ Prabodhananda Saraswati

tuṅgavidyā vraje yāsīt
sarva-śāstra-viśāradā
sā prabodhānanda-yatir
gaurodgāna-sarasvatī

The gopi Tungavidya, who was most learned in all the scriptures, has today become the sannyasi Prabodhananda, whose words are all used in the glorification of Lord Gauranga. (*Gaura-gaṇoddeśa-dīpikā* 163)

Venkata Bhatta lived in South India. He held a special position amongst the Brahmins as he was very learned in all the scriptures.

There was a Vaishnava of the Sri Sampradaya named Venkata Bhatta who respectfully invited the Lord to his house. (Chaitanya Charitamrita 2.9.82)

In his commentary to this verse of the Chaitanya Charitamrita, Srila Bhaktivinode Thakur has written: "Venkata Bhatta, Trimalla Bhatta and Prabodhananda Saraswati were previously acharyas of the Sri Sampradaya. Gopal Bhatta Goswami was the son of Venkata Bhatta."

Srila Bhaktisiddhanta Saraswati Goswami Thakur has also commented on the same verse: "Sri Venkata Bhatta was a Brahmin of the Sri Sampradaya who lived in Srirangam. Srirangam is situated in Tamil Nadu, where people do not use the names Venkata and Tirumalai (the name of Venkata's brother), so it is likely they came from elsewhere. This family had possibly moved to Srirangam not long before Mahaprabhu's visit there. Venkata Bhatta belonged to the Varagalai branch of the Ramanuja sampradaya. One of his brothers was the tridandi sannyasi, Prabodhananda, who acted as an acharya of the school. Venkata Bhatta's son was Gopal Bhatta Goswami."

These three brothers were originally worshipers of Lakshmi-Narayan, but were later converted to the worship of Radha and Krishna by the grace of Sri Chaitanya Mahaprabhu. Krishna Das Kaviraj Goswami has described this conversion in his Chaitanya Charitamrita.

Srila Prabodhananda Saraswati's disciple was his own nephew, Gopal Bhatta, one of the six Goswamis.

bhakter vilāsāṁś cinute prabodhā-
nandasya śiṣyo bhagavat-priyasya
gopāla-bhaṭṭo raghunātha-dāsaṁ
santoṣayan rūpa-sanātanau ca

Gopal Bhatta, the disciple of Prabodhananda who is dear to the Lord, has compiled these devotional activities to satisfy Raghunath Das, Rupa and Sanatan Goswamis. (Hari Bhakti Vilasa 1.2)

Srila Prabodhananda Saraswati wrote a number of books, including *Vṛndāvana-śataka*, *Navadvīpa-śataka*, *Rādhā-rasa-sudhā-nidhi* and *Caitanya-candrāmṛta*, which are especially loved by rasika devotees. Some of his other works are *Saṅgīta-mādhava*, *Āścarya-rasa-prabandha*, *Śruti-stuti-vyākhyā*, *Gīta-govinda-vyākhyāna* and *Kāma-bīja-kāma-gāyatrī-vyākhyāna*.

IS PRABODHANANDA PRAKASHANANDA?

In the third chapter of the *Madhya-khaṇḍa* of the Chaitanya Bhagavata, Srila Bhaktisiddhanta Saraswati Goswami Prabhupada makes the following observation: "Prakashananda was a teacher of the Mayavada doctrine and a sannyasi. During his discourses on the Veda, he would cut the Lord's divine and transcendental body into pieces. Some simplistic people say that this Prakashananda is the very same person as Venkata Bhatta's younger brother Prabodhananda, who lived on the banks of the Kaveri. This erroroneous belief has found its way into the Sahajiya text *Bhakta-māla* and even into the writings of many modern scholars." (*Gauḍīya-bhāṣya, Madhya-khaṇḍa*, 3.37)

The observations made here by Saraswati Thakur are quite true. In his dictionary, Ashutosh Deb states, "Prabodhananda was a Vaishnava philosopher, whose real name was Prakashananda Saraswati. Chaitanya Deva gave him the name Prabodhananda."

Furthermore, Haridas Das has also written in his *Gauḍīya Vaiṣṇava Abhidhāna*: "Some people hold that Prabodhananda is the Vaishnava name given to Prakashananda... It is quite clear from the last verse of the *Rādhā-rasa-sudhā-nidhi* that Prabodhananda had at one time been a Mayavadi sannyasi."

We would argue that the words to which Haridas Das refers—*māyāvādārka-tāpa-santapta* ("roasted by the burning sun of impersonalism")—are not acceptable as proof of Prabodhananda's former adherence to the impersonalist philosophy or of his having been a mayavadi at one time. Mahaprabhu and all of His followers argued against the impersonalist doctrines as much as they could because of its extreme opposition to devotion. In this spirit, Prabodhananda is simply glorifying Mahaprabhu's quality as the deliverer of the most fallen and drawing attention to just how far-reaching His mercy is. The Lord's deliverance of Sarvabhauma Bhattacharya and Prakashananda Saraswati are even greater feats of mercy than the salvation of sinners like Jagai and Madhai.

SARASWATI THAKUR'S INTRODUCTION TO CAITANYA-CANDRAMRTA

Srila Bhaktisiddhanta Saraswati Goswami Thakur has given an excellent account of Prabodhananda Saraswati's life in his introduction to the Chaitanya Math edition of *Caitanya-candrāmṛta*. Since we feel that we cannot improve on this description, we reproduce it here in full for the benefit of the reader:

In 1510 AD, Sri Krishna Chaitanya Mahaprabhu went to South India, ostensibly on pilgrimage. In fact, His real purpose was to show His mercy to His devotees. Starting from Puri in Orissa, he travelled southward to the Godavari River and then continued onward through various other holy places. Mahaprabhu found Himself in Srirangam on the Ekadasi of the waxing fortnight of the month of Asharh. The sannyasis of the Dashnami order to which He belonged normally follow the Chaturmasya vows, and so the Lord decided to spend this four-month period in the town of Srirangam.

Srirangam is the residence of many Vaishnavas of the Sri Sampradaya. The Vaishnavas of this school are strict in their practice, and as a result, the Smarta Brahmins throughout southern India find it difficult to live in villages where they have a strong presence. At the time Mahaprabhu visited Srirangam, it was a holy place inhabited exclusively by Vaishnavas of the Sri Sampradaya. He thus considered it to be a most favorable environment for the execution of His four-month vow and so he spent the period in visiting the temple of Ranganath and preaching about Krishna.

Three brothers, Tirumalai, Venkata and Prabodhananda had recently come from Mysore to live in Srirangam. They were not Tamils, but either from Andhra or Uttar Pradesh. The Lord was particularly merciful to this Brahmin family and spent the four months of the rainy season in their house. The Vaishnavas of the Sri Sampradaya are devoted to the worship of Lakshmi-Narayan. By Mahaprabhu's blessings, the Bhatta family developed a taste for Krishna rasa.

The middle brother, Venkata, had a five-year-old son, Gopal, who later became famous as one of the six Goswamis. The Lord's conversation with Venkata Bhatta is described in the ninth chapter of the Chaitanya Charitamrita's *Madhya-līlā*. Although we know nothing more about Tirumalai, we can surmise that he, like his brothers, was totally devoted to Sri Chaitanya Mahaprabhu.

The third brother, Prabodhananda, was unequalled in his attachment to Sri Chaitanya. It was through his pure teachings that Venkata's son Gopal Bhatta later became a great acharya of the Gaudiya Vaishnava school. Prabodhananda himself has a particularly elevated position amongst the followers of Sri Chaitanya. Kavi Karnapur identified him as Tungavidya in his *Gaura-gaṇoddeśa-dīpikā*. In the *Hari-bhakti-vilāsa*, he is identified as Gopal Bhatta Goswami's guru and as extremely dear to Lord Chaitanya. And in the *Bhakti-ratnākara*, the following passages about him are found:

> Everyone glorified Prabodhananda's virtues and he was thus given the title Saraswati, by which he was known everywhere. Sri Krishna Chaitanya is the Supreme Lord and the complete Divinity. Prabodhananda held him so dear that he knew nothing but the Lord, even in his dreams. Prabodhananda was greatly renounced; he was affection incarnate and handsome, as well as being a great poet and expert in singing, playing musical instruments and dancing. Everyone's joy increased on hearing him speak. These are some of the unlimited glories of Prabodhananda Saraswati. (*Bhakti-ratnākara* 1.149-153)

PRABODHANANDA COMES TO LIVE IN VRAJA

A few years after Mahaprabhu had returned to Puri, Prabodhananda entered into a deep understanding of Chaitanya Mahaprabhu's most intimate teachings. He left Srirangam and went to live in Kamyavan in the Mathura region. Gopal Bhatta also gradually developed an intense desire to come and live in Vraja and so he followed the path taken by his uncle and guru.

Many people ask the question, "If Prabodhananda was so dear to Chaitanya, why is his name not mentioned anywhere in Krishna Das Kaviraj Goswami's Chaitanya Charitamrita? Would Krishna Das not have included such a great personality's pastimes for the pleasure of the Vaishnavas?" We find an adequate response to this question in the *Bhakti-ratnākara*. Narahari Chakravarti writes:

> Some people have described the activities of Gopal Bhatta, while others have not. Those who cannot understand the reason for this engage in useless argument, with the result that they allow an offensive attitude to take root in them. Previously, great rasika devotee poets like Krishna Das Kaviraj Goswami, who were quite capable of describing these things did not do so in order that others would be able to do so in the future. Gopal Bhatta enthusiastically gave his approval to the writing of the Chaitanya Charitamrita but did not allow Krishna Das to write anything about him. Who knows why he did this? Most likely it was his great humility. But Krishna Das Kaviraj Goswami was not able to ignore his command.
>
> (*Bhakti-ratnākara* 1.209...223)

PRABODHANANDA AND SVAKIYA-RASA

Some Rupanuga Vaishnavas say that Prabodhananda's writing shows a tendency to the *svakīyā* doctrine. They thus do not show a great enthusiasm for studying his books in the conviction that Rupa Goswami's *parakīyā-vāda* is superior. We hold that anyone who is devoted to Chaitanya Mahaprabhu is blessed and so we simply follow Narahari Chakravarti, a neutral commentator, and avoid useless argument. We relish the writings of Prabodhananda which are filled with the sweetness of servitude to Krishna in the *pārakīyā* mood.

Prabodhananda's language contains philosophical weight and the sweetness of divine love in equal measure. Mahaprabhu's devotees take great pleasure in reading Prabodhananda's *Vṛndāvana-śataka*, an enthusiastic glorification of Vrindavan Dham. His *Navadvīpa-śataka* resembles this work, glorifying Nabadwip in the same spirit. His *Rādhā-rasa-sudhā-nidhi* is truly unequalled in the entire world. From a purely literary point of view, the *Caitanya-candrāmṛta* is not regarded as of the same caliber, nevertheless it is extremely dear to the devotees who are attached to the mellows of devotion to Lord Hari. One experiences a work as being superior or inferior according to one's taste, thus the transcendental moods of Vraja bhakti can only have an effect on readers who have accumulated pious activities in their previous lives.

In his notices of manuscripts, Professor Aufrecht attributes another book, *Viveka-śataka*, to Prabodhananda Saraswati. This manuscript was in the possession of the late Rama Das Sen of Berhampore. Aufrecht also lists *Saṅgīta-mādhava* as one of Prabodhananda's works. We managed to trace this work and published it in *Sajjana-toṣaṇī*, Vol. 18, 5-12.

The *Caitanya-candrāmṛta* was widely distributed in Bengal. Even those inimical to Chaitanya Mahaprabhu became purified upon reading it and experienced a change of heart. It thus goes without saying that those who are His devotees will be immersed in an ocean of indescribable ecstasy when they read it. Indeed, it is not surprising. If the Lord of Goloka comes and stays in someone's house and accepts his service for four whole months, would he not bestow the most rare form of love of Godhead upon his entire household? The blessed members of such a household would naturally possess an abundance of priceless love from which we insignificant living entities, to our great benefit, may hope to gain some leftover crumbs.

PRAKASHANANDA SARASWATI

Some people try to identify Prabodhananda with the mayavadi sannyasi Prakashananda Saraswati who lived in Benares. We do not find their arguments at all convincing for the following reasons:

Prakashananda Saraswati is first mentioned in the third chapter of the *Madhya-khaṇḍa* in the Chaitanya Bhagavata:

> The Lord constantly floated in the joys of devotion along with His followers in Nabadwip. One day, He heard a verse glorifying the Varaha avatar. Roaring ecstatically, He went to Murari Gupta's house. Murari glorified Him with hymns of praise and this satisfied the Lord. But He began to speak in anger against some portions of the Vedas: "The Vedas say that I have no hands, feet, face or eyes. This is the way that they make a mockery of Me. There is even a rascal in Kashi named Prakashananda who teaches people impersonalism, cutting up My body into little pieces. He states that the Veda does not accept that I have a body. Now his entire body has become infected with leprosy, yet he still does not accept My transcendental form. My body is completely pure, the essence of all sacrifices. Brahma, Shiva, and the other gods all glorify My form and activities. What audacity this rascal has to say that my body is false when one becomes purified and accumulates merit by coming into contact with it.
>
> (Chaitanya Bhagavata 2.3.35-40)

This event took place sometime between 1504 and 1509 AD. Mahaprabhu came to Srirangam in 1512, which is the first time that he met Prabodhananda and his brothers. These three brothers were Vaishnavas following Ramanuja in the Sri Sampradaya and thus accepted Narayan's eternality. Meanwhile, Prakashananda was a prominent follower of Shankar's doctrine, a mayavadi sannyasi. It is sheer madness for anyone to claim that that these two were one and the same person.

Again, in the Chaitanya Bhagavata, *Madhya-khaṇḍa*, the following mention is made of Prakashananda Saraswati:

> As He spoke, the Lord was suddenly possessed by the spirit of the Divinity. Grinding His teeth, He angrily spoke the following words: "That sannyasi Prakashananda is preaching in Kashi in a way that cuts My body into pieces. The rascal teaches Vedanta, but does not accept My transcendental form. I have infected his body with leprosy, but still he does not understand. How can this rascal say that My body, which is the reservoir of unlimited universes, is

false? I tell you truthfully, Murari, for you are My servant, that anyone who denies My transcendental form is destined for destruction. My lila and My works are all real; My abode is real. Anyone who denies them will be struck down. The glories of the Lord will destroy one's ignorance if one hears them, but this sinful professor calls it all false. Anyone who has so little affection for My holy fame will never be able to understand My descent."

(Chaitanya Bhagavata 2.10.31...44)

At this time, Prakashananda Saraswati was the leader of the ekadandi sannyasi followers of Shankara, whereas Prabodhananda was a tridandi sannyasi in the line of Ramanuja, who had moved to Srirangam from Mysore. Sri Vaishnavas who renounce family life never take the single staff (*ekadaṇḍa*), which is the mark of the Shankarites. Their custom is to take the triple staff (*tridaṇḍa*) and the title Rāmānujāryasvāmī. Prakashananda was a mayavadi living in Kashi, whereas Prabodhananda was a Vaishnava living in Kamyavan. One was a northerner, the other a southerner. One was an impersonalist and monist, the other a devotee who first followed Ramanuja's *viśiṣṭādvaita-vāda* and then converted to Mahaprabhu's *acintya-bhedābheda-vāda*. One was an enemy of Vishnu and the Vaishnavas and only after conversion became a devotee, the other was the guru of Gopal Bhatta Goswami, an eternal associate of Lord Chaitanya Mahaprabhu and acharya of the Gaudiya Vaishnava sampradaya. Anyone who calls Gopal Bhatta Goswami's worshipable guru and uncle a Mayavadi and enemy of Vishnu and the Vaishnavas, a conditioned soul rather than an eternally perfect devotee of the highest order, is engaging in offensive insults that are sure to lead the one who makes them to a hellish destination.

An extensive description of Prakashananda Saraswati's conversion is given in two places in the Chaitanya Bhagavata—*Ādi-khaṇḍa*, chapter 9, and *Madhya-khaṇḍa*, chapter 25. It is impossible to understand how someone who had been a Mayavadi from 1504 to 1509 could have then become a qualified dualist Vaishnava in South India in 1512, and then again become the leader of Kashi's Mayavadis in 1514. Therefore, any attempt to identify Prakashananda with Prabodhananda is evidence of extreme ignorance. It is no small cause of distress to see the tradition being distorted in this way.

As proof of his humility, Prabodhananda asked through Gopal Bhatta that his own activities not be described in the Chaitanya Charitamrita. Krishna Das Kaviraj Goswami was not able to disobey this order and so today we have this difference of opinion. If Prabodhananda had known that as a result of this silence people would later fall into confusion and identify him with someone who preached against Vishnu and the Vaishnavas, he would surely not have instructed Gopal Bhatta and Krishna Das Kaviraj Goswami in this way. Anyone who reads the *Bhakti-ratnākara* will understand. The author of that book writes:

Gaurachandra was the wealth of Tirumalai, Venkata, and Prabodhananda's lives. The three of them were worshipers of Lakshmi-Narayan whose preference changed to Radha and Krishna as a result of the Lord's mercy... The three of them wondered how they could possibly continue living in the Lord's absence; they wondered who would joke with them and who would accompany them to the Kaveri to bathe in the morning... After four months, when the Lord left, the three brothers began to cry. Mahaprabhu embraced the three brothers and tried to console them. Some people glorified Prabodhananda's virtues and thus he was known everywhere by his title, Saraswati. Sri Krishna Chaitanya is the Supreme Lord and Supreme Absolute Truth. Prabodhananda held him so dear that he knew nothing but the Lord, even in his dreams.

(*Bhakti-ratnākara* 1.83-4, 128-9, 133, 135, 149, 150)

Some people claim upon reading the *Chaitanya-candrāmṛta* that Prabodhananda had been a worshiper of Brahman, but if we accept this without adequate supplementary evidence, we fall into difficulty.

Srila Raghunath Das Goswami

dāsa-raghunāthasya pūrvākhyā rasa-mañjarī
amuṁ kecit prabhāṣante śrīmatīṁ rati-mañjarīm
bhānumaty-ākhyā kecit āhus taṁ nāma-bhedataḥ

Three different names are ascribed to Raghunath Das from his previous identity as a manjari in Krishna lila: Some say he was Rasa Manjari, others Rati Manjari, and yet others Bhanumati. (*Gaura-gaṇoddeśa-dīpikā* 186)

RAGHUNATH'S CHILDHOOD

Raghunath Das was born in around 1494 AD in the town of Saptagram in Hooghly district. His actual birthplace was in the village of Krishnapur, which is not far south of the current railway station named Adi Saptagram on the eastern bank of the ancient Saraswati River. Krishnapur is about a mile from Adi Saptagram station and approximately 1.5 miles from Trish Bigha station.[23]

Srila Raghunath Das Goswami was the son of Govardhan Majumdar. His mother's name is not known. Govardhan's older brother Hiranya had no male offspring. The two brothers belonged to the Kayastha caste and were the primary landholders in Saptagram. In those days, the borders of Saptagram stretched from the Jessore Bhairava creek almost up to the Rupa Narayan River. Raghunath lived in Saptagram Krishnapur, his uncle Kali Das, who was also Chaitanya Mahaprabhu's devotee, lived in Shankhanagara. Raghunath's family priest, Balaram Acharya and his guru, Yadunandan Acharya, lived in the town of Chandpur. Yadunandan was a intimate disciple of Advaita Acharya and a dedicated devotee of Lord Chaitanya Mahaprabhu who had also received the special blessings of Vasudeva Datta Thakur.

After delivering the prostitute sent to tempt him by Ramachandra Khan, Hari Das Thakur left Benapole and came to Chandpur where he stayed with Balaram Acharya. Srila Raghunath Das Goswami was just a young boy at this time, but he had the opportunity to see Hari Das Thakur and receive his blessings. Krishna Das Kaviraj Goswami says that these blessings were the cause of Raghunath's later being able to attain the association of Mahaprabhu in the last years of his life.

Raghunath Das was just a little boy engaged in studies when he had the darshan of Hari Das Thakur. Hari Das was merciful to him and this mercy was the reason that he later was able to attain the company of Lord Chaitanya.

(Chaitanya Charitamrita 3.3.168-9)

RAGHUNATH'S DESIRE TO JOIN THE LORD

Hiranya and Govardhan Majumdar had an annual income of 800,000 rupees. At that time, a rupee could buy about 650 lbs of rice, which means it had several hundred times the value of a rupee today. Even though Raghunath was the only heir to this great fortune, he was indifferent to riches from his childhood. He had his first opportunity to see Mahaprabhu when the Lord came to Shantipur after taking sannyas. As soon as he saw the Lord, Raghunath fell to his feet in a transport of divine love. Raghunath's father, Govardhan Majumdar, always served Advaita Acharya with faith and devotion and thus Advaita Prabhu was predisposed to show kindness to the young Raghunath. He thus made sure that Raghunath received the Lord's remnants for as long as he remained in Shantipur.

When the Lord departed for Puri, Raghunath returned to his home in Saptagram, but he had been transformed and was constantly feeling intense separation from the Lord. Seeing him in this condition, his father surrounded Raghunath by a guard of eleven men including two Brahmins, four servants and five guards. Even so, Raghunath tried on several occasions to run away in order to join the Lord, but each time was caught and brought back before realizing his objectives. Raghunath became progressively depressed as a result of this situation.

In 1513, when the Lord made His attempt to visit Vrindavan, but only managed to get as far as Kanair Natshala, He returned to Shantipur and again stayed there for a short period of time. Raghunath wanted to see the Lord and this time he begged his father to give him permission to go to Advaita's house. Govardhan was worried about the state of his son's mind and finally decided to let him go on the condition that he return quickly. He also sent a large entourage of guards to accompany him.

When Raghunath saw the Lord, it was as though he was given new life. He told the Lord of his intolerable situation and prayed to Him to tell him how he could break free from his material bondage. The all-knowing Lord could understand the depth of Raghunath's feeling and yet he tried to pacify him with the following instruction:

"Calm yourself and return home. Don't be foolish. It takes time to cross the ocean of material suffering. Don't make a show of "monkey renunciation" (*markaṭa-vairāgya*) simply for other people's benefit. Enjoy the worldly life in a moderate way without attachment. Be fixed on Krishna internally while externally dealing with the world in the appropriate fashion. It will not be long before Krishna delivers you."

(Chaitanya Charitamrita 2.16.237-9)

Srila Bhaktisiddhanta Saraswati Goswami Thakur has made the following comments on the word *markaṭa-vairāgya*: "To a superficial eye, monkeys are engaged in renunciation because they live naked in the forest without any fixed home. In fact, they are only interested in their own sensual enjoyment and have never given it up. Such show-bottle renunciation is called *markaṭa-vairāgya*, 'monkey-renunciation.' Real renunciation comes as a side-effect of pure devotion, and other types of renunciation which arise out of frustration with material pleasures or desires cannot last throughout one's life. Because of its temporary character, such renunciation is therefore called *phalgu*, or false. Such temporary renunciation, or monkey renunciation, is also known as *śmaśāna-vairāgya*, 'the renunciation of the cremation ground.'

"One may accept things which are absolutely necessary in order to serve Krishna without becoming absorbed in them or attached to them. If one lives in this way, he will not be under the influence of the karmic reactions resulting from the involvement with sense objects. In the *Bhakti-rasāmṛta-sindhu* (1.2.108), it is said:

yāvatā syāt sva-nirvāhaḥ
svīkuryāt tāvad arthavit
ādhikye nyūnatāyāṁ ca
cyavate paramārthataḥ

One who knows his purpose should accept only as much as he needs to maintain his existence. If he accepts more or less than that, he will fall from the supreme objective.

Sri Jiva Goswami glosses the word *sva-nirvāhaḥ* in his *Durgama-saṅgamanī* commentary with the words *sva-sva-bhakti-nirvāhaḥ*: a devotee should accept only those material things that will help him render service to the Lord, according to his own individual needs. In the *Bhakti-rasāmṛta-sindhu* (1.2.256), *markaṭa-vairāgya*, or *phalgu-vairāgya*, has been more clearly explained as follows:

> *prāpañcikatayā buddhyā*
> *hari-sambandhi-vastunaḥ*
> *mumukṣubhiḥ parityāgo*
> *vairāgyaṁ phalgu kathyate*

Phalgu-vairāgya is defined as the rejection by one desiring liberation of something which is related to the Lord in the understanding that it is something material.

(As I have written in *Vaiṣṇava ke?*): *śrī hari-sevāya jāhā anukūla, viṣaya boliyā tyāge haya bhūla*—"It is a mistake to renounce something which is favorable to the service of Lord Krishna, thinking it to be an ordinary material sense object."

> *anāsaktasya viṣayān*
> *yathārham upayuñjataḥ*
> *nirbandhaḥ kṛṣṇa-sambandhe*
> *yuktaṁ vairāgyam ucyate*

Yukta-vairāgya is defined as the attitude of one who is detached from the objects of the senses, but uses them only inasmuch as they have utility in the service of Lord Krishna.

[Once again, from Vaishnava ke?] *āsakti-rahita sambandha sahita viṣaya-samūha sakali mādhava*- "All sense objects which are used without personal attachment and in relation to Krishna are identical to Krishna."

Taking Mahaprabhu's instruction to heart, Raghunath returned home and gave up his feverish desire to renounce material life and instead engaged in his various duties with a sense of detachment. When Raghunath's parents saw him abandon all the external signs of renunciation, they were delighted and began to think that there was no necessity for such a tight guard around their son.

HIRANYA MAJUMDAR'S TAX PROBLEMS

In those days, there was an officer of the Shah with the title Chaudhuri or *nāyeb* who acted as an intermediary between the Shah and the zamindars. He collected taxes from the landowners and received a commission of 25% on them. Hiranya Majumdar, however, paid his taxes directly to the Shah, with whom he had a special agreement and thus cut out the middle man. Thus, on an income of 2,000,000 rupees, Hiranya was paying only 1,200,000 rather than 1,500,000—the difference which would normally have been paid to the Chaudhuri. Since he was losing a large amount of commission, the Muslim Chaudhuri, a Turk, became an enemy to the Majumdars.

Ever since returning from his meeting with Mahaprabhu, Raghunath was practicing *yukta-vairāgya* in accordance with the Lord's instructions. However, when he heard that Mahaprabhu had returned from Vrindavan, he started making preparations to join him in Puri. At that time, the Chaudhuri had started making complaints to the Shah about Hiranya and Govardhan out of anger at being cheated out of his percentage of the tax revenue. Fearful of arrest, the two brothers went into hiding.

When the minister came to investigate the Chaudhuri's complaints, he arrested Raghunath, since his father and uncle were not present. The Chaudhuri came daily to rebuke and threaten Raghunath, asking him to reveal their whereabouts. Finally he decided to have Raghunath beaten, but when he saw his calm, lotus-like face, he was unable to continue. In fact, although he verbally chastized him, the Chaudhuri was afraid to cause him any real harm because Raghunath belonged to an influential family of the Kayastha class. He knew that the Kayasthas were intelligent and could plot against him, causing him worse problems.

Raghunath himself was looking for a way to extricate himself from the situation, and spoke to the Chaudhuri in a sweet voice: "My father and uncle are like your brothers. The behavior of brothers is difficult to understand—sometimes they fight amongst themselves, sometimes they are loving to each other. Today you are arguing, but tomorrow, I am sure that you will be reconciled with each other. I am your son as much as I am my father's and therefore you are my protector. It is not right for one such as yourself to punish his dependent. I need say no more, for you know the scriptures and are practically a living saint, a pīr."

The Chaudhuri was affected by Raghunath's sweet words and began to cry as he was overcome by affection for him. He said, "From now on, I consider you to be my son. I will find an excuse to have you freed today. Have your uncle meet with me and make arrangements so that I can get my share of the revenues."

Raghunath was able to appease the Chaudhuri by his sweet and diplomatic behavior and thus bring the dispute between him and his uncle to an end. In the meantime, Raghunath's father was making arrangements for his son's marriage to an extremely beautiful girl in order to insure his commitment to the family.

THE DANDA MAHOTSAVA

A year later, Raghunath once again became anxious to see Mahaprabhu and repeatedly ran away from home in an effort to go to Puri. Each time, he was caught by his father and returned home. Raghunath's mother thought that her son was going mad and told her husband to place him under guard again. Govardhan responded in defeated tones:

"He has as much wealth as Indra, the king of the gods, and his wife is as beautiful as the heavenly courtesans. If these things have not been able to capture his spirit, then how will mere ropes be able to do so? The father who gives life to a child cannot interfere with the effects of his previous lives' actions. Sri Chaitanya Chandra has given his blessings to this boy. Who can keep prisoner one who was been made mad by Lord Chaitanya Mahaprabhu?" (Chaitanya Charitamrita 3.6.39-41)

While Raghunath Das was devising a plan for how he would be delivered from his entanglements, he heard that Nityananda Prabhu had made an auspicious appearance in the town of Panihati. Thinking that Nityananda was the deliverer of the most fallen and that by his mercy he would surely be able to find his freedom, he went across the Ganges to Panihati where he found the Lord sitting under a tree on a wooden seat, surrounded by his associates. As soon as Raghunath saw him from a distance, he fell down like a rod. The merciful Lord Nityananda immediately had him brought close to him and, understanding the deep-rooted desires of Raghunath's heart, arranged for him to perform a service to the Vaishnavas so that he could realize them.

"Like a thief, you don't come near me, but simply try to run away. Now that I have caught you, I shall punish you. I want you to feed all my followers chipped rice and yogurt." When he heard Nityananda's command, Raghunath's mind was filled with joy.

(Chaitanya Charitamrita 3.6.50-1)

The festival which Nityananda ordered Raghunath to put on is still celebrated as the Panihati Chira-dadhi Mahotsava. Nityananda Prabhu and a manifestation of Sri Chaitanya Mahaprabhu Himself celebrated the festival, eating on the banks of the Ganges just as though they were cowherd boys on the banks of the Yamuna River. Sri Chaitanya Mahaprabhu, Nityananda Prabhu, their associates, numerous Brahmins and countless men and women from the area enjoyed a feast of milk and chipped rice and yogurt and chipped rice. The opportunity to serve the Lord and His devotees in this way was something that could not come about except for some great fortune.

On the following day, Raghunath Das Goswami emotionally asked Nityananda through Raghava Pandit how he could possibly gain freedom from his material entanglements and find the association of Mahaprabhu. Like an ocean of mercy, Nityananda Prabhu placed his feet on Raghunath's head and said:

"You arranged this feast on the banks of the river and Mahaprabhu was merciful to you and came here Himself to enjoy it. He blessed you by accepting the offering of chipped rice and yogurt. Then, after watching the devotees' dancing, He took prasad in the evening. Lord Gauranga came here just to deliver you and now He has removed any impediments that remained. He will turn you over to Svarupa Damodar and making you his confidential servant, he will keep you by his side. Go home now and forget your worries. You will soon be able to go to the Lord without any difficulties."

(Chaitanya Charitamrita 3.6.139-143)

After discussing with Raghava Pandit, Raghunath gave a large sum of money as dakṣiṇā to be paid to Nityananda and his associates. He himself felt as though his life had been fulfilled after receiving Nityananda Prabhu's blessings. Upon returning to his house, he never again entered the inner quarters, but remained outside where he slept in the Durga Mandap. Nevertheless, there was always a guard posted near him to prevent him from running away.

RAGHUNATH ESCAPES

Though Raghunath knew that the devotees from Bengal were preparing their annual trip to Puri, he was afraid of joining them because he knew that he would easily be caught. One day, about an hour before dawn, Yadunandan Acharya came by the house while Raghunath was sleeping on the Durga Mandap. He told Raghunath that a disciple who performed the puja had abandoned his service and needed to be persuaded to take it up again as there was no replacement.

Raghunath accompanied his guru while all the guards were still sleeping. After walking a ways with Yadunandan Acharya, however, Raghunath told him to return to his home, saying that he would go alone to the disciple's house and convince him to come and perform his duties. He told him not to worry and bid him goodbye. With no guards or servants around him, Raghunath realized that he had a golden opportunity to make his escape.

Meditating on Mahaprabhu's lotus feet, he started to walk toward the east. He avoided the main roads for fear of being caught and even the smaller ones that ran through the villages. Despite the difficult route through the jungle, he walked thirty miles on the very first day, finally taking rest in a milkman's cowshed that evening. The milkman saw that he had not eaten for the entire day and gave him some milk.

When Govardhan heard that his son had run away, he immediately sent a group of ten servants with a letter for Shivananda Sen who was already on his way to Puri with the devotees, telling him to send Raghunath back. They caught up with the group of pilgrims at a place called Jhankra, but were disappointed to find that Raghunath was not with them. Meanwhile, Raghunath was walking at great speed towards Puri, completely oblivious to his own fatigue and hunger.

Raghunath arrived in Puri after only twelve days, having stopped to eat only three times along the way and resting only infrequently. He came upon Mahaprabhu, who was sitting with Svarupa Damodar, and paid his obeisances to the Lord from a certain distance. Mukunda Datta informed the Lord that Raghunath had arrived and was paying his obeisances. The Lord told him to approach and Raghunath fell at His feet. The Lord embraced him, His heart melting with compassion for the exhausted young man. He said, "Nothing is more powerful than Krishna's mercy. It has dragged you out of the deep latrine of sense gratification." (Chaitanya Charitamrita 3.6.193)

Raghunath answered the Lord mentally, thinking, "I know nothing about Krishna. I believe that it was You who pulled me out of that hole."

Mahaprabhu's maternal grandfather, Nilambar Chakravarti knew Raghunath's father and uncle and used to call them bhāyā because they were younger than he. They too called him dādā (older brother) because he was their elder and a Brahmin. Knowing that this relationship existed between them, Mahaprabhu joked with Raghunath, saying:

> "Your father and uncle are like worms in the latrine pit of sense gratification. They think the suffering that comes from sense gratification is happiness. Even though they believe in Brahminical culture and contribute to it, they are not pure Vaishnavas, only imitation Vaishnavas. The nature of the sense objects is that they make one blind; they make one engage in activities which result in material bondage. It is not possible to properly describe Krishna's mercy which has delivered you from such bondage."
>
> (Chaitanya Charitamrita 3.6.197-200)

Srila Bhaktisiddhanta Saraswati Goswami Thakur has written the following about Krishna's mercy and the suffering caused by the poison of sense gratification: "Krishna's mercy is more powerful than the results of one's previous activities. It was this powerful compassion of the Lord which pulled Raghunath out of the latrine of sensual existence. A living entity who is attached to sense gratification does not have the strength to give it up. For the living being who has become a pure devotee of Krishna, however, sense enjoyments are like a ditch of stool. Mahaprabhu knew that Raghunath was completely free from any attachment to sense gratification. Nevertheless, he said this to him as a teaching to the conditioned souls."

(*Anubhāṣya* 6.9.193)

"Sense objects (*viṣaya*) bring great distress to their so-called enjoyer (*viṣayī*). Even so, those whose brains are completely immersed in the objects of sense gratification and are entangled in the whirlpool of material existence consider these sources of distress to be happiness. The objects of material sense gratification should be discarded in the same way that one abandons an outhouse, and one whose mind is possessed by the desire for these objects of gratification is like a maggot who feeds off the stools in the latrine. This is how the transcendentalist sees the materialistic person who is trying to extract pleasure from inert matter. He has nothing but disdain for materialistic pleasures which he sees being exactly like the pleasure a maggot extracts from the taste of rotting excrement."

(*Anubhāṣya* 6.9.197)

RAGHUNATH'S RENUNCIATION

Mahaprabhu noticed that Raghunath was dirty and weak after his journey and so, after accepting him as His own son and servant, entrusted him to Svarupa Damodar, telling him to take responsibility for him and to see to his wellbeing. He was thenceforth to be known as Svarupa's Raghunath to distinguish him from Raghunath Vaidya and Raghunath Bhatta, who were also living in Mahaprabhu's association in Puri at that time. The Lord also told Govinda to take care of Raghunath with great affection. He then told him to go and take his bath in the ocean and go to see Lord Jagannath, after which he was to join Him for lunch. When Govinda gave Raghunath the remnants of the Lord's plate to eat, Raghunath was overjoyed.

Things went on like this for five days—Raghunath taking the Lord's remnants each day, but on the sixth day, he stopped taking the Lord's maha prasad. From that day on, he went to the Jagannath temple and took darshan of the Lord's flower offering, after which he would stand at the Lion's Gate and beg maha prasad. At night, after they had finished their duties, Jagannath's servants would pass by on their way home and would customarily give prasad to any hungry Vaishnavas who waited there. In this way, renounced Vaishnavas could keep body and soul together. This type of renounced attitude was particularly noticeable amongst Mahaprabhu's devotees.

When the Lord asked about Raghunath and learned that he was no longer taking prasad in the same way as before, but begging by the Singha Dwar, He was satisfied to see that he was taking the renounced way of life so seriously. He said:

> "That's very good. He is taking the life of a renunciate seriously. A renunciate should always be engaged in repeating the names of the Lord and should keep his body and soul together through begging. Anyone who takes the renounced order and then becomes dependent on others cannot achieve his ends and Krishna will ignore him. One who becomes a renunciate and then lusts for tasty foods will never attain his spiritual goal, and will simply become the slave of his tastebuds. A vairagi's duty is to always chant the names of Lord Krishna and fill his belly with spinach leaves, fruits and roots. One who runs here and there looking for good things to eat becomes attached to his sex organs and his belly and will never attain Krishna."
>
> (Chaitanya Charitamrita 3.6.222-7)

Srila Bhaktisiddhanta Saraswati Goswami Thakur has underscored Krishna Das Kaviraj Goswami's statement that the vairagi's only duty is to chant the names of the Lord. He has written the following: "Examining them impartially, both materialistic non-devotees and pure Vaishnavas can see that Mahaprabhu's associates are not attached to the gratification of their material senses. They are indifferent to anything which cannot be used in the service of Krishna. The reasons for such renunciation are incomprehensible to the ordinary materialistic person, for their service is without any external motive and it cannot be interrupted by any mundane impediment. When Lord Gaurasundar sees a devotee engaged in this kind of devotional service, completely indifferent to sense objects which are outside the scope of his service needs, He feels great love for such discrimination.

"The various rituals which are described in the *Hari-*

bhakti-vilāsa are meant for the wealthy householder and not for the vairagi who has renounced everything to take exclusive shelter of the Holy Name. One who chants the holy names in the morning, in the middle of the night, at midday and at sunset—in other words throughout day and night—is certain to cross over the ocean of material existence. Those pure devotees who are fixed exclusively on the devotional service of the Lord and chant his names and remember Him with love have no duty to perform other than kirtan and smaraṇa."
(*Anubhāṣya* 3.6.223, translation of Hari Bhakti Vilasa 20.366, 379, 382).

Srila Raghunath Das Goswami would never speak to the Lord directly, but asked Govinda or Svarupa Damodar to submit any question or request to the Lord on his behalf. One day he asked the Lord through Svarupa Damodar to instruct him personally on his duties. When the Lord heard this, he told Raghunath that Svarupa Damodar knew far more than He did and that he should take instruction from him about the goal of life and how to attain it. When Raghunath's eagerness to hear from him directly did not abate, the Lord said, "If he has faith in My words, then let him follow these instructions:

"Do not listen to gossip nor engage in gossip yourself. You should not eat very palatable food, nor should you dress very nicely. Always chant the holy name of Lord Krishna without any expectation of honor, offering all respect to others. Mentally render service to Radha and Krishna in Vrindavan."(Chaitanya Charitamrita 3.6.236-7)

The Bengali devotees arrived in Puri for Rathayatra and met Raghunath, who was particularly fortunate to receive Advaita Prabhu's blessings. Shivananda Sen told him that his father had been looking for him. After staying four months in Puri, the devotees returned to Bengal and Shivananda gave news of Raghunath to Govardhan Majumdar, telling him of his determined ascetic spiritual practices. Raghunath's parents were distressed to hear of his lifestyle and sent a Brahmin, two servants and four hundred rupees to Shivananda for Raghunath. The following year, Shivananda took these servants and the money to Puri with him and informed Raghunath that his father had sent them. Raghunath would not accept them, but thinking of his father's benefit, he took some of the money and used it to pay for Mahaprabhu's meals twice a month. After doing this for two years, Raghunath abandoned this practice also. In response to Mahaprabhu's question about why Raghunath had stopped inviting Him, Svarupa Damodar said that Raghunath had decided that since his father was a materialistic man, Mahaprabhu was not really pleased to eat the food purchased with his money. By accepting such money his own mind was becoming contaminated and his only gain was some fame and status. Furthermore, he thought that Mahaprabhu was only accepting his invitations out of kindness because Raghunath was so foolish that he would be unhappy if he refused, but that in fact he was secretly not very pleased by it. Mahaprabhu was greatly satisfied to hear this conclusion and said:

"When one eats food offered by a materialistic person, one's mind becomes contaminated. If the mind is contaminated, one is unable to remember Krishna. The food of a materialistic person is infected by the mode of passion and both the person who offers it and the one who accepts it are mentally contaminated. I accepted Raghunath's invitation for many days because of his enthusiasm. I am glad that he has realized all this and given up this practice on his own initiative." (Chaitanya Charitamrita 3.6.278-80)

Srila Bhaktisiddhanta Saraswati Goswami Thakur has commented on the above events as follows: "People who are egotistical and possessive are generally materialistic persons who try to enjoy the world for their own sense gratification. Such persons see their money as a tool for achieving such sense gratification. If they attempt to serve the Lord, the guru or the Vaishnavas, who are beyond the material energy, their only gain will be an increase in material prestige and not the true benefits of such service. One who seeks true auspiciousness should therefore try to serve the Supreme Personality of Godhead by full surrender to His lotus feet and then engaging whatever money one has honestly earned in the spiritual service of Krishna, the spiritual master and the Vaishnavas using his body, mind, words, and heart." (*Anubhāṣya* 3.6.275)

"Certain materialistic persons who are intoxicated by high birth, riches, learning or physical beauty, may make a show of deity worship, offer the prasad from that worship to Vaishnavas. Due to their ignorance, they are not aware that because they lack devotion, the Lord does not accept their offerings. Because of the taint of the sense enjoyer's false pride which contaminates such offerings, it is often seen that the pure Vaishnava is indifferent to such apparent service to the deity. In other words, a pure Vaishnava who has renounced the life of sense enjoyment does not accept such service. Rich materialistic sense gratifiers are so foolish because of their sense of identification with the body and mind that they become angry with the Vaishnavas and offended by their behavior. (*Anubhāṣya* 3.6.276)

"Non-devotees and Prakrita Sahajiyas are considered to be materialistic, or *viṣayīs*. Because they offer food without devotion, an aspiring devotee will be contaminated by their association through eating their food. The result of such flaws in association (*saṅga-doṣa*), one will develop the same mentality as they. If one engages in even minimal association with materialists or Sahajiyas, who are materialists in the guise of Vaishnavas, through any of the six kinds of association (exchanging gifts, food or confidences) with even a drop of hidden affection, the result will be that the transcendental devotional service of Lord Krishna is transformed into sense gratification and this will cause the aspiring devotee's falldown. The conclusion is that one whose mind is fixed on the pleasures of the bodily senses and contaminated by the sense objects is too impure to be able to serve Krishna through the process of transcendental remembrance or *smaraṇa*."
(*Anubhāṣya* 3.6.278)

Srila Bhaktivinode Thakur has also written about the *rājasika* character of a materialistic person's dinner invitations. He says, "Invitations to dinner are of three kinds, *sāttvika, rājasika* and *tāmasika*. The invitation of a pure devotee is in the mode of goodness, that of a pious materialistic person is in the mode of passion, while the invitation of a very sinful person is in the mode of darkness."

(*Amṛta-pravāha-bhāṣya*, 3.6.279)

Raghunath Goswami's asceticism grew stronger with each passing day. He stopped begging at the Lion's Gate and started going instead to an almshouse. When Mahaprabhu heard this news from Govinda, He asked Svarupa Damodar what the cause was for this change. Svarupa Damodar answered that Raghunath was finding that a lot of time was being wasted standing in front of the Singha Dwar and was going to the almshouse every day at noon instead. Mahaprabhu praised Raghunath's decision, saying, "Begging by the Singha Dwar resembles the behavior of a prostitute."

A prostitute stands around and waits for some man to come and give her some business, a beggar cannot remain indifferent as he waits for someone to be kind to him. Going for handouts at the almshouse does not present the same kind of problem. One simply has to go at the proper time and receive enough to keep his body alive. This is useful if one wishes to use one's time in chanting the Holy Names.

The sannyasi Shankarananda Saraswati sent Mahaprabhu a *guñja-mālā* and a Govardhan Shila from Vrindavan. Mahaprabhu cherished the two objects, taking the necklace of gunja beads to be identical to Radharani and the stone from Govardhan to be identical to Krishna. Mahaprabhu would hold the Govardhan Shila to His head, to His eyes and to His heart, and this would bring him great pleasure. After worshiping the necklace and the stone for three years, He decided one day to give them to Raghunath as a sign of His satisfaction with his devotion. Raghunath felt honored and delighted by the Lord's gift, and taking them to be the direct representations of Sri Sri Gandharvika-Giridhari, he worshiped them with water and tulasi leaves. When engaged in such loving service, he would go into a devotional trance. After his disappearance, the Govardhan Shila was placed in the Gokulananda temple where it is still being served.

It is said of Raghunath Das Goswami's ascetic vows that they were like lines drawn in stone. He spent 21 plus hours a day engaged in chanting Krishna's names and in *smaraṇa*, only one and a half hours for sleep and food. He only ate enough to keep body and soul together. He allowed no delicious foods to ever touch his tongue and wore only a piece of torn cloth and a quilt.

Finally, he started going at night to gather the prasad which the vendors outside the temple threw away near the Singha Dwar after it started to go so bad that even the Tailaṅgī cows would not eat it. He would wash it to take out the dirt with which it had become mixed until he reached the hard core of the grains which had not cooked. This is what he would eat, only adding a little salt. One day, Sri Svarupa Damodar Goswami saw Raghunath doing this and came and asked him for some of this prasad, comparing it to the nectar of the gods. Even Mahaprabhu, when He heard about it from Govinda, came and took a handful of Raghunath's prasad, though Svarupa Damodar prevented Him from taking a second.

"What is this all about? You are eating such nice things and not giving any to Me?" Saying this, the Lord snatched a morsel from Raghunath and ate it. As He was about to take another Svarupa Damodar caught Him by the hand and said, "It is not fit for you," and took it away from Him. (3.6.322-3)

Srila Raghunath Das Goswami has himself summarized these experiences in his verses called *Caitanya-stava-kalpa-vṛkṣa* ("The desire tree of Chaitanya Mahaprabhu's glories"), which can be found in the collection called *Stavāvalī*.

mahā-sampad-dāvād api patitam uddhṛtya kṛpayā
svarūpe yaḥ svīye kujanam api māṁ nyasya muditaḥ
uro-guñjā-hāraṁ priyam api ca govardhana-śilāṁ
dadau me gaurāṅgo hṛdaya udayan māṁ madayati

By His mercy, Sri Gauranga took pleasure in delivering me even though I am a fallen soul, the lowest of men, from the blazing forest fire of great material opulence and entrusted me to His personal associate, Svarupa Damodar. He gave me the cherished gunja garland that He wore on His chest as well as His Govardhan Shila. And now He awakens within my heart and makes me mad after Him.

(Verse 11)

RAGHUNATH GOES TO VRINDAVAN

Raghunath remained under Svarupa Damodar's tutelage as long as he stayed in Puri, thus gaining direct access to Mahaprabhu's confidential service and association. In all, he remained there for sixteen years until the Lord and His chief confidant disappeared to the eyes of this world.

When this event took place, Raghunath felt that he could no longer live in their absence and decided to go to Vrindavan to commit suicide by jumping from Govardhan Hill. When he arrived in Vraja, he met Rupa and Sanatan Goswamis. They spoke to him for a long time and finally persuaded him not to put an end to his life. They adopted him as their third brother and kept him with them. Rupa and Sanatan were enriched by hearing the nectarean pastimes of Lord Sri Chaitanya Mahaprabhu from Raghunath.

Raghunath Das Goswami's separation from Mahaprabhu and Radha-Krishna became so intense that he gave up eating solid food altogether, only drinking whey to sustain himself. He would pay a thousand prostrated obeisances, chant 100,000 Holy Names, serve Radha and Krishna mentally both day and night, recount the glorious pastimes of Lord Chaitanya Mahaprabhu and bathe three times a day without fail in Radha Kund. This was the exemplary standard of bhajan set by Raghunath in which he served Their Lordships for more than 22 hours a day, sleeping only an hour and a half, if at all.

Raghunath's renunciation may superficially be compared to that of the Buddha, but when examined more closely it will be observed that there are some unique characteristics in Raghunath's asceticism. The external meaning of renunciation is detachment from sense gratification, but its true meaning is attachment to the Supreme Person. Raghunath's strong attachment to the lotus feet of Radha and Krishna meant that he was completely and naturally detached from anything which was not connected to his worshipable Lordships.

RADHA KUND

Sri Raghunath Das Goswami lived a long life. Srinivas Acharya had the chance to receive Raghunath's blessings before leaving Vrindavan to return to the East with the Goswamis' books. Srinivas was astounded by his powerful asceticism and deep absorption in love. Raghunath Das Goswami wrote three books: *Stavāvalī*, *Sri Dāna-carita* (*Dāna-keli-cintāmaṇi*) and *Muktā-carita*.

He lived in Radha Kund, where he performed his most intense devotional practices. He was blessed there by Nityananda Prabhu's widow, Jahnava Devi, when she visited Radha Kund.

When Mahaprabhu Himself visited the village of Ariṭ, He displayed His pastime of bathing in a rice field by which He indicated the presence of Radha Kund and Shyama Kund. Until then, the two ponds had still not been excavated, nor was it finished with steps and stones. Raghunath thought it would be a good idea to have this work done, but he had some reservations about getting involved in this kind of work. However, one day, a rich merchant who was on pilgrimage to Badri Narayan with the intention of donating a large sum of money to the temple there. Badri Narayan appeared to him in a dream and told him to fund Raghunath's vision of a developed Radha Kund and Shyama Kund. The merchant came back to Vraja and found Raghunath in the village of Arit and recounted the story of the dream to him. Raghunath thus supervised the excavation of the ponds and the subsequent building of stone step walkways.

Five trees stood on the banks of Shyama Kund, which were said to be the five Pandavas. Raghunath had the intention of cutting down these trees so that Shyama Kund could be made perfectly rectangular. Before this could happen, however, Raghunath had a dream in which King Yudhisthira appeared to him and told him that the five Pandavas were present in Radha Kund in the form of these trees. Raghunath immediately stopped the workers from cutting them down. This is why Shyama Kund was not built as a perfect rectangle.

OTHER LEGENDS ABOUT RAGHUNATH IN VRAJA

Another story is told about Raghunath Das Goswami. It is said that when he read Rupa Goswami's play, *Lalita-mādhava*, he was submerged in an ocean of separation. Though he was permanently in Radha's association at Radha Kund, he was unable to tolerate even the idea of a moment's separation, what to speak of the actual intense feelings of Krishna's absence. When he read *Lalita-mādhava*, which has separation from Krishna as its primary subject matter, this mood became so strong that he became doubtful that he would even be able to survive. When Rupa saw Raghunath's response to his play, he wrote another short work named *Dāna-keli-kaumudī* which is full of humor and amusing banter. He gave this book to Raghunath and took back his copy of *Lalita-mādhava*. When Raghunath read *Dāna-keli-kaumudī*, he forgot his feelings of separation.

At first, when staying by Radha Kund, Raghunath had no fixed shelter. He occasionally stayed with Gopal Bhatta Goswami whose cottage was situated on the banks of the Manasa Ganga in Govardhan. One day he took bath in the Manasa Ganga and then went to sit under a tree surrounded by unkept thickets and began to worship the Lord in a devotional trance. While he was meditating, a tiger came there to drink water. Sanatan Goswami was also present there at the time and observed Raghunath as he remained unmoved even though exposed to such danger. He instructed Raghunath to build a cottage in which to live and engage in his devotional activities.

Srila Raghunath Das Goswami had special affection for a certain Vrajavasi whose name was Das. Raghunath's daily nourishment consisted of only a leaf bowl of whey. This Vrajavasi was distressed to learn that Raghunath ate so little, thinking that it was impossible for him to keep alive on such a small amount. One day when in the village known as Sakhi Sthali, he was overjoyed to see a silk cotton tree with huge leaves. He had a bigger sized bowl made with these leaves in which he put whey for Raghunath and then brought it to him.

Raghunath was quite astonished to see such a large leaf-bowl and asked him where he got it. When he heard the name of Sakhi Sthali, he immediately threw down the bowl and the whey. Sakhi Sthali is the home of Chandravali, Radharani's primary rival for Krishna's love. Chandravali's sakhis, like Shaivya and Padma, are constantly looking for ways to take Krishna away from Radha's bower and bring him to that of their girlfriend. Just as Radharani is distressed by these actions, so are her girlfriends. Raghunath was a member of Radharani's entourage and so it was his role to constantly think of how to bring happiness to Her and Her girlfriends. As soon as he heard the name of Sakhi Sthali mentioned, he was transported by anger. This mood is the ultimate stage of love which envious people who are burdened by material lust can never understand. In the *Bhakti-ratnākara*, it is written:

> After calming down, Raghunath said to Das, "That is Chandravali's place. You shouldn't ever go there." Das Vrajavasi calmed down and recognized that these were the symptoms of spiritual perfection in what was apparently a spiritual aspirant. All these devotees are eternally perfected souls. Anyone who doubts it must be considered fallen.
> (*Bhakti-ratnākara* 5.572-4)

There is one other extraordinary legend about Raghunath Das Goswami recounted in *Bhakti-ratnākara*. One day he was suffering from indigestion. Vitthalnath came with two doctors from Ballabhpur to cure Raghunath Das. After examining him, the doctors said that the indigestion had been caused by eating rice and milk. Vitthalnath was astonished to hear this diagnosis and said, "This is impossible. This man never eats anything but whey." Raghunath then spoke up, saying that he had indeed eaten milk and rice in the course of his meditation on the pastimes of Radha and Krishna.

Sri Raghunath Das Goswami left his body on the banks of Radha Kund where his samadhi tomb stands. This took place on the *śuklā dvādaśī* tithi of the month of Ashwin, in the year 1586.

[23] Saptagram was made up of seven villages: Saptagram, Bamshi Bati, Shivpur, Basudevapur, Nityanandapur and Shankhanagar. It was the main trade center on the Ganges in Bengal in the 15th and 16th centuries. The modern town of Triveni grew out of Saptagram.

Srila Jiva Goswami

According to the *Gaura-gaṇoddeśa-dīpikā* (195), Srila Jiva Goswami was Vilasa Manjari in his previous identity in Vraja. In verse 203 of the same book, it is stated that he was the son of Vallabha and a scholar of exemplary character (*suśīlaḥ paṇḍitaḥ śrīmān jīvaḥ śrī-vallabhātmajaḥ*). According to the *Gauḍīya Vaiṣṇava Abhidhāna*, Jiva was present in this world from 1511 to 1596 (1433-1518 Śaka), but some other sources propose that Jiva's lived from 1533 to 1618.

JIVA'S EARLY LIFE

Srila Jiva Goswami appeared in the village of Ramakeli in the district of Maldah as the son of Anupam Mallik (Vallabha) who had made his residence there in order to serve in the government. The name of Jiva's mother is unknown. Narahari Chakravarti has given Jiva's genealogy going back seven generations. This list, as explained by Srila Bhaktisiddhanta Saraswati Goswami Thakur, has been given here in this volume in the chapter on Srila Rupa Goswami. Jiva Goswami's father's original name was Vallabha, but Mahaprabhu gave him the name Anupam.

Mahaprabhu met Anupam and his brothers Rupa and Sanatan for the first time when he came to Ramakeli in 1513. By his will, a spirit of renunciation took root in Rupa and Sanatan upon meeting the Lord, which led to their abandonment of all worldly duties and possessions not long thereafter. They then set off in an effort to be reunited with Mahaprabhu in Vrindavan. The same spirit of renunciation took hold in Jiva Goswami's heart at this time also, as has been vividly described by Narahari in *Bhakti-ratnākara* as follows:

> Jiva's mind became distracted from the time that his two uncles went to Vrindavan. He abandoned his jewels and fine dress, his comfortable bed and his various amusements. It was as though nothing interested him any more. He could no longer bear hearing news of political and other mundane affairs. (*Bhakti-ratnākara* 1.686-8)

Narahari summarizes Jiva's early life as follows: In a dream, Jiva had a vision of Mahaprabhu dancing in the midst of sankirtan. He was overwhelmed by feelings of divine love and soon thereafter left his home in Bakla Chandradwip. He had some companions who went with him as far as Fateyabad, but from there he continued alone to Nabadwip. There he met Nityananda Prabhu in the home of Srivasa Pandit and received his blessings. Nityananda Prabhu told him at that time that he should go to Vrindavan:

> With fatherly affection, Nityananda touched Jiva's head with his feet. He showed incomparable mercy toward Jiva, lifting him from the ground and embracing him tightly. Transported by divine ecstasy, Nityananda Prabhu said, "I rushed here from Khardaha for your sake alone." He said other things like this to pacify Jiva and then made Srivasa Pandit and the other devotees give their blessings to Jiva. After keeping Jiva with him there for some time, Nityananda Prabhu sent him off to the West... He said, "Hurry off now to Vraja. That is the place the Lord has given over to your family."
> (*Bhakti-ratnākara* 1.765-9, 772)

It is not clear whether Jiva ever met Mahaprabhu directly even though there is a hint in *Bhakti-ratnākara* that Jiva was a baby when the Lord came to Ramakeli. Thus, Jiva demonstrated an interest in devotion to the Supreme Lord from his early childhood. Even when playing with his friends, he was only interested in games that were connected to the worship of Krishna.

> When Jiva was a little boy, he refused to play games that had no relation to Krishna with the other boys. He made images of Krishna and Balaram and would worship them with flowers and sandalwood paste and dress and decorate them. He would gaze upon them with unblinking eyes, looking for all the world like a golden doll himself, sitting motionless on the floor. When he paid obeisance to the deities, his eyes filled with tears. He would offer their Lordships sweets and then take the prasad and distribute it to his friends. (*Bhakti-ratnākara* 1.719-23)

JIVA GOES TO VRAJA

By Nityananda's grace, Jiva was able to visit all the sacred sites in Nabadwip Dham. After completing his tour of the dham, he travelled to Benares where he studied all the scriptures with Madhusudan Vachaspati. Then he went on to Vrindavan where he remained under the tutelage of Rupa and Sanatan Goswamis.

Srila Bhaktisiddhanta Saraswati Goswami Thakur has given the following summary of Jiva Goswami's life in his *Anubhāṣya* to the Chaitanya Charitamrita: "After the disappearance of Rupa and Sanatan, Jiva became established as the topmost teacher of doctrine in the sampradaya. He engaged everyone in the worship of Krishna through teaching the truths given by Mahaprabhu Himself. He would occasionally perform Vraja Dham parikrama with the other devotees and sometimes would go to visit Vitthalnath in Mathura.

"Krishna Das Kaviraj Goswami wrote the Chaitanya Charitamrita while Jiva was still alive. Not long thereafter, when Srinivas, Narottam and Dukhi Krishna Das came from Bengal, he taught them and gave them the titles Acharya, Thakur and Shyamananda, respectively. He then sent them back to Bengal with all the scriptures that had been written by the Goswamis, with instructions to preach the religion of the Holy Names and love of Krishna. He received the news of the loss of the scriptures and later of their retrieval. He later gave the title Kaviraj to both Ramachandra Sen and his brother Govinda. Jahnava Devi and other devotees came to Vrindavan during his lifetime. Whenever Bengali devotees came to Vraja, Jiva arranged for prasad and lodgings during their stay."

(*Anubhāṣya* 1.10.85)

The loss of the scriptures refered to in the above paragraph took place when agents of King Bir Hambir of Vana Vishnupur stole them. Later, when the king heard Srinivas Acharya speak on the Bhagavatam, he was converted to Vaishnavism and took initiation from him. Srinivas thus recovered the books. All this is described in full in this volume in the chapter of Srinivas Acharya (page 204).

JIVA'S WRITINGS AND CONTROVERSIES

In the *Bhakti-ratnākara*, a list of twenty-five works ascribed to Jiva has been given:

(1) *Harināmāmṛta-vyākaraṇa*
(2) *Sūtra-mālikā*
(3) *Dhātu-saṅgraha*
(4) *Rādhā-kṛṣṇārcana-dīpikā*
(5) *Gopāla-virudāvalī*
(6) *Rasāmṛta-śeṣa*
(7) *Mādhava-mahotsava*
(8) *Saṅkalpa-kalpa-vṛkṣa*
(9) *Bhāvārtha-sūcaka-campū*
(10) A commentary on *Gopāla-tāpanī Upaniṣad*
(11) A commentary on *Brahma-saṁhitā*
(12) A commentary on *Bhakti-rasāmṛta-sindhu*
(13) A commentary on *Ujjvala-nīlamaṇi*
(14) A commentary on *Yogasāra-stavaka*
(15) *Agnipurāṇa-stha-gāyatrī-bhāṣya*
(16) *Padma-purāṇokta Kṛṣṇa-pādapadma-cihna*
(17) *Sri Rādhikā-kara-pada-sthita-cihna*
(18) *Gopāla-campū*, *Pūrva* and *Uttara* divisions
(19) *Krama-sandarbha*
(20) *Tattva-sandarbha*
(21) *Bhāgavata-sandarbha*
(22) *Paramātma-sandarbha*
(23) *Kṛṣṇa-sandarbha*
(24) *Bhakti-sandarbha*
(25) *Prīti-sandarbha*

Srila Bhaktisiddhanta Saraswati Goswami Thakur has given the following warning in his *Anubhāṣya* to those inexperienced persons who might be deprived of Krishna prema through the influence of ignorant and offensive Sahajiya teachings: "Three slanderous ideas about Jiva Goswami are current amongst the ignorant Prakrita Sahajiyas. Anyone influenced by these calumnies, which are fundamentally inimical to Krishna, the guru and the Vaishnavas, will become increasingly offensive and end up losing his taste for service to the Supreme Lord.

"(1) It is said that a certain *dig-vijayī* scholar, on a mission to amass mundane prestige, came to Rupa and Sanatan to get their signature as an admission of defeat in debate. Jiva's gurus conceded defeat without any argument and the arrogant scholar began to slander them as nothing more than ignorant fools. He then asked Jiva to also sign such an admission of defeat. Jiva, however, decided to take on the puffed-up Brahmin in debate in order to silence his scurrilous tongue. In this way, he preserved the integrity of his spiritual master's reputation and demonstrated the ideal behavior of one who is *guru-devatātmā*, (one who recognizes his spiritual master to be his worshipable deity and source of life). Some ignorant Sahajiyas, however, say that Sri Jiva's behavior went contrary to Mahaprabhu's teaching of being humbler than a blade of grass and of giving respect to others while demanding none for one's self. Indeed, they say that Rupa Goswami chastised Jiva for this very reason and ostracized him for some time, and only when Sanatan later interceded on Jiva's behalf did he accept him again into his association.

"Only when these enemies of the spiritual master and the Vaishnavas receive Krishna's mercy and begin to see themselves as their eternal servant, will they also receive Jiva's blessings and be able to understand what it really means to be 'humbler than a blade of grass' and 'a giver of respect to all'. Only then will they be eligible to chant the Holy Names in the proper way.

"(2) Some other foolish Sahajiyas say that when Jiva first read the Chaitanya Charitamrita, with its clear and brilliant explanation of the divine devotional sentiments of Vraja, he was afraid that it would hamper his own scholarly reputation. He therefore threw the manuscript down a well in a spirit of mean-mindedness. Upon hearing of Jiva's action, Krishna Das Kaviraj Goswami was greatly shocked and immediately gave up his body. Fortunately, Krishna Das's disciple Mukunda had made a copy of the original manuscript and thus it was preserved and later published far and wide. Had Mukunda not done so, the Chaitanya Charitamrita would have been lost forever.

This is another contemptible bit of invention based on an inimical attitude to the guru and Vaishnava. It has no basis in reality and there is no possibility of its being true.

"(3) According to other sense-obsessed fornicators, Srila Jiva Goswami should not be accepted as an authority because, in his treatises, he opposed the idea that the gopis of Vrindavan were married to other men (the *pārakīyā-vāda*), but rather supported the *svakīyā-vāda*. They say that he cannot be accepted as a rasika bhakta, or a devotee who is knowledgeable in the divine sentiments:

"The fact is that during Jiva's lifetime, some of his followers demonstrated a preference for the *svīyā-vāda*. Jiva recognized their limitations and so, for their benefit and for the benefit of those in the future who would be unable to comprehend the transcendental nature of the *pārakīyā-vāda* and would themselves take up adulterous relationships in imitation of Krishna, he gave credence to the *svakīyā* doctrine. This is a sign of his acting appropriately as an acharya. One should not take this as evidence of his being opposed to the transcendental *pārakīyā-vāda*, however, for he is the topmost of Rupa Goswami's followers and one of Krishna Das Kaviraj Goswami's spiritual teachers."

(*Anubhāṣya*, 1.10.85)

RUPA'S MERCY TO JIVA

Narahari has shown how Rupa Goswami instructed Jiva, punished him and then blessed him, in a story told in the fifth wave of *Bhakti-ratnākara*:

One hot summer's day, while Rupa was writing *Bhakti-rasāmṛta-sindhu* and Jiva was fanning his perspiring body, Vallabha Bhatta came by to see Rupa Goswami. After reading some of Rupa's introductory verses, he offered to make a few corrections. When Vallabha went to the Yamuna to take a bath, Jiva followed him on the pretext of going to fetch water. In fact, he was angry because he considered Vallabha's proposal to be arrogant. He asked him what fault he had found in Rupa's verse. Vallabha told him and Jiva immediately showed him the flaws in his argument. A debate ensued in which Jiva countered every one of Vallabha's objections. When he came back to Rupa's hut, Vallabha told him how impressed he was with Jiva's scholarship, recounting the entire episode. Rupa gently rebuked Jiva, telling him to return to Bengal and to come back to Vrindavan only when he had calmed down.

Thus banished from his presence, Jiva left Rupa Goswami's dwelling, but rather than going back to the family home as he had been told, he went to Nanda Ghat, a nearby village. Hoping to regain his guru's favor, he began to practice rigorous austerities, worshiping Krishna intensely while fasting or eating only a bare minimum. As a result of such severe practices, his body became weak and sickly. One day, Sanatan Goswami happened to come to Nanda Ghat and discovered him in this condition. He was moved and took Jiva back with him to Rupa and appealed to his brother to forgive him. Rupa and Jiva were thus reconciled and Jiva once again began to receive Rupa's affectionate blessings.

Jiva Goswami's appearance day is on Bhadra *śuklā dvādaśī*, his disappearance day is Paush *śuklā tṛtīyā*. His deity, Radha-Damodar, is still being worshiped in the Radha-Damodar temple in Vrindavan. His samadhi tomb is on the grounds of the Radha-Damodar temple and his bhajan kutir is preserved in Radha Kund, near Lalita Kund.

VRINDAVAN DAS THAKUR

vedavyāso ya evāsīd
dāso vṛndāvano'dhunā
sakhā yaḥ kusumāpīḍaḥ
kāryatas taṁ samāviśat

Veda Vyasa became Vrindavan Das Thakur. Krishna's friend Kusumapida also entered into him for the sake of the Lord's pastimes. (*Gaura-gaṇoddeśa-dīpikā* 109)

Veda Vyasa described Krishna lila in the Srimad Bhagavatam. Non-different from Vyasa, Vrindavan Das described Mahaprabhu's lila in his Chaitanya Bhagavata. This book was first called *Caitanya-maṅgala*, but when Lochan Das later gave the same name to his biography of the Lord, it was dubbed "Chaitanya Bhagavata."

VRINDAVAN DAS'S MOTHER, NARAYANI

Vrindavan Das was born on the *kṛṣṇā dvādaśī* of the month of Vaishakh in 1429 of the Śaka era (1507 AD). Some say he was born in Mamgachi in the Nabadwip area, others say his birthplace was in Kumarahatta. His father was Vaikunthanath Vipra, who originally came from Sylhet; his mother was Narayani Devi. Narayani was the daughter of Srivasa Pandit's elder brother, Srinalina Pandit. Kavi Karnapur has also mentioned her name in his *Gaura-gaṇoddeśa-dīpikā*:

ambikāyāḥ svasā yāsīn
nāmnā śrīla-kilimbikā
kṛṣṇocchiṣṭaṁ prabhuñjānā
seyaṁ nārāyaṇī matā

"Kilimbika, who used to eat Krishna's remnants, was the younger sister of Krishna's nurse Ambika (Srivasa's wife, Malini). In Mahaprabhu's lila, she became Narayani."

Narayani also achieved fame because Gaurasundar bestowed His mercy on her when He gave her His remnants. Narayani was only a small child of four when the Lord displayed His divine form in the *mahā-prakāśa* in Srivasa Angan, but the Lord still made her intoxicated with the ecstasy of prema.

Whether born in Mamgachi or in Kumarahatta, Vrindavan Das spent part of his childhood with his mother in Mamgachi, at the home of his maternal grandparents where Narayani was married. Vrindavan Das's Gaura-Nitai deities are still worshiped at the Mamgachi home. When his father died, he and his mother moved to Srivasa's house where they received Mahaprabhu's special blessings. Vrindavan Das later moved to the village of Denur in the Matresvara precinct of Burdwan district. Thus Denur is considered to be his Sripat.

VRINDAVAN DAS WRITES CHAITANYA BHAGAVATA

It is well known that Vrindavan Das received copious blessings from Nityananda Prabhu, and he is therefore said to have been his initiated disciple.

> Vrindavan Das is the recipient of Nityananda's mercy. He is the original Vyasa of Chaitanya's pastimes.
> (Chaitanya Charitamrita 3.20.82)

Vrindavan Das wrote Chaitanya Bhagavata in 1535 AD. Krishna Das Kaviraj Goswami, the author of Chaitanya Charitamrita, praised him and his work in the following words:

> Vrindavan Das, the son of Narayani, wrote the *Chaitanya-maṅgala*. Veda Vyasa described Krishna's life in the Srimad Bhagavatam and Vrindavan Das is the Vyasa of Chaitanya lila. (Chaitanya Charitamrita 1.11.54-5)

> Veda Vyasa told the story of Krishna's pastimes in the Bhagavatam. Vrindavan Das Thakur performed the duties of Vyasadeva in recounting the pastimes of Chaitanya. His *Chaitanya-maṅgala* annihilates all misfortune. From it, I learned the wonders of Lord Chaitanya and Nityananda and came to know all the subtlest doctrines of devotional service to Krishna. Vrindavan Das Thakur has summarized the essence of the Srimad Bhagavatam's teachings in his *Chaitanya-maṅgala*. If even an atheist or a Muslim should listen to *Chaitanya-maṅgala*, he immediately becomes a great Vaishnava. An ordinary human being could not have composed such a sublime work; Lord Chaitanya Himself has spoken through the mouth of Vrindavan Das. I offer millions of obeisances unto the lotus feet of Vrindavan Das Thakur, who has delivered the entire universe through his book. He was born in the womb of Narayani who eternally enjoys Sri Chaitanya's remnants. How wonderful is his description of the activities of the Lord! Simply by hearing them, the three worlds have become sanctified!
> (Chaitanya Charitamrita 1.8.34-42)

In the Chaitanya Bhagavata, Vrindavan Das Thakur primarily narrates Mahaprabhu's early life, such as His childhood, His student life, His chastisement of the Kazi, His departure from Nabadwip, as well as some aspects of His life in Puri. He then became so absorbed in describing Nityananda Prabhu's lila that he only gave an abbreviated account of Mahaprabhu's later life. Krishna Das later elaborated on these undescribed activities in his Chaitanya Charitamrita. Krishna Das wrote:

> Vrindavan Das is the authorized biographer of Sri Chaitanya Mahaprabhu and equal to Srila Vyasadeva. He has described the Lord's pastimes in such a way that they become sweeter and sweeter. He was afraid of excessively enlarging his book and so left some parts of Mahaprabhu's life untold. I shall try as far as possible to fill in these empty spaces. (Chaitanya Charitamrita 1.13.48-9)

VRINDAVAN DAS'S CRITICISMS OF VAISHNAVA APARADH

Vrindavan Das showed infinite mercy on the fallen souls by warning them:

eta parihāre-o je pāpī nindā kare
tabe lāthi māroṅ tār śirera upare

"If someone still blasphemes the Vaishnavas even after being told how objectionable it is, I will kick him in the head."

These same words are repeated several times throughout the Chaitanya Bhagavata.[24] Some foolish and arrogant persons misunderstand such statements and criticize Vrindavan Das for having made them. Such criticism leads them to be mired in the bog of Vaishnava aparadh.

In this connection, the remarks of Srila Bhaktisiddhanta Saraswati Goswami Thakur, founder of the Sri Chaitanya Math and all the Gaudiya Maths, are well worth studying: "'I am ready to kick the heads of those envious and hellish persons who blaspheme Nityananda Prabhu, if by so doing I will be able to forever prevent them from repeating their attempts to show disrespect for the Supreme Lord. Not only that, but if by so doing I can bring about a clear conception of the truth, I will be performing them the greatest service.'

So says Vrindavan Das, the incarnation of Vyasa and acharya of the Vaishnava faith. If even a single fleck of dust should fall from Vrindavan Das' foot onto the head of a sinful blasphemer, then that person will be blessed and all his sinful conditioning will inevitably be eradicated. With these words the Thakur reveals compassion for even the most atheistic blasphemer with the unswerving faith appropriate to a servant of Nityananda Prabhu, the supreme guru. He tells such people that though they should be the object of indifference due to their foolishness, nevertheless, he and other compassionate Vaishnavas like him who practice and preach the Lord's doctrines unselfishly and disinterestedly act for their welfare despite their ignorance of the truth of Nityananda, their insistence on rushing headlong on the path to hell and their reluctance to act in their own real self-interest. The compassion manifested in Vrindavan Das's statement is beyond the comprehension of those who do not know what is truly in their own self-interest. Anyone who follows in the footsteps of Vrindavan Das and both practices and preaches the Vaishnava religion will always be engaged in an effort to bring about everyone's ultimate well-being. Though he may make a show of wanting to punish the enemies of the Lord, he in fact harbors a compassion toward them that knows no limit."

(*Gauḍīya-bhāṣya*, 1.9.225)

Vrindavan Das Thakur's disappearance day is the *kṛṣṇā daśamī* of Vaishakh. There is some dispute as to the exact year of his disappearance, which was likely 1511 Śaka (1589 AD).

[24] 1.9.225, 1.17.158, 2.11.63, 2.18.223 and 2.23.522.

Kavi Karnapur (Sri Puri Das)

Kavi Karnapur is considered to be a branch of Sri Chaitanya. His father was Mahaprabhu's dear associate, Shivananda Sen. Karnapur himself identifies his parents in *Gaura-gaṇoddeśa-dīpikā*:

purā vṛndāvane vīrā dātī sarvāś ca gopikāḥ
nināya kṛṣṇa-nikaraṁ sedānīṁ janako mama
vraje bindumatī yāsīd adya sā jananī mama

The go-between Vira, who previously brought all the gopis to Krishna, is my father. My mother was known as Bindumati. (*Gaura-gaṇoddeśa-dīpikā* 176)

PARAMANANDA DAS OR PURI DAS

Karnapur did not give his own identity in *Gaura-gaṇoddeśa-dīpikā*, but from what he has said of his own parents' identity, we can surmise that he too was an associate of Krishna in Vraja. From the *Vaiṣṇavācāra-darpaṇa*, we learn:

Kavi Karnapur was Gunachura Sakhi in Vraja. He is a branch of Chaitanya who lived in Kanchra Para. He was given the name Puri Das and accumulated great spiritual power from Mahaprabhu when he placed the Lord's big toe in his mouth.

Karnapur was born in 1527 in the town of Kanchan Palli, or Kanchra Para. His father named him Paramananda Das, Paramananda Sen or Puri Das. He was the youngest of Shivananda Sen's three sons. His older brothers were named Chaitanya Das and Rama Das. All three brothers were devotees of Lord Sri Chaitanya.

Shivananda Sen's entire family was blessed with the Lord's unlimited mercy. The Lord Himself showed his other associates just how dear this family was to him when he ordered that as long as Shivananda and his family stayed in Puri, they should receive His remnants.

(Chaitanya Charitamrita 3.12.53)

Kavi Karnapur received the name Paramananda Das from Mahaprabhu Himself. The Lord also jokingly called him Puri Das. Krishna Das recounts that he was born as a result of Mahaprabhu's blessing:

The Lord asked Shivananda Sen the youngest son's name and Sen answered, "Paramananda Das." The previous time Shivananda Sen had visited the Lord, the Lord had said to him, "This time, when your son is born, name him Puri Das." Shivananda's wife was pregnant at the time and she gave birth after Shivananda returned home. They named the child Paramananda Das in accordance with the Lord's wishes, but the Lord jokingly called him Puri Das.

(Chaitanya Charitamrita 3.12.45-49)

MAHAPRABHU GIVES THE EPITHET KAVI KARNAPUR

The next year, when Shivananda Sen brought the baby to Mahaprabhu, the Lord showed the child much mercy by placing his big toe in his mouth. When Puri Das was only seven years old, the Lord himself gave him the title Kavi Karnapur upon hearing the wonderful poetry that the child was capable of composing. Krishna Das Kaviraj describes all these things in the sixteenth chapter of the *Antya-līlā*.

One year, when Shivananda and his wife were in Puri for the Rathayatra, they came with Puri Das to see the Lord. The child paid obeisances to Mahaprabhu, and the Lord said to him, "Say the name of Krishna! Say 'Krishna'!" Though the Lord asked him repeatedly to chant, the boy refused to utter the Holy Name. His embarrassed father also tried to get him to chant, but little Puri Das was steadfast in his refusal. Mahaprabhu was astonished at his stubborn attitude and said, "I have made everyone in the universe, even the non-moving beings, chant the names of Krishna, but I am unable to make this little child do so. What on earth could be the reason?"

Svarupa Damodar suggested: "You have instructed him in Krishna's name. Because it is forbidden to repeat the mantra one has received from the guru aloud, he will only chant it mentally and not reveal it publicly. I would guess that this is what he is thinking."

The Lord was happy to see that such a young boy was aware of this scriptural injunction. In his *Anubhāṣya*, Srila Bhaktisiddhanta Saraswati Goswami Thakur has explained: "The mantra which one has received from the guru is not to be revealed to anyone else, otherwise it will lose its potency. We have seen this previously from the story about Gadadhar Pandit."[25]

This is why Puri Das would not repeat the mantra that had been given him by Mahaprabhu. Mahaprabhu then asked Puri Das to recite a verse in order to make him break his silence. The child recited the following verse of his own composition:

śravasoḥ kuvalayam akṣnor
añjanam uraso mahendra-maṇi-dāma
vṛndāvana-ramaṇīnāṁ
maṇḍanam akhilaṁ harir jayati

All glories to Hari, the ornament for all the beauties of Vrindavan—a blue lotus for their ears, black collyrium for their eyes, and a necklace of blue sapphires to decorate their breast. (Chaitanya Charitamrita 3.16.74)

All those who were present were charmed by the lovely verse. A small boy of seven who had barely commenced his education was yet able to recite a verse of such quality! Gods like Brahma and Shiva are unable to understand Mahaprabhu's mercy, what to speak of an ordinary jiva!

Though Kavi Karnapur received the mantra of Krishna's name from Chaitanya Mahaprabhu, he nevertheless followed the social custom of taking initiation from Srinath Chakravarti, a sub-branch of Advaita Acharya on the Chaitanya tree. Karnapur paid his obeisances to Srinath Chakravarti in his introduction to *Ānanda-vṛndāvana-campū*. Some people say that Srinath Chakravarti's deities are still being worshiped in Kumarahatta or Kanchra Para.

In another introductory verse to *Ānanda-vṛndāvana-campū*, Kavi Karnapur glorified Chaitanya Mahaprabhu as his family deity, saying that Mahaprabhu adopted Shivananda Sen's entire family as His own.

The following is a list of Kavi Karnapur's compositions: *Caitanya-caritāmṛta-mahākāvya, Ānanda-vṛndāvana-campū, Alaṅkāra-kaustubha, Caitanya-candrodaya-nāṭaka, Gaura-gaṇoddeśa-dīpikā, Bṛhad-gaṇoddeśa-dīpikā, Ārya-śataka, Āhnika-kaumudī*, a commentary on the tenth canto of the Srimad Bhagavatam, *Caitanya-sahasra-nāma* and *Keśavāṣṭaka*. His earliest book was *Caitanya-caritāmṛta-mahākāvya*, which he completed in 1542. He was still writing books in 1576 AD, the date of the *Gaura-gaṇoddeśa-dīpikā*.

Kavi Karnapur was dear to the Lord and became a writer of books in which he revealed the Lord's blessings to Sanatan Goswami. (*Bhakti-ratnākara* 1.657)

[25] Page 45. This story is found in Chaitanya Bhagavata 3.8.122ff.

SRI LOCHAN DAS THAKUR

FAMILY LIFE

Lochan Das Thakur was born in 1523 in Kogram, in the Katwa block of Burdwan district. This village is about ten miles north of Guskara train station. The Thakur's home is situated near the Ajaya River.

His birth tithi is given by some as the first day of the fortnight of the waxing moon in Paush. He was born in the Rarha clan of the physician caste (*vaidya*). His father's name was Kamalakar Das, his mother's Sadanandi. Lochan Das studied at his maternal grandfather's house. He displayed devotion for Mahaprabhu from his childhood.

Lochan Das was married at a very early age, according to the customs of that epoque. Since he had been married so young, his wife first remained with her parents in the village of Amedpur Kakuta. As he grew older, Lochan showed a highly renounced attitude to life and spent all his time discussing Krishna katha with other devotees of Gauranga. As the time approached when his wife was to join him, her family began to worry because of Lochan Das's indifference to material life. They approached his guru Narahari Sarkar and told him of their disquiet. As a result, Narahari ordered Lochan Das to go to his in-laws' home.

When Lochan arrived in Amedpur, he was unable to remember where their house was, since it had been so long since he had visited. He asked a young girl in the street for directions, addressing her as "mā," or "mother." When he arrived at his in-laws' house, he found out that the girl whom he had addressed as "mother" was in fact his wife. From that day on, he always looked upon his wife as a mother, worshiping Guru and Gauranga in an attitude of renunciation.

THE CAITANYA-MANGALA

Narahari Sarkar Thakur, Mahaprabhu's famous associate from Srikhanda, was very affectionate to Lochan Das and gave him initiation. Lochan Das enthusiastically took up residence with his guru in Srikhanda. His guru taught him the art of kirtan and later ordered him to write Mahaprabhu's holy biography. Lochan Das took this order seriously and wrote the *Caitanya-maṅgala*, the events of which are based on Murari Gupta's *Caitanya-carita*.

The word *maṅgala* means auspicious and this title reflects the fact that hearing Mahaprabhu Sri Chaitanya's divine pastimes is the most auspicious activity for all the living beings. Vrindavan Das Thakur's biography of the Lord was first named *Caitanya-maṅgala* and was only later known as Chaitanya Bhagavata. Lochan Das gives an indication of this in the introductory portion of his book:

I attentively pay my obeisances to Vrindavan Das Thakur; his Bhagavata's songs have enchanted the entire universe. (*Sūtra-khaṇḍa*, 1.35)

Some people believe that Lochan Das and Krishna Das Kaviraj Goswami gave the name Chaitanya Bhagavata to Vrindavan Das's book. In the *Caitanya-maṅgala*, Lochan Das prays for his guru's blessings as follows:

Narahari Das Thakur is the proprietor of my life, and out of the hope of attaining his lotus feet, I desire to sing the glories of Gauranga, even though I am the lowest of the low. This is my ambition. (Ibid., 1.9)

I offer my reverences to Narahari Das, the ocean of Gauranga's qualities. Other than him, I have no friend in the three worlds. (Ibid., 1.33)

My lord and master is Narahari Das. I prostrate myself in humility to him. May he fulfill my desires. (Ibid., 1.61)

Lochan Das wrote the *Caitanya-maṅgala* in Eastern Bengal's *pañcālī* style, completing it in 1537 AD. There is a legend that he wrote the book while sitting on a stone under a flower tree. In his new Bengali dictionary, Ashutosh Deb has underlined Lochan Das's contribution by stating that he was the first to write Bengali poetry using moric metres as well as being one of Bengal's earliest historical writers. The original manuscript of the *Caitanya-maṅgala* purported to be in the personal library of Pran Krishna Chakravarti of Kandra near the Guskara train station.

Other titles attributed to Lochan Das are *Prārthanā*, *Durlabha-sāra*, *Dhāmālī*, and Bengali verse translations of Ramananda's *Jagannātha-vallabha-nāṭaka* and the *Rāsa-pañcādhyāya*.

According to *Bhakti-ratnākara*, Lochan Das was present at Narahari Sarkar Thakur's disappearance festival and greeted guests by giving them sandalwood and garlands.

LOCHAN DAS' SONGS GLORIFYING NITYANANDA

In *Caitanya-maṅgala*, Lochan Das describes his guru Narahari as Mahaprabhu's dearest associate. He does not describe Nityananda's glories as extensively. Fearful that he may have committed an offense by neglecting Nityananda Prabhu, he later wrote a few songs in his praise. These songs are particularly well appreciated by the devotees.

(1)

nitāi guṇa-maṇi āmāra nitāi guṇa-maṇi
āniyā premera banyā bhāsāla avanī
premera banyā laiyā nitāi āilā gauḍa-deśe
ḍubila bhakata-gaṇa dīna-hīna bhāse
dīna-hīna patita-pāmara nāhi bāche
brahmāra durlabha prema sabākāre jāce
ābaddha karuṇā-sindhu nitāi kāṭiyā mohān
ghare ghare bule prema amiyāra bāna
locana bale mora nitāi je bā nā bhajila
jāniyā śuniyā sei ātma-ghātī haila

Nitai is a jewel of virtue! My Nitai is a jewel of virtue. He brought the deluge of love of God and flooded the world.

Nitai brought the deluge of love of God to Gauda Desh and inundated the devotees. The lowly and deprived were also washed away in the flood.

Nitai never excluded the lowly and deprived, nor the sinful and atheistic. He insisted that everyone take the gift of love, which is beyond the reach of even gods like Brahma.

Nitai released the floodgates that held back the ocean of compassion, going from door to door to give everyone the nectar of divine love.

Lochan Das says that anyone who has not worshiped Nitai has knowingly committed suicide.

(2)

akrodha paramānanda nityānanda rāy
abhimāna-śūnya nitāi nagare beṛāy
adhama patita jīver dvāre dvāre giyā
harināma mahāmantra dena bilāiyā
jāre dekhe tāre kahe dante tṛṇa kari
āmāre kiniyā laha bhaja gaura-hari
eta bali nityānanda bhūme paṛi jāy
sonāra parvata jena dhūlāte loṭāy
hena avatāre jāra rati nā janmila
locana bale sei pāpī ela āra gela

Completely free of anger, Lord Nityananda is the embodiment of supreme joy. He wanders throughout the town without any pride or arrogance.

He knocks on every fallen soul's door and bestows the Maha Mantra of the Holy Names on him.

Placing straw between his teeth, he says to everyone he sees, "Worship Gaura Hari and you will purchase me and make me your slave."

Then he falls to the ground in an ecstatic fit, looking like a golden mountain rolling in the dust.

Whoever lacks faith in such a compassionate incarnation is a sinner who will die having made nothing of his life, says Lochan Das.

(3)

Sri Gaura Nityānander Dayā

parama karuṇā, pahuṅ dui jana,
nitāi gauracandra
saba avatāra sāra-śiromaṇi
kevala-ānanda-kanda

These two lords, Nitai and Gaurachandra, are most compassionate. Of all the incarnations of Godhead, They are the most perfect, for They are the unique source of joy.

bhaja bhaja bhāi caitanya nitāi
sudṛḍha viśvāsa kari
viṣaya chāṛiyā se rase majiyā
mukha bala hari hari

Pray, O brothers! Pray with great faith to Chaitanya and Nitai. Give up the objects of sense gratification, absorb yourself in the flavors of Their divine mood, and use your tongue to sing the names of Hari!

dekho ore bhāi tribhuvane nāi
emono dayāla dātā
paśu pākhī jhure pāṣāṇa vidare
śuni jāṅra guṇa-gāthā

Just look, O my brothers! There are no more compassionate benefactors than Gaur-Nitai anywhere in the three worlds. Even the birds and beasts' hearts melt and stones crumble when they hear Their virtues.

saṁsāre majiyā rahili paṛiyā
se pade nahila āśa
āpana karama bhuñjāye śamana
kahaye locana-dāsa

I have fallen into the worldly life, completely absorbed in mundane pursuits, and have never aspired to attaining Them. The god of judgment is making me suffer the consequences of my acts, so sings Lochan Das.

Srila Lochan Das Thakur was present on the occasion of Sri Narahari Sarkar Thakur's disappearance festival. In *Bhakti-ratnākara* , it is said that he came there with Yadunandan Thakur, bringing garlands of flowers and sweet-scented sandalwood.

GAURA-NAGARA DOCTRINE CONDEMNED

Followers of certain heterodox groups or *apasampradāyas* say that the Gaura-nāgara doctrine is found in the *Caitanya-maṅgala.* But this is not true. Vrindavan Das Thakur writes in his Chaitanya Bhagavata: *gaurāṅga nāgara hena stava nāhi bale*—"No one should praise the Lord by calling him the golden playboy."

Srila Bhaktisiddhanta Saraswati Goswami Thakur comments: "Gaurasundar is Krishna who has been endowed with Radha's bodily hue and Her mood of love. Thus He never abandoned the qualities of the heart of Radha and the other gopis, the character of the *āśraya* of devotion in the erotic mood. This means that He never acts like the *viṣaya* (object) or bhoktā (enjoyer) of *madhura-rasa* by looking at other women in the spirit of a playboy."

(*Gauḍīya-bhāṣya* 1.15.30)

Lochan Das ended his pastimes in this world in 1589 AD. A brick samadhi at his Sripat marks the place where his remains are buried.

Srila Krishna Das Kaviraj Goswami

Krishna Das Kaviraj Goswami is the author of the Chaitanya Charitamrita, but he has only given us a little information there about himself. In his introduction to the original Gaudiya Math edition of Chaitanya Charitamrita, Srila Bhaktisiddhanta Saraswati Goswami Thakur wrote the following about Krishna Das's antecedents: "We do not know who Krishna Das's parents were, not even their names. Despite recent claims that their names have been discovered, no concrete evidence can be found to substantiate them.[26] Krishna Das is a spiritual name, and not one that he used in his family life.

"Krishna Das has given us some autobiographical information in the fifth chapter of the *Ādi-līlā*, from which we learn that he was born in Jhamatpur, which is near the Salar railway station. This village lies four miles west of Naihati in the Katwa block of Burdwan district. To this day, Krishna Das' Gaura-Nitai deities are still worshiped in his hometown, but there do not seem to be any descendants of his family still living there.

"Krishna Das was ordered to go to Vrindavan in a dream by Nityananda Prabhu. He spent the remainder of his life in Vraja Dham and his samadhi tomb can be seen on the grounds of the Radha Damodar temple."

(*Bhūmikā*, ii.)

There is a village near Naihati named Jhamatpur. Nityananda Prabhu appeared to me there in a dream

(Chaitanya Charitamrita 1.5.181).

Srila Prabhupada Saraswati Goswami has established Krishna Das's dates by collating information from several sources. He concludes that he was probably born in about 1520 AD and died in about 1616 or 1617. Vrindavan Das Thakur appeared sometime after 1510 AD. Krishna Das's magnificent biography of Chaitanya Mahaprabhu was meant to serve as an appendix to his work.

KRISHNA DAS' VARNASHRAM STATUS

There is some difference of opinion about Krishna Das's caste. Once again, Srila Prabhupada, Bhaktisiddhanta Saraswati Thakur, has discussed this point: "Supporters of different ideas claim that Krishna Das was born in one of the three upper castes (Brahmin, Kayastha or Vaidya). Kavirāja is a title given to those who have proven themselves by composing literary works that have achieved renown for their quality in learned circles. Since this title is also given to Ayurvedic physicians, some people hold that Krishna Das was a Vaidya. It is difficult to contradict those who claim that he is a Brahmin on the basis of his extraordinary mastery of the scriptures and other branches of learning, of which Chaitanya Charitamrita is an eloquent testimonial. Nor is the view that he was a Kayastha altogether illogical, as he reveals a soft spot for that caste when he praises its intelligence and managerial talents in the chapters about Raghunath Das Goswami's early life."
(*Bhūmikā*, iii.)

From this above discussion, we can see that Krishna Das may have been born in any of these three castes. Whatever the case, a Vaishnava is a superior human being no matter in what caste he takes his birth.

All scriptures state that a Vaishnava is still the best of humankind. It it does not matter in which caste he takes birth. That most sinful person who judges a Vaishnava in terms of his race or his caste will be born repeatedly in the lowest forms of life. (Chaitanya Bhagavata 2.10.100-2)

There is no unanimous opinion about Krishna Das' marital status, either. Some say that he was a lifelong brahmachari when he went to Vrindavan, for had he left a wife and family, he would likely have mentioned it when telling of his renunciation. Srila Prabhupada writes in this connection, "After arriving in Vrindavan, Krishna Das became totally absorbed in Hari katha and indifferent to talk of his previous family life. This behavior is appropriate for someone in the third or fourth station of life and completely committed to devotional service. The Chaitanya Charitamrita is the composition of someone who has reached the status of a paramahaṁsa and is completely beyond the four ashrams. He was known as Kaviraj Goswami to his spiritual family. His spiritual identity in Vraja lila is Ratnarekha Manjari, or Kasturi Manjari according to others."

From Krishna Das' statements in the Chaitanya Charitamrita, we also learn that he had a brother. He does not name him, but Haridas Das writes in the *Gauḍīya Vaiṣṇava Abhidhāna* that he was called Shyama Das Kaviraj.

KRISHNA DAS'S VISION OF NITYANANDA PRABHU

In the course of his glorification of Nityananda Prabhu in the Chaitanya Charitamrita, Krishna Das describes the crucial event in his life. He had organized a 24-hour kirtan at his house and amongst those invited was Lord Nityananda's dear associate, Minaketan Rama Das, who also lived in Jhamatpur.

Minaketan was a great Vaishnava who was constantly in a state of devotional trance as he chanted the name of Nityananda Prabhu. While in his ecstatic moods, he would sometimes slap people and sometimes hit them with his flute. In general, his ecstatic behavior was the cause of some astonishment amongst Krishna Das' guests and most came to pay their obeisances and offer him their respects. Only Gunarnava Mishra, who had been engaged at the festival as a pujari, did not demonstrate a respectful attitude. This behavior was an indication that Gunarnava Mishra had no faith in Nityananda Prabhu. Rama Das became angry and criticized Mishra, saying:

"Just look! This is a second Romaharshan Suta, who did not come forward to show respect when he saw Balaram!" (Chaitanya Charitamrita 1.5.170)

Gunarnava Mishra was pleased to have been chastised by Rama Das and simply continued in the performance of his service to the Deity. At the end of the kirtan festival, when Gunarnava Mishra had left, however, Krishna Das Kaviraj's brother got into an argument with Minaketan Rama Das about what had happened. Krishna Das' brother had strong faith in Chaitanya Mahaprabhu, but lacked similar faith in Nityananda. Upon hearing this, Rama Das was deeply wounded and he became so angry that he broke his flute and left. The result of this curse was that Krishna Das' brother was doomed to lose whatever devotion he had. In this argument, Krishna Das Kaviraj took the side of Nityananda Prabhu's associate and rebuked his brother:

"These two brothers (Chaitanya Mahaprabhu and Nityananda Prabhu) are one body, equal in every respect. If you do not accept the divinity of Lord Nityananda, you will meet with ruin. To have faith in one while disrespecting the other is as logical as taking the half of a hen that lays the eggs. Better you should be an atheist and deny the divinity of both rather than a hypocrite who believes in one and not the other."
(Chaitanya Charitamrita 1.5.175-7)

The Lord is influenced by His devotees and He gives great importance to even the slightest display of attachment, bestowing upon them all that they desire. Krishna Das writes that by taking the part of Nityananda Prabhu's associate and chastizing his brother, he won the blessings of Nityananda Prabhu himself. Nitai came to him in a dream and ordered him to go to Vrindavan.

"O Krishna Das! Have no fear. Go to Vrindavan, for there you will attain all things." After saying this, he indicated the way to Vrindavan by waving his hand and then disappeared with his associates.
(Chaitanya Charitamrita 1.5.195-6)

In contrast, a person who shows all the customary virtues, yet holds devotees in contempt, is eternally deprived of the Lord's blessings. A good example of this is the zamindar Ramachandra Khan, who committed offenses to Hari Das Thakur as a result of which he incurred Nityananda Prabhu's displeasure. Not only did this Ramachandra lose his family and possessions, but his house was razed to the ground, leaving him with nothing. Only a fool who lacks discrimination would be so bold as to behave unjustly toward a saintly person.

With words of profound humility, Krishna Das Kaviraj Goswami proclaims the glories of Nityananda Prabhu:

> I am more sinful than Jagai and Madhai and lower than a maggot in stool. Whoever hears my name loses the results of his virtuous deeds, and whoever utters my name commits a sin. Other than Nityananda, could anyone in this world show mercy to one as abominable as me? Nityananda is the incarnation of mercy; he is so intoxicated by ecstatic love that he does not discriminate between the good and the bad. He delivers anyone who falls down before him. Therefore he has delivered such a sinful and fallen person as me. (Chaitanya Charitamrita 1.5.205-9)

KRISHNA DAS WRITES THE FINAL PASTIMES OF THE LORD

Without the mercy of Vishnu and the Vaishnavas, it is impossible to describe their glories. It is for this reason that Krishna Das Kaviraj Goswami begins each chapter of the Chaitanya Charitamrita with invocations to Mahaprabhu and His associates like Nityananda Prabhu, Advaita Acharya, and concludes each chapter with a prayer for service to the feet of Rupa and Raghunath Goswamis. He has thus shown how important it is to avoid any disrespect or offense to the Vaishnavas.

> The activities of Sri Chaitanya Mahaprabhu are by nature wonderful and sweet. When described by Vrindavan Das Thakur, they become a shower of nectar. To describe them again would not only be repetition, but a display of arrogance, for I do not possess his powers. I shall thus only present a synopsis of those events already described fully by Vrindavan Das in his *Caitanya-maṅgala*. In this book, I shall do my best to fully describe only those incidents mentioned in his outline that he did not develop. I therefore offer respectful obeisances unto the lotus feet of Vrindavan Das Thakur, praying that I will not offend his lotus feet by my action. (Chaitanya Charitamrita 2.4.5-9)

> Just as Vyasadeva compiled Lord Krishna's pastimes in Srimad Bhagavatam, Thakur Vrindavan Das depicted Lord Chaitanya's pastimes.... I offer millions of obeisances unto the lotus feet of Vrindavan Das Thakur who has delivered the entire universe through his book.
> (Chaitanya Charitamrita 1.8.35,40)

> Vrindavan Das is the authorized biographer of Sri Chaitanya Mahaprabhu and equal to Srila Vyasadeva. The way he has described the Lord's pastimes makes them more and more delectable. Afraid that it would become too voluminous, Vrindavan Das left some events out of his book. I shall try as far as possible to fill in these gaps.
> (Chaitanya Charitamrita 1.13.48-9)

H. H. Bhakti Promode Puri Goswami Maharaj, the president of the editorial board of *Chaitanya Vāṇī* magazine, explains the above statements in his foreword to the Sri Chaitanya Gaudiya Math edition of the Chaitanya Charitamrita:

> "Vrindavan Das Thakur wrote an elaborate outline of Mahaprabhu's lila at the beginning of the Chaitanya Bhagavata, but as he became absorbed in describing Nityananda's activities, many events mentioned in the outline were left out of the final version of the book. Mahaprabhu's devotees in Vrindavan were afraid that these pastimes would be forgotten and so they approached Krishna Das Kaviraj, asking him to write down a full version of these events. Krishna Das then went to the deity of Madana Mohan and asked for permission to do as he had been asked. In front of all the prominent contemporary members of the Gaudiya community in Vrindavan, Madana Mohan's garland fell from his neck. This was taken by all present as a sign of the Lord's approval and they let out a joyous cheer. Madana Mohan's pujari picked up the garland and placed it on Krishna Das's chest. Accepting it as a symbol of the Deity's wishes, Krishna Das began to write his biography of the Lord. Thus he has written in great humility:

> "Chaitanya Charitamrita is being dictated to me by Madana Mohan. My writing is like the repetition of a parrot. I write as Madana Gopal orders me, just as a wooden marionette is made to dance by a puppeteer."
> (Chaitanya Charitamrita 1.8.78-9)

In writing Chaitanya Charitamrita, Krishna Das made use of Svarupa Damodar's notes, which Raghunath Das Goswami had memorized. Srila Bhaktivinode Thakur has described this as follows:

"Sri Svarupa Damodar Goswami wrote an outline in Sanskrit (*kaṛcā*) of Mahaprabhu's later activities. He had Raghunath memorize these verses and told him to preach them throughout the world. These verses were not written down anywhere else, however. The Chaitanya Charitamrita is the gist of Svarupa Damodar's *kaṛcā*.

> With the blessings of Sri Chaitanya Mahaprabhu, though I am an insignificant living being, I have summarized in writing everything that Svarupa Damodar recorded in his notes about the Lord's pastimes, as well as everything that I heard from the mouth of Raghunath Das.
> (Chaitanya Charitamrita 3.3.267-68)

Lord Chaitanya Mahaprabhu's glorious name, form, qualities and activities all manifest in Krishna Das Kaviraj's heart, which he then published in the Chaitanya Charitamrita. He himself stated this fact in various places throughout the book:

I am now an old man and an invalid. My hand trembles as I write and my memory fails me. I am going blind and deaf, but still I manage to write and this is a great wonder.
(Chaitanya Charitamrita 2.2.89-90)

While Srila Bhaktisiddhanta Saraswati Goswami Thakur was once glorifying the supremacy of Chaitanya Charitamrita to his disciples, he instructed them as follows: "If all the books in the world were destroyed, leaving only Srimad Bhagavatam and Chaitanya Charitamrita, then people would still be able to achieve the ultimate goal in life. And even if the Srimad Bhagavatam were lost, leaving only the Chaitanya Charitamrita, there would still be no loss to humanity, for that which has not been revealed in the Bhagavatam is found in Chaitanya Charitamrita. The supreme absolute truth is Sri Chaitanya Mahaprabhu, the combined form of Radha and Krishna. The Chaitanya Charitamrita is His sound incarnation. The divine mystery of Radharani's divine status and glories are found therein. Can there be any doubt, therefore, of the supreme status of this piece of transcendental literature?"

This statement underscores the supremely special status of Krishna Das Kaviraj Goswami himself. His three books, Chaitanya Charitamrita, *Govinda-līlāmṛta* and a commentary on *Kṛṣṇa-karṇāmṛta*, are all priceless works. *Govinda-līlāmṛta* describes in detail Lord Krishna's activities over a twenty-four-hour period. Narottam Das Thakur has therefore stated:

kṛṣṇadāsa kavirāja, rasika bhakata mājh
jeṅho kailā caitanya-carita
gaura-govinda-līlā, śunite galaye sila
tāhāte nā haila mora cita

Krishna Das Kaviraj Goswami stands out amongst the devotee literati, for he is the author of the biography of Chaitanya Mahaprabhu. Even the stones melt on hearing his descriptions of Gaura and Govinda's lila. Alas, my mind has still not been attracted by these works.
(*Prema-bhakti-candrikā*)

Krishna Das was honored with the title *kavirāja*, "king of poets"–for his *Govinda-līlāmṛta*. He is also respected in the Vaishnava world as the best amongst the followers of Rupa Goswami.

THE AUTHORITATIVENESS OF THE CHAITANYA CHARITAMRITA

From the illustrious commentator Vishvanath Chakravarti's *ṭīkā* to the Chaitanya Charitamrita, we can understand a little better just how dear Krishna Das Kaviraj Goswami was to Radharani, and by the same token, how the deepest and most esoteric truths of the Divinity were revealed to him, showing that every word he wrote is to be taken as the supreme spiritual truth. H.H. Bhakti Promode Puri Goswami Maharaj has recounted the following anecdote in his Chaitanya Charitamrita foreword: "While Vishvanath Chakravarti was writing his commentary on the Chaitanya Charitamrita, *Madhya-līlā* 21.125, he was unable to understand why Kaviraj Goswami had written that the *kāma-gāyatrī* mantra consists of 24 1/2 syllables rather than 25. He became so distraught by his inability to comprehend that he finally took a vow to starve to death by the banks of Radha Kund. As he dozed off in the middle of the night, the daughter of Vrishabhanu appeared to him in a dream and said, 'O Vishvanath! Get up. Krishna Das has indeed written correctly. He is My dear girlfriend, who brings Me much pleasure. I have blessed him so that he can understand the most intimate things about Me. Do not doubt anything he has written. In the book named *Varṇāgama-bhāsvat*, it is written that whenever the syllable *ya* is followed by the syllable *vi*, it is considered to be only half a syllable.'"

In the *Bhakti-ratnākara* it is mentioned that Srinivas Acharya met Krishna Das Kaviraj, Raghunath Das Goswami and Sri Raghava when he arrived in Vrindavan
(*Bhakti-ratnākara* 4.392).

On the grounds of Krishna Das Kaviraj's home in Jhamatpur is a small temple containing Nityananda's footprints. Local legend has it that Krishna Das received Nityananda's mercy, in the form of mantra initiation, at this very spot. According to the *Prema-vilāsa*, however, Krishna Das took initiation from Raghunath Das Goswami. In the temple there is a wooden sandal that is said to have belonged to Krishna Das. His cottage and samadhi tomb are in Radha Kund. He disappeared after Raghunath Das Goswami, on the *śuklā dvādaśī* tithi of the month of Ashwin.

[26] According to Ashutosh Deb's Bengali Dictionary and Haridas Das's *Gauḍīya Vaiṣṇava Abhidhāna*, Krishna Das's parents were named Bhagirath and Sunanda.

SRI JAHNAVA DEVI

śrī-vāruṇī-revata-vaṁśa-sambhave
tasya priye dve vasudhā ca jāhnavī
śrī-sūrya-dāsasya mahātmanaḥ sute
kakudma-rūpasya ca sūrya-tejasaḥ

anaṅga-mañjarīṁ kecij jāhnavāṁ ca pracakṣate
ubhayaṁ tu samīcīnaṁ pūrva-nyāyāt satāṁ matam

Balaram's wives Varuni and Revati became Vasudha and Jahnavi, the two wives of Nityananda Prabhu, in Chaitanya lila. Both of them were the daughters of Surya Das, who was as effulgent as the sun. He was Kakudman, the father of Revati, in his previous birth. According to another opinion, Jahnava was the incarnation of Ananga Manjari. Both these opinions are possible, as we have shown that more than one identity can be joined in associates of Chaitanya Mahaprabhu.
(*Gaura-gaṇoddeśa-dīpikā* 65-6)

Jahnava's father was Surya Das Sarkhel. According to the *Gauḍīya Vaiṣṇava Abhidhāna*, her mother's name was Bhadravati. Surya Das' Sripat is in the village of Shaligram, which is not far from Nabadwip, close to the Muragacha station on the Eastern Railway. Surya Das was the third son of Kamsari Mishra. His older brothers were Damodar and Jagannath, his younger brothers, Gauri Das, Krishna Das Sarkhel and Nrisingha Chaitanya.

Surya Das Pandit made his home in Shaligram, not far from Nabadwip. He held an important post in the service of the king of Gauda, as a result of which he was given the title Sarkhel (commander) and earned a large amount of money. Surya Das and his brothers were all very pure in their character and they had a spotless reputation. His virtues are innumerable. His daughters were Vasudha and Jahnava. (*Bhakti-ratnākara* 12.3875-8)

Surya Das Sarkhel and Krishna Das were brothers who both had great faith in Nityananda and were filled with love for Krishna. (Chaitanya Charitamrita 1.11.25)

Surya Das Sarkhel was a magnanimous devotee whose brother was Gauri Das Pandit. Gauri Das took his permission to come and live in Ambika on the banks of the Ganges. (*Bhakti-ratnākara* 7.330-1)

NITYANANDA PRABHU'S WEDDING

Narahari Chakravarti Thakur has written about Jahnava Devi's holy life at length in his *Bhakti-ratnākara*. Every manifestation of Vishnu-tattva has three energies which are known as Sri, Bhū, and Nīlā or Līlā. Nityananda Prabhu is also Vishnu-tattva and possesses these three energies. In the 12th Taraṅga of the *Bhakti-ratnākara*, Lord Nityananda's wedding is described as taking place according to human custom. The essence of that description is as follows.

A certain kayastha named Krishna Das, the son of Harihor of Borgachi, a village near Shaligram, took the responsibility of seeking a wife for Nityananda Prabhu. A certain elderly Brahmin from Shaligram saw that Surya Das was worried about finding a suitable husband for his two daughters and made the following suggestion: "In the village of Ekachakra in Rarhadesh are a couple named Harai Pandit and Padmavati Devi. They were Vasudeva and Rohini in their previous roles in Krishna lila. Balaram has appeared as their son, Nityananda. Nitai travelled to all the places of pilgrimage and performed many austerities and became a great scholar before coming to Nabadwip and becoming Chaitanya Mahaprabhu's dearest associate. He is the eternal husband of your two daughters."

In a dream, Surya Das also had a vision of Nityananda as Balaram with Vasudha and Jahnava standing to his left and right in their forms as Revati and Varuni. When Surya Das took the Brahmin's advice seriously and offered the two girls to Nityananda's lotus feet, Nityananda Prabhu mercifully gave him the same vision directly. Surya Das fainted in ecstasy.

He saw Vasudha and Jahnava as Varuni and Revati, whose forms were more effulgent than mountains of gold and kunkum. Standing to the left and right of Balaram, they were decorated in magnificent jewelry and bedecked in fine, colorful clothes. Nityananda revealed this magnificence to his devotee in order to give him joy, and Surya Das completely forgot himself in his ecstasy. (*Bhakti-ratnākara* 12.3908-10)

The *adhivasa* rituals on the eve of the wedding were conducted in the house of Krishna Das Sarkhel in Shaligram. All the Brahmins of Borgachi and Shaligram were present there.

The fortunate Surya Das Sarkhel gave his two daughters away to Nityananda Prabhu according to the religious rites and popular custom. (*Bhakti-ratnākara* 12.3983)

At Sachi Mata's request, Nityananda Prabhu stayed for some time in Nabadwip after his wedding in Shantipur. He then moved to Saptagram where he stayed with Uddharan Datta, and then established a permanent residence on the banks of the Ganges in Khardaha.

Jahnava Devi herself had no sons, but Nityananda's other Shakti, Vasudha Devi, gave birth to Virabhadra (or Virachandra) Goswami and Ganga Devi, who are the incarnations of Kshirodakashayi Vishnu and the river Ganges, respectively. According to the *Gaura-gaṇoddeśa-dīpikā* (69), Ganga Devi's husband Madhavacharya is an incarnation of King Santanu, who married the goddess Ganga Devi in the Mahabharata.

JAHNAVA DEVI'S GLORIES

Virabhadra Goswami was inundated with Jahnava Mata's mercy, becoming her direct initiated disciple. Nityananda Das writes in his *Prema-vilāsa* that when Virabhadra saw Jahnava in a four-armed form, his mind was changed and he decided to accept her as his diksha guru.

Without the mercy of Nityananda Prabhu's energy, Jahnava Devi, no one is able to cross over the ocean of material life, nor can one obtain the service of Nityananda Prabhu and enter into the loving service of his worshipable Gaura Hari and Radha-Krishna. Bhaktivinode Thakur has written in his *Kalyāṇa-kalpa-taru*:

"O Jahnava Devi! Be merciful today to your servant and deliver me from my pain. Give me a place in the boat of your lotus feet so that I can be sure to cross over the ocean of birth and death. You are Nityananda's energy, you are devotion to Krishna and my guru. Please give this servant the desire tree of your lotus feet. How numerous are the fallen souls that you have saved? So this fallen beggar seeks a place at your feet.

The Mahajan Krishna Das, in the song that begins *jaya rādhe jaya kṛṣṇa jaya vṛndāvana*, has prayed for Jahnava Devi's mercy after glorifying Krishna's name, abode and associates: "Remembering Jahnava Devi's lotus feet, the lowly Krishna Das sings the names of the Lord."

JAHNAVA DEVI'S TRAVELS

Jahnava was present when Narottam Das Thakur put on a great Deity-installation festival at Kheturi village on Chaitanya Mahaprabhu's appearance day. Indeed, the installation of the deities took place under her direction. She also supervised and participated in the cooking of the first offering to the deities, which she personally made. She then served the prasad to the assembled mahantas.

> Early that morning, Jahnava Isvari rose in great delight, took her bath and did her mantra meditation. She then began to cook innumerable vegetable preparations with great enthusiasm. (*Bhakti-ratnākara* 10.686-7)

> All of Chaitanya Mahaprabhu's personal associates from Bengal were very happy to see Narottam Das. Jahnava Devi, the daughter of Surya Pandit and wife of Nityananda Prabhu, worshiped by the entire universe and expert in the distribution of the pearl of prema, was delighted to hear his name. Her joy increased when she observed his renunciation and uncommon love for Krishna. Jahnava mercifully came to Kheturi, making everyone happy by being there and giving her darshan to all. How can a person as fallen as I fully describe the compassionate nature of Srimati Jahnava Devi? (*Bhakti-ratnākara* 1.429-34)

Jahnava Devi's travels are described in the eleventh Taraṅga of *Bhakti-ratnākara*. While traveling from Kheturi to Vraja, she stopped in a prosperous village where she delivered some atheistic unbelievers and criminals and bestowed Krishna prema upon them. When she arrived in Vrindavan, she saw the samadhi of Gauri Das Pandit, which moved her to tears. When in Vrindavan, the leaders of the Vaishnava community such as Jiva Goswami, Gopal Bhatta Goswami, Lokanath Goswami, Bhugarbha Goswami, and Madhu Pandit all came to offer her their respectful greetings. In the company of these Vaishnavas, she visited the principle temples of Vrindavan—Madana Mohan, Govinda and Gopinath—before going to Radha Kund. There she met Raghunath Das Goswami, who was engaged in constant chanting of the Holy Names and whose body was emaciated by his austerities.

Jahnava remained in Radha Kund for three days, engaged in bhajan. She heard the sound of Krishna's flute while sitting on the banks of the kund and had a vision of Sri Krishna that overwhelmed her with waves of divine love. The ghat where Jahnava bathed and had this vision is known today as Sri Jahnava Ghat. She then took the company of Vaishnavas on a parikrama of Vraja Mandala. During this parikrama she heard Jiva Goswami lecture on *Bṛhad-Bhāgavatāmṛta*.

On the return journey to Gauda Desh, Jahnava visited numerous villages. She spent three or four days in Kheturi (Narottam Das's home), some time in Budhari (the home of Ramachandra Kaviraj in Murshidabad district), the place of Nityananda's birth in Ekachakra (Birbhum), Katwa (where Mahaprabhu took sannyas and where she met Yadunandan Acharya), Jajigram (Srinivas Acharya's home village), Srikhanda (the home of Raghunandan Thakur, son of Narahari Sarkar Thakur), Nabadwip, Ambika, Saptagram (where she visited Uddharan Datta's house) before finally returning to Khardaha. There she recounted the story of her entire voyage to Vasudha and Virabhadra Goswami.

By Jahnava Devi's mercy, Nityananda's dear associate Paramesvari Das Thakur was fortunate enough to see Gopinath united with Radharani in Vrindavan. When he returned to Khardaha and told Jahnava and Vasudha what he had seen, Jahnava was overwhelmed with feelings of prema. She instructed Paramesvari to go immediately to the village of Antpur and install deities of Radha and Gopinath there.

Jahnava Devi arranged for Virabhadra's marriage to Yadunandan Acharya's two daughters, Srimati and Narayani, who both became disciples of Jahnava.

Nityananda's Shakti, Srimati Jahnava Devi disappeared on the *śuklā navamī* tithi of Vaishakh.

SRI VIRACHANDRA PRABHU (VIRABHADRA)

saṅkarṣaṇasya yo vyūhaḥ
payobdhi-śāyi-nāmakaḥ
sa eva vīracandro'bhūc
caitanyābhinna-vigrahaḥ

> Kshirodakashayi Vishnu, the expansion of Sankarshan who sleeps on the ocean of milk, has become Virachandra, who is not different from Chaitanya Himself. (*Gaura-gaṇoddeśa-dīpikā* 67)

The Supreme Personality of Godhead, Sri Krishna, is the origin of unlimited expansions and incarnations. He is the *avatārī*. His first expansion is the root Sankarshan or Balaram. This same Balaram appeared with Lord Chaitanya as Nityananda Prabhu. Balaram's expansion Maha Sankarshan has his abode in the Vaikuntha planets, and he in turn expands as the *puruṣāvatāras* in the work of creation of the universe: first as Karanodakashayi Vishnu, who lies in the causal ocean, then as Garbhodakashayi Vishnu, who lies in the ocean within the individual universes, and finally as Kshirodakashayi Vishnu, who not only lies in the ocean of milk, but is the director of the individual universe and is present as the indweller of every living being within the universe. Also known as Aniruddha, Kshirodakashayi Vishnu appeared in the course of Mahaprabhu Sri Chaitanya's pastimes as Virabhadra Prabhu, the son of Lord Nityananda and his energy, Vasudha Devi.

Krishna Das Kaviraj Goswami has written in his Chaitanya Charitamrita that Virabhadra is the best of all the branches of the Nityananda trunk of the tree of devotional service that grew with Chaitanya Mahaprabhu's pastimes.

The best of all of Nityananda's branches is Virabhadra Goswami. The sub-branches which grew out of him are unlimited in number. (Chaitanya Charitamrita 1.11.56)

As with all Vishnu-tattvas, the three energies, Sri, Bhu (Bhakti), and Nila (Lila) Shakti, were all present in Virabhadra's life. Virabhadra's Sri Shakti was named Srimati, who appeared in the village of Jhamatpur in Hooghly district as the daughter of Yadunandan Acharya and Vidyunmala (Lakshmi).

Yadunandan's wife Lakshmi was extremely chaste and devoted to her husband. Two daughters were born to her, Srimati and Narayani, both of whom were startlingly beautiful. At Jahnava's behest, the fortunate Brahmin gave both of his daughters in marriage to Virabhadra.

(*Bhakti-ratnākara* 13.251-3)

Though Virabhadra belongs to the category of Vishnu-tattva, it is his lila to behave like a devotee:

The greatest branch coming out of the trunk named Nityananda is Virabhadra Goswami, who also has innumerable branches and sub-branches. It is not possible to describe them all. Although he is the lord of the creation, Virabhadra presented himself as a great devotee. Though transcendental to all Vedic injunctions, he strictly followed the Vedic religion. Though the power of God was operating within him, out of sight to the world, he showed no pride. He is the main pillar holding up the edifice of devotional service to Sri Chaitanya Mahaprabhu. It is by the glorious mercy of Sri Virabhadra Gosai that people all over the world now have the chance to chant the names of Chaitanya and Nityananda. I therefore take shelter of the lotus feet of Virabhadra Goswami, for by his mercy all desires are fulfilled.

(Chaitanya Charitamrita 1.11.8-12)

Sri Narahari Chakravarti Thakur has written the following about Virabhadra in his *Bhakti-ratnākara*:

Nityananda Prabhu had a single son, Virabhadra, who was an ocean of virtue and capable of purifying the world. There is no limit to his glories, so who can sufficiently glorify him? He is famed as the branch of Nityananda Prabhu... The root of all joy, he is sometimes known as Virabhadra and sometimes as Virachandra. If anyone sees him even once he will give up everything and make his lotus feet his all-in-all.

(*Bhakti-ratnākara* 9.413-4, 420-1)

Virabhadra took initiation from his aunt and stepmother, Jahnava Devi. In his *Anubhāṣya*, Srila Bhaktisiddhanta Saraswati Goswami Thakur has made the following comments, "Virabhadra Goswami had three disciples, who were later celebrated as his sons—Gopijanavallabha, Ramakrishna and Ramachandra. The youngest, Ramachandra, belonged to the Shandilya dynasty and had the surname Batavyala. He established his family at Khardaha, and its members are known as the Khardaha Goswamis. The eldest disciple, Gopijanavallabha, was a resident of a village known as Lata, near the Mankor railway station in the district of Burdwan. Ramakrishna lived near Maldah, in a village named Gayeshpur."

According to the thirteenth chapter of the *Bhakti-ratnākara*, Virabhadra took permission from his mother Vasudha to go to Vrindavan. Upon arriving there, he performed Vraja Dham parikrama with the blessings of Bhugarbha and Sri Jiva Goswamis.

The old Shyamasundar temple in Khardaha has a manuscript of the Bhagavatam that is said to have been hand copied by Virabhadra Prabhu. Some hold that this was actually written by Nityananda Prabhu himself. Virabhadra personally brought a piece of stone to Khardaha from which deities were carved. The landing site on the Ganges where this stone was unloaded and brought on shore is known as Shyamasundar Ghat. These deities, which are still worshiped in Khardaha, are named Shyamasundar, Radhavallabha, and Nandadulal. Virabhadra established the custom of celebrating the birth of Nityananda Prabhu at Khardaha. The current managers of the Khardaha temple tell many other legends about the life of Virabhadra Goswami.

The date of Virabhadra's appearance is usually given as Karttik *kṛṣṇā navamī*. The *Gauḍīya Vaiṣṇava Abhidhāna*, however, gives the date as Agrahayan *śuklā caturdaśī*.

Srila Gopal Guru Goswami

Gopal Guru Goswami's name is found in neither the Chaitanya Charitamrita nor the Chaitanya Bhagavata, but information about his life has been preserved in the histories of the Radha Kanta Math in Puri.

Gopal Guru was born in an Orissan Brahmin family. His father's name was Murari Pandit. His mother's name is unknown. While still a child, he had the opportunity to serve Mahaprabhu under the guidance of Govinda, the Lord's servant. His original name was Makaradhvaja Pandit, but Mahaprabhu used to affectionately call him Gopal.

Gopal Guru was the disciple of Vakresvara Pandit, one of the Lord's close associates living in Jagannath Puri.[27] This is confirmed in the book *Vakreśvara-carita*, where the following passage is found:

There are five branches in the lineage descending from Vakresvara Pandit—those coming from Chandrasekhara, Shankararanya Acharya, Govindananda, Devananda and

Gopal Guru, whose qualities are beyond description.

From the book *Guru-praṇālī* published by the Radha Kanta Math, we learn that Gopal Guru Goswami was the sakhi Manjumedha in Vraja lila.

HOW HE GOT THE NAME GOPAL GURU

There is a legend surrounding the addition of the word guru to Gopal's name. There was once a devotee in Puri who was particularly attached to the chanting of the Holy Names. As a matter of fact, the chanting had become automatic for him, so that his tongue muttered the names incessantly. One day Gopal saw this devotee on his way to the toilet, holding his tongue between his fingers because he did not wish to chant the Holy Name while engaged in an impure act. Gopal was just a lad, but he was able to understand why the devotee was doing this and so said to him, "What are you doing? Don't you know that there are no regulations governing the time and place for chanting the Holy Name? One should chant the Name in all times and circumstances, pure or impure. If you were not able to chant while defecating, how would you be able to have an auspicious death, should death suddenly come upon you at that time?"

Mahaprabhu overheard Gopal sharing this wisdom with the Vaishnava and was very impressed and He announced to all his devotees that Gopal was doing the work of a guru. From that day on, the young Makaradhvaja Pandit was known to the Vaishnavas as Gopal Guru. The name was appropriate, because he both preached and practiced and was thus factually acting as an acharya or guru.

It did not take long for his fame to spread through the Vaishnava world. Abhiram Thakur had the reputation of being able to verify whether a stone was a real Vishnushila or Shalagram Shila by paying his obeisances to it. If not real, it would crack or turn into dust. Only a pure Vaishnava would be able to tolerate his obeisances, otherwise they could prove fatal. When the Vaishnavas heard that Abhiram Thakur had come to Puri to test Gopal Guru, they were anxious for the boy for whom they felt great affection. Mahaprabhu realized that everyone was troubled and so he placed his foot on Gopal's forehead, thus creating the distinctive tilak marking that is used to this day by those in Gopal Guru's spiritual lineage. Even so, Gopal was still frightened and so he sat in the Lord's lap for protection. Abhiram's obeisances could thus do him no harm.

THE SERVICE OF RADHA KANTA DEVA

Maharaj Prataparudra's father Purushottam Deva brought several deities back from Kanchi with him after defeating that city's king. Among these deities was the mūrti of Radha Kanta. This deity was first placed in a small temple on the northwestern corner of Jagannath's Chatrabhoga temple, but later, Prataparudra's guru Kashi Mishra asked to be given the deity for his personal service. Kashi Mishra had bequeathed everything he possessed to Mahaprabhu as he had no children of his own. Mahaprabhu then gave the service of Radha Kanta, his temple and the surrounding gardens, etc., to Gopal Guru. His guru, Vakresvara Pandit, never sat on the gadi,"or, in other words, never acted as acharya, at Radha Kanta Math. Rather, he stayed absorbed in kirtan and danced in the company of Mahaprabhu.

The tithi marking Mahaprabhu's bestowal of Radha Kanta's service on Gopal Guru is celebrated on the *śuklā dvādaśī* of Magh. On this day, he also gave him the post of first acharya of the Radha Kanta Math and the occasion is marked annually by an abhishek of the present-day abbot of the Math.

Srila Bhaktivinode Thakur has written the following about Gopal Guru Goswami: "Vakresvara Pandit's disciple Gopal Guru Goswami is currently abbot of Mahaprabhu's own math in the house of Kashi Mishra in Purushottam. He has completely memorized the teachings of Sri Svarupa Damodar Goswami." (*Jaiva Dharma*)

Svarupa Damodar's method of worshiping in the *madhura-rasa* was spread through the world through two different lines: one through Raghunath Das Goswami which was carried through Krishna Das Kaviraj Goswami, the other through Vakresvara Pandit and Gopal Guru Goswami. Gopal Guru wrote two books on the subject, *Smaraṇa-krama-paddhati* ("A guidebook to the steps to remembering") or *Sevā-smaraṇa-paddhati* ("A guidebook to remembering and service") and *Gaura-govindārcana-paddhati* ("A guidebook to Gaura-Govinda's deity worship").

From the time of Gopal Guru, Kashi Mishra's house was known as Radha Kanta Math. During Kashi Mishra's lifetime, the deity of Krishna was worshiped alone. While Gopal Guru was in charge of the temple, however, a deity of Radha was placed at Radha Kanta's left side and a deity of Lalita on his right. Deities of Gauranga and Nityananda were also installed and the temple buildings repaired and enlarged during this time, between 1538 and 1548 AD.

In the Orissan language a small separate room situated on temple grounds is given the name *gambhīrā*. Bhaktivinode Thakur has written, "In the customary architecture of a temple in Orissa, the deity room itself has a verandah (alinda) facing it. Facing the verandah is a paved and covered area known as the *dālān*. A small room within this area is given the name *gambhīrā*." The Gambhira at Kashi Mishra's house marks the place where Mahaprabhu performed His meditation and where He slept. Gopal Guru kept Mahaprabhu's wooden shoes and a quilt, which was made either by Svarupa Damodar Goswami or Jagadananda Pandit, in the Gambhira where they are worshiped. The waterpot made of clay from the Vraja area which Mahaprabhu used is also kept there, along with a wooden waterpot that was placed there in later times.

From *Bhakti-ratnākara* (8.382, 389) we learn that when Narottam Das Thakur visited Puri, he came to Kashi Mishra's house and met Gopal Guru, who greeted him very affectionately.

MIRACULOUS EVENTS AT GOPAL GURU'S DEATH

A few accounts of miraculous events are told about Gopal Guru. When Gopal Guru grew old, he turned the responsibility for the Radha Kanta Math over to his disciple, Dhyana Chandra. When he died not long after, his successor was overcome with grief. He took his guru's body to the Svarga Dwar (The gate to heaven) on the Puri seafront, where bodies were formerly cremated.

While he and other disciples of Gopal Guru Goswami were at the cremation ground, some representatives of a government department barricaded the temple, claiming that the transfer of authority to Dhyana Chandra had been done without ministerial sanction. When Dhyana Chandra heard that this was going on, he fell at the lotus feet of his guru's body, tears flowing from his eyes. Gopal Guru's body was already on the funeral pyre, but the prayers of his dear disciple reached him and he was revived. He rose up, chanting the Holy Names in sankirtan.

As soon as the government representatives heard of this event, they became fearful and abandoned their effort to take over Radha Kanta Math. Gopal Guru returned to the temple and made a legal written transfer of ownership to his disciple before disappearing finally some time later on the Karttik *śuklā navamī*.

A year after Gopal Guru disappeared, when some devotees who had made the trip from Vraja for the Rathayatra returned home, they were amazed to see

Gopal Guru sitting under a Pakur tree in Vamsi Bata, chanting japa. They sent the message to Dhyana Chandra in Puri and he immediately hurried to Vrindavan to see his guru. He fell down at his feet and begged to be allowed to stay in Vraja, even though Gopal Guru told him to go back to Puri and take care of his responsibilities. Finally Gopal told Dhyana Chandra, "If you feel such separation from me that you are unable to tolerate it, then have an image of me made out of a neem tree and place it in front of the altar room of the temple and worship it." This was done and the statue of Gopal Guru Goswami is worshiped at the Radha Kanta Math to this day.

GOPAL GURU GOSWAMI'S SUCAKA KIRTAN

The following kirtan is sung on Gopal Guru's disappearance day.

āre mora gopāla guru bhakati kalapa taru
makara-dhvaja nāma jāṅhāra
śrī kṛṣṇa caitanya jāṅke gopāla baliye ḍāke
dekhi śiśu caritra udāra

gaurāṅgera sevā-rase sadāi ānande bhāse
gorā binu nāhi jāne ān
tileka nā dekhi jāṅre dhairaja dharite nāre
gorā jena gopālera prāṇ

gopāla śiśura prati śikṣā dila eka rīti
prabhu premāveśe ḍhuli ḍhuli
kahe sabe āre āre āji haite gopālere
ḍākibā gopāla guru bali

gopāle karuṇā dekhi sabāra sajala āṅkhi
sukhera samudra uchalila
sabe kahe anupāma śrī gopāla guru nāma
prabhu datta jagate vyāpila

gopālera guru-bhakti kahite nāhika śakti
sadāi prasanna vakreśvara
mahāmatta nija-gīte nāhika upamā dite
sarva cittākarṣa kalevara

dekhila sakala ṭhāṅi emana dayālu nāi
kebā nā jagate yaśa ghoṣe
sabe kaila prema-pātra haila vañcita mātra
narahari nija karma doṣe

O Gopal Guru, you are my devotional desire tree. Your name was previously Makaradhvaja, but Sri Krishna Chaitanya called you Gopal because your behavior as a child reminded him of Gopal Krishna.

You were always absorbed in the joy of serving Gauranga; indeed you knew nothing other than Him. You could not tolerate being separated from the Lord for even a moment; it was as if Gaura was Gopal's very life.

One day, Gopal was explaining some devotional practices to another child. The Lord was so ecstatic when He saw this that he said to everyone, "From today on, I will call Gopal 'guru'."

Tears filled the devotees' eyes when they saw how merciful the Lord was to Gopal; it was as though the ocean of joy was overflowing. Everyone said that Gopal Guru was an extraordinary name and, as the Lord had given it, they all used it.

I am incapable of describing Gopal's devotion to his guru, Vakresvara, who was always pleased with him. The incomparable Gopal Guru, whose appearance was attractive to everyone, was always intoxicated in singing his own devotional songs.

Everyone recognized that no one was as merciful as he. Who in the world did not sing his glories? He made everyone worthy of loving ecstasy; only I, Narahari, have been deprived of it because of my own misdeeds.

[27] See chapter about Vakresvara Pandit (page 61).

SRINIVAS ACHARYA

SRINIVAS'S BIRTH

Srinivas Acharya was born in 1530 AD, on the full moon day of the month of Vaishakh, in the village of Chakhandi, which lies just north of Agradwip in the district of Nadia. His father, Gangadhara Bhattacharya, was a Brahmin of the Rarha class. The *Bhakti-ratnākara* describes how this came about:

Gangadhara was overcome with grief when Mahaprabhu took sannyas in Katwa and he began to cry constantly while calling out the names "Ha Chaitanya! Ha Chaitanya!" When the other devotees saw him intoxicated in divine love for Mahaprabhu, they nicknamed him Chaitanya Das, a name that stuck with him for the rest of his life.

Chaitanya Das was indifferent to the things of this world, but one day he suddenly felt a strong wish to have a son and told this to his wife, Lakshmi Priya. She responded by telling him to go immediately to Puri to get Mahaprabhu's blessings. The couple left for Puri, first stopping for a few days in Jajigram at the house of Lakshmi Priya's father, Balaram Vipra.

When they arrived in Puri, Chaitanya Das and his wife paid their obeisances to Mahaprabhu. Before they could speak, however, the Lord Himself spoke, understanding their wish to have a son: "Jagannath Deva will surely fulfill all your desires."

The other devotees were curious about what desire Mahaprabhu was talking about and they asked his servant Govinda to find out. Before Govinda could ask anything, however, Mahaprabhu called him over and said in a deep voice, as if from a trance state: "Chaitanya Das desires to have a child. Indeed, his wife will soon give birth to a jewel of a son, who will be named Srinivas. He will be the manifest form of My love, and will be nondifferent from Me. He will increase everyone's enthusiasm for devotion. I will bring scriptures into the world through Rupa, Sanatan and others; through Srinivas, I shall distribute them. Srinivas is the embodiment of pure love for Me. All minds will be enthused upon seeing him."(*Bhakti-ratnākara* 2.120-3)

Once they had received Mahaprabhu's blessing, Chaitanya Das and his wife returned to his home and when the auspicious moment came, a son was born to them. Chaitanya Das immediately consecrated the child to Mahaprabhu.

The baby went through the early childhood rituals of the first feeding of solid food, name-giving, and hair-cutting. All the local associates of Mahaprabhu, such as Govinda Ghosh and the residents of Srikhanda, Narahari and Raghunandan, poured affectionate blessings on the child.

EARLY EDUCATION AND TRAVELS

Srinivas Acharya was devoted to his parents. He was fortunate to hear about Mahaprabhu's divine glories as well as Radha and Krishna's Vrindavan pastimes from Chaitanya Das. Father and son would go into an ecstatic state as they discussed these transcendental topics. His mother trained him in kirtan. He also studied grammar, literature and poetic theory from Dhananjaya Vidya Vachaspati, and quickly acquired mastery of these subjects.

Srinivas's father died while he was still quite younng. The loss of his father's association greatly affected Srinivas, but the other devotees made a concerted effort to console him and his mother in their grief.

Srinivas took his mother and moved from Chakhandi to his maternal grandfather's house in Jajigram where the villagers were overjoyed to see him. Shortly after moving to Jajigram, he went to visit Narahari Sarkar in nearby Srikhanda. From Narahari he learned that Mahaprabhu would shortly be ending his earthly pastimes. This news made Srinivas determined to see the Lord before it happened. He quickly returned to Jajigram and took permission from his mother to make the trip to Puri. He then joined the devotees on the annual pilgrimage. It was the fifth day of the waxing moon.

Before Srinivas arrived in Puri, however, the news that Mahaprabhu had indeed ended His lila reached the party of pilgrims. Srinivas Acharya fainted at hearing this report, and when he came back to consciousness, he decided to commit suicide. However, the Lord Himself appeared to him in a dream and told him to complete his journey to Puri. Once in Puri, Srinivas again had a dream in which he saw Jagannath, Subhadra and Balaram, as well as Chaitanya Mahaprabhu with His associates.

In Puri, Srinivas met Srila Gadadhar Pandit Goswami, the incarnation of Mahaprabhu's pleasure potency, and both of them were immersed in an ocean of ecstasy. He also met Ray Ramananda, Paramananda Puri, Shikhi Mahiti, Sarvabhauma Pandit, Vakresvara Pandit, Govinda, Shankar Pandit, and Gopinath Acharya, and received blessings from them all. Srinivas stayed in Puri for some time, hearing Srimad Bhagavatam from Gadadhar Pandit Goswami. Gadadhar then told him to return to Gauda.

When Srinivas arrived in Bengal, he learned that Advaita Acharya and Nityananda Prabhu had also wound up their earthly pastimes. Once again he determined to end his life, but the two Prabhus appeared to him in a dream to assuage his grief and persuaded him to give up his resolve.

When he arrived in Nabadwip, Srinivas was once again plunged into an ocean of despondency at the loss of Chaitanya Mahaprabhu. Vamsivadanananda Thakur saw him in this condition and approached Vishnupriya Devi and asked her to grant Srinivas an audience and to bless him. Srinivas Acharya was amazed to see the intense renunciation and deep faith of Mahaprabhu's widow. While in Nabadwip, he had a dream of Sachi Devi and received blessings from her, too. Srinivas then wandered throughout Bengal, going to all the Sripats of the associates of Mahaprabhu and Nityananda Prabhu, seeking their blessings. In this way he visited Shantipur, Khardaha, Khanakul Krishnanagar, and Srikhanda. Among the parshads he met were Murari Gupta, Srivasa Pandit, Damodar Pandit, Shuklambar Brahmachari, Gadadhar Das, Paramesvari Das, Jahnava Devi, Vasudha Devi, Virabhadra, Abhiram Thakur, Narahari Sarakar Thakur, and Raghunandan Thakur. All these great personalities witnessed Srinivas's intense devotion and instructed him to go to Vrindavan. Srinivas went to his mother and asked her for permission to make the trip. Lakshmipriya could not refuse him when she saw how eager he was to visit the land of Krishna and the Goswamis.

SRINIVAS ARRIVES IN VRAJA

Srinivas traveled north through Agradwip, Katwa, Maureshwar and Ekachakra, then west to Kashi, Ayodhya, and Prayag. He spent a long time visiting all these holy places before he finally arrived in Vraja. There he learned that Rupa Goswami, Sanatan Goswami, Kashisvara Pandit and Raghunath Bhatta Goswami had all disappeared. Raghunath Das Goswami, Gopal Bhatta Goswami and Jiva Goswami were still living, however. Srinivas met all three of them and received their blessings. He was initiated by Gopal Bhatta and took instruction in the Vaishnava scriptures from Jiva. In great affection for Srinivas, Jiva commended him to his deities, Radha Damodar. Srinivas met Raghunath Das and Krishna Das Kaviraj in Radha Kund and received their blessings. One day Sri Jiva heard Srinivas explain a verse from *Ujjvala-nīlamaṇi* and was so impressed by his erudition that he bestowed the title "Acharya" upon him. Jiva also gave the titles "Thakur" to Narottam and "Shyamananda" to Duhkhi Krishna Das. Jiva ordered Srinivas to tour all of Vraja's pilgrimage sites with Raghava Goswami.

THE RETURN TO BENGAL

After Srinivas had attained mastery of the Gaudiya Vaishnava scriptures, Sri Jiva and the other Vaishnavas in Vraja ordered him, Narottam and Shyamananda to take manuscripts of these invaluable books back to Bengal in an ox-cart. They set off on the *śuklā pañcamī* of Agrahayan month. It was a long and dangerous trip, but they were able to cover the greater part of the distance without any trouble. Upon arriving in the Hindu kingdom of Bana Vishnupur, they felt that the danger was over. However, a rumor had reached the capital of Vishnupur that a rich merchant was travelling to Puri with a valuable cargo of merchandise.

Bir Hambir, the ruler of Bana Vishnupur, was also the leader of a gang of highwaymen. When he heard that a cargo of great value was passing through his territory, he asked an astrologer to divine the truth of the rumors. The astrologer confirmed that the chest being carried on the ox cart was indeed of great value. The king immediately sent a group of robbers to steal the chest, thinking that it contained gold and jewels and certainly not a number of manuscripts. He specified to the robbers that they should kill no one.

The robbers first worshiped the goddess Chandi, then sent out a spy who returned to report that everyone in the group accompanying the oxcart was sleeping in exhaustion after eating their evening meal. The robbers felt that Chandi had mercifully given them a golden opportunity to make the raid. They swooped down and seized the oxcart and the books, and turned them over to the king of Vishnupur.

When Bir Hambir saw the large chest, he was delighted at the prospect of finding large booty inside. How disappointed he must have been to see nothing but books! He turned to the astrologer and asked him how he could have made such a mistake. The astrologer answered, "I can't understand it. Every time I made my calculations I came up with the same conclusion: this chest is full of priceless jewels! It is incredible, I don't know where my calculations could have gone wrong!"

The mere sight of the holy books had a purifying effect on the king, however, and he regretted having stolen them. Indeed, he desired to meet with the acharya who owned them, the *granthācārya*. That night he had a dream in which this spiritual master appeared to him and this pacified him somewhat.

The next morning, Srinivas, Narottam and Shyamananda awoke to find the chest of books missing. They searched everywhere, but when they failed to find any clue of the books' whereabouts, they felt so depressed that they considered killing themselves. Some local villagers saw the distressed condition of the three Vaishnavas and immediately suspected the robber king, Bir Hambir. Srinivas made further inquiries and was assured that he would be able to find more information from the king himself. The three Vaishnavas felt some hope and abandoned their suicidal intentions. Srinivas Acharya decided to remain in Vishnupur in the hope that he would be able to recover the manuscripts, but he sent Narottam to Kheturi and Shyamananda to Orissa.

THE CONVERSION OF BIR HAMBIR

While staying in Vishnupur, Srinivas heard from a Brahmin named Krishnavallabha that Bir Hambir liked to listen to Srimad Bhagavatam and daily attended classes. On the next day, Srinivas went with this Brahmin to the hall where the Bhagavata classes were held. The Brahmin introduced Srinivas to the king as a great Vaishnava, and the king indeed observed the characteristics of a great person in him and was attracted to him. The King expressed a desire to hear Srinivas speak on the Bhagavata and Srinivas agreed, thinking that this might be a good opportunity to recover the books. So he started to deliver lectures on the

Bhagavata on a daily basis. The King was enchanted by Srinivas's unprecedented explanations of the Bhagavata in his sweet voice.

Srinivas Acharya preached Mahaprabhu's dharma both through speaking on the Bhagavata and kirtan, while Narottam and Shyamananda primarily used the medium of kirtan. Each of them had his own particular style of singing kirtan, by which they intoxicated their listeners with devotional ecstasy. The styles that these three acharyas developed were named *manohara-sāhī*, *garāṇahāṭī*, and *reṇeṭī*. Unfortunately, these styles of kirtan are no longer extant.

Bir Hambir arranged for a secluded dwelling to be given to Srinivas Acharya. One day, when he had the opportunity to find the king alone in his apartments, Srinivas recounted the entire story of his journey from Vraja and the theft of the manuscripts. The King immediately confessed, showing great sorrow for his misdeed, and had the chest of books returned to its owner. Greatly relieved, Srinivas immediately sent messengers to Narottam, Shyamananda and Vrindavan with the good news. In the course of time, Bir Hambir and his entire entourage all took initiation from Srinivas and dedicated their entire lives and wealth to him. At initiation, Bir Hambir was given the name Chaitanya Das.

SRINIVAS'S MARRIAGE

After staying in Vana Vishnupur for some time, Srinivas Acharya returned to his maternal grandfather's house in Jajigram. Then he set off on another tour of Katwa, Nabadwip and other important towns in Bengal. Srinivas respected Narahari Sarkar of Srikhanda greatly and was also very devoted to his saintly mother. When Narahari heard Srinivas's mother express her desire to see her son married, he gave him the order to do so. Even prior to receiving this order, Srinivas had received the same command from Advaita Acharya in a dream. Though he felt somewhat ashamed, he realized that he could not ignore the wishes of Narahari, his mother and Advaita Prabhu. He thus agreed to get married and was wed to Ishwari, the devoted daughter of Gopal Chakravarti of Jajigram.

It is not always easy to understand the divine activities of Mahaprabhu's devotees. Only someone who is totally surrendered to the Lord and His devotees can comprehend their glories.

SRINIVAS'S PREACHING ACTIVITIES

Srinivas Acharya started to teach the Goswamis' books to his disciples in Jajigram. One of his most important disciples was Ramachandra Kaviraj, the son of Srikhanda resident Chiranjiva Sen. Srinivas gave Ramachandra the title kavirāja after hearing his poems. Narottam Thakur had a close friendship with Ramachandra Kaviraj and even wrote about it in one of his songs:

dayā kara śrī-ācārya prabhu śrīnivāsa
rāmacandra saṅga mate narottama dāsa

"O my master, Srinivas Acharya! Please be merciful to me. I, Narottam Das, beg you to give me the association of Ramachandra."

When Shuklambar Brahmachari, Gadadhar Das, Narahari Sarkar and Dvija Hari Das all ended their earthly activities, Srinivas Acharya once again felt overcome by grief and made another trip to Vrindavan. Ramachandra Kaviraj and Shyamananda Prabhu also joined him in Vraja on this occasion. Once again Srinivas met with Gopal Bhatta and Sri Jiva Goswamis, as well as with Bhugarbha and Lokanath Goswamis, and these great devotees encouraged him and diminished his feelings of loss.

When he returned to Gauda, Srinivas joined in the festivities occasioning the anniversaries of the departure of Gadadhar Das in Katwa, Narahari in Srikhanda and Dvija Hari Das in Kanchan Gariya. From there he went to Budhari village, where Ramachandra Kaviraj and Govinda Kaviraj hosted him in great opulence.

Narottam Das Thakur had also left Vrindavan on Lokanath Goswami's orders, returning to his home in Kheturi. On the full moon day of Phalgun, he established the worship of six sets of deities in the temple there: Gauranga, Vallabhi Kanta, Vraja Mohan, Sri Krishna, Radha Kanta, and Radha Raman. Srinivas Acharya performed the installation ceremony and the first puja.

Jahnava Devi was also present at this great event. After the festival, she went on to Vraja with her entourage. Upon her return, she met with Srinivas Acharya at Katwa and then went with him to Jajigram where she spent some time as his guest.

Srinivas Acharya made another trip to Nabadwip with Narottam and Ramachandra Kaviraj, performing the parikrama of the nine islands, each of which represents one of the limbs of devotional service.

When Raghunandan Thakur entered *nitya-līlā*, Srinivas Acharya went to Srikhanda to help conduct the funeral festival in his honor. He returned with a heavy heart to Jajigram, and from there went to see his disciples in Vana Vishnupur. The king and other residents of the town were excited by his visit and received him with great pomp. In Vishnupur, Srinivas received an order from Mahaprabhu in a dream to accept the hand of Gauranga Priya, the daughter of a certain Raghava Chakravarti. Raghava and his wife Madhavi had been searching for a suitable husband for their daughter with no success. They had simultaneously received the order to give their daughter in marriage to Srinivas in a dream. Srinivas thus married for a second time.

Pure devotees have no objective in life other than to fulfill the desires of the Supreme Lord. They are thus ready to do anything if it pleases the Lord. None of their activities has the slightest hint of material desire in it. Srinivas Acharya is the *āveśa* incarnation of Mahaprabhu, and only a person who has received his special blessings can describe his transcendental activities.

Srila Narottam Das Thakur

ākumāra-brahmacārī sarva-tīrtha-darśī
parama-bhāgavatottamaḥ śrīla-narottama-dāsaḥ

Narottam Das was a brahmachari throughout his entire life. He visited all the places of pilgrimage. He was on the highest platform of devotional achievement.
(*Bhakti-ratnākara* 1.279)

Narottam Thakur was Champaka Manjari in Krishna lila. Eternally assisting Rupa Manjari in her service to Radha and Krishna, Champaka Manjari was merciful to the conditioned souls of this earth and appeared as Narottam in the village of Kheturi, about twelve miles from Rampur Bowalia in the Gopalpur subdivision of Rajshahi district. This took place on the full moon day of the month of Magh sometime around the middle of the 15th century of the Śaka era.

Narottam was born on the *māghī pūrṇimā*. From that day on he thrived and grew like the waxing moon.
(*Bhakti-ratnākara* 1.281)

Narottam's father was Raja Krishnananda Datta, the zamindar of the Gopalpur area. His mother's name was Narayani Devi. Raja Krishnananda had a younger brother named Purushottam Datta, who had a son named Santosh. In order to show that His associates can take birth in any caste, Krishna had Narottam take birth in a kayastha family.

From his early childhood, Narottam began to show signs of his future greatness. Everyone was amazed to see his great intelligence and devotional demeanor. He was constantly absorbed in meditation on the wonderful qualities of Sri Chaitanya Mahaprabhu and Nityananda Prabhu. The Lord and His associates often appeared to him in his dreams.

As tears poured from his eyes, Narottam would offer prayers of surrender to Sri Krishna Chaitanya, Nityananda, Advaita and the other associates of the Lord. Finally, the Lord and His associates appeared to him in a dream and consoled him with kind words.
(*Bhakti-ratnākara* 1.285-6)

Mahaprabhu Leaves Prema Behind for Narottam

According to the *Prema-vilāsa*, when Mahaprabhu passed through Kanair Natshala, as he was dancing ecstatically in kirtan, he began to call out Narottam's name. When Nityananda asked him why he was calling out this name, Mahaprabhu answered, "My Lord, you do not know your own glories. When we were in Jagannath Puri, you shed tears out of divine love, day after day. I managed to capture your divine love and save it. Now I wish to place it here by the Padmavati River in safekeeping for Narottam Das."[28]

Mahaprabhu then went to the place known as Kutubpur on the Padmavati River, where He bathed and sang and danced in ecstasy. He then called out to the river, "O Padmavati! Take my love and keep it here. When Narottam comes and bathes here, give it to him."

Padmavati inquired, "How will I recognize him?"

Mahaprabhu answered, "You will have no trouble recognizing Narottam, for as soon as he enters your waters, they will overflow."

The place where Mahaprabhu placed prema for Narottam's sake was later given the name Prematoli. When Narottam was twelve years old, he had a dream in which Nityananda Prabhu told him to bathe in the Padmavati and take the prema that had been stored there for him. He went the next day to the Padma and as soon as he put his foot in the water, the river started to overflow. Padmavati then remembered Mahaprabhu's words and gave Narottam the prema she had guarded for all that time.

Narottam Leaves Home

As soon as he experienced the ecstasies of prema, Narottam's character, his appearance—everything about him changed. His parents noticed the transformation and did everything they could to bring him back to his normal state, but failed. Having drunk the wine of divine ecstasy, Narottam had become intoxicated and the bonds of family life could no longer hold him back.

Narottam began to wonder how he could escape from his material entanglements. Finally, one day when his father and uncle were away on official business, he practiced some deception on his mother and tricked his bodyguards so that he could leave his family for Vrindavan. It was the full-moon day of Karttik when this event took place.

According to others, Narottam waited to go to Vrindavan until after the death of his father when his cousin Santosh was given the responsibility for the zamindari. Even though he was the son of a rich zamindar, in his desire to unite with the Lord, he was ready to abandon the pleasures of the body in a moment. Day and night, walking barefoot, crying, forgetting to eat and drink until finally he fell unconscious under a tree. Then a golden-skinned Brahmin came and offered him a cup of milk and said to him in a sweet voice, "O Narottam, drink this milk. Your cuts and bruises will go away. Compose yourself, for everything will turn out well."

After saying this, the Brahmin vanished and the exhausted Narottam was finally able to rest. That night, he dreamt of Rupa and Sanatan Goswami. The two Goswamis placed their hands on his chest and fed him the milk that Mahaprabhu Himself had brought him. All of Narottam's fatigue disappeared.

Narottam Is Initiated by Lokanath Goswami

The *Prema-vilāsa* also describes how Narottam took initiation from Lokanath Goswami. Narottam was born on the full-moon day of Magh, his renunciation took place on the full-moon day of Karttik, and he was initiated by Lokanath on the full-moon day of Shravan.

Lokanath Goswami is considered to be a personal associate of Sri Chaitanya Mahaprabhu. Indeed, he was the first Gaudiya Vaishnava to be instructed by the Lord to go to Vrindavan, along with Bhugarbha Goswami. Lokanath set the standard for worship in a spirit of renunciation while in the Holy Dham. He was a *viviktānandī* Vaishnava, that is, a hermit one who worships the Lord in solitude. In this spirit, he had vowed not to take any disciples. Narottam Das too made a vow—to take initiation from no one other than Lokanath. Though he was the son of a raja, Narottam's desire to receive Lokanath's mercy was so great that he went in the middle of every night to clean the place he used as a toilet. He would also leave fine earth and water for him to clean himself afterward. This is described as follows in the *Prema-vilāsa*:

> Narottam went to the place where the Goswami performed his bodily functions and did a special job of cleaning it. He sifted the soil to make a fine, clean earth with which Lokanath could clean his hands. He would hide his coconut-leaf broom and take it out each night to sweep the place clean, his heart filled with joy. All these things he did as a regular service. He considered himself to be fortunate to have this service and that it made his body worthwhile. He would hold the broom to his chest, repeating, "This is where I will get the strength to attain my Lord's lotus feet." As he said these words, he cried and torrents of tears washed over his chest.
>
> Lokanath was astonished to see that his toilet area was daily being kept clean. He became curious to to find out who was doing it and so, one evening, he went and hid in the jungle, chanting japa the entire night in wait for the anonymous benefactor. At midnight, he saw someone engaged in cleaning the place and asked him who he was. When he found out that Narottam, the son of a raja, was doing this filthy task, he felt embarrassed and told him to desist. Narottam, however, immediately fell at Lokanath's feet and began to cry. When Lokanath saw Narottam's humility and pain, his resolve softened and he finally gave him initiation. Thus Narottam Das gave an outstanding example to the world of how one should engage in the service of one's spiritual master.

> "Narottam went there and engaged in whatever service was necessary to his guru, performing it with great enthusiasm. Lokanath was pleased by Narottam's service and showed him the greatest mercy by initiating him in the mantra. (*Bhakti-ratnākara* 1.345-6)

> Without caring for his youth or his looks, he left home on the full moon day of the month of Karttik. After wandering through many pilgrimage places, he finally came to Vrindavan where he became Lokanath Goswami's disciple. On the auspicious day of *śrāvaṇī pūrṇimā*, Lokanath initiated Narottam. (*Bhakti-ratnākara* 1.292-4)

Narottam Das was thus Lokanath's one and only disciple. Srila Bhaktisiddhanta Saraswati Goswami Thakur demonstrated similar perseverance and patience in service to his spiritual master in order to convince him to accept him as a disciple. Gaura Kishor Das Babaji, like Lokanath, had vowed to take no disciples. He refused Srila Prabhupada three times, but this did not break Prabhupada's will. When Gaura Kishor saw Srila Prabhupada's humility and intense desire, he finally relented and gave him mantra diksha. Srila Prabhupada was Gaura Kishor Das's only disciple.

After the disappearance of Rupa and Sanatan Goswamis, Sri Jiva Goswami became the Gaudiya Vaishnava sampradaya's undisputed intellectual leader throughout Mathura, Bengal and Orissa and the chief-minister of the universal court of Vaishnavas at Vrindavan—the Viśva-vaiṣṇava-rāja-sabhā. Srinivas Acharya, Narottam Das, and Duhkhi Krishna Das all studied the scriptures under Jiva, receiving detailed personal instruction from him. When their studies were completed, Jiva gave them the titles of Acharya, Thakur and Shyamananda, respectively.

NAROTTAM RETURNS TO BENGAL

After their studies were complete, Jiva sent his three students to Bengal with the Vaishnava scriptures. Sri Jiva heard the news that the books had been stolen in Bana Vishnupur and then later that they had been recovered. This story has been told in this book in the chapter on Srinivas (page 205).

> Lokanath Goswami considered Narottam's previous life as a wealthy zamindar to be particularly suitable for preaching in his home area of northern Bengal and thought that with his status he would be able to teach the standards of renounced devotional behavior. Out of compassion for that country's people, he ordererd Narottam to return to his home town of Kheturi. Srinivas was aware of Lokanath's intention, so when the books were stolen, he told Narottam to continue on his way to Kheturi. Srinivas Acharya said, "Go quickly to Kheturi and carry out Lokanath's orders."
>
> (*Bhakti-ratnākara* 7.119)

Anchorite devotees (*viviktānandīs*), being absorbed in the intimate service of the Lord on the transcendental platform, normally have no taste for engaging in any welfare activity which brings only temporary succor to materialistic persons, bound by Maya and absorbed in their bodily identification. Materialistic welfare activities are considered to be of great value only when there is a misunderstanding about the real goal of life—service to Krishna. Lokanath taught the world through his disciple, on the principle that "a housewife teaches the daughter-in-law by instructing the daughter." Though Narottam himself was distraught with separation from his spiritual master, he nevertheless took his order seriously and returned to Kheturi where he began preaching the doctrines of pure devotional service to the people of northern Bengal. Narottam's humility and sorrow were expressed in his *Prārthanā*,

aneka duḥkhera pare, layechile vraja-pure
kṛpa-ḍora galāya bāndhiyā
daiva-māyā balātkāre, khasāiyā sei ḍore
bhava-kūpe dileka ḍāriyā
punaḥ yadi kṛpā kari, e janāre keśe dhari
ṭāniyā tulaha vraja-dhāme
tabe se dekhiye bhāla, natubā parāṇa gela
kahe dīna dāsa narottame

"After I had suffered for such a long time, You finally tied the rope of mercy around my neck and dragged me to Vraja Dham. But now, the forces of fate and illusion have loosened that rope and You have thrown me back down the well of material existence.

If You would only be merciful to me and grab me by the hair, pulling me back into Vraja Dham. Then everything would seem right once again. If not, Narottam says, his life is over."

On Lokanath Goswami's orders, Narottam installed six sets of deities in his temple in Kheturi: Gauranga, Vallabhi Kanta, Vraja Mohan, Sri Krishna, Radha Kanta, and Radha Raman. The great festival which he held on that occasion is still remembered in the Vaishnava world.

Narottam arrived in the land of Gauda. He had been ordered by Lokanath to establish the deity service of both Gauranga and Krishna, to serve the Vaishnavas and to preach the congregational chanting of the Holy Names. He immediately dedicated himself to carrying out these orders. First he set about establishing the service of six sets of beautiful deities, whose names, taken together, bring joy to the heart of the devotees (*Bhakti-ratnākara* 1.422-6)

gaurāṅga vallabhī-kānta
śrī-kṛṣṇa vraja-mohana
rādhā-ramaṇa he rādhe
rādhā-kānta namo'stu te

THE GREAT FESTIVAL AT KHETURI

Prior to the Kheturi-mahotsava, Narottam Das Thakur travelled throughout Bengal and Orissa, visiting various places where Mahaprabhu had performed His pastimes, meeting the Lord's associates and receiving their blessings. Amongst the places he visited were Uddharan Datta's home in Saptagram; Khardaha, where he met Paramesvari Das and Nityananda's shaktis, Jahnava and Vasudha; Khanakula Krishnanagar, the home of Abhiram Thakur; Shyamananda's home in Nrisinghapur; the Sripats of Narahari and Raghunandan in Srikhanda; the birthplace of Nityananda Prabhu in Ekachakra Dham; and in Jagannath Puri, Gopinath Acharya's home, Hari Das Thakur's samadhi tomb, Gadadhar Pandit's place of worship, the Jagannath temple and Gundicha, the Jagannath-vallabha gardens, and Narendra-sarovara, etc.

Most of the living associates of Mahaprabhu and other leaders of the sampradaya came to Kheturi on the occasion of the festival organized by Narottam Das. A list of names has been given by Narahari Chakravarti in his books, *Bhakti-ratnākara* and *Narottama-vilāsa*. Among those who attended were Shyamananda Prabhu, Jahnava Devi, Paramesvari Das, Jahnava's uncle Krishna Das Sarkhel, Nityananda's son-in-law Madhava Acharya, Raghupati Vaidya, Minaketan Rama Das, Murari Chaitanya Das, Jnana Das, Mahidhara, Sri Shankar, Kamalakar Pippalai, Gauranga Das, Nakari, Krishna Das, Damodar, Balaram Das, Sri Mukunda, Vrindavan Das Thakur; Raghunandan Thakur and other devotees from Srikhanda; Srivasa Pandit's brothers Sripati and Srinidhi from Nabadwip, Advaita's sons, Achyutananda, Gopal Mishra and Krishna Mishra from Shantipur, and Hriday Chaitanya and other devotees from Ambika Kalna.

Srinivas Acharya acted as the officiating priest at the festival and performed the rituals installing the deities. In the kirtan led by Narottam that followed, Mahaprabhu and His associates appeared.

Who can describe the joy of that kirtan? Mahaprabhu Himself descended with all His associates in its midst just like lightning in a conglomeration of rainclouds.
(*Bhakti-ratnākara* 10.571-2)

The kirtan was amazing: you could see Nityananda Prabhu and Advaita Acharya overcome with ecstasy and Gaurachandra, encircled by the devotees. What wonderful compassion the Lord displayed on that day! Who can understand these wonderful pastimes? What blessings He poured on Narottam and Srinivas, for they and their companions found the fulfilment of all their desires!
(*Bhakti-ratnākara* 10.605-7)

After the Kheturi festival, Narottam's fame spread throughout the Vaishnava world. Prominent Brahmins like Ramakrishna Acharya and Ganga Narayan Chakravarti became his disciples.

NAROTTAM'S PREACHING ADVENTURES

Narahari Chakravarti extensively described Narottam's activities in his *Narottama-vilāsa*. One can understand his outstanding accomplishments by reading this book. Some of these are given here.

In Gopalpur village lived a Brahmin named Vipra Das. He had a poisonous snake living in his wicker grain-storage bin (*golā*). When Narottam visited Vipra Das's house, the snake vanished, and deities of Gaura and Vishnupriya appeared in its place. "Gaurasundar and His beloved Vishnupriya came out of the *golā* and climbed into Narottam's lap in plain view of everyone." (*Bhakti-ratnākara* 10.202) Everyone was quite amazed. These same deities are today being served in the town of Gambhila.

A certain Smarta Brahmin scholar blasphemed Narottam, calling him a Shudra. The result of this offense was that he was attacked by leprosy. After suffering for some time, he was given a vision of the Goddess in a dream. She told him to fall at Narottam Das's feet and beg for forgiveness, and it was only after he followed this advice that the Brahmin was freed from his terrible disease.

Hariram and Ramakrishna, the sons of Shivananda Acharya, were taking a goat and a buffalo to be offered as a sacrifice to the Goddess on the order of their father. They met Narottam and Ramachandra Kaviraj on the way and were attracted by their effulgent beauty. Narottam Thakur advised the two young Brahmins to abandon worship in the modes of passion and ignorance that entailed violence to animals and to worship the Supreme Lord without any desire. The brothers immediately let the goat and buffalo go and bathed in the Padma. They then took initiation from Narottam and dedicated their lives to the service of Lord Krishna and his devotees.

Shivananda Acharya became angry when he heard about this. He called a Smarta scholar from Mithila named Murari to come and defeat Narottam's Vaishnava philosophy. However, Hariram and Ramakrishna were given divine blessings by their guru and were able to defeat every one of the Smarta's arguments with scriptural evidence. Defeated, Shivananda Acharya went to pray to the Goddess. She appeared to him that night in a dream and rebuked him for his enmity toward the Vaishnavas and told him to cease all such behavior.

In the course of time, Ganga Narayan Chakravarti, Jagannath Acharya and other well-known Brahmins started to become Narottam's disciples. This caused a stir in the Smarta community and they went to complain to Raja Narasingha: "Narottam is a Shudra who makes disciples of Brahmins. He is using some kind of mystic powers or hypnotism to convert them. He should be stopped."

After discussing the matter with Raja Narasingha, it was decided that a scholar named Rupa Narayan should be summoned to debate Narottam. This Brahmin had won numerous debates of this sort and was known as a *digvijayī*. The Raja himself set off with Rupa Narayan and a number of other Brahmins toward the village of Kheturi. Ramachandra Kaviraj and Ganga Narayan Chakravarti were upset to see the wicked intentions of the Raja and his pundit. When they heard that the Raja and his entourage were resting overnight in Kumarapur village, they went in disguise as a potter and a pān-seller and set up stalls in the village market. When the Brahmins came through the market, Ramachandra and Ganga Narayan spoke with them in Sanskrit. The Brahmins were astounded that even ordinary stall-keepers in the village were able to speak in Sanskrit. Ramachandra and Ganga Narayan began a debate with the Brahmins, defeating every Smarta argument that they put forward and establishing the pure doctrine of devotional service.

The Raja and his Digvijayi Pandit were rendered speechless by the scholarship of the two ordinary stall-keepers. When they learned that the two men were disciples of Narottam Das, the Raja said to his pandit, "If Narottam's common disciples can defeat you in debate, there is no need of going to see him."

But once again, the Goddess appeared to Raja Narasingha and Rupa Narayan and ordered them to go to Narottam and pray for forgiveness for their offenses. The two of them did so and thus became devotees of Radha and Krishna.

TWO SONGS BY NAROTTAM

In the *Gauḍīya Vaiṣṇava Abhidhāna*, the following comments are found: "Narottam's ashram was in a place called Bhajantuli, about two miles from his capital city, Kheturi. Narottam did his preaching through kirtan. He created the style of kirtan known as *garāṇahāṭī*. He wrote two books, *Prārthanā* and *Prema-bhakti-candrikā*, which are the very life of the devotees. He has written songs that are appropriate for every devotional mood, and this touches the devotees' hearts. These two books are so popular that they have been published countless times. Narottam's influence can be appreciated even in distant Maṇipur where everyone agrees that the Vaishnava religion spread through his spiritual potency. His devotional songs are sung in every home throughout Manipur state.

Srinivas Acharya's disciple Ramachandra Kaviraj was Narottam's dearest companion. Narottam received news of Ramachandra's disappearance first; not long afterward he heard of Srinivas's disappearance, he wrote the following song in the mood of separation, which is capable of melting even a stone-like heart.

je ānila prema-dhana karuṇā pracura
hena prabhu kothā gelā ācārya ṭhākura
kāhāṅ mora svarupa rūpa, kāhāṅ sanātana?
kāhāṅ dāsa raghunātha patita-pāvana?
kāhāṅ mora bhaṭṭa-yuga, kāhāṅ kavirāja?
eka-kāle kothā gelā gorā naṭarāja?
pāṣāṇe kuṭiba māthā anale paśiba
gaurāṅga guṇera nidhi kothā gele pāba
se saba saṅgīra saṅge je kaila vilāsa
se saṅga nā pāñā kānde narottama-dāsa

"Where has Acharya Thakur, who out of great mercy for the world brought it the wealth of love, gone? Where are my Svarupa and Rupa, where is Sanatan? Where has Raghunath Das, the deliverer of the most fallen, gone? Where are Raghunath Bhatta and Gopal Bhatta? Where is Krishna Das Kaviraj? Where has the king of the dance, Gauranga, suddenly disappeared to? I will beat my head against the rocks or enter the flames of a fire—but where can I go to find that ocean of virtue, Gauranga? Deprived of the association of all these companions of the Lord, Narottam Das can do nothing but cry."

Narottam Das Thakur was the topmost of the followers of Rupa Goswami, Mahaprabhu's close associate. His devotion to Rupa Goswami can be recognized from the following song, which was much beloved by Srila Prabhupada:

śrī rupa manjari pada sei mora sampada
sei mora bhajana pūjana
sei mora prāṇa-dhana sei more ābharaṇa
sei mora jīvanera jīvana

sei mora rasa-nidhi sei mora vāñchā-siddhi
sei mora vedera dharama
sei vrata, sei tapa sei mora mantra japa
sei mora dharama karama

anukūla habe vidhi se pade haibe siddhi
nirakhiba ei dui nayane
se rūpa mādhurī-rāśī prāṇa-kuvalaya-śaśī
praphullita habe niśi-dine

tuwā adarśana ahi garale jārala dehi
cira-dina tāpita jīvana
hā hā prabhu kara dayā deha more pada-chāyā
narottama laila śaraṇa

Rupa Manjari's feet are my treasure; they are my worship, they are my ritual. They are what keep me alive, they are my ornament, they are the life of my life.

They are my ocean of nectar, they are the perfection of my desire, they are my Vedic religion. They are my vow, they are my austerity, they are the mantra that I chant on my beads. They are my religious duty.

When Fate is kind to me, I will find perfection by attaining Rupa Manjari's feet. Then I will be able to see the beauty of Radha and Krishna's form, the moon of the lily of my life, with my own eyes.

The snake of your absence has burned up my body with its poison; I have suffered this pain for so long. O my master, be merciful to me, give me the shade of your feet for I, Narottam, seek refuge there.

NAROTTAMASTAKA BY VISHVANATH CHAKRAVARTI

śrī-kṛṣṇa-nāmāmṛta-varṣi-vaktra-
candra-prabhā-dhvasta-tamo-bharāya
gaurāṅga-devānucarāya tasmai
namo namaḥ śrīla-narottamāya

I offer my repeated obeisances to Srila Narottam Das Thakur, the glorious follower of the divine Gauranga, who destroys the darkness of ignorance with the nectarean rays of Krishna's holy name, which emanate from his moon-like face.

saṅkīrtanānandaja-manda-hāsya-
danta-dyuti-dyotita-diṅ-mukhāya
svedāśru-dhārā-snapitāya tasmai
namo namaḥ śrīla-narottamāya

I offer my repeated obeisances to Srila Narottam Das Thakur, who is bathed in torrents of tears and perspiration and who lights up every direction with the effulgence of his teeth, revealed as he laughs out of the joy of Harinam sankirtan.

mṛdaṅga-nāda-śruti-mātra-cañcat-
padāmbujāmanda-manoharāya
sadyaḥ samudyat-pulakāya tasmai
namo namaḥ śrīla-narottamāya

I offer my repeated obeisances to Srila Narottam Das Thakur, whose body is covered with horripilation and whose lotus feet dance enchantingly, being set into motion as soon as he hears the sound of the mridanga.

gandharva-garva-kṣapaṇa-svalāsya-
vismāpitāśeṣa-kṛti-vrajāya
sva-sṛṣṭa-gāna-prathitāya tasmai
namo namaḥ śrīla-narottamāya

I offer my repeated obeisances to Srila Narottam Das Thakur, whose fame has spread through the songs he has written and whose dance and song, indeed, every action in kirtan brings shame to the Gandharvas.

ānanda-mūrcchāvanipāt-bhāta-
dhūlī-bharālaṅkṛta-vigrahāya
yad-darśanaṁ bhāgya-bhareṇa tasmai
namo namaḥ śrīla-narottamāya

I offer my repeated obeisances to Srila Narottam Das Thakur, who can be seen only by one who has unlimited good fortune, whose figure is decorated with the dust that covers it as he falls to the ground in an ecstatic faint.

sthale sthale yasya kṛpā-prapābhiḥ
kṛṣṇānya-tṛṣṇā jana-saṁhatīnām
nirmūlitā eva bhavanti tasmai
namo namaḥ śrīla-narottamāya

I offer my repeated obeisances to Srila Narottam Das Thakur, who rains down mercy wherever he goes, causing every person's desires, other than those for service to Krishna, to be uprooted.

yad-bhakti-niṣṭhā pala-rekhikeva
sparśaḥ punaḥ sparśa-maṇīva yasya
prāmānyam evaṁ śrutivad yadīyaṁ
tasmai namaḥ śrīla-narottamāya

I offer my repeated obeisances to Srila Narottam Das Thakur, whose commitment to devotion is like a line scratched in a stone, whose touch is like that of the philosopher's stone, and whose every word is as authoritative as those of the Veda.

mūrtaiva bhaktiḥ kim ayaṁ kim eṣa
vairāgya-sāras tanumān nṛloke
sambhāvyate yaḥ kṛtibhiḥ sadaiva
tasmai namaḥ śrīla-narottamāya

I offer my repeated obeisances to Srila Narottam Das Thakur, who appears to some as devotion itself incarnate, or as the essence of renunciation in human form—this is forever the opinion of the wise.

rājan-mṛdaṅga-karatāla-kalābhirāmaṁ
gaurāṅga-gāna-madhu-pāna-bharābhirāmam
śrīman-narottama-padāmbuja-mañju-nṛtyaṁ

bhṛtyaṁ kṛtārthayatu māṁ phaliteṣṭa-kṛtyam

May the dancing of Srila Narottam Das Thakur's lotus feet, which follows every beat of the drum and hand cymbals and which incarnates the beauty of his intoxication in the songs glorifying Gauranga, bring fulfilment to me, his servant, by bringing to fruition all his sacrifices.

[28] The Padmavati or Padma River is one of the branches of the Ganges that splits east from the Bhagirathi. It forms the current border between West Bengal and Bangla Desh for about 50 km. Rajshahi lies on the northern shore. Mahaprabhu would have been on the south shore, closer to Murshidabad.

Sri Ramachandra Kaviraj

svardhunyās tīra-bhūmau
sarajani-nagare gauḍa-bhūpādi-pātrād
brahmaṇyād viṣṇu-bhaktād
api suparicitāt śrī-cirañjīva-senāt
yaḥ śrī-rāmendu-nāmā samajani paramaḥ
śrī-sunandābhidhāyāṁ
so'yaṁ śrīmān narākhye sa hi kavi-nṛpatiḥ
samyag āsīd abhinnaḥ

Ramachandra, a king amongst poets, was born in the town of Sarajani on the banks of the Ganges as the son of Sunanda and Chiranjiva Sen, a well-known minister of the king of Gauda, a devotee of the Brahmins and Vishnu. Ramachandra was not in any way different from Narottam Das Thakur. (*Saṅgīta-mādhava-nāṭaka*, quoted at *Bhakti-ratnākara* 1.270)

Chiranjiva Sen was a resident of Srikhanda, whose wife's name was Sunanda. They had two sons, the older was Ramachandra, the younger Govinda. Ramachandra was a disciple of Srinivas Acharya who took the title Kaviraj. His siddha name was Karuna Manjari.
(Verses quoted in *Gauḍīya Vaiṣṇava Abhidhāna*.)

After the death of his father, Ramachandra went to live in Kumar Nagar with his maternal grandfather, Damodar Kaviraj, who was a disciple of Narahari Sarkar. Later he went with his younger brother Govinda to live in the village of Telia Budhari in Murshidabad district. This place has the distinction of being his Sripat.

Ramachandra's Wedding

Srila Bhaktisiddhanta Saraswati Goswami Thakur has written that Ramachandra was a lifelong renunciate and never married. Haridas Das, on the other hand, writes in his *Gauḍīya Vaiṣṇava Abhidhāna* that Ramachandra did get married, but never lived with his wife. Srinivas Acharya saw Ramachandra on the very day of his wedding and said a few words to him about the temporary nature of material life, thus awakening within him an indifference to the world such that he never took up the duties of householder life. This story has been taken from a book which is not accepted as authoritative by everyone. The following quote is taken from there:

[Srinivas Acharya said,] "Just look at how much enthusiasm everyone has for this wedding! They are spending so much money and for what? Just to purchase illusion and quarrel. You don't realize that Maya has placed a noose around your neck and so you take a great interest in the auspicious invocatory rituals. People celebrate weddings thinking that they are auspicious when they are not, and that they have been fulfilled when they have not."

The Kaviraj Title

Srinivas Acharya was so overcome with affection for Ramachandra that he gave him the diksha mantra and engaged him as his personal servant. Though Bir Hambir became Srinivas Acharya's disciple, Ramachandra acted as his siksha guru. Ramachandra also visited Vrindavan where he associated with Jiva Goswami and the other Vaishnavas, receiving their blessings. They were very pleased to hear his poetry, so much so that Jiva Goswami gave him the Kaviraj title. He thus became one of the eight Kavirajs (*aṣṭa-kavirāja*). He was Narottam Thakur's favored companion for preaching activities and spiritual association.

Paramananda Bhattacharya, an ocean of love, Jiva Goswami and the other residents of Vraja, listened to Ramachandra recite his own poetic compositions and they joyfully awarded him the title of *kavirāja*. Ramachandra Kaviraj was full of all virtues and Narottam Das' second self.
(*Bhakti-ratnākara* 1.267-9)

Kamsari Sen, Rama Sen, Ramachandra Kaviraj, and the three Kavirajs, Govinda, Sriranga and Mukunda, are Nityananda's branches. (Chaitanya Charitamrita 1.11.51)

Ramachandra wrote several books, including *Smaraṇa-camatkāra, Smaraṇa-darpaṇa, Siddhānta-candrikā*, and *Srinivāsa Ācāryera Jīvana-carita*.

Ramachandra in Vrindavan

Narahari Chakravarti has written an extensive description of Ramachandra and his visit to Vrindavan in the ninth wave of *Bhakti-ratnākara*. All the residents of Vraja who saw him were attracted by his physical beauty. When Ramachandra visited the Radha-Damodar temple with Jiva Goswami and saw Rupa Goswami's samadhi, he experienced ecstatic transformations that were a source of amazement to all. Gopal Bhatta Goswami, Lokanatha Goswami and Bhugarbha Goswami gave him their blessings. He went to bathe in Radha Kund and Shyama Kund and met Raghunath

Das Goswami there. When he payed obeisances to Raghunath, the venerable saint affectionately embraced him.

Ramachandra's friendship with Narottam Das Thakur has been immortalized by Narottam Das prayer to Srinivas Acharya for his association:

dayā kara śrī-ācārya prabhu śrīnivāsa
rāmacandra saṅga māge narottama dāsa

"Please be merciful, Prabhu Srinivas Acharya! Narottam Das begs for Ramachandra's association."
(*Prārthanā*)

yau śaśvad-bhagavat-parāyaṇa-parau saṁsāra-pārāyaṇau
samyak sātvata-tantra-vāda-paramau niḥśeṣa-siddhāntagau
śaśvad-bhakti-rasa-pradāna-rasikau pāṣaṇḍa-hṛn-maṇḍalāv
anyonya-priyatābhareṇa yugalī-bhūtāv imau tau numaḥ

I pay my obeisances to Narottam and Ramachandra, who are devoted to all those who have dedicated their lives to the Supreme Lord, who help people cross over the ocean of material life, who know all the scriptures completely and have understood all the transcendental doctrines, who most generously distributed bhakti-rasa and won the hearts of the atheists, who are deeply attached to each others' affectionate company. (*Saṅgīta-mādhava-nāṭaka*, quoted at *Bhakti-ratnākara* 1.277)

Ramachandra's disappearance day is the *kṛṣṇā tṛtīyā* in the month of Magh. He passed away in Vrindavan after the disappearance of Srinivas Acharya.

Sri Shyamananda Prabhu

Sri Shyamananda Prabhu was a servant of a servant of Subala in Krishna lila. He was the disciple of Hridayananda or Hriday Chaitanya, a disciple of Gauri Das Pandit who was Subala in Krishna lila.

yaṁ lokā bhuvi kīrtayanti hṛdayānandasya śiṣyaṁ priyaṁ
sakhye śrī-subalasya yaṁ bhagavataḥ preṣṭhānuśiṣyaṁ tathā
sa śrīmān rasikendra-mastaka-maṇiś citte mamāharniśaṁ
śrī-rādhāpriya-narma-marmasu ruciṁ sampādayan bhāsatām

Sri Shyamananda was known in this world as Hridayananda's dear disciple. He was the grand-disciple of Subala Sakha, one of the Lord's dearest friends. May he, the crest-jewel of the connoisseurs of divine love, appear day and night in my mind, bringing me an appreciation of the essence of the joys of Radha's beloved Krishna.
(*Śyāmānanda-śataka*)

Shyamananda Prabhu was born on the full moon day of Chaitra in 1456 of the Śaka era (1534 AD) in the town of Dharenda Bahadurpur, which is near the Khargapur railway station in Midnapore. His father was Sri Krishna Mandal and his mother, Durika. Krishna Mandal's hometown was Dandeshwar, which lies on the banks of the Subarnarekha River. The following statement is found in the *Gauḍīya Vaiṣṇava Abhidhāna*: "Sri Krishna Mandal used to live in a place called Ambua, near Dandeshwar. He formerly lived in Gauda (the part of Bengal which lies on the banks of the Bhagirathi River) and only later moved to Dandeshwar, just across the present-day border in Orissa. Shyamananda's disciples have established five principle seats in the towns of Dharenda, Bahadurpur, Rayni, Gopiballabhpur, and Nrisinghapur."

Shyamananda Prabhu was born in the Sadgopa subcaste, which fits in the category of jala-cala, (Brahmins who are permitted to only take water touched by its caste members). Of course, a Vaishnava is beyond the material qualities and may take birth in a family of any race or caste. If anyone thinks badly of Vaishnavas or judges them on the basis of their race or caste is they are destined for hell.

arcye śīladhīr guruṣu naramatir vaiṣṇave jāti-buddhir
viṣṇor vā vaiṣṇavānāṁ kali-mala-mathane pādatīrthe'mbubuddhiḥ
śrīviṣṇor nāmni mantre sakala-kaluṣahe śabda-sāmānya-buddhir
viṣṇau sarveśvareśe tad-itara-samadhīr yasya vā nārakī saḥ

Anyone who considers the deity to be nothing but stone, the guru to be an ordinary human being, or the Vaishnava to be a member of a particular caste or race, who takes the holy water which has washed Vishnu or the Vaishnava's feet and can destroy all the sins of the age of Kali, to be ordinary water, who thinks that the name or mantra of Vishnu, which destroys all evils, is the same as any other sound, or who takes Vishnu to be equal to anything other than him, has a hellish nature. (*Padma-purāṇa*)

One who takes birth in a low-class family is not disqualified from performing devotional service, nor is one born in a pure, high-class Brahminical family automatically qualified for such service. Whoever engages in the worship of the Lord is a great person; one who does not worship is rejected. (Chaitanya Charitamrita 3.4.66-7)

na me bhaktaś caturvedī
mad-bhaktaḥ śvapacaḥ priyaḥ
tasmai deyaṁ tato grāhyam
sa ca pūjyo yathā hy aham

Simply being a knower of the four Vedas does not make someone my devotee. Even an outcaste who is my devotee is dear to me. One should exchange gifts and food with such a devotee, for he is certainly as worshipable as I am. (*Itihāsa-samuccaya*, quoted in *Hari-bhakti-vilāsa*, 10.127.)

Shyamananda's parents had lost several children in childbirth and they vowed to surrender their next child to Vishnu if it survived. They had suffered so much grief in the loss of their previous children that they first named Shyamananda Duhkhi, or "unhappy," to ward off further distress.

Shyamananda's parents Durika and Sri Krishna Mandala made their home in Dandeshwar. His father was the best of the Sadgopa caste, of impeccable character. Krishna was everything to him, and Krishna's devotees very dear. We cannot describe his virtues for fear of increasing the volume of this book. He and his wife had previously lived in Dharenda-Bahadurpur and people say that Shyamananda was born there. Though his brothers and sisters had all been stillborn to his parents, nothing could stop him. Even so, his parents brought him up in sadness and they called him Duhkhi.

(*Bhakti-ratnākara* 1.351-5, 359)

Shyamananda Prabhu's parents performed the appropriate rituals such as the first eating of solid food and the cutting of hair when their time came. As he grew older, he studied Sanskrit grammar. His parents were overjoyed to see his talents and religious proclivities. Shyamananda listened carefully to devotees when they spoke of Gauranga and Nityananda's glories and liked to repeat them to others. Whenever he listened to the activities of Gaura-Nitai or Radha and Krishna, tears would flow in torrents from his eyes.

Shyamananda also served his parents devotedly and they told him to get initiated so that he could fully commit himself to the service of the Lord. Duhkhi agreed and told them that he wished to take diksha from Hriday Chaitanya in Ambika Kalna. Going there would also give him the chance to see the Ganges and bathe in it. His parents happily gave him permission to go.

When Duhkhi arrived in Ambika Kalna, he threw himself at the holy feet of Hriday Chaitanya, who upon becoming acquainted with him, happily gave him Krishna mantra. He gave Duhkhi the Vaishnava name "Krishna Das" and so he was known from then on as Duhkhi Krishna Das. Hriday Chaitanya ordered him to go to Vrindavan and take up a life of intense bhajan. Though Duhkhi Krishna Das did not like being separated from his gurudeva, he set off for Vraja, first visiting Nabadwip and other places in Gauda Mandala, where he sought the blessings of the Vaishnavas. After spending much time on pilgrimage, he finally arrived in Vrindavan where he became completely absorbed in the worship of Radha and Shyamasundar.

In Vrindavan, Duhkhi Krishna Das studied the Vaishnava scriptures under Sri Jiva Goswami, who was the leading scholar of the sampradaya. When Hriday Chaitanya heard of the enthusiasm with which Duhkhi Krishna Das was leading the devotional life in Vraja, he wrote a letter to Jiva Goswami in which he said that Duhkhi should consider Jiva to be an extension of himself. Just as he gave titles to his other prominent students, Jiva gave the name Shyamananda to Duhkhi Krishna Das. The reasoning behind this name was that he brought great joy (*ānanda*) to Radha and Shyamasundar.

Jiva Goswami sent Srinivas Acharya, Narottam Das Thakur and Shyamananda back to Bengal with the Vaishnava scriptures in 1504 of the Śaka era (1582-3 AD). The idea was to spread the teachings found in these books throughout Bengal and Orissa. We have already related the events that took place when Bir Hambir had these books stolen. Narottam went to northern Bengal and Shyamananda went to Orissa. The Midnapore district was previously under the rule of the Orissan king.

RADHARANI'S SPECIAL MERCY ON SHYAMANANDA

Even though Shyamananda Prabhu was Hriday Chaitanya's initiated disciple, his guru entrusted him to the care of Jiva Goswami Prabhu. Through the association of Jiva and service to him, Shyamananda developed a taste for serving Radha and Krishna in the conjugal mood. Hriday Chaitanya Prabhu himself was a disciple of Gauri Das Pandit, who was one of the twelve Gopals, Subala Sakha. He thus worshiped Gaura-Nitai in the mood of friendship. Those who think that Shyamananda committed an offense to his initiating spiritual master by abandoning his mood and trying to directly serve Krishna in a different attitude are wrong. The mood of friendship is contained within the conjugal mood. If a disciple makes further progress in spiritual life it enhances the reputation of his teacher.

An extraordinary incident, which took place in Vrindavan prior to being ordered by Jiva to return to Orissa, demonstrates how dear Shyamananda was to Radharani. One day, Shyamananda Prabhu was sweeping the Rasa Mandala in Vrindavan, absorbed in ecstatic trance. Suddenly, by Radharani's transcendental mercy, he found her ankle bracelet (nūpura) lying on the ground. In his excitement, he touched the ankle bracelet to his forehead, where it left a mark that is preserved to this day as the tilak marking of the disciplic descendants of Shyamananda. It is known as *nūpura-tilaka*.

SHYAMANANDA PRABHU'S PREACHING

Narottam Thakur and Shyamananda primarily preached the message of Mahaprabhu through kirtan. Shyamananda would enchant his listeners with his heartfelt singing of kirtan in the reṇetī style.

As a result of Shyamananda's preaching in Orissa, many Muslims also became his disciples. The most important of his innumerable disciples was Rasika Murari or Rasikananda. Rasikananda was the son of Achyutananda, the zamindar of Rohini village. He had another name, Murari, and was thus most commonly known as Rasika Murari. He was a very powerful preacher and his fame is still widespread through the villages of Orissa. More is told about him in the next chapter.

A list of some of Shyamananda's prominent disciples is given in the *Bhakti-ratnākara*:

> Shyamananda made disciples all over the place. A person can be purified by hearing their names: Radhananda, Purushottam, Manohara, Cintamani, Balabhadra, Jagadishwara, Uddhava, Akrura, Madhuvan, Govinda, Jagannath, Gadadhar, Anandananda, and Radha Mohan. Shyamananda was constantly immersed in the joys of kirtan in the association of these disciples. Poets have described his wonderful pastimes for the pleasure of everyone. (*Bhakti-ratnākara* 15.62-66)

Among Shyamananda's most notable disciples was a yogi named Damodar whom he converted to Vaishnavism. Narahari Chakravarti has written the following account of that conversion:

> Shyamananda mercifully flooded the yoga practitioner named Damodar with devotional rasa. After becoming his disciple, Damodar cried and chanted the names of Nitai-Chaitanya. Who could remain untouched by his ecstatic absorption? He danced, crying out, "Bhakti is the best of all!" After delivering Damodar, Shyamananda continued to travel, distributing the jewel of devotion to everyone.
>
> (*Bhakti-ratnākara* 15.55-8)

Shyamananda put on a large festival at Dharenda with Rasika Murari and Damodar that is still remembered today. When he left the world, Shyamananda turned over the service of Govinda at Gopiballabhpur. Shyamananda's disciples and their descendants still worship his deity Radha Shyamasundar in Vrindavan. This temple is still one of the principle pilgrimage sites in Vrindavan.

Shyamananda Prabhu lived the last part of his life in Nrisinghapur in Orissa where he continued preaching Vaishnavism. His earthly pastimes came to an end on the first day of the waning moon in the month of Asharh in 1552 of the Śaka era (1630 AD). To preserve his holy memory, the branch of the Gaudiya Math in Midnapore city was named Shyamananda Gaudiya Math.

Srila Rasikananda Deva Goswami

RASIKANANDA'S BIRTH

Rasikananda Deva Goswami was born in 1512 of the Śaka era (1590 AD) in the village of Rohini or Rayni in the Midnapore district. This village is situated at the confluence of the Subarnarekha and Dolanga rivers. His father's name was Raja Achyutananda and his mother, Bhavani Devi. The Subarnarekha River crosses back and forth across the present-day Bengal-Orissa border. Midnapore district used to be a part of the Orissan kingdom. Raja Achyutananda was an Orissan of the Karana caste, the equivalent of the Kayasthas in Bengal. A Vaishnava is beyond the material qualities and should not be judged in terms of his caste origins. Achyutananda and Rasikananda were born in the Karana caste in order to bless it.

We can assume that Rasikananda was a manjari in Krishna lila. Though his spiritual master Shyamananda had himself been initiated by Hriday Chaitanya Goswami, who worshiped the Lord in the mood of friendship, he later took shelter of the conjugal mood due to the association of the Vraja devotees led by Jiva Goswami. Shyamananda thus initiated Rasikananda into the worship of Radha and Krishna.

Rasikananda was also known by the name Rasika Murari. Mother Jahnava's disciple Nityananda Das wrote in his *Prema-vilāsa* that Shyamananda had two principle disciples, one named Rasikananda, the other Murari, both of whom lived in Rayni. But Narahari Chakravarti indicates clearly in *Bhakti-ratnākara* that both names refer to the same individual:

> In the village of Rayni lived the famous son of Achyutananda. He had two names: Rasikananda and Murari. Thus he was also known as Rasika-Murari. He became learned in the scriptures in his childhood.
>
> (*Bhakti-ratnākara* 15.27-8)

We learn from the *Bhakti-ratnākara* that when the son of Dasharath, Lord Ramachandra, was exiled from Ayodhya, he spent some time with Lakshman and Sita in the village of Barajita, not far from Rayni. He there established the Shiva linga named Ramesvara.

Achyutananda was a benevolent landowner who strictly followed religious principles and took good care of his subjects. His wife also had a good reputation as a faithful and loyal wife. Rasika Murari learned to expertly serve his parents, bringing them much satisfaction. *Bhakti-ratnākara* also notes that he had a devoted wife named Icchamayi Devi or Icchadei, from the village of Ghantashila on the banks of the Subarnarekha. This village also has a certain historicity as a place where the Pandavas stayed during their exile. It was in this village that Rasika Murari first met his guru, an event that has been elaborately described in the *Bhakti-ratnākara*.

RASIKA MURARI MEETS SHYAMANANDA PRABHU

Rasika Murari was anxious to find a spiritual master who could give him guidance on the mystical path. One day while in Ghantashila, he went to a solitary place to meditate. He had just entered into a very deep trance when he heard a voice from an unseen source say, "Murari! You need be anxious no longer. Your guru is Shyamananda and you will meet him here very shortly. Take shelter of him and your life will be successful."

Upon hearing this divine message, Murari began chanting the name of Shyamananda on his beads with joyful enthusiasm. He spent the entire night crying out of eager expectation to meet his guru, until finally at the end of the night, he had a dream vision of Shyamananda Prabhu who said to him, "Don't worry any longer, for you will meet me on this very day."

At dawn, Rasika Murari was on the lookout for his guru when he saw the tall figure of Shyamananda approaching him, as effulgent as the sun. Surrounded by disciples like Kishor Das, he was dancing in a state of absorption in divine love while chanting the names of Nityananda and Chaitanya. Rasika Murari had been waiting anxiously for so long to encounter his guru that he immediately fell down at his feet. Shyamananda affectionately lifted him up and embraced him. Then, after giving him the Radha-Krishna mantra, he offered him up to Chaitanya and Nityananda Prabhus. This whole story demonstrates how we can find a guru through sincere prayers.

RASIKANANDA BECOMES A POTENT PREACHER

Rasikananda Deva Goswami fully committed himself in body, mind and soul to the service of his guru. Indeed, he served him so well that in a short time he was recognized as Shyamananda's chief disciple, a very powerful preacher and initiating guru himself. In fact, it is a truism that a good disciple becomes a good teacher. A spiritual master may have innumerable followers who call him their guru, but are disciples in name only. Only a true disciple who has dedicated himself completely to his spiritual master is imbued with all the powers of the guru. Shyamananda invested Rasikananda with such spiritual power that he was able to convert many criminals, atheists, Muslims, and other fallen spirit souls to the path of devotion, bestowing the jewel of prema upon them all.

On one occasion, a wicked Muslim tried to silence Rasika Murari by having him attacked by an intoxicated elephant, but Rasikananda was able to transform even the elephant into a disciple and engage him in the service of Vishnu and the Vaishnavas. All who witnessed this amazing event were overwhelmed with astonishment at Rasika Murari's spiritual power and the evil Muslim zamindar himself came and surrendered to him.

Shyamananda turned the service of his personal Govinda deity in Gopiballabhpur over to Rasikananda. He delivered unlimited living beings without any consideration of their caste or religious background. Rasikananda remained constantly intoxicated in Harinam sankirtan. Who will not be overcome with emotion on reciting his virtues? (*Bhakti-ratnākara* 15.81-6)

The *Prema-vilāsa* corroborates this account in the 19th chapter: "He delivered many criminals and Muslims."

The Raja of Mayurbhanj in Orissa, Vaidyanath Bhanj, was also attracted to the transcendental power of Rasikananda and became his disciple. Other important disciples were Ganapati, the zamindar of Patashpur in Midnapore, Sri Bhima and Srikara, zamindars of Dharenda, and Ahmed Beg, the son-in-law of Ibrahim Khan, the governor of Orissa.

Rasikananda Deva Goswami wrote a number of works, including *Śyāmānanda-śataka*, *Bhakta-Bhāgavatāṣṭaka*, and *Kuñjakeli-dvādaśaka*.

RASIKANANDA'S DISAPPEARANCE

It is said that just prior to Rasikananda's disappearance in AD 1652, he went with seven of his disciples to a village named Bansdaha near Jaleswar. Mahaprabhu passed through this village when travelling to Puri with Nityananda (Chaitanya Bhagavata 3.2.263-4)

Rasikananda and his party walked from there to Remuna, chanting kirtan the whole way. When they arrived in the courtyard of the famous Khirchora Gopinath temple, Rasikananda suddenly merged into the body of the Gopinath deity. His disciples also left their bodies in the same place. Rasika Murari's flower samadhi and those of his seven associates are still maintained in the courtyard of the Khirchora Gopinath temple. An annual festival lasting twelve days is held in Remuna to celebrate his disappearance. This takes place on *Śiva-caturdaśī* in the month of Magh.

Visvambharananda Deva Goswami, the author of the celebrated *Āstikya-darśana*, was Rasikananda's descendant.

SRI GANGA MATA GOSWAMINI

HARI DAS PANDIT GOSWAMI

Ganga Mata Goswamini was initiated by Hari Das Pandit Goswami into the line of Gauranga's Shakti, Srila Gadadhar Pandit Goswami. Krishna Das Kaviraj Goswami himself has described Pandit Hari Das's character in his Chaitanya Charitamrita:

Sri Hari Das Pandit was the head priest of the Govinda temple. His virtues and good fame are known all over the world, for he was gentle, tolerant, peaceful, magnanimous, grave, sweet in his words, and very sober in his endeavors. He was respectful to everyone and worked for the benefit of all. Diplomacy, envy and jealousy were unknown to his heart. The fifty general qualities of Lord Krishna were all present in his body... Pandit Hari Das' spiritual master was Gadadhar Pandit's disciple Ananta Acharya. Ananta Acharya was always absorbed in love of Godhead, magnanimous and advanced in all respects. He too was a reservoir of all good qualities, whose greatness cannot be fathomed by anyone.

(Chaitanya Charitamrita 1.8.54-7, 59-60)

Srila Bhaktisiddhanta Saraswati Goswami Thakur writes in his *Anubhāṣya*: "During the advent of Lord Sri Krishna, Ananta Acharya was Sudevi, one of the eight gopis, as is stated in the *Gaura-gaṇoddeśa-dīpikā*, verse 165: *anantācārya-gosvāmī yā sudevī purā vraje*. According to the disciplic succession descending from him at the famous Ganga Mata monastery in Puri, he is known as Vinoda Manjari. One of his disciples was Hari Das Pandit Goswami, who is also known as Sri Raghu Gopal and as Sri Rasa Manjari. He had two important disciples: Lakshmi Priya and her niece, Ganga Mata, who was the daughter of the Raja of Puntiya."

More is learned about Ganga Mata's holy life from Haridas Das's *Gauḍīya Vaiṣṇava Abhidhāna* and from Sundarananda Vidyavinoda, who has given a detailed account of her life in his *Sri Kṣetra*.

SACHI DEVI GOES TO LIVE IN VRAJA

Ganga Mata Goswamini's original name was Sachi Devi. She was born in Puntia, which is in the Rajshahi district of present-day Bangladesh. Her father was an important zamindar or raja, whose name was Naresh Narayan. Sachi Devi was indifferent to family life and devoted to Krishna from her early childhood. Her parents saw this and wanted to see her married as soon as possible, but Sachi told them that she refused to accept any mortal as her husband. When she announced her determination to remain unmarried in this way, her parents were troubled but could do nothing to change her mind. When her mother died, Sachi Devi left home and set out on a pilgrimage which led her first to Puri and then to Vrindavan.

Upon her arrival in Vrindavan Dham, she met Hari Das Pandit Goswami and felt as though making contact with him had made her entire pilgrimage worthwhile. She became anxious to take initiation from him, but he hesitated at first because of her wealthy family background. Later, however, when he saw her asceticism and unswerving determination to engage in pure devotional activity, he gave her initiation in the eighteen-syllabled mantra. This event took place in the Govindajī temple on the Chaitra *śuklā ekādaśī*.

After having received these blessings from her guru, she began to engage in intense bhajan, subsisting through madhukarī, (by begging for morsels of bread from door to door). After a year of this intense devotional activity, she was told by her spiritual master to live in Radha Kund with her spiritually advanced aunt and god-sister, Lakshmi Priya, who regularly chanted three lakhs of Names every day. As a part of their regular spiritual practice, the two of them daily circumambulated Govardhan together.

After several years of such practice at Radha Kund, when Sachi had become very advanced in her devotional life, her guru sent her to Purushottam Kshetra to recover the home of Sarvabhauma Bhattacharya, which had fallen into disrepair. Taking the command of her spiritual master as her all in all, Sachi Devi went to Jagannath Puri and took the *kṣetra-sannyāsa* vow. At that time, all that remained of Sarvabhauma's house was a single run-down building that housed his Damodar Shalagram Shila.

Even while she had lived at home in Puntia, Sachi Devi had studied the scriptures. In Vrindavan, furthermore, she had thoroughly studied the Bhagavata Purana. In order to salvage Sarvabhauma's residence, she set out to preach. Her transcendental qualities and discourses on the Bhagavata made such an impression on the public that she began to attract large audiences. It did not take long before her fame had spread so widely that the king of Orissa himself, Mukunda Deva, came to listen to her speak on the Bhagavata. He too became a devoted follower after being impressed by her devotional qualities and her learning.

THE SVETA GANGA

According to the *Utkala-khaṇḍa*, there was a King Sveta in the Treta Yuga who was a devotee of Jagannath. He made arrangements for Jagannath's bhoga just as Indradyumna had done. One morning he came to the temple and saw the offerings being made to Jagannath by the gods—thousands and thousands of wonderful gifts that were beyond the power of any mortal to give. King Sveta became disturbed at the insignificance of his own offerings and stood at the temple door, his head hung in shame. As he was meditating on his own insignificance, he had a second vision in which he saw Lakshmi Devi herself taking his food offerings and feeding them to both sets of Jagannath deities[29] who were eating them with great enthusiasm. The King immediately thought himself consummated by this vision and he continued to serve Jagannath with unflagging enthusiasm. Jagannath eventually granted him the boon of being liberated in a spot which faces Matsya Madhava, halfway between Akshaya Bata and the ocean, and was subsequently named Sveta Madhava in his honor. The pond excavated here was also named Sveta Ganga (the white Ganges). On the banks of this pond, deities of Sveta Madhava, Matsya Madhava and the nine planets are still worshiped.

One night, the king of Orissa, Mukunda Deva, had a dream in which Jagannath Deva appeared to him and told him to give Sachi Devi the tract of land bordering on this Sveta Ganga. The next morning, the King joyfully came to see Sachi Devi and told her about the dream. Though she had no interest in increasing her worldly possessions, Sachi Devi decided to accept the King's gift for the sake of her guru-given mission to improve the condition of Sarvabhauma's house. Prior to that she had to beg for the necessary articles to serve the deities. Wherever there is true devotion to the Lord, the trouble which one accepts in service is not seen as trouble, but rather as special opportunity and a source of joy.

HOW SACHI CAME TO BE KNOWN AS GANGA MATA

Not long afterward, a miraculous occurrence took place. One *kṛṣṇā trayodaśī*, an opportune moment came for the Maha Varuni Ganges bath. Many people who seek to accumulate pious credits make the trip to the Ganges for this auspicious occasion. Indeed, many of Sachi Devi's friends asked her to accompany them, but she could not abandon her *kṣetra-sannyāsa* vows nor her service to the deities, so she was obliged to plead that it was impossible for her to go.

Even though she really did not want to go, Jagannath Deva himself made arrangements for her to bathe in the Ganges. That night he appeared to her in a dream and told her to take bath in the Sveta Ganga in the middle of the night. Sachi Devi followed his instructions, but as soon as she entered the water, she had a vision of Ganga Devi herself. She was carried away in a strong river current that came from nowhere and suddenly found herself inside the Jagannath temple. At the same time, she continued to see herself bathing in the Ganges amongst her friends from Puri. She not only saw the Ganges and all those who were immersed in its waters, but she could hear the joyful noise of the bathing crowds.

She seemed to not be the only one there. The temple gatekeepers awakened on hearing this commotion and called Lord Jagannath's pujaris. They in turn gave a report to the King himself who ordered them to open the temple doors. When they finally flung the doors open, they saw no one but Sachi Devi standing there alone. Jagannath's pujaris were confused and at first did not know what to do. They assumed that Sachi Devi had broken into the temple with the intention of robbing the Deities' valuables and that they had caught her red-handed, but by their suspicions they committed an offense to this great devotee. As a result, they were attacked by various diseases and distresses—so much so that the service to Jagannath was affected.

Jagannath Deva finally appeared to the King again and told him what had really happened. Being influenced by Sachi Devi's pure devotional attitude, Jagannath Himself had made the Ganges flow from his feet to bathe Sachi Devi directly in the currents of his *caraṇāmṛta*. The King and the other servants of the Lord could only be freed from their offenses if they apologized to Sachi Devi and took mantra initiation from her.

King Mukunda Deva went to Sachi Devi with his entourage, the temple guards and servants. They paid her their prostrated obeisances and begged for her forgiveness. Though the King and all the pujaris, etc., asked her for initiation, she only gave the mantra to the King in obedience to Jagannath's order. The King wanted to give a large amount of land as *guru-dakṣiṇā*, but Sachi Devi refused it. When the King continued to beg for an opportunity to render service, she finally said that every midday he could send two containers of mahā-prasādī rice and one of vegetables, a cloth and 160 paisa for the service of the Vaishnavas. From that day onward, Sachi was known as Ganga Mata and Sarvabhauma Bhattacharya's house as Ganga Mata Math and to this day, after the midday offering at the Jagannath temple, these same items are sent to the Ganga Mata Math.

Another of those who were blessed by initiation from Ganga Mata Goswamini was a certain Smarta Brahmin named Mahirath Sharma from Dhananjayapur.

RASIKA RAY

There was a deity of Krishna named Rasika Ray in the house of Chandra Sharma, a resident of Jaipur in Rajasthan. As a result of *sevāparādha*, offenses in the performance of service to this deity, this Brahmin had no descendants to continue the family line. Jagannath Deva appeared to him in a dream and told him to bring the deity to Puri and to give it to Ganga Mata if he wished to be rid of the effects of his offenses. The Brahmin did as he was told and appeared at Ganga Mata's door to offer her the service of Rasika Ray. At first she was not ready to accept, as it was impossible for her to give the kind of royal service that was due such a deity. Finally, the Brahmin simply hid the deity amongst the tulasi bushes and went away. Rasika Ray appeared to Ganga Mata in a dream and told her that he wanted her to accept and serve him. Having been so ordered, Ganga Mata joyfully took the deity in and organized a festival in his honor.

At present there are five pairs of deities in the Ganga Mata Math: Sri Sri Radha Rasika Ray, Sri Sri Radha Shyamasundar, Sri Sri Radha Madana Mohan, Sri Sri Radhavinoda and Sri Sri Radharaman. Other than these, the Damodar Shalagram Shila of Sarvabhauma Bhattacharya, a dancing figure of Sri Gauranga, and a Gopal deity are also present on the altar.

According to the information given by the Math, Ganga Mata was born on the *śuklā daśamī* of Jyestha in AD 1601 and entered the eternal pastimes in AD 1721. Branches of her Math are found in Jagannath Puri at the Haveli Math and Gopal Math, as well as the Gopal Math in Tangi village in Cuttack district.

Devotees of Krishna may be born in any race, in any caste, or indeed in either sex. They are still to be considered the best of human beings and worshipable by all. There are many examples of women who attained the supreme achievement of pure devotional service to the Lord, such as the wives of the Vedic Brahmins who due to the demands of bhakti ignored the orders of their less-advanced husbands to serve Krishna. In the Kaliyuga, also, as a result of the blessings of Hari Das Thakur, a prostitute was transformed into a renowned Vaishnavi and many great devotees went to seek audiences from her in order to receive her saintly association.

[29] Besides the three main deities, there is a second set of Jagannath deities present in the temple, known as the *vijaya-vigraha*.

Srila Vishvanath Chakravarti Thakur

viśvasya nātha-rūpo'sau
bhakti-vartma-pradarśanāt
bhakta-cakre vartitatvāt
cakravarty-ākhyayābhavat

Because he revealed the path of devotion, he is considered to be identical with the Lord of the Universe, Vishvanath; and because he was predominant in the circle of Vaishnavas, he held the title Chakravarti.

VISHVANATH'S BIRTH AND DISCIPLIC SUCCESSION

Vishvanath took birth in a family of Rarhiya Brahmins in the village of Devagram in Nadia district in about 1560 of the Śaka era (1638 AD). Some others suggest 1576 (1656) as his year of birth. The *Gauḍīya Vaiṣṇava Abhidhāna* identifies his father as Rama Narayan Chakravarti. His mother's name is unknown. He had two older brothers, Ramabhadra and Raghunath. His spiritual master was Radharaman Chakravarti, disciple of Krishnacharan Chakravarti. Krishnacharan Chakravarti was a disciple and, according to some, adopted son of Ganga Narayan Chakravarti. Vishvanath has summarized his guru parampara at the beginning of the *Rāsa-pañcādhyāya* section of his *Sārārtha-darśinī* commentary on the Srimad Bhagavatam.

śrī-rāma-kṛṣṇa-gaṅgā-caraṇān natvā gurūn uru-premṇaḥ
śrīla-narottama-nātha-śrīgaurāṅga-prabhuṁ naumi

In this verse, Radharaman Chakravarti's name is abbreviated as Rama, Krishnacharan's name as Krishna, and Ganga Narayan's name as Ganga. The word nātha refers to Lokanath Goswami, whose guru was Gauranga Mahaprabhu. Thus the entire disciplic succession of Vishvanath has been given in this one single verse.

VISHVANATH'S STUDIES AND WRITINGS

After completing his studies of grammar in Devagram, Vishvanath went to Saiyadabad in the Murshidabad district to study devotional scriptures from his guru. According to the *Gauḍīya Vaiṣṇava Abhidhāna*, Vishvanath was married. Although he was married according to the rites, he never showed the slightest attachment for family life. It is said that he taught his wife the Bhagavata, giving her a taste for its nectar, and instructed her to devote herself to the worship of the Lord before he left home.

Srila Vishvanath Chakravarti Thakur followed the example of Sri Rupa and went to live in Vrindavan where he could dedicate himself to devotional life. As a result of his commitment to following the orders of his spiritual master, he received many blessings from him. These blessings took shape in his good fortune to be able to live in various spots in Vraja-dham and write a great number of books on Gaudiya Vaishnava subjects, which are considered to be a great treasure by those in the sampradaya. All his books and his commentaries on the Bhagavad Gita and Bhagavata are written in a Sanskrit that is clear and simple, but at the same time full of the nectar of devotion.

In the Sri Chaitanya Gaudiya Math edition of the Bhagavad Gita, some remarks have been made about Vishvanath under the heading, "A description of the commentary." Those comments have been reproduced here:

Vishvanath has an important place in Gaudiya Vaishnava history as the guardian and chief teacher of the middle period between the life of Mahaprabhu and His associates and the modern period. Amongst Vaishnavas of our day, a saying has been preserved about three of his works: *kiraṇa-bindu-kaṇā, ei tin niye vaiṣṇava-paṇā*—Vishvanath's resumes of Rupa Goswami's *Ujjvala-nīlamaṇi* (*Ujjvala-nīlamaṇi-kiraṇa*), *Bhakti-rasāmṛta-sindhu* (*Bhakti-rasāmṛta-sindhu-bindu*), and *Laghu-bhāgavatāmṛta* (*Bhāgavatāmṛta-kaṇā*) are the source of transcendental joy for the Vaishnavas; studying them makes one a Vaishnava.

After the disappearance of Mahaprabhu's Vrindavan associates, Srinivas, Narottam and Shyamananda preserved their traditions and expanded the movement in Bengal. Vishvanath is the fourth descendant in the disciplic line from Narottam Das. Few acharyas of the Gaudiya Vaishnava school have been as productive as he. Besides producing a large corpus of books, Vishvanath also made other major contributions related to preaching and kirtan.

Rupa Kaviraj was excommunicated from Vaishnava society. He was the founder of the Ati-bari sect, an apasampradaya which taught that only renunciates were eligible to act as acharya, and that all householders are disqualified. He preached a distorted doctrine of raganuga bhakti that completely negates the value of vidhi-marga, minimizing the importance of hearing and chanting. To the benefit of the general public, Vishvanath has argued against this doctrine in the *Sārārtha-darśinī* commentary on the Third Canto of the Bhagavata. Rupa Kaviraj holds that no householder can take the Goswami title. Vishvanath counters this proposition by stating, on the basis of scripture, that any member of a dynasty of gurus who has the proper qualifications is entitled to be called a Goswami, in other words he can do the work of a guru or acharya. However, to call one's unworthy children "Goswami" simply for the purpose of accumulating wealth and disciples is opposed to the scriptural conclusions and is to be considered unlawful, even if born in a family with a tradition of acting gurus.

Vishvanath Chakravarti Thakur wrote Bengali songs under the pen name of Harivallabha Das. Some people say that this name was given to him when he took the vairagi dress. In all respects, Vishvanath is worthy of superlatives, whether in his expertise in philosophical discourse, his knowledge of the Vaishnava scriptures, or his poetic talent.

It is said of Vishvanath that when he was writing on the Bhagavata, it rained and water fell everywhere except the place where he was sitting. Thus, the ink did not run and the text remained intact.

The following is a list of books and commentaries written by Vishvanath: (1) *Vraja-rīti-cintāmaṇi*, (2) *Camatkāra-candrikā*, (3) *Prema-sampuṭa*, (4) *Gītāvali*, (5) *Subodhinī* commentary to *Alaṅkāra-kaustubha*, (6) *Ānanda-candrikā* commentary to *Ujjvala-nīlamaṇi*, (7) a commentary on *Gopāla-tāpanī Upaniṣad*, (8) *Sri-Kṛṣṇa-bhāvanāmṛta*, a *mahā-kāvya*, (9) *Sri-Bhāgavatāmṛta-kaṇā*, (10) *Ujjvala-nīlamaṇi-kiraṇa-leśa*, (11) *Bhakti-rasāmṛta-sindhu-bindu*, (12) *Rāgavartma-candrikā*, (13) *Aiśvarya-kādambinī*, which appears to have been lost, (14) *Mādhurya-kādambinī*, (15) *Bhakti-sāra-pradarśinī*, a commentary on *Bhaktirasāmṛta-sindhu*, (16) *Ānanda-candrikā*, a commentary on the *Ujjvala-nīlamaṇi*, (17) a commentary on the *Dāna-keli-kaumudī*, (18) a commentary on the *Lalita-mādhava*, (19) an incomplete commentary on Chaitanya Charitamrita, (20) a commentary on the *Brahma-saṁhitā*, (21) *Sārārtha-varṣiṇī*, a commentary on the Bhagavad Gita, (22) *Sārārtha-darśinī*, a commentary on the Srimad Bhagavatam.

He also wrote a number of small works which have been brought together in the collection known as *Stavāmṛta-laharī*: (1) *Guru-tattvāṣṭaka*, (2) *Mantra-dātṛ-gurvaṣṭaka*, (3) *Paramaguror aṣṭaka*, (4) *Parātparaguror aṣṭaka*, (5) *Parama-parātparaguror aṣṭaka*, (6) *Sri-Lokanāthāṣṭaka*, (7) *Sri-Narottamāṣṭaka*, (8) *Sri-Śacīnandanāṣṭaka*, (9) *Sri-Svarūpa-caritāmṛta*, (10) *Svapna-vilāsāmṛtam*, (11) *Sri-Gopāladevāṣṭaka*, (12) *Sri-Madana-mohanāṣṭaka*, (13) *Sri-Govindāṣṭaka*, (14) *Sri-Gopīnāthāṣṭaka*, (15) *Sri-Gokulānandāṣṭaka*, (16) *Svayaṁ-bhagavad-aṣṭaka*, (17) *Sri-Rādhā-kuṇḍāṣṭaka*, (18) *Jagan-mohanāṣṭaka*, (19) *Anurāgavallī*, (20) *Sri-Vṛndādevy-aṣṭaka*, (21) *Sri-Vṛndāvanāṣṭaka*, (22) *Sri-Radhika-dhyānāmṛta*, (23) *Sri-Rupa-cintāmaṇi*, (24) *Sri-Nandīśvarāṣṭaka*, (25) *Sri-Govardhanāṣṭaka*, (26) *Sri-Saṅkalpa-kalpa-druma*, (27) *Sri-Nikuñja-virudāvalī*, (28) *Sri-Surata kathamṛta*, and (29) *Sri-Śyāmakuṇḍāṣṭaka*.

VISHVANATH'S STUDENT BALADEVA

When Vishvanath Chakravarti Thakur was old and hampered in his ability to travel, the acharyas of the Ramanuja sampradaya in the Galta village of Jaipur attempted to convert the King of Jaipur to their school by denying that the Gaudiya school had any historical basis. They accused the Gaudiyas of not having a tie to any one of the four Vaishnava disciplic successions. They advised the King of Jaipur to take initiation from someone in the Ramanuja line. The King was confused by their arguments and asked Vishvanath, who was the most prominent acharya of the Gaudiya school at that time, to come to Jaipur and answer the questions posed by the Ramanuja group. Due to his advanced age, Vishvanath was unable to go, but in his stead he sent his dear student, Baladeva Vidyabhushan, to defend the line.

One of the arguments of the Ramanujis was that the Gaudiya school had no commentary of its own on the Vedanta. Baladeva asked the accusers for some time—seven days according to some, three months according to others—to write a Gaudiya commentary on Vedanta. He was given the time and then he went to the Govinda temple and prayed to his guru and to the Lord to give him the power to write such a commentary. Govindaji's garland fell from around his neck and the pujaris placed it on Baladeva's chest. Baladeva took this as a sign that the Lord had given him authorization.

With the Lord's blessings, even the impossible becomes possible, and Baladeva undertook the writing of comments to the 500 sutras of the Vedanta Sutra, completing it in the limited time given him but without neglecting the subtle aspects of the divine aesthetics revealed in the pure devotional line of Gaudiya Vaishnava thought. When he went to Galta, the scholars of the other sampradayas were astonished by the quality of Baladeva's commentary. Because Govindaji himself had ordered its writing, the commentary became known as the *Govinda-bhāṣya*. It was after completing this commentary that Baladeva received the Vidyabhushan title.

Vishvanath established the service of Gokulananda, and the Gokulanandaji temple still stands in Vrindavan. Vishvanath left this world in Radha Kund in around 1630 of the Śaka era (1708 AD). The tithi was either the *śuklā* or *kṛṣṇā pañcamī* of the month of Magh.

SRILA BALADEVA VIDYABHUSHAN

The exact time and place of Sri Baladeva Vidyabhushan's birth are unknown. Perhaps historians will one day be able to firmly establish these facts beyond any doubt. From the little information that we do have about his life, we can conjecture that he was born in the 17th century of the modern era. Though we do not know the name of the exact village where he took birth, it was likely in the Balesore district of Orissa, somewhere near Remuna. From the date given in his commentary on Rupa Goswami's *Stava-mālā*, it is clear that Baladeva was still living after the Battle of Plassey in 1757.

We know that Baladeva studied in one of the villages of the Chilka Lake area in southern Orissa. There he learned grammar, poetics and logic, achieving expertise in all these subjects. He began his studies of Vedanta there, but in order to understand the commentaries in greater depth, he went to Mysore. He was there particularly impressed by the logical consistency of the Madhva *śuddha-dvaita* commentary on the Vedanta sutras. He thus became a disciple of that school and went to live in a Tattvavadi monastery. After taking sannyas, he moved to Purushottam Kshetra where he engaged many of the local scholars in debate, demonstrating the depth of his scholarship. His fame soon spread throughout the area.

Later, however, he met Radha Damodar Goswami, a scholar from Kanauj, under whose direction he studied Jiva Goswami's *Ṣaṭ-sandarbha* in great detail. When he was convinced of the supremacy of the Gaudiya Vaishnava philosophy, he took initiation from Radha Damodar Goswami.

He was thus initiated in Nityananda Prabhu's line. The following is his disciplic succession: (1) Gauri Das Pandit, (2) Hriday Chaitanya Prabhu, (3) Shyamananda Prabhu, (4) Rasikananda Deva Goswami, (5) Nayanananda Goswami, (6) Radha Damodar Goswami, (7) Baladeva Vidyabhushan.

Baladeva then continued his studies of the Gaudiya literature under Pitambar Das and later studied the *Bhāgavata Purāṇa* under Vishvanath Chakravarti. He also took the Vaishnava vairagi's dress, at which time he was given the name Ekanti Govinda Das.

BALADEVA'S WRITTEN WORKS

Baladeva was ordered by Vishvanath Chakravarti Thakur to go to Jaipur where he prayed to Rupa Goswami's Govindaji murti for the authorization to write a commentary on the Vedanta Sutra. He then composed the *Govinda-bhāṣya* and took it to Galta where he defeated the other sampradayas in debate, preserving the reputation of the Gaudiya school. After this episode, he was given the title Vidyabhushan. This story has been told in greater detail in the previous chapter on Vishvanath Chakravarti Thakur.

The following is a list of Baladeva Vidyabhushan's written works:

(1) A commentary on the Brahma Sutras, *Govinda-bhāṣya*
(2) *Siddhānta-ratnam*
(3) *Vedānta-syamantaka*
(4) *Prameya-ratnāvalī*
(5) *Siddhānta-darpaṇa*
(6) *Sāhitya-kaumudī*
(7) *Kāvya-kaustubha*
(8) *Vyākaraṇa-kaumudī* (which appears to have been lost)
(9) *Pada-kaustubha*
(10) *Vaiṣṇava-nandinī*, a commentary on the Tenth Canto
(11) A commentary on *Gopāla-tāpanī Upaniṣad*
(12) Commentaries on the *Īśa* and nine other *upaniṣads*
(13) *Gītā-bhūṣaṇa-bhāṣya*, a commentary on Bhagavad Gita
(14) *Nāmārtha-sudhā*, a commentary on the *Viṣṇu-sahasra-nāma*
(15) *Sāraṅga-raṅgada*, a commentary on the *Laghu-bhāgavatāmṛta*
(16) *Stavamālā-vibhūṣaṇa*, a commentary on *Stava-mālā*
(17) a commentary on Rupa Goswami's *Nāṭikā-candrikā*
(18) *Chandaḥ-kaustubha-bhāṣya*
(19) A commentary on Rasikananda's *Śyāmānanda-śataka*
(20) A commentary on *Candrāloka* (which appears to have been lost)
(21) *Kṛṣṇānandinī*, a commentary on *Sāhitya-kaumudī*
(22) *Govinda-bhāṣya-ṭīkā*, a commentary on his own *Govinda-bhāṣya*
(23) *Sūkṣmā*, a further clarification of his own *Siddhānta-ratnam*.

Other than these, it is claimed that Baladeva also wrote an *Aiśvarya-kadambinī* that is different from that written by Vishvanath Chakravarti Thakur. In the *Aiśvarya-kadambinī* by Vishvanath, there is a discussion of the dvaita and advaita doctrines, which is missing from Baladeva's work of that name.

It is said that Baladeva established the worship of the Vijaya Gopal deity in Galta. His two most prominent disciples were Uddhava Das and Sri Nanda Mishra.

In the succession of bona fide gurus which make up the Brahma-Madhva-Gaudiya-Saraswata sampradaya, Baladeva Vidyabhushan is to be remembered regularly. Simply demonstrating a connection through initiation to a family succession of initiating spiritual masters does not make one a bona-fide guru. One must demonstrate complete dedication to the supreme truth, *brahma-niṣṭhā*. Only a pure devotee can be called a bona fide guru. Therefore Bhakti Siddhanta Saraswati wrote, "I pay obeisances to Vishvanath and all his disciples like Baladeva, Baladeva's disciple Jagannath and his dearmost follower Bhaktivinode Thakur."

Sri Jagannath Das Babaji Maharaj

gaurāvirbhāva-bhūmes tvaṁ
nirdeṣṭā bhagavat-priyaḥ
vaiṣṇava-sārvabhauma
śrī-jagannāthāya te namaḥ

I offer my obeisances to you, Jagannath. Because you were the foremost Vaishnava of your era, you received the title Vaishnava Sarvabhauma. You are very dear to the Lord and through your divine vision, you designated the place where Mahaprabhu appeared in this world.

JAGANNATH DAS'S POSITION IN THE DISCIPLIC SUCCESSION

Throughout the world, any devotee who comes in the disciplic succession following Srila Bhaktisiddhanta Saraswati Goswami Thakur daily remembers Sri Jagannath Das Babaji Maharaj and prays for his mercy.

viśvanātha bhakta sātha, baladeva jagannātha
tāṅra priya bhakativinoda
mahā-bhāgavata vara, śrī-gaura-kiśora-vara
hari-bhajanete jāṅra moda
śrī-varṣabhānavī-varā, sadā sevya-sevā-parā
tāṅra dayita-dāsa nāma

[I offer respects to] Vishvanath along with his devotees, to Baladeva and to Jagannath, whose dear disciple is Bhaktivinode. Sri Gaura Kishor Das, the great devotee, whose great pleasure is the worship of the Lord. Radharani is the daughter of Vrishabhanu and is always fixed in service to her Lord. I am the servant of him who is dear to her.

There is also a Sanskrit version of the disciplic succession, where Jagannath is mentioned in the following way:

vaiṣṇava-sārvabhaumaḥ śrī-
jagannātha-prabhus tathā
śrī-māyāpur-dhāmnas tu
nirdeṣṭā sajjana-priyaḥ

Next in the line is Jagannath Prabhu, known as Vaishnava Sarvabhauma. Very dear to the saintly, he designated the dham of Sri Mayapur.

There are four dark ages in the history of Bengal Vaishnavism: (1) preceding the appearance of Chaitanya Mahaprabhu; (2) following the disappearance of the six Goswamis; (3) after the disappearance of Srinivas Acharya, Narottam Das Thakur, Shyamananda, and Rasikananda Deva Goswami; and (4) following the disappearance of Vishvanath Chakravarti Thakur and Baladeva Vidyabhushan.

One should not think that the Madhva-Gaudiya disciplic succession following in the spirit of Rupa Goswami has been disrupted on account of these periods of darkness. Sometimes spiritual masters in the disciplic succession are individual performers of solitary bhajan (*viviktānandī*), and sometimes they are preachers who delight in increasing the size of the congregation (*goṣṭhyānandī*). To an untrained eye, it seems that one can measure the strength of an acharya by the number of disciples he makes, but this is not an appropriate criterion for judgement.

Baladeva Vidyabhushan's disciple was Uddhava Das or Uddhara Das. This Vaishnava had a disciple also named Uddhava Das, who gave the renounced order to Madhusudan Das. This Madhusudan Das was famed throughout the Vaishnava world as Siddha Madhusudan Das Babaji from Surya Kund. Madhusudan Das gave the *paramahaṁsa-veṣa* (Babaji initiation) to Jagannath Das Babaji. Srila Bhaktisiddhanta Saraswati Goswami Thakur wrote: "All of these Vaishnavas adopted the lifestyle of the paramahaṁsa, preaching the path of pure devotion by their example. They are thus the objects of the greatest faith and reverence in the Gaudiya Vaishnava Sampradaya."

From this statement of Srila Prabhupada, we learn that all these *bhajanānandī*s not only practiced the anchorite life of solitary worship, but engaged in preaching activities as well, serving as acharyas.

JAGANNATH DAS'S LIFE IN VRINDAVAN

Jagannath Das was born in a respectable family in Tangail district in what is today Bangladesh, in around 1780 AD. According to some people he was born into a family of Varendra Kayasthas in Taras village in Pabna district. The names of his parents are unknown.

After taking the *pāramahaṁsa-veṣa*, Jagannath Das Babaji set an exemplary standard of intense bhajan in Nabadwip and Vrindavan, so much so that he was accepted by all the *bhajanānandī* Vaishnavas as their leader. He remained in this world for more than a century.

While Jagannath Das was engaged in bhajan in Vraja, a certain professional speaker on the Bhagavata from Katwa decided to move to Vrindavan to make his living, looking for gold and glory. Even though he gave excellent discourses on the Bhagavata, the renounced Vaishnavas showed no enthusiasm for them. When he inquired into the reasons that they were not coming to listen to him, Jagannath and the other Vaishnavas told him any discourse on the Bhagavata given by someone who has other goals in mind cannot be called a true explanation of the Bhagavata. His words can have no beneficial effect on anyone, not even himself. Indeed, such discourses have a negative effect on the consciousness of the listeners. The Vaishnavas led by Jagannath Das thus advised the professional speaker to give up the business of giving Bhagavata discourses as a means of making his living. By their grace, this money-minded Vaishnava was completely transformed and he gave up his false pride in learning and high birth. He became a great devotee with such humility that he paid prostrated obeisances to every creature residing in the Holy Dham.

Babaji Maharaj was himself a dedicated and intense *bhajanānandī*, but he did not believe that disciples who were unqualified and filled with material desires should be allowed to act in ways detrimental to service to Vishnu and the Vaishnavas on the pretext of engaging in the service of the Holy Name. He engaged less qualified disciples who had taken the renounced order in working the garden next to his cottage, so that he could offer vegetables to the Deity and the Vaishnavas. If the senses are not engaged in the service of Vishnu and the Vaishnavas, one does not develop the qualifications necessary to chant properly and it is impossible to experience the power of the Holy Name. When an individual engages the senses and sense objects in relation to the body and bodily relations, then attachment for these naturally arises. When we are fixed in the consciousness that our very self, including our body and senses, belong to the Lord, and we engage our senses in the service of the Lord and his devotees, then our feelings of love and possessiveness for him increase.

JAGANNATH DAS MEETS BHAKTIVINODE THAKUR

Jagannath Das Babaji met Bhaktivinode Thakur for the first time in 1880 AD. Their second meeting took place in the village of Amlajora in Burdwan district in 1891. On this occasion, they spent the entire night (it was Ekadasi) discussing Krishna katha. Jagannath Das Babaji encouraged Bhaktivinode Thakur to preach Gaura's name and abode.

The Thakur gave the following account of this eventful night in his *Sajjana-toṣaṇī* magazine: "After spending the whole night in the Ekadasi vigil, people from the entire village gathered together at eight in the morning to go on nagara sankirtan through its streets. With the venerable Jagannath Das Babaji Maharaj at the head of the group, they made their way to the Prapannashram. It is impossible to describe Babaji Maharaj's ecstatic transformations during this kirtan. Though he is over a hundred years old, he dances like a lion, sometimes singing out the couplet,

nitāi ki nāma eneche re nāma eneche nāmer hāṭe,
śraddhāra mūle nāma diteche re

'What divine name is this that Nitai has brought? He has brought the Name to the marketplace and is selling it for the price of faith!'

"As Babaji Maharaj sang, he cried and fell to the ground in ecstasy. I then saw something transpire which I had never seen before. All present were affected by his mood: their eyes filled with tears and their hairs stood on end, and even though they could barely sing, they remained absorbed in the kirtan and danced wildly."

Srila Bhaktivinode Thakur has also written about Jagannath Das Babaji in his autobiography: "In 1892, Jagannath Das Babaji and many other Vaishnavas participated in the sankirtan festival in Godrum and then in Sri Mayapur. In the month of Magh in 1299 (Bengali), Babaji Maharaj came from Kuliya-Nabadwip with his associates to Bhaktivinode Thakur's residence, Surabhi Kunj, in Godrumdwip. A great sankirtan festival was held there on Wednesday, the 27th of Magh."

BABAJI MAHARAJ DESIGNATES MAHAPRABHU'S BIRTH SITE

A physically powerful Vrajavasi named Bihari Das Babaji was Jagannath Das Babaji Maharaj's personal servant. He used to place Babaji Maharaj in a large wicker basket and carry him from place to place. Even though Babaji Maharaj was very aged, his sight was still good. His eyelids drooped, however, covering his eyes, and he had to lift them in order to see. It is said that Bihari Dasji carried Babaji Maharaj in the wicker basket as far as the birthplace of Chaitanya Mahaprabhu. Upon arrival, Babaji Maharaj got out of the basket and began to dance madly, singing the names Jaya Sachinandan Gaura-Hari. Everyone was amazed to see the old Babaji dance in this way. Through his divine vision, Babaji Maharaj pointed out the site of Mahaprabhu's birth and then later the site where the Kazi broke a mridanga. This place is now known as Kholabhangar Danga and is, of course, the site where Mahaprabhu had His all-night kirtanas—Srivasa Angan.

Srila Bhaktivinode Thakur described these events in *Sajjana-toṣaṇī* as follows: "At eleven o'clock in the morning on Thursday, the 20th of Phalgun, 1299 of the Bengali era (1892 AD), devotees filled three boats on the west bank of the Ganges in Nabadwip town. The great devotee Jagannath Das Babaji Maharaj was carried in a palanquin. By the time the party reached Mayapur it was impossible to count the number of people who had gathered. Dwarika Babu and a party of devotees carrying colorful flags were waiting for the renounced Vaishnavas with a joyous kirtan at Mahaprabhu's *janma-sthāna*. When all these devotees had gathered in the raised area where Mahaprabhu appeared and started to dance, it was such a wondrous sight as had likely not been seen in Nabadwip Dham for nearly four hundred years. Later the devotees sat down and, after discussing the matter, decided that deity service should be established both at the birthplace and at Srivasa Angan. Jagannath Das Babaji Mahashay proposed that Jagannath and Sachi Devi should be worshiped in one building and Mahaprabhu with Lakshmi Devi and Vishnupriya standing on his either side in another. On the other hand, deities of the Pancha Tattva should be consecrated in Srivasa Angan."

In those days, there was a large kadamba tree at the Mayapur *janma-sthāna*. Babaji Maharaj came and danced under this tree. Sri Gaura Kishor Das Babaji also used to sit under that tree, chanting the Holy Name in deep trance.

Jagannath Das Babaji spent the last years of his life in a cottage in Koladwip named Bhajan Kutir. This is where Babaji Maharaj's samadhi tomb is now situated. As a service to Jagannath Das, Srila Bhaktivinode Thakur had a concrete veranda built for this cottage.

BABAJI MAHARAJ IN CALCUTTA

Babaji Maharaj also came to visit Srila Bhaktivinode Thakur in his house, Bhakti Bhavan, in Ram Bagan in Calcutta. There he also met Srila Bhaktisiddhanta Saraswati Goswami Thakur, upon whom he showered unlimited affection. When he learned that Saraswati Thakur was an expert in astrology, he asked him to make an almanac based on the Vaishnava calendar. Later, the Chaitanya Math began publishing the *Navadvīpa-pañjikā* in accordance with Babaji Maharaj's wishes.

Though Babaji Maharaj would not allow anyone to take his photograph, Srila Bhaktivinode Thakur was able to arrange to have one taken when he came to visit Bhakti Bhavan. This photo is familiar to all disciples of the Gaudiya Maths, as it appears on their altars. It shows Babaji Maharaj sitting on a wooden seat with his worshipable Giridhari deity on his chest. If Srila Bhaktivinode Thakur had not gone to this trouble, we would be eternally deprived of knowing what Jagannath Das Babaji looked like.

Babaji Maharaj deeply loved Bhaktivinode Thakur. We have heard that he later gave his Giridhari to Bhaktivinode and that this deity is still being served in Bhakti Bhavan.

BABAJI MAHARAJ'S DISAPPEARANCE

When approaching the end of his sojourn in this world, Babaji Maharaj became hunched and tiny looking. Nevertheless, he would still dance in kirtan, and when he did, he stretched to his full height of six feet. When absorbed in the ecstatic mood of kirtan, he would sometimes jump five or six feet into the air. With his tall figure and long arms, he made people think of Mahaprabhu.

Jagannath Das's disappearance took place on the *śuklā pratipad* of the month of Phalgun, Monday, February 25, 1895. Srila Bhaktivinode Thakur wrote of it in *Sajjana-toṣaṇī* (22,2): "At ten o'clock in the morning, in the Bhajan Kutir in Koladwip in Nabadwip town, the old general of the Vaishnavas went to his eternal abode. Siddha Babaji Mahashay went to the spiritual world, leaving this world in darkness. Our mundane eyes will no longer be able to behold his ecstatic dancing in kirtan. May he bestow his blessings on us from his place in the eternal abode."

Rasavihari Goswami of Puruniya in Burdwan district was Jagannath Das's initiated disciple. Rasavihari Goswami in turn initiated the independent King of Tripura, Raja Ishan Chandra Manikya Bahadur. Rasavihari Goswami's deity,

Rasaviharijiu, is worshiped to this day in the Raja's palace.

SRI-SRILA-JAGANNATHASTAKAM

rūpānugānāṁ pravaraṁ sudāntaṁ
śrī-gauracandra-priya-bhakta-rājam
śrī-rādhikā-mādhava-citta-rāmaṁ
vande jagannātha-vibhuṁ vareṇyam

I venerate Jagannath, the best of the Vaishnavas, the foremost of the followers of Srila Rupa Goswami, the king of Gauranga's dear devotees, who takes pleasure in remembering Radhika and Madhava.

śrī-sūrya-kuṇḍāśrayiṇaḥ kṛpālor
vidvad-vara-śrī-madhusūdanasya
preṣṭha-svarūpeṇa virājamānaṁ
vande jagannātha-vibhuṁ vareṇyam

I venerate Jagannath, the best of the Vaishnavas, who was the dearest associate of Sri Madhusudan Das Babaji, the most merciful resident of Surya Kund.

śrī-dhāma-vṛndāvana-vāsi-bhakta-
nakṣatra-rāji-sthita-soma-tulyam
ekānta-nāmāśrita-saṅgha-pālaṁ
vande jagannātha-vibhuṁ vareṇyam

I venerate Jagannath, the best of the Vaishnavas, who stood out from the rest of the devotees of Sri Dham Vrindavan just like the moon amongst the stars. He was the protector of the assembly of Vaishnavas who are uniquely dedicated to the chanting of the Holy Name.

vairāgya-vidyā-hari-bhakti-dīptaṁ
daurjanya-kāpaṭya-vibheda-vajram
śraddhā-yuteṣv ādara-vṛttimantaṁ
vande jagannātha-vibhuṁ vareṇyam

I venerate Jagannath, the best of the Vaishnavas, effulgent with devotion to Hari, endowed with knowledge and renunciation, a veritable thunderbolt to those who are wicked and pretenders, and ever affectionate to the faithful.

samprerito gaura-sudhāṁśunā yaś
cakre hi taj-janma-gṛha-prakāśam
devair nutaṁ vaiṣṇava-sārvabhaumaṁ
vande jagannātha-vibhuṁ vareṇyam

I venerate Jagannath, the best of the Vaishnavas, who was directed by Gauranga Himself to point out the place where He appeared on this earth. He is worshiped by even the gods as the sovereign of the Vaishnavas on this earth.

sañcārya sarvaṁ nija-śakti-rāśiṁ
yo bhakti-pūrṇe ca vinoda-deve
tene jagatyāṁ hari-nāma-vanyāṁ
vande jagannātha-vibhuṁ vareṇyam

I venerate Jagannath, the best of the Vaishnavas, who infused the devoted Bhaktivinode Thakur with all of his own potency, and through him unleashed the flood of Harinam throughout the universe.

śrī-nāma-dhāmnoḥ prabala-pracāre
īhāparaṁ prema-rasābdhi-magnam
śrī-yoga-pīṭhe kṛta-nṛtya-bhaṅgaṁ
vande jagannātha-vibhuṁ vareṇyam

I venerate Jagannath, the best of the Vaishnavas, always immersed in the ocean of sacred rapture and engaged in forcefully preaching the Holy Names and the Lord's abode. He danced ecstatically in the Yoga Pith at Mayapur.

māyāpura-dhāmani sakta-cittaṁ
gaura-prakāśena ca moda-yuktam
śrī-nāma-gānair galad-aśru-netraṁ
vande jagannātha-vibhuṁ vareṇyam

I venerate Jagannath, the best of the Vaishnavas, who is totally attached to the holy dham of Mayapur, who is joyful from the vision of Gauranga, whose eyes flow with tears from the chanting of the Holy Names.

he deva he vaiṣṇava-sārvabhauma
bhaktyā parābhūta-mahendra-dhiṣṇya
tvad-gātra-vistāra-kṛtiṁ supuṇyāṁ
vande muhur bhaktivinoda-dhārām

O Lord! O sovereign of the Vaishnavas! Through your devotion you have overcome even the heavens. I constantly venerate the most pious line of Bhaktivinode Thakur that has grown out from your body and works.

JAGANNATH DAS AND THE BABAJI COMMUNITY

His Holiness Bhakti Promode Puri Goswami, the chairman of the editorial board of *Chaitanya Vāṇī* magazine, wrote an article summarizing some of the important contributions made by Vaishnava Sarvabhauma Jagannath Das Babaji. This article was published in the book *Sri-Sarasvatī-Jayaśrī*, published by the Bagh Bazaar Gaudiya Math in 1948.

On Sept. 28, 1922, after the Calcutta Gaudiya Math's annual festival, Srila Prabhupada traveled to Vrindavan, where he arrived on Saturday, Sept. 30. Through the efforts of Dr. Balahari Das, he and his disciples stayed at the Ghosh family residence near the Lala Babu temple. On Oct. 3, Srila Prabhupada went for darshan of Rupa Goswami's beloved deities, Radha and Govinda. He and his disciples went to look at a few places, seeking a site to establish a math in Vrindavan.

On hearing of Prabhupada's arrival, Madhusudana Goswami Sarvabhauma came from Radha Raman Ghera to visit him. They discussed scriptural matters for two hours and Prabhupada presented him with the latest copy and a few back issues of *Gauḍīya* magazine. Madhusudana

Goswami was very pleased with the high caliber of discussion found in *Gauḍīya* and stated that one day it would be the guiding publication for all Gaudiya Vaishnavas.

On Oct. 4, Srila Prabhupada visited the Madana Mohan temple of Sanatan Goswami. On his way back, he visited the famous Pandit Ramakrishna Das Babaji in Madana Mohan Thor, a walled garden near the Radha Ballabha temple. In the discussion that followed, Pandit Babaji claimed that the chanting of the Holy Name is on the same level as any other devotional activity and that all the various songs, even those that contradict the Goswamis' teachings, are equivalent to the Maha Mantra. He also stated that unless one was educated in the study of logic, or *nyāya*, one could not be qualified for the study of Vedanta. He also argued that it was unnecessary to discuss mundane and spiritual matters.

Srila Prabhupada replied in accordance with the teachings of the Goswamis, as furthered by Vishvanath Chakravarti Thakur, Baladeva, Jagannath Das and Gaura Kishor Das Babaji. He said, "The Goswamis have taught that the chanting of the Holy Names is the primary devotional practice as well as being the goal of all such practice. Divine remembrance of the Lord and his pastimes comes naturally to one who is engaged in such chanting. High level discussions of spiritual truth characterized both Mahaprabhu and His followers, the Goswamis. If one does not have an acute sense of discrimination between the spiritual and mundane, then one equates the debauchery of the Sahajiyas with devotional activity. This is the royal road to self and mass deception.

"Siddha Jagannath Das Babaji's teachings were in line with those of Rupa Goswami: he would in no way embrace any snappy jingles that made a confusion of the divine sentiments. Offenses to the Holy Name can in no way be equated with the pure Name. The scriptures talk of the positive effects of chanting either with faith or without it, but this is not at all the same as chanting without giving up the ten offenses. It is self-deception to think that you can allow yourself to commit any one of the ten offenses, knowingly or unknowingly, and still chant the Holy Names effectively."

THE VISHVA VAISHNAVA RAJA SABHA

According to *Sarasvatī-jaya-śrī*, it was Jagannath Das Babaji who identified the *śuklā pañcamī* of the month of Magh, also known as *śrī-pañcamī*, as the birthday of Vishnupriya Devi, the wife of Sri Chaitanya Mahaprabhu. He told this to Bhaktivinode Thakur, and from him the custom was established throughout the Vaishnava world, so that everyone honors Vishnupriya Devi on this day.

Srila Bhaktisiddhanta Saraswati Goswami Thakur chose Vishnupriya Devi's appearance day to reinstitute the Vishva Vaishnava Raja Sabha or World Vaishnava Association. This was done in the midst of a kirtan on Feb. 5, 1919 at the Ultadanga Math, also known as the Bhaktivinode Asan. The following article appeared in *Amrita Bazaar Patrika*, a Calcutta English-language daily, on the following day, the 10th of February:

"On Wednesday last was celebrated with great eclat the Advent Ceremony of Sri Sri Vishnupriya Devi at the same Asan (1 Ultadanga Junction Road). The occasion was solemnized by the reinstitution of Sri Vishva Vaishnava Raja Sabha as inaugurated by no less a personage than Sri Jiva Goswami himself eleven years after the passing of Sri Sri Mahaprabhu and as given fresh impetus by Sri Bhaktivinode Thakur 33 years ago."

Srila Prabhupada gave an explanation of the history of the Vishva Vaishnava Raja Sabha, which was published in *Sajjana-toṣaṇī*, vol. 21, no. 9.

SRILA PRABHUPADA'S SVAPNA-SAMADHI

After the disappearance of Srila Bhaktivinode Thakur and Srila Gaura Kishor Das Babaji Maharaj, the grief-stricken Srila Prabhupada stayed in Mayapur in the place called Vraja-pattana (now a part of the Chaitanya Math grounds). He wondered, "How can I fulfill the desires of my gurus by preaching the pure doctrine of Sri Chaitanya Mahaprabhu throughout the world. Where will I find the power to do so? I have no followers to help me and no money to speak of. I have no great learning by which I can enchant the mundane. In short, I have no assets of any kind that qualify me to perform this difficult task. It seems that I shall not be able to fulfill the desires of my gurus."

Srila Prabhupada went into an apparent state of deep depression, thinking that it would be impossible for him to continue the preaching mission. His work on writing a commentary on Rupa Goswami's *Upadeśāmṛta* came to a halt after only eight verses.

One night, however, Prabhupada had a dream-like vision in which he saw all the members of the Pancha Tattva being led by Mahaprabhu in sankirtan, dancing toward the birthplace at the Yoga Pith in Mayapur, approaching the *Nāṭa-mandira* from the east. They were followed by the six Goswamis and by Vaishnava Sarvabhauma Jagannath Das Babaji, Bhaktivinode Thakur, Gaura Kishor Das Babaji and other members of the disciplic succession, all appearing in effulgent, divine forms. They consoled Prabhupada, saying, "Why are you worrying? Get the task of preaching pure devotion underway. Preach Mahaprabhu's message everywhere: spread service to *Gaura-dhāma* (Mahaprabhu's abode), *Gaura-nāma* (his name), and *Gaura-kāma* (his desire or work). All of us are at the ready to support you at every turn. We will help you at every moment in your efforts to preach pure devotional service. Countless people, unlimited wealth and extraordinary scholarship are all waiting for you to call on them. Whenever you need anything at all, it will come to you to be engaged in the service of the preaching mission. Simply go forward to preach the message of love of God as given by Sriman Mahaprabhu, giving it your total effort. No worldly force will be able to disrupt this effort. We are with you always."

The following morning, Srila Prabhupada came and told Paramananda Prabhu and some other faithful followers about his dream. From that day onward, he displayed an unbounded enthusiasm for the worldwide preaching of Mahaprabhu's message. He completed his *Anuvṛtti* of the *Upadeśāmṛta*, and started making great efforts to publish books on bhakti. These efforts have borne fruit inasmuch as those seeking service to the divine throughout India have been washed up in the flood of pure devotional preaching that he started. The flood has even begun to inundate the West. It thus seems to me that Srila Prabhupada is constantly repeating Mahaprabhu's instructions to all of us:

jāre dekho tāre kaho kṛṣṇa upadeśa
āmāra ājñāya guru hañā tāro ei deśa
ihāte nā bādhibe viṣaya taraṅga
punarapi ei ṭhāñi pābe mora saṅga

Instruct whomever you see in the religion of Krishna. Become a spiritual master on my order and deliver everyone in this land. Do this and you will never again be entangled in the waves of materialistic life. Indeed, you will have my company again, here in this very place."
(Chaitanya Charitamrita 2.7.128-9)

Srila Satchitananda Bhaktivinode Thakur

namo bhaktivinodāya
saccidānanda-nāmine
gaura-śakti-svarūpāya
rūpānuga-varāya te

I offer my obeisances to you, O Bhaktivinode! You are the form of eternity, knowledge and bliss, the incarnation of Gaura's potency and the best of the followers of Rupa Goswami.

BHAKTIVINODE'S SPIRITUAL IDENTITY

Srila Bhaktivinode Thakur's transcendental identity is revealed to the members of his spiritual family. He is the best of the followers of Rupa Manjari who is the leader of Lalita Sakhi's entourage. Lalita Sakhi is the foremost of Radharani's eight girlfriends. In various places in his own writings, Srila Bhaktivinode Thakur has indicated this divine identity:

yugala-sevāya, śrī-rāsa-maṇḍale,
niyukta kara āmāy
lalitā-sakhīra, ayogya-kiṅkarī,
vinoda dhariche pāy

Praying, "Engage me in the service of the Divine Couple in the circle dance," Bhaktivinode, the most unworthy servant of Lalita Sakhi, holds tight to your lotus feet.
(*Kalyāṇa-kalpa-taru*)

Bhaktivinode Thakur also gives his eternal spiritual identity as Kamala Manjari, the servant of Sri Rupa Manjari, in the song *Siddhi-lālasā* in his *Gīta-mālā*. Her kunja is in the bower of Lalita, Vrajananda Sukhada Kunj, where she sets the standard of worship to the Divine Couple.

varaṇe taṛit, vāsa tārāvalī,
kamala-mañjarī nāma
sāṛe bāro varṣa, vayas satata,
svānanda-sukhada dhāma

My bodily hue is like that of lightning and I wear a sari the color of a clear night sky sprinkled with stars. I am twelve and a half years old and I live in Svananda Sukhada Kunj.

THE NEED FOR BHAKTIVINODE'S APPEARANCE

After the disappearance of Sri Krishna Chaitanya Mahaprabhu, Svarupa Damodar, Ramananda Ray and the six Goswamis, Srinivas Acharya, Narottam Das and Shyamananda Prabhu, a dark age descended on the world of Gaudiya Vaishnavism. Those unable to understand the transcendental purity of Mahaprabhu's religion of love started numerous heretical sects or apasampradayas. Totaram Das Babaji named thirteen such heretical sects:

āul, bāul, kartābhajā, neṛā, daraveśa, sain
sahajiyā, sakhībhekī, smārta, jāta-gosāñi
atibāṛī, cuṛādhārī, gauranga-nāgarī
totā kahe ei teror saṅga nāhi kari

Educated upper class Bengali society was shocked and disgusted by the practices of these heretical sects and came to identify Mahaprabhu's religion with the lower classes, the uneducated and the immoral. People of the gentle classes thus had no understanding or faith in Mahaprabhu's true religion. The most munificent incarnation Sri Chaitanya Mahaprabhu took pity on these bewildered persons and in order to reclaim them for his path of divine love sent his eternal associate Srila Bhaktivinode Thakur into this world. Possessed of superhuman prowess, the Thakur wrote more than a hundred books in several different languages with the goal of defeating all the unorthodox views opposed to the true doctrines of Mahaprabhu's religion. The result was that many members of discerning society and others from all over the world came to recognize the unequalled value of Mahaprabhu's teachings. The founder of the Chaitanya Math and the worldwide Gaudiya Maths, Srila Bhaktisiddhanta Saraswati Goswami Thakur, based his mission on the books and teachings given by Srila Bhaktivinode Thakur and set into motion the fulfillment of Mahaprabhu's message, found in the Chaitanya Bhagavata:

pṛthivīte paryanta āche jata deśa-grāma
sarvatra sañcāra haibeka mora nāma

My name will pervade every village and country in the world. (Chaitanya Bhagavata 3.4.126)

Srila Bhaktivinode Thakur thus made an unequalled contribution to the ultimate, spiritual welfare of humankind. Srila Bhaktisiddhanta Saraswati Goswami Thakur wrote in his preface to the Jaiva-dharma: "Srila Bhaktivinode Thakur is an extremely dear associate of Sri Chaitanya Chandra. In the course of time, when those who preached the desires of Chaitanya Deva had left this world to enter the Lord's eternal pastimes, the sky over Bengal slowly darkened, covered by the thick clouds of sensual enjoyment and false renunciation. The sky was covered and the world was bereft of the rays of light coming from the sankirtan propagated by Sri Chaitanya Mahaprabhu. One by one, the sun, the moon and the unlimited stars of that sky faded from view, leaving only the occasional flash of lightning to disrupt the unending darkness of ignorance. Almost 350 years after the appearance of Chaitanya Mahaprabhu, Srila Bhaktivinode Thakur came to illuminate the Gaudiya sky.

"All the great virtues are present in the body of a Vaishnava. The good qualities of Krishna gradually develop in His devotees. All these transcendental qualities are the characteristics of pure Vaishnavas, and they cannot be fully explained, but I shall try to point out some of the most important. Devotees are always merciful; they are not bellicose. They are truthful, equal to all, faultless, generous, mild and clean. They are without material possessions, and they work for the welfare of all. They are peaceful, surrendered to Krishna, and desireless. They are meek, resolute, and completely control the six character flaws of lust, anger, greed and so forth. They eat only as much as required and are prudent, respectful, and free from false prestige. They are grave, sympathetic, friendly, poetic, expert and silent." (Chaitanya Charitamrita 2.22.75-80)

"All of these qualities of the devotee were perfectly displayed by Srila Bhaktivinode Thakur throughout his life of pure devotion. The ocean of compassion, Sri Gaura Hari, displayed this merciful nature to the conditioned souls in nine different ways. The same kind of distribution of mercy is seen in the life and work of Srila Bhaktivinode Thakur."

THE SAMPRADAYA'S DEBT TO BHAKTIVINODE THAKUR

Srila Bhaktivinode Thakur is the root of the daily activities in the Chaitanya Math, the Gaudiya Math, the Chaitanya Gaudiya Math, and its sister institutions. The Gaudiya Math institutions cannot be separated from Srila Bhaktivinode Thakur. These institutions are entirely indebted to his sublime contributions.

Srila Bhaktisiddhanta Saraswati Goswami Thakur has written, "Devotees in the line of Srila Rupa Goswami do not preach faith in their own powers, but rather attribute everything to the source of their spiritual strength. We also do everything for the sake of Sri Krishna Chaitanya, Sri Rupa, Srila Bhaktivinode Thakur and our divine spiritual master." (From *Patrāvalī*, Srila Prabhupada's letters, vol. 3, p. 89.)

Devotees of the Brahma-Madhva-Saraswata-Gaudiya sampradaya pay their respects daily to Srila Bhaktivinode Thakur as follows:

śuddha-bhakti-pracārasya
mūlībhūta ihottamaḥ
śrī-bhaktivinodo devas
tat-priyatvena viśrutaḥ

Srila Bhaktivinode Thakur is the transcendental personality who is the root of the preaching movement of pure devotion. He is renowned as one who is dear to Sri Chaitanya Mahaprabhu.

HYMNS TO SRILA BHAKTIVINODE THAKUR

Two of Srila Bhaktisiddhanta Saraswati Goswami Thakur's most prominent disciples, Srila Bhakti Rakshaka Sridhar Deva Goswami and Srila Bhakti Vicar Yayabar Goswami Maharaj wrote hymns in praise of Srila Bhaktivinode Thakur, the former in Sanskrit, the latter in Bengali. These have been given below:

vande bhaktivinodaṁ śrī-
gaura-śakti-svarupakam
bhakti-śāstra-jña-samrājaṁ
rādhā-rasa-sudhā-nidhim

I bow to Sri Thakur Bhaktivinode, Mahaprabhu's divine energies personified. He is the emperor of Vaishnava scholars and possesses the ambrosial treasure of Sri Radha's sacred rapture.

bhakativinoda prabhu, dayā koro more
tava kṛpā bale pāi śrī-prabhupādere
bhakati-siddhānta sarasvatī prabhupāda
jagate āniyā dile kariyā prasāda

sarasvatī kṛṣṇa-priya, kṛṣṇa-bhakti tāṅra hiyā
vinodera sei se vaibhava
ei gītera bhāvārtha, prabhupāda para-artha
ebe morā kari anubhava

O Bhaktivinode Prabhu, be merciful to me, for by your blessings I can attain Srila Prabhupada, Bhaktisiddhanta Saraswati. Out of compassion for the world, you brought him whose heart is filled with devotion to Krishna and who is his dear one. This is the glory of Bhaktivinode Thakur. The purpose of this song is to find complete dedication to Srila Prabhupada and this is what we now experience.

śrī-caitanya-janma-sthāna śrī-māyāpur
tomāra pracāre ebe jānila saṁsāra
śikṣāmṛta, jaiva-dharma, ādi grantha śata
sajjana-toṣaṇī-patrī sarva-samādṛta
ei saba grantha-patrī kariyā pracāra
lupta-prāya śuddha-bhakti karile uddhāra
jīvere jānāle tumi hao kṛṣṇa-dāsa
kṛṣṇa bhajo kṛṣṇa cinto chāṛi anya āśa
kṛṣṇa-dāsye jīva saba parānanda pāy
sakala vipad ha'te mukta haye jāy

The whole world has learned that Chaitanya's birthplace is in Mayapur on account of your preaching efforts. Your hundred books such as *Śrī-Caitanya-Śikṣāmṛta* and *Jaiva Dharma*, and your magazine, *Sajjana-toṣaṇī* are valued by all. You preached these books and magazines and by so doing were able to restore the religion of pure devotion that had almost been lost. You told the fallen souls that they were in truth servants of Krishna and you told them to worship Krishna, to think of Krishna and to give up all other ambition. Through service to Krishna, the living being finds full happiness in life and freedom from all danger.

āpani ācari dharma śikhāle sabāre
gṛhe kimbā dhāme thāki bhajaha kṛṣṇere
gadādhara-gaurahari-sevā prakāśile
śrī-rādhā-mādhava-rūpe tāṅdera dekhile
gosvāmi-gaṇera grantha vicāra kariyā
susiddhānta śikhāyeche pramāṇādi diyā
tāhā paṛi śuni loka ākṛṣṭa hailā
jaga-bhari tava nāma gāhite lāgilā
vyāsera abhinna tumi purāṇa prakāśa
śukābhinna prabhupāda śrī-dayita-dāsa

You taught everyone by your own example that they should worship Krishna, whether they are living as a householder or residing in the Dham. You consecrated deities of Gadadhar-Gauranga, seeing Radha and Madhava in them. You studied the scriptures of the Goswamis and preached the pure doctrines that you found there with the appropriate evidence. Those who heard and read these doctrines were attracted and began to sing your glories throughout the world. You are like Vyasadeva who published the Puranas, and Srila Prabhupada, Dayita Das, your son, is like Sukadeva.

vaiṣṇavera jata guṇa āchaye granthete
sakala prakāśa hailā tomāra dehete
śrī-gaura-maṇḍala mājhe śrī-bīranagar
tava āvirbhāva sthāna sarva-śubhaṅkara
vandi āmi nata-śire sei puṇya-kṣetra
mastake dhāraṇa kari se dhuli pavitra
tomāra kṛpāya īśodyāne sthāna pāi
bhāgavata-Mathe basi tava nāma gāi
tomāra dāsānudāsa yati yāyābāra
prārthanā karaye dhāma-vāsa nirantara

All the Vaishnava qualities described in the books are manifest in your body. You appeared in Gaura Mandal, in the village of Birnagar, a place that is auspicious for all. I worship that holy spot with my head bowed low, taking its dust on my head. By your mercy, I have found a place in Ishodyan, the divine garden of Mayapur, and here in the Bhagavata Math, I glorify your name. The servant of your servants, the sannyasi Jajabar, prays to you to grant him eternal life in the Holy Dham.

SRILA BHAKTIVINODE THAKUR'S FAMILY HISTORY

Just as the Supreme Lord Sri Krishna's highest perfection is in His activities in a human form, so similarly His eternal associates also act in human-like ways when they descend to the worldly platform for the benefit of the fallen living entities. Even though they appear to be ordinary human beings, they are in fact never touched by the illusory nature and always remain transcendental to it. They may be situated in householder life, but they are never entangled in material sensual desires like an ordinary conditioned soul because of their deep attachment and love for the Lord. They are simply engaged in a pastime whereby they imitate the activities of the rest of mankind for the sake of exchanging with them for the purposes of benefitting them. Those who have surrendered with sincerity to Vishnu and the Vaishnavas are able to recognize the nonmaterial character of these personalities.

The King Adishura invited Brahmins and other upper class Hindus to Bengal, amongst whom was the Kayastha Purushottam. His seventh and eighth generation descendants were Sri Vinayaka and Narayan, who became government ministers. His fifteenth generation descendant was Mahaprabhu's contemporary, Raja Krishnananda Datta, a devotee of Krishna. Nityananda Prabhu came to stay in his home with his entourage and bestowed profuse blessings on him. Descendants of Krishnananda Datta include Govinda Sharan Datta who founded the village of Govindapur. Kalighat, Sutanuti and Govindapur are the three villages that formed the central core of Calcutta.

Govinda Sharan Datta's grandson was Ramachandra. His grandson was Madana Mohan Datta, who donated Calcutta's Hedua Pukur to the municipality for public use. In 1774, Madana Mohan Datta also spent a great deal of his personal wealth to build steps at Gaya's Pretasila Tirtha and Chandranath Mountain. His grandson was Rajaballabh

Datta, whose son Ananda Chandra Datta was very religious and detached from material life. Ananda Chandra married Jaganmohini Devi, the daughter of the celebrated zamindar of Ula village in Nadia district, Ishwara Chandra Mustaufi.

Srila Bhaktivinode Thakur accepted Ananda Chandra Datta and Jaganmohini Devi as his parents and appeared in Ula-Birnagar in the home of his maternal grandfather. It was the 352nd year after the birth of Chaitanya Mahaprabhu, Sunday, Sept. 2, 1838; the tithi was *śuklā trayodaśī* in the month of Bhadra. His parents gave him the name Kedarnath.

BHAKTIVINODE THAKUR'S CHILDHOOD

Bhaktivinode composed his first poem when he was only two years old. This extraordinary display of talent gave an indication of his future vocation and the transcendental devotional songs he would write later in his life. Songs full of devotion for the Lord and sacred sentiment like his are not the result of any worldly scholarship or creativity, but are self-manifested in the eternally perfect associate of the Lord. The words of the residents of Vaikuntha are all not different from the object of their speech, the Supreme Lord. They can in no way be compared to any mundane sound vibration. Every word used by the Thakur is divine ambrosia that awakens the mood of love for the Lord and is full of the flavors of devotional sentiment.

At only six, he had learned all the details of the historical epics, Mahabharata and Ramayana. Is an ordinary six-year old capable of such a feat? Without divine mercy, it is impossible to understand the basis of all the devotional scriptures. They are not accessible to mere scholarship. The scriptures revealed their meaning in the heart of the Thakur on their own. We can thus conclude that there is a basic difference between his explanations of the scripture and those derived from mundane scholarly analysis.

According to his autobiography, Srila Bhaktivinode Thakur began researching astrological texts when he was only nine years old, but he left them to inquire into spiritual truth at the age of ten. Though he was naturally fixed in eternal transcendental understanding at every moment, he displayed these pastimes in order to exemplify the special character of human life. At this time, he began to mix with people in order to find out what preoccupied them and what guided them in life. He won over everyone he encountered with his sweet words and respectful attitude. As a result, no one ever felt angry or disappointed, even when he pointed out flaws in their argument. This was not within the capacity of an ordinary restless boy of ten years.

The following is Srila Bhaktivinode Thakur's account of several childhood events from his autobiography: "I would go whenever a festival was held at someone's house. There were often such religious festivals at the Brahmachari's residence. There was a nice temple on the outside, and inside a flower garden and an altar for fire-sacrifice. The Brahmachari worshiped according to the tantric cult. He kept a human skull in a small, hidden room. Some people said that if you gave water and milk to a human skull, it will smile. I took the skull down and gave it water, but I saw no smile.

"Nearby there was also an astrologer's house where I would listen to singing performances. One old carpenter was engaged to paint backdrops for the image during the Durga puja. I sat near him while he worked and asked him many questions, which he always answered. I asked, 'When does the spirit of the god enter into the image?' The carpenter answered, 'When I paint its eyes, the god will come and take up residence in the image.' The day that he was actually going to paint the deity's eyes, I eagerly came but I never saw the god actually appear. I said, 'Goloka Pal made this image. He first tied bundles of straw and then covered it with clay. You covered it with chalk and then painted it. There is no god anywhere in this statue at all, is there?' The old carpenter then said, 'When the Brahmins consecrate the deity then the god incarnates and enters the form.' I observed this consecration ceremony carefully, but I was never able to see any divine manifestation. I thought that the carpenter was a fairly wise fellow and so I went to his house and asked him to explain again. He then said to me, 'I have no faith in this worship of idols. My belief is that the Brahmins simply use this as a means of deception for taking money from gullible people.' The carpenter's words brought me great pleasure and I asked him to tell me something about the Supreme Lord. He said, 'Say what you will, I believe in nothing other than the one Supreme Lord, Paramesvara. The gods and goddesses are all imaginary. I worship the one God every day.' These words of the old man gave me faith.

"I became even more inquisitive. The Muslim footman Golam Khan used to guard the treasury. Once in response to my questions, he said, 'God's name is Khoda. At one time he was alone and there was no one and nothing but him. Then he took the dirt from his body and made a pancake out of it which he threw into the single ocean. The upper part of the pancake became the sky and the lower part became the earth. He then created humankind, starting with Adam and Eve. We are all the descendants of Adam and Eve.' After hearing this myth, I asked him, 'Who do you think Rama is?' He said, 'Rama and Rahim are one. That is Khoda.' Then I learned from him about a spell that chases ghosts. Golam Khan said, 'Ghosts are the descendants of Satan. They are afraid of the name of Rahim.' These teachings gave me great pleasure.

"My maternal uncle Parashuram Mustaufi was studying law at that time. At first, he had some faith in God, but later dismissed the idea. While he was a believer, my other uncles Raghu and Nashu were his followers. When he stopped believing in the personal god, he started calling Rama Mohana Ray his guru. I was very troubled because, being just an ignorant child, I was uncomfortable having a difference of opinion with him. Uncle Parashuram said, 'Everything in the world is a product of natural forces. There is no such thing as a God outside of nature.' When I heard this, I went to see some Bhattacharya in his school and asked him to respond to it. His answers caused me to become more confused. Though I was confused, I never gave up chanting the name of Rama."

From all these stories, we can draw the lesson that rather than entering into the confusing business of reasoning out an absolute conclusion about the relation betwen the divine and creation, one should simply chant the Holy Name with faith. At one point, Mahaprabhu also bound His books in their cloth wrappers and told His students to simply chant the Holy Name. All essential spiritual knowledge will be revealed through the Holy Name. Dogmatic spiritual truth is not arrived at through mental speculation, for by this method one is bound to arrive at a mistaken conception of God.

KEDARNATH'S MARRIAGE

When Srila Bhaktivinode Thakur was only eleven years old, his father died. According to the custom prevalent at that time, Kedarnath's mother arranged for her twelve-year-old son to be married to a five-year-old from nearby Ranaghat. Srila Bhaktivinode Thakur has the following to say about his marriage: "It was just like a doll's play-marriage. Because I would not be able to stay alone at my in-laws' house, my parents sent my nanny to accompany me." Though the Thakur had direct perception of the human predicament, he did nothing to protest the defects of the marriage system of the period.

STUDIES

At six years of age, Kedarnath went to study Sanskrit at the Tola of Vidya Vachaspati. Then at the age of seven, his grandfather sent him to study at Krishnanagar College. At that time, the college principal's name was Captain D. L. Richardson and the principle native professor was Ramtanu Lahiri. The next year, an English-language school was established in Ula in which Kedarnath was enrolled. While studying at Krishnanagar College, one of his fellow students was the King of Coochbihar, who was still a child at the time.

When his maternal grandfather died, he and his mother came to live in Calcutta at the family home at the corner of Beadon Street and Hedua in Bhawanipur. He recommenced his studies at the Hindu Charitable Trust School. After four years there, he was admitted to the Hindu School in 1856.

Srila Bhaktivinode Thakur was one of Ishwar Chandra Vidyasagara's first students, whom he held in great affection. One day, Bhaktivinode visited the great scholar in his house in Calcutta. Vidyasagara Mahashaya said to him, "Since none of us has ever seen God, it is best that we not talk about him." Though he was his student, Bhaktivinode Thakur did not refrain from speaking the truth to the venerated teacher. He asked, "Pandit Mahashaya, why then did you write in your [children's] book Bodhodaya that God is formless and pure consciousness. If you haven't seen God, then why have you written this about him? God is omnipotent. Don't you think that if He can do anything, then He has the power to maintain a form? The Supreme Lord is our eternal master, and I am his eternal servant. The natural affection that we have for the Supreme Lord is called bhakti, brahma-vidyā or para-vidyā in the Veda. This is real knowledge, the realization of which means that there is no dearth of any knowledge."

Those who are always engaged in a direct relationship with the absolute truth, the Supreme Lord, are immediately able to recognize any statement which goes contrary to the spiritual truth. There is a complete difference between knowledge that has been garnered from the reading of books and the knowledge which arises from the revelation of the self-effulgent truth.

Calcutta University was founded in 1856 and entrance exams held for the first time. Amongst Srila Bhaktivinode Thakur's fellow students were Satyendranath and Ganendranath Tagore, Tarak Nath Palit and Naragopal Mitra. Principal Clint, Reverend Duff, George Thompson, and Keshab Chandra Sen were attracted by the young man's mastery of the English language and literature. Toward the end of 1856, Kedarnath published an English poem, The Poriade, which was well-received in educated circles in Calcutta. All the Thakur's English poems were published in the paper, Library (Literary) Gazette. He delivered a lecture to the British Indian Society in 1856 on the evolution of matter which was much applauded.

During this time, the Thakur also studied the Brahmo Dharma, Christianity, the Bible, the Quran and many other religious traditions and books. He considered Christianity superior to the Brahmo religion because of its acceptance of God's eternal personality. In 1857, the Sepoy Mutiny broke out. Kedarnath spent some of this time travelling and lecturing.

THE PREDICTION OF GRANDFATHER KRISHNAVALLABHA

In 1858, Kedarnath started from Bengal to reach Nilachala. On the way back to Calcutta, he stopped at Chutigram, where his grandfather Krishnavallabha Datta was living. His grandfather prophetically stated that Kedarnath would be a great Vaishnava. Immediately upon making this prediction, his life airs passed out through the top of his head. From there he moved on to Puri to be present at the time of Lord Jagannath's Chandan Yatra. Kedarnath remained in Puri for a few more days before continuing through Cuttack, Bhadrak, and Midnapore to Calcutta.

THE TITLE BHAKTIVINODE

On Ishvarachandra Vidyasagar's recommendation, Kedarnath Datta took a job teaching at the Cuttack Government Secondary School and shortly thereafter, the headmaster's position at a school in Bhadrak in 1860. During this time, he wrote a book on the various religious institutions of Orissa, *Maths of Orissa*, which Sir William Hunter made much use of as a reference in his work *Orissa*. He also wrote a work named *Sri-Caitanya-gītā* under the pen name Satchitananda Premalankar. He was given the title Bhaktivinode by the Sri Gaudiya Goswami Sangha on the 400th anniversary of Mahaprabhu's appearance (1885). From this time on, Kedarnath Datta was known in Vaishnava society as Sri Satchitananda Bhaktivinode Thakur.

TRAVELS AND PREACHING

The Thakur also taught at a school in Midnapore. One day a follower of the Brahmo religion, Rama Narayan Basu, heard him speak at a literary society meeting on the truth of religion and was deeply moved. During his time in Midnapore, the Thakur's first wife died and he married for a second time, to Bhagavati Devi. From Midnapore, he went to Burdwan to preach. While there, he published an English book, *Our Wants*, in 1863. He was involved in the arguments between the Brahmo Samaj and Christians and tried to mediate between the two religions. In two lectures he showed the problems with both groups' positions. While in Burdwan, he started a group called the *Bhrātṛ-samāja*. At one of the meetings of this group, he gave a learned speech on the soul which attracted the attention of a certain Mr. Heiley.

From Burdwan, the Thakur went to Chuadanga and Ranaghat before going to live temporarily in Chapra in Bihar. While living there he made his first visit to Vrindavan, travelling by train through Kashi, Mirzapur, Prayag, Agra, etc. While in Chapra, the Thakur studied Urdu and Persian and mastered these languages. He also gave a speech on Gautama while there.

From Chapra, he went to Purniya and then, in 1868, to Dinajpur where he was engaged as Deputy Magistrate. In Dinajpur, he found that there was a dispute between Hindus and Brahmos in which he intervened, giving a speech on *The Bhagavata: Its Philosophy, Its Ethics and Its Theology*.

In June of 1868, he visited Rupa and Sanatan's home in Ramakeli as well as Rajmahal, etc. Thereafter he returned to Calcutta, where he undertook research to find copies of Chaitanya Charitamrita and Srimad Bhagavatam. After much work, he finally found copies at the Bot Tola publishing house. With these valuable editions, he went to Purushottam Dham. He was engaged as a director of the temple to oversee its management. He lived in Puri continuously for over five years, from 1869-1874.

PUNISHING BISHIKISHAN FOR DECEPTION

In Srila Bhaktivinode Thakur's life we find that he personified the description of a Vaishnava as one who is more gentle than a rose, yet more terrible than the thunderbolt. Although he was generally kind and sympathetic, he gave no quarter to dishonesty in the name of religion. One event in his life which took place while he was in Orissa is an indication of this. In 1871, a member of the Khandait caste and the Atibari sect named Bishikishan who had gained some mystic powers through yogic practices proclaimed himself to be an incarnation of Mahavishnu. He was staying with his acolytes at the edge of the jungle near the town of Bhubaneshwar. He announced that on the 14th of Chaitra, he would reveal a four-armed form and destroy all the foreigners, restoring the true religion. His announcement was written in Orissan verse:

banere achi biṣakiṣaṇa
guptare achi na jānai āna
tera mīnare ārambhiba raṇa,
caturbhuja hoi nāśiba mleccha-gaṇa

In the forest am I hiding and no one else knows me, but on the 13th of Mīna I will begin the war. Taking on a four-armed form, I will destroy the Mlecchas.

Through his mystic powers, he had been able to cure incurable diseases and these powers had won for him a large following. One day he announced that on the full-moon day he would perform the *rāsa-līlā* and invited the girls of a nearby village to come and join him. The Chaudhuris of the Bhringar clan found that he had polluted their womenfolk and went to complain en masse to the district commissioner, Mr. Ravenshaw. The Commissioner gave the task of investigating the matter to Bhaktivinode Thakur, who went personally into the jungle to meet with Bishikishan. Bishikishan told Bhaktivinode that he was the living Mahavishnu and that Jagannath Deva was nothing but a lifeless wooden statue. He tried in various ways to flatter the Thakur and to win him over. When he saw that Bishikishan had no intention of stopping his efforts to deceive the people, Bhaktivinode had him arrested and brought back to Puri.

The Thakur proceeded to investigate the background of Bishikishan by going to many villages and Buddhist *vihāras* in the Khandagiri area of Puri district. After accumulating a mass of evidence showing the extent to which this yogi was cheating people, he had him brought to court. While the case was being heard, the yogi used his mystic power to cause Bhaktivinode and his family to be attacked by various illnesses, in an effort to intimidate him, but without success. The Thakur was determined to see Bishikishan punished for conspiracy to rebellion and gave him a sentence of one and a half years. Bishikishan went for 21 days without food or drink and then left his body.

In the months that followed, another rascal in Jajpur proclaimed himself to be the incarnation of Brahma, while someone else in Khorda said that he was a manifestation of Balaram. Bhaktivinode Thakur quickly thwarted their efforts to cheat the populace.

OTHER ACTIVITIES OF THE THAKUR IN PURI

While living in Puri, Srila Bhaktivinode Thakur took the opportunity to study the Bhagavata, the Six Sandarbhas of Jiva Goswami, the *Govinda-bhāṣya, Siddhānta-ratnam* and *Prameya-ratnāvalī* of Baladeva Vidyabhushan. He also studied Rupa Goswami's *Bhakti-rasāmṛta-sindhu* in great detail. By making a display of intense study, he demonstrated the necessity of cultivating an understanding of the scriptures in order to learn the truths about pure devotion contained therein. Mahaprabhu indicated that one of the five principle limbs of devotional service is hearing the Bhagavata. Jiva Goswami indicated that this is the best of all devotional activities. In order to proclaim this same truth, Srila Bhaktivinode Thakur founded a regular group for discussion of the Bhagavata, Bhagavata Samsad, which was held in the Jagannath-vallabha gardens in Puri.

Many of the leading Vaiṣhnavas in Puri such as Nityananda Das, Paramananda Das, Narayan Das Mahanta, Harihara Das Mahanta of Uttara Parshva were attracted to hearing the Bhagavata from his lips. Just as Mahaprabhu performed the pastime of hearing Bhagavata from Srila Gadadhar Pandit Goswami, Srila Bhaktivinode Thakur also listened to discourses given by Sri Gopinath Pandit.

A certain renounced Vaishnava, Raghunath Das Babaji of Hati Akhra, objected to the Thakur's speaking on Bhagavata and was attacked by disease. After Jagannath appeared to him in a dream and ordered him, he went and begged Srila Bhaktivinode Thakur for forgiveness, after which he was cured.

When the Thakur went to the Jagannath temple, he did not sit in the Mukti Mandapa, where Mayavadi scholars discussed their philosophy. He would sit by the Lakshmi temple where Mahaprabhu's footprints are enshrined and discussed devotional doctrines there. Many of the Mayavadis were attracted by his discourses and soon the place became known as the Bhakti Mandapa or the Bhakti Prangan.

During this time, Srila Bhaktivinode Thakur studied Krishna Das Kaviraj Goswami's Chaitanya Charitamrita and Narahari Chakravarti's *Bhakti-ratnākara*, but he did not accept Jayananda's *Caitanya-maṅgala* as being authoritative. He associated with a siddha Vaishnava named Svarupa Das Babaji, discussing scripture with him. He also wrote the Sanskrit work, *Datta-kaustubha* and began writing the Sanskrit verses of *Sri-Kṛṣṇa-saṁhitā*.

THE BIRTH OF BHAKTISIDDHANTA SARASWATI

A wealthy family in Puri had leased land along the Grand Road from the Dakshina Parshva Math and built a house on it. Srila Bhaktivinode Thakur and his family resided in this building, which is not far from the Jagannath temple, next to the Narayan Chata. This house was reclaimed in 1974 by His Divine Grace Bhakti Dayita Madhava Goswami Maharaj and now houses a Chaitanya Gaudiya Math with a beautiful temple building.

At 3:30 on Friday, February 6, 1874, on the *kṛṣṇā pañcamī* of Magh, an effulgent and beautiful child was born to Bhagavati Devi in this home, while the Thakur and other family members sang the names of the Lord. Everyone was amazed to see that the child's umbilical cord was wrapped around his body like a sacred thread. He was named after the divine energy of Jagannath Deva, Vimala Devi, as Bimala Prasad (Vimalā-prasāda). His first solid food was Jagannath's maha prasad. This child grew up to become the founder of the Chaitanya Math and the worldwide Gaudiya Maths, Srila Bhaktisiddhanta Saraswati Goswami Thakur Prabhupada.

Srila Bhaktivinode Thakur was Jagannath Deva's own man. It was thus by Lord Jagannath's arrangement that he was brought to Puri to see to the smooth management of his service. After the birth of Srila Bhaktisiddhanta Saraswati Goswami Thakur, the preaching of Mahaprabhu's message spread over the entire planet. This gave meaning to the words written by Vyasadeva in the *Padma-purāṇa, hy utkale puruṣottamāt*, "out of Purushottam in Orissa."

Ten months after Bimala Prasad's birth, Bhaktivinode Thakur was reposted to Ranaghat, so he and his family returned to Bengal, travelling overland by palanquin.

BHAKTIVINODE'S INCOMPARABLE CONTRIBUTION

Veda Vyasa and the scriptures he wrote are the foundation of the Sanatan Dharma. He himself practiced and preached the means by which humankind can attain the supreme peace. He compiled and divided the Veda, wrote the eighteen Puranas and the Mahabharata including the Bhagavad Gita, but remained unsatisfied. Finally, while at Badarikashram, Narada Muni instructed Vyasa Deva to glorify the activities of Sri Krishna in order to attain his pleasure. After he had written the twelve cantos of the Srimad Bhagavatam, Veda Vyasa finally found the peace he had been looking for.

Mahaprabhu Sri Chaitanya preached the Bhagavata religion found in this text. After the disappearance of Mahaprabhu and His associates, however, the path of pure devotion slowly became covered with thorns until Bhaktivinode Thakur appeared to write many books and to preach the pure doctrine of devotional service to Krishna. Through his tireless efforts, all the heretical doctrines were shown to be empty, and the path of supreme auspiciousness and compasision was again revealed to the world. These efforts can only be said to constitute an unequalled and certainly unsurpassed contribution. No one can spread the message of pure devotion without being empowered by Krishna Himself. Were Bhaktivinode Thakur not a direct associate of Gauranga Mahaprabhu and Sri Krishna, he would never have been able to make such a show of empowerment.

Externally, Bhaktivinode Thakur was a householder with family obligations, a government servant engaged in the administrative service, but despite these responsibilities he was still able to write over a hundred books in several different languages. One cannot fail to be impressed by this monumental achievement. Every word he wrote is scripture; every word awakens the spirit of devotion to the Lord beyond the grasp of the material senses and mind. No mundane scholars could ever achieve the kind of synthesis he did. His every thought was perfectly rational and never unsound. His writings are a permanent display of compassion to the fallen souls. His Divine Grace Bhakti Dayita Madhava Maharaj used to say to his disciples, "You need do nothing other than translate Bhaktivinode Thakur's books into the world's various languages. By doing so, you will perform the greatest act of welfare for the people of the world." Whatever the Gaudiya Math and its numerous branches throughout the world have achieved is built on the foundation established by Srila Bhaktivinode Thakur.

BHAKTIVINODE'S TRAVELS AND PREACHING ACTIVITIES

After the birth of Srila Bhaktisiddhanta Saraswati Goswami Thakur, Srila Bhaktivinode Thakur returned to Bengal. From then on he engaged in preaching the doctrine of pure devotional service, travelling throughout India. We will give a brief summary here of all the places he visited between 1877 and 1910, whether for pilgrimage or preaching. He went to Amta in the Uluberiya subdivision, to Abhiram Thakur's Sripat in Khanakul Krishnanagar, Shyampur, Bhadrak in Orissa, Naral in Jessore district, Calcutta, Prayag, Vrindavan (where he met Jagannath Das Babaji for the first time), Sri Radha Kund, Sri Govardhan (where he broke up the Kanjhara dacoit gang that was harassing pilgrims to the Dham), Mathura, Lucknow, Faiyedabad, Goptar Ghat, Ayodhya and Benares.

Bhaktivinode then returned to Calcutta, where in 1882 he started construction on Bhakti Bhavana at 181 Maniktola Street. While digging the foundations for the building, a murti of Kurma Deva was found. Srila Bhaktivinode Thakur gave this deity to Srila Bhaktisiddhanta Saraswati Goswami Thakur and taught him how to worship it. He also visited Mayapur for the first time.

The Thakur was then engaged as Deputy Collector in the Barasat subdivision. Then he was transfered to Srirāmapur (1884) Vaidyanātha, Bākipur, and Gaya, where he saw the steps on Pretasila constructed by his great-grandfather, Madana Mohan Datta. He returned to Naral, Barasat, Memari, Kulingram, Bandel, and Saptagram. In Kulīnagram he lectured on the Holy Name, distinguishing between the pure name, *nāmābhāsa* and *nāmāparādha*. There he also gave Srila Bhaktisiddhanta Saraswati Goswami Thakur initiation in the Holy Name and the Nrisingha mantra.

In 1885, Bhaktivinode established the Chaitanya Yantra printing press in Calcutta. In 1886, he helped establish the Vishva Vaishnava Raja Sabha at the Durga Mandap of Rama Gopal Basu in Krishna Singher Gali off Bethune Road. There he gave lectures on Chaitanya Charitamrita and *Bhakti-rasāmṛta-sindhu*. At this time he also had a meeting with the famous Ramakrishna Paramahamsa, during which he countered his impersonal philosophy and explained the truth of pure devotion.

THE DISCOVERY OF MAHAPRABHU'S BIRTHPLACE

In 1887, Bhaktivinode Thakur visited Tarakeshwar, where the most important Shiva linga in Bengal has its temple. While there, Shiva appeared to him in a dream and said, "You want to go to Vrindavan, but there is much work left to do in Nabadwip Dham, which is nearby. What have you done there?"

Later that year, the Thakur was transfered to Krishnanagar, just a few miles from Nabadwip. He thus had the occasion to visit Kuliya, where the modern city of Nabadwip stands. He was staying at the Ranir Dharma Shala (guest house) overlooking the Ganges. At about ten o'clock at night, he went on the roof to cool off after a hot day and saw an illuminated building on the other side of the river. His son Kamala Prasad was accompanying him and also saw this light. On inquiry, they learned that the light was coming from a place known as Ballal Dighi. On going later to Ballal Dighi, they learned from the elderly residents of the village that this was Chaitanya Mahaprabhu's birthplace. Intrigued, Bhaktivinode Thakur began to research old maps and documents and was able to establish conclusively that Mahaprabhu's birthplace was indeed at Ballal Dighi.

Bhaktivinode Thakur continued to maintain his Calcutta home where he installed the Giridhari Shila given him by Jagannath Das Babaji. In 1888 he purchased a property in Godrumdwip, which he named Surabhi Kunj. While stationed at Krishnanagar, he was also able to visit his birthplace at Ula.

In 1889, Bhaktivinode was transferred to East Bengal in the Netrakona subdivision in Mymensingh District. There he visited Narayan Ganj, Mymensingh city, the Garo Hills where he blessed the people of the Hajong tribe, and Gowalanda. Though he was able to visit Calcutta during this period, he was soon transfered to Tangail and then to Burdwan. He visited Shantipur, Kalna, Baghna Para, Koigram, and Denur, the site of Vrindavan Das Thakur's Sripat.

In May 1890, he visited Kuliya again where he met Jagannath Das Babaji at his bhajan kutir. He rendered service to Babaji Maharaj by arranging for a concrete veranda to be built for him. While in Burdwan, he also performed kirtan with the devotees of Amlajora village and visited Gopalpur, Raniganj and Barakar.

In 1890, Srila Bhaktivinode Thakur was again posted in Raniganj in East Bengal and then in Dinajpur in 1891. When in Calcutta, he met the famous newspaper publisher, Sisir Kumar Ghosh, who considered him a guru, even calling him "the seventh Goswami." Sisir Kumar Ghosh would come regularly to visit him at Bhakti Bhavan and at the Thakur's direction, started chanting japa and wearing a tulasi mala around his neck. He was not able to accept the principles of Vaishnava behavior in their entirety, however.

During this period Bhaktivinode also visited Midnapore, where he discoursed with Sitanath Mohapatra and other devotees, Ghatal in Midnapore district and Kayapat Badna Ganj in Hooghly district. From there he returned to Krishnanagar, staying once again in Surabhi Kunj. He arranged for some large assemblies to be called in Krishnanagar at which he spoke. A number of Englishmen, including Messrs. Mulrow, Wallace and Butler, were regular attendants at these meetings.

At Amlajora on March 9, 1892, he participated in a *Harivasara* (Ekadasi) program at which Jagannath Das

Babaji was present. From there he travelled to Vrindavan, stopping at Bāksar (Bihar) and Prayag. He was in Vraja from March 21 to 29, during which time he managed to visit Bilvavan, Bhandiravan, Mathavan, Man Sarovar, Mathura, Gokula, Madhuvan, Talavan, Kumudavan, Bahulavan, Radha Kund, Govardhan, etc. He then returned to Calcutta via Kanpur and Allahabad.

In Calcutta, Bhaktivinode Thakur once again engaged in preaching the message of Sri Chaitanya Mahaprabhu at Bhakti Bhavan, as well as continuing to hold assemblies at Krishnanagar. In Magh 1399 (February, 1893), he held a kirtan festival at Godrumdwip at which Jagannath Das Babaji was the guest of honor. Later that spring, on the 20th of Phalgun (March, 1893), Jagannath Das indicated the exact spot where Mahaprabhu had first appeared in this world.

At this time, the Thakur had an argument with a certain member of a Goswami family who held that one of Mahaprabhu's closest associates was a Shudra. Srila Bhaktivinode Thakur was very displeased when he heard this and warned him with the words:

vaiṣṇava-caritra, sarvadā pavitra,
jei ninde hiṁsā kari
bhakativinoda, na sambhāṣe tāre,
thāke sadā mauna dhari

A Vaishnava's character is always spotless. I, Bhaktivinode, always remain silent and never speak to those who criticize Vaishnavas out of spite.

Also at about this time, Srila Bhaktivinode Thakur wrote down his guru-paramparā and hung it on the outside of Bhakti Bhavan. He also did some preaching of Mahaprabhu's religion of love in Bihar, in the towns of Sasaram, Nasirganj and Dihiri.

In January of 1894, Srila Bhaktivinode Thakur held another large meeting at the A.B. School in Krishnanagar. At this meeting it was decided that deities should be installed at Mahaprabhu's birthplace. At the same time, the Nabadwip Pracharini Sabha was formed to publicize the newly discovered birthsite. Nafar Chandra Pal Bhakti Bhushan, the zamindar of Natudaha in Nadia district, was elected executive secretary of the Sabha. Dwarika Babu, Nafar Babu, and other members of the Sabha decided that a thatched cottage would be constructed on the site and would house deities of Gaura and Vishnupriya. These deities were consecrated on Friday, March 21, 1894 (Chaitra 9, 1300 Bengali), on the Phalguni Purnima, in the midst of a rousing kirtan held during a lunar eclipse. A committee was formed (Sri Mayapur Seva Samiti) for the maintenance of the deities. This committee had many distinguished Vaishnava members including Shyamlal Goswami, Sasibhushan Goswami, Radhikanath Goswami, Bipina Bihari Goswami, Mahamahopadhyaya Pandit Ajitanath Nyayaratna, Mahendranath Bhattacharya Vidyaranya, Satya Jivan Lahiri, Raja Vanamali Ray Bahadur of Taras in Pabna district, Sisir Kumar Ghosh, Matilal Ghosh, Jatindranath Chaudhuri, Mahendranath Majumdar, the advocate Kishorilal Sorkar, Nalinakha Datta, Kanailal Dey Bahadur, Deputy Magistrate Navin Chandra Sen, and Jagatchandra Ray.

BHAKTIVINODE RETURNS TO PURI

On October 4, 1894, Srila Bhaktivinode Thakur retired from government service and came to live permanently in Surabhi Kunj in Godrumdwip where he continued his practice of giving discourses on the Vaishnava scriptures. Some time after the disappearance of Jagannath Das Babaji in February of 1896, he accepted the invitation of the independent Raja of Tiperrah (Tripura), Birchandra Devavarma Manikya Bahadur, to go to Agartola. He went there with Bhaktisiddhanta Saraswati in July 1896 and enchanted the Raja with his discourses on pure devotional service. Later in the same year, he took Bhaktisiddhanta Saraswati to Karshiyang in the Himalayan foothills, then in 1898 to Benares and Prayag.

In 1899, Srila Bhaktivinode Thakur purchased another property in Godrum on which Svananda Sukhada Kunj would be built. When this building was finished, he came to perform his bhajan there. Gaura Kishor Das Babaji was a regular visitor, coming to hear the Thakur's Bhagavata lectures, and it was here that Srila Bhaktisiddhanta Saraswati Goswami Thakur met his guru for the first time.

In 1900, Bhaktivinode Thakur travelled with Bhaktisiddhanta through Balesore, Remuna, Bhubaneswara, and Sakshi Gopal to Puri. Srila Bhaktisiddhanta Saraswati Goswami Thakur displayed a deep desire to engage in bhajan near Hari Das Thakur's samadhi on the beach and his father arranged with Puri's sub-registrar, Jagabandhu Pattanayak, for him to be given the service of the Giridhari Asan of the Satasan Math. In March of 1901, they came to Puri again and in 1902 the construction of Bhakti Kuti was begun. During this time, the Raja of Cossimbazar, Manindra Chandra Nandi, took instruction in devotional service from the Thakur.

In 1903, Bhaktisiddhanta Saraswati would regularly read and give discourses at Bhakti Kuti on Chaitanya Charitamrita in the presence of the Thakur. The famous Radharaman Charan Das Babaji came to visit Bhaktivinode Thakur during this time and they discussed devotional doctrines. Srila Bhaktisiddhanta Saraswati Goswami Thakur found Charan Das's activities and teachings to be heterodox and showed how by reference to the scriptures. Later, after Srila Bhaktivinode Thakur had returned to Nabadwip, Charan Das indicated his desire to participate in the Nabadwip parikrama inaugurated by the Thakur, but unfortunately left his body before he was able to do so.

THE THAKUR RETURNS TO GODRUMDWIP

In 1906, Srila Bhaktivinode Thakur gave a lengthy discourse on Mahaprabhu's teachings at the house of zamindar Jatindranath Ray Chaudhuri in Taki, 50 km east of Calcutta. On February 26, 1906, the Thakur came to Calcutta again and from there returned to Svarupa Ganj in Godrumdwip where he engaged in his devotional activities at Svananda Sukhada Kunj. While there, a certain Tarak Brahma Goswami of Jessore came to him and asked him to accept his Radha-Madhava deities for Mahaprabhu's birthplace. Tarak Brahma Goswami moved to the birthplace with his wife and family, but after a short time it became clear that his behavior was at odds with the standards expected of them and they were obliged to leave. On April 29, 1906, however, the Sri Dham Pracharini Sabha decided to award an annual stipend of 500 rupees to the temple for the service of Sri Sri Radha-Madhava.

In 1908, Srila Bhaktivinode Thakur took the dress of a renounced Vaishnava, a *bhāgavata-paramahaṁsa*, in order to dedicate his life to deeply relishing the sacred nectar of Radha and Govinda's intimate pastimes.

On March 25, 1910, which was again a *Phalguni Purnima* (the appearance day of Lord Chaitanya Mahaprabhu), Jagadish Bhakti Pradip, at that time still a householder, visited Bhaktivinode Thakur at Mayapur and five days later received initiation from him at Godrumdwip. Another disciple, Krishna Das Babaji, was also living with the Thakur at Svananda Sukhada Kunj at that time.

Srila Bhaktivinode Thakur preached that the rules of the *Daiva-varṇāśrama dharma* should always be followed. Thus, he upheld the directives of the *Sat-kriyā-sāra-dīpikā* in giving the sacred thread to Jagadish Bhakti Pradip (who after taking sannyas from Srila Bhaktisiddhanta Saraswati Goswami Thakur became Bhakti Pradip Tirtha Maharaj), Sitanath Mohapatra Bhakti Tirtha, Vasanta Kumar Ghosh and Manmathanath Ray.

In this connection, it is worth examining the following words written by the Thakur: "The Varnashram dharma current in today's society is quite distinct from the transcendental religion of exclusive devotion to Krishna. The practice of Varnashram dharma on its own does not result in full surrender to the Lord. The ultimate instruction of the Bhagavad Gita is to discard all the principles related to the varnas and ashrams, in short, all activities based on bodily identification, and to engage in cultivation of devotional activities based on the natural emotional constitution of the soul, which is pure and without ulterior motive. Dedicated scholars such as Raghavachari have no understanding of Gaudiya Vaishnavism's glorious concept of pure devotion."

BHAKTIVINODE SENDS BHAKTISIDDHANTA TO BALIGHAI

In 1910, while still at Svananda Sukhada Kunj, Srila Bhaktivinode Thakur was engaged in writing his *Sva-niyama-dvādaśaka* when he suddenly became extremely ill. Srila Bhaktisiddhanta Saraswati Goswami Thakur and other dear disciples and followers gathered around him, afraid that he was about to enter the *nitya-līlā*. Even in this state of extreme physical discomfort, however, the Thakur's enthusiasm for preaching Lord Chaitanya's message was unabated. Though unable to walk, he indicated that he wished to be taken from place to place on horseback so that he could continue to spread Mahaprabhu's teachings.

Three years before the Thakur's disappearance, Srila Bhaktisiddhanta Saraswati Goswami Thakur approached his father and vowed to him that though he felt himself to be an unworthy servant, he would take up the ultimate welfare work of defeating all heterodox doctrines that go against pure devotional service. Bhaktivinode Thakur was delighted to hear his son's determination and when Gopiballabhpur's Sri Vishvambharananda Deva Goswami invited him to participate in a conference in Balighai, Midnapore, he sent Srila Bhaktisiddhanta Saraswati Goswami Thakur and Suresh Chandra Mukhopadhyaya in his place. The conference, the theme of which was to establish orthodox doctrines in certain areas of theology, took place from Sept. 8-11, 1911. Many respected and well-reputed scholars of the sampradaya were present, including Madhusudan Goswami Sarvabhauma of the Radha Raman Ghera in Vrindavan.

Srila Bhaktisiddhanta Saraswati Goswami Thakur gave a talk on the distinctions between a Vaishnava and a Brahmin, clearly demonstrating a great amount of research, and left the assembly of scholars enchanted and speechless. A year later, when Madhusudan Goswami visited Srila Bhaktivinode Thakur at Bhakti Bhavan, he enthusiastically proclaimed Srila Bhaktisiddhanta Saraswati Goswami Thakur to be Bhaktivinode's worthy successor in his work of protecting the Gaudiya Sampradaya.

In 1913, Bhaktisiddhanta Saraswati started writing his commentary on the Chaitanya Charitamrita, which was meant to accompany Bhaktivinode Thakur's *Amṛta-pravāha-bhāṣya*. He read several passages of the *Anubhāṣya* to the Thakur, giving him indescribable pleasure.

BHAKTIVINODE THAKUR'S ENTRY INTO THE ETERNAL PASTIMES

A few days before his disappearance, Srila Bhaktivinode Thakur left Godrumdwip to come to Bhakti Bhavan. On June 23, 1914, on the disappearance day of Gaura Shakti, Srila Gadadhar Pandit Goswami, in his Calcutta home, Srila Bhaktivinode Thakur entered the midday pastimes of Sri Sri Radha and Govinda at Radha Kund. Six years later, his wife Bhagavati Devi, the worshipable Mata Thakurani, went to join him on exactly the same tithi.

Srimad-Bhaktivinode-viraha-daśakam

(Ten verses describing the feelings of separation from Srila Bhaktivinode Thakur written for the occasion of his disappearance day by His Grace Bhakti Rakshaka Sridhar Deva Goswami in 1936)

hā hā bhaktivinoda ṭhakkura guro dvāviṁśatis te samā
dīrghād-duḥkha-bharād aśeṣa-virahād duḥkhīkṛtā bhūr iyam
jīvānāṁ bahu-janma-puṇya-nivahākṛṣṭo mahī-maṇḍale
āvirbhāva-kṛpāṁ cakāra ca bhavān śrī-gaura-śaktiḥ svayam

Alas! Alas! O my guru Bhaktivinode Thakur! For twenty-two long years the world has been burdened with the grief of your separation. You, the personification of Sri Gauranga's energy, mercifully appeared in this world after being attracted by the living beings' many lifetimes of pious activities.

dīno'haṁ cira-duṣkṛtir na hi bhavat-pādābja-dhūli-kaṇā-
snānānanda-nidhiṁ prapanna-śubhadaṁ labdhuṁ samartho'bhavam
kintv audārya-guṇāt tavāti-yaśasaḥ kāruṇya-śaktiḥ svayaṁ
śrī-śrī-gaura-mahāprabhoḥ prakaṭitā viśvaṁ samanvagrahīt

Being most fallen and possessing nothing but sinful activity in my past, I have not been able to attain the joyful treasure of bathing in the dust of your lotus feet, which brings all auspiciousness to the surrendered. Even so, you are deservedly renowned for your magnanimity. You are the personification of Lord Sri Chaitanya Mahaprabhu's compassionate powers and have appeared in this world in order to bestow his divine blessings upon it.

he deva! stavane tavākhila-guṇānāṁ te viriñcādayo
devā vyartha-manorathāḥ kim u vayaṁ martyādhamāḥ kurmahe
etan no vibudhaiḥ kadāpy atiśayālaṅkāra ity ucyatāṁ
śāstreṣv eva na pāraye'ham iti yad gītaṁ mukundena ca

O Lord! The gods led by Brahma are frustrated when they endeavor to glorify your unlimited virtues. What then can lowborn humans such as we accomplish? This is no rhetorical exaggeration, as some scholars may claim, for even Mukunda himself has said the same to the gopis in the Bhagavata (10.32.22).

dharmaś carmagato'jñataiva satatā yogaś ca bhogātmako
jñāne śūnya-gatir japena tapasā khyāti-jighāṁsaiva ca
dāne dāmbhikatānurāga-bhajane duṣṭāpacāro yadā
buddhiṁ buddhimatāṁ bibheda hi tadā dhātrā bhavān preṣitaḥ

You were sent by the Lord when even the most intelligent people's wisdom had been ruined by religious activities that seek only bodily pleasures, by constant ignorance, by yoga that has sense enjoyment as its goal, by the idea that the goal of knowledge is the void, by the desire to destroy individual consciousness through prayer and austerity, by arrogant pride in giving charity, and by immoral practices spread in the name of *rāgānuga-bhajana*.

viśve'smin kiraṇair yathā himakaraḥ sañjīvayan nauṣadhīr
nakṣatrāṇi ca rañjayan nija-sudhāṁ vistārayan rājate
sac-chāstrāṇi ca toṣayan budha-gaṇaṁ sammodayaṁs te tathā
nūnaṁ bhūmi-tale śubhodaya iti hlādo bahuḥ sātvatām

Just as the moon gives life to the world's vegetation, revitalizes the constellations and spreads its own nectar with its rays, so did your auspicious appearance on Earth bring fulfillment to the holy scriptures, joy to the intelligent and abundant ecstasy to the Vaishnavas.

lokānāṁ hita-kāmyayā bhagavato bhakti-pracāras tvayā
granthānāṁ racanaiḥ satām abhimatair nānāvidhair darśitaḥ
ācāryaiḥ kṛta-pūrvam eva kila yad rāmānujādyair budhaiḥ
premāmbodhi-vigrahasya bhavato māhātmya-sīmā na tat

Wishing to bless everyone in the world, you demonstrated how to preach devotion to the Supreme Lord through writing a multitude of books, all appreciated by the saintly. The glorious achievements of all the previous acharyas such as Ramanuja cannot match yours, for you are the embodiment of the ocean of prema.

yad-dhāmnaḥ khalu dhāma caiva nigame brahmeti saṁjñāyate
yasyāṁśasya kalaiva duḥkha-nikarair yogeśvarair mṛgyate
vaikuṇṭhe para-mukta-bhṛṅga-caraṇo nārāyaṇo yaḥ svayaṁ
tasyāṁśī bhagavān svayaṁ rasa-vapuḥ kṛṣṇo bhavān tat-pradaḥ

You came to give the Supreme Person, Krishna Himself, whose body is the blissful form of absolute divinity, the effulgence of whose abode is known in the Veda as Brahman, whose mere partial expansion is the goal of the great yogis' austere practices, who is the source of Narayan, whose lotus feet are surrounded by the most advanced, bee-like liberated souls in Vaikuntha.

sarvācintya-maye parātpara-pure goloka-vṛndāvane
cil-līlā-rasa-raṅginī parivṛtā sā rādhikā śrī-hareḥ
vātsalyādirasaiś ca sevita-tanor mādhurya-sevā-sukhaṁ
nityaṁ yatra madā tanoti hi bhavān tad-dhāma-sevā-pradaḥ

You bestowed service to the completely inconceivable divine abode of Goloka Vrindavan, which lies beyond the other spiritual worlds, where Radha, surrounded by Her sakhis, whose pleasure is in the transcendental nectar of spiritual pastimes, constantly and joyfully serves in the erotic mood, Sri Hari, who is also worshiped in other moods like parenthood.

śrī-gaurānumataṁ svarūpa-viditaṁ rūpāgrajenādṛtaṁ
rūpādyaiḥ pariveśitaṁ raghu-gaṇair āsvāditaṁ sevitam
jīvādyair abhirakṣitaṁ śuka-śiva-brahmādi-sammānitaṁ
śrī-rādhā-pada-sevanāmṛtam aho tad dātum īśo bhavān

You are perfectly competent to give the nectar of service to Radharani's feet, which was approved by Gauranga Mahaprabhu, which was understood by Svarupa Damodar, adored by Sanatan Goswami, distributed by Sri Rupa Goswami, relished and enjoyed by Raghunath and the rest of Sri Rupa's followers, and which is held aloft by even Suka, Shiva and Brahma.

kvāhaṁ manda-matis tv atīva patitaḥ kva tvaṁ jagat-pāvanaḥ
bho svāmin kṛpayāparādha-nicayo nūnaṁ tvayā kṣamyatām
yāce'haṁ karuṇā-nidhe varam imaṁ pādābja-mūle bhavat-
sarvasvāvadhi-rādhikā-dayita-dāsānāṁ gaṇe gaṇyatām

I am a wicked-minded fallen soul, so far from you who purify the entire universe. O Master! Please forgive all my offenses out of your great compassion. I beg you, O ocean of mercy, to grant me this boon: that I may be included amongst the followers of Srila Bhaktisiddhanta Saraswati Goswami Thakur, for whom your lotus feet are everything.

SRIMAD-BHAKTIVINODE-DASAKAM

(This poem, also by Srila B.R. Sridhar Maharaj, was published in *Gauḍīya* magazine, July 1939, 7.47)

amanda-kāruṇya-guṇākara śrī-
caitanya-devasya dayāvatāraḥ
sa gaura-śaktir bhavitā punaḥ kiṁ
padaṁ dṛśor bhakti-vinoda-devaḥ

O ocean of unlimited compassion, you are the incarnation of Chaitanya Deva's mercy. You are the energy of Gauranga. O Lord Bhaktivinode, when will you again be visible to me?

śrīmaj-jagannātha-prabhu-priyo ya
ekātmako gaura-kiśorakena
śrī-gaura-kāruṇya-mayo bhavet kiṁ
nityaṁ smṛtau bhakti-vinoda-devaḥ

When will Bhaktivinode Prabhu, the embodiment of Mahaprabhu's blessings, remain fixed in my memory? He is dear to Jagannath Prabhu and is not different from Gaura Kishor Das Babaji.

śrī-nāma-cintāmaṇi-sampracārair
ādarśam ācāra-vidhau dadhau yaḥ
sa jāgarūkaḥ smṛti-mandire kiṁ
nityaṁ bhaved bhakti-vinoda-devaḥ

When will Bhaktivinode Prabhu, who gave us the example of how to act by preaching the jewel of the Holy Name, remain alive in the temple of my memory?

nāmāparādhai rahitasya nāmno
māhātmya-jātaṁ prakaṭaṁ vidhāya
jīve dayālur bhavitā smṛtau kiṁ
kṛtāsano bhakti-vinoda-devaḥ

When will Bhaktivinode Prabhu, most merciful to all living beings, take his place in my mind after revealing the glories of the Holy Name, void of any offenses?

gaurasya gūḍha-prakaṭālayasya
sato'sato harṣa-kunāṭyayoś ca
prakāśako gaura-jano bhavet kiṁ
smṛtyāspadaṁ bhakti-vinoda-devaḥ

When will I remember Bhaktivinode Prabhu, the member of Gauranga's entourage who revealed his hidden birthplace, to the joy of the saintly and the envious reaction of the wicked?

nirasya vighnān iha bhakti-gaṅgā-
pravāhanenoddhṛta-sarva-lokaḥ
bhagīratho nitya-dhiyāṁ padaṁ kiṁ
bhaved asau bhakti-vinoda-devaḥ

Like King Bhagiratha, he saved the entire world by destroying all impediments and allowing the Ganga of pure devotion to flow. When will Bhaktivinode Prabhu be the permanent object of my meditation?

viśveṣu caitanya katha-pracārī
māhātmya-śaṁsī guru-vaiṣṇavānām
nāma-grahādarśa iha smṛtaḥ kiṁ
citte bhaved bhakti-vinoda-devaḥ

When will I remember Bhaktivinode Prabhu, who preached the message of Chaitanya Mahaprabhu throughout the world, glorified the guru and the Vaishnavas and set the example for chanting the Holy Name?

prayojanaṁ sann abhidheya-bhakti-
siddhānta-vāṇyā samam atra gaura-
kiśora-sambandha-yuto bhavet kiṁ
cittaṁ gato bhakti-vinoda-devaḥ

When will Bhaktivinode Prabhu, himself the representative of prayojana-tattva, appear in my mind, accompanied by Gaura Kishor Das Babaji, the personification of sambandha-tattva, and by Bhaktisiddhanta Saraswati, the incarnation of abhidheya-tattva?

śikṣāmṛtaṁ sajjana-toṣaṇīṁ ca
cintāmaṇiṁ cātra sa-jaiva-dharmam
prakāśya caitanya-prado bhavet kiṁ
citte dhṛto bhakti-vinoda-devaḥ

When will Bhaktivinode Prabhu, who made people conscious of Sri Chaitanya Mahaprabhu through his publications *Caitanya-śikṣāmṛta*, *Sajjana-toṣaṇī*, *Harināma-cintāmaṇi*, and *Jaiva Dharma*, be held constantly in my mind?

āṣāḍha-darśe'hani gaura-śakti-
gadādharābhinna-tanur jahau yaḥ
prapañca-līlām iha no bhavet kiṁ
dṛśyaḥ punar bhakti-vinoda-devaḥ

When will Bhaktivinode Prabhu appear to us again? Being non-different from Gaura-Shakti Gadadhar Pandit, he left the material world on the same day as he, the dark-moon-day of Asharh month.

SRI GODRUMA-CANDRA-BHAJANOPADESA

("Instructions to worship the Moon of Godrum." These verses written by Srila Bhaktivinode Thakur were published posthumously for the first time in 1950 in *Gauḍīya* magazine, 18.47-8, pp. 757-8)

yadi te hari-pāda-saroja-sudhā-
rasa-pāna-paraṁ hṛdayaṁ satatam
parihṛtya gṛhaṁ kali-bhāva-mayaṁ
bhaja godruma-kānana-kuñja-vidhum

If your heart wishes to always drink the nectar of Hari's lotus feet, then abandon your home, which is filled with the spirit of Kali, and worship the moon of Godrum's forest bowers.

dhana-yauvana-jīvana-rājya-sukhaṁ
nahi nityam anukṣaṇa-nāśa-param
tyaja grāmya katha-sakalaṁ viphalaṁ
bhaja godruma-kānana-kuñja-vidhum

All the joy you get from wealth, youth, life and power is temporary and susceptible to destruction at any moment. Give up all your useless mundane discourses and worship the moon of Godrum's forest bowers.

ramaṇī-jana-saṅga-sukhaṁ ca sakhe
carame bhayadaṁ puruṣārtha-haram
hari-nāma-sudhā-rasa-matta-matir
bhaja godruma-kānana-kuñja-vidhum

O friend! The joys of intercourse with beautiful women are ultimately a source of fear, for they prevent the achievement of life's goals. Become intoxicated with the nectar of the Holy Names and worship the moon of Godrum's forest bowers.

jaḍa-kāvya-raso nahi kāvya-rasaḥ
kali-pāvana-gaura-raso hi rasaḥ
alam any kathady-anuśīlanayā
bhaja godruma-kānana-kuñja-vidhum

The relishing of poetic sentiments is not the sacred rapture of devotional poetry. Real sacred rapture is found in the sentiments connected to the purifier of the age of Kali, Gaura. Give up the study of all other subjects and worship the moon of Godrum's forest bowers.

vṛṣabhānu-sutānvita-vāma-tanuṁ
yamunā-taṭa-nāgara-nanda-sutam
muralī-kala-gīta-vinoda-paraṁ
bhaja godruma-kānana-kuñja-vidhum

Worship the moon of Godrum's forest bowers, the son of Nanda, the playboy who sports on the Yamuna's banks with the daughter of Vrishabhanu at His left side, joyfully playing wonderful songs on His flute.

hari-kīrtana-madhyagataṁ svajanaiḥ
pariveṣṭita-jāmbunadābha-hariṁ
nija-gauḍa-janaika-kṛpā-jaladhiṁ
bhaja godruma-kānana-kuñja-vidhum

Worship the moon of Godrum's forest bowers, the ocean of mercy for His own companions from the land of Gauda; He dances in the midst of the kirtan, surrounded by these associates, His effulgent form appearing to be of refined gold.

girirāja-sutā-parivīta-gṛhaṁ
nava-khaṇḍa-patiṁ yati-citta-haram
sura-saṅgha-nutaṁ priyayā sahitaṁ
bhaja godruma-kānana-kuñja-vidhum

Worship the moon of Godrum's forest bowers, whose house is surrounded by the daughters of the king of mountains, who is the Lord of the abode of nine islands, who steals the minds of the sannyasis and who, in the company of His beloved, is praised by the heavenly hosts.

kali-kukkura-mudgara-bhāva-dharaṁ
hari-nāma-mahauṣadha-dāna-param
patitārta-dayārdra-sumūrti-dharaṁ
bhaja godruma-kānana-kuñja-vidhum

Worship the moon of Godrum's forest bowers, who has taken the mood of the hammer-wielding chastiser of the Kali-dog, who makes a gift of the great panacea of the Holy Name, and whose form is soaked in tearful compassion for the fallen.

ripu-bāndhava-bheda-vihīna-dayā
yad abhīkṣṇam udeti mukhābja-tatau
tam akṛṣṇam iha vraja-rāja-sutaṁ
bhaja godruma-kānana-kuñja-vidhum

His mercy makes no distinction between friend and foe. Though His bodily hue is not black, He is the son of the King of Vraja. Worship the moon of Godrum's forest bowers.

iha copaniṣat-parigīta-vibhur
dvija-rāja-sutaḥ purṭābha-hariḥ
nija-dhāmani khelati bandhu-yuto
bhaja godruma-kānana-kuñja-vidhum

Worship the moon of Godrum's forest bowers—He whose glories are sung in the Upanishads and is now a son of the best of Brahmins with a golden bodily hue, playing in His own dham with His eternal associates.

avatāra-varaṁ paripūrṇa-phalaṁ
para-tattvam ihātma-vilāsa-mayam
vraja-dhāma-rasāmbudhi-gupta-rasaṁ
bhaja godruma-kānana-kuñja-vidhum

Worship the moon of Godrum's forest bowers, who is the best of the incarnations of the Supreme, who brings the ultimate fruit of spiritual life, who is the Supreme Truth come into this world out of His own pleasure and who relishes a taste hidden in the ocean of rapture that is Vraja Dham.

śruti-varṇa-dhanādi na yasya kṛpā-
janane balavad-bhajanena vinā
tam ahaituka-bhāva-pathā hi sakhe
bhaja godruma-kānana-kuñja-vidhum

Learning or high birth are useless in bringing about His mercy without intense bhajan. O friend, worship the moon of Godrum's forest bowers without any fruitive desire.

api nakra-gatau hrada-madhya-gataṁ
kam amocayad ārta-janaṁ tam ajam

avicintya-balaṁ śiva-kalpa-taruṁ
bhaja godruma-kānana-kuñja-vidhum

This same Lord also once liberated a distressed demigod from a crocodile body within the lake known as Goradaha. He is the unborn one, possessing inconceivable power, and is truly a desire tree of pure auspiciousness. Just worship the beautiful moon of Godrum's forest bowers.

surabhīndra-tapaḥ-parituṣṭa-mano
vara-varṇa-dharo harir āvirabhūt
tam ajasra-sukhaṁ muni-dhairya-haraṁ
bhaja godruma-kānana-kuñja-vidhum

When His mind was pleased by the austerities of Indra and Surabhi, He appeared in a golden form before them. Worship the moon of Godrum's forest bowers, who brings unlimited pleasure and who disturbs the calm minds of the silent sages.

abhilāṣa-cayaṁ tad abheda-dhiyam
aśubhaṁ ca śubhaṁ ca tyaja sarvam idam
anukūlatayā priya-sevanayā
bhaja godruma-kānana-kuñja-vidhum

Give up all your desires for sense enjoyment. Give up the idea .that you are identical with the Lord. Abandon both auspicious and inauspicious works. Only worship the moon of Godrum's forest bowers with acts compatible with His pleasure and by serving those dear to Him.

hari-sevaka-sevana-dharma-paro
hari-nāma-rasāmṛta-pāna-rataḥ
nati-dainya-dayā-paramāna-yuto
bhaja godruma-kānana-kuñja-vidhum

Become fixed in the religion of serving the servants of Hari. Be fixed in drinking the nectar of the Holy Names. Always be fixed in respect, humility and compassion. Worship the moon of Godrum's forest bowers.

vada yādava mādhava kṛṣṇa hare
vada rāma janārdana keśava he
vṛṣabhānu-sutā-priyanātha sadā
bhaja godruma-kānana-kuñja-vidhum

Sing the names of Yadava, Madhava, Krishna and Hari. Sing the names of Rama, Janardana and Keshava. Always sing the name of the dearest lord of the daughter of Vrishabhanu. Worship the moon of Godrum's forest bowers.

vada yāmuna-tīra-vanādri-pate
vada gokula-kānana-puñja-rave
vada rāsa-rasāyana gaura-hare
bhaja godruma-kānana-kuñja-vidhum

Sing the name of the Lord of the forests by the Yamuna banks. Sing the name of the sun that lights up the gardens of Gokula. Sing the name of Gaura Hari, the alchemist of sacred rapture. Worship the moon of Godrum's forest bowers.

cala gaura-vanaṁ nava-khaṇḍamayaṁ
paṭha gaura-hareś caritāṇi mudā
luṭha gaura-padāṅkita-gāṅga-taṭaṁ
bhaja godruma-kānana-kuñja-vidhum

Go live in Gauranga's forest with its nine divisions. Study Gaura Hari's life. Roll about in the dust by the banks of the Ganges marked with Gauranga's footprints. And worship the moon of Godrum's forest bowers.

smara gaura-gadādhara-keli-kalāṁ
bhava gaura-gadādhara-pakṣa-caraḥ
śṛṇu gaura-gadādhara-cāru kathaṁ
bhaja godruma-kānana-kuñja-vidhum

Remember always the enchanting pastimes of Gaura-Gadadhar. Become a follower of Gaura-Gadadhar. Always listen to the enchanting topics of Gaura-Gadadhar. Worship the moon of Godrum's forest bowers.

A LIST OF BHAKTIVINODE THAKUR'S WRITTEN WORKS

Other than the titles already mentioned, Srila Bhaktivinode Thakur wrote numerous works from 1866 to 1907 which are listed here as far as possible.

(1) *Balid-e-registry* (Urdu), 1856.
(2) Speech on Gautam (English), 1856.
(3) Speech on the Bhagavatam (English), 1869.
(4) *Garbha-stotra-vyākhyā* (Bengali), 1870.
(5) "Reflections" (English), 1871.
(6) "Slokas of Hari Das Thakur's Samadhi" (English), 1871.
(7) "Jagannath Mandir of Puri" (English), 1871.
(8) "Akhras of Puri" (English), 1871.
(9) *Vedāntādhikaraṇa-mālā* (Sanskrit), 1872.
(10) *Datta-kaustubham* (Sanskrit), 1874.
(11) *Datta-vaṁśa-mālā* (Sanskrit), 1876.
(12) *Bauddha-vijaya-kāvyam* (Sanskrit), 1878.
(13) *Sri-Kṛṣṇa-saṁhitā* (Sanskrit and Bengali), 1880.
(14) *Kalyāṇa-kalpa-taru* (Bengali songs), 1881.
(15) *Sri-sajjana-toṣaṇī* (Bengali monthly magazine) from 1881-1898.
(16) Review of *Nitya-svarūpa-saṁsthāpana* (English), 1883.
(17) *Srimad Bhagavad Gītā*, with Vishvanath Chakravarti's commentary, and *Rasika-rañjana* translation (Bengali), 1886.
(18) *Sri-Caitanya-śikṣāmṛta* (Bengali), 1886.
(19) *Sammodana* commentary to *Śikṣāṣṭaka* (Sanskrit), 1886.
(20) *Manaḥ-śikṣā padyānuvāda* (Bengali), 1886.
(21) *Daśopaniṣac-cūrṇikā* (Sanskrit), 1886.
(22) *Bhāvāvalī*, verses and commentary (Sanskrit), 1886.
(23) *Prema-pradīpa* (Bengali novel), 1886.
(24) *Viṣṇu-sahasra-nāma* with Baladeva's commentary (Sanskrit), 1886.
(25) Published Satyarāja Khan's *Sri-Kṛṣṇa-vijaya*, 1886.
(26) *Caitanyopaniṣat* with *Caitanya-caraṇāmṛta* commentary

(Sanskrit), 1887.
(27) *Vaiṣṇava-siddhānta-mālā* (Bengali), 1888.
(28) *Sri-Āmnāya-sūtra* (Sanskrit sutras, Bengali explanation), 1890.
(29) *Sri-dhāma-navadvīpa-māhātmya* (Bengali), 1890.
(30) *Siddhānta-darpaṇa* translation (Bengali), 1890.
(31) *Srimad Bhagavad Gītā*, Bengali translation (*Vidvad-rañjana-bhāṣya*) and Baladeva's Sanskrit commentary (Bengali), 1891.
(32) *Sri-Harināma* (Bengali), 1892.
(33) *Sri-Nāma* (Bengali), 1892.
(34) *Sri-Nāma-tattva* (Bengali), 1892.
(35) *Sri-Nāma-mahimā* (Bengali), 1892.
(36) *Sri-Nāma-pracāra* (Bengali), 1892.
(37) *Sriman-Mahāprabhura Śikṣā* (Bengali), 1892.
(38) *Tatta-viveka* (Sanskrit verses and Bengali commentary), 1893.
(39) *Śaraṇāgati* (Bengali songs), 1893.
(40) *Śoka-śātana* (Bengali song), 1893.
(41) *Jaiva Dharma* (Bengali), 1893.
(42) *Tattva-sūtra* (Sanskrit and Bengali), 1894.
(43) *Īśopaniṣat Vedārka-dīdhiti-vyākhyā* (Bengali), 1894.
(44) *Tattva-muktāvalī* or *Māyāvāda-śata-dūṣaṇī* (Sanskrit and Bengali), 1894.
(45) *Amṛta-pravāha-bhāṣya* on Chaitanya Charitamrita (Bengali), 1895.
(46) *Sri-Gaurāṅga-smaraṇa-maṅgala-stotra* (Sanskrit), 1896.
(47) "Life and Precepts of Sree Chaitanya Mahaprabhu" (English), 1896.
(48) *Sri-Rāmānuja-Upadeśa* (Bengali), 1896.
(49) *Artha-pañcaka* (Bengali), 1896.
(50) Bengali translation of *Brahma-saṁhitā*, 1897.
(51) *Kalyāṇa-kalpa-taru* (Revised), 1897.
(52) Translation and commentary on *Kṛṣṇa-karṇāmṛta* (Bengali), 1898.
(53) Translation and commentary on *Upadeśāmṛtam* (Bengali), 1898.
(54) Bhagavad Gita with Madhva's commentary (Bengali), 1898.
(55-56) Sanatan Goswami's *Bṛhad-Bhāgavatāmṛta* in two volumes (Bengali translation), 1898.
(57) Narahari Thakur's *Bhajanāmṛta* (Bengali translation), 1899.
(58) *Navadvīpa-bhāva-taraṅginī* (Bengali verse), 1899.
(59) *Sri-Harināma-cintāmaṇi* (Bengali verse), 1900.
(60) *Tattva-vaṁśa-mālā* (Bengali)
(61) *Bhāgavatārka-marīci-mālā* (compilation and Bengali translation), 1900.
(62) *Sri-saṅkalpa-kalpadruma* (Bengali translation), 1900.
(63) *Padma-purāṇa* (edited), 1901.
(64) *Bhajana-rahasya* (collection of verses and Bengali verse translation), 1902.
(65) *Vijana-grāma o sannyāsī* (Bengali verse, revised edition), 1902.
(66) *Sri-Kṛṣṇa-saṁhitā* (Sanskrit and Bengali, revised), 1903.
(67) *Sat-kriyā-sāra-dīpikā* (edited), 1903.
(68) *Sri-Caitanya-śikṣāmṛta* (revised and expanded), 1905.
(69) *Prema-vivarta* (Bengali), 1905.
(70) *Sva-niyama-dvādaśakam* (Sanskrit verse), 1906.
(71) *Sri-Nimbārka-daśa-ślokī* (Bengali trans. and comment), 1907.
(72) *Sri-Gītimālā* (Bengali songs), 1907.
(73) *Sri-Gītāvalī* (Bengail songs), 1907.
(74) *Hari katha* (Bengali verse), 1850.

Srila Bhaktivinode Thakur wrote *Sri-Kṛṣṇa-saṁhitā* and *Kalyāṇa-kalpa-taru* and started publishing the monthly magazine, *Sajjana-toṣaṇī*, while living at Naral in Jessore district, from 1878 to 1881. He published an English edition of *Sajjana-toṣaṇī* in 1883 while in Barasat. Then, in 1886, when in Serampore, he published his translation-commentary to the Bhagavad Gita, *Rasika-rañjana*, along with Vishvanath's commentary, *Sārārtha-darśinī*. While in Serampore, he also wrote *Caitanya-śikṣāmṛta*, the *Sammodana-bhāṣya* commentary to Mahaprabhu's *Śikṣāṣṭaka*, and a book named *Bhaktivinode*. In 1887, while in Sambalpur, he published *Caitanyopaniṣat* after receiving a unique manuscript from a disciple named Madhusudan Das. Later in the same year, while living in Krishnanagar, he started work on *Āmnāya-sūtra* and also published his *Navadvīpa-māhātmya*. In 1896, after returning to Calcutta from Tripura he published his English *Life and Precepts of Sree Chaitanya Mahaprabhu* and the Sanskrit *Gaurāṅga-smaraṇa-maṅgala-stotra*.

[30] *Bhakti-vinoda* or taking delight in devotional service is the ultimate goal of prema, *sambandha* is the relationship with Mahaprabhu (*gaura-kiśora*) and the devotional processes established by the doctrine, or *bhakti-siddhanta* are the *abhidheya-tattva*.

[31] This incident is recounted in Jagadananda's *Prema-vilāsa*, chapter 15.

[32] This incident is described in Bhaktivinode's *Navadvīpa-dhāma-māhātmya*.

Srila Gaura Kishor Das Babaji

namo gaura-kiśorāya
sākṣād vairāgya-mūrtaye
vipralambha-rasāmbhodhe
pādāmbujāya te namaḥ

I bow to your lotus feet, Srila Gaura Kishor Das Babaji, the embodiment of renunciation and the ocean of sacred rapture in separation.

EARLY LIFE

Paramahamsa Srila Gaura Kishor Das Babaji Maharaj was born into a vaishya family on the banks of the Padma River in Bagayan village in Faridpur district in what is now Bangladesh. The names of his parents are unknown. His given name was Vamsi Das. He was born sometime in the middle of the nineteenth century. He is important to us because he was the diksha guru of Srila Bhaktisiddhanta Saraswati Goswami Prabhupada, founder of the Chaitanya Math and the worldwide Gaudiya Maths.

Vamsi Das's parents had him married at an early age, according to the custom of the time, but he always remained detached from householder life. His main interest was always in worshiping the Lord. When his wife died, he left home and went to Vrindavan where he took the *paramahaṁsa-veṣa* from Bhagavata Das Babaji (a disciple of

Srila Jagannath Das Babaji Maharaj) and took the name Gaura Kishor Das Babaji.

GAURA KISHOR COMES TO NABADWIP

After being initiated into the Babaji order, Gaura Kishor Das spent thirty years in Vraja engaged in intense religious practice. He also travelled outside of the Vraja area, visiting northern India and Bengal. While in the East, he met many of the leading Vaishnavas of Bengal and Orissa, such as Svarupa Das Babaji of Puri, Bhagavan Das Babaji of Kalna and Chaitanya Das Babaji of Kuliya.

In 1893, after the birthplace of Chaitanya Mahaprabhu was consecrated at the Sri Mayapur Yoga Pith, Jagannath Das Babaji Maharaj ordered Gaura Kishor Das to stay in Nabadwip. This is where he remained for the rest of his life. He saw all the residents of Nabadwip with transcendental eyes, considering them to be divine beings. He thus accepted *madhukarī* from them, cooking everything in a rejected clay bowl. It is said that sometimes he would subsist on nothing but Ganges water and mud. Often he would go for long periods without eating, chanting the Holy Names constantly. He set the standard for those in the renounced order who live the life of solitary worship, remaining completely independent of others.

Mahaprabhu's personal envoy, Srila Bhaktivinode Thakur was extremely impressed by Gaura Kishor's extraordinary renunciation, pure devotion, and attachment to the Lord. Gaura Kishor would often go to Bhaktivinode's home in Godrumdwip, Svananda Sukhada Kunj, where he would listen to him give readings of the Bhagavata and discuss Vaishnava theology with him.

SARASWATI THAKUR MEETS BABAJI MAHARAJ

Babaji Maharaj never accepted service from anyone. He constantly chanted the Holy Name, sometimes counting the names on a tulasi mala, at other times by making knots on long strips of an old cloth. His favorite texts were Narottam Thakur's *Prārthanā* and *Prema-bhakti-candrikā*, which he considered to be his all-in-all. His renunciation resembled that of Raghunath Das Goswami and he possessed the same attachment to Krishna.

In 1898 AD, Gaura Kishor Das Babaji Maharaj met Srila Bhaktisiddhanta Saraswati Goswami Thakur for the first time at Svananda Sukhada Kunj in Godrumdwip. Saraswati Thakur was enchanted by Babaji Maharaj's heartfelt emotional kirtan. He wrote the kirtan down and later taught it to his own disciples. The song describes Raghunath Das Goswami's ecstatic separation from Radha.

kothāy go premamayi rādhe rādhe
rādhe rādhe go, jaya rādhe rādhe
dekhā diye prāṇa rākha rādhe rādhe
tomāra kāṅgāla tomāya ḍāke rādhe rādhe
rādhe vṛndāvana-vilāsini rādhe rādhe
rādhe kānu-mano-mohini rādhe rādhe
rādhe aṣṭa-sakhīra śiromaṇi rādhe rādhe
rādhe vṛṣabhānu-nandini rādhe rādhe
(gosāñi) niyama kare sadāi ḍāke rādhe rādhe
(gosāñi) ekabāra ḍāke keśī-ghāṭe rādhe rādhe
ābāra ḍāke vaṁśī-baṭe rādhe rādhe
(gosāñi) ekabāra ḍāke nidhuvane rādhe rādhe
ābāra ḍāke kuñja-vane rādhe rādhe
(gosāñi) ekabāra ḍāke rādhākuṇḍe rādhe rādhe
ābāra ḍāke śyāma-kuṇḍe rādhe rādhe
(gosāñi) ekabāra ḍāke kusuma-vane rādhe rādhe
ābāra ḍāke govardhane rādhe rādhe
(gosāñi) ekabāra ḍāke tāla-vane rādhe rādhe
ābāra ḍāke tamāla-vane rādhe rādhe
(gosāñi) maline vasana diye gāya,
vrajera dhulāya gaṛāgaṛi jāya, rādhe rādhe
(gosāñi) mukhe rādhā rādhā bale
bhese nayanera jale, rādhe rādhe
(gosāñi) vṛndāvane kulākuli
kende beṛāya rādhā bali, rādhe rādhe
(gosāñi) chāpānna daṇḍa rātri dine, jāne nā
rādhā-govinda bine, rādhe rādhe
tāra para cāri daṇḍa śuti thāke svapne
rādhā-govinda dekhe, rādhe rādhe

Where is the abode of all love? Radhe Radhe! Glories to Radha! Show Yourself to me, Radha. Give me life once again. I have become a beggar for You, Radha, and I am calling You. O Radha, you cavort in Vrindavan, You enchant Krishna's mind, You are chief amongst the eight sakhis, and are the daughter of Vrishabhanu.

Raghunath Das Goswami regularly, constantly calls out to You, Radha. He calls for You in Keshi Ghat, in Vamsi Bata, Nidhuvan, Kunjavan, in Radha Kund and Shyama Kund, in Kusumavana and Govardhan, in Talvan and Tamalvan. He calls out wearing only a worn and dirty cloth and rolling in the Vrindavan dust. The names of Radha on his lips, his eyes are filled with tears. He wanders through every part of Vraja, calling Radha's name. Night or day, for twenty-three hours he thinks of nothing but Radha and Govinda, and when he sleeps, he dreams of Radha and Govinda.

GAURA KISHOR INITIATES SRILA PRABHUPADA

In January 1900, Srila Bhaktisiddhanta Saraswati Goswami Thakur took initiation from Gaura Kishor Das Babaji on the instructions of Srila Bhaktivinode Thakur. Bhaktisiddhanta Saraswati was Babaji Maharaj's only disciple. Babaji Maharaj was an anchorite who had sworn not to take any disciples, but he was forced to change his decision when he saw Saraswati Thakur's determination and devotion.

The story is told that Srila Prabhupada asked Gaura Kishor Das Babaji Maharaj several times to give him initiation. The first time he asked, Babaji Maharaj told him, "If Mahaprabhu tells me to, I will."

The second time Babaji Maharaj told him that he had forgotten to ask Mahaprabhu. Srila Prabhupada did not give up and came a third time, Babaji Maharaj said,

"Virtuousness, scholarship and other qualities are not the means to attain the Lord. They do not give you any right to initiation."

Though he had been turned away by Gaura Kishor Das Babaji repeatedly, Srila Prabhupada did not abandon his resolution. Ramanujacharya was turned away eighteen times before receiving the mercy of Gosthipurna. Srila Prabhupada showed his qualities of patience and determination and continued to come before Babaji Maharaj. He humbly entreated him to give him initiation until finally Babaji Maharaj's heart melted, and out of great affection, he mercifully initiated Srila Prabhupada by sprinkling the dust of his lotus feet on his head.

Gaura Kishor Das Babaji would never allow any materialistic persons touch his feet. If they did so, he would make a show of anger, saying, "You are doomed!" Most people were thus afraid to attempt it. On this occasion, however, he himself offered the dust of his feet to his dear disciple and smeared it on his body. From Srila Prabhupada's disciples, it is heard that he was turned away twelve times before Babaji Maharaj became compassionate and initiated him at his thirteenth request. Others say that it happened on the fourth time. This story reminds one of Narottam's initiation by Lokanatha Goswami. Unswerving dedication to the guru is the sign of a disciple. Afterward, Babaji Maharaj, judging Srila Prabhupada to be eminently qualified for the task, blessed him and ordered him to preach Mahaprabhu's message all around the world.

SRILA PRABHUPADA DESCRIBES HIS GURU

Srila Prabhupada wrote the following words about his guru, with exemplary humility, in order to show the world the definitive path to auspiciousness: "In order to complete the gaping needs that I felt, I was busily trying to get my hands on everything under the sun. I thought that possessions would fulfill my needs. Over time, I had indeed accumulated a great number of rare possessions, but I was not able to rid myself of the sense of being unfulfilled. I had encountered many personalities who were reputed to be great saints, but saw various deficiencies in every one of them and so was unable to give them my full respect. Fortunately, the supremely merciful Sri Gauranga Mahaprabhu allowed two of His dearest companions to show their kindness to me. I was egotistically so self-absorbed that I had completely lost any sense of where my wellbeing could be found. Even so, due to past pious activities, I was able to get the association of Srila Bhaktivinode Thakur who was my ever wellwisher. My Prabhu often came to visit him and sometimes stayed overnight at his house. Out of mercy to me, Srila Bhaktivinode Thakur introduced me to him. From the time that I first met my Prabhu, my stubborn egoism started to diminish. Previously, I used to think that everyone who took birth in a human body was filled with the same faults that I had, but upon seeing my Prabhu's divine character I realized that there truly were flawless Vaishnavas in this world who matched the ideal."

Srila Prabhupada further wrote, "Many people who saw Gaura Kishor Das Babaji, whether innocent or experienced, young or old, learned or ignorant, or proud of their being advanced devotees, were not able to truly see him. This is the divine power of Krishna's devotees. Hundreds of people came to him seeking help in fulfilling their material desires and he would give them advice, but this was a kind of deception. There are countless persons who take on the dress of a saintly person and make a show of acting like a saintly person, but on closer analysis are far from the standard. My Prabhu was not a cheater like them. It is clear from his spiritual activities that he identified complete honesty with the truth. His sincere affection was incomparable; it proved that the attainment of spiritual powers is a deception. He showed no enmity for those who opposed him or disagreed with him; similarly, he made no particular external show of affection for those who were objects of his compassion. He used to say, 'I neither love nor hate anyone in this world; everyone is the object of my respect.'

"Amazingly, Prabhu would be surrounded by people with no understanding—fakers and materialists inimical to the path of pure devotion who thought themselves to be recipients of such a saintly person's mercy, but continued to engage in sensual activities. Prabhu never openly rejected any of these people, but he never openly accepted any of them, either."

BABAJI MAHARAJ'S DISAPPEARANCE

Babaji Maharaj was an expert judge of character and had highly-developed foresight and clairvoyance, often foretelling events in the distant future.

On the 30th of Karttik in 1322 (Bengali—1915 AD), Paramahamsa Srila Gaura Kishor Das Babaji entered the eternal pastimes of the Lord. At the time, he was residing at Ranir Dharma Shala in Kuliya. When Srila Bhaktisiddhanta Saraswati Goswami Thakur received the news of his disappearance, he was overcome with feelings of separation from his guru and immediately hurried to the site of his departure. He was heart-broken to see that *mahāntas* (abbots) of various *ākhaṛās* (ashrams) were busily arguing about where and how to bury his body. The idea of the Babajis was to lay claim to any future samadhi temple as such a temple would be an attractive pilgrimage site and a possible source of money-making. Srila Prabhupada alone stood up and spoke out against this rascaldom. As things heated up, Nabadwip's chief of police, Jatindranath Singh Ray Bahadur, came to maintain the peace.

At that time, Srila Prabhupada had not yet taken tridandi sannyas. The Babajis argued that as they had taken the renounced order, they had the right to perform the last rites for one of their order. As this was not the case for Srila Prabhupada, he had no rights. Srila Prabhupada displayed his spiritual strength and stated that he was Babaji Maharaj's one and only disciple. He then asked them if there was any amongst them who had not had illicit sexual relations in the previous six months, in the previous three months, one month, or even in the previous three days. He who had so done would be doomed if he touched Babaji Maharaj's divine remains.

When he heard Srila Prabhupada make this challenge, Jatindra Babu asked how anyone could prove whether or not he had had illicit sexual relations. Srila Prabhupada answered that he would take anyone who came forward at his word. When the Babajis recognised the great spiritual purity emanating from Srila Prabhupada, they slowly slunk away, one by one. The chief of police was embarrassed at this sight and he payed his obeisances to Srila Prabhupada and then left himself.

Some residents of Kuliya told Srila Prabhupada what Babaji Maharaj had said about his last desires. Apparently, he had stated that he wished his body to be dragged through the streets of Nabadwip so that it would be covered by the dust of the holy dham. Srila Prabhupada replied, "This is my gurudeva. Even Krishna is honored to carry him on His shoulders and carries Him like a crown upon His head. He said these things to confound the pride of the materialists with his humility. We may be inexperienced fools and offenders, but we should still make an effort to understand his intention. When Hari Das Thakur entered his eternal pastimes, Lord Gauranga took his body to His chest and danced with it. What a precedent He set for honoring the perfected soul's departure! We would rather follow Mahaprabhu's example and carry Siddha Baba's divine remains on our head."

On the first day of Agrahayan in Kuliya's Nuton Chora, Srila Prabhupada performed the samadhi rites for Srila Gaura Kishor Das Babaji according to Vaishnava Smriti injunctions. A certain Poddar Mahashaya of Lohagara in Jessore district gave the land for the samadhi, renouncing any claims on the property. Later, however, he reneged on his promise and came to live there himself and engaged in various illicit activities on the site. During the Ganges floods one season, the samadhi temple was washed into the river. On the 5th of Bhadra, 1339 Bengali (1932 AD) Srila Bhaktisiddhanta Saraswati Goswami Thakur retrieved some of the remains from the Ganges bed and took them to the Chaitanya Math where he established a samadhi temple on the banks of Radha Kund. The site was consecrated on the 2nd of Ashwin, 1339 and in the course of time, a small temple housing a mūrti of Gaura Kishor Das Babaji was constructed there. The mūrti's *nitya-sevā* has continued ever since.

BABAJI MAHARAJ'S TEACHINGS

Srila Bhaktisiddhanta Saraswati Goswami Thakur recounted some events from Gaura Kishor Das Babaji's life that are full of import for the practitioner of devotional life.

(1) On one occasion, a certain Babaji came to visit Srila Gaura Kishor Das Babaji with some of his followers in tow. These acolytes began glorifying their guru to Babaji Maharaj, "Our Prabhu is so merciful. He takes so much trouble to travel from place to place to deliver the poor, fallen souls. If he did not travel, what would be the destiny of these forsaken places?" Babaji Maharaj immediately became cross and answered, "If someone makes a pretense of delivering the world when in fact he is only interested in making money and garnering prestige, he not only does no one any good, but falls down for having cheated others."

(2) One day, a few devotees were describing the expertise of a particular lecturer on the Bhagavata. Babaji Mahashaya knew that this individual received money for his services. He said, "This fellow does not explain the Bhagavata or the scriptures of the Goswamis. He is simply speaking on the sense-gratificatory scriptures. He isn't chanting 'Gaura, Gaura!' or 'Krishna, Krishna!', but 'Money! Money!'. It has nothing to do with bhajan. The end result is that the true Vaishnava religion is obscured. Nothing good can come from it; indeed, the world will be harmed by such preaching."

(3) One day Babaji Mahashaya was chanting japa late at night when he suddenly jumped up and exclaimed, "Did you see that? Did you see? A professional speaker on the Bhagavata has gone to Pabna district and has just made a chaste widow break her vows! What a shame! These rascals are giving Mahaprabhu's religion a bad name." He spoke as if he were personally witnessing the event.

(4) The owner of the Nabadwip Dharma Shala was a certain Girish Babu. One day, his wife offered to build a cottage for Babaji Maharaj. He answered, "I have no problem sleeping under the straw shelter on a boat. The only problem I have is that so many rascals are constantly coming to me asking me to bless them. They disturb my chanting. They don't really want my blessings because they don't really want what is best for them, but still they come to disrupt my chanting the Holy Name. If you give me your brick outhouse, I will be able to chant in peace. No one will come to bother me there." When he realized that Babaji Mahashaya was serious, Girish Babu immediately had the outhouse purified with cowdung and brought in a mason to completely redo the building.

(5) One day during the cold season, a devotee made a gift of a quilt to Babaji Mahashaya, but rather than wrapping himself in it, he simply draped it over the tiny bamboo shelter under which he slept. When asked why he did that, he answered that the cold would go away simply upon seeing the quilt.

(6) One day the Raja of Cossim Bazaar, Sir Manindra Candra Nandi Bahadur, invited Babaji Maharaj to his palatial residence for a Vaishnava assembly. Babaji Mahashaya answered, "If you want my association, leave all your riches and come and live under a bamboo shelter like mine. You won't have to worry about food. I will beg enough to feed the both of us. If I go to stay in your palace, it won't be long before I start desiring to enjoy sense gratification. I will start thinking about how I can accumulate a property for myself. Then before you know it, I will become your enemy. If you want to preserve our friendship and if you wish to be kind to me as your Vaishnava friend, then you will come to the Dham and join me in worshiping the Lord and eating *madhukarī*."

GAURA KISHOR DAS BABAJI'S FAVORITE SONG

Narottam Das Thakur's songs were much beloved of Babaji Maharaj. He was often heard to sing one of them in particular. In his view, all Vaishnava teachings are contained in this one song:

gaura pahū nā bhajiyā moinu
prema-ratana-dhana helāya hārāinu

I have invited my spiritual death by not worshiping Lord Chaitanya. I have carelessly cast away the treasure of love for Krishna.

adhane yatana kari dhana teyāginu.
āpana karama-doṣe āpani ḍubinu

I have rejected the real purpose of my life and given my attention to worthless things. I am drowning because of my own misdeeds.

sat-saṅga chāṛi kainu asate vilāsa
te-kāraṇe lāgila je karma-bandha-phāṅsa

Disregarding the association of the holy, I have amused myself in the company of the wicked. Is there any wonder that the noose of karmic reaction is dangling around my neck?

viṣaya viṣama viṣa satata khāinu
gaura-kīrtana-rase magana nā painu

I have constantly drunk the most dangerous poison of sense gratification and so could not absorb myself in the taste of Mahaprabhu's divine sankirtan.

keno vā āchaye prāṇa ki sukha lāgiyā
narottama dāsa kena nā gela mariyā

What pleasure keeps me still alive today? Narottama Das wonders, "Why have I not died from this misery?"

Srila Vamsi Das Babaji

Srila Vamsi Das Babaji

The Paramahamsa Avadhuta

This article is based on other articles that previously appeared in the old *Gauḍīya* magazine and various statements made by Srila Bhaktisiddhanta Saraswati Goswami Thakur and his disciples who knew Vamsi Das Babaji personally.

Srila Vamsi Das Babaji appeared in the village of Majidpur in the Jamalpur district of Bangladesh, not far from the city of Jamalpur. Before the partition of India, this city was formerly in the district of Mymensingh. According to Haridas Das, his father's name was Sanatan Malobrahma and he was previously known as Bhairava.

Babaji Maharaj came to Nabadwip from East Bengal. He was a paramahamsa Vaishnava who acted in the manner of an avadhuta. The word avadhuta refers to one who has shaken free from all worldly feeling and obligation. He does not care for social conventions, particularly Varnashram Dharma, and he is quite eccentric in his behavior. Nityananda Prabhu is often characterized as an avadhuta.

Vamsi Das lived in Nabadwip under a tree on the banks of the Ganges, demonstrating a very high standard of renunciation. Srila Bhaktisiddhanta Saraswati Goswami Thakur was attracted by his Vaishnava behavior and his disregard for the rules and regulations of society at large. Srila Prabhupada himself paid his obeisances to Babaji Maharaj from a distance, but did not allow his disciples to associate with him. For though Babaji Maharaj was a paramahamsa Vaishnava, an ordinary beginner in devotional practice would likely misunderstand his indifference to the rules and regulations and end up committing offenses at his feet.

The primary purpose of the rules and regulations is to bring pleasure to Sri Sri Radha and Govinda. A practitioner who has not yet overcome his mundane conditioning may very well judge an advanced Vaishnava according to rules and regulations which were designed to help him advance to the next level of spiritual realization. If he measures a perfected soul by the standards that have been set for the beginner, there is a possibility of committing offenses that could result in falldown from the devotional path.

It is said that Babaji Maharaj had two cloth bags. He kept his Nitai Gaura deities in one, Radha Govinda in the other. He would regularly worship them, taking them out of the bags and serving them mentally with mantras. Then, when he had finished, he would place the deities back in their bags. On occasion he would leave them outside so that people could look at them. Once in a while, he would offer tobacco to Radha and Govinda in a hookah—but not to Nitai Gauranga. Many people would come bringing offerings of rice, fruits, vegetables, flour, or bananas, but Babaji Maharaj would ignore them. When he noticed an accumulation of such offerings, he would mentally offer them to his deities and then distribute the remnants to whoever happened to be present. Who can understand such enigmatic behavior?

Babaji Maharaj was tall enough to be able to pick fruits for his puja from the high branches of a tree without making use of ladders or other paraphernalia. On one occasion, he fell from a tree and from that time on he took on the guise of a lame person. He only wore a kaupin, a strip of cloth covering his private parts, and left his hair and beard uncut and unkept.

BABAJI MAHARAJ'S VOYAGE TO VRAJA

Babaji Maharaj did not stay exclusively in the Nabadwip area, but travelled to many holy places where he also performed his spiritual practices. He embodied the verse *kṛṣṇa-bhakti-rasa-bhāvita-matiḥ*, and wherever he went he always remained immersed in the ocean of Krishna rasa. Everything reminded him of Krishna lila, but especially the peepal or baṭa tree. Whenever he saw a peepal tree, he would sit under it, taking it to be the Vamsi Bata under which Krishna played his flute to attract the gopis. Once he had stationed himself there, it would be difficult to get him to move.

On the 12th of Phalgun, 1347 (Monday, Feb. 24, 1941), Vamsi Dasji left Koladwip or present day Nabadwip city and headed for Vrindavan. Sometimes he walked, sometimes travelled by ox-cart, and othertimes by rail. He first went to Katwa where he stayed for two days under a baṭa tree near the train station. Then he took the train to Bhagalpur where he stayed for one day under a baṭa tree near the station and for four days by the Ganges. Then he travelled on to Gaya where he remained on the banks of the Phalgu River for three days. He also stayed on a boat in the Ganges near Dasasvamedha Ghat in Benares for three days, spent another three days in Ayodhya by the Sarāyū including three hours under a baṭa tree, at the Triveni confluence at Prayag for ten days, two days at the Vishram Ghat in Mathura, eight days at the Vamsi Bata in Vrindavan, nine days at the Madhyachura on the banks of the Yamuna, one day at the Govindaji temple, two days at Kalidaha, eight days under a tamal tree on the east bank of Surya Kund at Nandagram, two days at Pavan Sarovar, four days at the foot of a pīlu tree, and then another nine days at Vamsi Bata Ghat in Vrindavan. Everywhere he went, he remained absorbed in chanting the Holy Names and meditating on Krishna's form and pastimes. After three months, he returned to Nabadwip Dham, in the month of Jyestha.

Those who travelled with Vamsi Das recounted that when wandering through Vraja Mandala, he would sometimes sing songs about Krishna's lila, sometimes glorify Nabadwip Dham, sometimes laugh madly. Sometimes, he would babble incoherently, and oftentimes he would remain completely silent. When visiting a temple, he was often seen muttering confidentially to the deities, disclosing some personal sentiment to them. All in all, his companions were charmed by his devotional absorption.

In the old *Gauḍīya* weekly magazine, further accounts of Babaji Maharaj's travels were given. It is stated there that between 1943 and 1947, he travelled to Ambika Kalna, Kharagpur, Baleshwar, Soro, Bhadrak, Khorda Road and Purushottam. Afterwards, he again visited Gaya, Kashi, Saidpur, Patna, Munger, etc.

After travelling to all these places, some devotees from his birthplace in Majidpur invited him to come for a visit. He acquiesced to their enthusiasm, but found little pleasure in going. He said that it was a place the Pandavas had neglected.

HIS DIVINE GRACE MADHAVA MAHARAJ'S ENCOUNTER WITH BABAJI MAHARAJ

The founding acharya of Sri Chaitanya Gaudiya Math, my spiritual master, *nitya-līlā-praviṣṭa* Om Vishnupada Srimad Bhakti Dayita Madhav Goswami Maharaj told his disciples a story about a personal encounter he had with Vamsi Das Babaji. Gurudeva founded an ashram in Midnapore city, the Shyamananda Gaudiya Math, with the help of two of his godbrothers, H. H. Bhakti Vichar Jajabar Maharaj and H. H. Bhakti Kumud Santa Maharaj. On one occasion, Babaji Maharaj was travelling and passed through Midnapore. When Gurudeva received the news that Babaji Maharaj was coming with a group of devotees by ox-cart, he immediately sent a disciple to invite him to visit the Math. Babaji Maharaj promised the disciple that he would come and so Gurudeva started to make preparations to receive the party of pilgrims. However, after the midday offering and arati, no one from Vamsi Das's party came. Srila Gurudeva waited for some time and finally took a number of his disciples and went looking for him.

When Vamsi Das had entered the city with his party, he had seen a peepal tree and had taken it to be Vamsi Bata. He had camped there and made arrangements for making an offering to his deities and feeding his party there. When he saw Gurudeva, Babaji Maharaj remembered his affection for Srila Prabhupada and offered him some sweet rice prasad, which Gurudeva accepted respectfully. I often heard Gurudeva say how delicious the sweet rice tasted that day.

H. H. BHAKTI PROMODE PURI MAHARAJ'S REMINISCENCES

My siksha guru, H. H. Bhakti Promode Puri Goswami Maharaj, also told us a few anecdotes about Vamsi Das Babaji, incidents that he had witnessed personally: "Once, a pile of fruit intended for the service of the deities had accumulated at Babaji Maharaj's cottage by the Ganges and Baba would not let anyone lay a finger on it. One day, however, a cow managed to enter the cottage and ate all the fruit. Though they tried, no one was able to drive the cow away. Meanwhile Babaji Maharaj watched and laughed, clapping his hands. Out of curiosity I asked Baba's disciple, whose name was Purna or Punya, why Baba was laughing. He said, 'Last night a thief stole all the deity's pots and pans, dishes and utensils. Now a cow has come and eaten all the fruit. So Baba is beside himself with joy and is laughing and saying, "One thief gives and another thief takes away!"' Krishna is the supreme thief.

"Babaji Maharaj never allowed anyone to touch his feet, except once, on the day after Phalguni Purnima, when everyone was remembering Jagannath Mishra's celebration of Gauranga's birth. Babaji Maharaj was so ecstatic that he forgot his rule and became as generous as a desire tree. So I was fortunate enough to get the dust of his lotus feet on that day. Another time, I also had the good fortune of getting his prasadi leftovers.

"Babaji Maharaj enjoyed hearing devotional songs. One day, he heard someone singing Bhaktivinode Thakur's couplet, *tyajiyā śayana sukha, vicitra pālaṅka, kabe vrajer dhulāya dhūsara habe aṅga*—'When will I give up the pleasure of sleeping in a comfortable bed and roll in the dust of Vrindavan?' Babaji Maharaj said, 'You are only singing a song. It only bursts open for those who have burst open.' In other words, we only sing the songs of the Mahajans, but we feel no emotion. When the dust of the holy places covers our bodies, we only think of brushing it off. We have no real idea of its value.

"Another day, however, someone started singing one of these new-fangled, invented mantras that contradicts siddhanta and divine sentiment. Babaji Maharaj said, 'That name is not allowed here.'

"One gentleman often came to visit Babaji Maharaj and kept asking him for his mercy. One day, Baba finally became impatient; he took off his kaupin and handed it to the gentleman and said, 'You want my mercy? Here it is—take it.' The visitor was frightened by the manner in which Baba challenged him. We have heard that all perfections come from the grace of the Vaishnavas, but we do not have the sincerity necessary to really take their blessings when they are given. What is the use of repeatedly imploring them to be merciful if we don't mean it?

"We had an elderly godbrother named Gokula Das Babaji. His original home was not far from that of Babaji Maharaj. Gokula Das Baba went frequently to see Vamsi Das Baba, and when they got together, they would joyfully converse about Krishna in their Mymensingh dialect."

VAMSI DAS'S TEACHINGS

Babaji Maharaj was normally occupied with his devotional activities; he minded his own business and spoke little. He would talk to his deities, sometimes laughing, sometimes crying desperately, but he did not speak much to others. Many people would come to see him and often they would ask him questions. Mostly he remained silent, and if he took any notice at all, he would usually answer indirectly. If he did give spiritual instruction, he would rarely cite scripture, but always spoke from his personal realization. In two or three short phrases, he was often able to make a deep impression on the listener.

Once, he had a regular visitor who kept asking him, "How can we attain God?" Babaji Maharaj just remained silent, giving the questioner no answer. One day, he suddenly looked at this visitor and asked him, "What do you want?" The fellow replied, "I want to find God." Babaji Maharaj answered in one word, "Cry."

Those who visited him occasionally reported the short answers that he gave to their questions. Some of these were noted down and are given here.

Q: Baba, what should we do?
A: Worship Nitai and you will get Gaura. Your unhappiness will go away and you will begin to feel real joy.

Q: How can we become free from the demands of the senses?
A: *śuniyā govinda-rab, āpani palābe sab, siṁha-rabe jathā kari-gaṇ*—"They will all flee at the sound of Govinda's name just as the deer flee at the sound of the lion's roar." (*Prema-bhakti-candrikā*—Narottam Das)

Q: Baba, is there no happiness in this world, then?
A: There is no joy here, unless you worship Gaura-Nitai. That is our eternal world, while this world of yours is an illusion. Happiness in this world is like the laughing or crying of a dreaming baby.

Q: How can we tell if we have received the blessings of Krishna or the Vaishnavas?
A: *je kare tomāra āśa, tāre koro sarva-nāśa*—"You ruin everything for those who aspire to attain you." *kāhāke-o ṭākā dey, kāhāro ṭākā nei*—"To some He gives money, while He makes others penniless." *Tomā sthāne aparādhe nāhi paritrāṇa*—"There is no pardon for offenses to your (Vaishnava Thakur's) feet." How can you stop it, if it comes? Who else will deliver you? If I try to explain, who will understand me? I haven't got the slightest bit of attachment to the Vaishnavas.

Q: How can I get Krishna's mercy?
A: You will get his mercy by crying. Who really cries? If you shed tears of love, you will get the Lord's mercy. *Mukhe bali hari, kāje anya kari, prema-vāri cokhe elo nā*—"I recite Hari's names, but I act otherwise. So the tears of love do not well up in my eyes."

Q: How can we be happy? In renunciation or in enjoyment?
A: There are saintly persons on the Sarayu who chant the names of Sita Rama. They are happy; they know no distress. Those who stay with King Duryodhana know no joy. Those who were with Yudhisthira are happy. Happiness and distress—enjoyment and renunciation—are twins. Some people enjoy and some renounce.

Q: Have you ever been to Mayapur?
A: Yes. Some call it Mayapur, some call it Nabadwip. There are buildings all over the Mayapur temple site and the deity is worshiped under a neem tree. I once went to Mayapur with a torn wrapper and a waterpot. Sachinandan Gosai (Mahaprabhu) came and took my waterpot. I sat down and waited and a few minutes later Sachinandan Gosai came and gave it back. Then I came back here.

Babaji Maharaj's disappearance day was the Shravan *śuklā caturthī*.

[33] According to Haridas Das, Vamsi Das Babaji never locked his doors, even though he was asked to do so by his wellwishers. His house was thus regularly robbed. When asked why he didn't lock his doors, Vamsi Das said that it was Gaura-Nitai's responsibility to protect their own house and possessions. Sometimes he would chastise the deities for not stopping the thieves when he found that the pots or foodstuffs had been stolen.

(Gaudiya Vaishnava Jivana, Vol 2, 327.)

Prabhupada Srila Bhaktisiddhanta Saraswati Goswami Thakur

APPEARANCE IN PURI DHAM

On Friday, February 6, 1874 (Magh 25, 1280 Bengali, 1795 Śaka), at 3:30 P.M., in the home of Srila Bhaktivinode Thakur, Om Vishnupada Srila Bhaktisiddhanta Saraswati Goswami Thakur appeared from the womb of Bhagavati Devi as an effulgent, golden-skinned child. It was *kṛṣṇā pañcamī* of the month of Magh. This house, named Narayan Chata, is situated not far from the Jagannath Temple on the Grand Road in Puri and was constantly reverberating with the sound of Harinam. Those who saw the newborn child were amazed to see that his umbilical cord was wrapped around his shoulder like a natural Brahmin thread. Srila Bhaktivinode Thakur named the child after Jagannath Deva's *parā śakti*, Vimala, calling him Vimalā-prasāda (Bimala Prasad).

THE CHILD'S PREFERENCE

Six months after the appearance of the child, it was time for the Rathayatra festival. That year, by Jagannath's desire, the cart stopped in front of Bhaktivinode's house and simply would not move forward. Jagannath remained motionless before the Narayan Chata for three whole days. Under Bhaktivinode Thakur's direction, a kirtan festival was held in front of the Deity for the entire three-day period. During one of these days, the six-month old baby came before Jagannath in the arms of his mother, he grabbed Jagannath's feet and took the garland from around the Deity's neck. Bhaktivinode gave the child Jagannath prasad for the *anna-prāśana* ritual in which a child eats its first solid food.

The child stayed in Purushottam Dham for ten months after his birth, after this he went with his mother in a palanquin by land to Ranaghat in Bengal. He went through his entire childhood in the midst of an extended festival of Harinam sankirtan.

INITIATION IN HARINAM AND NRISINGHA MANTRA

While Srila Bhaktivinode Thakur was living in Serampore, he came back one day from a visit to Puri with a garland of tulasi leaves which had been used by Jagannath. He gave it to Bimala Prasad, who was a seventh grade student at the time, and initiated him in the chanting of the Holy Name and the Nrisingha mantra. While he was in the fifth grade, the boy had invented a type of phonetic writing he called Bicanto, or *vikṛnti*. Srila Bhaktivinode Thakur read him the *Chaitanya-śikṣāmṛta*, which he was writing at the time.

WORSHIP OF KURMA DEVA

In 1881, Srila Bhaktivinode Thakur started construction of Bhakti Bhavan in Calcutta's Ram Bagan district. During the digging of the building's foundations, a small deity of Kurma was found. Srila Bhaktivinode Thakur taught his seven-year-old son the rules for worshiping a deity and the Kurma mantra, after which Bimala Prasad started to regularly wear tilak and to perform the deity's puja. In 1885, Bhaktivinode Thakur founded a centre for publishing Vaishnava literature named "The Vaishnava Depository" at Bhakti Bhavan. From this time, the boy started to gain experience with the printing press and helped with proofreading and other tasks. Srila Bhaktivinode Thakur also resumed publishing his monthly magazine *Sajjana-toṣaṇī* in that year. Bimala Prasad also travelled with his father to many of the Sripats of some of Mahaprabhu's associates, such as Kulinagram and Saptagram, where he heard his father lecture on the doctrines of the Holy Name.

BIMALA PRASAD RECEIVES THE TITLE SIDDHANTA SARASWATI

When Bimala Prasad was a fifth grade student, he began to show a natural talent for mathematics and astrology. He went to study the astrological texts with the great scholar Mahesh Chandra Churamani from the Siyakhala village on the Tarakeshwar railway line. In a very short time he mastered the arts of calculating astrological charts. Later he went on to advanced studies of astrology with Aloya resident, Sundar Lal Pandit.

Churamani Mahashaya was astounded by the talents of the fifteen year old boy. From this young age, he was called Sri Siddhanta Saraswati by his teachers. After taking sannyas in 1918, he took on the name Parivrajakacharya Sri Bhaktisiddhanta Saraswati. At other times, he identified himself as Varshabhanavi Dayita Das.

THE WORLD VAISHNAVA ASSOCIATION

In 1885, 399 years after the appearance of Sri Chaitanya Mahaprabhu, Srila Bhaktivinode Thakur formed the Vishva Vaishnava Sabha or World Vaishnava Association at the home of Rama Gopal Basu in Krishna Singh Gali, which is today known as Bethune Row. The association organized the 400th anniversary celebrations of Mahaprabhu's appearance the following year. Some of its well-known members were Madan Gopal Goswami, Nila Kanta Goswami, Bipin Bihari Goswami, Radhika Nath Goswami and Sisir Kumar Ghosh. Sri Saraswati Thakur attended the Association's weekly meetings every Sunday in the company of his father, and carried his father's copy of *Bhakti-rasāmṛta-sindhu* for him. He would listen attentively to the discussion of scripture which took place at these meetings.

DISTASTE FOR BAD COMPANY AND MATERIAL LEARNING

While Saraswati Thakur was a student, he never mixed with children who had behavior problems. Thus from his very earliest life, the determination to avoid *asat-saṅga* and to associate exclusively with saintly persons was evident in his character. In the early years of high school, he spent more time studying astrology and Vaishnava scriptures than the prescribed curriculum. In fact, he had a hard time maintaining interest in his school textbooks. He felt it was unnecessary to even touch these books once outside the school grounds, where he would only read Narottam's *Prārthanā* and *Prema-bhakti-candrikā* and the books written by his father.

THE AUGUST ASSEMBLY

While still a student, Saraswati Thakur published *Sūrya-siddhānta, Bhakti-bhavana-pañjikā*, and other books related to astrology. In the afternoons, he would go to Calcutta's Beadon Square and engage in debate with other students about religion, politics and other subjects. In 1891, this debating society took the name "The August Assembly" and all its members took the vow to never get married. People of all ages, including many highly educated and respected members of society, attended the Assembly's meetings.

AT THE SANSKRIT COLLEGE

In 1892, Saraswati Thakur was admitted to the Calcutta Sanskrit College. There once again, instead of studying the books which were on the curriculum, he took to systematically reading all the books in the library. He studied the Veda with the scholar Prithvidhar Sharma. A few years later, in 1898, when teaching Sanskrit at the Saraswata Chatushpathi in Bhakti Bhavan, he studied *Siddhānta-kaumudī* with the same Prithvidhar Sharma, and rapidly went through the entire text. Prithvidhar Sharma advised him to devote his life to the study of *Siddhānta-kaumudī* and Sanskrit grammar, but Saraswati Thakur disagreed with him, saying that human life is meant for worshiping the Supreme Lord and not for studying grammar manuals with their verb roots and conjugations, nor for reading mundane poems.

SARASWATI THAKUR ABANDONS MUNDANE LEARNING

While studying at the Sanskrit College, Saraswati Thakur also came into public disagreement with the opinions of the renowned scholar from Kashi, Bapudeva Shastri and the professor Panchanan Sahityacharya.

We can see parallels in the life of Saraswati Thakur and Sri Chaitanya Mahaprabhu, for Saraswati Thakur first engaged in the delights of study and debating during his student life but then turned to exclusively chanting and preaching the Holy Names. In his autobiography, he wrote, "'If I go on to study at the university, my family will inevitably harass me to get married. On the other hand, if I present myself to the world as a useless fool, no one will try to interest me in that kind of life.' This was the reasoning that led me to quit the Sanskrit College. I then started looking for an honest means of making my livelihood with minimum effort so that I could lead a life of devotion to the Lord."

IN TRIPURA

In 1895, Saraswati Thakur took a job with the royal family of Tripura, which was then an independent state. He was engaged as associate editor of the royal family's history, *Rāja-ratnākara*. While there, he had the opportunity to study many important books held in the royal library. When the Maharajah, Virachandra, left this world on December 11, 1896, his son Radha Kishor Manikya Bahadur was placed on the throne. The new Maharajah engaged Saraswati Thakur as Sanskrit and Bengali tutor for the crown prince, Vrajendra Kishor. Later, he sent Saraswati Thakur to Calcutta with various responsibilities. When Saraswati Thakur expressed a desire to permanently leave the employ of the royal family in 1905, the Maharajah gave him a full pension equal to the salary he had been earning. Saraswati Thakur continued to receive this pension until 1908.

SARASWATA CATUSHPATHI

In 1897, the Saraswata Catushpathi Sanskrit school was established at the Bhakti Bhavan. Many educated and important people came there to study astrology including Lala Hara Gauri Shankar, Dr. Ekendranath Ghosh, M.B., Satkori Chattopadhyaya Siddhanta Bhushan, Shyamlal Goswami (the noted scholar of the Nityananda family), Sarat Chandra Jyotir Vinode, etc. From the Saraswata Catushpathi, Saraswati Thakur published the monthly magazines *Jyotirvid* and *Bṛhaspati*, as well as many ancient astrological works.

ON PILGRIMAGE WITH SRILA BHAKTIVINODE THAKUR

In October of 1898, Saraswati Thakur set off on a pilgrimage with Srila Bhaktivinode Thakur during which they visited Kashi, Prayag, and on the way back, Gaya. While in Kashi, he met Rama Mishra Shastri, with whom he discussed many aspects of the Ramanuja sampradaya. On this occasion also, Saraswati Thakur began to show the spirit of renunciation which ran throughout his life. Starting in 1897, he had begun to follow the rules of Chaturmasya according to the Vaishnava scriptures, cooking *haviṣyānna* (boiled food without salt or spices) himself which he would eat directly off the floor without using a plate and sleeping on the ground without a pillow.

AN INVESTIGATION OF THE SRI SAMPRADAYA

Saraswati Thakur first started his study of the Ramanuja sampradaya while in Bengal and he published books and articles as the results of his research. In 1898, he wrote about Srinath Muni, Yamunacharya and other acharyas of this school in a series of articles which appeared in *Sajjana-toṣaṇī*. Prior to this, he had books in the four South Indian languages provided to him by Sundareshwar Shrauti, from which he learned about the Ramanuja and Madhva schools.

In 1899, he wrote articles on spiritual matters in the weekly magazine, *Nivedana*, and in 1900, he published a book, *Baṅge Sāmājikatā* ("Bengali Social Customs"), a study of religous and social behavior in Bengal, which was the fruit of a great deal of research.

FIRST ENCOUNTER WITH HIS GURU

In 1897, Srila Bhaktivinode Thakur established his place of worship in Navadwip's Godrumdwip area, near the Saraswati River, and called it Svananda Sukhada Kunj. It was there, in 1898, that Saraswati Thakur first saw his future guru, Srila Gaura Kishor Das Babaji Maharaj. He was attracted by the extraordinary character of this Vaishnava paramahamsa, who was indifferent to all social conventions, and later, in the month of Magh (January-February), 1900, on the order of Srila Bhaktivinode Thakur, took *bhāgavatī dīkṣā* from him.

SATASAN MATH AND BHAKTI KUTI

In March of 1900, Saraswati Thakur accompanied Srila Bhaktivinode Thakur on a trip to Baleshwar and Remuna, where he had darshan of Kshirachora Gopinath. Then they travelled on to Bhubaneshwar and Puri. On this occasion, Saraswati Thakur deepened his attachment to the holy city of Puri. When he expressed a wish to establish a Math near the samadhi of Hari Das Thakur, the local sub-registrar, Jagabandhu Pattanayaka and other prominent citizens asked him to take over the service of one of the seven seats of the Satasan Math, that of Giridhari. In 1902, Srila Bhaktivinode Thakur himself started construction of a residence not far from Hari Das Thakur's samadhi and named it Bhakti Kuṭī. During this time, Cossim Bazaar's Maharajah, Manindra Chandra Nandi Bahadur, in mourning at the loss of a loved one, came to live in a tent on the beach near to this site. He came frequently to hear Bhaktivinode Thakur and Saraswati Thakur speak on the Vaishnava scriptures. Saraswati Thakur also regularly read and spoke on the Chaitanya Charitamrita in the presence of his father.

COLLECTING MATERIALS FOR MANJUSA

While in Puri, Saraswati Thakur engaged in collecting materials for his book *Vaiṣṇava-mañjuṣā*. He was introduced to the abbot of the Govardhan Math, Madhusudan Tirtha, with whom he had many philosophical discussions. Tirtha Swami held Saraswati Thakur in high esteem. Other people whom he met in Puri and with whom he engaged in scriptural discussions included Vasudeva Ramanuja Das and Damodar Ramanuja Das of Samadhi Math; Raghunandan Ramanuja Das of Emar Math, Jagannath Das of the Jamayet (Ramanandi) sampradaya's Papudia Math, Omkara Japi Vriddha Tapas of Svargadwarer Chata, the scholar Sada Shiva Mishra, the lawyer Harish Chandra Basu, Bihari Das Pujari of Ganga Mata's Math, Radha Kanta Math's abbot Narottam Das, Ananta Charan Mahanti, etc.

During this time, he would preach door to door to prominent people in Puri, out of which many difficulties and dangers arose. Problems also came up in the responsibilities which he had accepted at the Giridhari Asan of Satasan Math. Saraswati Thakur showed the same attitude as Prahlad Maharaj, however, demonstrating exemplary fortitude and turning a deaf ear to the foul-mouthed accusations made against him. In these circumstances, Srila Bhaktivinode Thakur advised him to go to Mayapur and worship in solitude, just as Ramanuja had done at Tirunarayanpur.

MAHATMA VAMSI DAS

When he arrived in Nabadwip, Saraswati Thakur was introduced to Vamsi Das Babaji by Srila Bhaktivinode Thakur. Not long afterward, Charan Das Babaji, along with Kalna's Vishnu Das and many others, accompanied Saraswati Thakur on a kirtan party to Mahaprabhu's birthplace in Mayapur to participate in the Dola Purnima festival there. The following year, Charan Das Babaji announced to Srila Bhaktivinode Thakur that he wished to take a party on a tour of Nabadwip Dham every year. Unfortunately, his disappearance in 1906 made it impossible for him to carry out this wish.

WINNING AN ASTROLOGICAL DEBATE

On January 2, 1902, Saraswati Thakur engaged in a

debate with an accomplished student of Bapudev Shastri. Ray Bahadur Rajendra Candra Shastri, President of the Royal Society, presided over the debate in which Saraswati Thakur so badly defeated his opponent that the latter's professor passed stool and urine in the assembly out of shock.

MORE PILGRIMAGES

In January of 1904, Saraswati Thakur visited Sita Kund and Chandranath. In December of the same year he went to Puri and on February 23, 1905, he went on a pilgrimage to South India. He visited Singhachalam, Rajahmundry, Madras, Perembadur, Tirupati, Conjeevaram, Kumbhakonam, Srirangam, Madurai, etc., before returning to Calcutta and Sri Mayapur. In Perembadur, he learned the scriptural rules and regulations surrounding Vaishnava tridandi sannyas from a member of that order in the Ramanuja sampradaya.

THE VOW TO CHANT A BILLION HOLY NAMES

While staying in Mayapur in 1905, Saraswati Thakur began preaching the message of Chaitanya Mahaprabhu and, following in the footsteps of Hari Das Thakur, he undertook a vow of chanting a billion (ten crores) of Holy Names, chanting a minimum of three lakhs (300,000) every single day. In 1906, Rohini Kumar Ghosh, the nephew of Justice Chandra Madhava Ghosh, had an extraordinary dream telling him to go to Saraswati Thakur and take initiation from him. Rohini Kumar Ghosh thus became his first initiated disciple.

In 1909, Saraswati Thakur had a cottage, Vraja-pattan, built on the site of Chandrasekhara's house where he continued to engage in his vrata, visualizing himself on the banks of Radha Kund.

VICTORIOUS IN DEBATE

A crisis arose for the Vaishnava world in 1911. The Smarta Brahmins were engaged in a concerted attack on the Vaishnava religion and its acharyas. Those who claimed descendence from Nityananda Prabhu and other associates of Chaitanya Mahaprabhu had taken the side of the Smartas in the hope of extracting some advantage from the alliance. Srila Bhaktivinode Thakur was bed-ridden at the time, so when an assembly of hundreds of scholars and paṇḍitas was called in Midnapore at Balighai village to debate the issues, he sent Saraswati Thakur in his place. In the debate presided over by Vishvambharananda Deva Goswami, Vrindavan scholar Madhusudan Goswami invited him to speak. Saraswati Thakur read an article and gave a discourse on the distinction between Brahmins and Vaishnavas which completely destroyed the arguments of the materialistic karmi Smartas.

In the same year, at Bara Akhra in Nabadwip town, a debate was held on the Gaura mantra. Saraswati Thakur established on the basis of the Atharva Veda's *Caitanyopaniṣad* and other scriptural evidence that a special mantra for worshiping Gauranga Mahaprabhu was eternally valid.

On March 23, 1912, Saraswati Thakur went to a religious conference held at Cossim Bazaar where he gave a speech, establishing the characteristics of pure devotional service and criticizing the materialistic ambitions and sycophancy of those who claimed to be the leaders of the Gaudiya Vaishnava religion. In order to demonstrate non-cooperation with the so-called leaders of the school, he fasted for the four days he was there before returning to Mayapur where he resumed taking prasad.

PILGRIMAGE THROUGH THE GAUDA MANDALA

On November 4, 1912, Saraswati Thakur took a small group of devotees on a tour of Srikhanda, Jajigram, Katwa, Jhamatpur, Akai Hat, Chakhandi, Dain Hat and other places where Mahaprabhu's associates had had their homes. In every place he preached the gospel of pure devotional service.

THE PUBLICATION OF ANUBHASYA

In April of 1913, Saraswati Thakur established a publishing house named Bhagavata Yantralaya in Calcutta's Kalighat area. The first book printed was Chaitanya Charitamrita with his *Anubhāṣya* commentary. Others which followed were the Bhagavad Gita with Vishvanath's commentary and the *mahā-kāvya*, *Gaura-kṛṣṇodaya* of the Orissan poet, Govinda Das.

After Srila Bhaktivinode Thakur's disappearance on June 23, 1914, Saraswati Thakur took over the editorship of *Sajjana-toṣaṇī*, the monthly magazine founded by his father. In January of 1915, the press was moved to Vraja-pattana in Mayapur and more books continued to be printed. On June 14, 1915, the *Anubhāṣya* commentary to Chaitanya Charitamrita was completed at Vraja-pattana. In July of 1915, the printing press was again moved to Krishnanagar, and *Sajjana-toṣaṇī* and various books written by Srila Bhaktivinode Thakur were published from there.

THE DISAPPEARANCE OF GAURA KISHOR DAS BABAJI

On November 17, 1915, *utthāna ekādaśī*, Srila Gaura Kishor Das Babaji entered into his eternal pastimes. Saraswati Thakur performed his last rites according to the prescriptions of Gopal Bhatta's *Saṁskāra-dīpikā*, establishing the samadhi of his guru in the Nutan Chora neighborhood of old Kuliya (the present-day town of Nabadwip).

SARASWATI THAKUR TAKES TRIDANDI SANNYAS

On March 7, 1918, on the occasion of Sri Chaitanya Mahaprabhu's appearance day, Saraswati Thakur took Tridandi sannyas in Sri Mayapur. Although as an eternally perfected soul, he had already achieved the goals of the renounced order, he took this step in order to preach the

gospel of Lord Chaitanya everywhere without restriction, to crystallize the conception of the *daiva-varṇāśrama* social system, and to demonstrate the transcendental character of the paramahaṁsa (Babajī) dress taken by his gurus, Jagannath Das, Satchitananda Bhaktivinode Thakur and Gaura Kishor Das Babaji.

On the same day, he consecrated the deities of Guru-Gauranga and Radha-Govinda at the house of Chandrasekhara Acharya and established the Sri Chaitanya Math. The Sri Chaitanya Math became the headquarters for the branch Gaudiya Maths throughout the world, the flagship of which is situated in Calcutta.

At the end of March, Saraswati Thakur gave an exhaustively researched lecture on Vaishnava philosophy in the Krishnanagar town hall. In May, he went to Daulatpur and other places to deliver Hari katha.

VISIT TO SRI KSHETRA

On June 2, 1918, Saraswati Thakur and a group of devotees left Calcutta for Puri. They stopped at Sauri, Kuamara and other places along the way to preach. As they followed the route Mahaprabhu had taken to Puri, Saraswati Thakur was overcome with ecstatic feelings of separation from the Lord. The party stopped at Remuna where they saw Gopinath and then at Baleshwar where he gave a lecture on Mahaprabhu's *Śikṣāṣṭaka* to the town's Hari Bhakti Pradayini Sabha. He was welcomed to Baleshwar by the Subdivisional Magistrate, Ray Saheb Gaura Shyama Mahanti and other distinguished personalities of the town. At Cuttack, he was invited by Diwan Bahadur Sri Krishna Mahapatra to stay at his home and preach on the Bhagavata there. Then in Puri, the party stayed at Bhakti Kuti and performed parikrama of Sri Kshetra Mandala. Once again, Saraswati Thakur was in a state of ecstatic separation the whole time.

The former Collector and present Deputy Magistrate of Puri, Atal Bihari Maitra, had heard Saraswati Thakur explain Chaitanya Charitamrita and Srimad Bhagavatam. In a great meeting held on the grounds of Hariballabh Basu Ray Bahadur's house, Shashi Bhavana, Saraswati Thakur gave a lecture on the difference between personal and impersonal conceptions of the Absolute Truth. He wrote a Sanskrit poem of a few verses about the memorial to Mahaprabhu's lotus feet enshrined in the Jagannath temple.

SILENCING ENEMY TONGUES

In August and September of 1918, a spokesman for a group of atheists with little philosophical knowledge sent a list of 29 questions challenging the Vaishnava faith and its acharyas. Saraswati Thakur silenced these critics with answers based on logic and scripture. The questions and his answers were published in a pamphlet named *Pratīper praśnere pratyuttara*, "Answering the enemy's questions."

BHAKTIVINODE ASAN AND VISHVA VAISHNAVA RAJA SABHA

To increase the preaching activity in Calcutta, in November of 1918, Saraswati Thakur established a center at 1 Ultadingi Junction Road, which he named Sri Bhaktivinode Asan. From there, he travelled to various towns in Jessore and Khulna districts. On February 5, 1919, he reestablished the World Vaishnava Association under the name Vishva Vaishnava Raja Sabha at the Bhaktivinode Asan. On June 27, 1919, he consecrated a deity of Srila Bhaktivinode Thakur at Svananda Sukhada Kunj in Godrumdwip. The first month-long kirtan festival was held at the Bhaktivinode Āsana from August 18 to September 18, 1919.

PREACHING IN EAST BENGAL

On October 4, 1919, on the appearance day of Madhvacharya, Saraswati Thakur set off on a preaching trip to north and eastern Bengal. In April of 1920, he and the other leaders of the Vishva Vaishnava Raja Sabha sent a letter with seven questions to the Maharaj of Cossim Bazaar's annual convocation of Vaishnava scholars, challenging them to clarify the distinction between pure and blemished devotion.

Six years to the day after the disappearance of Srila Bhaktivinode Thakur, on June 23, 1920, Saraswati Thakur's mother Bhagavati Devi left for her eternal abode.

THE FIRST GAUDIYA MATH

On September 6, 1920, deities of Guru and Gauranga, Radha and Govinda, were installed at the Bhaktivinode Asan and the first Gaudiya Math was established at that time.

VAISNAVA MANJUSA

At the request of Srila Bhaktivinode Thakur and Sisir Kumar Ghosh, Saraswati Thakur had been working on the compilation of a Vaishnava encyclopedia, for which he had travelled throughout India. In October of 1920, he came to Cossim Bazaar at the invitation of Maharaj Sir Manindra Chandra Nandi Bahadur, to whom he described the scope of this Vaishnava encyclopedia. The Maharaj agreed to donate a monthly stipend for the publication of the encyclopedia, but in the end was unable to fulfill his commitments.

Saraswati Thakur left Cossim Bazaar and went with his party to Saidabad, Nowallis Para, Kheturi and other places in the area that had been blessed by the touch of Mahaprabhu's associates. Everywhere he went, he preached Mahaprabhu's message.

THE FIRST SANNYAS DISCIPLE

On November 1, 1920, Saraswati Thakur initiated Srila Bhaktivinode Thakur's disciple Jagadish Bhakti Pradip, *Vaiṣṇava-siddhanta-bhūṣaṇa*, *Sampradāya-vaibhavācārya*, B.A., into the renounced order as a Tridandi sannyasi. He was thus the first member of the order in the Vishva Vaishnava Raja Sabha and was known thenceforth as Tridandi Swami Bhakti Pradip Tirtha Maharaj.

On March 14, 1921, Saraswati Thakur revived the annual parikrama or tour of Nabadwip Dham. At the end of March, he left again for Puri on a preaching trip. Meanwhile, H. H. Bhakti Pradip Tirtha Maharaj published a book *Ācāra o Ācārya* ("Standards of conduct and the spiritual master") which caused a great stir amongst the caste Goswamis, most of who were acting as professional gurus.

PREACHING AND ESTABLISHING MATHS IN EAST BENGAL

Afterwards, Saraswati Thakur visited Dhanbad, Katrasgarh and Dhaka. In Dhaka, he spoke on the Bhagavata's *janmādy asya* verse for an entire month, explaining it in thirty different ways. On October 13, 1921, he established the Madhva Gaudiya Math in Dhaka. On October 31, deities were installed and a great feast held in their honor. From Dhaka, he went on to Mymensingh for preaching.

After this, he returned to Nabadwip where he reestablished the worship of Gaura Gadadhar at Champa Hati. He also performed a deity installation at the birthplace of Vrindavan Das Thakur in Modadrumdwip. Then he returned to Calcutta to preach there and in the surrounding area.

SRI PURUSHOTTAM MATH

According to Veda Vyasa, *hy utkale puruṣottamāt*, the pure message of the Vaishnava religion would spread out of Jagannath Puri. In order to do honor to this prediction, Saraswati Thakur established the Sri Purushottam Math at Bhakti Kuti on June 9, 1922, installing a deity of Gauranga Mahaprabhu. Then, in the spirit of Mahaprabhu, he and his followers participated in the cleaning of Gundicha, performed the parikrama of Jagannath Puri and went to Alalanath during Jagannath's *anavasāra* period when he is taken off the temple altar. He instituted an annual memorial festival at the Purushottam Math in honor of Srila Bhaktivinode Thakur and Srila Gadadhar Pandit Goswami.

Saraswati Thakur also sent disciples to Cuttack, Baripada, Kuamara, Udala, Kaptipada, and Nilgiri, to preach Mahaprabhu's gospel of pure devotion.

GAUDIYA MAGAZINE

On August 19, 1922, the monthly magazine and organ of the Gaudiya Math, the *Gauḍīya*, was published for the first time from the Bhagavata Press.

VISIT TO VRAJA MANDALA

On September 28, 1922, Saraswati Thakur left for Vrindavan with the intention of establishing a preaching centre. Accompanied by his disciples, he visited Mathura, Vrindavan, Radha Kund, and other important holy sites connected to Krishna's pastimes. He gave a speech on Mahaprabhu's teachings and the Vaishnava religion at an assembly of learned Vaishnavas at Lala Babu's temple in Vrindavan town.

On his return to Bengal during the month of Karttik, Saraswati Thakur came to Dhaka where he once again outlined the true character of devotional service. After this he went to Kuliya and revealed the site where Mahaprabhu forgave Devananda Pandit and Chapal Gopal their offenses. From there, he went on to the Santal Paragana to preach Hari katha.

THE CONSTRUCTION OF THE TEMPLE AT THE CHAITANYA MATH

On the appearance day of Chaitanya Mahaprabhu, March 2, 1923, work began on the construction of a temple at the Chaitanya Math. It was to be built according to Saraswati Thakur's original idea of having deities of Guru-Gauranga and Radha-Govinda installed in the main deity room, while placing images of the founders of the four sampradayas (Lakshmi, Brahma, Rudra, the four Kumaras) and their acharyas (Ramanuja, Madhva, Vishnuswami, Nimbarka) in shrines on the temple's four corners.

IN PURI

After preaching in West and East Bengal, Saraswati Thakur returned again to Puri for the annual festival and, emulating the pastimes of Mahaprabhu in separation from Krishna, danced in front of the Rathayatra cart. He also preached to large numbers of devotees, including Raja Manindra Candra Nandi, Shashimohana Goswami of Bhadrak, etc. He sent preachers to Mayurbhanj and Madras to spread Mahaprabhu's gospel and himself took a party of devotees to Amlajora in Burdwan and then to Banari Para in Barisal district.

PREACHING THE BHAGAVATA

In 1923, just before the annual festival at the Gaudiya Math in Calcutta, the Gaudiya Printing Works was established and the first fascicules of the Srimad Bhagavatam were published with the *Gaura-kiśorānvaya* (word by word translation), *Svānanda-kuñjānuvāda* (translation), and the *Ananta-gopāla-tathya* and *Sindhu-vaibhava* commentaries.

VYASA PUJA

On February 24, 1924, on the tithi commemorating the 50th anniversary of Saraswati Thakur's appearance in the world, the first Vyasa Puja in his honor was held at the Calcutta Gaudiya Math. The speech that he gave on that occasion stands as an immortal jewel in the history of Vaishnava literature.

Not long thereafter, on the occasion of Mahaprabhu's appearance day, the first edition of the Chaitanya Bhagavata was published from the Madhva Gaudiya Math in Dhaka.

TRIDANDI MATH AND SARASWATA ASAN

On July 9, 1924, Saraswati Thakur established the Tridandi Math in Bhubaneshwar in Orissa. From there he went to preach in the Madras presidency where he established the Saraswata Asan. There he gave extensive instruction to his disciples from Bhaktivinode Thakur's books. In the first part of September of the same year, many distinguished persons came to hear him speak, including Raut Ray of Mayurbhanj, His Excellency General Jang Bahadur of Nepal, Justice Manmathanath Mukhopadhyaya, etc.

In October, he set foot in Dhaka for the fifth time and spoke extensively on Madhvacharya's life and the Madhva sampradaya, giving a learned explanation of the differences between the Madhva and Gaudiya doctrines, especially underlining Madhva's vision of Varnashram Dharma.

AT BENARES HINDU UNIVERSITY

On December 16, Saraswati Thakur came to the Benares Hindu University to lecture on the place of Vaishnavism in the world's religions. Amongst those in the audience who greeted his lecture with enthusiasm were the director of the Department of Western Philosophy, Pramath Nath Tarkabhushan and Professor Phani Bhushan Adhikari, M.A. Afterwards, he and his followers went to places in Kashi visited by Mahaprabhu, then to Prayag, where he indicated the exact spot where Rupa Goswami had taken instruction from Mahaprabhu, and then to Arail, where Mahaprabhu had met with Vallabhacharya.

PILGRIMAGE THROUGH GAUDA MANDALA

On January 29, 1925, Saraswati Thakur took a large group of devotees on a tour of Gauda Mandala to visit the various sites made holy by Mahaprabhu and His associates. Overcome with divine inspiration, he lectured on pure devotion in all these places.

In the same year, during the Nabadwip Parikrama, deities of Radha Govinda were carried on the back of an elephant through the streets of Koladwip. The envious leaders of those in the guru business incited a number of ruffians to throw bricks at the deities and the devotees who were accompanying them, including Saraswati Thakur, at Porama Tola. One witness of the event was quoted in the next day's (Phalguna 24, 1331) Ananda Bazaar Patrika as saying, "Today I witnessed the same pastime that was enacted about four hundred years ago when Nabadwip's constables, two thugs named Jagai and Madhai, tried to do injury to Nityananda Avadhuta."

MADAN MOHAN MALAVIYA

On April 17, 1925, Pandit Madan Mohan Malaviya, the leader of the Hindu Mahasabha, a nationalist organization, came to the Calcutta Gaudiya Math and heard Saraswati Thakur explain the Daiva Varnashram system according to the book, *Āgama-prāmānya*.

Saraswati Thakur sent preachers to Sylhet and other places.

BHAGAVATA JANANANDA MATH

In 1926, a three-day sacrifice to the Holy Name was performed to commemorate the appearance of Nityananda Prabhu. This subsequently became an annual tradition. In April of the same year, a Math was founded in Chirulia (Midnapore), and given the name Bhagavata Janananda Math. Now possessed of an increasing number of Tridandi sannyasis, Saraswati Thakur sent them throughout India to preach the message of pure devotion, while he himself spoke and lectured through Midnapore. This is the time when the large-scale expansion of the Gaudiya Math really started.

TRAVELING AND PREACHING THROUGH INDIA

In the beginning of November 1926, Saraswati Thakur started on a trip throughout India, when he would meet with various learned persons to discuss scriptures and gather information. He was also, of course, preaching Krishna consciousness to the people in large assemblies. The acharyas of many schools acclaimed him as the leading acharya of the Gaudiya Vaishnava school. The Mahanta of Nathdwar, Gokulanath Goswami Maharaj of Bombay, the abbot of the Udipi monastery of the Madhva sampradaya and the abbot of the Salimabad seat of the Madhva sampradaya all received him with the honor due the spiritual master of a Vaishnava sampradaya.

While on this trip, Saraswati Thakur established a Math in Naimisharanya called Paramahamsa Math. Upon his return, he opened the Paravidya Pith school in Mayapur, as well as the newly completed 29 towered temple at the Chaitanya Math. Deities of the acharyas and Radha Govinda were installed there.

THE HARMONIST

In 1927, Saraswati Thakur started publishing *Sajjanatoṣaṇī* in three languages—English, Sanskrit and Hindi. The English edition was given the name *The Harmonist*. On September 17, 1927, in Dumurkonda in Manbhoom district, the Chaitanya Gaudiya Math was founded.

At the end of September, Saraswati Thakur set out again on a preaching tour of northern India. In 1928, during the Gaudiya Math festival period, he spoke at Calcutta's Albert Hall and other public places, giving access to Mahaprabhu's message to the common people. The fourth edition of the Chaitanya Charitamrita was published. On September 26, the foundations of the Bagh Bazaar Gaudiya Math were laid near the banks of the Ganges. On October 7, he went with a large party of devotees to Assam, where he spoke in Shillong to several large assemblies. Amongst those who came to hear him explain the unexcelled doctrines of Chaitanya Mahaprabhu was the prince Saradindu Narayan Ray.

AT KURUKSHETRA FOR THE SOLAR ECLIPSE

On November 4, in order to experience the mood of separation that was experienced by the gopis and by Mahaprabhu during the Rathayatra, Saraswati Thakur went with a party of devotees to Kurukshetra at the time of a solar eclipse. Hundreds of thousands of pilgrims who had also come there had the good fortune to hear the Gaudiya Math devotees singing the names of Gaura. Deities of Gauranga were installed at the Sri Vyasa Gaudiya Math and a spiritual diorama exhibition (the Bhagavata Pradarshini) was opened.

THE OPENING OF THE EKAYANA MATH

On December 30, the great scholar Pramath Nath Tarka Bhushan came to the Gaudiya Math and heard an extended explanation of the Daiva Varnashram system from Saraswati Thakur.

In January of 1929, Saraswati Thakur established the Ekayan Gaudiya Math in Krishnanagar. At the opening ceremony, he gave a lecture with an original explanation showing that the single path of exclusive devotion (*ekāyana*) is the trunk and the various other paths (*bahvāyana*) are the branches of the Vedic tree.

On January 14, 1929, Saraswati Thakur met Professor Albert E. Suthers of Ohio State University, and explained to him how the Vaishnava religion was extended and perfected Christianity. On January 16, Saraswati Thakur was in New Delhi to open the Delhi Gaudiya Math, creating the opportunity for Mahaprabhu's gospel to be spread to thousands of respectable people in India's capital.

A SPEECH IN THE KRISHNANAGAR TOWN HALL

On March 30, 1929, Saraswati Thakur gave a lecture on the Holy Name in the Rama Gopal Town Hall building. In May of the same year, he was in Puri where he started Gaurasundar's Chandan Yatra festival. At the same time, he started repair work on the Alalanath temple. On August 12, he spoke at Calcutta's Albert Hall on the Gaudiya philosophy.

SHRINES OF MAHAPRABHU'S FOOTPRINTS

It was Saraswati Thakur's wish to establish 108 shrines throughout India as memorials to the places Mahaprabhu had sanctified by the touch of His feet. These shrines or *pāda-pīṭhas* would house prints of Gaurasundar's feet stamped in marble. For this purpose, he went to Kanair Natshala on October 13, 1929, and to Mandara two days later. From there he went on to Rajmahal, Bhagalpur, Nalanda and Rajgiri, to preach Mahaprabhu's message. Then he went on to Kashi where he discoursed on Mahaprabhu's teachings to Sanatan Goswami.

He was welcomed by many educated and respectable people to Kashi, Faizabad, Ayodhya, Naimisharanya, Karauna, Misrikh, Sitapur, and Lucknow. Many seekers of the truth were initiated by him into the religion of pure devotion. The widely-renowned bar-at-law, Mr. A. P. Sen, the professor Dr. Radha Kumud Mukhopadhyaya, Dr. Radha Kamal Mukhopadhyaya, Dr. A. N. Sen Gupta, and many other highly regarded citizens came to hear him speak.

THE SRI MAYAPUR POST OFFICE

On June 1, 1929, a temporary post office was opened at Sri Mayapur and made into a permanent branch in October. During this time, Saraswati Thakur had his devotees establish the "Lord's garden" (Ishodyan) that Srila Bhaktivinode Thakur had desired in Mayapur. He also had electricity brought to Mayapur and electric lights placed on the pinnacle of the Chaitanya Math temple.

MAHA MAHOPADHYAYA HARAPRASAD SHASTRI

On January 8, 1930, the great scholar Dr. Haraprasad

Shastri visited Saraswati Thakur and discussed many matters with him regarding the history of the various Vaishnava sampradayas including the Gaudiya, the dates of many acharyas, the Pancharatra, and Sri Chaitanya.

In the middle of January, Saraswati Thakur went to the Purna Kumbha Mela in Prayag. He engaged the Chaitanya Math's preachers in talking about Mahaprabhu's teachings to Rupa Goswami. He installed deities of Radha Govinda, the life and soul of Sri Rupa Goswami, at the confluence of the three rivers, Triveni. By the grace of the best of Rupa Goswami's followers, the pilgrims who came to Prayag to bathe in the confluence of the holy rivers were fortunate to be able to hear the message of pure devotion.

EXHIBITION IN SRI DHAM MAYAPUR

From February 3 to March 17, 1930, Saraswati Thakur held an unprecedented spiritual diorama exhibition in Nabadwip-Mayapur. It was opened by the famous chemist, Dr. Prafulla Chandra Roy. On February 18, on the occasion of his Vyasa Puja, a shrine to the acharya's feet was inaugurated at the Chaitanya Math.

On May 4, Mr. I. H. Napier came to hear about Indian spiritual philosophy from Saraswati Thakur. On May 25, Saraswati Thakur went to Chatrabhoga, a place that Mahaprabhu visited on his way to Puri and blessed many seekers of the truth. In July, he went to the Satchitananda Math in Cuttack and spoke on Krishna to both learned and general audiences. On August 22, he travelled to Allahabad where he stayed with his entourage at the house of retired Sessions Judge, Manomohan Sannyal. He spoke there for several days, attracting Mr. Sannyal to Chaitanya Mahaprabhu's lotus feet. He also resolved many of the questions asked by educated citizens of the town, especially Professor Dr. P. K. Acharya.

SPIRITUAL ASSEMBLY

On October 5, 1930, the move with the devotees and deities was made from the Ultadingi Junction Road Math to the new buildings at Bagh Bazaar. At the same time, a festival was held in honor of Radha Madan Mohan, Radha Govinda and Radha Gopinath. A transcendental diorama exhibition was also opened and a great spiritual conference was called at the same time. The chief contributor to the construction of the temple, Jagabandhu Bhakti Ranjan, died on November 19 of the same year.

On December 25, Saraswati Thakur was in Jajpur; on the 26th, in Kurmakshetra; on the 27th in Singhachalam; Kovvur on the 29th and on the 31st in Mangalagiri. In all these places, he installed shrines of Chaitanya Mahaprabhu's lotus feet and preached His gospel. Sir P. S. Shivasvami Iyer, K.C.S.I., Dr. U. Ramrao, and P. N. Subrahmanya Iyer were among the distinguished persons who were attracted by Saraswati Thakur's preaching.

THE BHAKTIVINODE INSTITUTE

On April 3, 1931, Saraswati Thakur opened the Bhaktivinode Institute in Sri Mayapur, and to the large assembly of people present for the occasion, spoke on the difference between material and spiritual knowledge. On May 3, he went to Darjeeling to preach in that district. On June 28, he officially accepted responsibility for the management of the Sripat of Nityananda Prabhu's associate, Mahesh Pandit, in Chakdaha. At the opening ceremonies, he spoke to a large crowd of seekers.

On July 12, he installed the deity of Gauranga named Gaudiyanath at the Brahma-Gaudiya Math in Alalanath. Five days later, he set the foundations of the Purushottam Math temple on land that had been donated by the Maharajah of Mayurbhanj. From there he went on to Cuttack where he spoke on Krishna at the Satchitananda Math. He sent a party of preachers to Simla in northern India.

On July 30, he spoke Hari katha to an audience including the well-known professor Kalidas Nag of Calcutta University at the Bagh Bazaar Gaudiya Math. On September 5, Honorable Justice Manmath Nath Mukhopadhyaya came to listen to Saraswati Thakur speak at the Gaudiya Math.

THE SPIRITUAL EDUCATION EXHIBITION IN CALCUTTA

At the time of the Gaudiya Math's annual festival, on September 6, Saraswati Thakur opened a spiritual education exhibition (*Sat-śikṣā Pradarśinī*) in Calcutta. Over the next few weeks, some of the prominent people who came to hear him speak were Dr. Dinesh Chandra Sen Ray Bahadur, Biraj Mohan Mazumdar, Vice Principal of Institutional College, Dr. Magnus Hirschfeld, the German scholar and world-traveller, and Dr. Stella Kremrisch of Calcutta University.

Saraswati Thakur spoke at the Gaudiya Math's many festivals. On September 29, he spoke on the nature of spiritual sound to the principal of the Calcutta Medical College, Colonel Dvarakaprasad Goyel, I.M.S., and the American traveller and scholar, A. J. Jacobs. On October 11, in Prayag he met Allahabad University Vice Chancellor, Dr. Ganganath Jha, Allahabad District Commissioner, Vinayak Shankar Mehta, I.C.S., and answered their questions on spiritual life.

THE HINDI MAGAZINE, BHAGAVATA

On October 16, Saraswati Thakur was welcomed to Benares by its distinguished citizens and stayed and spoke at the Maharajah's Mint Palace. On the 19th and 20th, he spoke at length on Vaishnava philosophy and Krishna lila to Vasanta Kumar Chatterjee, Deputy Accountant General of Bengal and man of letters. From there he went on to Lucknow on Oct. 31, and then to Naimisharanya, where on November 9, he introduced the new Hindi fortnightly, *Bhāgavata*, published from the Paramahamsa Math.

On November 14, Saraswati Thakur sent preachers to

New Delhi to tell the Viceroy, Lord Willingdon, about the Math's preaching activities. On November 17, he established the annual festival at the Delhi Gaudiya Math and spoke to many distinguished personalities about the life of Chaitanya Mahaprabhu. He also gave a speech about bhakti at the Gurudwar Bungalow Saheb Hall in New Delhi. On November 29, a great spiritual assembly in the garden of Honorable Council of State member, Ray Bahadur Lala Jagadish Prasad, at which Saraswati Thakur gave a speech. Then on November 30, he went with his entourage to Sukaratala, the place where Suka first narrated the Bhagavatam, and himself spoke from the Bhagavatam.

On December 6, he installed Radha-Govinda deities in the Delhi Gaudiya Math. On the 9th, he came to Calcutta to speak at the first annual memorial service in honor of Jagabandhu Bhaktiranjan, the builder of the Bagh Bazaar Gaudiya Math buildings. The Honorable Justice Manmath Nath Mukhopadhyaya presided over the assembly. On the 13th, Mr. Mukhopadhyaya visited Mayapur where he again heard Saraswati Thakur speak. He also visited the Dham and the Bhaktivinode Institute.

PREACHING IN MADRAS

On January 10, 1932, Saraswati Thakur went with a party of twenty devotees to Madras. A large group of devotees and dignitaries, including Madras Corporation President, T. S. Ramaswami Iyer, the Honorable T. Rajan, Mr. S. V. Ramaswami Mudaliyar, the honorable Diwan Bahadur, G. Narayan Swami Chetiyar, C.I.E. (Companion of the Indian Empire), and T. Punurulla Pillai, etc., greeted him at the Basin Bridge Station and accompanied him in a huge sankirtan procession back to the Gaudiya Math which at that time was situated in the North Gopalpura neighborhood. In the assembly which followed, the honorable Diwan Bahadur Kumarswami Reddiyar offered a speech in which he indicated the depth of his esteem for the acharya, Saraswati Thakur.

On January 14, Madras High Court Justice, Diwan Bahadur Sundaram Chettiyar visited Saraswati Thakur at the Madras Gaudiya Math and was satisfied by answers to his questions on spiritual matters. On January 23, deities were installed in the Madras Gaudiya Math. On the same day, the cornerstone for a new Math was laid in the Raipetta district. On January 24, a huge meeting was held with many important personalities as guests, including Sir P. S. Shivaswami Iyer. Saraswati Thakur spoke and attracted many of these people to Mahaprabhu's teachings. On January 27, the governor of Madras Presidency, Sir George Frederick Stanley, laid the cornerstone for the Sri Krishna Kirtan Hall at the Madras Gaudiya Math.

On January 29, Madras City Corporation gave an official welcome to Saraswati Thakur. He gave a speech of thanks in the Corporation's Rippon Building.

On the 30th, Saraswati Thakur went to the town of Eluru in the West Godavari district, where he was greeted by a huge sankirtan party of townspeople. He received an official letter of welcome from the Janardana Prarthana Samaj. He gave a speech and then initiated and inspired a large number of people from that region in the practice of pure devotional service. On his 58th birthday, he wrote a speech that was sent to Calcutta to be read at the Vyasa Puja festivities there.

Saraswati Thakur returned to Mayapur before the 1932 Nabadwip Parikrama. On the occasion of Mahaprabhu's appearance day, he laid the cornerstone for a new temple building at Advaita Acharya's house. He gave a speech at the annual meeting of the Sri Dham Pracharini Sabha as well as instituting the examinations for *Bhakti-śāstrī* and *Bhakti-vaibhavācārya* degrees. On April 3, he presided over the annual award-giving ceremony at the Bhaktivinode Institute where he gave a speech on "Altruism and Extended Altruism."

MADRAS, UDAGAMANDALAM, MYSORE AND KOVVUR

On May 23, 1932, Saraswati Thakur returned to Madras. This time he had the opportunity to explain the particularities of the Gaudiya Vaishnava sampradaya to the religious leaders and scholars of the Shankar, Ramanuja and Madhva schools. On May 25, he spoke to a group of questioners led by Prof. K. Panchapagesan of Pudukottai College, and was able to settle their doubts. On May 29, he was welcomed to Combatoire by its citizens. He spoke there and on the banks of the Bhavani River to the people of the town of Mettuppalaiyam. From there he went to Udugamandalam in the Nilgiri Hills, where he stayed at the Rangavilas Bhavan. He stayed there long enough to revise Prof. Nishikanta Sannyal's English book, *Shri Krishna Chaitanya*, as well as completing his own English translation of *Brahma-saṁhitā*, his *Gauḍīya-bhāṣya* commentary on the Chaitanya Bhagavata, and a short English book on the life of Ramananda Ray.

While in Udagamandalam, several distinguished people came to visit Saraswati Thakur and had the opportunity to hear his teachings through his principal disciples. They included Sir Kishan Prasad, G.C.I.E. (Knight and Grand Commander of the Indian Empire), prime minister to the Nizam of Hyderabad, Hyderabad zamindar Dhanraj Girji, Sir P. S. Shivaswami Aiyar, and the honorable Diwan Bahadur, P. Muniswami Naidu.

On June 17, the Maharajah of Mysore, Sir Krishnaraj Vadhiyar, G.C.S.I. (Knight and Grand Commander of the Star of India), G.B.E. (Grand Cross of the British Empire) invited Saraswati Thakur and his disciples to Mysore where they stayed as his guests in the Rama Mandira and tirelessly preached the Chaitanya gospel throughout the area. On the way from Udagamandalam to Mysore, Saraswati Thakur visited various places such as the Lingayat temple to Kantheshwar and the Madhva Math, etc., in Nanjangud. On June 19, Saraswati Thakur visited Krishnaraj Sagar and Srirangapattanam (20 km north of Mysore).

In the morning of June 20, Saraswati Thakur visited the Mysore Sanskrit College and spoke to the professors on Krishna bhakti. That afternoon he was invited to the Maharajah's palace where he gave a discourse on Chaitanya Mahaprabhu and answered the Maharajah's questions.

From there, Saraswati Thakur went to Kovvur, the place on the banks of the Godavari where Mahaprabhu met with Ramananda Ray for the first time. On July 5, he installed deities at the Ramananda Gaudiya Math. Hundreds of thousands of people come around that time to take bath in the Godavari on the occasion of the *Puṣkara-yoga* and were blessed by the chance to hear the chanting of Gauranga's names. Saraswati Thakur spoke on the gradual process of spiritual life and its ultimate goal to the educated people of the locality.

GAURA KISHOR DAS'S SAMADHI IS TRANSFERRED

By August 16, Saraswati Thakur had returned to Calcutta and Sir Deva Prasad Sarvadhikari came to hear him speak on "Sri Chaitanya prema." On the 28th, during the annual festival held at the Gaudiya Math, he gave a lecture entitled "Relative Worlds."

On August 21, 1932, upon hearing that the samadhi tomb of his guru Srila Gaura Kishor Das Babaji Maharaj, was about to fall into the Ganges, Saraswati Thakur sent disciples to arrange to have his transcendental remains transferred in their entirety to the Chaitanya Math in Mayapur.

In the beginning of September, publication of a monthly magazine in the Assamese language, *Kīrtana*, was begun out of the town of Dhuburi on Saraswati Thakur's orders. On September 3, Saraswati Thakur gave a lecture entitled "The Ultimate Goal of Life" at the Calcutta Gaudiya Math. On the 4th, Calcutta University professor Suniti Chatterjee and Nadia District Magistrate T. C. Ray came to the Gaudiya Math to hear him speak. On Sept. 11, he gave a lecture on the Vedanta. These three lectures were later published. Then on the 16th, Saraswati Thakur came to Mayapur to inaugurate the samadhi temple of Gaura Kishor Das Babaji.

VRAJA MANDALA PARIKRAMA

On October 9, the appearance day of Sri Madhvacharya, Saraswati Thakur and countless devotees undertook the 84 kros pilgrimage tour of Vraja Mandala. Stopping at every place where Krishna had engaged in his pastimes, Saraswati Thakur and his disciples preached in various different languages for the benefit of devotees coming from many different places. He himself lectured on Rupa Goswami's *Upadeśāmṛta* to a large assembly of Vraja residents and scholars.

On November 4, after finishing the parikrama, he went to Hardwar-Mayapur where he laid the cornerstone for the Sri Saraswata Gaudiya Math. Then on Nov. 21, in Prayag, the cornerstone for the Sri Rupa Gaudiya Math was laid at his invitation and in his presence by the governor of the United Provinces, Sir William Malcolm Haley. On the 24th, deities of Radha and Govinda were installed in the Sanatan Gaudiya Math in Benares.

On November 27, the second annual memorial festival in honor of Jagabandhu Bhakti Ranjan was held, with Sir Manmath Nath Ray Chaudhuri Raja Bahadur presiding at the meeting. On December 4, Krishnanagar College professor Sudhendu Kumar Das and Vishvambhar Vyakarana-tirtha, Vedanta-shastri of Radha Kanta Math in Puri came to Mayapur where they learned much about the different Vaishnava sampradayas throughout India.

A SPIRITUAL EDUCATIONAL EXHIBITION IN DHAKA

On December 12, Saraswati Thakur came to Dhaka to open a diorama exhibition. He remained there for longer than a month, until January 30, 1933, during which time many of the most respectable members of the learned community came to see him and hear his teachings. A diorama exhibition with the theme of spiritual education—unprecedented in Dhaka—was opened on January 6. His lecture on that occasion, entitled "Exhibition Speech," created a change in the ideas of his listeners about the true nature of religion and its doctrines.

On February 2, Saraswati Thakur returned to the Calcutta Gaudiya Math, where he explained the difference between *eka-daṇḍa* sannyas and *tri-daṇḍa* sannyas after being questioned on the subject by Satishchandra De, dean of Narasingh College in Howrah, and Professor Ranada Charan Chakravarti. On the 8th, Saraswati Thakur went to Sri Mayapur to celebrate Nityananda's appearance day, Vyasa Puja and the appearance day of Sri Chaitanya Mahaprabhu.

PREACHING ENVOYS TO EUROPE

On Mahaprabhu's appearance day, 1933, Prof. Nishikanta Sannyal's English-language book, *Shri Krishna Chaitanya*, was released for distribution. After this event, Saraswati Thakur decided that it was now time to preach Mahaprabhu's message in Europe. He selected three leading disciples for the service: H. H. Bhakti Pradip Tirtha Maharaj, H. H. Bhakti Hridoy Bon Maharaj, and Sambidananda Das, M. A., Bhakti-Shastri. On March 18, in a meeting presided over by Jatindranath Basu, M.L.C [Member of Legislative Council], Saraswati Thakur gave a farewell speech called "My Message" (*Āmār kathā*), in which he praised these three disciples, bidding them bon voyage before they left to carry out the European mission.

The first news of results of their preaching in London was received at the beginning of May: a centre had been opened at 39 Drain Gardens, Kensington, S.W. 10. On May 31, Saraswati Thakur answered inquiries on spiritual matters sent from London by the Marquess of Ludian and Lord Zetland, a former governor of Bengal. On June 15, Lord Zetland presided over a meeting of the Society for the Study of Religion at Bedford Square, in which Saraswati Thakur's disciples spoke on the glories of Sri Chaitanya Mahaprabhu.

On June 23, a meeting was held at the London Gaudiya Math in honor of Srila Bhaktivinode Thakur. Many distinguished guests, including the Honorable Justice Bistrow, came there to hear about Bhaktivinode's teachings. In the month of July, Saraswati Thakur received letters from several distinguished British citizens thanking him for the great work the Gaudiya Math had undertaken in Great Britain. They included Lord Irwin's private secretary, Mr. R. A. Butler, the Marquis of Ludian, Sir Stanley Jackson, and Times editor, Mr. Brown.

On July 5, former Viceroy of India Lord Irwin, his wife and representatives of the Joint Select Parliamentary Committee heard from the Gaudiya Math missionaries about their objectives in preaching Mahaprabhu's message in Europe. At 4 P.M. on July 20, the Secretary of State for India, Sir Samuel Hoare, introduced the Gaudiya Math preachers to Emperor George V and Empress Mary. The preachers had the opportunity to offer their respects to the emperor and tell him the purpose of the Gaudiya Mission. On July 14, they met with the head of the Church of England, the Archbishop of Canterbury, the Most Reverend Cosmo Gordon Lang. Then on October 7 and 8, a large meeting was held for the professors and students of Oxford University, in which the Gaudiya Vaishnava doctrine of the Holy Names was explained.

The Gaudiya Math's European preachers gave lectures on Chaitanya Mahaprabhu's gospel at the Eastbourne Theosophical Society on November 24-25, then at the Deutsch Akademi in Munich, Germany, on December 10; at Humboldt House in Berlin on December 12; Koningsburg on the 14th, at the Institut de la Civilisation Indienne in Paris. On December 20, the London Gaudiya Math moved to 3 Gloucester House, Cornwall Gardens, S.W. 7.

PREACHING ACTIVITY IN BOMBAY AND OTHER CITIES

While this was going on, Saraswati Thakur opened the Sri Krishna Kirtan Hall in Madras. From there he went to Bombay, where he met with the Nepali professor, Sanjiva Kumar Chaudhuri, M.A., and answered his three sincere questions.

Not long afterward, he opened the Gaudiya Math's Bombay office in the Jangu Villa on Babul Nath Road. While staying there, he made great efforts to preach Mahaprabhu's message in the large city. On May 20, in response to a question by a distinguished relative of Dadabhai Naroji, he gave his resolution of the problem of the movement for the admission of untouchables into Hindu temples.

Meanwhile, on June 16, Saraswati Thakur spoke on the uniqueness of the Srimad Bhagavatam at the Krishnanagar Town Hall. The occasion was a memorial meeting in honor of Srila Bhaktivinode Thakur which was presided over by Khitipati Nath Mitra and Dinanath Sannyal Ray Bahadur.

On July 3, Saraswati Thakur installed deities of Gaurasundar and Radha-Govinda in the newly finished temple at the Tridandi Gaudiya Math in Bhuvanesvar. This was followed by a kirtan festival.

In August, on the occasion of a solar eclipse, a spiritual diorama exhibition was held for the second time at Kurukshetra. During the time of the Bagh Bazaar Math's annual festival, a large kirtan procession was taken through many Calcutta neighborhoods. On August 12, Saraswati Thakur spoke on "The ultimate goal of human life," on the 20th, on "The uniqueness of Sri Chaitanya Mahaprabhu," and on the 27th, in English on "The Vedanta, its morphology and ontology". On September 7, he went by motor launch to Nabadwip, bringing sankirtan to various places along the Ganges.

On October 27, Saraswati Thakur made his auspicious entrance into the city of Patna to preach Mahaprabhu's message to the local populace. Some of the distinguished people who came to hear his instructions were Amarendranath Das, Ray Bahadur; Ganesh Chandra Chand, the government archeological superintendent for the region of Bihar, Orissa, and Chota Nagpur; barrister, P. R. Das; advocate Nabadwip Chandra Das; District and Session Judge, Shivapriya Chatterjee. On November 14, Darbhanga Maharaj, Sir Kameshwar Singh Bahadur, K.C.S.I., opened the diorama exhibition in Patna, attracting some of the most distinguished citizens of that town.

On November 19, the third annual memorial meeting for Jagabandhu Bhaktiranjan was presided over at the Gaudiya Math by Sir Vijaya Prasad Singh Ray. At the end of November, the *Bhakti-sandarbha*, edited by Saraswati Thakur, was published in its entirety. On November 24, he spoke Hari katha in Tetiya Palli near Nrisingha Palli in Nabadwip Dham. On November 26 and 27, he took part in a sankirtan festival at the Ekayana Math in Krishnanagar. By his grace, there was also preaching activity in Amarshigram in Midnapore at this time as well.

During this time, preaching activity was also being conducted in Karachi, now in Pakistan. On December 24, the spiritual exhibition was opened in Benares in the Michir Pokra neighborhood by Saraswati Thakur's supporter, District Magistrate and Collector, Mr. Pannalal, I.C.S. (Indian Civil Service).

THE MAHARAJAH OF TRIPURA VISITS THE GAUDIYA MATH

On January 15, 1934, the King of the independent state of Tripura, Viravikram Kishor Devavarma Manikya Bahadur, visited the Calcutta Gaudiya Math with his entourage. He showed his reverence for the Acharya and at a great assembly that evening, and gave a speech praising the work of the Gaudiya Math. On February 2, Kumar Bahadur Radhika Ranjan Chakravarti, B.A., his private secretary and retinue came to visit Saraswati Thakur and to receive his instructions.

On February 4, on his 60th birthday, the Vyasa Puja ceremony was held and printing of a book written by his disciples in glorification of his life, *Saraswati Jayaśrī*, was begun. On the same day in London, a meeting in honor of the Acharya was held at Grosvenor House in London's Park Lane, presided over by Lord Zetland.

On February 25, in Modadrumdwip, the new temple at Vrindavan Das Thakur's birthplace was inaugurated. That year, the Nabadwip Dham parikrama and festival celebrating the appearance of Chaitanya Mahaprabhu were held as usual, temple buildings at the site of Srivasa Angan and Gaura Kishore Das Babaji's samadhi were consecrated, three devotees were initiated into the Tridandi Sannyas order, and Saraswati Thakur gave regular lectures in the Bhakti Vijaya Bhavana as well as at the annual meeting of the Nabadwip Dham Pracciharini Sabha. Amongst the notable visitors to the Chaitanya Math during this time were Rajarshi Kumar Sharadindu Narayan Ray and Ray Bahadur Ram Prasad Chanda, who came on February 19, and visited many of the holy places in Mayapur besides coming to see the Acharya.

On March 5, Saraswati Thakur headed a large preaching party that went to Chanchuri Puruliya in Jessore, the home village of the Gaudiya Math temple manager, Maha Mahopadeshak Acharyatrika Kunja Bihari Vidyabhushan Mahashaya. He spent five days there constantly preaching the message of Lord Chaitanya.

THE NEW TEMPLE AT THE MAYAPUR YOGA PITH

On March 18, foundations were laid for the proposed temple at the birthplace of Chaitanya Mahaprabhu, as well as for a smaller temple at Murari Gupta's house. Three months later, at 10 A.M. on June 13, the four-armed form of Vishnu known as Adhokshaja was found in the ground while digging the foundations for the new temple at the Yoga Pith, made possible by the donations of Sakhicharan Ray Bhakti Vijaya. This was the same deity worshiped by Jagannath Mishra in his home.

THE GAUDIYA MISSION SOCIETY IN LONDON

On April 2, Saraswati Thakur established a shrine to Mahaprabhu's lotus feet in Chatrabhog. The villagers there awarded him special recognition and he gave a speech in response. On April 8, he gave sannyas to several disciples. On the 20th he went to Puri from Calcutta.

On April 24, in Westminster's Caxton Hall, a general meeting presided over by Lord Zetland was held to inaugurate the foundation of the Gaudiya Mission Society.

On May 6, the archeologist Ram Prasad Chanda Ray Bahadur gave a lecture on "Nabadwip at the time of Lord Chaitanya" at a meeting presided over by Jatindranath Basu, M.L.C.

IN PURI

Throughout the month of May, Saraswati Thakur met with a number of important people and spoke to them about Krishna. They included the chief lecturer of the Ayurveda department at the Puri Sanskrit College, Ananda Mahapatra, the novelist Sachishchandra Chattopadhyaya, the abbot of Emar Math, Gadadhar Ramanuja Das, Hanuman Khuntiya, Ray Bahadur Gaura Shyama Mahanti, Radha Shyama Mahanti, Professor Junakar of Dhaka University, Puri Deputy Magistrate Revatinath Chathopadhyaya and Magistrate Narendranath Datta Ray Bahadur, the founder of the Bodhana Ashram, Girija Prasanna Mukhopadhyaya, Khagendranath Mitra Ray Bahadur, professor at Calcutta University.

On June 27, the Gopinath deity was consecrated by Saraswati Thakur at the Alalanath Brahma Gaudiya Math along with festive kirtan. The revised and expanded edition of the book *Brāhmaṇa o Vaiṣṇava* was released on this day.

On July 12, he installed a deity of Gaura Kishor Das Babaji in Mayapur. On August 13, he preached to the son of the illustrious O. N. Mukherjee, Jamini Nath Mukhopadhyaya. On the 14th, he installed deities at the Patna Gaudiya Math.

At the annual Gaudiya Math festival, once again Harinam Sankirtan was held in the streets of Calcutta. On September 1, on the day of Krishna Janmashtami, the book *Sarasvatī Jayaśrī* was released. On September 4, the English language fortnightly *Harmonist* was published in a new format.

On September 16, Saraswati Thakur spoke at the Gaudiya Math on Radhashtami in an assembly presided over by Dvarakanath Mitra, M.A., D.L. Countless visitors to the temple heard Saraswati Thakur speak on Krishna conscious topics.

THE MONTH OF KARTTIK IN MATHURA

Starting October 17, Saraswati Thakur spent the month of Karttik observing the vrata in Mathura with a large group of disciples and followers. During this time, he set the example of discussing Radha and Krishna's *aṣṭakālīya-līlā*. On October 29, he discovered the place in Mathura city, in the Satghara neighborhood where Rupa Goswami would come for darshan of Gopal.

In the third week of October, Saraswati Thakur's representative preachers visited several German universities to preach the message of pure devotion.

On November 1, Saraswati Thakur and his party visited Chandra Sarovar, Parasauli, Gauri Tirtha, and Paitha Gram, and he was inspired to talk on the lilas which took place in these spots. On November 17, he gave Tridanda sannyas to a brahmachari disciple.

On November 29, at the Rmjendra Bhavan in New Delhi, he spoke on "The duty of human life" and "Mahaprabhu's mercy and His teaching" to an audience that included N. Chatterjee and Dr. J. K. Sen.

CHAITANYA-SIKSAMRTA IS TRANSLATED INTO TELUGU

On December 6, Raja Bhupendra Narayan Singh Bahadur presided over the fourth annual memorial assembly in honor of Jagabandhu Bhaktiranjan. At this time, on his order, Saraswati Thakur's Andhra disciple, Y. Jagannath, B.A., published Bhaktivinode's *Śrī Chaitanya-śikṣāmṛta* in the Telugu language. Meanwhile, the English edition of *Jaiva Dharma* was also in publication.

THE GOVERNOR OF BENGAL VISITS MAYAPUR

On January 15, 1935, the Governor of Bengal, Sir John Anderson, came to visit the birthplace of Sri Chaitanya Mahaprabhu in Mayapur and, after hearing about the site from Saraswati Thakur, himself gave a speech.

Saraswati Thakur's 61st birthday was celebrated with Vyasa Puja on February 23 in his birthplace, Puri, amidst the sand dunes near the ocean. A huge assembly was held at which the Maharaj of Puri, Gajapati Ramachandra Deva Bahadur presided. The following day, Saraswati Thakur led a parikrama around Puri and gave a lecture for the occasion. In preparation for the Dol Purnima festivities, Sakhi Charan Ray Bhakti Vijaya had electric lights installed in the Yoga Pith temple building. On March 4, Sir. B. L. Mitra came to hear Saraswati Thakur speak on Chaitanya Mahaprabhu.

On March 20, Dol Purnima, the birthdate of Chaitanya Mahaprabhu was marked by the inauguration of the newly finished temple. The Maharajah of Tripura, Sir Viravikrama Kishor Devavarma Manikya Bahadur, came to Mayapur for the occasion and officially opened the temple doors.

PREACHING TOUR IN EAST BENGAL

On March 24, the Gaudiya Math Acharya went with a party of devotees to Deruli in Khulna district where he addressed several massive gatherings. On March 31, the Maharaj of Burdwan, Sir Vijaya Chand Mehtab came to the Calcutta Gaudiya Math and heard the Acharya speak.

On April 8, Saraswati Thakur came to Dhaka and placed the foundation for the proposed new temple building of the Madhva Gaudiya Math in Narinda Palli. The residents of Dhaka and Narain Ganj welcomed him and eulogized him.

On April 12, Saraswati Thakur installed deities at the Jagannath Gaudiya Math in Mymensingh. He stayed there until the 15th at "Shashi Lodge" on the invitation of Maharaj Shashi Kant Acharya and was able to preach to many learned and distinguished citizens of the district.

FOUNDING THE GAYA GAUDIYA MATH

On April 19, Saraswati Thakur travelled to Gaya where he visited all the places that Mahaprabhu had been to and constantly spoke to many educated and respectable people. On the 22nd, he established the Gaya Gaudiya Math. On April 30, he sent a few preachers to East Bengal and Burma. On May 31, he was in Darjeeling with a group of devotees, and spoke constantly on topics related to Krishna. Then on June 9 and 10, in large assemblies presided over by Sir Jadunath Sarkar and Colonel Upendranath Mukhopadhyaya, he had his leading disciples speak. On June 9, he spread Chaitanya's gospel on the Indian Broadcasting Service's radio network.

On June 28, at the Calcutta Gaudiya Math, he received Cooch Bihar Maharani Indira Devi, the princesses Ela Devi and Gayatri Devi, Prince Indrajitendra Narayan Bahadur, and the French intellectual Maximilian Poitiers, PhD, all of whom heard from the Acharya about Vaishnava philosophy.

On July 8, he installed deities at the Bombay Gaudiya Math on Proctor Street and in a meeting held at the People's Jinnah Hall spoke on the Bhagavata and Pancharatra. At this time, Saraswati Thakur's disciple Sambidananda Das, M.A., Bhakti Shastri, *Pratna-tattva-viśārada*, received his doctorate from the University of London in Vaishnava history and literature. From the end of July to the middle of August, the Acharya was preaching in different places in the Nabadwip area.

PREACHING THE GOSPEL OF LORD CHAITANYA ON THE RADIO

Every Sunday beginning with the annual Gaudiya Math festival, street sankirtan was held and programs about Janmashtami, Nandotsava, Radhashtami and Bhaktivinode Thakur's appearance day were given on the radio. Then, from Balaram's appearance day, the Acharya spoke on the Bhagavata for sixteen consecutive days. During the festival itself, at the great assembly presided over by Cossim Bazaar Maharajah, Sachindra Nandi Bahadur, he spoke on "Devotion and worldly indifference."

In Calcutta on September 18, the people of Calcutta welcomed and gave a special letter of appreciation to returning preacher Bhakti Hridoy Bon Maharaj and two German devotees, who arrived from London.

On September 21, the full moon day of the month of Bhadra, On April 2, Saraswati Thakur gave a lecture inspired by the completion of the Gaudiya Math publication of the entire twelve volumes of the Bhagavata.

NIYAMA-SEVA IN RADHA KUND

From October 1 to 7, Saraswati Thakur was on a preaching engagement in New Delhi. Then, from the 8th, he spent more than a month in Radha Kund to keep the vows for the month of Karttik (*niyama-sevā*). During this time, he spoke daily on the Upanishads, Chaitanya Charitamrita, Srimad Bhagavatam, as well as circumambulating the kund, and hearing and chanting about Krishna's *aṣṭakālīya-līlā*. A committe was founded to improve opportunities to serve the holy dham of Vraja named the Vraja Dham Pracharini Sabha.

On November 4, Saraswati Thakur installed deities at the Kunja Bihari Math at Radha Kund, and two days later, Srila Bhaktivinode Thakur's *puṣpa-samādhi* memorial and *bhāva-sevā* at Vraja Svananda Sukhada Kunj.

On November 7, he travelled to Śeṣashayi in the Punjab and then on to Delhi where he preached at the annual festival on the 10th. On the 11th, he was in Gaya where he stayed, telling the good news of Mahaprabhu's mercy to the people of that town until the 15th. On the 13th, he installed deities in the Gaya Gaudiya Math. During this period, the preaching activity in Burma was meeting with great success.

On Dec. 23, the Maharajah of Tripura, Viravikrama Kishor Devavarma Manikya Bahadur, presided over the fifth annual memorial festival to Jagabandhu Bhaktiranjan. After the assembly, the Acharya met with Dr. Henry Hand and Mr. S. V. Rossetto of California, barrister S. N. Rudra, retired judge Lalita Mohan Basu and others, preaching to them about transcendent knowledge which exists beyond sense perception.

DIORAMA EXHIBIT AT PRAYAG

On December 27, Saraswati Thakur travelled to Patna where he spoke at the Gaudiya Math. On the 30th, he went on to Allahabad where he spoke on Mahaprabhu's teachings to Rupa Goswami.

On January 7, 1936, he opened the transcendental diorama exhibition at Prayag, after which he gave the presidential speech in English before an assembly of learned persons.

A DEVOTIONAL LIBRARY AND SOCIETY FOR PROMOTING DAIVA VARNASHRAM

On January 11, Saraswati Thakur returned to Mayapur, where he remained for a full two months, preaching daily to the devotees living at the Chaitanya Math and the birthsite of Gauranga Mahaprabhu.

On February 12, in celebration of his 62nd birthday, he established the Thakur Bhaktivinode Research Institute or the *Kṛṣṇānuśīlanāgāra* ("Library for Krishna Culture"), and the Daiva Varnashram Sangha. The Vyasa Puja was held at Srivas Angan. The appearance day of the Acharya was also celebrated in London with the London Gaudiya Mission Society chairman, The Right Honorable Sir Sadilal, presiding.

Starting from February 25, Saraswati Thakur started establishing deities of the *viṣaya* and *āśraya-vigrahas* of each of Nabadwip's nine islands. On March 1, he went to Suvarṇa Bihār where he established the Suvarna Bihari Math and installed deities there. On March 5, he opened the Sarvabhauma Gaudiya Math in Vidyanagar, also installing deities there. On the 7th, the Rudradwip Gaudiya Math was opened along with deity service.

On March 8, the appearance day of Sri Chaitanya Mahaprabhu, on the Acharya's direction, the Burmese education minister, Dr. Bame, opened the Rangoon office of the Gaudiya Math at 29 Brooking St. At the London Gaudiya Math also, the devotees gave speeches in honor of Mahaprabhu's appearance, with Dr. Parhi presiding.

On March 15, the Acharya travelled to Assam where deities were insalled at the Gaudiya Math. The residents of Sarbhog gave him a warm welcome and bestowed honors on him.

THE HUNDRED-DAY KIRTAN FESTIVAL IN ORISSA

On March 27, Saraswati Thakur travelled to Cuttack where he preached to distinguished people of that town. From March 29, he stayed at Chatak Parvat in Puri, establishing a residence for devotees and a temple with deities of Radha and Govinda. In a speech before many learned people of the city, he inaugurated a hundred-day sankirtan festival. On May 4, he celebrated Nrisingha Chaturdashi at Alalanath, at the Brahma Gaudiya Math. On May 30, he initiated several brahmachari preachers into the order of Tridandi sannyasa.

BALIYATI, GODRUM, DARJEELING AND BOGRA

On June 7, Saraswati Thakur went to Dhaka where he stayed at the home of Supati Ranjan Nag M.A., B.L., where he spoke on Krishna consciousness to an audience of distinguished persons. He also initiated a number of truthseekers into the service of Lord Sri Krishna Chaitanya.

On June 9, he arrived in Baliyati village in Dhaka district, accepted the welcome of the villagers and gave a speech in thanks. On June 10, he installed deities of Radha-Govinda in the newly constructed Gadai Gauranga Math temple. On the 13th and 14th, he had his sannyasi preachers and one of his German disciples speak at Dhaka University and the Dhaka Bar Library.

On June 19th, he returned to Mayapur and celebrated the 22nd anniversary of Srila Bhaktivinode Thakur's disappearance at Svananda Sukhada Kunj in Godrumdwip. He spoke on renouncing the company of non-devotees and held a sankirtan festival. On the same day, the Gaudiya Math devotees gave the opportunity to thousands of pilgrims who had assembled at Kurukshetra for the solar eclipse to hear Mahaprabhu's gospel by visiting the diorama exhibition, Sat Siksha Pradarshini.

On the 27th, Saraswati Thakur went to Darjeeling where he stayed at the Gaudiya Math office. He spoke and had his disciples speak Hari katha to their distinguished guests. He installed Radha Govinda deities there on July 19, taking the opportunity to speak himself to the assembled guests.

On July 24, he came to Bogra on the insistent invitation of its people. He was given a warm welcome and at the local Hindu Sabha meeting he spoke on the need for preaching Gaudiya Vaishnavism in northern Bengal, which had previously been blessed by Narottam Das Thakur.

THE PURUSHOTTAM VRATA IN VRINDAVAN

After celebrating the appearance day of Balaram and Janmashtami in Calcutta, Saraswati Thakur decided to spend the month of Purushottam (the supplementary month irregularly added to the Hindu calendar to balance the lunar and solar years, also known as *mala-māsa*) in the Mathura area. He left Calcutta on August 12. He first stayed in Mathura Cantonment at "Shivalaya." From there, he went to Vrindavan where he stayed at Madhumangala Kunj, giving daily Bhagavatam classes. He inaugurated a place of worship in Govardhan. He returned to the Calcutta Gaudiya Math on September 9 for the annual festival.

THE GAUDIYA SANGH PRESIDENT SENT TO GREAT BRITAIN

On October 16, Saraswati Thakur spoke for nearly an entire hour to Dr. Shivapada Bhattacharya, M.B. On the 23rd, he gave a speech in the Sārasvata Śravaṇa Sadana in which he bestowed the responsibility for preaching Mahaprabhu's message in Great Britain and America on Bhaktisaranga Prabhu. He blessed him and gave him instructions in the worship of Gomatī, Shalagram and Govardhan Sila.

INTIMATIONS OF SARASWATI THAKUR'S DEPARTURE

On October 24, he left for Puri. On November 1, Saraswati Thakur's dear disciple Tridandi Swami Bhakti Srirupa Puri Maharaj's life on this earth came to an end.

While at Chatak Parvat, Puri's nondifferent manifestation of Govardhan hill, he celebrated the appearance of Madhvacharya and performed Govardhan Puja, which he worshiped with the hymns composed by Rupa and Raghunath Goswamis. He also observed a festival of separation from his dear lord, Srila Gaura Kishor Das Goswami Maharaj. Each day, his disciples and guests were refreshed after bathing in the holy waters of his discourse. While in Puri, he constantly warned everyone, "Worship the Lord without duplicity, for not much time is left." He constantly repeated two prayers written by Rupa and Raghunath:

pratyāśāṁ me tvaṁ kuru govardhana pūrṇām

O Govardhan, fulfill every one of my wishes!
(Rupa Goswami's first *Govardhanāṣṭakam*)

nija-nikaṭa-nivāsaṁ dehi govardhana tvam

O Govardhan, please give me residence somewhere near to You.
(Raghunath Das's *Govardhana-vāsa-prārthanā-daśakam*)

Srila Prabhupada returned to Calcutta on December 9, preaching to his disciples without cessation during the entire voyage.

SRILA PRABHUPADA'S FINAL INSTRUCTIONS

On December 27, several days prior to the setting of the blazing sun of the Gaudiya Vaishnava sampradaya, Om Vishnupada Srila Bhaktisiddhanta Saraswati Goswami Thakur spoke to a gathering of his closest disciples, at which time he said the following words:

"I have disturbed many people because I felt myself obliged to speak the unadulterated truth. I have told everyone to worship Hari without hypocrisy and because of this some people have perhaps considered me to be their enemy. So I have caused many people anxiety by telling them to give up other desires and hypocrisy and to sincerely serve Krishna. Some day they will be able to understand what I was getting at.

"All of you please preach the message of Rupa and Raghunath with great enthusiasm. The ultimate object of our desires is to become specks of dust at the lotus feet of the followers of Rupa Goswami. Remain united in following the *āśraya-vigraha* in order to satisfy the transcendental senses of the one, non-dual Supreme Truth. Make your way through this impermanent, transitory life in whatever way you can, keeping the goal of worshiping the Lord foremost in your minds. Don't abandon this goal, even in the face of hundreds of dangers, insults, or persecutions. Don't lose your spirit if you see that the majority of people cannot accept the principle of selfless service to the Supreme Lord. Never abandon your bhajan, hearing and chanting Krishna katha, the sum and substance of your devotional life. Please always chant the name of the Lord, being humbler than a blade of grass and more tolerant than the tree.

"This body is like the aging cow which in ancient times was meant to be offered up in sacrifice. Only we desire to offer the body to Krishna in the sacrifice of the Holy Name established by Sri Krishna Chaitanya and His associates. We do not seek to become heroes performing great works or religious deeds; our true being and our identity is that of a speck of dust at the lotus feet of Sri Rupa Prabhu, life after life. The stream which flows from Srila Bhaktivinode Thakur will never be dammed up. Remember this and vow to double your efforts to fulfill Srila Bhaktivinode Thakur's desires. Amongst you are many capable and worthy individuals. We seek nothing for ourselves; our only motto is:

ādadānas tṛṇaṁ dantair idaṁ yāce punaḥ punaḥ
śrīmad rūpa-padāmbhoja-dhūlḥ syāṁ janma-janmani

Taking grass between my teeth, I pray repeatedly that I may become a speck of dust at Sri Rupa Goswami's lotus feet, birth after birth.

(Raghunath Das Goswami, *Muktā-carita.*)

"While living in the world, we encounter many difficulties; but there is no need for us to be bewildered by these difficulties—nor need we make any effort to remove them. What is necessary is for us, while we are still here, is to learn what will remain after we have removed all those difficulties—what will be the nature of our eternal life. There are so many things which we want or don't want, but we have to come to terms with this duality of attractions and repulsions. The more we distance ourselves from Krishna's lotus feet, the more these things will draw us in. We can only begin to comprehend the exquisite taste of service to Krishna's lotus feet after transcending these worldly attractions and repulsions and being attracted by His holy name. The doctrines of Krishna bhakti seem startling at first, perhaps even perplexing. Knowingly or unknowingly, every human being is struggling to eliminate the adventitious elements in life which interfere with his direct experience of eternal fulfillment. Our only obligation is to go beyond duality and to enter the world of that eternal fulfillment.

"We have no attachment for anyone in this world, nor any hostility. Whatever arrangements we make in this world last but a moment, while the need to search out the supreme fulfillment is equally unavoidable for everyone. May all of you work united and in harmony toward the same goal: to earn the right to serve the root *āśraya-vigraha.* May the current of ideas propagated by Rupa Goswami flow throughout the world. May we never under any circumstances become indifferent to the seven-tongued sacrificial flame of the Holy Name. If our attraction to it remains ever-increasing, we will achieve all perfection. Remain faithful to Rupa Goswami's followers and preach Rupa and Raghunath's teachings enthusiastically and fearlessly."

SARASWATI THAKUR'S LAST DAY

In the morning of the day on which he disappeared, Srila Prabhupada asked Tridandi Swami Bhakti Rakshaka Sridhar Maharaj to sing Narottam Das' song, *śrī rūpa mañjarī pada*, and Navina Krishna Vidyalankara to sing the song *tuhuṅ dayā sāgara tārayite prāṇī* from Bhaktivinode Thakur's translation of the *Śikṣāṣṭaka*. Prabhupada expressed satisfaction and thanks to Bhakti Sudhakar Prabhu (Nishikanta Sannyal) for his service. He also told Patna's Vrajeshwari Prasad Prabhu to remain enthusiastic in his service.

At about four o'clock in the afternoon, he called Sakhi Charan Ray Bhakti Vijaya to tell him that he was very fortunate because of the service he had rendered to Sri Mayapur. Later in the afternoon, he said to Bhakti Viveka Bharati Maharaj, "You are a competent person. Take care of the mission. It is best if love and rapture are seen as having the same meaning. Narottam Das Thakur adopted Rupa and Raghunath's understanding. It is best if we live according to that understanding."

Then Srila Prabhupada said to everyone, "I give my blessings to all who are present here and to those who are absent. Remember always that our only duty and religion is to propagate the service of the Bhagavata and of Bhagavan."

ENTERING THE ETERNAL ABODE

At about 5:30 A.M., on Thursday, January 1, 1937, a *kṛṣṇā caturthī*, Srila Prabhupada entered the eternal abode, joining Radha and Krishna in the predawn pastimes (*niśānta-līlā*) of their eternal 24-hour cycle of activities in Vraja. At the end of every night, Radha and Krishna lie intertwined in embrace, becoming as one body. It is at this moment, when their united form of Gaurasundar is eternally manifest, that Vārṣabhānavīdayita Das, their servant, joined them.

namaste gauravāṇī-śrī-
mūrtaye dīna-tāriṇe
rūpānuga-viruddhāpa-
siddhanta-dhvānta-hāriṇe

Obeisances to you who are the incarnation of Gauranga Mahaprabhu's gospel, the deliverer of the fallen and the destroyer of the darkness of unorthodox doctrines which oppose the conclusions given by Rupa Goswami and his followers.

The announcement of Prabhupada's departure published in *Gauḍīya* magazine

Last Narayan 4, 450 of the Chaitanya era, at the end of the Thursday night, Paush 16, 1343 of the Bengali calendar, on Friday morning, January 1, 1937, Paramahaṁsa Parivrājakācārya Om Vishnupada Srila Bhaktisiddhanta Saraswati Goswami Prabhupada joined the eternal activities of Radha Govinda in the first hour of their eternal twenty-four hour cycle of activities. This is the same hour that his own guru, Om Vishnupada Gaura Kishor Das Babaji entered into *nitya-līlā*. Srila Prabhupada was the great acharya of the Gaudiya Vaishnava sampradaya and its only protector, ninth in descent from Sri Chaitanya Mahaprabhu, and the best of the followers of Svarupa Damodar and Sri Rupa Goswami.

The meaning of entering the lila at this hour is understood clearly by those who are intimate with him for it is directly experienced in their hearts, but a hint can be given here. At the end of the night, Radha and Krishna are locked in an unbreakable embrace, *gāḍhāliṅgana-nirbhedam āptau*. Jayadeva Goswami has indicated this situation with the word *naktam* in the first verse of *Gīta-govindam* which begins *meghair meduram ambaram*. When Radha and Krishna are joined together like this, they take on their combined form of Gaurasundar. It is this auspicious moment that Varshabhanavi Dayita Das chose to make his entry into their pastimes.

Srila Prabhupada is like the sun of the Gaudiya sampradaya, as he is identical with its acharyas Rupa and Svarupa Damodar. But now that this sun of Sri Chaitanya Mahaprabhu's sampradaya has set, darkness has descended not only on the preachers of the Gaudiya Math, but on the entire world. It seems that the direct light of guileless devotion will once again be hidden from the view of the world's people. Our only hope is that this luminary amongst spiritual teachers sufficiently inspired his followers with such a desire to serve the feet of the Lord—with such ever-fresh enthusiasm, and instilled in them such ideals of practice and preaching—that the stream which passed through Svarupa and Rupa and then through Bhaktivinode Thakur will continue to gather force and flow into the world. In our hearts, we consider nothing else to be possible even in our worst imaginings. From the blessings that he gave just before passing on, we know that by adhering faithfully to his teachings and propagating them, we will be able to get his direct, personal association and will be able to find all the strength we need. Furthermore, by preaching fearlessly, with an independent spirit, and with the force of character that comes of sincere service and fidelity, we will be able to preach the gospel of Gaurasundar, our master's master, throughout the world. By so doing, we are assured that his blessings will continue to rain down on us even more profusely. This faith is the sole lampost illuminating the path of pure devotion, which is strewn with countless obstacles.

We, the Gaudiya's writers, are today without shelter, as we will no longer be able to show our articles to him who was the preserver of Rupa and Raghunath's tradition. Srila Prabhupada would eagerly read every article which was to be published in the Gaudiya. He would give us blessings and show the deepest satisfaction with our efforts. Now, even though he will no longer be able to do this directly, we will not be entirely devoid of his blessings nor of the spiritual strength arising from his mercy. We are not without succour, for he left us the gift of service to those who know the doctrines of pure devotion as taught by Bhaktivinode Thakur, and through this service we shall gain the capacity to understand his most confidential desires and doctrines.

PRABHUPADA'S EULOGY OF SRILA BHAKTIVINODE THAKUR

Srila Prabhupada wrote the following words in *Sajjana-toṣaṇī* after the disappearance of Om Vishnupada Srila Bhaktivinode Thakur:

"The purpose of *Sajjana-toṣaṇī* remains unchanged. Thakur Mahashaya has entered the *nitya-līlā*, but by his blessings this magazine will continue to bring joy to the pious through Hari katha, just as before.... Some think, accepting the opinion of the material sensualists, that the cause of bhakti is advanced by eliminating the idea of pure devotion; others tarnish pure devotion's beauty by accepting the facile path of the materialistic devotees as the standard.

"Srila Bhaktivinode Thakur sang in his *Kalyāṇa-kalpa-taru*,

bhakti-bādhā jāhā ha'te se vidyāra mastakete
padāghāta kara akaitava
sarasvatī kṛṣṇa-priyā kṛṣṇa-bhakti tar hiyā
vinodera sei se vaibhava

'Fearlessly stomp on any learning which causes obstacles on the path of devotion. The goddess of learning, Saraswati, is dear to Krishna, and her heart is full of devotion to the Lord. Such devotion is my wealth and glory.'

"Srila Prabhupada, Bhaktivinode Thakur, and Gauranga Mahaprabhu can neither condone words which contradict devotional service, nor any which compromise with it. This, we have repeatedly recognized, is the extraordinary characteristic of those teachings. Chaitanya-Saraswati (Srila Prabhupada) who is most dear to Krishna, as Bhaktivinode's wealth and expansion refer to the wealth extended from the lotus feet of the original *āśraya-vigraha*, Srimati Radharani. The daughter of Vrishabhanu has expanded as Mahaprabhu's gospel through Bhaktivinode. Thus, service to Gaura's teachings in obedience to the guru is identical with the service of Radha Govinda, and service to the gopis and Sri Gopinath in the wake of Sri Rupa Manjari.

"Illuminated by the lamp of devotion, we can see the path which leads to the bower where the Gauranga of Bhaktivinode's teachings sports. It reveals those words of Gauranga, the everlasting order of his goddess of learning which enters into the ears of eternally conditioned souls like ourselves: 'Be the servant of Svarupa and Rupa's followers and always chant the Holy Name.'

We pray to remain constantly dedicated to the glorification of that abode of virtue, Gauranga, who is Krishna himself residing in that message-bower, with single-minded commitment and great gusto. On this day, we pray to all the Vaishnavas who are obedient to the preceptors in the line of Svarupa and Rupa for this blessing."

SOME OF SRILA PRABHUPADA'S TEACHINGS

1. Chaitanya Mahaprabhu has revealed our supreme worshipable object in His *Śikṣāṣṭakam*: *paraṁ vijayate śrī-kṛṣṇa-saṅkīrtanam*. (From *Patrāvalī*, vol. 3, page 38)

2. Only Krishna, the object of devotion (*viṣaya-vigraha*), is the enjoyer (*bhogī*); everyone else is the enjoyed (*bhogya*). (Ibid., 58)

3. Everyone but the worshiper of Hari is a suicidal fool. (Ibid., 76)

4. One of the Math resident's chief duties is to learn tolerance. (Ibid., 88)

5. The followers of Rupa Goswami do not place their faith in their own powers, but rather attribute all glory to the fountainhead of those powers. (Ibid., 89)

6. Taking the Holy Name and the direct experience of God are one and the same thing. (*Patrāvalī*, vol. 2, page 3)

7. Those who follow a jumbled syncretic religious path cannot engage in the service of the Lord. (Ibid., 13)

8. True service to Sri Mayapur will be achieved through the establishment of printing presses, the distribution of devotional literature and the establishment of Nam Hatta preaching centres. (Ibid., 51)

9. Join together and cooperate in the common purpose of serving Hari. (Ibid., 53)

10.A holy place is there where the topics of Krishna are being discussed. (Ibid, 82)

11. We perform neither pious works nor engage in sinful activity; we are neither learned nor ignorant. We are simple carriers of genuine devotees' sandals, initiated in the mantra, *kīrtanīyaḥ sadā hariḥ*. (Ibid., 104)

12. My advice is that you not calumniate other people's nature, but rather that you rectify yourselves. (Ibid., 106)

13. In the principles set forth by Mahaprabhu, I cannot find the principles of the Kshatriyas, Vaisyas, Shudras or Muslims. From His teachings, I understand that He adopted the highest standards from the principles of the seers, the Rishis. Following in His footsteps, we also will adopt this religion of the Bhagavata based on Brahminical moral principles. (*Patrāvalī*, vol. 1, page 27)

14. Our ultimate duty is to serve the residents of Vraja in their mood of separation after Krishna has parted for Mathura. (Ibid., 46)

15. The *Mahābhāgavata* knows that everyone is his guru; and that is why he is guru to the whole world. (Ibid., 58)

16. If I seek the path leading to the ultimate good, I must ignore the countless voices of popular wisdom and listen to that of the realized souls—the *śrauta-vāṇī*.
(Lecture, Asharh 22, 1333 Bengali era, 1926 AD)

17. The truly beneficial should also be pleasing.
(Lecture, Karttik 2, 1333)

18. A confidential devotee is greedy for nothing but service to the followers of Rupa Goswami.
(*Sajjana-toṣaṇī*, 19.10, 380)

19. If, in order to carry out the orders of a Vaishnava guru, I must act arrogant or impolite, or even if I must go to hell for all eternity, I agree to sign the contract. I am arrogant enough to say that on the strength of my guru's lotus feet, I have the knock out punch for all of the world's spurious philosophies. (Lecture, Asharh 25, 1334 (1927))

20. Other than the ear, there is no route to a vision of the non-material Supreme Entity.
(Lecture, Phalgun 18, 1334)

21. Once we are bereft of a protector, everything around us will turn into a hostile force ready to attack. Our only protection is the Hari katha of a genuine saintly person.(Ibid.)

22. A flatterer is neither a guru nor a preacher.
(Lecture, Chaitra 12, 1334)

23. Better to take birth as an animal or bird, a worm or an insect, rather than be a hypocrite. Only one who is free from hypocrisy can attain auspiciousness.
(Lecture, Phalgun 18, 1334)

24. Simplicity by another name is Vaishnavism. The servants of a Vaishnava on the highest platform of realization are unpretentious. This means that they are the best of Brahmins. (Ibid.)

25. The most charitable person considers it his only duty to reform the misleading tastes and tendencies of the conditioned souls. If one single person can be rescued from Mahāmāyā's fortress, then we will have done a charitable work of more importance than opening a hundred million hospitals. (Ibid.)

26. Every selfless welfare worker in the Gaudiya Math should be prepared to expend 200 gallons of his own blood to nourish the spiritual body of every person in this human society. (Chaitra 12, 1335)

27. The Gaudiya Math's volunteer workers struggle with great effort from dawn to dusk to collect money. Every last farthing of this money is used for the satisfaction of Krishna's senses, and thus brings an end to material sense gratification which, based on an error, is a source of suffering. (Ibid.)

28. Those whose tendency to serve the Supreme Lord is not constantly awakened before one who knows the self are not desirable company, however pleasing their association may be. (*Patrāvalī*, Vol. 1, 73)

29. Preaching which is not backed up with practice should be considered to be nothing more than an aspect of karma.
(Speech, Oct. 23, 1936)

30. We have not established the Math to provide fuel for the sense-enjoyer or material for the philosopher to cleverly speculate on. Our assets are not measured in the one or two rupees we collect for the benefit of the Math. If we are able to do some real good for someone, then he or she will contribute to the Math which does everything for the service of Krishna. (*Patrāvalī*, 3, 70)

31. Srila Bhaktivinode Thakur identified himself as the sweeper in the marketplace of the Holy Name. This is a transcendental lila, and the work that takes place in cleaning up the material world has countless aspects in which

we are engaging our hundreds of followers. Though this and our refusal to imitate the undesirable example of non-devotees may make us unattractive to the worldly, it is through this work that our ultimate good will be achieved. (Introduction to *Gauḍīya-kaṇṭha-hāra*)

32. As one serves the Lord and his devotees, one's entanglement in family duties diminishes. (*Patrāvalī*, 3, 74)

33. Our basic disease is nothing but the accumulation of things devoid of any relation to Krishna. (Ibid., 83)

34. We have not come to this world to be brick-layers or carpenters; we have simply come to be Lord Chaitanya's menial servants. (Lecture, November 8, 1936)

35. We will not remain much longer in this world. If this body should drop while we are engaged in chanting the Holy Names, our life will have been worthwhile. (Ibid.)

36. The only thing we want in our life is the dust of the lotus feet of Rupa Goswami, who made the desires of Lord Chaitanya a reality on this earth. (Ibid.)

"BRINGING IN THE NEW YEAR"

The following is a translation of, *Hāyanodghāta*, the last article by Srila Prabhupada published in *Gauḍīya* magazine, in Vaishakh of 1936.

Gauḍīya magazine today enters its fifteenth year. For fourteen years, *Gauḍīya* has sung Goloka's incomparable glories just as Lakshman served Rama during his exile. May the readers and hearers of *Gauḍīya* find eternal ecstasy in joyfully relishing the fruits born by this fifteen-year-old tree. We ask that everyone join us in praying for Lord Gaurasundar's mercy so that *Gauḍīya's* message will soon spread to America. This message is being discussed in Europe, particularly in London, so why should America be left behind?

May Bhaktivinode Thakur's songs and transcendental literature, which contain the same essence as those of Narottam Das Thakur, be distributed in huge numbers throughout Bengal, Orissa and Assam. The translations of *Śaraṇāgati* into Tamil and *Caitanya-śikṣāmṛta* into Telugu will certainly help the people of those regions find direction to the highest spiritual truth.

May the Tridandi sannyasis of the Gaudiya Math bring joy to *Gauḍīya* magazine. May Gaudiyas in every stage of life find firm faith in the service of Lord Chaitanya.

pṛthivīte jata kathā dharma nāme cale
bhāgavata kahe tāhā paripūrṇa chale

Whatever is called religion in this world is said by the Bhagavatam to be a complete fraud.

May this statement become the standard by which religions all over the world be measured. May the world's intelligentsia come to adore *Jaiva Dharma* and *Sri Caitanya Śikṣāmṛta*. May they then raise the victory flag of the truly non-sectarian religion and learn that Sri Krishna Chaitanya, Harinam and the book Bhagavata are identical with each other. May the Bengali devotees along with the rest of the world's people hear, chant and study the Bhagavata. May this institution for Rupa Goswami's followers be eternally engaged in Chaitanya Mahaprabhu's service. May all fraudulent conclusions about spiritual life disappear like a fog from the heart of the human race with the rising of the sun of the Srimad Bhagavatam.

ARTICLES BY SRILA PRABHUPADA PUBLISHED IN GAUDIYA

YEAR I (1922-3):

Sri-kṛṣṇa-janma – "The birth of Krishna"
Madhura-lipi – "A sweet letter" (*)
Loka-vicāra – "Public opinion" (*)
Paramārtha – "The highest purpose"
Purāṇa-saṁvāda – "The message of the Puranas"
Nīti-bheda – "Ethical differences"
Ruci-bheda – "Differences in taste"
Sri Jīva Gosvāmī – "Sri Jiva Goswami"
Gauḍīye Prīti – "Affection for *Gauḍīya* magazine" (*)
Durgā-pūjā – "Durga puja"
Śāradīyā vāhana – "Durga's carrier" (*)
Je dike bātās – "Whichever way the wind blows"
Marute secana – "Drying in the wind"
Smārtera Kāṇḍa – "The tricks of the Smartas"
Vicāra Ādālata – "The courthouse"
Sevāpara Nāma – "The Name devoted to service"
Tridaṇḍi Bhikṣu Gīti – "The song of the Tridaṇḍi Sannyasi"
Sri Madhva Janma-tithi – "The appearance day of Madhvacharya"
Varṇāśrama – "Varnashram"
Aprakaṭa-tithi – "Disappearance Days"
Vraje Bānara – "Vraja's monkeys"
Sāmājika Bheda – "Social differences"
Cyuta-gotra – "The fallible family line"
Nṛmātrādhikāra – "The heritage of every human being"
Bhṛtaka-śrotā – "A hired audience"
Vaiṣṇava o abhṛtaka – "The Vaishnava and one not hired"
Dīkṣā-vidhāna – "Initiation regulations"
Āsurika pravṛtti – "Demonic tendencies"
Sri Baladeva Vidyābhūṣaṇa – "Sri Baladeva Vidyabhushan"
Sadācāra-smṛti – "Scriptures prescribing saintly behavior"
Pañcarātra – "The Pancharatra"
Nigama o āgama – "Vedic and Tantrik scriptures"
Viśvanātha Cakravartī – "Visvanath Chakravarti"
Vaiṣṇava darśana – "Vaishnava philosophy"
Varṇāntara – "Changing caste"
Paricaye praśna – "A question about identity"
Asatye ādara – "An attachment for untruth"
Ayogya santāna – "An unworthy son"
Aśūdra dīkṣā – "Initiation for non-Shudras"
Pūjādhikāra – "The right to perform deity worship"
Anātma-jñāna – "Knowledge of the non-self"
Nija paricaya – "One's own identity"
Vaṁśa-praṇālī – "Family disciplic lineages"
Gaura-bhajana – "Worshiping Mahaprabhu"

Dhānyā o Śyāmā – "Rice and wild rice"
Tṛtīya janma – "The third birth"
Avaidha sādhana – "Illegitimate practices"
Vaija-brāhmaṇa – "The Vaidya caste's claims to Brahminhood"
Pracāre bhrānti – "Mistakes in preaching"
Bhāgavata-śravaṇa – "Listening to the Bhagavata"
Math ki? – "What is a Math?"
Āche adhikāra – "We have the right"
Sridhar Swami – "Sridhar Svami"
Vyavahāra – "Behaviors and custom"
Kaminā – "Ignobility"
Śakti-sañcāra – "Finding the energy"
Varṣa-parīkṣā – "Annual exam"
Ekajāti – "One race"
Ihaloka Paraloka – "This world and the next"

SECOND YEAR, (1924-1925)

Varṣa-praveśa – "The new year"
Brahmaṇya-deva – "The Lord of Brahminical society"
Guru-bruva – "So-called spiritual masters"
Kīrtane vijñāna – "A scientific approach to chanting"
Āvirbhāva tithi – "Appearance days"
Mathera utsava – "Math festivals"
Gosvāmi-pāda – "Goswami status" (*)
Kṛṣṇe bhoga-buddhi – "The enjoyer mentality directed to Krishna"
Dīkṣita – "The initiated person"
Gauḍīya bhajana-praṇālī – "The process of performing bhajan in the Gaudiya sampradaya"
Sri-vigraha – "The divine form"
Jābālā katha – "The story of Jabala"
Smārta o Vaiṣṇava – "Smarta Brahmins and Vaishnavas"
Sāmājika ahita – "Unbeneficial acts to society"
Prakṛta bhoktā ke? – "Who is the real enjoyer?"
Gauḍīyera veṣa – "The Gaudiya dress"
Pratisambhāṣaṇa – "A speech in response to an honor"
Sūtra-vidveṣa – "Enmity of the Sutras"
Sāmayika-prasaṅga – "Essays on timely subjects"

(Nos. 42-4, 49-50)

THIRD YEAR (1924-1925):

Gauḍīya hāsapātāla – "Gaudiya hospitals"
Sāmāyika prasaṅga – "Essays on timely subjects" (No. 7)
Bhāgavata-vivṛti – "Explanations of the Bhagavatam"
Sri Kulaśekhara – "Sri Kulashekhar"
Meyeli Hinduwānī – "Effeminate Hinduism"

FOURTH YEAR (1925-1926):

Madhura lipi – "A sweet letter"
Sri Vyāsa-pūjā abhibhāṣaṇa–"Address on the occasion of Vyasa Puja"
Prāpta-pātra (rahasya) – "Receipt of a mysterious letter"
Aśrauta-darśana – "Philosophy without revelation"
Vedānta-tattva-sārer upodghāta – "Introduction to the *Vedānta-tattva-sāra*"

FIFTH YEAR (1926-1927)

Patrāvalī – Collected letters.
Darśane bhrānti – "Philosophical Errors"
Vaiṣṇava-śrāddha-vyavasthā – "Sraddha regulations for the Vaishnava"
Ālocaker ālocanā – "Criticizing the critics"
Nyākābokār svarūpa – "The description of a real simpleton"

SIXTH YEAR (1927-1928)

Māna-dāna o hāni – "Offering respects and its dangers"
Pratinivedana – "A counter-request"
Paramārtha – "The spiritual goal of life"
Gaudapur – "The city of Gauda"
Āsal o nakal – "Real and counterfeit"
Ahaituka dhāma-sevaka – "A selfless servant of the Dham"
Sarva-pradhān vivecanār viṣay – "The most important thing to consider"
Bhāi Kutārkik – "Brother quibbler"
Kṛṣṇa-bhakta nirbodh nahen – "A devotee of Krishna is not a fool"
Prācīn Kuliyay śahar Navadvīp – "The city of Nabadwip is in old Kuliya"
Kapaṭatā daridratār mūl – "The source of all poverty is deceitfulness"
Ekaścandra – "Ekashchandra" (*)
Puṇyāraṇya – "Punyaranya"
Goṛāy galad – "A basic error"
Nīlācale Srimad Satchitananda Bhaktivinode – "Bhaktivinode in Puri"

SEVENTH YEAR (1928-1929)

Sāmāyik prasaṅga – "A timely subject"
Virakta jaghanya nahe – "The renunciate is not contemptible"
Āmi ei nai, āmi sei – "I am not this one, I am he"
Vyavasādārer kapaṭatā – "The duplicity of the merchants"
Haṁsajātir itihāsa – "The story of the swans"
Patrāvalī – "Letters"
Mantra-saṁskāra – "The sacrament of receiving the mantra" (*)
Bhoga o bhakti – "Sense enjoyment and devotional service"
Sunīti o durnīti – "Good and evil policies" (*)
Kṛṣṇa-tattva – "Krishna, the ultimate truth"
Sridhāma vicār – "Conclusions about the Holy Dham"
Ekāyana-śruti o tad-vidhān –"The Ekayana scriptures and their prescriptions"
Pratīcye Kārṣṇa sampradāya –"The school of devotion to Krishna in the West"
Vijñapti – "An announcement" (*)
Pañcarātra – "Pancharatra"
Nīlācale Srimad Bhaktivinode – "Bhaktivinode Thakur in Puri"
Tīrtha Pāṇḍharapur – "The holy site of Pandharpur (Maharasthra)"
Manikya bhāskar – [An article praising the king of Tripura
Vaiṣṇava-smṛti – "Scriptures governing the rules of Vaishnava behavior"
Mahānta Guru-tattva – "The doctrine of the highly elevated guru"
Boṣṭam Pārlāmeṇṭ – "The parliament of the so-called Vaishnavas
Alaukik Bhakta-caritra – "The transcendental life of a devotee saint"

EIGHTH YEAR (1929-1930)

Sridhāma Māyāpur kothāy? – "Where is Sridham Mayapur?"

Gauḍācale Sri Bhaktivinode – "Bhaktivinode Thakur in Bengal"
Sātvata o asātvata – "Sātvata devotees of Krishna and non-Sātvatas"
Bhārata o paramārtha – "The supreme goal of life and India" (*)
Paramārther svarūpa – "The nature of the supreme goal of life"
Patrāvalī – "Collected letters"
Vyāsa-pūjāya pratyabhibhāṣaṇa–"Speech in response to the Vyasa-puja offerings"
Prācīna Kuliyaya Dvārabheṭ – "Charging admission to Nabadwip's temples"
Śikṣaka o śikṣita – "The teacher and the taught"
Viṣayīr Kṛṣṇa-prema – "The ecstatic lecturer"
Āśramer veṣa – "The appropriate dress of the different stages of life"

NINTH YEAR (1930-1931)

Sri-bhakti-mārga – "The holy path of devotion"
Pāramārthik sammilanīr sabhāpatir abhibhāṣaṇa – "The presidential address at the spiritual Conference"
Bhava-rogīr Hāsapatāl – "A hospital for those with the material disease"
Jagabandhur Kṛṣṇānuśīlan – "Jagabandhu's way of serving Lord Krishna
Patrāvalī – "Collected letters"

TENTH YEAR (1931-1932)

Gauḍīya mahimā – "In praise of *Gauḍīya* magazine"
Patrāvalī – "Collected letters"
Sat-śikṣārthīr vivecya – "What every honest student should consider"
Nimbabhāskara – "Nimbarka"
Ajña o vijñer narma katha – "The conversation of a fool and a wise man"
Vaiṣṇava-vaṁśa – "The Vaishnava dynasty"
Vārṣika abhibhāṣaṇa – "Speech made at Madras on the occasion of the Vyasa Puja"
Kanph-ucor vicāra – "The philosophy of Confucius"
Patra – "A letter"

ELEVENTH YEAR (1932-1933)

Ekādaśa prārambhikā – "Entering the eleventh year of Gauḍīya"
Patrāvalī (1) – "Letters"
Vaiṣṇave jāti-buddhi – "Ascribing caste to a Vaiṣṇava"
Mādhukara bhaikṣya – "Begging from door to door"
Pradarśaker abhibhāṣaṇ – "The exhibitor's speech"
Patrāvalī (2) – Letters
Duṣṭi-vaiklavya – "Distress from wrongdoing"
Āmāra Kathā – "My message"
Sat-śikṣā pradarśinī – "The spiritual education exhibit"
Kṛṣṇa bhakti-i śoka-kāma-jāḍyāpahā – "Devotion to Krishna is the only way to get rid of suffering, desire and lethargy"
Kṛṣṇe matir astu – "May you always think of Krishna"

TWELFTH YEAR (1933-1934)

Kṛpāśīrvāda – "Merciful blessings"

THIRTEENTH YEAR (1934-1935)

Sva-para maṅgala – "Auspiciousness for oneself and for others"
Vaikuṇṭha o guṇa-jāta jagat – "The difference between Vaikuntha and the world born of nature's modes"
Bhogavāda o bhakti – "Hedonism and devotion"

FOURTEENTH YEAR (1935-1936)

Nava-varṣa – "The new year"
Patrāvalī – "Letters"
Baṛa āmi o bhāla āmi – "I am great and I am good"
Tad-vana vāstava-vastu – "The factual substance" (*)

FIFTEENTH YEAR (1936-1937)

Hāyanodghāta – "Bringing in the new year"
Patra – "A letter"

Other than these, Srila Prabhupada wrote many other articles, letters, autobiographical accounts, diaries, commentaries, explanations, books and literature. All of these have been preserved in the *Gauḍīya* head office. Srila Prabhupada also wrote many articles which were published in *Nadīyā Prakāśa* and *The Harmonist*.

MAGAZINES AND NEWSPAPERS FOUNDED BY PRABHUPADA

(1) *Sajjana-toṣaṇī* or *The Harmonist* – Srila Sarasvati Thakur restarted publication of this magazine in March of 1915 after Bhaktivinode Thakur's disappearance.
(2) *Gauḍīya* – a Bengali weekly published from the Calcutta Gaudiya Math, starting August 19, 1922.
(3) *Dainik Nadiyā Prakāś* – A Bengali daily published from Mayapur start ing March 1926. At first it appeared twice a week in English and Bengali editions. From February 29, 1928, however, it was made into a daily at Srila Prabhupada's wish.
(4) *Bhāgavata* – A Hindi monthly published from the Naimisharanya Paramahamsa Math, starting in 1931.
(5) *Kīrtana* – An Assamese monthly published from Goalpara Prapannashram, starting in 1932.
(6) *Paramārthī* – Orissan fortnightly, published from the Cuttack Satchitananda Gaudiya Math, starting in 1932.
(7) *Bṛhaspati* or *Scientific Indian* – A monthly in English and Bengali on astrological matters. First appeared in October, 1896.
(8) *Jyotirvid* – A monthly magazine devoted to astrological matters. Published from Manik Tola Street in Calcutta. The first issue came out in April, 1901.
(9) *Nivedana* or *Signboard* – A weekly published starting in 1899.

PRINTING PRESSES ESTABLISHED BY SRILA PRABHUPADA

(1) Bhagavata Yantra, Krishnanagar – In 1913, Chaitanya Charitamrita was published here with Srila Prabhupada's *Anubhāṣya* commentary. In 1914, the Bhagavata Yantra was moved to Mayapur. It was moved back to Gowari Krishnanagar in July of 1915.

(2) Gaudiya Printing Works, Calcutta. 1923.
(3) Nadia Prakash Yantralaya, Sri Dham Mayapur, 1928.
(4) Paramarthi Printing Works, Cuttack, 1936.

MATHS AND PREACHING CENTERS ESTABLISHED BY SRILA PRABHUPADA

(1) Sri Chaitanya Math, Sridham Mayapur, Nadia.
(2) Sri Gaudiya Math, P.O. Bagh Bazaar, Calcutta.
(3) Sri Yoga Pith Mandir, Sridham Mayapur, Nadia.
(4) Advaita Bhavan, Sridham Mayapur, Nadia.
(5) Srivasa Angan, Sridham Mayapur, Nadia.
(6) Chand Kazi's Samadhi, Sridham Mayapur, Nadia.
(7) Sri Murari Gupta's Sripat, Sridham Mayapur, Nadia.
(8) Paravidyapith, Sridham Mayapur, Nadia.
(9) Thakur Bhaktivinode Institute, Sridham Mayapur, Nadia, 1931.
(10) Thakur Bhaktivinode Research Institute, Sridham Mayapur, Nadia, 1931.
(11) Jayadeva Gaudiya Mathalaya. Srinathpur, Nadia.
(12) Svananda Sukhada Kunj. Godrum. P.O. Swarup Ganj, Nadia.
(13) Suvarṇa Bihar Gaudiya Math. Nadia.
(14) Sri Kunj Kutir. Krishnanagar, Nadia.
(15) Tetiya Kunj Kanan, P.O. Krishnanagar, Nadia.
(16) Sri Bhagavata Asan, Krishnanagar, Nadia.
(17) Sri Gaura Gadadhar Math. Champa Hati, P.O. Samudra Garh, Burdwan.
(18) Sri Modadrum Chatra, Maugachi, P.O. Jannagar, Burdwan.
(19) Sarvabhauma Gaudiya Mathalaya, Vidyanagar, Burdwan.
(20) Sri Rudradwip Gaudiya Math, P.O. Sri Mayapur, Nadia.
(21) Sri Ekayan Math, Govindapur, P.O. Hanskhali, Nadia.
(22) Sri Mahesh Pandit's Sripat, Kanthalpuli, P.O. Chakdaha, Nadia.
(23) Sri Madhva Gaudiya Math. Dhaka.
(24) Gopalji Math, Kamlapur, P.O. Dhaka.
(25) Sri Gadai Gauranga Math, Baliyati, P.O. Dhaka.
(26) Sri Jagannath Gaudiya Math, Bara Bazaar, P.O. Mymensingh.
(27) Amaljora Prapannashram Math, P.O. Rajbandh, Burdwan.
(28) Sri Chaitanya Gaudiya Math, Ḍumurkondā, P.O. Chirkunda, Manbhoom (Bihar).
(29) Sri Bhagavata Janananda Math, Chirulia, P.O. Basudevpur, Midnapore.
(30) Amarshi Gaudiya Math, P.O. Amarshi, Midnapore.
(31) Brahmanpara Prapannashram Math. Brahmanpara, P.O. Maju, Howrah.
(32) Darjeeling Gaudiya Math, August Villa, Darjeeling.
(33) Ranaghat Gaudiya Mathasan, Nadia.
(34) Punra Sri Gaudiya Math, 24 Paraganas.
(35) Goalpara Prapannashram, Assam.
(36) Sarabhoga Gaudiya Math, P.O. Chakchaka, Kamrup (Assam).
(37) Sri Purushottam Math, Chatak Parvat, Puri.
(38) Bhakti Kuti, Swarga Dwar, Puri.
(39) Tridandi Gaudiya Math, P.O. Bhubaneshwar, Puri.
(40) Sri Brahma Gaudiya Math, Albar Nath, P.O. Brahmagiri, Puri.
(41) Satchitananda Math, Bansgali, P.O. Oriya Bazaar, Cuttack.
(42) Baleshwar Gaudiya Math Pith.
(43) Sri Ramananda Gaudiya Math, P.O. Kavoor, West Godavari.
(44) Madras Gaudiya Math, P.O. Raipetta, Madras.
(45) Patna Gaudiya Math, P.O. Bankipur, Kadamkua.
(46) Danapur Gaudiya Mathalaya.
(47) Gayā Gaudiya Math, Ramna Road, Gaya.
(48) Sri Sanatan Gaudiya Math, 42 Faridpur, Benares City, U.P.
(49) Sri Rupa Gaudiya Math, Allahabad, U.P.
(50) Sri Paramahamsa Math, P.O. Nimsar, Naimisharanya, Sitapur, U.P.
(51) Bhagavata Path Shala, Naimisharanya, U.P.
(52) Sri Vyasa Gaudiya Math, Kurukshetra, Thaneshwar, Karnal (H.P.)
(53) Sri Saraswata Gaudiya Math, Hardwar, Saharaṇapur, U.P.
(54) Sri Krishna Chaitanya Math, Purana Sahar, Sri Dham Vrindavan, Mathura, U.P.
(55) Sri Mathura Gaudiya Mathalaya, Vishram Ghat, Mathura, U.P.
(56) Sri Kunja Bihari Math, Radha Kund, Mathura, U.P.
(57) Sri Vraja Svananda Sukhada Kunj, Radha Kund, Mathura, U.P.
(58) Sri Radha Kund Gosthabati, Radha Kund, Mathura, U.P.
(59) Sri Sanketa Vihari Math, P.O. Varshana, Mathura, U.P.
(60) Sri Nandagram Gaudiya Mathalaya, Mathura, U.P.
(61) Barshana Gaudiya Mathalaya, Mathura, U.P.
(62) Sri Gosthavihari Math, Sesh Shayi, P.O. Hodol, Gurgaon (Punjab)
(63) Delhi Gaudiya Math, 43 Hanuman Road, New Delhi.
(64) Bombay Gaudiya Math, Kalyan Das Building, Gwalior Trunk Road.
(65) London Gaudiya Mathalaya, 3 Gloucester House, Cornwall Gardens, S.W.7, London.
(66) Rangoon Gaudiya Mathalaya, 224 Lewis St., Rangoon (Burma).

SHRINES TO MAHAPRABHU'S FEET ESTABLISHED BY SRILA PRABHUPADA

(1) Mandara. October 13, 1929.
(2) Kanair Natshala. October 15, 1929.
(3) Jajpur. December 25, 1930.
(4) Kurmakshetra. December 26, 1930.
(5) Singhachalam. December 27, 1930.
(6) Kavoor. December 29, 1930.
(7) Mangalagiri. December 31, 1930.
(8) Chatrabhoga. April 2, 1934.

OTHER PREACHING INSTITUTIONS FOUNDED BY SRILA PRABHUPADA

(1) Sri Bhaktivinode Asan, founded in Calcutta in November, 1918.
(2) Sri Vishva Vaishnava Raja Sabha, first established by Rupa and Sanatan Goswamis, and then reestablished on Febraury 5, 1919, in Calcutta.
(3) Sri Saraswata Asana, July 1924.
(4) Gauḍiya Sampadaka Saṅgha (The editorial board of *Gauḍīya*, August 15, 1925.
(5) Nikhila Vaishnava Sammilanī, March 18, 1927. This meeting of Vaishnavas was held annually on Gaura Purnima in Mayapur.
(6) Paramarthika Alochana Sammilanī. A nine-day meeting held at the Calcutta Gaudiya Math, starting October 24, 1930.
(7) London Gaudiya Mission Society. Established in London for preaching in Europe at a meeting on April 24, 1934, with India Secretary, Lord Jutland, presiding.
(8) Sri Vraja Dham Pracharini Sabha. ("Society for the Promotion of Vraja Dham") Established October 9, 1935 at Radha Kund.
(9) Bhaktivinode Research Institute. Founded at Mayapur on February 12, 1936.
(10) Daiva Varnashram Sangha. ("Association for Promoting the Spiritual Varnashram Social System"). Established at Mayapur on February 12, 1936.

SPIRITUAL DIORAMA EXHIBITIONS

(1) Kurukshetra Gaudiya Pradarshani. Opened on November 4, 1928.
(2) Sri Dham Mayapur-Navadwip Pradarshani. February 9, 1930.
(3) Calcutta Gaudiya Math Paramarthika Pradarshani. November 5, 1930.
(4) Calcutta Gaudiya Math Sat-siksha Pradarshani. September 6, 1931.
(5) Dhaka Sat-siksha Pradarshani. January 6, 1933.
(6) Kurukshetra Gaudiya Pradarshani. August 21, 1933.
(7) Patna Paramarthika Pradarshani. November 14, 1933.
(8) Kashi Paramarthika Pradarshani. December 24, 1933.
(9) Prayag Sat-siksha Pradarshani. January 7, 1936.
(10) Kurukshetra Sat-siksha Pradarshani. June 19, 1936.

SRILA BHAKTI DAYITA MADHAVA GOSWAMI MAHARAJ

nama oṁ viṣṇupādāya rūpānuga-priyāya ca
śrīmate bhakti-dayita-mādhava-gosvāmi-nāmine

Obeisances to Srila Bhakti Dayita Madhava Goswami Maharaj, the representative of Lord Vishnu and one who is dear to the followers of Rupa Goswami.

kṛṣṇābhinna-prakāśa-śrī-mūrtaye dīna-tāriṇe
kṣamā-guṇāvatārāya gurave prabhave namaḥ

Obeisances to you, Lord and guru, who are the personification of the quality of forgiveness, who [as guru] are the manifestation of Krishna meant to deliver the most fallen.

satīrtha-prīti-saddharma-guru-prīti-pradarśine
īśodyāna-prabhāvasya prakāśakāya te namaḥ

Obeisances to you, whose religious principle is to act on your affection for your guru and your godbrothers, for which you revealed the spiritual power of the Lord's Garden (Ishodyan) in Mayapur.

śrī-kṣetre prabhupādasya sthānoddhāra-sukīrtaye
sārasvata-gaṇānanda-saṁvardhanāya te namaḥ

Obeisances to you, who increased the joy of those devoted to Srila Bhaktisiddhanta Saraswati Goswami Thakur by recovering his birthplace in Puri, for which you are justly renowned.

śrī-bhakti-dayitaṁ nāmācārya-varyaṁ jagad-gurum
vande śrī-mādhavaṁ deva-gosvāmi-pravaraṁ prabhum

I worship my lord, Srila Bhakti Dayita Madhava Goswami Maharaj, teacher of the Holy Name and spiritual master to the universe.

APPEARANCE OF BHAKTI DAYITA MADHAVA GOSWAMI MAHARAJ

Tenth in the preceptorial line from Sri Krishna Chaitanya, Paramahamsa Parivrajakacharya Om 108 Sri Srimad Bhakti Dayita Madhava Goswami Maharaj Vishnupada, one of the dearest associates of Prabhupada 108 Sri Srila Bhaktisiddhanta Saraswati Goswami Thakur, the founder of the Chaitanya Math and Gaudiya Maths throughout the world, was himself the founder of the Chaitanya Gaudiya Math throughout India and my own spiritual master. He appeared in this world at 8:00 A.M. on Friday, Agrahayan 3, 1311 (Bengali), or November 18, 1904, Utthan Ekadasi, in the village of Kanchanpara in the Madarīpur subdivision of Faridpur district in East Bengal.

Utthan Ekadasi is the tithi that marks the end of the Chaturmasya period, when Vishnu wakes up from his four-month long sleep. It is thus a day that brings joy and auspiciousness to the world. Similarly, the appearance on that tithi of the most compassionate dear associate of Lord Hari, our most worshipable Srila Bhakti Dayita Madhava Goswami Maharaj, had the effect of bringing joy and good fortune to the world's conditioned souls who are suffering from the three-fold miseries. It is also significant that our *parameṣṭhī-guru*, the incarnation of extreme renunciation, Paramahamsa Vaishnava Srila Gaura Kishor Das Babaji, entered the eternal pastimes on this same tithi.

GURUDEVA'S BIRTHPLACE AND FAMILY

Kanchanpara village is in a pure and beautiful area on the banks of the Padma near its mouths in the precinct of Bhedara Ganj. The Padma River is sometimes called the Kirtinasha River, "the river that destroys all glories," because its annual flooding washes away so many villages and towns. Further upstream, however, there is a place called Prema Tali where Nityananda Prabhu once bathed, depositing divine love of God there for Narottam Das Thakur.

The village was prosperous and home to a large number of Brahmins. It was also the residence of my gurudeva's maternal uncles, who were of a prominent wealthy family in the area. Though they were talukdars or subsidiary landholders, they were given respect equal to that of zamindars. The British rulers of the day decorated them with the title "*Rāja-cakravartī*"; thus, although the family name was Bandyopadhyaya, their home came to be known as "Chakravarti Bari." The village is known to Madhava Maharaj's disciples as "Gurudeva's *mātulālaya*."

The following is known about Srila Gurudeva's paternal family. His grandfather's name was Chandra Prasad Devasharma Bandyopadhyaya, his father, Nishikanta. They lived in the village of Bharakar in the precinct of Tangibari in the Bikrampur subdivision of Dhaka district. Both Srila Gurudeva's father and grandfather were well known in the district as pious men. Srila Gurudeva's mother, Shaibalini Devi, was an extremely devoted woman who dedicated herself to the service of God, the Brahmins and holy men.

Srila Gurudeva lost his father at the age of four, after which his mother took him and returned to her brothers' home which is where he was raised. His uncles' great affection for him played an important part in his upbringing. The name given him by his father was Sri Heramba Kumar Bandyopadhyaya, but he was popularly known by his nickname Ganesh.

GURU MAHARAJ'S CHILDHOOD

Srila Gurudeva began to display extraordinary qualities from a very early age. Under no circumstances would he tell a lie. He would furthermore explain the moral value of truthfulness to his friends and companions. Everyone was impressed by the young lad's character.

Even when very young, Srila Gurudeva showed little interest in material enjoyments. He distinguished himself from the other children by his desire to lead an orderly and disciplined life. He not only set an example in this way, but encouraged the other children to do the same. He always tried to alleviate the sufferings of others and bring them happiness, even if it meant undergoing some difficulty himself. People who observed the extent of his generosity and wisdom were convinced that he would grow up to become a man of extraordinary virtue.

I personally heard from Srila Gurudeva's mother that whenever she gave him some special delicacy or sweet, he would only eat whatever was left after he had called his friends and distributed it amongst them.

At school, his teachers were astonished to hear Srila Gurudeva say things that showed a level of wisdom beyond his years. The following story can serve as an example: One day, he and some of his fellow students were playing the way boys of that age do. They were engaged in various competitions of speed and strength, including a running race. Srila Gurudeva was a good runner and quickly took the lead, but tripped on a root and fell with great force, causing him to bleed profusely. When the schoolteachers and other guardians heard what had happened, they rushed to the scene and applied medicines to his cuts and bruises. They also said many things to calm him, but he answered, "You need not worry on my account. I will get better soon. The Lord does everything for our good. I could have injured my eyes, ears or broken my nose, but nothing serious like that happened. I no doubt committed so many sins in previous lives that I should have suffered a more serious accident, but God is so merciful that he did not allow it to happen." When Srila Gurudeva's school teachers heard him say these things, they immediately realized that he was no ordinary child.

While in high school, Srila Gurudeva started a library for the benefit of his poorer classmates and lent books to them without cost. Throughout his youth, Srila Gurudeva was a natural leader as a result of his tall, handsome figure, his charismatic personality, his extraordinary honesty and patience. He never had to apply, or stand for election to leadership positions; wherever he chose to participate, others would unfailingly be impressed by his qualities and acclaim him as their leader. What is more, they were satisfied with his performance afterwards. In truth, leadership is the result of an individual's depth of character, exemplary behavior and competence. Tall and strong, Srila Gurudeva also excelled in sports and was regularly made captain of his teams. He also participated in dramatic presentations. There was no area in which he did not excell and thus he was always involved in directing the affairs of any group in which he participated. He even played a role in the independence movement.

BEGINNINGS OF A SPIRITUAL CALLING

Srila Gurudeva was exemplary in his devotion to his mother. She would read to him and have him read various scriptures to her, so that he became conversant with religious issues and imbued with faith in God. She made him read the Bhagavad Gita daily, so that by the age of eleven, he had memorized all of its 700 verses.

Srila Gurudeva finished his primary and secondary education in Kanchanpara and Bhatagram. Then for higher education he went to Calcutta. While in Calcutta he began to feel great separation from the Lord. He was staying with a relative and childhood friend named Narayan Chandra Mukhopadhyaya, who later took sannyas from him and was given the name Bodhayan Maharaj. Narayan Chandra recounted that he often saw Srila Gurudeva calling out the names of the Lord and crying in the middle of the night. He would eat only *haviṣyānna* (an unspiced khichuri) once a day. In this state of absorption in the Lord, he one day had a dream in which Narada Muni came to reassure him. Narada gave him a mantra and told him that by chanting it he would achieve all perfection. Upon awakening, however, try as he might Srila Gurudeva was unable to recall the mantra in its entirety. The loss of this mantra bewildered and distressed him immeasurably. His irritation with household life reached an intolerable degree and he became determined to leave it behind. With this in mind, he went to ask the blessings of his widowed mother who at that time was living in Gosain Durgapur in Nadia district. She made no effort to oppose his wishes. So, with an intense desire to have the company of the Supreme Lord, Srila Gurudeva set off for the Himalayas. Just as iron filings attracted by a magnetic force cannot be thwarted, the individual soul who has been attracted to the Supreme Soul allows nothing of this world, whether friends or family, to interfere with his calling.

SRILA GURUDEVA GOES TO HARDWAR

Srila Gurudeva's passionate desire for the Lord brought him first to Hardwar and from there into the mountains. High up in the Himalayan jungle, he fasted for three days from food and water, all the time calling out anxiously to the Lord. When he had practically lost all awareness of the external world, he was given a divine order to seek out a spiritual master. He was also told that his guru would appear to him in the very place that he had left.

Taking the divine order as his imperative, Srila Gurudeva came down from the mountain to the holy town of Hardwar on the banks of the Ganges, where he decided to stay for a few days. While there, he met a saintly person to whom he recounted all that had happened on the mountain. When he asked this sadhu for advice, he was told to return home and that he would meet a bonafide spiritual master there.

Srila Gurudeva made up his mind that he would return to Calcutta after spending a few more days in the pilgrimage town, but his stay in Hardwar was disturbed when a rich businessman and his wife from North India came there on pilgrimage. The couple, which was childless, saw the handsome figure of Srila Gurudeva when bathing in Brahma Kund, and was attracted to him. They gave him a gift of fruit and sweets and insisted that he visit them in their lodgings. Out of courtesy, Srila Gurudeva acceded to their request.

At their place of residence, the couple once again fed him copiously and generally treated him with great affection. Finally, they proposed that he become their adopted son, which meant that he would eventually inherit their substantial wealth. Srila Gurudeva was unprepared for such an offer and began to think, "I came here with the intention of abandoning family life. Now Maya has devised another way to ensnare me."

Srila Gurudeva politely refused their proposal and left their home, but the businessman and his wife were so enamored of him that they came each day and repeatedly put pressure on him to accept their offer. One who has a sincere eagerness to attain to the Supreme Lord, however, cannot be swayed by any amount of material temptation. Someone filled with desires for sense enjoyment would have found it impossible to resist such an opportunity to become heir to a fortune, but Srila Gurudeva had no such yearnings. Because of his sincere aspiration to worship the Lord, he considered the couple's invitation to be dangerous and rejected it out of hand. Consequently, he found it impossible to remain in Hardwar and returned to Calcutta without any further delay. These events took place sometime around 1925.

SRILA GURUDEVA MEETS SRILA PRABHUPADA

That same year, Srila Gurudeva came to visit Mayapur for the first time with Narayan Chandra Mukhopadhyaya and some other friends. When they saw Srila Bhaktisiddhanta Saraswati Goswami Thakur, they were attracted by his superhuman personality. During a lecture they attended, Srila Prabhupada said that it was alright to visit the deity form in the temple, but that one had to learn to see it first. One cannot really see it with eyes that are blinded by material desire, but only with the eyes of love. Srila Gurudeva and his party watched on that same day as Srila Prabhupada initiated Dr. S.N. Ghosh and his wife.

After returning to Calcutta, Srila Gurudeva started visiting the Gaudiya Math on Ultadanga Road to hear Srila Prabhupada speak Hari katha. Understanding that through service to the Vaishnavas one could clear the road to the Lord and receive his mercy, or perhaps wishing to teach that same principle to the world, Srila Gurudeva sent much money and material for the Math without any fanfare. During this period, he also spent much of his time in studying the scriptures.

After hearing the Vaishnava doctrines from Srila Prabhupada, he became convinced of their rationality and superiority over other religious dogmas. He took shelter of Srila Prabhupada and on September 4, 1927, on Radhashtami, received initiation in the Holy Name and the mantra at the Ultadanga Math. After initiation he was known as Hayagriva Das Brahmachari. Acharya Das Deva Sharma was the officiating priest at the Vaishnava fire sacrifice.

LIFE AND SERVICE IN THE GAUDIYA MATH

Not long after being initiated, Srila Gurudeva decided to commit himself completely to the service of Krishna and His devotees by moving into the Math. He thus took the great vow of remaining a lifelong celibate or *naiṣṭhika-brahmacārī*. It was not long before Srila Gurudeva was counted amongst Srila Prabhupada's leading disciples as a result of his dedicated service to his guru, unflagging enthusiasm and competence in a variety of services. Srila Prabhupada used the words "volcanic energy" to describe Srila Gurudeva's unflinching resolve, application and success in all endeavors entrusted to him.

Srila Gurudeva was one of the leading collectors, whose service was essential for maintaining Srila Prabhupada's vast movement and especially the efforts made toward preaching Mahaprabhu's message in the West. Anyone who saw Srila Gurudeva's golden form and heard him speak Hari katha could not fail to be attracted. Many people came forth spontaneously and made donations to him.

On Srila Prabhupada's order, Srila Gurudeva spent a long time at the Madras Gaudiya Math, where he was chiefly responsible for the purchase of land and construction of the temple, nat mandir and residences. During this time he was particularly encouraged by his senior godbrothers, H. H. Bhakti Rakshaka Sridhar Maharaj and H. H. Bhakti Hridoy Bon Maharaj. In the course of collecting funds for this project, Srila Gurudeva met with the leading citizens of Madras and became closely acquainted with many of them.

SRILA PRABHUPADA'S ADVANCE MAN

In order to awaken consciousness of the Lord amongst the people at large, Srila Prabhupada travelled to Calcutta, Dhaka, Patna, Allahabad, Benares and other important places throughout India. He organized preaching festivals as well as parikramas of Vraja and Nabadwip Dhams, established preaching centres and Maths, spreading the message of Sri Chaitanya Mahaprabhu in various cities, putting on programs and sending out street sankirtan parties. He also established shrines of Mahaprabhu's feet (*pāda-pīṭhas*) in many of the places the Lord had visited, restored other holy sites, published transcendental books, magazines and newspapers in a variety of languages in order to spread the message of pure devotion. Srila Gurudeva was a leading participant in all of these preaching programs.

Srila Prabhupada generally sent Srila Gurudeva as the advance man to do groundwork for these events. He had complete faith that whatever task he gave him would be carried out to completion. Srila Gurudeva was one of the principle devotees charged with building the Ramananda Gaudiya Math in memory of Mahaprabhu's intimate associate Ramananda Ray. He was involved in purchasing land in Andhra Pradesh, near Goshpad Tirtha in Rajahmundry district, where Ramananda's meeting with Lord Chaitanya took place, and supervising the construction of the buildings.

Anyone, no matter how important a person, who met Srila Gurudeva—with his handsome features and imposing physique, pleasant manner, extraordinary personality, facility with modern reasoning and ability to convince by means of irrefutable scriptural evidence—would become enchanted and quite happy to do anything requested of him. Srila Gurudeva's entire being—his meditation, his thoughts, his japa, everything—was fully devoted to fulfilling Srila Prabhupada's desires. Today's volunteer workers cannot even imagine the extent of his commitment to service, for which he gave up eating and sleeping, working through the night if necessary to achieve his goals.

Srila Gurudeva's sincere, single-minded allegiance to his spiritual master is an example to be followed by everyone. He never undertook any task without the express direction of his spiritual master. As a result of his full surrender to Srila Prabhupada's lotus feet, he came to inherit his divine potency for spreading Lord Chaitanya's mission in its entirety.

SRILA PRABHUPADA'S VISIT TO ASSAM

We can know the degree to which Srila Prabhupada trusted Srila Gurudeva and considered him to be a responsible servant and intimate associate from comments he made in March of 1936, on the occasion of the installation of Sri-Sri-Guru-Gauranga-Gandharvika-Giridhara deities at the Sarbhog (Assam) Gaudiya Math.

The Sarbhog Gaudiya Math in Assam's Kamrup district, near Barpeta was one of the 64 Maths and preaching centres established during Srila Prabhupada's lifetime. Srila Prabhupada sent Srila Gurudeva along with his senior godbrother, H. H. Bhakti Rakshaka Sridhar Maharaj, Janaki Vallabha Das Brahmachari and others to make preparations for the Deity installation ceremony. At that time, the Math was under the direction of Srila Gurudeva's senior godbrother, H. H. Tridandi Swami Bhakti Vijnan Ashram Maharaj. Srila Gurudeva's party arrived in Sarbhog only a few days before the festival date and was shocked to find that little or nothing had been done in preparation for Srila Prabhupada's coming and the installation of the Deities.

Srila Gurudeva's nature was such that he would never lose enthusiasm or stop working until his desired goals were achieved. He immediately brought all his efforts to bear on finding temporary quarters for Srila Prabhupada and the other devotees who would be coming with him.

When Srila Prabhupada arrived at the Sarbhog rail station at 6:30 AM on Sunday, March 15, 1936, he was greeted by a large party of devotees and local citizens. Noteworthy amongst those who accompanied him were Kunja Bihari Vidyabhushan Prabhu, Paramananda Vidyaratna Prabhu, Vasudeva Prabhu, Kirtanananda Brahmachari, Sajjana Maharaj, and Krishna Keshava Brahmachari. On each of the three days that Srila Prabhupada remained in Sarbhog, thousands of men, women and children were satisfied with varieties of maha prasad.

On the following day, Srila Prabhupada ordered Tridandi Swami Bhakti Rakshaka Sridhar Maharaj to make the final arrangements for Sri-Sri-Guru-Gauranga-Gandharvika-Giridhara's installation rituals, over which he was to officiate. As a part of these arrangements, Sridhar Maharaj dressed the deities and decorated them with flower garlands and other ornaments. At the auspicious moment at 10 o'clock in the morning, upon being told that everything was ready, Srila Prabhupada entered the temple room, took darshan of the garlanded deities and paid his prostrated obeisances to them. On seeing that they were already decorated, he said, "The deities have already been installed." On hearing this, Sridhar Maharaj immediately became remorseful, thinking that he had committed an offense by doing something that Srila Prabhupada had intended to do himself. Despite his faux pas, the installation of the deities was performed in great splendor according to the regulations of the Vaishnava Smritis and in the midst of joyous sankirtan.

At the end of the installation ceremony, Ashram Maharaj repeatedly asked Srila Gurudeva to tell Srila Prabhupada that Nimananda Brahmachari had not carried out his duties. Srila Gurudeva was reluctant to do anything that would be displeasing to Srila Prabhupada, and so at first refused. Upon being pressed, however, he felt obliged to do as he was asked out of respect for his senior godbrother.

Later that day, Srila Gurudeva followed Srila Prabhupada when he went out for a walk, fanning him to keep insects away. As they were talking, he told Prabhupada of Ashram Maharaj's complaint. As soon as Srila Prabhupada heard it, he became angry and chastised Srila Gurudeva who felt extremely sorry at having displeased him. Srila Prabhupada, however, seeing the effect his words had on Srila Gurudeva, immediately changed his mood and began to praise him affectionately. Srila Gurudeva was not happy at hearing such praise, either, because he took it to mean that Srila Prabhupada felt he would not be able to take criticism. However, Srila Prabhupada took the opportunity to give him many valuable personal instructions that showed the extent to which he held his disciple dear.

Srila Prabhupada first said, "Why do you want so much? And why do you let it bother you that much? It is not proper to expect so much service from this person. Your service to your spiritual master and all its details are your responsibility alone. You should be grateful if anyone else contributes to it in any way. Krishna's 'major domo' is Srimati Radhika. She knows that she alone is entirely responsible for Krishna's pleasure. If anyone comes forward to help her, she is filled with gratitude."

Here, it is apparent that Srila Prabhupada was saying that it was up to Srila Gurudeva to take full responsibility for his service in its entirety. If anyone should assist him in the fulfilment of that responsibility, he should be grateful. From this statement it is clear that Srila Prabhupada considered him to be a confidential associate. Because of this affectionate relationship and the physical similarity of Srila Gurudeva to the tall, light-skinned Srila Prabhupada, people often mistook him to be his son.

Srila Gurudeva often recounted the story of the Sarbhog Gaudiya Math when he wished to give an example of the process of surrender to his disciples. We have already stated that Srila Sridhar Maharaj humbly felt as though he had committed an offense for having garlanded the deities in the place of Srila Prabhupada. Sridhar Maharaj asked Srila Gurudeva to approach Srila Prabhupada and ask him for forgiveness on his behalf, that he made the mistake unintentionally. Having been so entreated by Sridhar Maharaj, Srila Gurudeva wrote a letter to Srila Prabhupada in which he prayed for forgiveness on Sridhar Maharaj's behalf. Prabhupada answered that a surrendered soul never commits offenses. The Lord never sees the faults of one who is surrendered to him, always forgiving him, for the surrendered person has given up everything for the service of the Lord without any ulterior motive. On the other hand, someone who has ulterior motives and is not surrendered must fear offenses at every moment.

SRILA GURUDEVA DOES NOT GO TO ENGLAND

Srila Prabhupada was eager to preach Mahaprabhu's message in the western world and had chosen Srila Gurudeva as one of his missionaries because of his competence. He and two other godbrothers had their photos taken and passports made in preparation for the trip. When everything was ready, Rajarshi Saradindu Narayan Ray said to Srila Prabhupada, "England is a land full of heavenly nymphs. I don't think it is a good idea to send handsome young men there to preach. It would be better to send a more mature disciple."

Srila Prabhupada thought the Rajarshi's suggestion had merit and so decided to send H. H. Bhakti Pradip Tirtha Maharaj in Srila Gurudeva's place. He gave Srila Gurudeva the responsibility of collecting money for the preaching mission.

Srila Gurudeva was afraid that Srila Prabhupada would not remain in the world much longer and had been worried that if sent to England he may never see him again. He was thus relieved when Srila Prabhupada changed his mind about sending him there on the Rajarshi's advice.

MEETING WITH PANCHANAN TARKARATNA

Srila Prabhupada recognized that Srila Gurudeva possessed a great talent for persuading others with his humble and respectful manner of defeating their arguments. As a result, on October 4, 1936, he decided to send him to Bengal's leading religious scholar, Panchanan Tarkaratna of Bhattapara in Naihati. Panchanan Tarkaratna was very proud of being a Brahmin and a learned scholar and had forcefully criticized the Daiva Varnashram system preached by Srila Prabhupada. Srila

Prabhupada was afraid that his criticisms could cause untold harm to countless people seeking the ultimate good and thus gave Srila Gurudeva the responsibility of trying to change his opinion. Panchanan Tarkaratna was reluctant to give proper respect to anyone not born in the Brahmin caste. For this reason, Srila Prabhupada told Gurudeva to go without tilaka or Vaishnava dress and give his identity as a high-caste Brahmin.

On the given day, at 8:30 in the morning, Srila Gurudeva came to Panchanan Tarkaratna's house accompanied by Praphulla Candra Chattopadhyaya of Naihati's Kanthalpara. He first met with the pandit's highly qualified son, Sri Jiva Nyayatirtha, and then spent two hours in scriptural discussions with him. Srila Gurudeva often recounted the experience that he had to his disciples: "It is true that Panchanan Tarkaratna possessed vast learning. He had memorized large numbers of verses from scripture, but in some cases was not able to come to logical conclusions or to resolve contradictions. In his arguments he would go down a blind alley and not be able to give a proper answer when questioned."

When asked how such a great scholar could end up this way, Srila Gurudeva would answer, "Pandit Mahashaya had never had the opportunity to associate with a pure devotee or a real saintly person. Only by following a pure devotee or through associating with saintly persons can one arrive at the right conclusions."

Srila Gurudeva's long conversation with Panchanan Tarkaratna resulted in an article that headlined the *Gauḍīya*, the Math's Bengali weekly, 15.13-15 (1936).

SRILA GURUDEVA MEETS DR. C.V. RAMAN

The following events took place in 1930 while Srila Prabhupada was still present. A month-long festival was being held at the Calcutta Bagh Bazaar Gaudiya Math for Janmashtami. Each day a different dignitary was invited to sit as honorary chairman of the evening meeting. Some students of world-renowned scientist C.V. Raman were amongst those who came regularly to listen to the lectures of the Gaudiya Math preachers. One day, these students came to see Srila Prabhupada and complained that every day a different distinguished person was being made honorary chairman, but their professor, whose fame had spread throughout the world, had not even been invited.

Srila Prabhupada answered that he had no objection to making Dr. Raman honorary chairman one evening. He asked Srila Gurudeva to take charge of inviting him. Srila Gurudeva first went to Dr. Raman's house but did not find him there. The scientist's wife sent him with an orderly to Dr. Raman's laboratory on Circular Road. There, Srila Gurudeva met with him on the second floor where he was sitting in a corner of a huge loft, engaged in his research activity. Dr. Raman spoke neither Bengali nor Hindi and so their conversation took place in English.

Upon being asked by Dr. Raman the reason for his coming, Srila Gurudeva answered, "A large month-long religious gathering is being held by the Bagh Bazaar Gaudiya Math at Janmashtami. On each day, a different dignitary of the city is invited to grace the chairman's seat, and we humbly invite you to do the same."

Dr. Raman answered, "I do not believe in your Keshto-Bishtu. I have no faith in anything that cannot be confirmed by direct sensory experience. I cannot waste my valuable time with imaginary things. I would gladly attend any conference dealing with science or education, but not a religious one."

Srila Gurudeva said, "Your own students have been coming regularly to listen to the Math's swamijis speak. It was their desire that you be honored in the same way that so many other Calcutta community leaders have been. I have been asked by my Gurudeva to invite you, so please accept our invitation."

Dr. Raman then challenged Srila Gurudeva: "Can you show me your God? If you can show him to me, I will go."

One side of the lab room in which the conversation was being held was a windowless, doorless wall, on the other side of which lay the whole of north Calcutta. Srila Gurudeva asked, "I can see nothing on the other side of this wall, but if I say that there is nothing there, will that be true?"

Dr. Raman answered, "Perhaps you cannot see what is there, but you could with the appropriate instruments."

Srila Gurudeva then asked him, "There is a limit to what your instruments can do. You can only see as far as they allow you. Can you say that there is nothing beyond these limits?"

Dr. Raman replied, "Never mind. I will not waste my time on this. I will not give my attention to anything that is not within my sense experience. I will only spare my valuable time if you can actually show me your God. Can you do it?"

Srila Gurudeva: "If your students were to say to you that they will study your scientific findings only if you can show them the truth of what you have realized through your experiments, what would you say?"

Dr. Raman: "I would make them realize it!"

Srila Gurudeva: "Can you make them realized before teaching them?"

Dr. Raman: "No, I would first have to show them the process by which I have come to realize the truth. They will have to follow that process if they want to have the same realization. First they will have to earn their B.Sc. degree, then their M.Sc. Then they will have to study with me for another five years. Then I will be able to make them understand."

Srila Gurudeva: "If this is true for you and your scientific knowledge, then can the seers of ancient India not say exactly the same thing? Follow their process and see whether you experience God's existence or not. You are not able to show the scientific truths you profess to your students until they have adopted your process. Similarly, if you want to experience or understand God, you have to follow the process by which that is accomplished. If it does not happen, then you can deny its value. But how can you deny its value without having experimented?"

Dr. Raman could not answer. After a few moments of silence, he said, "I know nothing about Krishna. If I go, I will be able to say nothing. You would be better off inviting someone who knows something about these matters."

Srila Gurudeva's quick-wittedness and presence of mind was such that it was impossible to get away with an illogical statement in his presence. Such capacity does not come with simple book-learning. Only one who has surrendered himself to his spiritual master and has come to direct realization of the truth through his mercy can display such divine power. To such a person, a display of intelligence without any basis in realization cannot get very far.

AFTER THE DISAPPEARANCE OF SRILA PRABHUPADA

Srila Prabhupada instructed all of his disciples to follow him in preaching the message of Sri Rupa and Raghunath Goswamis, and that they should work together to achieve this one purpose. From the superficial point of view of a short-sighted pessimist, the events that followed Srila Prabhupada's disappearance seem to have contradicted his wishes, but whatever comes about as a result of the all-auspicious Lord Hari's desire is for the good of everyone. If we are unable to see the truth of this basic tenet of spiritual life we become incapable of recognizing the order which exists in creation and become unhappy as a result. Nothing takes place contrary to the will of the Lord; one who believes that he is all-auspicious must also accept that whatever takes place is somehow directed toward the fulfilment of some larger, auspicious purpose. The short-sighted are only able to realize this after much water has flowed under the bridge.

Mahaprabhu said, "My name will be preached in every town and village throughout the world." In order to bring this prophecy to fruition, it was his will and that of his *prakāśa-mūrti*, Srila Prabhupada, who is non-different from him, that those leading disciples who had been enriched by their blessings should be inspired to work to that end independently. Srila Prabhupada did not wish that those worthy disciples of his who had attained the qualifications to act as acharya should be restricted or limited in their activities. As a result of their being empowered by him to spread Mahaprabhu's message, the movement has today been acknowledged and adopted by many persons throughout the world, fulfilling the Lord's prediction. If Prabhupada's disciples were ordinary flawed living beings who disregarded the wishes of their spiritual master, then such widespread successes would not have been possible. When those hapless people who are ignorant of the overall intention of the Supreme Lord praise one of Srila Prabhupada's disciples and condemn another, they fall from the path of spiritual life and into the mire of Vaishnava aparadh.

All of Srila Prabhupada's associates tried or are trying to sincerely follow his orders to the extent of their abilities. As a result of these sincere efforts, great numbers of wayward souls have been attracted to the teachings of Lord Chaitanya Mahaprabhu and have accepted the discipline of Vaishnava *sad-ācāra*. They have been engaged in the worship of Lord Krishna according to the doctrines of pure devotional service and have thus made their lives successful.

OPENING THE SHYAMANANDA GAUDIYA MATH

In 1942, just prior to taking the tridandi sannyas vows, Srila Gurudeva worked together with his godbrothers, particularly H. H. Tridandi Swami Bhakti Kumud Santa Maharaj and H. H. Tridandi Swami Bhakti Bichar Jajabar Maharaj, to establish a math in the city of Midnapore. This center was named the Shyamananda Gaudiya Math in honor of Shyamananda Prabhu who first preached Mahaprabhu's message in this area. As a result of the preaching efforts of these godbrothers, many men and women of the city became attracted to Mahaprabhu's message, took up the regulative principles of Vaishnava *sad-ācāra* and the path of devotional service as ordained by Sri Chaitanya. The Gaudiya Math's good name spread throughout the region and many wealthy citizens of Midnapore city took up the task of establishing a permanent branch there. With their help, land and a large two-storey building were purchased in the Shiva Bazaar area for the Math.

Srila Gurudeva told the story of how one of the chief donors, Govardhan Piri, came into contact with the Math and the amazing change in his life as he renounced all sinful activity to engage in the service of Krishna and the devotees. When Srila Gurudeva was in search of donations for the establishment of the Math, he suggested going to visit Govardhan Piri, but local people counselled him not to. They described him as a great miser who would not give a paisa to a poor person in need. They told Srila Gurudeva that if he went to see him, he was sure to be insulted.

Srila Gurudeva answered, "A sadhu shouldn't be bothered by the fear of insults, nor should he seek praise. If Govardhan Piri is a miser, then the sadhus should make an effort to see that he changes his ways. There is no need to change a good person. We can see the real results of preaching when bad people change and become good."

One day, Srila Gurudeva went to Govardhan Piri's office and was greeted cordially and given a suitable seat. When he heard from Srila Gurudeva that he was trying to open a preaching centre through which the ultimate good for the jivas could be achieved through spreading Sri Chaitanya Mahaprabhu's teachings, Govardhan Babu responded by saying that his family had worshiped Radha and Krishna for generations and that they continued to serve the deities in his home. He invited Srila Gurudeva to come to his rooftop temple and take darshan of them. Srila Gurudeva was very pleased to see the beautiful Radha Krishna deities and said, "Radha and Krishna are the object of our worship. As yet we have no deities in our preaching centre. We would be very grateful if you gave us these deities for our temple."

Govardhan Babu answered, "These are our family deities and they have a great deal of land in their name. It is impossible for us to part with them. However, if you want to purchase deities for your temple, I will pay the cost."

Srila Gurudeva told him that the Gaudiya Math always imported images of Radha and Krishna from Jaipur, but Govardhan Babu was not deterred and continued to agree to bear all the expenses. When Srila Gurudeva returned to the ashram and told his companions about Govardhan Babu's offer, they were all dumbfounded. Govardhan Babu paid not only for the deities, but for their service, their dress and ornaments, the installation ceremony and the feast which followed it. He also began coming regularly to hear Hari katha in the temple. In time, as a result of the association of devotees, he came to realize that materialistic life was without substance and gave up all sinful practices. Understanding that true happiness could only be found in worshiping the Lord, he took initiation in the Holy Name and the mantra and adopted a regulated Vaishnava life.

When the local people saw the amazing change in Govardhan Babu's behavior, they were astonished and overjoyed. One day his wife came to the Math and in an outburst of emotion, fell at Srila Gurudeva's feet and said, "Ever since you came, my husband has been returned to me. All our family problems have disappeared."

We cannot say how many people's lives were affected by coming into contact with Srila Gurudeva and having sweet dealings with him. This is only a single small example of how one person's life was completely changed.

SRILA GURUDEVA TAKES SANNYAS

Immediately prior to taking sannyas, Srila Gurudeva went on a preaching tour of Bankura and Midnapore districts, visiting Kether Danga, Onda, Jhanti Pahari, Bankura city, Gardevata, and other places. People everywhere were impressed by his personality, his upstanding character and his powerful Hari katha, and became attracted to the gospel of Lord Chaitanya Mahaprabhu. Accompanying him on this trip were Krishna Keshava Brahmachari, Rama Govinda Brahmachari, Kunjalal Prabhu, Hari Govinda Prabhu and other godbrothers. Helping the preaching work in Kether Danga and Onda were Radha Govinda Sit and Avinash Pal, respectively.

Although Srila Prabhupada had intended to give Srila Gurudeva Tridandi sannyas, he never did so because of the important role he played in fundraising. Not long after Srila Prabhupada's disappearance, however, a large group of Gurudeva's godbrothers appealed to him to take the renounced order. Amongst them were Kunja Bihari Vidyabhushan Prabhu, H. H. Bhakti Prakash Aranya Maharaj, H. H. Bhakti Sarvasva Giri Maharaj, H. H. Bhakti Svarupa Parvata Maharaj, H. H. Bhakti Prasun Bodhayan Maharaj, Krishna Keshava Brahmachari, and Sundar Gopal Brahmachari. They convinced him that if he wished to fully commit himself to the fulfillment of Srila Prabhupada's command to preach Mahaprabhu's message, it was incumbent on him to take sannyas. Thus, at the age of 40, he took sannyas according to the Vaishnava rituals from H. H. Bhakti Gaurava Vaikhanasa Maharaj on the grounds of the Tota Gopinath temple. It was the Phalguni Purnima of 1944, the 457th anniversary of Mahaprabhu's appearance. He was thenceforth known as Parivrajakacharya Tridandi Swami Srimad Bhakti Dayita Madhava Goswami Maharaj. Amongst the godbrothers present on that occasion were Kunja Bihari Vidyabhushan Prabhu, Paramananda Vidyaratna Prabhu, H. H. Parvat Maharaj, and H. H. Bodhayan Maharaj.

After taking sannyas, Srila Gurudeva returned to the Shyamananda Gaudiya Math in Midnapore where he was greeted with great pomp by the members of the Vishva Vaishnava Raja Sabha. The Vishva Vaishnava Raja Sabha presented him with a special certificate in which they praised him for the ways that he gave great joy to Srila Prabhupada—through his fearlessness, his saintly courage, his ability to enchant people when speaking on religious topics, and above all, his affection for the devotees.

Of all of Srila Gurudeva's virtues, his attachment to his spiritual master and his affection for his godbrothers were exemplary. After Srila Prabhupada's disappearance, whenever any of his godbrothers were faced with hardship, he would immediately step forward to give them a helping hand without considering his own happiness or distress. Many of Prabhupada's worthiest disciples were unable to come to terms with the turmoil in which the Math found itself after his disappearance and either returned to householder life or considered doing so. Srila Gurudeva took a lot of trouble to find such devotees, seeking them in their homes and persuading them to return to the Math and a life of service to the Lord. Some of those he brought back subsequently took the role of acharya!

Devotees are the worldly manifestation of Krishna; affection for them accurately demonstrates the extent of one's affection for Krishna. Similarly, the guru's disciples are the manifestations of the guru himself and affectionate behavior to them demonstrates the depth of one's love for the guru. Srila Gurudeva's exemplary love for his godbrothers was evident to the very last days of his presence in this world.

PREACHING ACTIVITIES IN EAST PAKISTAN

After Srila Gurudeva took sannyas, just prior to Indian independence (1947) and afterward, he went on an extended preaching tour throughout India and East Pakistan (modern Bangladesh). Accompanying him were Mihir Prabhu, Sankarshan Prabhu, Krishna Keshava Brahmachari, Trailokya Prabhu, Mahendra Prabhu, Sri Brahma, Pyari Mohan Brahmachari, Yajneshwar Das Babaji Maharaj, and others. Some of the important places he visited in Dhaka and Mymensingh districts were Baliyati, Nawabganj, Kalakopa village, Jamuki, Pakulla, and Churain.

While in Jamuki-Pakulla in Mymensingh district, Srila Gurudeva gave a lecture in a pandal set up at the local high school. He often talked about this event later. More than a thousand people of both Hindu and Muslim faiths were present in the audience that gathered that day. Many students and teachers from the school also came. Several local policemen gave Srila Gurudeva a friendly warning that following the partition of India and Pakistan, the situation was tense for Hindus in the Muslim-dominated country. He was told to be careful about what he said and did because the government was watching him. If complaints were made that something he said went against Pakistan's interests, he could be jailed. After having received this warning and seeing the large numbers of police officers present in the crowd, Srila Gurudeva started to worry about the difficulties a devotee would have to face if put in prison, where contact with untouchable foodstuffs would be inevitable. Seeking to avoid any possibility of trouble, he requested the listeners to save their questions for which he would leave fifteen to twenty minutes at the end of his discourse. He furthermore said he would entertain further inquiries on matters not related to his lecture in his quarters at another time. He asked that no one interrupt the lecture to ask questions, for it would disrupt the proceedings and cause distress to the other listeners.

Despite this request, however, after Srila Gurudeva had been speaking for half an hour, a mullah stood up and asked, "What is the reasoning behind the Hindu custom of worshiping idols (*but-parastī*)?" Many of the people in the audience were irritated by the interruption and told him to hush up and Srila Gurudeva not to answer, but Srila Gurudeva welcomed the mullah's question by praising it, saying that it was deserving of an answer from which everyone present could profit. Furthermore, by answering it he would not wander from the subject under discussion, but would rather enrich it.

He then proceeded to deal with the mullah's question as follows. He said that before answering him, he wished to ask him a question: "Do you believe in God (*khudā*)?" The mullah said, "Of course I do." Srila Gurudeva then asked, "Do you believe in Khuda's omnipotence?" The mullah loudly declared, "Khuda is all-powerful!" Srila Gurudeva then laughed and said, "There you have your answer."

Not realizing the implications of the word "omnipotent," the mullah was at first confused by Srila Gurudeva's answer. So Gurudeva started to clarify by asking, this time with the help of an example: "Is God powerful enough to take a Mymensingh elephant and to push him through the hole of the smallest needle without even harming a hair on his body?"

When the mullah remained silent, Srila Gurudeva continued, "Perhaps Maulvi Saheb does not know the extent of Khuda's powers. The fact is that nothing is impossible for the omnipotent Lord. *Kartum akartum anyathā kartuṁ yaḥ samarthaḥ sa eva īśvaraḥ*. He can do whatever he wishes, not do something if he does not wish to do it, or undo or change whatever he has done. The Supreme Lord is all-powerful and nothing is beyond his abilities. The omnipotent Lord is not limited to the powers that we ascribe to him. That is not what is meant by omnipotence. The *sarva-śaktimān* is one who possesses all powers imaginable and unimaginable. Once we have accepted that the Supreme Lord is omnipotent, we cannot say, 'He can do such and such, but not this or that.' So, in accordance with his wishes, the supremely powerful Lord can appear in any form he desires, at any time, with his full complement of powers. If you say that he cannot, then there is no point in claiming that he is all-powerful.

"Any figure that a man may create out of the five elements, or any entity that he imagines with his material mind—whether with form or formless—is all material. That is what we call a *putul* or an idol. There is no regulation in the Sanatan Dharma for the worship of such idols. What is ordained, rather, is service to the Lord's deity form or *śrī-vigraha*. The *śrī-vigraha* is that form which the all-powerful Supreme Lord feels obliged to accept as a result of his devotee's love for him. There is a gulf of difference between an idol and the Lord's deity form. Even though the Lord's deity form is purely spiritual, *cid-ānanda-maya*, a materially conditioned soul is unable to recognize him, just as he would be unable to recognize the Lord if he appeared incarnate directly before him. One can only perceive the Lord's divine form with the eyes of pure devotion. A vision of the Lord which has not been earned is not a true vision of the Lord."

PREACHING IN ASSAM

After East Pakistan, Srila Gurudeva took his party into Assam, recalling that Srila Prabhupada had once directly ordered him to preach there, for the Assamese people are simple and have faith in sadhus. To fulfill Prabhupada's order, Srila Gurudeva first went to Sarbhog near Barpeta in Kamrup district. Accompanying him were Bhuvana Prabhu, Uddharan Prabhu, and Krishna Keshava Brahmachari Prabhu.

Because of the problems in the Gauḍiya Math subsequent to the disappearance of Srila Prabhupada, Srila Gurudeva stayed at the house of Krishna Keshava Brahmachari's brother rather than in the Math. As there had been torrential rains and extensive flooding in the area, the devotees had to put all their bedding in an ox-cart and walk through knee-deep water to get there. As the veranda and ground floor of the house were under water, the party had to construct a bamboo platform on which to sleep, while another such platform served as a toilet. Even in these difficult circumstances, Krishna Keshava Prabhu's devout mother daily cooked meals for the Vaishnavas.

The war with Japan was at its height during this period and the Japanese army had already conquered Burma and crossed the border into Assam. The British Indian government's War Ministry had ordered many homes throughout Assam to be requisitioned for quartering Indian army troops. Krishna Keshava Brahmachari's family home was one of those taken over for this purpose and Srila Gurudeva and his party was obliged to stay in some village not far from Sarbhog. This is just a small example of how Srila Gurudeva was prepared to accept any difficulty to follow the orders of his own spiritual master and to bring auspiciousness to those who had forgotten Krishna.

Srila Gurudeva preached in these untoward circumstances for seven days before moving to Sarbhog where he stayed in Gopal Prabhu's house. While there, he gave daily Bhagavatam lectures at the house of a local high school teacher and leading citizen, Chinta Haran Patgiri. Those who became Srila Gurudeva's disciples during his preaching activities in Sarbhog were Gopal Das Adhikari and his wife, Shivananda Das Adhikari, Khagen Das Adhikari, and Achyutananda Das Adhikari.

A local youth named Kamala Kanta Goswami was a regular attendant at Srila Gurudeva's Bhagavata lectures. He was so attracted by Mahaprabhu's teachings that he decided to leave home and join his preaching party. Shivananda Prabhu and his nephew enthusiastically invited Srila Gurudeva to visit their village, Bhavanipur Tapa, where he stayed for a few days. Kamala Kanta Goswami accompanied the Vaishnava group to Tapa, but when his father, Ghana Kanta Goswami, found out, he came there, severely chastised him, and took him back home.

Ghana Kanta was conditioned to believe in the superiority of Brahmins. He did not accept the rationale behind the Daiva Varnashram taught by the Gaudiya Math. He considered that his son had lost his caste status by eating the food of the devotees and instructed him to remain outside the house until he had atoned. Kamala Kanta had been born in a very high caste, but after hearing the pure scriptural doctrines from Srila Gurudeva about the differences between a Vaishnava and a Brahmin, about the superiority of the Vaishnava and about how a Vaishnava can be born in any race or caste, he could not understand what fault there was in taking food that had been cooked and served by Vaishnavas who followed the religious practices prescribed in the scriptures. He could not approve of his father's attitude, which was disrespectful to the Vaishnavas, and in order to avoid offenses, he left home again the very next day and came back to Tapa to surrender to Srila Gurudeva. Though Kamala Kanta wanted to take initiation, Srila Gurudeva worried that his father and family might cause trouble, and thought it better to not give him Harinam and mantra on that occasion.

In Tapa, several wealthy Marwari businessmen were attracted to Srila Gurudeva and took great care to serve the

Vaishnavas and to help the preaching of Mahaprabhu's gospel. Shivananda Prabhu was very renounced, even though married. He gave his worthy son, Lokesh, to Srila Gurudeva to be fully engaged in the service of Guru and Gauranga. It is rare to see a father give his own son over to devotional service in this way. Shivananda Prabhu's nephew Sri Lohita and son Lokesh were initiated in the Holy Name at the house of Tularama Babu in Tapa. Just before leaving for Calcutta, Srila Gurudeva also initiated Kamala Kanta Goswami, Ram Prasad and Bhavananda in the Holy Name. He gave full initiation to Sri Lohita, Lokesh and Kamala Kanta when they arrived in the Midnapore Math. They were given the names Lalita Charan Brahmachari, Lokanath Brahmachari and Krishna Prasad Brahmachari, respectively. All three of these devotees later took sannyas from Srila Gurudeva and were known thereafter as Tridandi Swami Srimad Bhakti Lalita Giri Maharaj, Tridandi Swami Srimad Bhakti Suhrid Damodar Maharaj, and Tridandi Swami Srimad Bhakti Prasad Ashram Maharaj.

BHAGAVATA DISCOURSES AT THE CHIEF MINISTER'S HOUSE

Before returning to Calcutta, Srila Gurudeva spent a few days in the Assamese capital, Gauhati. Through the efforts of Krishna Keshava Brahmachari and Chinta Haran Patgiri, he had the opportunity to meet many of Assam's leading citizens and preach to them. Amongst these people were Assam's chief minister, Gopinath Bardalai, Durgeshwar Sharma, Kumudeshwar Goswami, Bhuvana Goswami, Kanakeshwar Goswami, Rohini Chaudhuri, Navina Bardalai, Girija Das, Dhiren Deb, Charitra Babu, Narendra Babu, and others.

Arrangements were made for Srila Gurudeva to speak on the Bhagavata at the Chief Minister's house. The people who came there to hear him speak the pure doctrines of the Bhagavata were enchanted. One day after Gurudeva's lecture, Gopinath Bardalai came to him with great enthusiasm and praised his explanation of siddhanta. He said, "Upon hearing your *Bhāgavata-pāṭha*, I am convinced that your objectives and those of Mahatma Gandhi are the same. You give so many examples from scripture and explain everything logically, and then you tell people to chant the names of Krishna. Gandhiji also ends his speeches, in which he talks about so many different things, by engaging everyone in '*Rām-dhun*.' So both of you have the same goal—to make people chant the names of God. I don't see any difference between your messages. What do you think of this opinion?"

Srila Gurudeva recognized that Gopinath Bardalai had great faith and affection for him. He did not wish to disturb his mind by saying something that would hurt him, so he decided to instruct him according to his level of understanding. He said, "If you don't mind, then I will tell you what I think."

The Chief Minister said, "I have been illuminated by all your valuable instructions. I have never heard such a learned discourse on the Bhagavata from anyone else before. How could I mind if you say anything at all for my benefit. Speak freely and say whatever you wish to say."

Guru Maharaj then said, "Before I entered the Math, I used to take part in the Independence movement. Gandhi's Sabarmati Ashram used to publish an English newspaper called *Young India*, which I often read. I remember once that Gandhiji told his audience in a speech that he was ready to abandon even the chanting of the Holy Name for the sake of his country. As far as I can remember, his exact words were, 'I can even sacrifice *Rām-dhun* for my country.'

"We, on the other hand, say exactly the opposite: 'We can sacrifice our country for *Rām-dhun*.' Our worshipable Lord Rama is not there for us and our ends. Everything exists for him. Western philosophers have defined the Absolute by saying, 'The Absolute is for itself and by itself.' We do not have an 'It-God'. Our Lord is the Supreme Person, the 'He-God.' So we prefer to say, 'The Absolute is for Himself and by Himself.' The unlimited universes come out of Him, they exist within Him, and they are maintained by Him. So their existence is uniquely to fulfill His ends. If anyone wishes to worship the Lord, he must have a proper theological understanding."

Gopinath Bardalai was so influenced by Srila Gurudeva's powerful personality that he told him he wanted to abandon householder life and live in the Math, dedicating his entire life to the service of the Lord. Unfortunately, his associates would not let him leave politics. Not long afterward he died and so was never able to do as he had wished. Politics are so entangling that once one has gotten involved in them, it is very difficult to extricate oneself.

As a result of the influence Srila Gurudeva had on all these important people in Gauhati, he became well-known both in the city and outside it. After completing his preaching activities there, he returned to Calcutta.

BHAKTI BALLABH TIRTHA MAHARAJ TAKES SHELTER

In 1947, Srila Gurudeva returned to Assam, this time to Goalpara. He was invited by the Gaudiya Math householder, Radha Mohan Das Adhikari. Accompanying Srila Gurudeva this time were Krishna Keshava Brahmachari, Uddharan Brahmachari, Madhavananda Vrajavasi, and Ratharurha Das Brahmachari. Srila Gurudeva and his companions headquartered in Radha Mohan Das's house and held meetings in various parts of the town. The regular Harisabha in Goalpara held a special assembly at which the town's leading barrister, Khiroda Sen, was made president. Amongst the other important people who were present were the local district attorney, Kamakhya Charan Sen and the pleader for the Mechpara estate, Priya Kumar Guha-Ray.

Kamakhya Charan Guha-Ray, son of Dhirendra Guha-Ray, first met Srila Gurudeva at Radha Mohana's house in Goalpara. He later took initiation and became known as Krishna Ballabh Brahmachari, and after sannyas, Tridandi Swami Bhakti Ballabh Tirtha Maharaj. He came with his friend Devavrata (Rabi) to ask some questions about spiritual life, as he wished to establish clearly by what method he could attain the Lord. When he first saw him sitting on an elevated seat and paid his obeisances to him, Kamakhya Charan felt Srila Gurudeva's blessings being showered on him, and his entire body erupted with horripilation.

He asked him the following question: "When I chant the Holy Name, I feel as though I will see the Lord any minute. Then I will have to leave my home and family, giving up all the love I feel for them. This troubles me so much that I stop chanting. Please give me some advice so that I won't stop chanting when thoughts like this start bothering me."

Even though the question did not show any great intellectual depth, Srila Gurudeva praised it to encourage the questioner. He then said, "A few geese used to live by a lake which was really nothing more than a stinking, stagnating little waterhole. They lived quite happily there, eating the plentiful snails, clams, worms and shrimp. One day, they saw a flock of their cousins, the swans, flying overhead. The large birds looked so beautiful with their sparkling white wings that the geese began to think that the place where they were heading must surely be much more wonderful than their waterhole. If they could only live there, surely they would become as beautiful as the swans and be as happy as they.

"The swans had been to the sea and were now on their way to Man Sarovar for the summer. One of them saw the geese looking at them so pitifully and felt compassion for them. He came down to land near the geese who were astonished by the swan's beauty. They asked him if he could take them with him to his home. The swan said that he had come precisely for that reason, to take them away from this putrid place. But when he told them to follow him, the poor geese pleaded that they were unable to fly very far. The swan felt so sorry for them that he told them to climb on his back and that he would carry them.

"The geese then started to wonder whether they would be able to find the snails, clams, worms and shrimp they were used to eating once they were at Man Sarovara. The swan answered that such disgusting things were not available there and that they lived on lotus stems. The geese began to shriek as if with one voice, 'Then how will we survive?' And so they decided not to go at all.

"The geese's attachments to other things kept them from going to live in a beautiful place like Man Sarovar. Similarly, our attachment to this perishable body and everything connected with it is an impediment to our going to join the Lord. The Lord is all-auspicious and free from any material defects, he is the embodiment of ultimate joy, and so is his abode. There is no place there for the despicable aspects of transitory material life. Anyone who is unable to abandon his attachments to things unconnected to the Lord and wishes to hang on to those things are unable to attain him. The Lord and Maya are opposites. Supreme auspiciousness cannot be had unless one is freed from material wants through the association of advanced devotees."

tato duḥsaṅgam utsṛjya
satsu sajjeta buddhimān
santa evāsya chindanti
mano-vyāsaṅgam uktibhiḥ

An intelligent person should therefore avoid bad company and associate only with devotees. With their realized instructions, such saints can cut through the knots of material attachments. (SB 11.26.26)

Radha Mohan Prabhu was Srila Bhaktisiddhanta Saraswati Goswami Prabhupada's initiated disciple. He had stayed as a brahmachari in the Gaudiya Math for a while before entering householder life. People of the region held him in high esteem because of his knowledge of Vaishnava philosophy, his dedicated worship, high standards and personal character. In Goalpara he was known as Ram Mohan Da. He worked as a clerk in the office of Kamakhya Charan's uncle, and so had the opportunity to shower his affection and kindness upon him by showing him the devotional path. He was thus the *vartma-pradarśaka guru* who brought Bhakti Ballabh Tirtha Maharaj to the Gaudiya Math. Because of his interest in the ultimate spiritual benefit of others, he had to face much opposition and criticism. Srila Gurudeva's letters for Kamakhya were sent to Radha Mohan's address. The affection of Radha Mohan's pious wife and family for Kamakhya could never be repaid.

In his letters, Srila Gurudeva advised Kamakhya to study Srila Bhaktivinode Thakur's *Jaiva Dharma* in order to eradicate all doubts. As a result of reading this book, Kamakhya Charan indeed found that the doubts which he had harboured for so long were effaced. In another letter, Gurudeva said that if he planned to follow a life of contemplation, the *nivṛtti-mārga*, and dedicate his life to the worship of the Lord, then it made no sense to take a government job. On the other hand, if he wished to follow the path of action, the *pravṛtti-mārga*, and worship the Lord while staying at home, he should take the job. Kamakhya realized that it would not be possible for him to engage in pure devotional service in his family environment and so he made up his mind to leave.

PREACHING ACTIVITIES IN HAULI

My parama gurudeva, Srila Bhaktisiddhanta Saraswati Goswami Thakur, visited Goalpara on only one occasion. He ordered his householder disciple, Nimananda Prabhu, to establish a Gaudiya Math near the banks of the Brahmaputra River, in a beautiful spot on Hulukanda Hill. The math was given the name Prapannashram and was considered a branch of the Gaudiya Math. In the course of time, however, due to the unavailability of personnel and other problems, the institution was lost. Later, Goalpara resident Sarat Kumar Nath offered to give a building and land for the establishment of a math in the town. Srila Gurudeva understood that this was Srila Prabhupada's desire and so he accepted the offer. He thus established a branch of the Chaitanya Gaudiya Math there in 1969.

Some of the places Srila Gurudeva visited while preaching in Assam were Bijanī, Bhatipara, Hāulī, and Barpeta. In Hāulī a great meeting was held where thousands of men and women, both of the Hindu and Muslim faiths were present. As usual, Srila Gurudeva asked the audience to save its questions for the end. Here again, however, a Muslim scholar interrupted to ask, "Has anyone ever seen the soul or God? What is the proof that you are not simply deceiving everyone when you talk about the soul and God?"

The audience asked Srila Gurudeva not to answer as the question had been asked in a challenging manner, but he thought that if he did not respond, the ignorant would think that he had no answer. He saw that the maulvi was carrying a book and he asked him what its name was. The Maulvi called the book a *kitāb* and gave its name. Though Srila Gurudeva knew several languages, including Bengali, Assamese, Hindi and English, and though his eyes were in perfect condition, he said he could not read the book's title from where he was sitting. He asked the Maulvi if he was not deceiving him by giving him some false name. How could he prove that it was not so?

The Maulvi asked the people sitting around him to confirm that the title he had given was indeed correct. Srila Gurudeva said, perhaps the group was in collusion to deceive him. Maulvi Saheb was surprised by his statement and asked him what he saw. Srila Gurudeva said that it looked like a bunch of scribbles. The maulvi replied that he evidently did not know Urdu, and Srila Gurudeva confessed that indeed he did not. The Maulvi then asked him, if he did not know Urdu how could he expect to know what was written there? He would first have to learn Urdu, then he would be able to confirm that he had been told the book's correct title.

Srila Gurudeva then took the maulvi's own words to explain to him what he was getting at. "Even if someone knows many languages, he won't be able to understand Urdu unless he has learned it. Even if one has good eyesight, unless he knows Urdu, he will neither be able to recognize what sounds are represented by its script, nor what the meaning of those sounds is. The same thing goes for understanding the soul and the Supersoul. Even if one has great learning and experience in this world, unless he has specifically earned the qualifications to experience the Lord, he will not be able to experience him.

"There are two kinds of vision, one based on knowledge (*veda-dṛk*), the other on simple sensual capabilities (*māṁsa-dṛk*). The physical eye can only see physical objects and nothing else. Things which are beyond matter and the senses are self-revelatory and can only be seen with his blessings. The truth is revealed in the heart of the surrendered soul."

A few people took shelter of Srila Gurudeva in Hauli. They became fixed in Vaishnava practices and took the vow to worship the Lord according to the teachings of Lord Chaitanya Mahaprabhu. Most noteworthy amongst these was Rameshwar Varman, who was known after initiation as Rameshwar Das Adhikari.

MORE PREACHING IN ASSAM

Remembering Srila Prabhupada's instructions, Srila Gurudeva returned to Assam nearly every year with a force of disciples and godbrothers in all stations of life. The immense efforts paid off as hundreds of men and women took to following the regulative principles and became his disciples.

In some places, conditions were extremely unfavorable. Nevertheless, Srila Gurudeva remained undisturbed and continued to preach fearlessly. The great devotees who have completely surrendered to Krishna go wherever they wish without any worry. Nothing can impede their tendency to serve the Lord. Because their service has no basis in personal desire, it is unstoppable.

tathā na te mādhava tāvakāḥ kvacid
bhraśyanti mārgāt tvayi baddha-sauhṛdāḥ
tvayābhiguptā vicaranti nirbhaya
vināyakānīkapa-mūrdhasu prabho

O Madhava, O Lord, those who have given themselves to You, who are fixed in friendship with You, never fall from the path in that way. Being protected by You, they can fearlessly step over the heads of armies of opponents.
(Srimad Bhagavatam 10.2.33)

Srila Gurudeva wandered from village to village simply to bring the greatest good to every living being, to turn them toward Krishna. Despite the difficulties, he travelled, sometimes by foot and sometimes by oxcart, in order to deliver the Lord's message. Some of the places he visited were Goalpara, Dhubarī, Basugaon, Bilasīpara, Kashiketra, Sidali, Agiya, Depalchong, Bardamal, Lakshmipur, Krishnai, and Dudhnai in Goalpara district; Gauhati, Sarbhog, Chakchaka Bazaar, Ketaki Bari, Hauli, Barpeta, Barpeta Road, Pathshala, Tihun, Bijani, Rangia, Nalbari, Jalaha Ghat, Bhatipara, Unnikuri, and Amingaon in Kamrup and Barpeta districts; Tezpur, Tangla, Bindukuri, Rangapara, Dhekiajuli, and Mangaldai in Darranga district; Silchar and Hailakandi in Cachar district; Sibsagar, Lakhimpur, and other important towns in eastern Assam, and Shillong in Meghalaya state.

Most Assamese tribals are traditionally followers of the Bhagavata religion. Many Vaishnava acharyas such as Shankar Deva, Madhava Deva, Damodar Deva and Hari Deva preached the Bhagavata throughout Assam. The topmost leader or *satrādhikārī* of Shankar Deva's school at that time, Narayan Deva Mishra, had great faith in our worshipable Srila Gurudeva. Narayan Deva Mishra was the priest when Srila Gurudeva came to Barpeta to preach in a vast assembly at the local school and college. He was especially attracted by Srila Gurudeva's scholarship and his force of character and invited him to his home. While in Barpeta, Srila Gurudeva stayed either at the house of Amiya Kanti Das and Hare Krishna Das, who were later initiated and given the names Aghadaman Das and Hari Das. When Srila Gurudeva went to Barpeta from Hauli in 1945, Krishna Keshava Brahmachari, Gopal Krishna Das Adhikari, Trailokyanath Vrajavasi, Madhavananda Vrajavasi and Bhuvana Mohan Das Adhikari were in his party.

Another important individual who was attracted by Srila Gurudeva's personality was Jiveshwar Goswami of Tihun. He confessed to Srila Gurudeva that he had been disenchanted with the Gaudiya Math after hearing one of its fiery householder preachers criticize another religious denomination and its doctrines. He praised Srila Gurudeva, saying that though he said basically the same things, he did so in a way that was pleasing and he felt none of the same disturbance that he did before. Such sweetness of expression was only possible for a transcendental personality of extraordinary character.

As a result of his tremendous preaching efforts, Srila Gurudeva was able to open three maths in Assam—the first in Tezpur, then Gauhati and finally in Goalpara.

No mundane efforts can diminish the glory of a true guru or devotee. For the benefit of the world's conditioned souls, Mahaprabhu took Srila Gurudeva out of a restrictive situation so that he could act freely to spread his gospel of pure devotional service everywhere. Though Srila Gurudeva left the Chaitanya Math at a fairly advanced age, he was able to organize a great preaching effort throughout India by which countless men and women were attracted to the pure devotional religion which had been practiced and taught by Sri Krishna Chaitanya Mahaprabhu. In a very short time, he was able to establish major centres throughout India. Without the divine power invested in him by the Supreme Lord, this would never have been possible for him to take on such responsibilities. Just as a wisp of cloud cannot hide the sun, no amount of envious disruptions can hold back the brilliant manifestation of a bonafide guru. Anyone who tries to do that will fall into the swamp of *vaiṣṇavāparādha*.

CALCUTTA

Two distinguished residents of Calcutta, Manikantha Mukhopadhyaya and the president of the Homeopathic Factory, Dr. S. N. Ghosh, were influenced upon hearing Srila Gurudeva's vigorous delivery of Hari katha. They came forward at a time when Srila Gurudeva was in apparent difficulty and became his right and left-hand men, taking the responsibility for the management and improvement of all the temples that he had established. Later, Calcutta lawyer Jayanta Kumar Mukhopadhyaya was attracted by Srila Gurudeva's effulgence, character and words to take up much of the responsibility of running the Sri Chaitanya Gaudiya Math.

OTHER PREACHING ACHIEVEMENTS

One of Srila Gurudeva's extraordinary achievements was to pierce the fortress of impersonalist philosophy in the Punjab and in Hyderabad. Hundreds of men and women in these places accepted the pure doctrines of Mahaprabhu's religion and Vaishnava *sadācāra*, and took the vow of worshiping the Lord in the manner ordained by Mahaprabhu.

Atul Krishna Goswami of the Radha Raman temple in Vrindavan held a high opinion of Srila Gurudeva, saying that he had never seen a "gigantic spiritual personality" of equal stature.

As a result of his force of personality, Srila Gurudeva acquired the land and buildings on the birthsite of his own spiritual master, Srila Bhaktisiddhanta Saraswati Goswami Thakur, in Puri. He established centres in Sector 20-B in Chandigarh and in the Tripura capital of Agartola, where he took over the service of the Jagannath temple. He was the chief organizer of the India-wide festivities celebrating Srila Prabhupada's 100th birthday, in which all of his godbrothers took part.

It seems that no personality of any significance, whether president, state governor, judge, minister, barrister, lawyer, vice-chancellor, professor, mayor, chief commissioner, doctor, inspector general of police, wealthy citizen, Westerner or member of other religious denominations participating in interfaith conferences, was not attracted to Srila Gurudeva once he came into contact with him. A full account of his transcendental activities and contributions can be found in his full biography, which has been published as a separate volume.

His extraordinary and exemplary character, his warmth and affectionate behavior, his outstanding tolerance and forgiveness were qualities which attracted educated and influential people, many of whom through his instigation left material life to take Tridandi sannyas and to dedicate their lives to the service of Krishna and the devotees. It was for this reason that the Chaitanya Gaudiya Math could have such wide results in such a short time.

SRILA GURUDEVA'S GURU PUJA LECTURE

Srila Gurudeva gave the following lecture to his disciples in his evening class in the Calcutta temple at 35 Satish Mukherjee Road, on November 12, 1967. It was Utthan Ekadasi, his appearance day:

"Today, Utthan Ekadasi, is also the tithi when we worship our predecessor acharya, Srimad Gaura Kishor Das Babaji Maharaj, for it is his disappearance day. You have heard a great deal about Babaji Maharaj's transcendental activities and teachings from the venerable Puri Maharaj. As I utter his name, I beg for his blessings, and I also pray for the blessings of my Guru Maharaj, who is non-different from him.

"Coincidentally, this also happens to be my own birthday. Those who love me have taken this opportunity to give me their profuse blessings. Who is such a fool that he will not accept blessings when they are given? Who will not take the opportunity to make spiritual advancement when it comes? I therefore humbly accept all of your blessings. May every one of my senses be constantly engaged in the service of Krishna and His devotees by your mercy.

"It is the custom for those in the renounced order to worship the guru on their own birthday. So, today, I make this my personal duty. I have three types of gurus: (1) The word *gu-ru* means 'the destroyer of ignorance.' The embodiment of unlimited knowledge is the Lord Himself, whose appearance destroys all ignorance. The Lord Himself is thus the root of the truth that is guru. (2) The second is he who personally attracted me and engaged me in the service of the Lord, who is himself another form of the Lord—he who founded the worldwide Chaitanya Maths and Gaudiya Maths, my Gurudeva, *nitya-līlā-praviṣṭa* Prabhupada Srila Bhaktisiddhanta Saraswati Goswami

Thakur. (3) Thirdly, all the Vaishnavas are my gurus.

"What do the Vaishnavas do? Just as it is the guru's job to constantly engage the disciple in the service of the supreme object of service, the Lord, similarly the Vaishnavas keep us engaged in the service of our worshipable Lord. It is impossible for anyone to get away with anything. If you deviate in any way, they will catch you. So, I also include my disciples amongst my gurus.

"Today my disciples performed kirtan and worshiped me as their guru. By listening to their kirtan, I worshiped them. If by listening I had any untoward motives, if I had tried to 'pocket' it, then there would have been no puja. Just as kirtan is a devotional activity, so listening is also a devotional activity, śravaṇa. However we express it, they are all my masters, whom I must serve. But even though they are my masters, the objects of my service, the great affection I have for them makes me instruct them, take care of and protect them in the same way that Yashoda and Nanda punished Gopal, instructed and took care of him. When Yashoda bound little Gopal to the mortar, she did not do so because she considered him to be the 'object of her service', she did it because she considered him to be her child. The object of service can be both the one who protects and the one who is protected, the one who takes care and the one who is taken care of. Therefore both attitudes are found in a pure devotee.

"Srila Prabhupada called his disciples prabhu; he called even his most insignificant disciples prabhu and used the polite form of the pronoun, *āpni*. He used the more intimate pronouns, tui and tumi, with only very few of his disciples; he was never condescending. But he would chastise and instruct even those disciples whom he addressed as prabhu, using the respectful pronoun āpni. When one calls someone prabhu, or 'master', is it not paradoxical to then discipline him? Some might even consider it to be a kind of hypocrisy. But this is not hypocrisy on his part: when he calls his disciple 'master', he means it. On the other hand, when the other mood comes on him, he disciplines his disciple. In one way of looking at things, the spiritual master is disciplinarian, in another, he is the disciple's dearmost friend and well-wisher.

"I am most grateful to all those who have blessed me today. May the result of their blessings be that my every thought and instinct be directed toward the service of Krishna and His devotees. And if anyone was really worshiping me, then he should know that he has in fact worshiped my spiritual master, who is the real object of worship. Service to the guru is service to God. I never saw anything in my guru other than the desire to achieve the pleasure of the Lord. He never for a moment thought that anything other than devotion to Krishna was in the true interest of the conditioned souls. Had he thought thus, he would not have been able to keep someone like me in the Math.

vāco-vegaṁ manasaḥ krodha-vegaṁ
jihvā-vegam udaropastha-vegam
etān vegān yo viṣaheta dhīraḥ
sarvām apīmāṁ pṛthivīṁ sa śiṣyāt

A sober person who can tolerate the urges of speech, the mind and anger, as well as the urges to taste nice food, to fill the belly and to satisfy the genitals, is qualified to become master of the entire world. (*Upadeśāmṛta*, 1)

"Those who have controlled the six urges are qualified to discipline others. Srila Bhaktivinode Thakur considered the above instruction to be directed towards householders and not to renunciates, but in fact, unless one has already been able to control the six urges, he is not qualified to leave the householder āśrama. Why then did Srila Prabhupada make me a tyāgī, when I have not been able to master the six urges? Perhaps I can make a mistake, but he certainly could not have made one. As my well-wisher, as my protector and master, why did he keep me in the Math? The reason is that he knew with certainty that there is no other way for anyone to achieve the ultimate good without associating with Vaishnavas and engaging in the service of the Supreme Lord.

"Through association with the devotees, by hearing the scriptures, one is able to experience the greatness of the Lord. This gives him the impetus to serve the Lord. There is no guarantee that simply by superficially controlling the senses one will become a devotee. There are many eunuchs in the world who would have become devotees if that were the case. Such sense control or renunciation has no standing unless there is love for the guru, Krishna and Radha. Without love for Krishna, without service to my Lord, then all this renunciation is not worth a plugged nickel, it is false renunciation.

"A renunciate or celibate who has no interest in service to the Lord is nowhere near as dear to us as someone who has dedicated himself to the Lord's service who is by far superior. This is because even though at first he may be somewhat erratic in controlling his senses, through the higher taste his senses will ultimately be completely mastered and he will have no interest in anything but Krishna. Nothing else will enchant him.

viṣayā vinivartante nirāhārasya dehinaḥ
rasa-varjaṁ raso'py asya paraṁ dṛṣṭvā nivartante

Although a person of gross corporeal consciousness may avoid sense objects by external renunciation, his eagerness for sense enjoyment remains within. However, inner attachment to sense objects is spontaneously denounced by the person of properly adjusted intelligence, due to his having had a glimpse of the all-attractive beauty of the Supreme Truth. (Bhagavad Gita, 2.59)

"One may fast, but does that stop one from desiring food? Even if one stops sense activities, the tendency to engage in such activities is not stopped. When one experiences a higher taste, however, one loses one's interest in the lower taste. When one has the experience of the joys of love for Krishna, then the inferior pleasures of the world cease to hold any charm. This is called *yukta-vairāgya*. This is why Narada instructed Yudhiṣṭhira: *tasmāt kenāpy upāyena manaḥ kṛṣṇe niveśayet*: 'O Maharaj Yudhiṣṭhira! Engage your mind in Krishna by any means possible.' (Srimad Bhagavatam 7.1.32)

"I may be renounced, but my mind is still accepting and rejecting thoughts and desires constantly. So, I am associating with my mind, not with Krishna. What benefit can come of that? It is of no benefit to me to associate with someone who simply praises and flatters me. It is far more beneficial to find the company of someone who will discipline me, who will instruct me and show me my mistakes.

"Devotion to Krishna has no relation to worldly learning or ignorance. If it did, then scholars and pandits would all be devotees. Whoever has realized that the ultimate goal of life is Krishna's pleasure alone does not need to waste his time in studies. I remember an event which took place when I was at the Madras Gaudiya Math, where I spent about ten years of my life. Through the efforts of Sripad Sridhar Maharaj, Sripad Bon Maharaj, other venerable godbrothers and myself, we were able to build the Madras temple. Ramachandra Aiyar, the son of the man who had donated the land for the temple, Sadashiva Aiyar, advised us to learn Tamil so that we could preach to the general populace of the city. He even took steps to help us learn. I had been studying Tamil for only three days when a telegram came telling me to go to Puri. When I saw Prabhupada, I told him that it would take about six months to learn Tamil. Srila Prabhupada said, 'Krishna bhakti is not transmitted by language. Through it, you may be able to transmit learning or scholarship, but that is all. Love for Krishna is communicated by one who possesses love for Krishna. Preach in whatever languages you already know. I don't advise you to lose your valuable time learning other languages.'

"The Math is there for culturing one's inherent love for Krishna. Through such culture, one feels happiness and he communicates that happiness to others. One who loves Krishna loves every single living being. Devotion to the Lord is awakened by associating with saintly devotees: *saṅgena sādhu-bhaktānāṁ īśvarārādhanena ca*
(Srimad Bhagavatam 7.7.30).

"I may be incapable, but my worshipable Lord is not. If any of you engage me in the service of Krishna and His devotees, then my worshipable Lords, Srila Prabhupada, Mahaprabhu and Radha Krishna, will surely give you their combined blessings. May all of you be successful, may Srila Prabhupada be pleased with you all."

REGISTRATION OF SRI CHAITANYA GAUDIYA MATH

In order to assure the proper management of the Sri Chaitanya Gaudiya Math, Srila Gurudeva had the society officially registered according to the Registration of Societies, West Bengal Act XXVI of 1961. This was done on August 9, 1976. Not long thereafter, he wrote the following letter:

"To the members and associates of the Sri Chaitanya Gaudiya Math, as well as to all my disciples:

"My physical condition is worsening, and I do not know where I will be when I leave my body. In view of my imminent departure, I make the following submission to my disciples, whether renounced or householder, as well as to my affectionate godbrothers, that I have registered all of my Maths and temples according to the Society Registration Act. The society has twelve trustees. None of these trustees can be changed unless it is proved that they have committed a serious fault contrary to the principles of pure devotion or some act which is against the interests of the Math and its preaching activities. If one of the trustees leaves of his own will, then someone else must be chosen to replace him according to the rules. I have chosen Tridandi Swami Bhakti Ballabha Tirtha Maharaj to be president and acharya of the Sri Chaitanya Gaudiya Math after my departure. I will be happy if everyone works toward the maintenance of the institution, preaching pure devotion and maintaining its principles under his leadership.

The humble petitioner,
Tridandi bhikshu, Sri Bhakti Dayita Madhava,
Dec. 12, 1976."

SRILA GURUDEVA'S LAST INSTRUCTIONS

The following lecture was delivered at the Calcutta Sri Chaitanya Gaudiya Math on the morning of Saturday, Dec. 30, 1978. Tridandi Swami Bhakti Ballabh Tirtha Maharaj told Srila Gurudeva that an inexperienced Western devotee had come to Calcutta from Chandigarh in order to receive personal instructions from Srila Gurudeva himself. The devotee had been there for several days, but since the doctor had forbidden Gurudeva to talk excessively, he had had no opportunity to hear him speak. It would be nice if Gurudeva could say something to him. Our most worshipable Srila Guru Maharaj then started to speak, directing his words to the Western devotee who had taken shelter of him.

EXCLUSIVE DEVOTION TO KRISHNA

"I am not well and the doctor has warned me not to speak too much. It is quite possible that I will not stay much longer in this world. I am telling you that to engage in a proper practice of devotional service, you must be fixed in the worship of your desired form of the Lord. When a woman is not faithful to her husband, when she loves someone else, she cannot give herself to his service. Infidelity and exclusive devotion cannot go together. For this reason, a faithful and devoted wife will never allow anyone to take the place of her husband, nor will she criticize anyone else. She will not condemn her brother-in-law, her mother-in-law or her father-in-law, nor anyone else who is related to her husband, but will rather give each of them his or her due respect. In the same way, if you wish to advance in devotional service, worship Krishna alone. Do not criticize the other gods and goddesses, but think of them as servants of Krishna and give them their due respect in that consciousness. But be careful to never give them the place which is due to the ultimate object of your devotion. I am giving you this instruction. Take responsibility for it. Give this matter a little thought. You are a competent person, you are highly qualified, but you don't understand this tradition yet.

"In the Gaudiya sampradaya, in the line from Chaitanya Mahaprabhu, in the religious tradition of devotion to Krishna, dedicated devotees worship Krishna exclusively. If you put other gods and goddesses on the same level as Krishna, you are making a mistake. Not all gods and goddesses are equal, nor all incarnations of Vishnu. *Ete cāṁśa-kalāḥ puṁsaḥ kṛṣṇas tu bhagavān svayam.* After discussing all the different incarnations, Matsya, Kurma, Rama, Nrisingha, etc., Veda Vyasa says that none of these incarnations is Krishna Himself. Some of them are expansions, some are partial manifestations, but Krishna is the Supreme Personality of Godhead.

jāṅr bhagavattā haite anyer abhagavattā
svayaṁ bhagavān śabder tāhātei sattā

The epithet *svayaṁ bhagavān* can only be used for Him from whom the characteristics of Godhead are derived.

(Chaitanya Charitamrita 1.2.88)

"No one is equal to Krishna. Everyone should keep this in mind and worship Krishna exclusively and with dedication. Devotion will not increase by making a great sound and fury. Everyone should remember this. We will not condemn any other gods or goddesses, but will pray to them to give us the blessing that we remain fixed on our supreme object of worship, Krishna.

INSTRUCTIONS FOR THE MATH AFTER HIS DEPARTURE

"I have registered the Math. The Math is no one's personal property. But that doesn't mean that I am going to leave this place a mess, with everyone in charge. If I do that, all my life's efforts will have been wasted. I have therefore devised a management scheme, which is necessary for the proper running of the Math after I am gone. One person will be named Acharya; he will be the head man or president.

"When I am gone, one person will take my place. Who will that be? My spiritual master did not like the idea that there should be a vote to decide the matter. To elect an acharya is not in accordance with the principles of Hari bhakti. God Himself will decide who is the acharya. The acharya is the person who is most dear to the Lord. Who will make that decision? The proper arrangement is that the Lord Himself says, 'This person is the one who is most dear to me.' Therefore the rule of the disciplic succession is that the choice should come from above. The correct process is that the order should be given from higher up. From the worldly point of view, everyone can get together to elect a leader, but the correct process is that the Lord Himself indicates which devotee is filled with love for Him, and He makes him the acharya. This is the process approved by scripture.

"When Srila Prabhupada was ill, he asked the solicitor, Mr. J. N. Basu, to write up a constitution. We heard that the constitution could be made according to one of two methods, by nomination or by election. Finally, the constitution was written according to the latter method. But Srila Prabhupada did not like it and he rejected it. I and two or three others were personally present when it happened. You cannot decide who is a sadhu, an acharya or realized soul, by taking a vote on the matter. Someone will say one thing, another something else and the debate will simply go on.

Therefore the proper method is that the Lord Himself will choose which person should be honored with the position of acharya. The scripture enjoins us to respect this process.

"This process is not followed only in the Gaudiya sampradaya; it can be seen in every Vaishnava sampradaya, the Ramanuja, Madhva, Nimbarka and Vishnuswami lines. This is the way that the disciplic succession is maintained. Therefore, the process ordained in the disciplic succession must be followed. I have therefore discussed with my senior godbrothers who are a part of the Gaudiya Math brotherhood, and I have decided to make Sriman Bhakti Ballabh Tirtha my successor and president in my absence....

"When I have gone, that does not give you all a license to behave just as you please. The defining characteristic of a Vaishnava is following a devotee. The Lord's blessings follow the blessings of the devotee. When a devotee is merciful to someone, the Lord's mercy follows. This is the essence of my instruction to you, please follow it. I have written about this in more detail elsewhere.

"It will not be correct if you try to expel someone from the Math as soon as there is some discord. That will result in chaos. You must first try to explain and clarify the situation. If that still doesn't work, then give the devotee who is causing problems some money and a letter and send him to another Math. Do not act impetuously, but try to work together by following the person who has been made leader. It is not proper to ignore his commands and do as one pleases. One has to follow the directions of the temple commanders. All their commands are being given for the service of the Lord, bear that in mind.

THREE IMPEDIMENTS TO DEVOTIONAL SERVICE

"I want to say one more thing. We have come here to engage in devotional service to Krishna. There are three principle impediments we have to watch out for.

"The first is the desire for sense gratification. The first obstacle to devotional service is *kanaka*, gold—the greed to accumulate lots of money. Your attention, your attachment, should be fixed on Krishna's lotus feet. If you become attached to anything else, you will fall down. You should not think that because outsiders will not understand, you should save money for a rainy day. Mendicants beg, that is their dharma. But they should turn whatever money they collect over to the Math on the same day.

"The temple managers should note that they must arrange for treatment if any temple devotee falls ill. If necessary, they should borrow money, but they must see that the devotee is taken care of. I can remember a time in the Math when we didn't even have money for groceries. So I borrowed money from someone without telling any of the devotees and went and bought food from the market. Only Uddharan Prabhu knew about it. Uddharan Prabhu would also go to a householder's place and borrow money from him. The householder was Govinda Babu. If Govinda Babu didn't have any money, he borrowed it from his wife. Later I paid all the money back. How many people know about that?

"Sripad Goswami Maharaj, Sripad Nemi Maharaj and I did all the collecting. I would put on a waistcoat and go out to collect. Then I would come back and give all the money to the temple. Srimad Bhakti Pradip Tirtha Maharaj, Jajabar Maharaj and Sridhar Maharaj would accompany me. Whenever they needed something I would buy it, but I never spent the temple collection money for myself.

"When I was at the Calcutta Math, I would go to Kunja Da and ask, "Is there any cloth in the Math? If there is, let me have one." But I would never ask him for anything that I did not need, just for pleasure. None of you should horde money that was collected in the name of the temple. That will disrupt your devotional life. It doesn't really matter to the Math if you decide to hold some of the money for yourself, because Krishna will take care of the Math and the devotees. But if you try to build up a savings account with that money, your spiritual life will go to hell and you will not last long in devotional service. So please don't set money aside for your personal use; give everything to the temple manager. If there is any problem, tell the temple manager. The desire for money is an obstacle to devotional service.

"The next obstacle is association with women. Both direct association and subtle association cause problems. It goes without saying that you don't engage in gross sexual activity, but you shouldn't even think about it, because we have given up everything to come here and engage in the service of the Lord.

"The third obstacle is the desire for personal aggrandizement. Srila Prabhupada wrote:

kanaka kāminī pratiṣṭhā bāghinī
chāṛiyāche jāre sei to vaiṣṇava
sei anāsakta, sei śuddha bhakta,
saṁsāra tathāya pāy parābhava

'Someone who has given up the tigresses of gold, women, and fame is a true Vaishnava. He is unattached and a pure devotee. He has overcome the illusory power of the material world.'

"Prabhupada here compares the desires for wealth, women and fame to a tigress. The desire for fame and good reputation are very strong and problematic, but even someone who does not seek fame finds that it comes to him of its own accord when he engages in true service to the Lord. People naturally give him their respect. People will always give respect to a true devotee.

pratiṣṭhāra bhaye purī gela palāñā
kṛṣṇa-preme pratiṣṭhā cale saṅge gaṛāñā

Madhavendra Puri ran away, afraid of being distracted by fame, but when one has love for Krishna, fame flows alongside him. (Chaitanya Charitamrita 2.4.147)

"So, avoid these three obstacles. It is not an easy thing to do, for they draw the mind. The conditioned soul lives for money, women, and fame. They are anarthas that remain to a greater or lesser extent in the mind of the practitioner, but we should not tolerate their presence there or approve of them.

"Tirtha Maharaj cannot always stay here. So Jagamohana Prabhu has to run the Math. Don't be offended if I am rough with you. Forgive me. I only wish to serve the Vaishnavas. I want to serve all of you.

"Worship the Lord with unflinching dedication. Don't stop worshiping Him, no matter what situation you are in. This is my prayer to you, my appeal and my instruction. Chant the Holy Name in all circumstances. Worship Krishna always. Always respect the best Vaishnava, and don't hesitate to do so. May all auspiciousness follow you all."

vāñchā-kalpa-tarubhyaś ca
kṛpā-sindhubhya eva ca
patitānāṁ pāvanebhyo
vaiṣṇavebhyo namo namaḥ

I offer my respectful obeisances unto all the Vaishnava devotees of the Lord. They are just like desire trees which can bestow all that is wished for, they are oceans of compassion who purify the fallen souls.

SRILA GURUDEVA'S DISAPPEARANCE

On Tuesday, February 27, 1979 (Govinda 26, 492 of the Chaitanya era; Phalgun 14, 1386 Bengali), at 9 A.M., in the midst of the singing of the Holy Names, Srila Gurudeva entered the eternal pastimes of the Lord, during his morning lila with Radha. He left his godbrothers and disciples in an ocean of grief. It was also the disappearance day of Jagannath Das Babaji and Rasikananda Deva Goswami. Srila Gurudeva was in his own room at the Calcutta Math, situated at 35 Satish Mukherjee Road. At four o'clock in the afternoon on the same day, the devotees left Calcutta with his body in the accompaniment of the Holy Names and came to Mayapur, where he was placed in samadhi according to the scriptural directions. The officiating priest at his funeral was H. H. Bhakti Promode Puri Maharaj, and on March 1, 1979, a festival of mourning was held in his honor at the headquarters of the Chaitanya Gaudiya Math at Ishodyan in Mayapur.

On Thursday, March 22, 1979, a memorial assembly was held in the sankirtan hall at the Calcutta Math on Satish Mukherjee Road, under the direction of H. H. Parivrajakacharya Tridandi Swami Bhakti Hridoy Bon Maharaj. The guest of honor was the publisher of the Amrita Bazaar Patrika, Tushar Kanti Ghosh. Many of Srila Gurudeva's godbrothers and leading citizens of Calcutta were present at the assembly.

A LIST OF MATHS AND INSTITUTIONS ESTABLISHED BY SRILA GURUDEVA

Here is a list of the many Maths, schools, libraries, free clinics, and printing presses—the great drums of the modern sankirtan movement established by our gurudeva. This list is given in chronological order.

(1) 1942. Shyamananda Gaudiya Math, Midnapore (W.B.). This temple was established by Srila Gurudeva with the help of his two godbrothers, H. H. Bhakti Bichar Jajabar Maharaj and H. H. Bhakti Kumud Santa Maharaj.

(2) 1948. Sri Gaudiya Math, Tezpur (Assam).

(3) 1953. Sri Chaitanya Gaudiya Math. Paltan Bazaar, Gauhati-8 (Assam).

(4) 1955. Sri Chaitanya Gaudiya Math. 86A Ras Bihari Avenue, Calcutta-26.l

(5) 1956. Sri Chaitanya Gaudiya Math. Ishodyan, Sri Mayapur, Nadia (W.B.).

(6) 1956. Sri Chaitanya Gaudiya Math. Sarveshwar Haveli, Vrindaban (U.P.).

(7) 1960. Sri Chaitanya Gaudiya Math. Goari Bazaar, Krishnanagar, Nadia (W.B.).

(8) 1960. Sri Chaitanya Gaudiya Math. Mathura Road, Vrindaban (U.P.).

(9) 1961. Sri Chaitanya Gaudiya Math. 35 Satish Mukherjee Road, Calcutta-26. The new temple was opened in 1967.

(10) 1961. Sri Gaudiya Sevashram. Madhuvana Mahauli, Mathura (U.P.)

(11) 1962. Sri Chaitanya Gaudiya Math. Urdu Gully, Patharghati, Hyderabad (A.P.).

(12) 1962. Srila Jagadish Paṇdit's Sripat. Jashra, Nadia (W.B.).

(13) 1967. Sri Vinoda Vani Gaudiya Math. 32, Kaliya Daha, Vrindaban (U.P.).

(14) 1969. Sri Chaitanya Gaudiya Math. Goalpara (Assam).

(15) 1970. Sri Chaitanya Gaudiya Math. Sector 20A, Chandigarh.

(16) 1972. Sri Chaitanya Gaudiya Math. Divan Deori, Hyderabad (A.P.)

(17) 1974. Sri Chaitanya Gaudiya Math. Grand Road, Puri (Orissa).

(18) 1975. Sri Chaitanya Gaudiya Math. Gokula Mahaban, Mathura (U.P.).

(19) 1976. Sri Chaitanya Gaudiya Math. Sri Jagannath Mandir, Agartala (Tripura).

(20) 1977. Sri Chaitanya Gaudiya Math. 187, D.L. Road, Dehradoon (U.P.).

SCHOOLS

(1) 1946. Sri Chaitanya Saraswata Catushpathi. Shyamananda Gaudiya Math, Midnapore.

(2) 1959. Sri Siddhānta Saraswati Prathamik Vidyalaya. Ishodyan, Sri Mayapur (Nadia).

(3) 1959. Sri Gaudiya Sanskrit Vidyapith. Ishodyan, Sri Mayapur (Nadia).

(4) 1961. Sri Chaitanya Gaudiya Vidyamandir. (Primary and secondary). 86A Ras Bihari Avenue, Calcutta-26.

(5) 1967. Sri Chaitanya Gaudiya Paschatya Bhasha Sikshalaya (Western languages school). 86A Ras Bihari Avenue, Calcutta-26.

(6) 1968. Sri Chaitanya Gaudiya Sanskrit Mahavidyalaya. 86A Ras Bihari Avenue, Calcutta-26.

(7) 1972. Sri Chaitanya Gaudiya Sanskrit Vidyalaya Sector 20-B, Chandigarh.

(8) 1972. Sri Chaitanya Gaudiya Antahpradeshik Bhasha Sikshalaya (Indian languages school). Sector 20-B, Chandigarh.

LIBRARIES (GRANTHAGARA)

(1) 1970. Sri Chaitanya Gaudiya Math Granthagar (for comparative religious studies). 86A Ras Bihari Avenue, Calcutta-26.

(2) 1972. Sri Chaitanya Gaudiya Math Granthagar. Sector 20-B, Chandigarh.

FREE CLINICS (DATAVYA-CHIKITSALAYA)

(1) 1959. Sri Chaitanya Gaudiya Math Datavya Chikitsalaya. Ishodyan, Sri Mayapur, Nadia.

(2) 1972. Sri Chaitanya Gaudiya Math Datavya Chikitsalaya. Sector 20-B, Chandigarh.

(3) 1978. Sri Chaitanya Gaudiya Math Datavya Chikitsalaya. Grand Road, Puri (Orissa).

PRINTING PRESS

(1) 1964. Sri Chaitanya Vani Press. 26/1, Prince Golam Mohammad Road, Tollygunge, Calcutta-33. Was moved in 1966 to 34/1A, Mahim Haldar Street, Calcutta-26.

MONTHLY MAGAZINE

(1) 1961. *Sri Chaitanya Vāṇī Patrikā*. 35 Satish Mukherjee Road, Calcutta-26.

OTHER TEMPLES THAT CAME
UNDER SRILA GURUDEVA'S MANAGEMENT

(1) 1955. Sarbhog Sri Gaudiya Math. P.O. Chakchaka Bazaar. Kamrup (now Barpeta), Assam.
(2) 1955. Sri Gadai Gauranga Math, P.O. Baliati, Dhaka district, Bangladesh.

HIS DIVINE GRACE A.C. BHAKTIVEDANTA SWAMI PRABHUPADA

His Divine Grace A. C. Bhaktivedanta Swami Prabhupāda was a rasika-acharya, an expert in relishing the mellows of pure devotion as taught by Sri Chaitanya Mahaprabhu. Such a capacity to relish hearing and chanting of the Godhead's transcendental name, form, attributes, and pastimes is uncommon. The great Srimad Bhagavatam (6.14.5) informs us:

muktānām api siddhānāṁ
nārāyaṇa-parāyaṇaḥ
sudurlabhaḥ praśāntātmā
koṭiṣv api mahā-mune

"Out of thousands of perfected souls, it is very rare to find one that is a pure devotee of God."

Perfection, or self-realization, is indeed a noteworthy accomplishment, yet it pales in comparison to unalloyed devotion. One need not fully surrender to God to achieve liberation from the flawed existence of material life. Any number of techniques may be employed in this attempt, but absolute humility of heart is not a requirement. Pure devotion, on the other hand, acknowledges no technique, while humility and absolute surrender are the stage on which the drama of divine love is eternally performed. His Divine Grace had such humility, such surrender, although he was at the same time often very demanding, insisting on a high standard from his disciples. His assertiveness was all on behalf of Godhead and therefore justified. It was an example of the dynamic face of humility, not an abstract, sterile humility, but the concrete and productive humility of doing God's bidding.

Srila Prabhupāda came to America in 1965 "as an aggressor." Aggression against illusion is the highest service to humanity. The cost of this war is absolute humility, for souls in this world are often less than thankful, unaware as they are of their own self-interest. The reward, however, is great. It is the dignity of the soul. This was the work of His Divine Grace: to bring dignity to all souls, and he did so with all of the humility at his command. It has been said that what Mohammed did with the sword, what Christianity did with wealth, he did with a humble heart—inundating the entire planet with love of God. The day will come when all men, women, and children from all races, countries, and creeds sing his praise.

For twelve years, beginning in 1965 until he disappeared from mortal vision in 1977, His Divine Grace circled the globe transplanting what was thought by many to be an Indian religion onto foreign soil. He demonstrated practically that Gaudiya Vaishnavism is not a product of a particular culture, but the dharma of the soul. He took the living conception of what he called Krishna consciousness and extended its life beyond what the greatest

Srila A.C. Bhaktivedanta Swami Prabhupada

Gaudiya thinkers and practitioners of the time imagined even remotely possible. Deep realization lies within the ability to adapt the spiritual reality to diverse material circumstances, making it accessible to one and all. This is the work of an acharya, who teaches both by precept and example. The acharya is not frozen in time. He is melted in love of Godhead, and flows without restriction to anyone and everyone who shows even the slightest interest in pure devotion. This was the work of His Divine Grace. He left a legacy of love, not law, for any and all of his immediate followers to embrace and continue. He gave to all, and looked for one—one who could actually understand his message.

Who was His Divine Grace? Founder Acharya of the International Society for Krishna Consciousness, father, friend, and śaktyāveśa avatar (empowered incarnation of a particular potency of God), nityānandāveśa, the empowerment of Sripad Nityananda Prabhu. The Lord Himself in His most merciful disposition, can only describe what we could see of him with the outer eye attuned to the spiritual mind. The inner truth of Srila Prabhupāda's eternal form and personality will forever remain concealed to those who fail to embrace not merely the form, but the substance of all that he taught and all that he exemplified. The darshan (spiritual revelation) of his inner identity is his prerogative. May His Divine Grace mercifully bestow that most precious vision upon all who follow him with steadfast intelligence.

Srila Bhakti Rakshaka Sridhar Deva Goswami Maharaj

Srila Bhakti Rakshaka Sridhar Deva Goswami Maharaj was born in Hapaniya, West Bengal, in 1895. The pastimes of his youth were spent in learning and he naturally excelled in every subject that he took up. From his childhood, his tendency was towards the culture of faith in God and the study of the Vedas, Upanishads, and other scriptures. He received the sacred thread according to his family tradition when fourteen years old, and his affinity for the divine world kept on increasing. In his early years he was especially attracted to Lord Ramachandra, but later, when he came in contact with the doctrine of Sri Chaitanya Mahaprabhu, he began to read Bhagavad Gita and developed an attraction for Lord Krishna.

After completing his primary and secondary education, Srila Sridhar Maharaj entered Krishnanath College in Berhampore (District Murshidabad), Bengal. After four years of study, he graduated with a Bachelor of Arts degree in philosophy. For some time Srila Sridhar Maharaj was searching for a sadhu from whom he could take initiation, but could not find anyone to his liking. Then, by the grace of the Almighty, Srila Sridhar Maharaj met his eternal guide and preceptor Srila Bhaktisiddhanta Saraswati Thakur, and in 1927 became his initiated disciple.

In 1930 Bhaktisiddhanta Saraswati Thakur awarded Srila Sridhar Maharaj sannyas and bestowed upon him the name Bhakti Rakshaka, meaning "guardian of devotion." Bhaktisiddhanta Saraswati Thakur saw in Srila Sridhar Maharaj the ability to perfectly protect the Gaudiya Vaishnava line from misrepresentation and misconception. After reading Srila Sridhar Maharaj's Sanskrit compositions glorifying Bhaktivinoda Thakur, Bhaktisiddhanta Saraswati Thakur remarked, "Now I am satisfied that, after I leave, there will be at least one man who can represent my conclusions (*bhakti-siddhānta*)."

Srila Sridhar Maharaj was recognized for his vast understanding and realization of the shastra and thus his guru also awarded him the title *śāstra-nipuṇa*, meaning one who is very expert or intelligent in understanding the meaning of shastra. Not only was Srila Sridhar Maharaj recognized by his guru for his advancement in Krishna consciousness, but he was also recognized by many of his affectionate godbrothers for his seniority. Many of them, such as Srila A. C. Bhaktivedanta Swami Prabhupāda, Srila Bhakti Prajñāna Keśava Maharaj, Srila Bhakti Saranga Goswami Maharaj, Srila Bhakti Dayita Madhava Maharaj, Srila Bhakti Promode Puri Goswami Maharaj and many others, considered him to be their siksha guru.

Once in a letter Srila A. C. Bhaktivedanta Swami Maharaj commented as follows: "What Sripad Sridhar Maharaj has directed, I take it on my head. He is my ever well-wisher. After the departure of Prabhupada (Saraswati Thakur) it is appropriate that I should accept his direction. I got direction from him that I shall live in this country forever."

Sometime after the passing away of Bhaktisiddhanta Saraswati Thakur in 1936, Srila Sridhar Maharaj established his own temple, Sri Chaitanya Saraswata Math, on the banks of the sacred Ganges in Nabadwip Dham, the holy land of Sri Chaitanya Mahaprabhu. Having deeply assimilated the teachings of Sri Chaitanya, Srila Sridhar Maharaj began composing original texts. His first work, *Śrī-śrī-prapanna-jīvanāmṛta*, was a comprehensive scriptural study of *śaraṇāgati* (surrender). Srila Sridhar Maharaj composed numerous songs, prayers, and commentaries in Bengali and Sanskrit. Among these important works are his commentaries on Bhaktivinoda Thakur's *Śaraṇāgati*, Bengali translations of Bhagavad Gita and *Bhakti-rasāmṛta-sindhu*, and his own original Sanskrit poem summarizing Chaitanya lila, *Prema-dhāma-deva-stotram*. An outstanding contribution to the Rupanuga Gaudiya Sampradaya is Srila Sridhar Maharaj's commentary on Gayatri mantra, *Gāyatrī-nigūḍhārtha*, following the siddhanta of Srimad Bhagavatam.

The senior members of the Gaudiya Vaishnava community deeply appreciated all the literary works of Srila Sridhar Maharaj. The well-known, if not famous, disciple of Saraswati Thakur, Srila Akinchana Das Babaji Maharaj, used to say, "I find the writings of Sripad Sridhar Maharaj to be not different from those of Narottama Das Thakur."

Many enlightened souls have proclaimed the greatness of the *Gāyatrī-nigūḍhārtha* as the supreme wealth of the Gaudiya Vaishnavas. Srila Bhakti Promode Puri Goswami Maharaj wrote: "Sridhar Maharaj's explanation

Srila Bhakti Rakshaka Sridhar Dev Goswami

of Brahma-gayatri, the mother of all the Vedas, indicating how it is centred on the meditation of Srimati Radharani, was revealed to him in the depth of his realization. It is the result of Paramaradhya Sri Srila Prabhupada (Bhaktisiddhanta Saraswati Thakur)'s divine grace on him. This explanation is deeply appreciated by those fortunate, intelligent devotees who are aware of the relishable beauty of pure devotional service.

"Parama-pujyapada Sridhar Deva has presented the world with this most beautiful, full-fledged explanation of Gayatri, the mother of Sruti, after realizing the deepest meaning of Srimad Bhagavatam. He has shown us the treasure of the most beautiful opulent wealth of the supreme reality: that the loving adoration of *vareṇya bhargo*, who is the supreme loving worshiper, ecstasy giver and internal potency of the supremely worshipable Sri Lila Purushottam Deva, is the best way to attain the grace of Sri Krishna. Gayatri is the benevolent source of pure devotional inspiration and intelligence required to attain the grace of Sri Krishna, the Divine Lord of this universe, and is the exclusive meaning of the expression *śavalāc chyāmalaṁ prapadye* (Upanishads)."

In the *Gāyatrī-nigūḍhārtha* Srila Sridhar Maharaj has written:

bhv-ādes tat-savitur-vareṇya-vihitaṁ kṣetra-jña-sevy-arthakam
bhargo vai vṛṣabhānu-jātma-vibhāvaikārādhana-śrī-puram
bhargo jyotir acintya-līlana-sudhaikārādhana-śrī-puram
bhargo dhāma taraṅga-khelana-sudhaikārādhana-śrī-puram
bhargo dhāma sadā nirasta-kuhakaṁ prajñāna-līlā-puram
devasyāmṛta-rūpa-līlā-rasadhera radha-dhiḥ-preṣiṇaḥ
devasyāmṛta-rūpa-līlā-puruṣasya radha-dhiḥ-preṣiṇaḥ
devasya dyuti-sundaraika-puruṣasyārādhya-dhiḥ-preṣiṇaḥ
gāyatrī-muralīṣṭa-kīrtana-dhanaṁ rādhā-padaṁ dhīmahi
gāyatrī-gaditaṁ mahāprabhu-mataṁ rādhā-padaṁ dhīmahi
dhīr ārādhanam eva nānyad iti tad rādhā-padaṁ dhīmahi

"With all of your thoughts and heart's desire, fully engage yourself in the pure devotional service and worship of *bharga*, the supreme goddess Srimati Radharani, who is the unlimited origin and possessor of the *svarūpa-śakti* of Krishna, the Supreme Beautiful Godhead (*deva*). Being the ultimate and all-harmonizing potency of Krishna, She remains His eternally unexcelled beloved servitor. In order to fully enrich and promote His *līlā-vilāsa*, She manifests Herself in variegated congenial forms. It is She who manifests Herself as *dhāma* (Goloka) the abode of Krishna, in the form of beautiful effulgence (*saundarya-jyotiḥ*) and opulence (*vaibhava*), adorning and glorifying Him all around. It is She who extends Herself as *līlā-śakti* (the potency principle which promotes the bliss giving pastimes of Sri Krishna in variegated colorful, tasteful, mystically opulent and beautiful ways). She is the unlimited ocean of Love of Krishna personified (*mahābhāva-svarūpiṇī*). Therefore adore Her as the supreme goal of life, who gives venerable, blessed intelligence, realization and taste of enhanced loving worship towards Her and Her eternal beloved deva, Sri Krishna, the all fulfillment of life.

"The sound of Gayatri is none other than the divine flute song of Krishna. This flute song is naturally filled with Radha-prema and dedicated to serve pleasure unto Her. What is the special characteristic of this all-attractive flute song in the life of devotional aspirants? It deeply attracts all souls to the unending beauty, glories and qualities of His eternal beloved Srimati Radharani, and situates them correctly in their own respective positions in Her eternal ecstatic service. Krishna's flute song thus deeply inspires the devotees to embrace an artist-servitor in the divine service-concert of His eternal consort Srimati Radharani through harmonious service performance. The innermost meaning of this flute song for all devotees is *rādhā-padaṁ dhīmahi,* which means to wholeheartedly embrace and engage yourself in the service of the lotus feet of Srimati Radharani with all devotional love. The highest and innermost instruction of Sri Chaitanya Mahaprabhu is *rādhā-padaṁ dhīmahi.*"

Krishna is *deva*, the Supreme Personality of Godhead, who reveals His pastimes of love in the eternal Goloka Vrindavan surrounded by His devotees imbued with wonderful love of God. The honorific suffix *deva* was given to Srila Sridhar Maharaj's name, as Sridhar *deva* Goswami, due to his ability to reveal the inner meaning of the Supreme Lord's divine pastimes of love to the sincerely aspiring devotee. The way that Srila Sridhar Maharaj spoke of the Supreme Lord's pastimes was absolutely wonderful. His voice and every movement were filled with divine love for Godhead. He was, as one disciple exclaimed, "beauty, sweetness, and charm in motion."

At an advanced age, in his fully matured stage of realization, Srila Sridhar Maharaj spoke extensively before devotees who had come from around the world to hear the teachings of Bhaktisiddhanta Saraswati Thakur and the great predecessor acharyas from him. These talks were recorded on audio and videotape and transcribed. They continue to be published by Sri Chaitanya Saraswata Math and Srila Sridhara Maharaj's many affectionate followers and admirers.

During the last days of his manifest pastimes, Srila Sridhar Maharaj remained always absorbed in deep moods of devotional separation and hankering for the divine service of Sri Sri Radha Govinda. Then in 1988, on the Amavasya, or the dark moon night, of the month of July, Srila Sridhar Maharaj withdrew his manifest presence from this earthly plane to enter the nitya lila (eternal pastimes) of the Supreme Lord.

At present the teachings of Srila Sridhar Maharaj are being spread throughout the world through the noble efforts of his many loyal and dedicated followers. Gaura Haribol!

Srila Bhakti Promode Puri Goswami Maharaj

In the early years of this century, Srila Prabhupada Bhaktisiddhanta Saraswati Goswami Thakur set into motion a devotional revival that rapidly spread through Bengal, India, and eventually the world. He put into question the very foundations of present-day theistic thought in a way that has little comparison anywhere in the spiritual record, East or West. Through him, the world was awakened to the teachings of Sri Chaitanya Mahaprabhu and the movement of pure devotion, *śuddhā bhakti*.

In orchestrating this modern bhakti revolution, Srila Prabhupada gathered some of the greatest spiritual luminaries in contemporary history into his circle. Such a convergence of exalted spiritual personalities can only be compared to the coming together of Sri Chaitanya's direct followers in the sixteenth century. One of the devotional giants who entered Srila Prabhupada's orbit was His Divine Grace Srila Bhakti Promode Puri Goswami Maharaj.

We cannot describe the life of Srila Puri Goswami Maharaj without emphasizing his contribution to the spiritual movement in which he was so integrally involved. The depth of his accomplishments cannot be fathomed outside the context of Sri Gaudiya Math. With his fellow godbrothers, he shared an indomitable faith in the service of his Guru and the message of Sri Chaitanya Mahaprabhu. This service was the sole purpose and highest aspiration of his being. This conviction led him to spend his entire life in the pursuit of Srila Prabhupada and Mahaprabhu's pleasure and the fulfillment of their desires. If we examine his life in this setting, we will see more than just numbers, dates, places and names. We will see how he embodied the very life current that his spiritual preceptors came to give to the world.

Srila Puri Goswami Maharaj took birth in the village of Ganganandapur in Jessore district (in present-day Bangla Desh), on October 8, 1898. His parents, Tarini Charan Chakravarti and Srimati Ram Rangini Devi, named him Sri Promode Bhushan Chakravarti. During his childhood, he met his *vartma-pradarśaka* guru (one who opens the door to the path of devotion), Srila Bhakti Ratna Thakur, a godbrother and siksha disciple of Thakur Bhaktivinoda, the legendary architect of the present Gaudiya Vaishnava movement. Through Bhakti Ratna Thakur he was introduced to Sajjana-toṣaṇī, Bhaktivinoda Thakur's own Vaishnava periodical, which was filled with Bhaktivinoda's commentaries and holy teachings. In this way Srila Puri Maharaj became familiar with the seminal works of the *śuddhā bhakti* tradition, such as Chaitanya Charitamrita, Chaitanya Bhagavata and the Srimad Bhagavatam. It was also through Bhakti Ratna Thakur that he first learned of his future guru, Srila Bhaktisiddhanta Saraswati Goswami Prabhupada.

Srila Puri Maharaj was still a young university student when he first came before Srila Prabhupada at the Yoga Pith in Sri Mayapur in 1915. It was a significant occasion, as Srila Prabhupada's diksha guru, Paramahamsa Thakur Srimad Gaura Kishor Das Babaji, had entered his eternal abode only the day before. Srila Puri Maharaj often recounted that as soon as he saw Srila Prabhupada and paid his obeisances to him for the first time, he knew in his heart that this was his spiritual master. Some years later, on the auspicious day of Sri Krishna Janmastami in 1923, he accepted both Harinam and mantra diksha from Srila Prabhupada and was given the name Pranavananda Brahmachari.

At the time, Sri Gaudiya Math was rapidly establishing itself as a bona fide manifestation of Indian religious culture and transforming the caste-conscious socio-religious world of Hinduism. Srila Prabhupada Saraswati Thakur was bringing together his intimate associates to share the wealth of Sri Krishna sankirtan. He had accepted *tridaṇḍī* sannyas in 1918 and by the early 1920's had already assumed a formidable position in the Bengali spiritual firmament. He was fearless when it came to upholding true religious principles. The students and practitioners of the Gaudiya Math aligned themselves with this attitude and led most exemplary lives of devotion, imbued with austerity, discipline and in-depth scriptural learning. This high standard of religious life was the hallmark of Sri Gaudiya Math and would be the thread that guided all of Srila Prabhupada's disciples, including Srimad Puri Goswami Maharaj.

The keystone of success in devotion is to perfectly hear the holy words spoken by one's spiritual preceptor. Srila Prabhupada would often say, "All that is required of you is that you lend me your ears." Srila Puri Maharaj was fully committed to this maxim. He had the great good fortune to associate closely with Srila Prabhupada for thirteen years and during that time he served him personally by recording his lectures and conversations, which were later published. The greater part of Srila Prabhupada's spoken words we are left with today come from the transcriptions of these notes. At the same time, Srila Puri Maharaj cultivated a deep knowledge of the Vaishnava scriptures, with the result that he became a veritable storehouse of the wealth of the preceptorial line coming from Sri Chaitanya and his followers. This led him to become one of the most prolific writers and influential teachers in all of Gaudiya Vaishnava history. His writings reflect the disciplined eye of a scholar who expresses with grace and directness the purest scriptural conclusions supported by his own uncommonly profound realization.

Following Srila Prabhupada's directives, Srila Puri Maharaj edited, wrote for, published and helped distribute countless spiritual publications. He was initially inspired and directed by Srila Prabhupada to start writing and contributing articles to the Gauḍīya magazine, the backbone of the Gaudiya Math's missionary work. For seven years he served as a proofreader and as one of its primary editors. In 1926, he was charged with running the world's only daily Vaishnava newspaper, Dainika Nadiyā Prakāśa. He held this service for two years, publishing all of his preceptor's daily discourses along with articles by fellow students and other contemporaries. His service and learning did not pass unnoticed by Srila Prabhupada who awarded him the titles of mahā-mahopadeśaka (great instructor) and pratna-vidyālaṅkāra (keeper of the wisdom of the ancient scriptural lore).

After the disappearance of his Gurudeva in 1937, Srila Puri Maharaj continued his vocation of spreading the teachings of Sri Chaitanya through the Gauḍīya magazine, first out of the Bagh Bazaar Gaudiya Math and then later the Sri Chaitanya Math in Mayapur. After he founded the Sri Chaitanya Gaudiya Math, Srila Puri Goswami Maharaj's godbrother, Srimad Bhakti Dayita Madhava Maharaj, invited him to head the editorial board of Chaitanya Vāṇī magazine in 1964. Puri Maharaj served in this capacity for thirty-three years, furthering his life's work of preserving the teachings of his spiritual lineage. Through Chaitanya Vāṇī, he continued to make a deep impact on the devotional world.

In all, Srila Puri Maharaj's wisdom is embodied in over sixty years of writings on Vaishnava philosophy and theology. He penned a rich variety of texts, bringing the Bhagavata dharma to life through hundreds of poems, essays, narratives, diaries, editorials and personal letters, thus creating a storehouse of the wealth of pure devotion for his disciples and the world at large.

In 1942, Srila Prabhupada appeared to Srila Puri Maharaj in a dream vision and imparted to him the sannyas mantra, ordering him to accept the renounced order. After accepting *tridaṇḍī* sannyas from his godbrother Bhakti Gaurava Vaikhanasa Maharaj in Champahati in August of 1946, he toured parts of India with other godbrothers such as Bhakti Hridoy Bon Maharaj and Bhakti Dayita Madhava Maharaj. In the meantime, he continued to write and lecture with dedication. At the behest of his godbrother Tridandi Swami Bhakti Vilasa Tirtha Maharaj, he also served for seven years as chief pujari for the Yoga Pith temple, the birthsite of Sri Chaitanya Mahaprabhu.

Srila Puri Maharaj took up a more solitary life of worship in the 1950's. He moved to a humble cottage on the banks of the Ganges in Ambika Kalna. The king of Burdwan was extremely impressed by his saintly ascetic character and, on the appearance day of Srimati Radharani in 1958, presented him with the ancient Ananta Vasudeva temple in Kalna.

In 1989, at the age of 91, Srila Puri Goswami Maharaj established the Sri Gopinath Gaudiya Math in Ishodyan, Sri Mayapur, for the service of their divine lordships, Sri Sri Gaura-Gadadhar, Jagannath Deva, Radha-Gopinath and Lakshmi-Narasingha Deva. In the following years, he established other temples in Jagannath Puri, Vrindavan, Calcutta and Midnapore.

Srila Puri Maharaj taught through his every action. He excelled in all aspects of devotional practice and there was perhaps no area in which he did not exhibit utmost expertise, diligence and foresight. This ranged from his encyclopedic knowledge of scripture, to maintaining the printing press, to his beautiful singing of kirtan. He was especially recognized for his sensitivity and attention to detail in the performance of deity worship and devotional rites and was thus widely called upon to be the head priest in most of the Gaudiya Math's deity installations and ceremonial functions. He was rarely known to rest; his service was an uninterrupted flow. Even in his later years, he would remain awake, writing and chanting through the night while all his youthful disciples were still asleep. When his personal servants came in the morning, they would inevitably find him awake and chanting the Holy Name, arisen before everyone else in the ashram.

Srila Bhakti Promode Puri Maharaj had outstanding love for his godbrothers and was inspired in his glorification of others. He found richness in everyone he met. He had the quality of making one feel so much wanted and their life so much valued. At the same time, he paid the least attention to himself. He was an emblem of humility and simplicity, and his generosity of spirit and kindness touched the hearts of the whole Vaishnava community. Among his lifetime, intimate companions were Srila Bhakti Rakshaka Sridhar Deva Goswami Maharaj, Srila Bhakti Prajñāna Keśava Maharaj, and Srila Akinchana Krishna Das Babaji Maharaj. Toward the end of his sojourn in this world, he was honored by the Gaudiya Vaishnava community for his learning, long life of service and devotion and made president of the World Vaishnava Association in 1995.

"He has love for his Guru; and let it be known that his life is one with his words." This tribute, coming from Srila Prabhupada himself, is the most revealing statement about Srila Puri Goswami Maharaj's personality and qualities. He gave credit for all of his accomplishments to the mercy of his Gurudeva alone. Through the blessings of Srila Bhaktisiddhanta Saraswati Goswami Thakur, Srila Bhakti Promode Puri Maharaj attracted the hearts of so many to the Bhagavata religion. People from so many different backgrounds and countries found in him a true spiritual guide and shelter. He upheld the principles of pure Vaishnavism and delineated the path of *śaraṇāgati*. He so embodied pure devotion and service to his spiritual master that one of his disciples once remarked that he was able to "silently lay down Srila Prabhupada's entire siddhanta."

We are greatly indebted to His Divine Grace for his gift–a lifetime of pure devotion, spanning over a century, which we can aspire for, learn from, and discuss about for our own spiritual nourishment. Srila Puri Maharaj departed this world for the eternal abode in the predawn hours of Narayan Chaturdasi, October 21, 1999, one day before the Rasa Purnima. His divine body was transported from Jagannath Puri to the Gopinath Gaudiya Math in Ishodyan and there placed in his eternal samadhi shrine. Prior to his departure from this world, Srila Puri Goswami Maharaj appointed his intimate disciple, Sripada Bhakti Bibudha Bodhayan Maharaj as his successor and president-acharya of Sri Gopinath Gaudiya Math.

In years to come as more of his words and vision are translated, the world outside of Bengal and India will come to know the spirit of the true Vaishnava religion that he tirelessly shared. May the gentle rain of nectar of his perfect teachings continue to bring auspiciousness into this world.

Swami Bhakti Ballabha Tirtha Maharaj

His Holiness Srila Bhakti Ballabh Tirtha Maharaj was born in 1924 in Assam, India, on Rama-navami, the most auspicious appearance day of Lord Ramachandra. Having been brought up in a pious environment, he developed a strong inclination to search for truth, which led him to take up the study of philosophy at Calcutta University.

After completing his MA in philosophy in 1947, he came in contact with his spiritual master, Srila Bhakti Dayita Madhava Goswami Maharaj, and immediately became attracted by his divine and powerful personality. Srila Madhava Maharaj was one of the foremost followers of the illustrious preceptor of the pure devotional school of bhakti yoga, Srila Bhaktisiddhanta Sarasvati Goswami Thakur. From that time onward, Srila Tirtha Maharaj completely dedicated his life to the service of his guru. Soon he became secretary of the devotional institution Sri Caitanya Gaudiya Math, which has over twenty ashrams in India alone. As one of Madhava Maharaj's first sannyas disciples, he took the vow of renunciation in 1961.

After the disappearance of Srila Madhava Goswami Maharaj in 1979, Srila Tirtha Maharaj was appointed his successor as acharya of the Math. During his lifetime, he received the blessings and intimate association of many of Srila Bhaktisiddhanta's prominent followers, such as Srila Bhakti Promode Puri Maharaj, Srila Bhakti Hridoy Bon Maharaj, Srila Bhakti Rakshaka Sridhar Maharaj, Akinchana Krishna Das Babaji Maharaj and many others.

For the last five decades, Srila Bhakti Ballabh Tirtha Goswami Maharaj has been engaged in preaching the philosophy of Sri Caitanya Mahaprabhu to counter the modern trend toward violence and cruelty, and to bring about unity of hearts among all, irrespective of race, creed or religion. Srila A.C. Bhaktivedanta Swami Maharaj had requested Srila Tirtha Maharaj to accompany him to the USA just prior to his launching of the Krishna consciousness movement in the west in 1965. As he was engaged in the service of his gurudeva as secretary of Sri Caitanya Gaudiya Math at that time, Srila Tirtha Maharaj humbly declined. Since 1997, however, at the request of Srila Bhakti Promode Puri Maharaj, he has been traveling the globe several months a year, enlivening all who come in contact with his humble, sweet personality, extraordinary kirtan and message of divine love. To date, his preaching travels outside India have taken him around the world, including the UK, Holland, France, Spain, Italy, Austria, Germany, Slovenia, Russia, the Ukraine, Australia, Singapore, Malaysia, Indonesia, Hawaii and throughout the continental US. Everyone is attracted by his eloquent, insightful and, most of all, purely devotional discourses.

During his US tour in 1997 His Holiness Srila Tirtha Maharaj addressed the United Nations' "World Peace Prayer Society," and "World Conference on Religion and Peace" in New York City, offering them a succinct outline for world peace based upon the spiritual tenets of the ancient Vedas. His preaching programs over the past years have also included many interesting dialogues with prominent Catholic, Protestant, Jewish, Hindu and Baha'i theologians, in such diverse settings as universities, interfaith groups, churches, Hindu temples and a wide variety of metaphysical and private educational centers. All are invariably won over by his gentle and affectionate nature, combined with his resolute faith in Guru, Vaishnava and Bhagavan. He has also spoken on the sublime teachings of Sri Caitanya Mahaprabhu on many radio and television programs, including a thought provoking interview on BBC radio in 2000, which was broadcast worldwide.

In addition to his role as acharya of Sri Caitanya Gaudiya Math, Srila Bhakti Ballabh Tirtha Maharaj serves as the acharya of GOKUL (Global Organization of Krishnachaitanya's Universal Love), which he founded in 1997. He has also served as vice-president of the World Vaishnava Association (WVA). Working eighteen hours a day, he is incessantly engaged in the service of humanity as a teacher of Vedic wisdom and the philosophy of bhakti yoga. He is presently engaged in writing articles and books in his native languages as well as in English. To date, his English publications include the books *Śuddha Bhakti*, *Sages of Ancient India*, *A Taste of Transcendence* and *Sri Chaitanya: His Life and Associates*.

Sri Krishna Chaitanya Prabhu Nityananda

Sri Advaita Gadadhara Srivas

Adi Gaura Bhakta Vrinda